KU-777-861

FUNDAMENTAL CONCEPTS IN COMMUNICATION

USTRATH

FUNDAMENTAL
CONCEPTS
IN COMMUNICATION

Pierre Lafrance
The Johns Hopkins University

Prentice-Hall International, Inc.

This edition may be sold only in those countries to which
it is consigned by Prentice-Hall International. It is not to
be re-exported and it is not for sale in the U.S.A., Mexico,
or Canada.

Tables 7-3 and 7-4 are adapted from R.E. Blahut, *Theory and Practice of Error Control Codes*,
© 1983, Addison-Wesley Publishing Co., Inc. Reading, Mass, Tables 5.3 and 7.1. Reprinted
with permission.

© 1990 by Prentice-Hall, Inc.
A Division of Simon & Schuster
Englewood Cliffs, New Jersey 07632

All rights reserved. No part of this book may be
reproduced, in any form or by any means,
without permission in writing from the publisher.

Printed in the United States of America
10 9 8 7 6 5 4 3 2 1

ISBN 0-13-344615-8

Prentice-Hall International (UK) Limited, *London*
Prentice-Hall of Australia Pty. Limited, *Sydney*
Prentice-Hall Canada Inc., *Toronto*
Prentice-Hall Hispanoamericana, S.A., *Mexico*
Prentice-Hall of India Private Limited, *New Delhi*
Prentice-Hall of Japan, Inc., *Tokyo*
Simon & Schuster Asia Pte. Ltd., *Singapore*
Editora Prentice-Hall do Brasil, Ltda., *Rio de Janeiro*
Prentice-Hall, Inc., *Englewood Cliffs, New Jersey*

UNIVERSITY OF STRATHCLYDE
15 MAR 1995
UNIVERSITY LIBRARY

D
621.38
LAF

ADM

To
John William Strutt
In memoriam

CONTENTS

CONTENTS

PREFACE

*Le savant doit ordonner; on fait
la science avec des faits comme
une maison avec des pierres;
mais une accumulation de faits
n'est pas plus une science qu'un
tas de pierres n'est une maison.*

Henri Poincaré (1854–1912)

What Poincaré said about science applies as well to engineering, and, especially, to engineering texts. Within the field of engineering, the communication discipline has continued to grow at an increasing rate through the past decades. This growth can be attributed to major theoretical developments (viz., Shannon and information theory), significant technological advances (viz., digital communications), and a healthy dose of synergism between the two. Naturally, this growth has encouraged the continuing publication of a number of excellent texts in areas related to communications.

So why write yet another communication text?

The need for a new book arose when I began teaching a graduate course, "Fundamental Concepts in Communication," at the Johns Hopkins University. The intent of this course is to prepare students for a professional environment in which they will be responsible for applying their engineering skills to a growing and constantly changing variety of communication systems. Such an ambitious objective could have been met by a very busy two-semester survey course covering all of the standard topics and as many applications to modern communication systems as time and patience allowed.

I have opted instead for a different approach, which has evolved into this book. I have attempted to describe the few essential concepts that define the field of communication. The underlying theme is that there are fundamental principles and performance limits in communication systems. These limits have their origins in physics and mathematics and, therefore, are technology independent. This book should be well suited to the upper-level undergraduate student, the graduate student who wants to take only one course in communication, the practicing engineer whose academic training did not include communication, and a growing number of scientists entering the communication field with good mathematical credentials, but without prior exposure to a formal engineering education. It is for this diverse audience that this book was written.

My goal has been to gather a well-ordered description of the mathematical and physical foundation of communication. The text contains examples to illustrate the utility of the material presented as well as to provide a welcome counterpoint to what could otherwise be considered tedious mathematical reading. The result is a book that can be used as an upper-level undergraduate or beginning graduate text in communication theory; it is also a good reference text for the practicing engineer.

This book is a succinct presentation of what I consider to be the essential topics in communication. I have, therefore, chosen to avoid a common practice in communication texts, which is to present, usually in several chapters, a review of probability, stochastic processes, Fourier analysis, etc. The reader is assumed to approach the present material already having been exposed to the usual mathematical and engineering background. The book assumes that the reader is comfortable with linear vector spaces, probability, statistics, and some rudiments of random processes. Variational techniques are used at times to provide elegant derivations of results. The reader not familiar with this may skip these derivations.

Throughout this text, the usual derivations introducing certain topics are supplemented by alternative treatments that are not usually found in most communication texts. This gives readers with differing backgrounds several points of view from which to approach a new idea, and promotes an interdisciplinary approach to communication.

I would like to thank the Johns Hopkins University's Applied Physics Laboratory for a three-month Stuart S. Janney Fellowship, which allowed me to write parts of this book.

FUNDAMENTAL CONCEPTS IN COMMUNICATION

INTRODUCTION
TO COMMUNICATION

Felix qui potuit rerum cognoscere causas.

Vergil

1

While it is possible to study communication engineering by investigating various specific systems, one eventually realizes that there are fundamental rules that govern their performance. There are universal mathematical principles that apply to communication systems. This means that communication can be studied "in the abstract," without reference to any specific system or technology. This is one of the triumphs of the mathematical theory of communication[†] advanced by Claude Shannon.

The motivation for studying the mathematical foundation of communication is its universality. The theory applies to all communication systems and is not affected by any particular technology. Technological advances reflect efforts to more closely approximate the theoretical performance bounds described by the theory rather than to introduce fundamental changes to the theory. A study of communication theory provides a set of timeless tools with which to understand, design, and evaluate communication systems.

It is therefore appropriate to begin our study of communication with a definition of its essential elements. This chapter first loosely defines these elements in nonmathematical terms in order to develop an intuitive feeling for the mathematical developments that follow. Then a chapter-by-chapter introduction to the topics covered in this book follows, where these principles are identified with areas of electrical engineering, physics, and mathematics, which will be covered in some detail.

This chapter encapsulates the various concepts upon which communication theory is based and points to the interrelationships between these ideas. Admittedly, some technical terms are used without the benefit of a precise definition (viz.,

---

[†] The phrase "theory of communication," as used in this book, also includes related disciplines such as information theory and coding.

information, channel, capacity). These terms are precisely defined in later chapters. For a first reading of Chapter 1, we trust that the reader's intuition will supply a sufficient understanding of these terms.

1.1 THE SCOPE OF COMMUNICATION

Communication systems are forever evolving toward increased complexity and better performance. However, one thing about them remains unchanged. Their basic objective is the transformation of information issuing from certain sources into a form that, to some degree, withstands the effects of noise while being transmitted or stored on a *channel*.

Figure 1-1 shows the elements of a generic digital communication system. The information originates as a signal from a source, either continuous or discrete. The process of encoding this information for transmission onto, and later retrieval from, a channel involves two conceptually distinct processes. First, the information stream from the source must be transformed into a set of symbols, a process called *source coding*. Source coding maps the source information into a set of symbols from a finite alphabet. Then this information must be impressed on the physical channel. The appropriate mapping for this depends on channel properties.

The only requirement for source coding is that the process must be reversible. The original information must be uniquely recoverable from its coded transcription. While there are several ways of encoding an information source, parsimony is always the goal for economy of design. Encoding an information source into as few symbols as possible results in a more efficient and economical utilization of finite channel resources such as time, bandwidth, and energy. The mathematical measure of a source's information content and the efficiency with which it can be encoded, therefore, form an important part of the mathematical theory of communication.

The physical channels used to transmit or store information all have fundamental limitations that restrict their *capacity,* which measures the amount of information that can be reliably transmitted over the channel. A measure of channel capacity, expressed in the same units as those used to describe the information rate of a source, can be used to compare source rate to a channel's capacity. One of the more significant results of information theory is that information can be transmitted over a channel with arbitrarily small probability of decoding error provided the channel capacity exceeds the source information rate by however small an amount as we may choose. The search for techniques that approach this ideal but theoretically achiev-

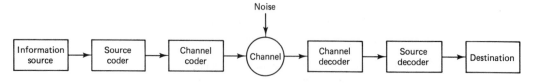

Figure 1-1.   The components of a generic digital communication system.

able performance constitutes the topic of *channel coding*, and its implementation involves what are now known as *error-control codes*.

There are occasions when one is forced to exceed channel capacity and, therefore, incur some unavoidable amount of distortion. This topic is the subject of *rate-distortion theory*, which provides not only bounds on the minimum distortion, but also a rationale for constructing algorithms that result in acceptable trade-offs between information transmission and distortion.

1.1.1 Defining Communication

Communication, at its simplest level, involves the symbolic representation of thoughts, ideas, quantities, and events we wish to record for later retrieval or transmit for reception at a distant point. Operationally, this involves the transformation of one set of quantities (thoughts, ideas, quantities, or events) into others (symbols) that are somehow more suited for transmission or recording over a degrading medium and the recovery of estimates of the original quantities at the receiving point. The goal of communication is to achieve the maximum information throughput across a channel with fixed capacity.

It is a tribute to human ingenuity that many ways have been devised to accomplish this. Communication systems form—some would even say define—an important part of human civilization. A complete list is outside the scope of this work, but we mention a few major categories, not listed in any particular order.

- Speech may have been one of the first complex communication bridges between humans. This remarkable means of transmitting ideas is, for the most part, taken for granted. The systematic representation of thoughts, things, events, and even abstract relations by mutually agreed upon acoustic modulations occupying about four kilohertz of spectrum has not only facilitated interactions between humans, but also made possible the passing of information from one generation to the next. The acoustic medium over which we vocalize is remarkably linear (at least over the range of engineering parameters accessible to humans) and introduces little in the way of distortion, save for attenuation over long distances and, in some occasional instances, annoying multipath echoes. Noise and interfering signals can, at times, present difficulties, however.

- Written language occupies a special place among communication systems. Aside from its ability to enable the keeping of records more faithfully than memory would, it is a powerful tool of mass communication, and a cornerstone of civilization. The ability to represent ideas by written symbols, together with the technology to reproduce and disseminate them with ease, has played a major role in spreading knowledge.

  Written language is amenable to scientific study with the tools of communication engineering and information theory. This is because written language itself represents a convenient level of symbolic mapping that uses a finite number of symbols, viz., letters or ideograms. This is a very useful starting point for additional mappings for the purposes of data compression, transmission, or storage.

- One of the challenges to human creativity has been to devise reliable means of communication that extend beyond an individual's immediate sensory environment. Many schemes have been devised for the transmission of information over long distances. Drums, smoke signals, semaphores, and lights are all methods that have been successfully used to encode and transmit messages. Without direct contact between one another, communicators become more vulnerable to the limitations of the communication channel between them. It is here that we begin to face seriously the need for good coding schemes. It is also here that problems of channel limitations must be reckoned with.

- Electrical communication, by which we mean to include all electromagnetic ways of representing and transmitting information, presents some of the greater challenges to the communication engineer. Electrical waveforms are used to represent and transmit a variety of analog and digital information sources. This great versatility is accompanied with another useful property: the great speed with which electrical waveforms can be transmitted over wires or as electromagnetic waves. Electrical waveforms make possible the implementation of systems that force us to consider the performance limits predicted by communication theory.

The design of a communication system requires the efficient transmission of information from a source with known statistical properties, at a given information rate, over a channel with known limitations. It also requires the ability to recover the information at the receiving end with minimal distortion. Communication theory is the study of systems that provide mappings between an information source and a symbol alphabet suitable for conveying this information over a noisy channel.

There are two fundamental problems in communication. First, communication involves a mapping, or coding, that transforms the output of an information source into a set of symbols for transmission or storage over a channel. The first problem involves finding ways to achieve as efficient a source coding as possible. Implied here is also the development of a performance measure that defines what is achievable in source coding efficiency. The physical nature of the channel imposes limitations on its ability to carry information. The second problem involves finding ways of transmitting the source information on a channel while incurring as little distortion as possible.

1.1.2 Reversible Mappings: There and Back Again

One of the advantages of communication theory is that it makes possible a discussion of communication system performance without actually having to invoke any of the details of the particular technology involved. The reason for this is that, fundamentally, communication involves mappings between sets of waveforms and symbols It is therefore sufficient to study the properties of these mappings and the conditions under which they can accurately and efficiently represent information-bearing signals. These representations must have sufficient latitude to represent whatever class of signals is of interest.

EXAMPLE

The keyboard with which this book was originally written has 58 keys. Assuming all keys are used with equal frequency, this keyboard can be considered to be a discrete information source producing $\log_2 58 = 5.86$ bits of information for every source symbol (i.e., for every keystroke). Since some of these keys can be used in combinations, the information source rate is actually somewhat higher. The keyboard itself does not change this information, but merely transforms it into a format compatible with the channel, which, in this case, is the magnetic disk on which the text is stored. The information symbols, however, do not occur with equal probability. Also, some keystroke combinations occur frequently while others never do. The result is that there is, on average, less than 5.86 bits of information per source symbol. The information content of a source H_s, measured in bits per source symbol, can be calculated from the statistical properties of the source symbols. It represents the minimum average information rate a code must have in order for the decoding to be unique. A code with a smaller rate would result in unavoidable distortion, whereas a code with larger rate would not be as efficient and would result in wasted channel resources. The aim is to find a code for the information source that comes as close as possible to H_s bits per symbol. One of the major results of information theory is an existence proof for codes with rates that, on the average, come arbitrarily close to H_s.

EXAMPLE

Speech is a good example of a continuous information source. Figure 1-2 shows a typical example of a speech waveform. The figure shows 50-millisecond segments of several vowels. Voiced sounds such as these form almost periodic waveforms consisting of segments that closely repeat over intervals called pitch periods. Although there is a gradual change in the waveform from one pitch period to the next, there is a considerable similarity between adjacent pitch periods. Another feature of voiced sounds is that the waveform itself varies smoothly from point to point. These observations suggest that speech signals are far from being random. The sample-to-sample and pitch-period-to-pitch-period correlations imply a certain redundancy that can be exploited by an encoder. Considerable savings in transmitted data rates can be achieved by coders that can "compress" data by removing the predictable (and hence redundant) component of a signal, and allocating coding resources only to the remaining random information-bearing component.

One of the remarkable results of information theory is that it is possible to discuss these mappings and messages in some detail without making any reference to their physical nature. This allows us to divorce the mathematical aspects of communication from its technological and implementation aspects. It also allows the development of a detailed and general mathematical theory of communication.

A requirement of source coding is the reversibility of the operations applied to the information-bearing signal. We require that the original sequence of source information symbols be uniquely recoverable, or at least recoverable with minimum

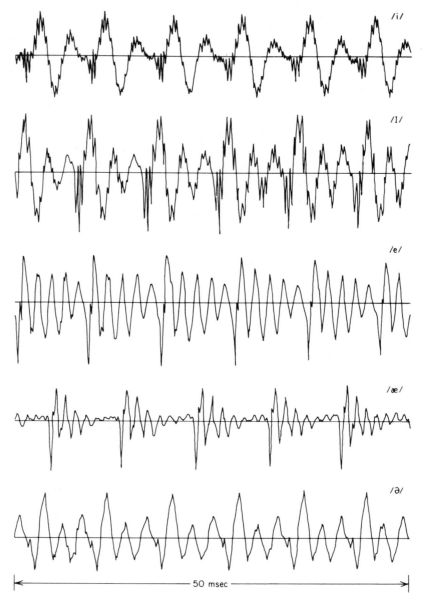

Figure 1-2. Examples of speech waveforms. (From Lawrence R. Rabiner and Ronald W. Schafer, *Digital Processing of Speech Signals*, pp. 46–47, © 1978 Bell Laboratories, Inc. Adapted by permission of Prentice-Hall, Inc., Englewood Cliffs, NJ, and Bell Laboratories, Inc.)

distortion, from the coded waveform used to represent it. Viewed this way, the mathematics of coding is essentially a mathematics of reversible mappings from one set of waveforms or symbols to another. We note in passing that this reversibility criterion applies not only to the coding procedure, but to any signal-processing operation used along the way. There are important results due to Shannon concerning the existence of reversible coding for channels whose capacity is at least as large as the source information rate.

A desirable property of coding is that it be parsimonious with respect to its use of channel symbols. The economical implications of coding efficiency provide an incentive to develop codes that come as close as possible to the performance limit imposed by the information content of the sources. While a deterministic knowledge of the source symbols is precluded, a statistical description of the information source can be exploited in the design of codes that, in some well-defined sense, best match the information source to the symbol alphabet representing it. This requires a quantitative definition of information that, in turn, opens the way to important coding theorems.

Once information-bearing physical parameters have been expressed as a suitable set of signals through the intermediacy of transducers such as keyboards, analog-to-digital converters, etc., we no longer need be concerned with the physical parameters themselves, but merely with their mathematical representation.

EXAMPLE

Source coding can map the information from a source into a different yet equivalent set of symbols. The judicious application of information theoretic principles to source coding can result in superior performance. A particularly striking example of this emerges in the comparison of some of the techniques that are used to record music for entertainment, a technology currently undergoing profound changes. For decades, analog "coding" has been used to provide a mapping between the details of the acoustic waveform and the physical engravings having the same characteristics, i.e., that accurately mimic the compressions and rarefactions of the original acoustic waveforms. These engravings are then stored on disks and are decoded by a mechanical probe that senses the changing local topography of the portion of the disk passing under them.

This brute-force approach, although tremendously practical and popular, has always been plagued by noise caused by dust, scratches, and by having to rely on the mechanical stability of turntables. A slightly more sophisticated coding involves representing the acoustic waveform by the analog magnetization of suitably prepared surfaces that themselves are subject to stretching, breaks, etc. and depend on sophisticated and bulky mechanical systems for their operation.

This technology is now being supplanted by digital compact disks, where analog acoustic information is represented by discrete digital symbols. Furthermore, sophisticated error-correcting codes are used to protect this information against a certain amount of physical damage to the disks. Here the waveforms used by the system are very different from the form of the original information source. The physical details of an information source are irrelevant to the communication engineer. Only its unique representation by mathematical symbols matters.

Source coding can be viewed simply as a transformation from one set of signals to another. One of the immediate concerns, if this goal of information representation is to be achieved, is that the systems used to represent the information generated by a source have sufficient latitude (e.g., bandwidth and dynamic range in the case of waveforms) to faithfully represent this information. "Latitude" in this context is measured by the total number of distinguishable *system states* Ω. A system's capacity to store information is then measured by the logarithm of Ω, a quantity that must be commensurate with the information source *entropy H_s*.

1.1.3 Physical Channel Constraints

An understanding of channel limitations is essential to the design of a communication system. Channels are physical systems used to store or carry information. That information must be coded into a form that is compatible with the physical limitations of the channel. Typical channels are the 3.5-kHz telephone channel with a 30-dB dynamic range; radio propagation channels that are subject to static, propagation phenomena, and atmospheric noise; magnetic recording media that, although generally reliable, are subject to error-inducing flaws; fiber-optics cables with their dispersion properties; and computer memories. As physical systems, communication channels have constraints that limit their capacity to store or carry information. Rather than studying the detailed physics of the systems that make up communication channels, it is possible to model channel limitations with a property called capacity.

All physical systems are limited by the finite speed with which they can respond to an input or excitation. This is another way of saying that physical systems have finite bandwidths. This limits the rate at which information can be passed through a channel.

1.1.4 Noise and Uncertainty

An essential attribute of a communication system is the ability to recover the original information from the transmitted waveform. This is done by a decoding operation that associates a particular symbol with every received waveform. Were it not for noise, this could be done unambiguously.

Measurements over channels can introduce noise in a communication system. For example, a radio channel is subjected to thermal noise and to the vagaries of atmospheric electrical discharges. These static bursts give rise to electrical signals that can cause decoding errors at the receiver. Noise limits the accuracy with which a signal can be recovered from a channel. This, in turn, limits the amount of information that can be stored on the channel.

Some form of noise is always introduced by the channel or at the point where the signals are read or measured. The presence of noise on the channel is an unavoidable consequence of physics. This noise is measured together with the intended signal, resulting in a certain uncertainty in the measured value. One consequence of noisy measurements is that the structure of the optimal receiver is dictated by the necessity to implement detection as a statistical inference process.

A very common form of noise is thermal in origin. Thermal noise is caused by the random motion of electrons in the resistive elements of an electrical circuit. At most frequencies of interest in engineering, the power spectral density of thermal noise is proportional to the absolute temperature and, therefore, can never be totally eliminated.

Recovering information from a channel involves a process of measurement that is subject to various forms of inaccuracies. The limitations that noise imposes on the performance of a communication system play a major role in the development of a theory of communication. When noise is added to the received waveform, there is the possibility that the decoding operation will result in an error, i.e., that the symbol associated with the received waveform is not the symbol that was sent by the transmitter. This points to the need for some care in selecting a coding operation that minimizes these errors. The selection of waveforms for communication over noisy channels is an important part of communication engineering. The idea is to construct waveforms such that the "distance" between different symbols is as large as possible so that noise will mostly result in a received waveform that is in some sense "close" to the intended symbol. Decoding is then reduced to measuring "distances" in a suitably defined signal space and selecting the symbol that is "closest" to a symbol code word. This, of course, is *maximum-likelihood decoding*. Signal theory provides us with useful measures of distance: the *Euclidian metric* in *Hilbert space*, and the *Hamming distance* in codes defined over finite fields.

The study of the physics of random processes falls within the purview of statistical mechanics. This discipline has developed an extensive formalism for describing the statistical behavior of systems of interacting elements with a large number of degrees of freedom. What engineers call a noise waveform is essentially a mathematical representation for a measurement made on a random system possessing a large number of degrees of freedom. We can, therefore, expect that the tools of statistical mechanics can be used to describe important noise-waveform properties. It turns out that this is the case and that this formalism blends quite well with signal-theory concepts. These topics motivate a discussion of thermal noise not usually found in communication texts.

1.1.5 Statistical Estimation

An important consequence of the presence of noise in communication systems is that decoding must be implemented as a statistical inference process. Statistical detection theory is a fundamental part of communication.

The application of statistical detection theory to communication is based on determining which transmitted message results in a maximization of the likelihood of the waveform that was in fact transmitted. This requires an a priori knowledge of the statistics of all possible messages to be transmitted and a statistical characterization of the channel noise properties. Detection can thus be reduced to a problem of statistical hypothesis testing.

This is accomplished by forming the *likelihood ratios* linking the received waveform to all possible transmitted waveforms, declaring as decoded that symbol that corresponds to the largest likelihood ratio. Aside from providing a rational mathematical approach to decoding, the likelihood ratio can be used to describe the form of the optimal detection processor for the particular signal and noise statistics involved.

Statistical estimation and the processing of signals for detection are intimately linked. A fundamental signal property used in distinguishing between different waveforms in the detection process is the metric distance between waveforms. Decoding fundamentally boils down to evaluating some metric between the received waveform and signals corresponding to the various statistical hypotheses. In fact, matched filtering can be shown to be a consequence of minimum metric decoding in the presence of additive noise.

When the noise is additive, spectrally white, and has Gaussian statistics, the probabilistic approach to detection leads to matched filtering. Matched filters, by guaranteeing a maximum signal-to-noise ratio, result in a minimum probability of decoding error for interference caused by additive white Gaussian noise processes. An alternative and instructive view of matched filtering is that it provides a metric distance between the measured and reference waveforms. Its output can be regarded as leading to an implementation of detection based on minimum metric decoding when the noise has Gaussian statistics.

1.1.6 Performance Limits

For many engineering applications, a singularly useful description of a system's performance is the specification of the conditions under which it ceases to perform.

Examples of performance limits abound in communications. These limits delineate the achievable from the impossible. There are two basic types of limitations in communications. Some limitations are inherent in the mathematical theory and have something to do with the signals, their representations, and the properties of the channels over which they are sent. These represent bounds that cannot be exceeded under any set of circumstances. We call these *fundamental* limitations. There are also limitations imposed by technology. Technological limitations are pushed back every year. This book limits itself to the fundamental limitations of communication.

We shall encounter several forms of fundamental performance limits. Shannon's coding theorems tell us that it is possible to find codes that come arbitrarily close to matching the rate of an information source and that it is possible to enjoy error-free communication, provided the transmission rate does not exceed channel capacity. These are fundamental limits. Clearly, then, means of calculating such quantities as source information rate and channel capacity must play an important role in communication theory.

In many instances, we are forced to exceed channel capacity and pay a price in signal distortion. There are important theorems that bound the minimum distortion and that can be used to develop a quantitative rationale for design trade-offs. This is the realm of rate-distortion theory. This theory provides important tools with which to calculate design trade-offs.

Very powerful methods exist for coding that enable a system to detect and even correct some of the errors incurred during reception. While the theory of error-control coding can at times seem involved, there are remarkably simple (and powerful) rules that can tell us something about the number of errors that can be fixed by a code. Thus, a code with *minimum distance* d_{min} can be used to correct up to t errors per code word, where

$$2t + 1 \leq d_{\min}$$

This is true regardless of the decoding procedure. It is a fundamental property of linear block codes.

The topic of error-control coding is usually formally developed within the framework of the algebraic properties of waveforms in Galois fields. The development of algebraic coding theory is a subject of some mathematical sophistication. The fundamental concepts, however, are very simple and are a direct extension of what has been discussed thus far, but must be recast in the terminology of finite fields.

Another example of a fundamental performance limit is the interesting appearance of the time–bandwidth product in several diverse areas of electrical engineering. We first encounter the time–bandwidth product in signal theory, where it is a measure of the dimensionality of signal spaces. We shall see that the gain of a matched filter is equal to twice the waveform's time–bandwidth product. This then places a limit on the processing gain achievable, for example, in spread spectrum systems. It also appears in the expression for the maximum imaging resolution achievable with synthetic aperture radar. A knowledge of a waveform's dimensionality is important to determine the maximum performance achievable in these examples.

An important physical limit that turns up in this context is the minimum cost of gaining one bit of information by making a measurement in thermal noise:

$$\mathscr{E}_{\min} = k_B T \ln 2 \text{ joules per bit}$$

where $k_B = 1.38054 \times 10^{-23}$ J/K is Boltzmann's constant, and T is the temperature in degrees Kelvin. This limit dictates performance bounds for distant space probes transmitting information back to Earth.

1.2 A GUIDED TOUR OF THE BOOK

In order to introduce the fundamental features of communication in their most general form, it is necessary to adopt a presentation style that is somewhat different from the usual sequence of topics one is likely to encounter in most communication texts. Both communication and noise waveforms can be described as abstract vectors in suitably defined linear vector spaces. This approach has the advantage of highlighting the algebraic properties of the waveforms without regard to the details of the particular fields used to represent them. This makes for an easier discussion of the fundamental properties of waveforms, be they real or complex signals in Hilbert space, or code words over Galois fields.

Detection is described as the outcome of a process that measures the metric distances between waveforms in these abstract signal spaces. Minimum metric decoding is introduced as a way of distinguishing between different waveforms. The similar mathematical definitions for the Euclidian metric and for waveform energy provide a useful link between mathematical and physical descriptors of an important performance characteristic of communication waveforms. The concepts of metric distance and energy appear in several places in communication theory, providing a bridge between the physical and philosophical aspects of this discipline. For example, the total number of distinguishable band-limited waveforms of limited duration in additive Gaussian noise—the information capacity of such an ensemble of waveforms—is limited by the amount of noise energy per waveform coordinate (degree of freedom). This, in turn, defines the minimum metric distance between any two such distinguishable waveforms.

The advantages of the general formalism become evident when communication performance can be attributed to such general waveform properties as norms and metrics rather than to their detailed wave shapes in either the time or the frequency domains. The advantage of this approach is that it highlights those features that describe fundamental performance limits of communication systems, independent of the particular representation chosen.

Signal theory is introduced in Chapter 2. This is done to provide, at the outset, a common frame of reference with which to describe communication waveforms. The basic idea behind signal theory is that waveforms can be described by suitable vectors in a multidimensional linear vector space. Processing and coding operations can then be represented by transformations that map a signal from one space to another. A fundamental signal property is its time–bandwidth product, a quantity that is associated with the approximate number of signal space dimensions necessary for representing a waveform. The formalism of finite-dimensional linear vector spaces is developed only to the extent to which it is needed in this book. The reader is encouraged to consult more advanced mathematical texts for a more detailed discussion. This formalism is introduced to allow the development of the concepts and fundamental performance behavior of communication signals. Later in the book, these same concepts, by then familiar, easily carry over to Galois fields to provide a discussion of error-control codes.

Chapter 2 opens with a description of signal space as a linear vector space. Two important concepts are discussed: waveform degrees of freedom and the Euclidian metric. The concept of waveform number of degrees of freedom is one that keeps turning up in several discussions of communication and detection performance. This is usually expressed by twice the time–bandwidth product and is intimately related to the dimensionality of the space in which the signals are represented. The concept of waveform degrees of freedom will be revisited in later chapters, where such topics as matched filtering gain, waveform and processing complexity, and information capacity are discussed.

The other important concept, the Euclidian metric, is first introduced as a formal mathematical entity as a measure of distance between waveforms. This metric appears under a variety of guises in signal analysis and communications. We encounter it in least-squares optimization as well as in maximum-likelihood detection, where it is used to measure the distance between a received waveform and various possible signaling waveforms. A detection strategy based on distances in signal space leads quite naturally to the more usual topics of matched filtering and correlation processing.

The Euclidian metric may be more familiar to engineers as the square root of the energy of the difference between two signals. This interpretation is further exploited in Chapter 3, where the statistical physics of noise is compared to the mathematical description of noise waveforms, and sets the stage for viewing signal detection as a physical measurement process. The equivalence between energy and metric distance is used in several discussions, where it provides a bridge between the mathematical measure of distance in signal space and the more familiar notion of signal energy.

Specific signal representations are introduced through a discussion of waveform sampling and reconstruction. A general proof for the sampling theorem is accompanied with a discussion relating sampling to information-preserving representations of the waveform in a suitable vector space.

Matched filtering is introduced as an optimum (in the sense of signal-to-noise ratio maximization) processing technique for signals in additive noise. The usual general derivation of the complex matched filter for complex signals in colored noise is given. This is then followed with a frequency-domain interpretation of matched filtering, where complex signal phasors are aligned on the real axis and summed. This alternative explanation, not usually found in textbooks, demonstrates both the optimal nature of matched filtering as well as giving a measure of its sensitivity to the effects of time delays and frequency offsets. Matched filtering turns out to be the processing implied by minimum metric detection in additive white Gaussian noise, where the symbol that is declared as detected corresponds to the signaling waveform that is nearest, in the metric sense, to the received waveform. The signal-to-noise ratio gain of a matched filter is shown to be equal to the number of waveform degrees of freedom, a fundamental signal theoretic quantity, and is independent of the details of the waveform.

Chapter 3 presents a discussion of noise and of processing for detection in the presence of additive noise. Thermal noise, because of its importance and ubiquity, plays a central role in the theory of communications. Noise waveforms, as described with the tools of signal theory, bear a striking resemblance to kinetic systems having a large number of degrees of freedom. This is no surprise since thermal noise is generated by such systems, viz., thermally agitated electrons. Chapter 3 is interdisciplinary in approach, combining material from statistical physics, mathematics, and communication engineering.

The law of large numbers is introduced in Chapter 3 as a purely mathematical theorem from the theory of probability. Later, this simple, yet surprisingly powerful, result reappears in successively more complex forms, including coding theorems.

An entire section is devoted to the central limit theorem. Particular attention is given to the cases in which it applies and also those to which it does not. The central limit theorem simplifies the analytical solution of many detection problems, and the temptation to use it sometimes exceeds the need for prudence. There are times when the central limit theorem is not applicable. For example, problems involving very small tail probabilities (false-alarm rates) should be approached with caution. A discussion of the Chebyshev inequality and of the Chernoff bound is presented both to ease subsequent analyses as well as to provide tools to test the applicability of the central limit theorem.

The mainstay of communication engineering revolves around the important theorems of information theory and coding. Chapter 4 discusses four principal topics: entropy, source coding, channel capacity, and coding for the channel. This chapter begins with a discussion of the related concepts of randomness and information. Hartley's logarithmic measure of information capacity leads naturally to Shannon's measure of information content for the information source generating an ensemble of messages: entropy. The mathematics of conditional and mutual information is then developed as necessary background for the definition of channel capacity.

Shannon's fundamental theorem guaranteeing the existence of codes that come arbitrarily close to matching a source information rate is introduced as a consequence of his interpretation of the law of large numbers. The ensemble of all possible messages of length M independent symbols issuing from a source with entropy $H_s = -\sum_k p_k \log p_k$ per symbol can be divided into two categories. One set of messages turns out to be much more likely than the other in the limit of large M. In fact, there is a set of approximately 2^{MH_s} equiprobable messages that tend to occur frequently, whereas the remaining messages occur with a probability that tends to zero as M grows large. This is then applied to the coding of discrete and continuous information sources by realizing that code words need be assigned only to the more likely sequences. Any distortion under this scheme can be made as small as one likes by encoding larger and larger messages. Good performance is realized only at the cost of higher coding complexity.

Communication channels are introduced as physical systems with limited information-carrying capacity. Channel capacity is formally introduced as the maximum value of the mutual information between the channel input and output. Channel capacity can also be discussed in terms of the number of distinguishable waveforms it can support, leading to an interesting geometrical interpretation of capacity using signal-space concepts. A few simple but useful channel models are then presented.

Signal detection is introduced in Chapter 5 as a statistical inference process associated with a limited resolution measurement in the presence of noise. Some emphasis is given to the minimum metric approach to detection, which leads to matched filtering in the presence of additive noise. The concept of minimum metric detection is revisited later in Chapter 7, where error-control coding is discussed.

Detection is described as a statistical attempt to maximize the likelihood with which the symbols of a given alphabet were sent, consistent with the signal that has been received. The maximum-likelihood formalism is developed and then applied to situations found in communications. The form of the optimal detection waveform processing implied by maximizing the likelihood ratio is introduced and applied to both single sample detection and to continuous waveforms.

For completeness, detection based on the Neyman–Pearson constant false-alarm rate (CFAR) approach is introduced. The discussion of CFAR is then generalized to include binary detection, viewed as target or preamble information passing through a CFAR channel with crossover parameters defined in terms of the probabilities of detection and false alarm.

Coding performance for coherent and noncoherent communications in additive white Gaussian noise is the subject of Chapter 6. Performance is measured by the probability of decoding errors. In parallel sections, the decoding performance for coherent and noncoherent coding is presented as a function of signal-to-noise ratio and coding complexity level, as measured by the number of bits per code word. These discussions lead to the minimum amount of energy per bit required for

detection in additive Gaussian noise. The last section in the chapter introduces the bandwidth expansion factor as a measure of how efficiently channel resources are utilized by a particular coding scheme.

Chapter 7 introduces error-control coding as a means of approaching coding rates close to channel capacity. Rather than relying heavily on algebraic properties of Galois fields, fundamental concepts introduced earlier in the book are applied to waveforms that happen to be expressed over finite fields. Emphasis is placed on waveform dimensionality, on the Hamming metric, and on code structure based on weight distributions. The minimum distance between code words is used to bound the code's error-detection and -correction capability.

This chapter discusses the mathematical aspects of error-control codes. Very long vectors received over the discrete memoryless channel have some error patterns that are much more probable than others, leading to efficient decoding approaches. Coding performance can be measured in terms of information throughput or residual decoding error rate. The price paid is in terms of redundancy and algorithmic complexity. Approaches to design trade-offs are discussed.

An elementary discussion of the algebraic structure of codes, and especially of cyclic codes, is presented as an introduction to readers who wish to pursue further studies in this field.

No text on communication would be complete without a chapter on rate-distortion theory. This is the subject of Chapter 8. The first section presents some theoretical results leading to distortion bounds for discrete memoryless and Gaussian sources. This is then followed by a section illustrating how rate-distortion theory can be used in practice. Examples are shown for analog-to-digital quantization and for the subband coding of speech signals.

SIGNAL THEORY

'Tis further from London to
Highgate than from Highgate to
London. [An example of a non-
commutative metric.]

Anonymous

2

Communications involve the transmission, reception, and processing of signals. Some aspects of signal theory are essential to an understanding of communications. The traditional engineering approach to signal detection as applied, for example, to radar and communication systems has been to derive the form of the optimal signal processor whose output, when suitably thresholded, maximizes the likelihood of correct detection. For linear processing in the presence of additive noise, this naturally leads to the matched filter, which maximizes the signal-to-noise ratio. Operationally, this is a two-step process. First, the signal is processed, often by filtering, to improve the signal-to-noise ratio. Then decision parameters are formed by sampling the outputs of these filters, and a detection decision is made based on the relative energies of these samples. The performance of communication waveforms is determined by the statistics of the decision parameters, i.e., of the statistics of their energies.

Although these topics are all discussed, the traditional approach is eschewed because it often gives the impression of being applicable only to continuous modulated waveforms. Error-control codes, which form an important part of communication, can often be perceived as being totally separate, and often mathematically alien, entities. This is encouraged by the description of these codes in finite algebraic fields and employs mathematical approaches that are not usually included in the engineer's tool kit.

We wish to emphasize the essential sameness between continuous waveforms and codes used for communication. The mathematical background presented in this chapter will hopefully allow the reader to make an easy transition from Chapters 5 and 6, where continuous communication waveforms are discussed, to Chapter 7. By then familiar concepts will simply be extended to signal spaces that happen to be defined over finite fields of scalars.

We also point out some of the fundamental properties of signals that play an important part in communications. For example, the time–bandwidth product of a signal is essentially a measure of signal complexity, of the number of degrees of freedom or coordinates used to describe the signal. This dimensionless quantity can be used as a universal benchmark to compare the performance of different waveforms. As will be seen, it is a direct measure of the achievable gain in matched filtering or of radar resolution. The concept of distance or metric measure in signal space is introduced here and will be found later in the book to be important in defining the performance of communication waveforms.

The chapter closes with a discussion of matched filtering as a signal-processing operation to be performed when noise is added to a signal. In this chapter, matched filtering is treated purely from a signal-processing point of view. It is the linear filtering operation that results in the largest output signal-to-noise ratio, a desirable feature for the identification of a signal buried in noise. In Chapter 5, a statistical inference approach to signal detection will lead us to rediscover the matched filter as the optimal processor for a signal in additive Gaussian noise.

2.1 LINEAR ALGEBRA OF SIGNAL SPACES

This section introduces some results from the theory of linear vector spaces. The algebraic structure of linear vector spaces is essential for the description of communication signals. This structure is identical for widely dissimilar signals. To emphasize this fact, we summarize important results in very general terms and illustrate these results with examples from continuous as well as discrete signals.

Many of the results in this chapter are established theorems from modern algebra and the theory of linear vector spaces. These are presented without proof. The reader interested in more detail than space allows here is referred to [Bl 83, Bl 85a, Li 83, Mc 72, Pe 72, St 80] for a readable presentation of modern algebra and to [Ch 70, Fr 69, Ha 74] for vector spaces. For an introduction to the calculus of variations, one could do far worse than to consult the excellent discussions found in [La 70] and [We 74].

2.1.1 Groups, Rings, and Fields

The study of modern algebra begins with a discussion of groups. A *group* consists of a set of elements $G: \{ a, b, c \ldots \}$ together with a composition operation called addition[†], denoted by "$+$", that satisfies the following four properties:

1. For every a and b in G, element $c = a + b$ is also in G. This is the closure relation.

2. There is an *identity* element i in G for which $i + a = a + i = a$ for every element a in G.

[†]The composition operation for groups is general and not restricted to ordinary arithmetic addition. Real and complex numbers do form groups under arithmetic addition. However, other groups with elements that are not necessarily numbers and with very different composition laws also exist.

3. For every element a in G, there exists an *inverse* element a_- also in G for which $a + a_- = a_- + a = i$.

4. For every a, b, and c in G, the following associativity rule holds: $(a + b) + c = a + (b + c)$.

Despite the suggestive notation, the elements of a group (or of other algebraic structures to be introduced shortly) need not be numbers and the composition operation need not be an arithmetic operation. This generality makes modern algebra a very powerful tool.

The identity element of a group is always unique. It is often called "zero" and is commonly denoted by 0. The inverse of any element is also unique. An important property of a group is the number of elements it contains. There are two possibilities: group may contain a finite or infinite number of elements. The number of elements of a group is called the *order* of the group. Groups having a finite order are called *finite groups*.

Note that the composition operation for groups is not necessarily commutative. Groups for which the operation is commutative, i.e., for which $a + b = b + a$ for all a and b in G are called *abelian* or *commutative* groups. The groups we encounter in signal theory are abelian.

In some cases, some subset of the elements of a group themselves satisfies all of the group properties. In particular, the subset is closed under group addition. Such a subset is then called a *subgroup*, since it inherits all of the other group properties from the parent group from which it is derived. It is easy to find many examples of different groups.

EXAMPLE

The real numbers form a group under ordinary arithmetic addition. The identity element is zero (0) and the inverse of an element a is simply its negative $-a$. The integers also form a group under arithmetic addition and are a subgroup of the real numbers. These groups have infinite orders. Real numbers under arithmetic addition form a group that contains an uncountably infinite number of elements; this group has an order of infinity denoted by $\aleph_1$†, the number of points on the real line. The even integers form a subgroup of A of order $\aleph_0$ under arithmetic addition.

EXAMPLE

The real numbers form a group under ordinary arithmetic multiplication. The identity element is one (1); the inverse of an element is its reciprocal. Note that the integers are not a subgroup of the multiplicative group for real numbers because a multiplicative inverse does not exist for every integer. In fact, integer 1 is the only element having a multiplicative inverse, namely itself.

---

†The symbol $\aleph$ (the Hebrew letter aleph) is used to denote the order of infinity. Thus, $\aleph_0$ is equal to the number of integers, and $\aleph_1$ is the number of points on a line. For a brief but enlightening discussion, see [Ga 61].

EXAMPLE

One-dimensional translations by a fixed increment Δ in either direction form a group with elements $\{0, \pm\Delta, \pm2\Delta, \pm3\Delta, \ldots\}$. This discrete translational group has infinite ($\aleph_0$) order. Note that there is a one-to-one relationship between the discrete translational group and the group formed by the integers under arithmetic addition. In fact, we find no distinguishing features between these two groups other than notation. Whenever such a one-to-one relationship can be established between the elements of two groups, we say that such groups are *isomorphic*, meaning that they share the same structure. Similarly, the continuous translation group defined by arbitrary displacements in one dimension is isomorphic to real numbers under arithmetic addition.

EXAMPLE

Groups are not restricted to numbers and arithmetic operations performed on them. A good example of a group that involves no arithmetic operation is provided by permutations. Consider a finite set $\{a_k\}$ of elements in some order. A rearrangement of these elements results in a different permutation.

For example, $\{a_1, a_2, a_3\}$, $\{a_2, a_1, a_3\}$, and $\{a_3, a_2, a_1\}$ are three different permutations of the same three elements. There are $n! = n(n-1)(n-2)\cdots 2\cdot 1$ permutations of n different elements so that the order of this finite group is $n!$. Note that the elements of the permutation group are not the $\{a_k\}$, but rather the rules that change the order in the $\{a_k\}$. A listing of the $\{a_k\}$ in different permutation orders can be used to label the permutations. However, any other set of $n!$ distinct labels will also do just as well.

Finite groups have the interesting property that repeated application of the composition operation between an element of a finite group and itself produces a cyclic sequence. For notational convenience, we represent the composition operation by "multiplication", and denote it by juxtaposition. Exponential notation becomes very useful in this and other applications. Thus, when the composition operation is applied between group element α and itself, we obtain a group element denoted by α^2. Successive multiplications by α generate the sequence α^3, α^4, α^5 and so on.† In general, these elements are distinct. However, since the group is finite, the sequence must eventually repeat itself. One can easily show (see Prob. 2.1) that the sequence thus generated is a finite group, and is called a *cyclic group*. Writing the elements of this group, we must eventually return to element α after some finite number of applications of the composition operation. The elements of the cyclic group thus generated are described by the following periodic sequence:

$$\ldots, \alpha^3, \alpha^4, \alpha^5, \ldots, \alpha^{n-2}, \alpha^{n-1}, \alpha^n, \alpha^{n+1}, \alpha^{n+2}, \ldots$$

---

†The exponents 2, 3, 4, 5, . . . appearing in this notation are simply reminders that the composition operation has been applied 2, 3, 4, 5, . . . numbers of times. Confusion sometimes arises, especially in groups or other algebraic structures where the elements α themselves are numbers. The exponents are not members of any group, but simply count the number of applications of the composition rule.

There must come a point where $\alpha^n = 1$ (the identity element), so that a typical cycle of the group can be written as

$$\alpha^0 = 1, \; \alpha^1 = \alpha, \; \alpha^2, \; \alpha^3, \; \alpha^4, \; \alpha^5, \; \ldots, \; \alpha^{n-1} \tag{2.1}$$

We say that this cyclic group is of order n, and is generated by the element α. This group, in fact, is completely defined by element α, which is called the *generator* for the group. Since all of the elements of a cyclic (or of any) group are distinct, n is the smallest number for which there results $\alpha^n = 1$. We call α an *element of order n* of the group. In general, different elements have different orders, and, consequently, generate cyclic groups of different lengths. Of particular interest are *primitive elements*, which, if they exist, generate all of the elements in the original group.

EXAMPLE

The N complex roots of unity $a_k = e^{2\pi jk/N}$, with $k = 0, 1, 2, \ldots, N - 1$ form a cyclic group of order N under complex multiplication. A finite-order multiplicative group results since the index k can be calculated modulo N owing to the cyclic nature of the complex exponentials:

$$a_{k+N} = e^{2\pi j(k+N)/N} = e^{2\pi jk/N} = a_k \tag{2.2}$$

This group can be conveniently represented graphically for $N = 12$ in Fig. 2-1(a). The elements $a_k = e^{2\pi jk/12}$ are the 12 complex roots of unity, and are represented by equispaced points on the unit circle. For this group, element $a_1 = e^{\pi j/6}$ is primitive.

Another interpretation of this group is suggested by Fig. 2-1(a). The same group structure is shared by rotations in increments of $\pi/6$ radians. This finite rotation group and the multiplicative group of the 12 complex roots of unity are,

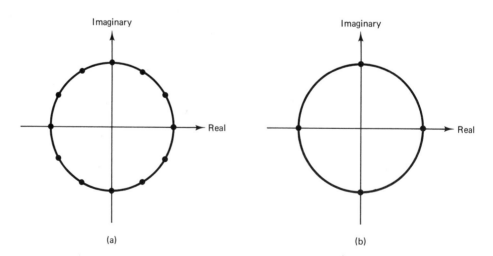

Figure 2-1. (*a*) Multiplicative group of order 12 for the complex roots of unity. (*b*) Subgroup of order 4.

therefore, isomorphic. They have identical group properties that differ only in notation.

If N is a composite integer, it can be written in the form $N = ab$, with $a \neq 1$ and $b \neq 1$. In this case, the following subgroups can be formed: $\{b_k = e^{6\pi j\, k/12}\}$, which is a multiplicative subgroup of order 4, and $\{c_k = e^{8\pi j\, k/12}$, which is a multiplicative subgroup of order 3. The group $\{b_k = e^{6\pi j\, k/12}\}$ is shown in Fig. 2-1(b). The original multiplicative group of N complex roots of unity under complex multiplication has as many subgroups as there are factors of N.

Groups are very general algebraic structures and form the starting point for introducing other entities. Just as a group is a set of elements closed under one operation, an algebraic *ring* is a set of elements closed under two operations. Rings are defined by the following conditions:

1. A ring is an abelian group under the operation of "addition", denoted by " $+$ ".
2. There is an operation called "multiplication" and denoted by juxtaposition. The ring is closed under multiplication. That is, the product ab is an element of the ring for all a and b in the ring.
3. Associativity holds for all elements of the ring: $a(bc) = (ab)c$.
4. Distributivity holds for all elements of the ring: $a(b + c) = ab + ac$ and $(b + c)a = ba + ca$.

As was the case for groups, the terms "addition" and "multiplication" as used here have a more general meaning than the familiar arithmetic operations. These names have been chosen because group "addition" and ring "multiplication" have a similar structure to their arithmetic counterparts. By definition, the elements of a ring form a commutative group under addition. Multiplication need not be commutative, but if it is, for all elements in the ring, we say that we have a *commutative ring*. A ring need not contain a multiplicative identity, but if it does, it is known as a *ring with identity* and the identity is often called "one" and denoted by 1.

A ring element need not have a multiplicative inverse, but when it does, it is called a *unit*. The element 0 does not have a multiplicative inverse. The multiplicative inverse of an element α is denoted by α^{-1}. There are several examples of rings. The reader is urged to verify that the following satisfy all of the conditions for being rings.

EXAMPLE

The real numbers under arithmetic addition and multiplication form a commutative ring, where all elements except zero are units. The set of all integers Z also form a ring under addition and multiplication; the units in this ring are ± 1.

EXAMPLE

Polynomials with real coefficients form a ring under polynomial addition and multiplication.

EXAMPLE

The set of integers $\{0, 1, 2, 3, \ldots, m-1\}$ together with arithmetic addition and multiplication modulo m forms a commutative ring with identity. The introduction of arithmetic modulo m allows us to form a finite ring out of the ring consisting of all integers by restoring closure under addition and multiplication. An element of that finite ring is also a unit only if it is relatively prime to m. In other words, a ring element has a multiplicative inverse only if it has no factor in common with m.

EXAMPLE

The set of integers $\{0, 1, 2, 3, 4, 5\}$ together with arithmetic addition and multiplication modulo 6 forms a ring whose units are 1 and 5. Element 1 is its own inverse since $1 \cdot 1 = 1$ (modulo 6); similarly, element 5 is also its own inverse in that ring since $5 \cdot 5 = 25 = 1$ (modulo 6).

EXAMPLE

It is not necessary for an element of a ring to be its own inverse. In the ring defined by $\{0, 1, 2, 3, 4, 5, 6, 7, 8\}$ with modulo-9 addition and multiplication, we have $4 \cdot 7 = 28 = 1$ (modulo 9), so that 4 is the multiplicative inverse of 7, and vice versa.

At first glance, this may seem like a far-fetched way of introducing multiplicative inverses. However, all of the conditions that define a ring have been satisfied and the result is a legitimate ring, even though the operations may not be familiar. In fact, finite rings, where closure is maintained by remaindering, play a very important role in communication and signal processing.

Rings are algebraic structures in which one can perform addition, subtraction (since all elements have a unique additive inverse), and multiplication. Division is possible only when multiplicative inverses exist. Division and cancellation are, therefore, generally restricted over rings, if they exist at all. With cancellation, the equation $ac = ab$ implies $c = b$. In the ring of real numbers, division is unrestricted. In the ring of integers, it is possible only if the quotient is a rational number. In finite-integer rings, there are no multiplicative inverses other than for the unit 1. However, the ring $\{0, 1, 2, 3, \ldots, p-1\}$ together with addition and multiplication carried modulo p, where p is a prime number, allows unrestricted division and cancellation since every element except 0 has a multiplicative inverse.

We now introduce another algebraic structure called a field. A *field* is an abelian group under both addition and multiplication, and for which the distributive property

$$(a + b)c = ac + bc \tag{2.3}$$

holds. This definition is almost identical to that of a commutative ring with identity. There is, however, one very important difference: since a field is a group under multiplication, a multiplicative inverse exists for every nonzero field element. This means that division is unrestricted over a field.

EXAMPLE

Typical examples of very useful fields are the real numbers R, the complex numbers C, and the rational numbers Q. Although most of our experience is with these fields, our introduction to arithmetic probably was made with simpler algebraic structures. Children are introduced to arithmetic through the operation of addition over the set of integers and are, without being told, working with an additive group of infinite order. Multiplication introduces another group. Eventually, division is introduced and arithmetic settles over the field of real numbers for several years until complex numbers are introduced.

Fields with an infinite number of elements seem commonplace to us. So much so that when simpler algebraic structures are reintroduced, they may seem difficult to tackle at first. This has always been a bit of a paradox, and one of the aims of this chapter is to point out that the important thing about algebraic structures is their composition laws and the implications derived from them, rather than particular examples of rings or fields. We are already familiar with R and C, but there are other equally valid fields with similar algebraic structure, but defined over different and even finite sets of elements. One of the most important examples is that of finite (Galois) fields, which find application in the theory of coding. Other examples include integer and polynomial rings in digital signal processing.

EXAMPLE

A field with a finite number q of elements is called a *Galois field* and is denoted by GF(q). Galois fields come in many isomorphic forms, but the simplest to introduce consists of the set of integers $\{0, 1, 2, 3, \ldots, p - 1\}$, with p a prime number, and with addition and multiplication being defined modulo p. All fields must at least include 0 and 1, the additive and multiplicative group identities. The smallest Galois field is GF(2) and consists of the set $\{0, 1\}$ together with addition and multiplication modulo 2:

$$0 + 0 = 0 \qquad 0 \cdot 0 = 0$$
$$0 + 1 = 1 \qquad 0 \cdot 1 = 0$$
$$1 + 0 = 1 \qquad 1 \cdot 0 = 0$$
$$1 + 1 = 0 \qquad 1 \cdot 1 = 1$$

Field GF(p) contains p elements. Finite fields can be derived from the integer ring by defining all composition operations to be modulo p, a prime number. What is being done here is to start with a ring having an infinite number of elements (the integers) and transforming it into a finite ring by forcing closure by defining arithmetic to be modulo some integer. This ring can be made a field by taking that modulus to be a prime number.

EXAMPLE

The set of integers $\{0, 1, 2, 3, 4, 5, 6\}$ together with arithmetic addition and multiplication modulo 7 defines the Galois field GF(7). To this set correspond the additive inverses {0, 6, 5, 4, 3, 2, 1} and the multiplicative inverses {none, 1, 4, 5, 2, 3, 6}, respectively (0 has no multiplicative inverse in any field).

In general, a finite ring of order m can be built from the integers by doing addition and multiplication modulo m. The elements of this ring can be listed by enumerating all the positive integers from 0 to $m - 1$. This ring can be used to build a finite field by requiring m to be a prime number raised to some integer power. A Galois field GF(q) has q field elements; $q - 1$ of these are nonzero. Galois fields exist only for $q = p^n$, i.e., a prime raised to a power, and we therefore use the notational reminders GF(p) and GF(p^n).

We now consider polynomials. We have already mentioned that polynomials with real coefficients form a ring. We proceed to show that, just as was done with integer rings, finite fields can be derived from polynomial rings. However, before starting, we note a few facts about polynomials. A typical polynomial has the form

$$f(x) = a_n x^n + a_{n-1} x^{n-1} + \ldots + a_1 x + a_0 \tag{2.4}$$

The exponent of the highest-order term with a nonzero coefficient is called the *degree* of the polynomial. The above polynomial is of degree n. The ring property of polynomials is an attribute of its form, i.e., the sum of terms of the form $a_k x^k$. The a_k are scalars, and x is an independent variable that can be real, complex, and in general, an element from any field. A polynomial is an algebraic structure for mapping an indeterminate element x into an element $f(x)$ based on a particular function. This involves adding several terms of the form $a_k x^k$, each of which is the element x multiplied by itself k times and then multiplied by the element a_k, with addition and multiplication being understood in the general algebraic sense. We thus make a distinction between the polynomial itself and the algebraic structures from which the elements a_k and x are chosen. In general, we shall take a_k and x from some field. We note that the indices k appearing in the polynomial terms are not field elements, but convenient labels.

Having defined the concept of a field, it is now clear how polynomial rings can be constructed. First, it is important to see that a polynomial is defined over some given field, the elements of which are usually referred to as *scalars*. Different fields have different scalars and can be used to define different kinds of polynomials. We are already accustomed to polynomials over R or C. Polynomials can also be defined over finite fields. To define a polynomial ring, we must define addition and multiplication in the ring. These operations are simply borrowed from the field of scalars over which the polynomials are defined. The set of all polynomials of finite degree forms an abelian group under addition. This set is also closed under multiplication, but does not necessarily form a multiplicative group. Associativity and distributivity hold for all elements. This set is, therefore, a ring, the polynomial ring, and has a countably infinite number of elements.

A finite field can be derived from the polynomial ring. The procedure used is similar to that for generating finite fields from integer rings: we force closure over a finite field through the artifice of remaindering. In this case, the division and remainders are over polynomials instead of integers.

We first introduce some definitions and algebraic results without proof. These have to do with extending the concept of divisibility to polynomials. The result is an algebraic structure for polynomials that is identical to that of integers. Our goal is to introduce the reader to finite polynomial fields defined modulo certain prime polynomials. In the discussion that follows, we talk about polynomials over arbitrary fields. Important special cases are polynomials with coefficients from the field R of real numbers, polynomials with coefficients from the field C of complex numbers, and polynomials with coefficients from the Galois field GF(q). It sometimes helps to keep a specific example in mind, but the ring properties of polynomials are quite general.

We begin with a polynomial ring. Within this ring, addition, its inverse, and multiplication are valid operations between any pair of elements. Division however, is not. We say that a polynomial $f(x)$ is *divisible* by the polynomial $p(x)$ if there exists a polynomial $q(x)$ such that $f(x) = p(x)q(x)$. In this case, we say that both $p(x)$ and $q(x)$ divide $f(x)$. If a polynomial cannot be expressed as a product of other polynomials other than a scalar and itself, we say that it is an *irreducible* polynomial. Irreducible polynomials play the same role for polynomials as prime numbers do for integers. There is a unique factorization theorem for polynomials just as there is for integers. Just as a number can be uniquely factored (up to the order of the factors) into a product of prime numbers raised to some powers, one can express any polynomial as a product of a scalar field element and of irreducible polynomials raised to powers. A polynomial whose highest-degree-term coefficient is 1 is called a *monic* polynomial. An irreducible polynomial that is also monic is called a *prime* polynomial. We note in passing that whether a polynomial is irreducible or not depends on the field from which its scalars are chosen. A polynomial that is irreducible over one field may not be irreducible over another.

EXAMPLE

The polynomial $x^4 + x^3 + x + 1$ over GF(2) can be factored in the following way:

$$x^4 + x^3 + x + 1 = (x + 1)^2(x^2 + x + 1) \tag{2.5}$$

in terms of the irreducible polynomials $x + 1$ and $x^2 + x + 1$ over GF(2). Note that all polynomials in GF(2) are monic.

Constructing a finite polynomial ring is easy. Guided by the way a finite integer ring is built, we choose a modulus polynomial, say $q(x)$, over some finite field GF(p^n), and require polynomial multiplication to be carried modulo $q(x)$. Polynomial addition is carried term by term in GF(q). For definiteness, let $q(x)$ be of degree m:

$$q(x) = q_m x^m + q_{m-1} x^{m-1} + \cdots + q_1 x + q_0 \tag{2.6}$$

with scalars $\{q_0, q_1, \ldots, q_k, \ldots, q_m\}$ from GF(p^n). Next, we list all possible polynomials over GF(p^n) of degree less than m. To do this, we merely form all possible combinations of $\{q_0, q_1, \ldots, q_k, \ldots, q_{m-1}\}$ with each q_k taking on all possible values over the scalars in GF(p^n). There are p^{mn} such combinations, so that the order of the resulting ring is p^{mn}, i.e., the power of a prime number. Addition and multiplication in this ring are carried modulo $q(x)$.

In building a finite integer ring from the infinite ring of all integers, we simply chose some integer m and then listed all integers from 0 to $m - 1$. Addition, subtraction, and multiplication on that ring are defined modulo m to effect closure. Operations modulo m imply that for this ring, m is equivalent (mathematicians say *congruent*) to zero. Thus, $m + 1$ is congruent to 1, and so on, and, in this way, closure is maintained over the m ring elements.

With polynomials, the idea is very much the same. We can form a finite polynomial ring by starting with the infinite ring of polynomials of all degrees, just as we started with the infinite ring of all integers. We achieve closure on a finite ring by choosing any polynomial $q(x)$ of degree m and then listing all ring elements of degree $m - 1$ or less. This is done by substituting all possible combinations of scalars from GF(p^n) for the polynomial coefficients. Addition, subtraction, and multiplication on that ring are defined modulo $q(x)$. By this, we mean that $q(x)$ is congruent to zero, and write $q(x) = 0$, which implies that

$$q_m x^m + q_{m-1} x^{m-1} + \cdots + q_1 x + q_0 = 0 \tag{2.7}$$

Since the q_k are field elements, we can always divide through by q_m to obtain a monic polynomial, which, in turn, can be written in the form

$$x^m = r_{m-1} x^{m-1} + \cdots + r_1 x + r_0 \tag{2.8}$$

where $r_k = -q_k/q_m$. This expression can be used to reduce any polynomial of degree greater or equal to m to a polynomial of lesser degree, and, therefore, a member of the finite ring. Polynomials of degree less than m are not affected by this reduction.

If the polynomial $q(x)$ is prime over GF(p^n), then the resulting ring is also a field of polynomials of degree $m - 1$ or less over GF(p^n). Since all Galois fields of the same order are isomorphic, we can establish a one-to-one correspondence between each of these p^{mn} polynomials and the elements of the field GF(p^{mn}) derived from an integer ring. Elements of one finite field can be regarded merely as labels for another finite field of the same order.

Viewed in this light, the previous construction for GF(p^{mn}) leads us to an interesting procedure for building fields of high order from fields of low order. In building the polynomial field GF(p^{mn}), we can start with elements from GF(p^n), which are then substituted in all possible combinations in some prime polynomial of degree $m - 1$ over GF(p^n). Equivalently, one can build GF(q^n) from GF(q) by listing all polynomials over GF(q) and then reducing these modulo a prime polynomial of degree n over GF(q). The existence of prime polynomials is, therefore, a matter of some importance, and it is known that in every Galois field, there are prime polynomials of every degree. Table 2-1 lists some prime polynomials over GF(2).

EXAMPLE

We shall build the Galois field GF(2^3) from GF(2). Polynomials of degree 2 or less on GF(2) all have the form $f(x) = \alpha_2 x^2 + \alpha_1 x + \alpha_0$, and these are the only polynomials to be considered, since any polynomial of higher degree would have to be reduced modulo a prime polynomial of degree 3 anyway. With α_0, α_1, and $\alpha_2 \in$ GF(2), there are exactly $2^3 = 8$ distinct polynomials for $f(x)$, and these correspond to the elements of GF(2^3). Expressed as polynomials, they are

TABLE 2-1. SOME PRIME POLYNOMIALS
OVER GF(2)[a]

Degree	$p(x)$
1	$x + 1$
2	$x^2 + x + 1$
3	$x^3 + x + 1$
4	$x^4 + x + 1$
5	$x^5 + x^2 + 1$
6	$x^6 + x + 1$
7	$x^7 + x^3 + 1$
8	$x^8 + x^4 + x^3 + x^2 + 1$
9	$x^9 + x^4 + 1$
10	$x^{10} + x^3 + 1$
11	$x^{11} + x^2 + 1$
12	$x^{12} + x^6 + x^4 + x + 1$
13	$x^{13} + x^4 + x^3 + x + 1$
14	$x^{14} + x^{10} + x^6 + x + 1$
15	$x^{15} + x + 1$
16	$x^{16} + x^{12} + x^3 + x + 1$
17	$x^{17} + x^3 + 1$
18	$x^{18} + x^7 + 1$
19	$x^{19} + x^5 + x^2 + x + 1$
20	$x^{20} + x^3 + 1$
21	$x^{21} + x^2 + 1$
22	$x^{22} + x + 1$
23	$x^{23} + x^5 + 1$
24	$x^{24} + x^7 + x^2 + x + 1$

[a]These polynomials are also primitive (see text).
Source: Shu Lin and Daniel Costello, Jr., *Error Control Coding: Fundamentals and Applications*, ©1983, p. 29. Adapted by permission of Prentice-Hall, Inc., Englewood Cliffs, NJ.

$0, 1, x, x + 1, x^2, x^2 + x, x^2 + 1$, and, lastly, $x^2 + x + 1$. Any polynomial of higher degree over GF(2) reduces to one of these when reduced modulo the prime polynomial $x^3 + x + 1$. In this context, the field GF(q) is called the *base field* and the field GF(q^n) is called an *extension field* of GF(q).

The preceding construction of GF(2^3) from GF(2) is simple because it closely follows our recipe for building a finite field out of a ring. First, the ring elements are generated, and then each ring element is reduced modulo some prime quantity. There is another way of generating the elements of GF(q^n). Recall that a primitive element of a multiplicative group generates all nonzero elements of that group. One can, therefore, generate the nonzero elements of GF(q^n) by forming the $m = q^n - 1$ products, $\alpha^0, \alpha^1, \alpha^2, \ldots, \alpha^m$, of some primitive element α of GF(q^n). This is always possible since every Galois field has at least one primitive element.

There are special prime polynomials $p(x)$ over GF(q), called *primitive polynomials*, which have the property that in the extension field constructed modulo $p(x)$, the element of GF(q^n) represented by x is primitive. Constructing the extension field GF(q^n) from the base field GF(q) is very simple with primitive polynomials. All of the $q^n - 1$ nonzero elements are found by computing successive powers of x and reducing modulo $p(x)$ a primitive polynomial of degree n over GF(q).

All elements of GF(q) belong to a multiplicative group. A cyclic subgroup under multiplication can be formed by multiplying any element α by itself any number of times. Since GF(q) is of finite order, the sequence thus produced must repeat itself after some point. By previous reasoning, we end up with a multiplicative subgroup of order n if $\alpha^n = 1$, and we say that α is a field element of order n. If the order of some element is $q - 1$, then the multiplicative subgroup thus generated covers all nonzero elements of GF(q). Such elements are called *primitive elements*. In GF(q), there is at least one primitive element.

A polynomial over GF(q) can be evaluated not only at every element α of GF(q), but also at every element β of any extension field GF(q^n) of GF(q); all operations are performed in the extension field. This is because GF(q) is contained within GF(q^n). A particularly interesting case is the existence of field elements γ at which $f(\gamma) = 0$, i.e., at which a polynomial vanishes. The field elements for which $f(\gamma) = 0$ are called the *roots* of $f(x)$. Note that for $f(x)$ a polynomial over GF(q), the roots are not necessarily in GF(q), but may be in any extension field GF(q^n) of GF(q). This is not surprising. For example, the real polynomial $x^2 + 1$ has no real roots; its only roots are in the complex field, which is an extension of the real field.

2.1.2 Linear Vector Spaces

A proper discussion of signals begins with a definition of the mathematical structure of the signal spaces over which they are defined. The algebra of linear vector spaces is admirably suited for this. Rather than discussing specific signal spaces at first, we present a more general and abstract discussion because the fundamental algebraic structure of linear vector spaces applies equally well to a number of different vector spaces of practical interest.

The definition of a linear vector space involves the introduction of an abelian group of elements called vectors (**boldface** quantities), and of a set of elements called scalars, which form a field. The vectors satisfy the usual definition of an abelian group. A vector space consists of an abelian group of objects called *vectors* with respect to an operation called addition, and has the following properties:

1. Closure: for any two vectors **x** and **y** in the group, their sum **x** + **y** is also in the group.

2. Associativity: **x** + (**y** + **z**) = (**x** + **y**) + **z**.

3. Commutativity: **x** + **y** = **y** + **x**.

4. Identity: the group contains an element **0** (vector zero) such that **x** + **0** = **x** for any **x** in the group.

5. Additive inverse: for any **x** in the group, there is a unique element (−**x**) such that **x** + (−**x**) = **0**.

These five properties define an additive abelian group. There is also a set of scalars that form a field and an operation called scalar multiplication, such that the following properties hold:

6. Closure: for every scalar a and vector $\mathbf{x}$, there is a vector $a\mathbf{x}$ in the field.

7. Associativity: $a(b\mathbf{x}) = (ab)\mathbf{x} = ab\mathbf{x}$.

8. Identity: there exists a scalar element 1 (scalar one) such that $1\mathbf{x} = \mathbf{x}$ for any $\mathbf{x}$.

9. There is an element 0 (scalar zero) such that $0\mathbf{x} = 0$ for any $\mathbf{x}$ in the space.

10. Distributivity: $a(\mathbf{x} + \mathbf{y}) = a\mathbf{x} + a\mathbf{y}$ and $(a + b)\mathbf{x} = a\mathbf{x} + b\mathbf{x}$.

Properties 6 through 10 also hold when arbitrary scalars a, b, and c are substituted for vectors $\mathbf{x}$, $\mathbf{y}$, and $\mathbf{z}$. Vectors satisfying properties 1 through 10 are said to form a *linear vector space*.

Although we have referred to addition and multiplication, these operations need not represent the usual arithmetic sum and product rules. It happens, however, that in many useful instances, these operations coincide with their arithmetic counterparts. For simplicity, we adopt the usual notation $\mathbf{x} + \mathbf{y}$ for addition and $a \times \mathbf{x}$ or simply $a\mathbf{x}$ for multiplication.

EXAMPLE

The ordinary Euclidian space of geometry provides a good example of a linear vector space with which we are already familiar. Here the scalars are usually taken from the field R of real numbers. The vectors are physical vectors such as position, momentum, etc.

EXAMPLE

Complex functions form a linear vector space, where the scalars are from C. It is sometimes useful to view complex numbers as an ordered pair of real quantities that represent the real and imaginary part. This concept can be extended to include any set of ordered n-tuples, which also form a linear vector space.

EXAMPLE

The set of all polynomials with degree less than or equal to n forms a linear vector space. Here we can view the various terms of a polynomial as the elements of an ordered n-tuples. The order in the n-tuples is maintained by the various powers of the polynomial's independent variable.

EXAMPLE

The set of all n-tuples over GF(q) forms a linear vector space denoted by GF(q)^n. This space has q^n elements and plays an important part in defining the error-control codes to be studied in Chapter 7.

We note here something all vectors have in common. In general, all vectors can be represented as ordered sets of scalars. The previous examples differ only in notation. There are, therefore, two distinguishing features of vectors: the number n of scalars in these ordered n-tuples, and the field over which these scalars are defined. The number of scalars, later to be identified with the dimensionality of the space, can be either finite or infinite. Quite separate from the issue of vector-space dimensionality, the order of the fields from which the scalars are taken can be finite or infinite.

The type of scalar, i.e., the nature of the field from which these scalars are selected, has a profound influence on the nature of the resulting linear vector space. For example, complex scalars from C give rise to linear vector spaces that can be used to represent continuous complex functions and, therefore, can describe modulation waveforms. On the other hand, scalars selected from Galois fields give rise to discrete vectors that can assume only certain quantized values. The corresponding linear vector spaces are useful in describing certain error-control codes used in communication applications.

2.1.3 Linear Independence

A *linear combination* can be obtained by forming a sum of m scaled vectors:

$$\mathbf{y} = \sum_{i=1}^{m} a_i \mathbf{x}_i \tag{2.9}$$

A set of vectors $\{\mathbf{x}_i; i = 1, \ldots, m\}$ is said to be *linearly independent* if their linear combination vanishes (i.e., $\mathbf{y} = \mathbf{0}$) only if every scalar a_i is equal to zero. Linear independence is a collective property of m vectors in a linear vector space. This property implies that it is not possible to express a vector from that collection as a linear combination of the other vectors from that collection.

It can be shown that the set of all linear combinations forms a vector space, which is a *subspace* of the original linear vector space. The real vector space $\mathbf{R}$ is a subspace of the complex space $\mathbf{C}$. Any set of m linearly independent vectors $\{\mathbf{x}_i; i = 1, \ldots, m\}$ forms an m-dimensional subspace $\mathbf{M}$, and forms a *basis* for $\mathbf{M}$. We also say that the basis set forms a *coordinate system* for the linear vector space. Space $\mathbf{M}$ is the set of all possible linear combinations of the basis vectors and is said to be *spanned* by that set of basis vectors. Given a basis vector set $\{\phi_1, \phi_2, \phi_3, \ldots, \phi_m\}$ in some linear vector space, then any vector $\mathbf{x}$ can be written in the form of a linear combination involving some or all of the basis vectors:

$$\mathbf{x} = \sum_{k=1}^{m} a_k \phi_k \tag{2.10}$$

The scalars a_k quantify the composition of $\mathbf{x}$ in terms of the component vectors ϕ_k.

The vector $\mathbf{x}$ may also be expressed as an m-tuple:

$$\mathbf{x} = (x_1, x_2, \ldots, x_m)$$

where x_k is the component of $\mathbf{x}$ along the kth linear vector space coordinate. In general, x_k is not equal to a_k. However, it is always possible to express the x_k in terms of the a_k, and vice versa. This subject will be discussed in more detail in Sections 2.2.3 and 2.2.4.

The dimension of a linear vector space is the number of basis vectors that span the space. If the number of basis vectors in a space is finite, we say the space is *finite-dimensional;* otherwise, it is *infinite-dimensional*. The concept of linear independence can be extended by saying that an infinite number of vectors forms a linearly independent set if every finite subset is linearly independent. Note that a scalar is also a one-dimensional vector.

EXAMPLE

The set of n-tuples

$$(1, 0, 0, \ldots, 0)$$

$$(0, 1, 0, \ldots, 0)$$

$$(0, 0, 1, \ldots, 0)$$

.

.

.

$$(0, 0, 0, \ldots, 1)$$

forms a basis for the space of all real n-tuples. For example,

$$(a_1, a_2, \ldots, a_n) = a_1(1, 0, 0, \ldots, 0) + a_2(0, 1, 0, \ldots, 0)$$

$$+ \cdots + a_n(0, 0, 0, \ldots, 1)$$

EXAMPLE

The set of trigonometric functions $\sin(2\pi nx/L)$ and $\cos(2\pi nx/L)$ where $n = 1, \ldots, \infty$, forms a basis for real functions having convergent Fourier series defined over the interval $[0, L]$. The subspace spanned by these functions has a countably infinite dimension $\aleph_0$ and is denoted by $\mathbf{R}^\infty[0, L]$.

EXAMPLE

The set of complex exponentials $\exp(\pm 2\pi j nx/L)$, $n = 1, \ldots, \infty$, where $j = (-1)^{1/2}$ forms a basis for complex functions having convergent Fourier series defined over the interval $[0, L]$ in the linear complex space $\mathbf{C}^\infty[0, L]$ with dimensionality $\aleph_0$. The Fourier series representation of a periodic function expresses the function in terms of a discrete set of complex exponentials.

EXAMPLE

The set of complex exponentials $\exp(\pm 2\pi j vt)$ forms a basis for square integrable complex functions defined over the interval $(-\infty, \infty)$ in the linear complex space $\mathbf{C}^\infty(-\infty, \infty)$ with dimensionality $\aleph_1$. The Fourier transform representation of a function expresses the function in terms of a continuous set of complex exponentials.

2.1.4 Metrics

It is possible to impart a geometric interpretation to linear vector spaces by formally introducing the concept of "distance" between vectors. The concept of distance in linear vector spaces is fundamental to communication performance. The performance of a communication system depends on the distance between the waveforms used for signaling. These waveforms are simply vectors judiciously chosen from linear vector spaces. In communication theory, we work primarily with two types of linear vector spaces. One consists of continuous functions defined over a field of complex scalars. This vector space gives rise to the continuous waveforms of Chapter 6. The other consists of a subset of the discrete vectors defined over scalars from the finite field $GF(q)$, and yields the code words to be studied in Chapter 7.

    We first introduce the general concept of a metric distance, and then define two special distances: one for use with complex functions, and the other with discrete vectors from $GF(q)^n$, the n-dimensional linear vector space with scalars from $GF(q)$. Although signals from these two spaces look very different, their usefulness in communication is unified by the concept of a metric distance. Later, we will show that a large distance between signaling waveforms leads to good communication performance in the sense of minimizing the probability of receiver decoding errors. This is true regardless of the particular linear vector space from which the waveforms are selected, provided that the selection guarantees a minimum mutual distance between waveforms.

    To define a distance, we need a mapping that associates a unique real scalar d with a pair of vectors $\mathbf{x}$ and $\mathbf{y}$. Such a mapping $d:\{\mathbf{x}, \mathbf{y}\} \rightarrow R$ is a *metric* if it satisfies the following conditions:

1. $d(\mathbf{x}, \mathbf{y}) \geq 0$, with equality holding if and only if $\mathbf{x} = \mathbf{y}$;
2. $d(\mathbf{x}, \mathbf{y}) = d(\mathbf{y}, \mathbf{x})$;
3. $d(\mathbf{x}, \mathbf{z}) \leq d(\mathbf{x}, \mathbf{y}) + d(\mathbf{y}, \mathbf{z})$.

Note that these conditions satisfy the intuitive notion of distance. A metric is nonnegative, symmetric (commutative with respect to its arguments), and also satisfies the triangle inequality.

    A metric that plays an important role in signal theory is the *Euclidian metric*, defined as follows. Consider a pair of vectors $\mathbf{x}$ and $\mathbf{y}$ with scalars from C, expressed in a particular representation by the ordered m-tuples $\mathbf{x} = \{a_k, k = 1, \ldots, m\}$ and $\mathbf{y} = \{b_k, k = 1, \ldots, m\}$. The scalars a_k and b_k are the components of $\mathbf{x}$ and $\mathbf{y}$ with respect to some set of basis vectors. The Euclidian metric is defined by the expression

$$d_0(\mathbf{x}, \mathbf{y}) = \left[\sum_k (a_k - b_k)^2 \right]^{1/2} \tag{2.11}$$

where the sum is over all corresponding m components. When $\mathbf{x}$ and $\mathbf{y}$ are infinite-dimensional vectors, such as the functions $x(t)$ and $y(t)$, an equivalent definition of the Euclidian metric is

$$d_0[x(t), y(t)] = \left[\int [x(t) - y(t)]^2 \, dt \right]^{1/2} \tag{2.12}$$

where the integral is over all values of t.

Several properties of the Euclidian metric are worth emphasizing. First, it is identical with the intuitive concept of distance. This makes possible the visualisation of what would otherwise be an abstract concept. Second, when applied to real or complex waveforms, the square of the Euclidian metric $d_0^2(\mathbf{x}, \mathbf{0})$ between a vector and the origin (i.e., the zero vector) can be recognized as the square of the norm of that vector. Physically, that vector norm is associated with the *energy* or the *variance* of that vector. The Euclidian metric itself, $d_0(\mathbf{x}, \mathbf{y})$, is the root-mean-square error or difference signal between $\mathbf{x}$ and $\mathbf{y}$.

A set of vectors together with a particular metric is called a *metric space*. In a metric space, distance is measured with the particular metric associated with that space.

Code words are a subset of the n-tuples over some field. A collection of such n-tuples that satisfies the axioms of a linear vector space and certain metric properties is called a *linear code* and is a subspace of the metric space.

EXAMPLE

The following sixteen 7-tuples over GF(2) form a linear code. Note that the modulo-2 componentwise addition of any two code words results in another code word.

0 0 0 0 0 0 0	1 0 1 0 0 0 1
1 1 0 1 0 0 0	0 1 1 1 0 0 1
0 1 1 0 1 0 0	1 1 0 0 1 0 1
1 0 1 1 1 0 0	0 0 0 1 1 0 1
1 1 1 0 0 1 0	0 1 0 0 0 1 1
0 0 1 1 0 1 0	1 0 0 1 0 1 1
1 0 0 0 1 1 0	0 0 1 0 1 1 1
0 1 0 1 1 1 0	1 1 1 1 1 1 1

There are $2^7 = 128$ vectors in the space GF(2)^7. The code shown contains 16 elements. These 16 code words were chosen from GF(2)^7 based on a distance measure between all possible pairs of elements in GF(2)^7. The reason for this will be explained in Chapter 7. We must first introduce a metric for the discrete space GF(q)^n.[†]

[†]Do not confuse the notation GF(q^n) for the Galois field with q^n elements with GF(q)^n, the n-dimensional linear vector space over GF(q).

Just as we defined the Euclidian metric for a linear vector space over scalars from C, we now introduce a metric suitable for code words over GF(q). The general form of a vector in a discrete linear vector space is $\mathbf{x} = \{\alpha_1, \alpha_2, \ldots, \alpha_n\}$, where the α_k are scalars from GF(q). Consider two vectors: $\mathbf{x} = \{\alpha_1, \alpha_2, \ldots, \alpha_n\}$ and $\mathbf{y} = \{\beta_1, \beta_2, \ldots, \beta_n\}$ in GF(q)^n. We define a metric for that space by counting (i.e., assigning an element from the set of integers) the number of positions where corresponding scalars differ. That is, we compare α_k and β_k for all k running from 1 to n, and tally all instances where $\alpha_k \neq \beta_k$. Equivalently, we form the vector $\mathbf{z} = \{\gamma_1, \gamma_2, \ldots, \gamma_n\}$, where γ_k is 1 if $\alpha_k \neq \beta_k$, and 0 otherwise. The distance between $\mathbf{x}$ and $\mathbf{y}$ is then simply the *weight* of vector $\mathbf{z}$, where weight is defined as the total number of nonzero elements in the vector.

This may appear to be an imprecise way of defining a metric because distance is not a function of the particular values of the α_k and β_k. However crude the measure is, it can be verified that all of the properties of a metric are nonetheless satisfied.

The simplest example of such a metric is the *Hamming metric* in GF(q)^n, the linear vector spaces of n-tuples of scalars from GF(q). The Hamming metric is defined as the number of corresponding places in which two n-tuples differ. To compute the Hamming metric, one simply compares two vectors, $\mathbf{x}$ and $\mathbf{y}$, and counts the number of positions in which they differ. Over GF(2), the Hamming metric is simply

$$d_H(\mathbf{x}, \mathbf{y}) = \sum_{k=1}^{n} (a_k - b_k) \qquad (2.13)$$

where $\mathbf{x} = (a_1, a_2, \ldots, a_n)$, $\mathbf{y} = (b_1, b_2, \ldots, b_n)$, and subtraction is performed modulo 2. Note that in arithmetic modulo 2, addition and subtraction give the same result.

EXAMPLE

The Hamming metric between (1, 0, 1, 1, 0, 1) and (1, 0, 0, 1, 1, 0) is 3, since these two 6-tuples differ in three positions, namely, the third, fifth, and sixth.

EXAMPLE

The two 9-tuples $\{1\ 0\ 1\ 1\ 0\ 0\ 0\ 0\ 1\}$ and $\{1\ 0\ 0\ 1\ 0\ 1\ 1\ 0\ 1\}$ differ in the third, sixth, and seventh places. The Hamming distance between these two vectors is therefore 3. Alternatively, we can compute the difference vector

$$\{1\ 0\ 1\ 1\ 0\ 0\ 0\ 0\ 1\} - \{1\ 0\ 0\ 1\ 0\ 1\ 1\ 0\ 1\} = \{0\ 0\ 1\ 0\ 1\ 0\ 1\ 0\ 0\}$$

and note that the weight of the resulting vector is 3.

The Hamming metric can take on all possible integer values from the set $\{0, 1, 2, \ldots, n\}$ and is a mapping $d:\{\mathbf{x}, \mathbf{y}\} \to Z$ onto the set of nonnegative integers, which is a subset of R.

Closely associated with the concept of a metric is the *norm* of a vector. The norm of a vector $\mathbf{x}$ is denoted by $\|\mathbf{x}\|$ and satisfies the following properties:

1. $\|\mathbf{x}\| \geq 0$, with $\|\mathbf{x}\| = 0$ iff $\mathbf{x} = \mathbf{0}$;

2. $\|\mathbf{x} + \mathbf{y}\| \leq \|\mathbf{x}\| + \|\mathbf{y}\|$ (triangle inequality);

3. $\|\alpha\mathbf{x}\| = |\alpha| \|\mathbf{x}\|$ for any scalar α.

The norm is a measure of the "size" of a vector and maps vectors into R. To see this, we verify that $d(\mathbf{x}, \mathbf{y}) = \|\mathbf{x} - \mathbf{y}\|$ satisfies the properties of a metric, since

a. $\|\mathbf{x} - \mathbf{y}\| \geq 0$ with $\|\mathbf{x} - \mathbf{y}\| = 0$ iff $\mathbf{x} = \mathbf{y}$;

b. $\|\mathbf{x} - \mathbf{y}\| = \|(-1)(\mathbf{y} - \mathbf{x})\| = |-1| \|\mathbf{y} - \mathbf{x}\| = \|\mathbf{y} - \mathbf{x}\|$;

c. $\|\mathbf{a} + \mathbf{b}\| \leq \|\mathbf{a}\| + \|\mathbf{b}\|$ from the triangle inequality. Now let $\mathbf{a} = \mathbf{x} - \mathbf{y}$ and also let $\mathbf{b} = \mathbf{y} - \mathbf{z}$. Then,

$$\|\mathbf{a} + \mathbf{b}\| = \|\mathbf{x} - \mathbf{y} + \mathbf{y} - \mathbf{z}\| = \|\mathbf{x} - \mathbf{z}\|, \text{ and}$$

$$\|\mathbf{x} - \mathbf{z}\| = \|\mathbf{a} - \mathbf{b}\| \leq \|\mathbf{a}\| + \|\mathbf{b}\|,$$

$$\|\mathbf{x} - \mathbf{z}\| \leq \|\mathbf{x} - \mathbf{y}\| + \|\mathbf{y} - \mathbf{z}\|.$$

The quantity $d(\mathbf{x}, \mathbf{y}) = \|\mathbf{x} - \mathbf{y}\|$, therefore, behaves like a metric that measures the distance between $\mathbf{x}$ and $\mathbf{y}$. In particular, $\|\mathbf{x}\|$ is the distance between the vector $\mathbf{x}$ and the vector $\mathbf{0}$ (i.e., the origin), and we can consider $\|\mathbf{x}\|$ to be a measure of the size of $\mathbf{x}$.

The previous discussion is very general and does not depend on the particular type of metric chosen. It is however instructive to consider the norm of $\mathbf{x}$ expressed in terms of the Euclidian metric. Specifically, the square of the Euclidian norm of a function $x(t)$ is given by

$$\|x(t)\|^2 = \int_{-\infty}^{\infty} x^2(t) \, dt \tag{2.14}$$

which is immediately recognized as the energy $\mathcal{E}$ in the waveform $x(t)$. The equivalence between the square of the norm and waveform energy is a very useful relation in the mathematical theory of communication.

The Euclidian metric, or, equivalently, its square, plays a central role in many applications in communications and signal processing. It is introduced here in a formal way and is a concept that will be revisited throughout the book. It is an easily computable quantity that can conveniently be used to characterize a set of vectors.

In our study of communication, we shall find it useful to represent a vector $\mathbf{x}$ sometimes as an n-tuple and sometimes as a continuous function $x(t)$ of an independent variable. Which notation is used is often a matter of convenience, since, as we shall see, many functions $x(t)$ encountered in communication can also be expressed as an ordered set of scalars. Whichever notation is used, we shall always be dealing with metric spaces, although not always defined with respect to the same metric. We shall find that although we can represent various communication signals as different vectors in spaces endowed with dissimilar metrics, the performance of communication systems does not depend on the details of a particular metric space or the peculiarities of vectors described in that space. Rather, the fundamental nature of communication performance can be viewed as a property of the algebraic structure of such metric spaces in general. As special cases, we shall study the performance of signaling waveforms in linear vector spaces defined over fields of complex elements in Chapter 6 and of coding signals defined in code-word spaces based on Galois fields in Chapter 7.

For metric spaces defined over the fields C of complex scalars, we will concentrate on a particular linear vector space in our study of signals. This space will be formally introduced in the following section. To prepare for this definition, we must first develop some preliminary concepts.

A sequence of elements $\{x_1, x_2, x_3, \ldots, \}$ is said to *converge* to the value x if there exists a numbering index n_0 for which $d(x_n, x) < \epsilon$ for all $n \geq n_0$ and for any $\epsilon > 0$. In other words, there exists an index n_0 past which all elements x_n of the sequence are arbitrarily close, in the metric sense, to x. Such a convergent sequence is called a *Cauchy* sequence. Note that whether a sequence is Cauchy or not depends on the definition of the metric. Although we can use the Euclidian metric, Cauchy sequences exist for other choices of the metric. Metric spaces in which every Cauchy sequence converges to an element of the space are called *complete* metric spaces. Signal spaces defined over the fields R or C are complete metric spaces.

2.1.5 Inner Products

Consider a linear vector space defined over a field of complex scalars. We now introduce a new operation between vectors that maps a pair of vectors into the field of complex scalars. We shall call this mapping an *inner product* and denote it between $\mathbf{x}$ and $\mathbf{y}$ as $\langle \mathbf{x}|\mathbf{y} \rangle$ over the field C of complex numbers. Inner products are extremely useful for doing manipulations in signal space. When working with continuous functions, we shall use the equivalent notation $\langle x(t)|y(t) \rangle$ or, simply, $\langle x|y \rangle$. One can define an inner product $\langle \mathbf{x}|\mathbf{y} \rangle$ between any two vectors as follows. The inner product is a linear operation that provides a mapping from two vectors to a scalar from C. The inner product has the following properties:

1. $\langle \mathbf{x}|\mathbf{y} \rangle = \langle \mathbf{y}|\mathbf{x} \rangle^*$,

2. $\langle \mathbf{z}|a\mathbf{x} + b\mathbf{y} \rangle = a\langle \mathbf{z}|\mathbf{x} \rangle + b\langle \mathbf{z}|\mathbf{y} \rangle$,

3. $\langle \mathbf{x}|\mathbf{x} \rangle \geq 0$, with equality holding if and only if $\mathbf{x} = \mathbf{0}$,

4. $\langle a\mathbf{x}|\mathbf{y} \rangle = a^*\langle \mathbf{x}|\mathbf{y} \rangle$,

where the asterisk (*) denotes complex conjugation. Note that the inner product between two vectors is not, in general, commutative.

This notation for inner product was introduced by P. A. M. Dirac for the pre- and postfactors of an inner product, and finds application, for example, in quantum mechanics, where linear vector-space concepts are used extensively [Me 70, Sc 68] and where an efficient notation is essential. This notation is based on the noncommutativity of the inner product, since, in general,

$$\langle \mathbf{x} | \mathbf{y} \rangle \neq \langle \mathbf{y} | \mathbf{x} \rangle \tag{2.15}$$

where, for example,

$$\langle \mathbf{x} | \mathbf{y} \rangle = \int_{-\infty}^{\infty} x^*(t) y(t) \, dt \tag{2.16}$$

although the absolute value of these products is the same. Rule 2 shows that the inner product is linear with respect to the postfactor, but rule 4 shows that it is not, in general, linear with respect to the prefactor. We say that the inner product depends on the prefactor in an *antilinear* fashion. To avoid the apparent asymmetry, we think of the pre- and postfactors as being from two separate spaces, with each space being linear in itself but related to the other space in an antilinear way. These two spaces are not independent and are said to be *dual* to each other.

EXAMPLE

The most familiar example of an inner product is the dot product of vector analysis. In this case, we can represent a vector over the field of real numbers by an ordered *n*-tuple such as $\mathbf{x} = \{x_1, x_2, \ldots, x_n\}$ and $\mathbf{y} = \{y_1, y_2, \ldots, y_n\}$. The dot product between two such vectors is simply the scalar defined by

$$\mathbf{x} \cdot \mathbf{y} = x_1 y_1 + x_2 y_2 + \ldots + x_n y_n$$

EXAMPLE

An often encountered form of the inner product consists of operations of the form

$$\int_0^L f(x) \sin(2\pi n x/L) \, dx \qquad \text{and} \qquad \int_0^L f(x) \cos(2\pi n x/L) \, dx$$

where $f(x)$ is an arbitrary continuous function over $[0, L]$. The trigonometric functions $\sin(2\pi n x/L)$ and $\cos(2\pi n x/L)$ for $n = 0, 1, 2, \ldots$ form a basis over $[0, L]$ and the previous scalars can be thought of as representing projections of $f(x)$ over that basis. The resulting scalars can be thought of as being the scalar components of the vector $f(x)$. For functions that vanish outside the closed interval $[0, L]$ or that are periodic with period L, the previous inner products are the familiar Fourier coefficients of $f(x)$. In general, there is a countably infinite ($\aleph_0$) number of such scalars.

Note that the square root of the inner product $\langle \mathbf{x} | \mathbf{x} \rangle^{1/2}$ satisfies all of the properties of a norm. The inner product is, therefore, a norm. That is, we can define a norm by the inner product

$$\|\mathbf{x}\| = \langle \mathbf{x} | \mathbf{x} \rangle^{1/2} \tag{2.17}$$

The square root of the inner product $\langle(\mathbf{x}-\mathbf{y})|(\mathbf{x}-\mathbf{y})\rangle^{1/2}$ can, therefore, be used as a metric. A space where the inner product is used in this manner to define a metric is called an *inner-product space*. A complete inner-product space, i.e., one in which every Cauchy sequence converges, is called a *Hilbert space*.

We now introduce the extremely useful concept of orthogonality. Two vectors $\mathbf{x}$ and $\mathbf{y}$ are said to be *orthogonal* if their inner product vanishes, i.e., if $\langle\mathbf{x}|\mathbf{y}\rangle = 0$. Orthogonality has a familiar interpretation when applied to vectors such as force, velocity, displacement, etc. In these cases, we visualize orthogonal vectors as being perpendicular to one another. Equivalently, one can say that the projection of one vector onto another vanishes. The concept of orthogonality, however, is very general and can be applied in any vector space.

Although the only requirement of a set of basis vectors is that they be linearly independent, a particularly useful basis results when the basis vectors are mutually orthogonal, i.e., when $\langle\boldsymbol{\varphi}_k|\boldsymbol{\varphi}_m\rangle = 0$ for any $k \neq m$ in the set. In general, we then have

$$\langle\boldsymbol{\varphi}_k|\boldsymbol{\varphi}_m\rangle = \alpha_{km}\,\delta_{k,m} \tag{2.18}$$

where $\alpha_{km} = \alpha_{mk}$ is a real scalar that is symmetrical with respect to the value of the indices k and m, and where $\delta_{k,m}$ is the Kronecker delta, which is defined by

$$\delta_{k,m} = 1 \text{ when } k = m, \text{ and is zero otherwise}$$

When $\alpha_{kk} = 1$ for all k, we say that the basis is *orthonormal*, since the basis vectors are all normalized to unity. It is always possible to form an orthogonal set from a linearly independent set by a procedure known as Schmidt orthogonalization [Ar 85, Tr 76]. The orthogonal vectors thus obtained may then be normalized individually to form an orthonormal basis. One of the benefits of using orthonormal bases is that it is very easy to obtain the expansion coefficients for a vector expressed in terms of that basis. Consider a vector $\mathbf{x}$ written in terms of an orthonormal basis expansion:

$$\mathbf{x} = \sum_k a_k\boldsymbol{\varphi}_k \tag{2.19}$$

The expansion coefficient a_k can be obtained by taking the inner product $\langle\boldsymbol{\varphi}_m|\cdot\rangle$ of $\boldsymbol{\varphi}_m$ with each side of the last equation. Specifically, we can explicitly write the expansion as

$$\langle\boldsymbol{\varphi}_m|\mathbf{x}\rangle = \sum_k a_k\,\langle\boldsymbol{\varphi}_m|\boldsymbol{\varphi}_k\rangle = \sum_k a_k\delta_{k,m} = a_m \tag{2.20}$$

The simplification results from the collapse of the last summation due to the presence of the Kronecker delta. The geometric interpretation is that the coefficient a_m is simply the orthogonal projection of $\mathbf{x}$ onto the basis vector $\boldsymbol{\varphi}_m$. Without an orthogonal basis set, these coefficients must be obtained by solving the set of coupled linear equations:

$$\langle\boldsymbol{\varphi}_m|\mathbf{x}\rangle = \sum_k a_k\langle\boldsymbol{\varphi}_m|\boldsymbol{\varphi}_k\rangle \tag{2.21}$$

where the a_k are unknowns, and the inner products $\langle \varphi_m | \varphi_k \rangle$ are known constants. Note from this expression that $\mathbf{x}$ and the basis set $\{\varphi_k\}$ are from the same linear vector space $\mathbf{X}$. This linear combination defines a representation for $\mathbf{x}$ in terms of an n-tuple of coefficients $\{a_k\}$, where n is the dimension of the space spanned by the basis $\{\varphi_k\}$. The set of all n-tuples $\{a_k\}$ itself forms a linear vector space over the scalars of $\mathbf{X}$. For example, for vectors $\mathbf{x}$ defined in Hilbert space, the coefficients are, in general, complex and form n-tuples of complex scalars.

An important relation involving norms and inner products is the Schwarz inequality:

$$|\langle \mathbf{x} | \mathbf{y} \rangle|^2 \leq \langle \mathbf{x} | \mathbf{x} \rangle \langle \mathbf{y} | \mathbf{y} \rangle \tag{2.22}$$

where equality obtains only if $\mathbf{x}$ and $\mathbf{y}$ are colinear, i.e., if $\mathbf{x} = a\mathbf{y}$, where a is a scalar in the field [Ar 85, Tr 76]. The Schwarz inequality is an extremely useful identity in signal analysis. When $\mathbf{x}$ and $\mathbf{y}$ represent the functions $x(t)$ and $y(t)$, respectively, the Schwarz inequality takes the more familiar form:

$$\left[\int x^*(t) y(t) \, dt \right]^2 \leq \int x^*(t) x(t) \, dt \int y^*(t) y(t) \, dt \tag{2.23}$$

where the integrals run over the domain of $x(t)$ and $y(t)$.

Let both $\mathbf{x}$ and $\mathbf{y}$ be vectors from a linear vector space $\mathbf{H}$. When an orthonormal basis set is used for their representation, there results an equality between inner products in $\mathbf{H}$ and in $\mathbf{C}$. Expressing both $\mathbf{x}$ and $\mathbf{y}$ in terms of some orthonormal basis in $\mathbf{H}$, we have

$$\mathbf{x} = \sum_k a_k \varphi_k \qquad \text{and} \qquad \mathbf{y} = \sum_k b_k \varphi_k \tag{2.24}$$

Taking the inner product between $\mathbf{x}$ and $\mathbf{y}$, we have

$$\langle \mathbf{x} | \mathbf{y} \rangle = \sum_{k,m} a_k^* b_m \langle \varphi_k | \varphi_m \rangle = \sum_k a_k^* b_k \tag{2.25}$$

With the Euclidian metric, there is also an equality of distance in the two spaces. The square of the distance between $\mathbf{x}$ and $\mathbf{y}$ can be written as

$$d^2(\mathbf{x}, \mathbf{y}) = \|\mathbf{x} - \mathbf{y}\|^2 = \langle \mathbf{x} - \mathbf{y} | \mathbf{x} - \mathbf{y} \rangle = \sum_k (a_k - b_k)^2 = d^2(\mathbf{a}, \mathbf{b}) \tag{2.26}$$

where $\mathbf{a} = (a_1, a_2, \ldots, a_n)$ and $\mathbf{b} = (b_1, b_2, \ldots, b_n)$ are n-tuple representations of the vectors $\mathbf{a}$ and $\mathbf{b}$, respectively. We can represent continuous time signals as vectors in linear vector spaces of ordered n-tuples and still maintain the concept of distance.

EXAMPLE

The equality of corresponding inner products

$$\langle \mathbf{x} | \mathbf{y} \rangle = \sum_k a_k^* b_k \tag{2.27}$$

where $\{a_k\}$ and $\{b_k\}$ are the projections of $\mathbf{x}$ and $\mathbf{y}$, respectively, onto an orthonormal basis, is sometimes known by a different name in Fourier analysis. Fourier analysis provides a representation of functions $f(t)$ with respect to the basis of complex exponentials $e^{-2\pi j \nu t}$ over the field C. For example, function $f(t)$ and its Fourier transform

$$F(\nu) = \int_{-\infty}^{\infty} f(t) e^{-2\pi j \nu t} \, dt$$

satisfy a relation known as Raleigh's theorem:

$$\int_{-\infty}^{\infty} f^*(t) f(t) \, dt = \int_{-\infty}^{\infty} F^*(\nu) F(\nu) \, d\nu$$

over the field C of complex scalars. A similar relation for Fourier series goes by the name of Parseval's theorem.

The inner product between two vectors can be used to define a measure of distance. This fact finds important applications in the processing of signals for detection, since, as will be discussed in later chapters, detection is fundamentally a comparison of distances in some signal space. Often, these distances are not measured directly, but can be inferred by evaluating inner products. Consider again two vectors $\mathbf{x}$ and $\mathbf{y}$ in some linear vector space $\mathbf{X}$. The square of the distance between them can be written as

$$
\begin{aligned}
d^2(\mathbf{x}, \mathbf{y}) &= \|\mathbf{x} - \mathbf{y}\|^2 = \langle \mathbf{x} - \mathbf{y} | \mathbf{x} - \mathbf{y} \rangle \\
&= \langle \mathbf{x}|\mathbf{x} \rangle + \langle \mathbf{y}|\mathbf{y} \rangle - \langle \mathbf{x}|\mathbf{y} \rangle - \langle \mathbf{y}|\mathbf{x} \rangle \\
&= \langle \mathbf{x}|\mathbf{x} \rangle + \langle \mathbf{y}|\mathbf{y} \rangle - \langle \mathbf{x}|\mathbf{y} \rangle - \langle \mathbf{x}|\mathbf{y} \rangle^* \\
&= \|\mathbf{x}\|^2 + \|\mathbf{y}\|^2 - 2 \mathcal{R}e \langle \mathbf{x}|\mathbf{y} \rangle.
\end{aligned}
\tag{2.28}
$$

If distances are to be computed between vectors $\mathbf{x}$ and $\mathbf{y}$ such that the sum of the squares of the norms $\|\mathbf{x}\|^2 + \|\mathbf{y}\|^2$ is a constant, then the quantity $\mathcal{R}e\langle \mathbf{x}|\mathbf{y} \rangle$ can be used as an indication of distance between $\mathbf{x}$ and $\mathbf{y}$. This situation arises often when $\mathbf{x}$ is a fixed reference waveform and distances are to be computed between $\mathbf{x}$ and several other vectors $\mathbf{u}$, $\mathbf{v}$, $\mathbf{w}$, etc. having equal norms, i.e., where $\|\mathbf{u}\|^2 = \|\mathbf{v}\|^2 = \|\mathbf{w}\|^2$, etc.

Note that the inner product by itself cannot be used as a measure of distance because metrics and norms are defined as mappings over the field R of real numbers. An inner product is a mapping over the field C of complex numbers. The inner product $\langle \mathbf{x}|\mathbf{y} \rangle$ is a complex number whose real part can, according to Eq. (2.28), be used to measure distance.

Large values of $\mathcal{R}e\langle \mathbf{x}|\mathbf{y} \rangle$ correspond to small values of $d(\mathbf{x}, \mathbf{y})$, and vice versa. The inner product $\langle \mathbf{x}|\mathbf{y} \rangle$ is simply a zero-lag correlation, as can be seen when $\mathbf{x}$ and $\mathbf{y}$ represent the functions $x(t)$ and $y(t)$, respectively:

$$\langle \mathbf{x}|\mathbf{y} \rangle = \langle x(t)|y(t) \rangle = \int_{-\infty}^{\infty} x^*(t) y(t) \, dt \tag{2.29}$$

EXAMPLE

Consider two n-tuples $\mathbf{x}$ and $\mathbf{y}$ over GF(2). For example, these could be represented as

$$\mathbf{x} = (x_1, x_2, \ldots, x_k, \ldots, x_n)$$

and

$$\mathbf{y} = (y_1, y_2, \ldots, y_k, \ldots, y_n)$$

with $x_k, y_k \in \{0, 1\}$. These two n-dimensional vectors consist of

n_1 places in which x_k and y_k are both "1",
n_2 places in which x_k and y_k are both "0", and
n_3 places in which they differ,

with $n_1 + n_2 + n_3 = n$. The Hamming distance $d_H(\mathbf{x}, \mathbf{y})$ between $\mathbf{x}$ and $\mathbf{y}$ is simply the number of places in which $\mathbf{x}$ and $\mathbf{y}$ differ, i.e.,

$$d_H(\mathbf{x}, \mathbf{y}) = n_3 = n - n_1 - n_2$$

The correlation between two binary sequences is usually defined as

$$\rho(\mathbf{x}, \mathbf{y}) = \frac{\text{number of like places} - \text{number of unlike places}}{\text{total number of places}} = \frac{n_1 + n_2 - n_3}{n}$$

$$= 1 - 2\frac{n_3}{n} = 1 - \frac{2}{n}d_H(\mathbf{x}, \mathbf{y})$$

or

$$d_H(\mathbf{x}, \mathbf{y}) = \frac{n}{2}[1 - \rho(\mathbf{x}, \mathbf{y})] \tag{2.30}$$

Large positive correlations are associated with small metric distances, and large negative correlations are associated with large metric distances.

EXAMPLE

We have already shown that

$$d^2(\mathbf{x}, \mathbf{y}) = \|\mathbf{x}\|^2 + \|\mathbf{y}\|^2 - 2\,\mathcal{R}e\,\langle \mathbf{x}|\mathbf{y}\rangle \tag{2.31}$$

This suggests implementing metric measurements with an algorithm that calculates the correlation $\langle \mathbf{x}|\mathbf{y}\rangle$ for vectors having constant norm. This is precisely the approach followed in the implementation of certain optimal receivers, as will be studied in Chapters 5 and 6.

2.2 SIGNAL REPRESENTATIONS

2.2.1 Decomposition into Orthogonal Subspaces

We say that a space is spanned by n linearly independent basis vectors when any vector in the space can be expressed as a linear combination of the basis vectors. Another way of saying the same thing is that the vector space contains all possible linear combinations of the n basis vectors. The number of vectors in a linear vector space depends on the type of scalar field over which the field is constructed. In an infinite-dimensional space, it is immediately clear that an infinite number of vectors is possible. Most of our work will be limited to finite-dimensional linear vector spaces. Unless otherwise specified, a finite vector-space dimensionality is assumed in all that follows.

EXAMPLE

In a space with n dimensions with the basis $\{\varphi_1, \varphi_2, \ldots, \varphi_n\}$ and with scalars from the complex field C, a typical vector $\mathbf{x}$ can be written as

$$\mathbf{x} = \sum_{k=1}^{n} a_k \varphi_k \tag{2.32}$$

where the a_k are from C. Since there are infinitely many such scalars in C, an infinite number of vectors $\mathbf{x}$ can be constructed with respect to a fixed basis by substitution of all possible scalar values from C for the a_k.

By contrast, an n-dimensional linear vector space built on scalars from the Galois field $GF(q)$ can only have q^n elements, which accounts for all possible combinations of n vector components, each weighted by any one of a possible number q of scalars from the finite field.

Now consider an arbitrary n-dimensional linear vector space, which we denote by $\mathbf{X}(n)$, and a subspace $\mathbf{X}(m)$ of $\mathbf{X}(n)$ with $m < n$. The space of all vectors that are orthogonal to each vector of $\mathbf{X}(m)$ is called the *orthogonal complement* of $\mathbf{X}(m)$, and is denoted by $\mathbf{X}\perp (m)$. The dimension of $\mathbf{X}\perp (m)$ is $n - m$, and any vector from $\mathbf{X}(n)$ can be expressed as the sum of two vectors, one in $\mathbf{X}(m)$ and one in $\mathbf{X}\perp (m)$. It is clear that $\mathbf{X}(m)$ and $\mathbf{X}\perp (m)$ are each other's orthogonal complement, and that $\mathbf{X}\perp\perp (m) = \mathbf{X}(m)$. In this way, a linear vector space $\mathbf{X}(n)$ can be expressed as a *direct sum* of a subspace and its orthogonal complement. This is usually denoted by

$$\mathbf{X}(n) = \mathbf{X}(m) \oplus \mathbf{X}\perp (m) \tag{2.33}$$

In general, a number of subspaces can be mutually orthogonal, so that a linear vector space can be decomposed into a direct sum:

$$\mathbf{X}(n) = \mathbf{X}(p) \oplus \mathbf{X}(q) \oplus \ldots \oplus \mathbf{X}(r) \tag{2.34}$$

where $n = p + q + \ldots + r$. An easy way to form such a decomposition of $\mathbf{X}(n)$ into a direct sum over orthogonal complement subspaces is to start with the n orthogonal basis vectors of $\mathbf{X}(n)$ and selecting from these, without replacement, using p of these for a basis for $\mathbf{X}(p)$, q for a basis for $\mathbf{X}(q)$, and so on. This will result in mutually orthogonal subspaces $\mathbf{X}(p), \mathbf{X}(q), \ldots, \mathbf{X}(r)$ of $\mathbf{X}(n)$.

To motivate the reader's interest in the abstract concept of orthogonal complements, we briefly mention the context in which it occurs in signal analysis. All physical systems exhibit noise, which requires an infinite-dimensional linear vector space for its representation. However, communication signals are finite-dimensional. It is, therefore, useful to partition the noise-representation space into a signal subspace and its orthogonal complement. One of the limitations of physical instruments, including communication systems, is that they can represent signals only over a limited set of basis functions. Typically, a physical measurement yields information of a particular signal over a finite-dimensional subspace. It is therefore important to be able to describe such signals and to develop techniques for optimizing a system given that one has only access to a limited number of space dimensions.

Any vector may be represented by an n-tuple of its projections[†] onto a set of n basis vectors. Thus, the vector

$$\mathbf{x} = \sum_{k=1}^{n} a_k \boldsymbol{\varphi}_k$$

represented with respect to the basis set $\{\boldsymbol{\varphi}_1, \boldsymbol{\varphi}_2, \ldots, \boldsymbol{\varphi}_n\}$ could just as well have been described by the set of coefficients $\{a_1, a_2, \ldots, a_n\}$. Note that the values of these coefficients change with a change of basis. We assume that a particular basis set has been selected and that the expansion coefficients are taken with respect to that basis. Many equivalent choices are possible for a basis.

The next construct to be introduced in this section is that of a *direct product* between two vector spaces. Consider two different linear vectors spaces $\mathbf{X}(n)$ and $\mathbf{Y}(m)$ sharing a common field of scalars. A typical vector $\mathbf{x}$ of $\mathbf{X}(n)$ can be represented by the set $\{a_1, a_2, \ldots, a_n\}$ of expansion coefficients with respect to the basis set $\{\boldsymbol{\varphi}_1, \boldsymbol{\varphi}_2, \ldots, \boldsymbol{\varphi}_n\}$. Similarly, a vector $\mathbf{y}$ of $\mathbf{Y}(m)$ can be represented by the set $\{b_1, b_2, \ldots, b_m\}$ of expansion coefficients with respect to the basis set $\{\psi_1, \psi_2, \ldots, \psi_m\}$. One can form a new vector $\mathbf{z}$ that is represented by the set $\{a_1, a_2, \ldots, a_n, b_1, b_2, \ldots, b_m\}$. Sometimes $\mathbf{z}$ is written in the shortened notation $\mathbf{z} = \mathbf{xy}$. Clearly, $\mathbf{z}$ belongs to a linear vector space $\mathbf{Z}(n + m)$ of dimension $n + m$. We call this space the *direct product space* of $\mathbf{X}$ and $\mathbf{Y}$.

2.2.2 The Projection Theorem

In a Hilbert space $\mathbf{H}$, any complex function f can be represented exactly by the complex scalars $\{a_k; k = 1, 2, \ldots\}$, which are the expansion coefficients with respect to a basis $\{\psi_1, \psi_2, \ldots\}$[‡]:

$$f = \sum_k a_k \psi_k \qquad (2.35)$$

[†]The term *projection* implies an orthogonal basis, with $a_k = \langle \mathbf{x}|\varphi_k \rangle / \langle \varphi_k|\varphi_k \rangle$ interpreted in the geometric sense of a projection of $\mathbf{x}$ onto the vector φ_k. If the basis is not orthogonal, an n-tuple of coefficients can still be used to represent $\mathbf{x}$, but now the a_k are solutions to a set of linear equations and cannot be interpreted as projections. The coefficients a_k can always be called *expansion coefficients*, referring to the linear combination in terms of the basis functions; when the basis functions are orthogonal, the quantities a_k can also be interpreted as projections. Because of their convenience, orthonormal bases are often preferred.

[‡] We omit here our usual notation of using **boldface** characters to denote vectors from some linear vector space. Complex functions are vectors from Hilbert space. However, no ambiguity results from using roman type to denote vectors from a Hilbert space. We shall also, henceforth, refer to vectors from a Hilbert space simply as functions.

An important problem is that of finding an approximation $\tilde{f}$ to f over a subspace $\mathbf{M}$ of $\mathbf{H}$ with a finite number m of dimensions. Clearly, the function f cannot, in general, be represented exactly in $\mathbf{M}$, so that a strategy for finding the "best" approximation must be used. This strategy is very simple. Of all the functions in $\mathbf{M}$, we select that function $\tilde{f}$ that is closest, in the metric sense, to f. The best approximation to f is defined as the function $\tilde{f}$ that is closest to f in Hilbert space. Note that since we are in Hilbert space, the metric we use must be defined in terms of an inner product: $d^2(f, g) = \langle (f - g) | (f - g) \rangle$.

Of course, the approximation $\tilde{f}$ for f could, in principle, be obtained by substituting all possible functions g belonging to $\mathbf{M}$ in the inner product $\langle (f - g) | (f - g) \rangle$, keeping the function that minimizes that expression. There is, however, a theorem that can save us a lot of work.

The approximation $\tilde{f}$ can be written as a linear combination over a basis set that spans $\mathbf{M}$:

$$\tilde{f} = \sum_{k=1}^{m} a_k \phi_k \tag{2.36}$$

We can define an error function $e = f - \tilde{f}$ so that e^2 is the square of the distance between the functions f and $\tilde{f}$:

$$e^2 = d^2(f, \tilde{f}) = \langle (f - \tilde{f}) | (f - \tilde{f}) \rangle \tag{2.37}$$

Now require that $\tilde{f}$ be given by the $\{a_k\}$ that minimize e. We therefore set the m derivatives of e^2 with respect to the a_k to zero:

$$\frac{\partial e^2}{\partial a_k} = 0 \quad \text{for} \quad k = 1, 2, \ldots, m$$

This immediately leads to the expression

$$\langle f - \tilde{f} | \varphi_k \rangle = 0 \quad \text{for} \quad k = 1, 2, \ldots, m \tag{2.38}$$

There are two interesting interpretations of this result. The last expression can be written as

$$\langle f | \varphi_k \rangle = \langle \tilde{f} | \varphi_k \rangle \quad \text{for} \quad k = 1, 2, \ldots, m \tag{2.39}$$

For an orthonormal basis set $\{\varphi_1, \varphi_2, \ldots, \varphi_m\}$, the inner products $\langle \tilde{f} | \varphi_k \rangle$ are simply the expansion coefficients a_k, and these are simply obtained by projecting f onto the set $\{\varphi_1, \varphi_2, \ldots, \varphi_m\}$. As an algorithm, this is much simpler than finding $\tilde{f}$ by substituting all functions g of $\mathbf{M}$ in the distance measure $\langle (f - g) | (f - g) \rangle$.

The other interpretation, useful in providing insight in the derivation of some analytical results, is that the best approximation $\tilde{f}$ to f is that which causes the error function $f - \tilde{f}$ to be orthogonal to the φ_k. This result is true whether or not the basis is orthogonal, and is known as the projection theorem:

Theorem. For any function f in a Hilbert space $\mathbf{H}$, there is a unique function $\tilde{f}$ in $\mathbf{M}$, where $\mathbf{M}$ is a complete subspace of $\mathbf{H}$, such that $\|f - \tilde{f}\| \leq \|f - g\|$ for any function g in $\mathbf{M}$. Furthermore, $f - \tilde{f}$ is orthogonal to all functions in $\mathbf{M}$.

The projection theorem gives us a way of finding the best (i.e., minimum-squared-error norm) representation of f in $\mathbf{H}$ with vectors from $\mathbf{M}$. A proof of the projection theorem appears in [Fr 69] and also in [Tr 76].

EXAMPLE

The problem of finding a best approximation to a function f can always be approached by solving for the expansion coefficients a_k that cause the norm of the error function

$$e = f - \sum_k a_k \varphi_k$$

to be a minimum. The functions φ_k are usually chosen for mathematical convenience or to simplify the calculations. For example, the φ_k may span a subspace that corresponds to certain experimental measurements or they may be chosen for their simple analytic form.

Fourier representation automatically provides the best (minimum error norm) linear estimate. Here the set φ_k consists of the complex exponentials over C. This infinite set can be used to represent any continuous square-integrable complex function. When only a finite set is used, the projection theorem guarantees that the best a_k are given by the inner products $\langle f | \varphi_k \rangle$.

Let us generalize this by exploring a very interesting property of representations with respect to an orthogonal basis. Let $f(x)$ be some square-integrable function defined in an (infinite-dimensional) Hilbert space. The function $f(x)$ has the following representation with respect to the orthonormal basis set $\{\varphi_1(x), \varphi_2(x), \ldots\}$

$$f(x) = \sum_{k=1}^{\infty} \alpha_k \varphi_k(x) \qquad \text{where} \qquad \alpha_k = \int_{-\infty}^{\infty} \varphi_k^*(x) f(x)\, dx$$

We now seek an approximation $\tilde{f}(x)$ to $f(x)$ using only a finite subset S consisting of m of the $\varphi_k(x)$. We can express $\tilde{f}(x)$ as

$$\tilde{f}(x) = \sum_{\varphi_k \in S} \beta_k \varphi_k(x)$$

The problem is to find the best values for the β_k coefficients. These can be determined by requiring that the norm $\|f - \tilde{f}\|$ be minimized. That is, we require that the β_k minimize the quantity

$$\|f - \tilde{f}\|^2 = \int_{-\infty}^{\infty} \left[f^*(x) - \sum_k \beta_k^* \varphi_k^*(x) \right] \left[f(x) - \sum_k \beta_k \varphi_k(x) \right] dx$$

where the sum is over all values of k for which $\varphi_k(x) \in S$. By differentiating with respect to β_j and setting the result equal to zero, there results

$$\int_{-\infty}^{\infty} \left[f^*(x) - \sum_k \beta_k^* \varphi_k^*(x) \right] \varphi_j(x) \, dx = 0$$

from which

$$\int_{-\infty}^{\infty} f^*(x) \varphi_j(x) \, dx = \beta_j^*$$

and, therefore,

$$\beta_j = \int_{-\infty}^{\infty} f(x) \varphi_j^*(x) \, dx = \alpha_j$$

The important result here is that the entire set of representation coefficients $\{\beta_j\}$ does not have to be recalculated anew with each choice of m. Of course, the approximation gets better as m is allowed to increase, or even by substituting different choices for those elements of S that are used; but once the set S is chosen, the best representation in the minimum-squared-error norm sense is given by the corresponding projections of $f(x)$ onto the basis functions.

An important practical consequence of this is that it does away with the necessity of recomputing a whole new set of $\{\beta_k\}$ if m is changed. Only those β_k corresponding to new coordinates need be calculated. In this sense, the representation coordinates are independent. In contrast, if the basis set is not orthogonal, then the entire set of β_k is obtained as the solution to a set of m-coupled linear equations. This is not a fundamental difficulty, but does represent added computations. This is explored in more detail in the following section.

2.2.3 Normal Equations

The projection theorem states that the best approximation of f as a linear combination of vectors from an m-dimensional subspace $\mathbf{M}$ is simply the projection of f on $\mathbf{M}$. If the orthonormal set φ_k spans $\mathbf{M}$, then the minimum-error norm approximation results when the m expansion coefficients are given by $\langle f | \varphi_k \rangle$. This result can be generalized to the case where the φ_k are not necessarily orthonormal (although this is the most convenient case).

If we merely require that the functions φ_k be linearly independent, then all linear combinations

$$\sum_{k=1}^{m} a_k \varphi_k$$

cover the subspace $\mathbf{M}$ of $\mathbf{H}$. If a function f in $\mathbf{H}$ is to be represented by such a linear combination in $\mathbf{M}$, then the best a_k are given by the condition that the error function

$$e = f - \tilde{f} = f - \sum_{k=1}^{m} a_k \varphi_k$$

be orthogonal to each of the the φ_n, i.e., that $\langle e|\varphi_n \rangle = 0$ for each of the φ_n in **M**. This leads to the equation

$$\sum_{k=1}^{m} a_k \langle \varphi_n | \varphi_k \rangle = \langle \varphi_n | f \rangle \qquad (2.40)$$

which is a set of m linear equations for the a_k. These equations are called the *normal equations* and can be solved for the a_k when the φ_n are linearly independent, i.e., when they form a basis in the subspace **M**. The normal equations can also be written in matrix form:

$$\begin{vmatrix} \langle \varphi_1|\varphi_1 \rangle & \langle \varphi_1|\varphi_2 \rangle & \cdots & \langle \varphi_1|\varphi_m \rangle \\ \langle \varphi_2|\varphi_1 \rangle & \langle \varphi_2|\varphi_2 \rangle & \cdots & \langle \varphi_2|\varphi_m \rangle \\ \cdot & \cdot & \cdot & \cdot \\ \cdot & \cdot & \cdot & \cdot \\ \cdot & \cdot & \cdot & \cdot \\ \langle \varphi_m|\varphi_1 \rangle & \langle \varphi_m|\varphi_2 \rangle & \cdots & \langle \varphi_m|\varphi_m \rangle \end{vmatrix} \begin{bmatrix} a_1 \\ a_2 \\ \cdot \\ \cdot \\ \cdot \\ a_2 \end{bmatrix} = \begin{bmatrix} \langle \varphi_1|f \rangle \\ \langle \varphi_2|f \rangle \\ \cdot \\ \cdot \\ \cdot \\ \langle \varphi_m|f \rangle \end{bmatrix} \qquad (2.41)$$

2.2.4 Change of Basis

The theory of linear vector spaces allows equivalent representations to be related to one another by linear transformations. Such transformations, provided they be reversible, do not change the basic nature of a vector, but may be used to express it in equivalent coordinate systems. No new information is added to the signal, but the new representation may be more useful. A good example of this is the Fourier transform, which maps a signal between time and frequency representations.

The distinguishing requirement for a set of vectors to be a basis is that they form the largest set of linearly independent vectors in the space over a set of scalars from some specified field. There are, in general, many such sets, albeit all with the same number n of elements, in an n-dimensional linear vector space. The choice of a basis is not unique. The representation of a vector as an n-tuple of scalars that are the expansion coefficients with respect to some basis must include not only the scalars themselves, but also a mention of the basis used. The representation is then said to be with respect to that particular basis.

As far as the representation of vectors is concerned, all bases are mathematically equivalent. However, considerable simplification may occur with the choice of a particular basis. A vector may be obtained in one particular representation, but it may be desirable to express it with respect to a different basis. It is of analytical and practical importance to be able to change a vector's representation from an arbitrary basis set to another.

Let the vector $\mathbf{x}$ in the linear vector space $\mathbf{X}$ have the representation $\{a_k\}$ with respect to the basis $\{\varphi_k\}$:

$$\mathbf{x} = \sum_k a_k \varphi_k$$

It is desired to express $\mathbf{x}$ with respect to another basis $\{\psi_k\}$ in $\mathbf{X}$. We can formally regard $\mathbf{x}$ as belonging to two vector spaces. In the space $\mathbf{Y}$, $\mathbf{x}$ has the representation

$$\mathbf{x} = \sum_k b_k \psi_k$$

Of course, $\mathbf{X}$ and $\mathbf{Y}$ are really the same space, but we can always regard $\mathbf{Y}$ as a subspace of $\mathbf{X}$. This artifice enables us to use the projection theorem, which tells us that the best b_k in the minimum-error norm sense can be found by requiring that the error vector be orthogonal to every ψ_n:

$$\sum_k a_k \varphi_k - \sum_k b_k \psi_k \perp \psi_m \qquad \text{for all } \psi_m \text{ in } \mathbf{Y}$$

In this case, the error vector vanishes, since either basis set can be used to represent $\mathbf{x}$ exactly. This is really a special case of the projection theorem; the approximation we seek is an exact representation. The last expression implies that

$$\sum_k b_k \langle \psi_m | \psi_k \rangle = \sum_k a_k \langle \psi_m | \varphi_k \rangle$$

But the a_k are known quantities and the inner products $\langle \psi_m | \psi_k \rangle$ and $\langle \psi_m | \varphi_k \rangle$ are also known. The last expression can, therefore, be regarded as a set of normal equations for the coefficients b_k. If the $\{\psi_m\}$ form an orthonormal basis, then we have simply

$$b_m = \sum_k a_k \langle \psi_m | \varphi_k \rangle \tag{2.42}$$

where the inner product $\langle \psi_m | \varphi_m \rangle$ represents the projection of φ_k onto ψ_m. For this special case, the representation $\{b_m\}$ of $\mathbf{x}$ with respect to the orthonormal basis $\{\psi_k\}$ has a particularly simple interpretation. The component b_m is simply the sum of the projections of each component $a_k \varphi_k$ onto the coordinate ψ_m.

That it is always possible to solve the normal equations can easily be shown by using matrix notation and concepts from linear algebra. To do this, we repeat some of the previous steps. A vector expressed in a representation corresponding to a particular basis can easily be expressed in terms of another, equivalent, basis. Let $\mathbf{x}$ be a vector whose representation with respect to the orthonormal basis set $\{\varphi_k; k = 1, \ldots, n\}$ is the set of scalars $\{c_k; k = 1, \ldots, n\}$. Let another orthonormal basis set be $\{\psi_k; k = 1, \ldots, n\}$. The representation of $\mathbf{x}$ with respect to this new basis is

$$\mathbf{x} = \sum_{k=1}^n c_k' \psi_k$$

where the new coefficients $\{c'_k; k = 1, \ldots, n\}$ can be expressed in terms of the old basis. Taking the inner product of the above expression with φ_m gives

$$\langle \varphi_m | \mathbf{x} \rangle = c_m = \sum_{k=1}^{n} c'_k \langle \varphi_m | \psi_k \rangle \qquad (2.43)$$

If $\{c_k; k = 1, \ldots, n\}$ and $\{c'_k; k = 1, \ldots, n\}$ are considered to be the components of the n-dimensional vectors $\mathbf{c}$ and $\mathbf{c}'$, respectively, then the last expression can be written as

$$\mathbf{c} = \mathbf{A}\mathbf{c}'$$

where $\mathbf{A}$ is a matrix with elements $a_{mk} = \langle \varphi_m | \psi_k \rangle$. The vector $\mathbf{c}'$ can be expressed in terms of $\mathbf{c}$ provided $\mathbf{A}$ can be inverted:

$$\mathbf{c}' = \mathbf{A}^{-1}\mathbf{c}$$

We now prove that $\mathbf{A}$ is always invertible. To do so, we note that a necessary and sufficient condition for the invertibility of a square matrix is that the column be linearly independent. We therefore show that the columns of $\mathbf{A}$ are, in fact, linearly independent.

Since the basis vectors φ_k are by definition linearly independent, we must show that

$$\sum_{k=1}^{n} a_k \langle \varphi_m | \psi_k \rangle = 0$$

necessarily implies that $a_k = 0$ $(k = 1, \ldots, n)$. This linear combination can be written as

$$\langle \varphi_m | \sum_{k=1}^{n} a_k | \psi_k \rangle = 0$$

Since φ_m is nonzero, then the vector forming the inner product with φ_m must vanish:

$$\sum_{k=1}^{n} a_k \psi_k = 0 \qquad (2.44)$$

But since the vectors ψ_k form a basis, they must be linearly independent. The only way then that the last expression can be satisfied is for all of the coefficients a_k to vanish. This completes the proof.

2.3 THE DIMENSIONALITY OF CONTINUOUS SIGNALS

This section deals with signals in Hilbert space. In general, Hilbert space is an infinite-dimensional space of complex functions. Furthermore, any number of such functions can be mathematically defined over any finite interval in time or frequency. The purpose of this section is to develop the mathematics necessary to describe how signals can be approximated with the fewest number of Hilbert-space coordinates. One can distinguish between two signals $s_1(t)$ and $s_2(t)$ if the Euclidian metric distance between them [i.e., the energy in the difference signal, $s_1(t) - s_2(t)$] exceeds some threshold energy. Noise is always present in physical measurements and establishes a minimum separation between distinguishable signals.

This section develops the concept of signal dimensionality. Chapters 4, 5, and 6 will establish a minimum signal-to-noise energy (i.e., metric) ratio for signal distinguishability, and will interpret this result in a communication context.

2.3.1 Sampling and Reconstruction from Samples

We begin our discussion of sampling with a review of a few sampling theorems. These theorems are often first encountered in the study of digital signal processing, where it becomes necessary to sample continuous waveforms in order to produce sequences that can be digitally processed. There the mathematical properties of sequences are studied and related to equivalent properties of the original continuous waveform. One of the important results of that analysis is that, for band-limited waveforms, sampling at a sufficiently high rate guarantees that all of the properties of the continuous waveform are preserved in its samples. This result, although often taken for granted, is actually a remarkable statement about representing a continuous curve by discrete samples, which really amounts to discarding most of the function and keeping only a few isolated points.

Although it would be possible to approach this section with the processing of sampled signals in mind, we choose to take a more general view. Our discussion will be limited only to those cases where it is possible to represent a continuous waveform exactly by a sequence of discrete samples. This has obvious applications to digital signal processing, but is also the foundation for a powerful analytical tool, where a continuous function can be represented as a sequence of discrete samples, and provides us with some insight as to the structure of signals. The more general view is then to consider sampling as a method whereby a waveform is represented by a sequence of scalars.

Much has been written on sampling, and only the rudiments can be presented here. The immediate goal of this section is to establish a correspondence between how a signal may be sampled and the dimensionality of the space in which that signal is defined. The reader may wish to consult any of a number of excellent texts on digital signal processing [Cr 83, Op 75, Pa 77, Ra 75, Tr 76] for the usual treatment of sampling and reconstruction. A review paper on sampling [Je 77] is also recommended for an in-depth look at this process.

Fundamentally, there is but one sampling theorem, which is a statement of the fact that a vector can be uniquely represented with as many scalars as there are dimensions in the linear vector space in which the vector is defined. There are various statements of the sampling theorem, and these are discussed in what follows.

A function $f(t)$ is said to be *strictly band-limited* if its Fourier transform $F(\nu)$ has the property[†]

$$F(\nu) = 0 \qquad |\nu| > W \tag{2.45}$$

[†]Although we shall refer to t as "time" and to ν as "frequency", these are merely names that could be applied to a variety of other conjugate physical variables where Fourier transforms are involved.

where W is called the bandwidth of the signal. There is really no such thing as a strictly band-limited signal in nature. However, this mathematical model gives us considerable insight into what, in most practical cases, turns out to be a good approximation. For definiteness, we shall use the following symmetrical definition of the Fourier transform:

$$f(t) \leftrightarrow F(\nu): \begin{cases} F(\nu) = \int_{-\infty}^{\infty} f(t)e^{-2\pi j \nu t}\, dt \\ f(t) = \int_{-\infty}^{\infty} F(\nu)e^{2\pi j \nu t}\, d\nu \end{cases} \tag{2.46}$$

A strictly band-limited signal has its Fourier transform entirely contained within a finite bandwidth. Without loss of generality, we are considering strictly band-limited functions whose Fourier transforms have been translated in frequency to baseband in such a way that the highest frequency components are exactly at $\pm \nu$.

Since $F(\nu) = 0$ for $|\nu| > W$, the Fourier transform can itself be expanded in a Fourier series of period $2W$

$$F(\nu) = \sum_{k=-\infty}^{\infty} F_k e^{-2\pi j k \nu / 2W} \tag{2.47}$$

where

$$F_k = \frac{1}{2W} \int_{-W}^{W} F(\nu)e^{2\pi j k \nu / 2W}\, d\nu \tag{2.48}$$

Now consider the inverse Fourier transform of $F(\nu)$:

$$f(t) = \int_{-W}^{W} F(\nu)e^{2\pi j k \nu t}\, d\nu \tag{2.49}$$

By comparing this with Eq. (2.48), there results

$$F_k = \frac{1}{2W} f\left(t = \frac{k}{2W}\right) \qquad k = -\infty, \ldots, \infty \tag{2.50}$$

We have succeeded in representing a continuous function $f(t)$ by an infinite set of scalars F_k. Furthermore, these scalars are found by sampling $f(t)$ at regularly spaced intervals $\Delta t = 1/2W$. It now remains to show how $f(t)$ can be reconstituted from these samples.

Reconstructing the continuous function $f(t)$ from its samples is also called *interpolation*. We again emphasize that we are considering an interpolation scheme that exactly reproduces the original function $f(t)$. By starting with the Fourier series expansion for $F(\nu)$ given by Eq. (2.47) and expressing F_k in terms of samples of $f(t)$, there results

$$F(\nu) = \frac{1}{2W} \sum_{k} f\left(\frac{k}{2W}\right) e^{-2\pi j k \nu / 2W} \tag{2.51}$$

Summation over all allowable values of k is implied. Substituting Eq. (2.51) into Eq. (2.49),

$$f(t) = \int_{-W}^{W} F(\nu)e^{2\pi j \nu t}\, d\nu = \frac{1}{2W} \sum_{k} f\left(\frac{k}{2W}\right) \int_{-W}^{W} e^{2\pi j \nu (t - k/2W)}\, d\nu \tag{2.52}$$

The reconstruction of $f(t)$ from regularly spaced samples can, therefore, be expressed as

$$f(t) = \sum_k f\left(\frac{k}{2W}\right)\frac{\sin(2\pi W t - k\pi)}{2\pi W t - k\pi} \qquad k = -\infty, \ldots, \infty \qquad (2.53)$$

This interpolation formula, due to Whittaker [Wh 15], has the form of a convolution with the function

$$h(t) = \frac{\sin(2\pi W t)}{2\pi W t} \qquad (2.54)$$

The function $h(t)$ has the Fourier transform

$$H(\nu) = \begin{cases} \dfrac{1}{2W} & |\nu| \le W \\ 0 & \text{otherwise} \end{cases} \qquad (2.55)$$

Until now, we have made no mention as to whether $f(t)$ is real or complex. The derivation of the baseband sampling theorem was kept entirely general. Let us now examine what happens when we choose $f(t)$ to be real†.

If $f(t)$ is a real function, then the scalars F_k are also real. Furthermore, there is one such scalar for every dimension of the space in which $f(t)$ is defined. In this case, $f(t)$ is defined over a real function space with a countably infinite ($\aleph_0$) number of dimensions. That is, we can associate a real scalar F_k with each one of the integers.

If $f(t)$ is a real function, then $F(\nu)$ is Hermitian. The Fourier transform of a real function $f(t)$ is a complex function that has the following symmetry:

$$F(\nu) = F^*(-\nu) \qquad (2.56)$$

The Hermitian symmetry relation can be applied to the Fourier transform of $f(t)$, resulting in the condition

$$F_k = F_k^* \Rightarrow F_k \text{ is real}$$

Since $F(\nu)$ is band-limited and complex, it is defined in a linear vector space with $\aleph_0$ dimensions. The projection of $F(\nu)$ on each of the basis vectors is a complex scalar, and each one of these complex scalars can be associated with an integer. Since a complex scalar is equivalent to a pair of real numbers, it might at first appear as if we had twice as many real quantities as are needed to specify $f(t)$. However, the Hermitian symmetry of $F(\nu)$ implies that half of these real quantities can be expressed in terms of the other half.

If we now consider $f(t)$ to be a complex function, it can be represented by a set of complex scalars F_k, one for each of the dimensions of the linear vector space. In general, no symmetry rule relates these complex scalars.

We can summarize these results with the following theorem.

---

†A similar argument holds for $f(t)$, a purely imaginary function.

Theorem.   A function that is strictly band-limited such that its Fourier transform vanishes outside the interval $[-W, W]$ can be uniquely represented by samples spaced $1/2W$ apart in the time domain.

Now consider the case of a function $f(t)$ with finite bandwidth W centered at frequency ν_0. This situation arises, for example, at the output of the intermediate-frequency stage of a radio receiver. In fact, this provides the simplest example of a band-pass function, since, for that case, $f(t)$ is real.

The usual approach to introducing the band-pass sampling theorem for real functions exploits the fact that the Fourier transform of a real function exhibits Hermitian symmetry. The positive frequency components can be expressed in terms of the negative frequency components, and vice versa. This twofold redundancy in the Fourier spectrum allows an approach whereby either the positive or the negative frequency half of the Fourier transform may be discarded, and the remaining half is translated to baseband. No information about the original function is lost since the discarded half of the Fourier transform can always be regenerated from the remaining half. The resulting situation is then identical to that treated under the baseband sampling theorem.

A useful mathematical technique for expressing a real function in terms of its positive or negative frequency components is the Hilbert transform. The *Hilbert transform* $\hat{f}(t)$ of a function $f(t)$ can be defined as

$$\hat{f}(t) = \frac{1}{\pi} \int_{-\infty}^{\infty} \frac{f(\tau)}{t-\tau} d\tau = \left(\frac{1}{\pi t} \right) * f(t) \tag{2.57}$$

where the asterisk (*), used as an operator, denotes convolution. The Hilbert transform can, therefore, be considered to be a linear filter with impulse response

$$h(t) = \frac{1}{\pi t} \tag{2.58}$$

and with frequency-domain response

$$H(\nu) = \mathcal{F}[h(t)] = -j \; \mathrm{sgn} \; \nu \tag{2.59}$$

where $\mathcal{F}[\cdot]$ denotes Fourier transformation.

We now define a complex quantity $f_+(t)$, called the *analytic signal*, as

$$f_+(t) = f(t) + j\hat{f}(t) \tag{2.60}$$

The Fourier transform of the analytic signal is

$$F_+(\nu) = F(\nu) + j \, \mathcal{F}[h(t) * f(t)]$$

$$= F(\nu) + j \, H(\nu)F(\nu)$$

$$= (1 + \mathrm{sgn} \; \nu \,)F(\nu) \tag{2.61}$$

The analytic signal, therefore, only has positive frequency components. Its Fourier transform is equal to twice the Fourier transform of $f(t)$ for positive frequencies and vanishes for negative frequencies. By a similar argument, the analytic function defined by

$$f_-(t) = f(t) - j\hat{f}(t) \tag{2.62}$$

has only negative frequency components.

Complex demodulation can be used to translate $F_+(\nu)$ to baseband. This is accomplished with the shift theorem of Fourier analysis:

$$F_+(\nu + \nu_0) = \int_{-\infty}^{\infty} f_+(t)e^{-2\pi j(\nu + \nu_0)t} \, dt$$

which can be expressed as the Fourier transform of the product of the analytic signal $f_+(t)$ and of a complex exponential:

$$F_+(\nu + \nu_0) = \mathscr{F}\left[f_+(t)e^{-2\pi j \nu_0 t}\right] \tag{2.63}$$

The equivalent complex baseband function, denoted by $f_0(t)$, can now be recognized as

$$f_0(t) = f_+(t)e^{-2\pi j \nu_0 t} \tag{2.64}$$

The bandwidth of $f_0(t)$ is the same as the bandwidth of either the positive or the negative frequency portion of $F(\nu)$, namely W. This means that $F_0(\nu)$, the Fourier transform of $f_0(t)$, vanishes outside the interval $-\frac{1}{2}W \leq \nu \leq \frac{1}{2}W$. To be uniquely reconstituted from its samples, the complex function $f_0(t)$ must, therefore, be sampled at the rate of W complex samples per second. This is clearly equivalent to sampling the analytic function $f_+(t)$ at the rate of W complex samples per second and also equivalent to sampling $f(t)$ at the rate of $2W$ real samples per second. The effect of these transformations on the Fourier spectrum is shown in Fig. 2-2.

These results are all compatible with the Nyquist sampling theorem, which states that perfect reconstruction is possible provided (real) samples be taken at a rate equal to twice the signal's bandwidth. In the case of real band-pass signals,

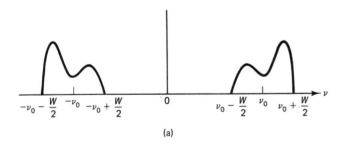

(a)

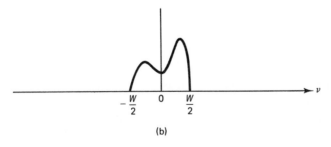

(b)

Figure 2-2. (*a*) Modulus of the Fourier transform of a real band-pass function. Note the symmetry between positive and negative frequency components. (*b*) Equivalent baseband spectrum obtained by eliminating the negative frequency components with a Hilbert transform, and complex demodulation of the positive frequency spectrum.

the samples are taken at half that rate from the corresponding complex analytic signal, but being complex samples, the same amount of information is present in the sampled representation. This is sometimes a source of confusion; it is important to state whether the samples are real or complex, and to keep track of how much information is required for perfect waveform representation.

Figure 2-3 shows how a real function $f(t)$ or its analytic function $f_+(t)$ may be sampled. $f_+(t)$ is a complex function whose real part is $f(t)$ and whose imaginary part is $\hat{f}(t)$, the Hilbert transform of $f(t)$. These two components appear on the right of the vertical dashed line in Fig. 2-3. The top channel carries $f(t)$ and the bottom channel, understood to be the imaginary component of the analytic signal, carries $\hat{f}(t)$, which is obtained from $f(t)$ by processing with a filter whose impulse response is given by Eq. (2.58).

We note in passing that the "$+$" that appears in Eq. (2.60) is simply the algebraic sign of the imaginary component of the analytic signal. It does not indicate arithmetic addition of the real and imaginary parts, which would be meaningless. A complex number is a 2-tuple vector over the real numbers, with addition defined componentwise. Thus, Eq. (2.60) should be read as a 2-tuple vector representation, with the symbol "j" acting as a delimiter to separate the two components. The complex function $f_+(t)$ in Fig. 2-3 requires two separate channels to carry its two (real and imaginary) components.

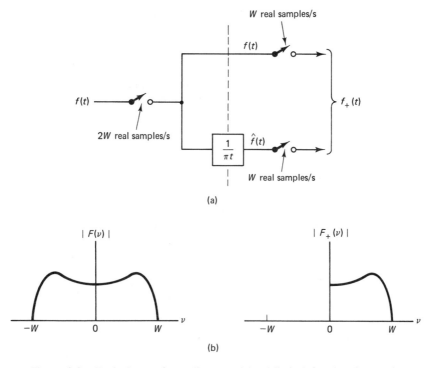

Figure 2-3. Equivalence of sampling a real band-limited function $f(t)$ or its analytic signal. (*a*) Time-domain sampling. (*b*) Magnitude of the spectrum.

The real function $f(t)$ in Fig. 2-3 is band-limited with bandwidth W, as shown in Fig. 2-3 (b). $f(t)$ can be represented by its (real) samples taken at the Nyquist rate of $2W$ samples per second. On the right side of the vertical dashed line, $f(t)$ is represented by its analytic signal $f_+(t)$, which has only positive frequency components. Each channel $f(t)$ and $\hat{f}(t)$ can be sampled at W samples per second, which is equivalent to a total of $2W$ real samples per second or W complex samples per second.

2.3.2 The Duration-Bandwidth Product

A signal can be uniquely represented by a set of independent parameters, the number of which is equal to the dimensionality of the linear space in which the signal is defined. The number of *degrees of freedom* of a vector is defined as the number of scalars needed to represent it with respect to any basis. This, of course, is the dimensionality n of the linear vector space. The examples discussed thus far involved spaces of infinite dimensionality. However, there are important cases for which a waveform can be considered to have a finite number of degrees of freedom.

Each of these n scalars represents an independent measurement made on the signal. The signal may thus be expressed as a point or vector in an n-dimensional signal space. That signal is said to have n degrees of freedom or coordinates. Each dimension in the space corresponds to an independent measurement, the measurement itself being given by the magnitude of the corresponding signal coordinate.

In the previous section, we found that a continuous real signal with bandwidth W can be uniquely represented by real samples spaced $0.5/W$ apart in time. The output of an ideal passband filter with bandwidth W produces a band-limited function with bandwidth W. It is tempting to jump immediately to the conclusion that a T-second segment of such a band-limited signal can be uniquely represented by exactly $2TW$ samples collected during that time interval. This would imply that a signal of duration T and bandwidth W is a vector in a $2TW$-dimensional space, since any such function can be represented by $2TW$ independent quantities. It would appear that in our discussion of sampling, we accidentally stumbled on a particularly simple (i.e., sampling) representation of signals in $2TW$-dimensional space. This, as we shall see, is only approximately true. A full treatment of this topic requires developments that are beyond the scope of this book. However, we shall attempt to sketch enough of the mathematics to make the picture clear.

First, we show that the concept of a function "with duration T and bandwidth W" is not a valid mathematical construct, although sufficiently good approximations exist to warrant the use of such loose terminology. The reader is reminded that time and frequency play dual roles in signal description, and that the two words may be interchanged without changing the truth of a statement. In fact, any pair of Fourier-conjugate variables may be substituted for time and frequency.

Before proceeding further, we need some definitions. First, we generalize the definition of a strictly band-limited function to include all functions whose Fourier transform is nonzero over a finite support and vanishes everywhere else. That is, the Fourier transform $F(\nu)$ of a function $f(t)$ may be nonzero over some disconnected segments of the frequency (ν) axis and vanish identically in between. The length of all such segments is called the bandwidth W and such a function is said to be strictly band-limited.

EXAMPLE

In frequency-division multiplexing, several communication signals with respective bandwidths W_1, W_2, . . . , W_n share a portion of the frequency spectrum. The individual signal power spectra are translated in frequency so that they occupy adjacent slots without overlapping. As a precaution against mutual interference, an unoccupied guard band is often placed between such channels. The overall spectrum looks as shown in Fig. 2-4. The total bandwidth actually occupied by the signals is simply $W = W_1 + W_2 + \ldots + W_n$, and does not include the gaps corresponding to the guard bands. Only that portion of the spectrum actually occupied by the signal contributes to the bandwidth. If the Fourier transform is identically zero elsewhere, then the signal is said to be strictly band-limited. The bandwidth of a signal $f(t)$ includes all segments of nonzero measure where $F(\nu)$ does not vanish.

A signal observed at the output of an ideal band-pass filter having bandwidth W is strictly band-limited with a bandwidth W. All signals we work with are band-limited because they are produced by or passed through systems that have finite response times. This is why we use such an abstraction: it corresponds very closely with what is commonly encountered in nature.

We also work with signals of finite duration. Many of the mathematical functions used to describe signals are defined over an infinite domain, but physical signals are all restricted to regions of finite support. This motivates the definition of a strictly time- (or duration-) limited signal to describe signals that are nonvanishing only over a finite, although possibly disconnected, time interval. Thus, it is tempting to join the two concepts and describe physically realizable signals as being both time- and bandwidth-limited. It is possible to have a strictly time-limited or a strictly band-limited signal, but not both. This is because time and frequency are related and the specification of the time behavior of a function also affects its frequency behavior. The two may not be specified independently.

All of the important properties of strictly band-limited and time-limited functions can be described in terms of functions that have no gaps in their time histories

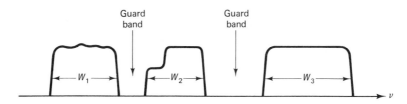

Figure 2-4.   The frequency spectrum of a frequency-division multiplexed signal.

or Fourier transforms. With no loss of generality, we shall consider a function $f(t)$ to be strictly time-limited if it vanishes identically outside a finite time interval T:

$$f(t) = 0 \qquad \text{for} \quad |t| > T$$

and strictly band-limited if its Fourier transform $F(\nu)$ vanishes identically outside a finite time interval W:

$$F(\nu) = 0 \qquad \text{for} \quad |\nu| > W$$

We reconcile this with the more general definition introduced earlier by admitting the possibility of such functions vanishing over finite portions of their domains. We shall restrict our discussion to signals having finite energy (i.e., finite norm):

$$\mathscr{E} = \int_{-\infty}^{\infty} f^*(t)f(t)\, dt = \int_{-\infty}^{\infty} F^*(\nu)F(\nu)\, d\nu < \infty \qquad (2.65)$$

A complex function $f(t)$ of a complex variable t that possesses a first derivative in some region of the complex plane is called an *analytic* function. A function that is analytic over the entire complex plane is called an *entire* function. A band-limited function is also an entire function. Note that the word "analytic" is used here with a different meaning than when we discussed the analytic signal in conjunction with Hilbert transforms.

The sampling theorem applies only to a strictly band-limited function. Such a function, by virtue of being analytic everywhere, must have infinite duration. Observing a strictly band-limited function through a finite time interval does not produce a function that is both strictly band-limited and strictly time-limited. Time truncation with however smooth a window results in an increase in bandwidth albeit possibly with very small Fourier components at very high frequencies. A function that starts out being strictly band-limited loses that property with the application of any time window that restricts its duration. Such a signal cannot be uniquely represented by samples spaced at the Nyquist rate.

This is true no matter in what order the limiting operations are performed on the signal. Thus, by starting with a time-limitation operation, the signal is strictly time-limited, but with a large bandwidth. Passing this time-limited signal through an band-pass filter results in a strictly band-limited signal, but one of greater duration than was applied at the input. This no longer corresponds to the original signal. It seems as if it is impossible to contain a signal in both time and frequency, although containment in any one domain is allowed.

The reason for this can be found in the mathematical properties of strictly band-limited functions. Time–frequency duality allows similar conclusions to be drawn about strictly time-limited functions. Only the band-limited case, therefore, has to be discussed.

Consider a band-limited complex function $f(t)$. The Fourier transform $F(\nu)$ of such a function exists and $f(t)$ can be expressed in terms of $F(\nu)$ through the inverse Fourier transform

$$f(t) = \int_{-W}^{W} F(\nu)e^{2\pi j \nu t}\, d\nu$$

The derivative of $f(t)$ can be obtained by differentiating the expression under the integral sign:

$$f'(t) = 2\pi j \int_{-W}^{W} F(\nu)\nu e^{2\pi j \nu t} \, d\nu$$

This integral always exists, owing to the finite limits of integration.

An important result from the theory of complex functions is that a function cannot be simultaneously band-limited and time-limited. This follows because band-limited functions are entire functions, and such functions must vanish identically over the entire t plane if they vanish over any finite region of it. In other words, imposing a time limitation on a band-limited function causes it to vanish over some region of the t plane. The only band-limited function for which this can be done is $f(t) = 0$.

By using suitably shaped time and frequency windows, approximate containment is possible, but the approximation prevents us from making a statement that the resulting signal is exactly $2TW$-dimensional. We can however say that the signal is "approximately $2TW$-dimensional", with caveats to be discussed throughout the remainder of this section. An eminently readable and thought-provoking paper in this area has been written by David Slepian [Sl 76].

The meaning (and, hence, practical implication) of the approximate dimensionality of continuous signals having finite bandwidth and limited duration should not be a troubling concept. What it means is that an exact representation of signals requires an infinite number of dimensions in Hilbert space. Practical limitations force us to use a finite number of coordinates to represent signals. We are, therefore, constrained to operate in a finite-dimensional subspace of Hilbert space, and, consequently, must be content with approximations of signals as best they can be represented in finite-dimensional subspaces. This situation is not all bad since these finite subspaces can be chosen so as to contain "most" (in a sense to be defined later) of these signals. In the next section, we will see that with the choice of the proper basis, the penalty for using such signal approximations can be minimized.

2.3.3 Prolate Spheroidal Wave Functions✳

According to the discussion thus far, we have seen that it is not possible to have a function that is both band-limited and time-limited. It is, however, possible to have either a strictly band-limited or a strictly time-limited function. It is, however, not possible to represent functions, even those that are band-limited or time-limited, in a finite-dimensional function space. This would be an attractive proposition since practical limitations confine us to the use of finite-dimensional spaces.

Since mathematics denies us the exact representation of signals with a finite number of coordinates, the next best thing to have is an approximate representation that is optimal in some sense. This will be the subject of this and the next section. Let us expand our mathematical vocabulary by introducing a couple of definitions. We will consider a function $f(t)$ to be *approximately time-limited at the level ϵ* if

---

✳Sections marked with this symbol (✳) are optional. The reader may skip over these.

$$\int_{-\tau}^{\tau} f^*(t)f(t)\, dt = \mathscr{E} - \epsilon$$

where $\mathscr{E}$ is the total signal energy (i.e., norm) defined by

$$\int_{-\infty}^{\infty} f^*(t)f(t)\, dt = \mathscr{E}$$

What this definition says is that a function is considered to be approximately time-limited if all but an amount ϵ of its total energy lies inside the interval $[-\tau,\ \tau]$. The smaller the fraction $\epsilon/\mathscr{E}$, the closer $f(t)$ is to being strictly time-limited. A function may be strictly band-limited and approximately time-limited. An interesting (and practical) mathematical problem is the search for functions $\varphi(t)$ that are strictly band-limited and that come as close as possible to being strictly time-limited. Specifically, we shall look for band-limited functions $\varphi(t)$ that have as much energy as possible in the interval $[-\tau,\ \tau]$. We, therefore, wish to maximize a quantity of the form

$$\int_{-\tau}^{\tau} \varphi^*(t)\varphi(t)\, dt \tag{2.66}$$

where

$$\varphi(t) = \int_{-W}^{W} \Phi(\nu) e^{2\pi j\, \nu t}\, d\nu \tag{2.67}$$

By substituting Eq. (2.67) into (2.66), there results

$$\int_{-\tau}^{\tau} dt \int_{-W}^{W} d\nu \int_{-W}^{W} d\nu'\, \Phi^*(\nu)\Phi(\nu') e^{-2\pi j\,(\nu - \nu')t} \tag{2.68}$$

which must be maximized. Doing the t integral first, we obtain

$$\int_{-\tau}^{\tau} e^{-2\pi j\,(\nu - \nu')t}\, dt = \frac{\sin[2\pi(\nu - \nu')\tau]}{\pi(\nu - \nu')}$$

We, therefore, want a $\Phi(\nu)$ that maximizes the expression

$$\int_{-W}^{W}\!\int \Phi^*(\nu)\Phi(\nu')\frac{\sin[2\pi(\nu - \nu')\tau]}{\pi(\nu - \nu')}\, d\nu\, d\nu' \tag{2.69}$$

where $\Phi(\nu)$ vanishes outside the interval $[-W,\ W]$. Maximizing Eq. (2.69) is equivalent to maximizing the square of its modulus. In doing so, we make use of the Schwarz inequality and conclude that the $\Phi(\nu)$ that maximizes Eq. (2.69) is given by

$$\Phi(\nu) = \alpha \int_{-W}^{W} \Phi(\nu')\frac{\sin[2\pi(\nu - \nu')\tau]}{\pi(\nu - \nu')}\, d\nu' \tag{2.70}$$

where α is any complex constant. Equation (2.70) is an integral equation for $\Phi(\nu)$. This equation can also be expressed in the t domain. This can be done by evaluating the inverse Fourier transform of the expression for $\Phi(\nu)$:

$$\varphi(t) = \int_{-W}^{W} \Phi(\nu) e^{2\pi j\, \nu t}\, dt = \alpha \int_{-W}^{W} d\nu'\Phi(\nu') \int_{-W}^{W} \frac{\sin[2\pi(\nu - \nu')\tau]}{\pi(\nu - \nu')} e^{2\pi j\, \nu t}\, dt$$

The integral over t can be rewritten as

$$\int_{-W}^{W} \frac{\sin[2\pi(\nu - \nu')\tau]}{\pi(\nu - \nu')} e^{2\pi j \nu t} \, dt = \int_{-\infty}^{\infty} \Pi(\nu/2W) \frac{\sin[2\pi(\nu - \nu')\tau]}{\pi(\nu - \nu')} e^{2\pi j \nu t} \, dt \tag{2.71}$$

where the function $\Pi(x)$ is defined by

$$\Pi(x) = 1 \qquad \text{for} -1/2 \leq x \leq 1/2$$

$$\Pi(x) = 0 \qquad \text{otherwise} \tag{2.72}$$

and has the Fourier transform

$$\Pi(x) \leftrightarrow \frac{\sin \pi y}{\pi y} = \operatorname{sinc} y \tag{2.73}$$

where the doubleheaded arrow indicates a Fourier transform pair in the conjugate variables x and y. The function $\Pi(x)$ and its Fourier transform are shown in Fig. 2-5.

The integral over t can now easily be evaluated by recognizing that

$$\Pi(\nu/2W) \leftrightarrow 2W \frac{\sin 2\pi W t}{2\pi W t}$$

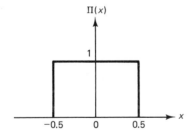

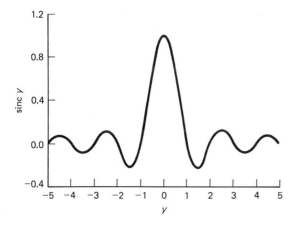

Figure 2-5. $\Pi(x)$ and its Fourier transform sinc (y).

and

$$\frac{\sin[2\pi(\nu - \nu')\tau]}{2\pi(\nu - \nu')} \leftrightarrow e^{2\pi j \nu' t} \frac{1}{2t} \Pi\left(\frac{t}{2\tau}\right)$$

The ν integral in Eq. (2.71) can, therefore, be solved by using the Fourier convolution theorem, and is equal to

$$W \frac{\sin 2\pi W t}{2\pi W t} * e^{2\pi j \nu' t} \Pi\left(\frac{t}{2\tau}\right)$$

where the asterisk (*) denotes convolution. The function $\varphi(t)$ we seek is, therefore, given by

$$\varphi(t) = \alpha W \int_{-W}^{W} \Phi(\nu') \frac{\sin 2\pi W t}{2\pi W t} * e^{2\pi j \nu' t} \Pi\left(\frac{t}{2\tau}\right) d\nu'$$

$$= 2\alpha W \frac{\sin 2\pi W t}{2\pi W t} * \int_{-W}^{W} \Phi(\nu') e^{2\pi j \nu' t} d\nu' \cdot \Pi\left(\frac{t}{2\tau}\right)$$

$$= \alpha \frac{\sin 2\pi W t}{2\pi W t} * \left[\varphi(t) \cdot \Pi\left(\frac{t}{2\tau}\right)\right]$$

$$= \frac{1}{2}\alpha \int_{-\infty}^{\infty} \varphi(x) \Pi\left(\frac{x}{2\tau}\right) \frac{\sin[2\pi W(t - x)]}{\pi(t - x)} dx$$

$$= \frac{1}{2}\alpha \int_{-\tau}^{\tau} \varphi(x) \frac{\sin[2\pi W(t - x)]}{\pi(t - x)} dx \qquad (2.74)$$

This expression can be written in the form

$$\int_{-\tau}^{\tau} \varphi(x) \frac{\sin[2\pi W(t - x)]}{\pi(t - x)} dx = \lambda \varphi(t) \qquad (2.75)$$

where λ is some complex constant. This integral equation for $\varphi(t)$ admits solutions only for certain values of λ. These values are denoted by $\{\lambda_k; k = 1, 2, 3, \ldots\}$ and are called the *eigenvalues*. The corresponding solutions are denoted by $\{\varphi_k(t); k = 1, 2, 3, \ldots\}$ and are called the *eigenfunctions*. The eigenfunctions for this particular eigenvalue problem are the prolate spheroidal wave functions [Sl 61, La 61, La 62].

We can recast this eigenvalue problem in dimensionless form by normalizing the time arguments (t and x) by the characteristic time τ:

$$\int_{-1}^{1} \psi(x) \frac{\sin[2\pi\beta(t - x)]}{\pi(t - x)} dx = \lambda \psi(t) \qquad (2.76)$$

where $\Psi(t) = \varphi(\tau t)$, and $\beta = \tau W$. In this form, the eigenfunctions depend only on the dimensionless parameter β, which is one-half the duration-bandwidth product.

We close this section with a few important properties of the prolate spheroidal wave functions. These properties are stated without proof. The eigenfunctions $\varphi_k(t)$ are all band-limited. This follows directly from their derivation, which was presented as a search among band-limited functions for special functions with the greatest energy concentration over a finite time interval. It also turns out that the $\varphi_k(t)$ are orthonormal on the interval $(-\infty, \infty)$:

$$\int_{-\infty}^{\infty} \varphi_k(t)\varphi_n(t)\, dt = \delta_{k,n} \qquad \text{for } k, n = 0, 1, 2, \ldots \qquad (2.77)$$

For any value of $c = 2\pi W \tau$, there is a countably infinite set of eigenfunctions $\{\varphi_k(t;c), k = 0, 1, 2, \ldots\}$ corresponding to the real positive eigenvalues

$$1 > \lambda_0(c) > \lambda_1(c) > \lambda_2(c) > \ldots$$

Figure 2-6(a) shows a graph of $\varphi_0(t;c)$ for $c = 1, 2,$ and 4. Figure 2-6(b) shows the behavior of the largest eigenvalue $\lambda_0(c)$ as a function of c. The largest eigenvalue $\lambda_0(c)$ is the fraction of the energy of $\varphi_0(t;c)$ contained in the interval

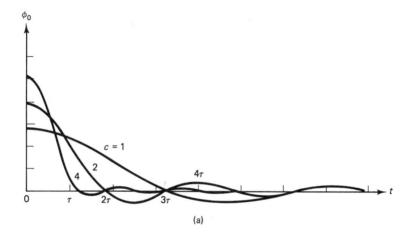

(a)

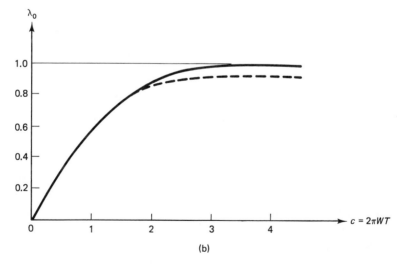

(b)

Figure 2-6.   (*a*) The first prolate spheroidal wave function $\phi_0(t;c)$. (*b*) The largest eigenvalue $\lambda_0(c)$, corresponding to $\phi_0(t;c)$. (Adapted from Reference [Fr 69]. Reproduced by permission from the author.)

$[-\tau, \tau]$. Among all functions band-limited on $[-W, W]$, $\varphi_0(t; c)$ contains the largest portion of its energy on $[-\tau, \tau]$. The dashed line in Fig. 2-6(b) compares this with the ability of $\Pi(\frac{1}{2}\nu/W)$ to concentrate energy on $[-\tau, \tau]$.

The functions $\varphi_k(t)$ form a complete set for band-limited functions. Any band-limited function $f(t)$ can be represented exactly in terms of a linear combination of the $\varphi_k(t)$:

$$f(t) = \sum_{k=1}^{\infty} a_k \varphi_k(t)$$

with

$$a_k = \int_{-\infty}^{\infty} f(t) \varphi_k(t) \, dt$$

Such an expansion in terms of the $\varphi_k(t)$ always converges to $f(t)$:

$$\lim_{n \to \infty} \left| f(t) - \sum_{k=1}^{n} a_k \varphi_k(t) \right|^2 = 0 \tag{2.78}$$

In addition to being orthonormal over $(-\infty, \infty)$, the $\varphi_k(t)$ are also orthogonal over $[-\tau, \tau]$:

$$\int_{-\tau}^{\tau} \varphi_k^*(t) \varphi_n(t) \, dt = \lambda_k \delta_{k,n} \qquad \text{for } k, n = 0, 1, 2, \ldots$$

The $\varphi_k(t)$ are also complete over $[-\tau, \tau]$: any time-limited function $g(t)$ can be expressed as

$$g(t) = \sum_{k=1}^{\infty} b_k \varphi_k(t)$$

with

$$b_k = \lambda_k^{-1} \int_{-\tau}^{\tau} g(t) \varphi_k(t) \, dt$$

Note, however, that such an expression does not necessarily vanish outside $[-\tau, \tau]$.

2.3.4 Approximate Signal Dimensionality❋

We are now ready to examine the problem of dimensionality for functions that are localized in duration as well as in bandwidth. Any function in a linear function space can be represented exactly by a linear combination of all of the basis functions for that space. The coefficients in that linear combination form a representation for the function and, in the case of an orthogonal basis set, can be interpreted as coordinate projections. In Hilbert space, the dimensionality is infinite, so that, in general, an infinite number of coefficients are required. Moreover, the choice of a particular basis set is not unique, and there are, in general, an infinite number of equivalent choices. Any representation of a function in terms of a linear combination must specify which basis set is used. In special cases, only a finite number of coordinates may be needed to represent a function.

Practical considerations restrict us to signals that are confined in time and frequency. The concepts of time-limited and band-limited functions have been developed to deal with this. However, these two concepts are reluctant to be united since a band-limited function must be entire and, therefore, cannot also be time-limited. The next best thing is a band-limited function that is as much time-limited as possible, i.e., a band-limited function with as much of its energy as possible localized within a finite-duration segment. Yet a function can have all of its energy contained within some bandwidth W and most of its energy within a duration T, so that it would appear, at least on an intuitive basis, that most of the signal energy can be contained in a few coordinates, leading to the concept of approximate dimensionality.

As it turns out, the subject of waveform dimensionality can be approached from two directions. The first (mathematical) approach is the subject of the Landau–Pollak theorem [La 62] and states that although functions have an infinite number of dimensions, it is possible to find an approximate representation that concentrates as much of a signal's norm in as few coordinates as possible, provided the prolate spheroidal wave functions are used for a basis. Sampling does not provide such a minimal representation, although, in some cases, it is a good approximation. The second (philosophical) approach, eloquently stated by Slepian [Sl 76], recognizes the inherent physical limitations of measuring equipment and the consequent inability to distinguish between two signals that are sufficiently similar, but differ by a small amount. This statement can be made more precise. Two functions are indistinguishable if the squared norm of their difference is smaller than the energy resolution of a measurement. Thus, functions are infinite-dimensional in a strict mathematical sense, but physical measurements can only distinguish between a finite number of them. For practical purposes, therefore, only a finite number of dimensions are of consequence. The mathematical and philosophical approaches yield identical results in terms of measurable quantities. These two approaches will be briefly discussed here. The reader is referred to the references for a more complete mathematical treatment.

Slepian, Landau and Pollak [Sl 61, La 61, La 62] give a thorough discussion of the representation of functions with duration and bandwidth limitations by a basis set consisting of the prolate spheroidal wave functions. In particular, they show that for a function $f(t)$ with unit total energy band-limited to bandwidth W, and whose energy is mostly concentrated in the closed interval $[0, T]$,

$$\int_0^T |f(t)|^2 \, dt = 1 - \epsilon \tag{2.79}$$

where $\epsilon < 1$; then

$$\inf_{\{a_k\}} \int_{-\infty}^{\infty} |f(t) - \sum_{k=0}^{2TW} a_k \Psi_k(t)|^2 \, dt < 12\epsilon \tag{2.80}$$

if the $\psi_k(t)$ are the prolate spheroidal wave functions. This important result, known as the Landau–Pollak theorem, says that the error incurred by using only $2TW + 1$

coordinates to represent a band-limited signal is upper bounded by 12ϵ, a quantity that can be made arbitrarily small by choosing T sufficiently large.

It is, therefore, possible to represent such functions $f(t)$ by $2TW + 1$ independent quantities to within an error having a Euclidian norm that is upper bounded by $(12\epsilon)^{1/2}$, where ϵ is the fraction of the energy of $f(t)$ falling outside the interval $[0, T]$. Within the validity of this approximation, $f(t)$ can be represented in an approximately $(2TW + 1)$-dimensional signal space provided the coordinates are the prolate spheroidal wave functions. For large duration-bandwidth products, the number of coordinates required is approximately $2TW$. For small values of TW, the error incurred by using only $2TW + 1$ coordinates to represent a function can be substantial.

EXAMPLE

The square pulse function $\Pi(t)$ shown in Fig. 2-5 has the Fourier transform

$$\Pi(t) \leftrightarrow \frac{\sin \pi \nu}{\pi \nu} = \text{sinc } \nu \tag{2.81}$$

$\Pi(t)$ has a duration $T = 1$, unit norm, and its first spectral null is at $\nu = 1$, which is customarily taken to be the bandwidth. The fraction ϵ_1 of the waveform energy not contained in the bandwidth that extends up to the first null is

$$\epsilon_1 = 1 - 2 \int_0^1 \frac{\sin^2 \pi \nu}{(\pi \nu)^2} \, d\nu \approx 0.0972$$

which indicates that approximately 90 percent of the waveform's energy is contained within the main spectral lobe. According to the Landau–Pollak theorem, using only three prolate spheroidal wave functions to represent a square pulse results in an approximation error norm that is upper bounded by $(12\epsilon_1)^{1/2} = 1.08$, which is on the same order as the function itself. If the bandwidth is made to extend to the next lobe, the fraction ϵ_2 of the waveform energy not contained in the main and first lobes is $\epsilon_2 = 0.0501$, and the resulting error norm is bounded by 0.78, still a large quantity. This poor fit is the result of the abundant spectral leakage exhibited by the sinc function.

EXAMPLE

The triangular function $\Lambda(t)$ shown in Fig. 2-7 has the Fourier transform

$$\Lambda(t) \leftrightarrow \frac{\sin^2 \pi \nu}{(\pi \nu)^2} = \text{sinc}^2 \nu \tag{2.82}$$

and exhibits considerably less spectral leakage than $\Pi(t)$. This waveform has a norm of 2/3, and a duration $T = 2$. Choosing $W = 1$, which corresponds to a bandwidth extending up to the first null as in the previous example, we have $\epsilon_1 = 0.0020$ and $(12\epsilon)^{1/2} = 0.15$, which is considerably smaller than what was obtained with $\Pi(t)$. Similarly, choosing $W = 2$ results in $\epsilon_2 = 0.0003$ and $(12\epsilon_2)^{1/2} = 0.06$.

In Section 2.3.1, we saw that a band-limited function $f(t)$ can be represented by its uniformly spaced samples, with the reconstruction being given by Eq. (2.54)

$$f(t) = \sum_k f\left(\frac{k}{2W}\right) \frac{\sin(2\pi W t - k\pi)}{2\pi W t - k\pi} \qquad k = -\infty, \ldots, \infty$$

This is simply a convolution with the Whittaker interpolation function

$$h(t) = \frac{\sin 2\pi W t}{2\pi W t}$$

The reconstruction formula can also be considered an orthogonal expansion with respect to the basis functions (sometimes called the sampling functions):

$$g_k(t) = \frac{\sin(2\pi W t - k\pi)}{2\pi W t - k\pi} \qquad (2.83)$$

since the $g_k(t)$ are orthogonal:

$$2W \int_{-\infty}^{\infty} g_k(t)g_n(t)\, dt = \delta_{k,n}$$

The function $g_k(t)$ goes to zero very slowly, so that a very large number of samples is required to approximate a band-limited function. Truncation in general results

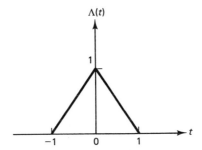

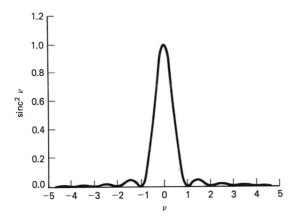

Figure 2-7. $\Lambda(t)$ and its Fourier transform $\text{sinc}^2 = \nu$.

in an appreciable error norm, which Landau and Pollak have shown to be on the order of the fourth root of ϵ. Since $\epsilon < 1$, the sampling functions give a poorer approximation than the prolate spheroidal wave functions.

Recall that the functions $\varphi(t)$ that are strictly band-limited on a frequency interval of width W and that concentrate as much energy on the closed time interval $[-\tau, \tau]$ are the solutions to the eigenvalue equation

$$\int_{-\tau}^{\tau} \varphi(x) \frac{\sin [2\pi W (t - x)]}{\pi (t - x)} \, dx = \lambda \varphi(t) \tag{2.84}$$

We now look for the asymptotic form of $\varphi(t)$ as W remains fixed and as $\tau \to \infty$. We shall denote this asymptotic form by $\xi(t)$. This limiting process lets us study the asymptotic form of the prolate spheroidal wave functions for the case of band-limited functions with very large duration-bandwidth product. It will turn out that $\xi(t)$ has a particularly simple form: it coincides with the sampling functions. Taking the limit as $\tau \to \infty$, we obtain the following integral equation for $\xi(t)$:

$$\int_{-\infty}^{\infty} \xi(x) \frac{\sin [2\pi W (t - x)]}{\pi (t - x)} \, dx = \lambda \xi(t) \tag{2.85}$$

It can be shown that the solutions to this equation are of the form

$$\xi(t) = \frac{\sin (2\pi W t - k\pi)}{2\pi W t - k\pi} \tag{2.86}$$

with $\lambda = 1$ (see Prob. 2.13).

The significance of this is that the representation of long $(T \gg 1/W)$ segments of band-limited functions can be approximated in a $2WT$-dimensional linear function space, provided the representation is with respect to the prolate spheroidal wave functions. It is in this sense that, many times throughout this book, we consider functions to be defined in a finite $2TW$-dimensional linear function space.

When T is much longer than $1/W$, the basis functions asymptotically approach the Whittaker interpolating functions. With this choice of basis, the representation of a function is simply given by its $2TW$ samples, uniformly spaced according to the Nyquist criterion. This result is of special importance in digital signal-processing systems, where band-limited functions are sampled.

2.4 MATCHED FILTERING

The detection of signals in noise must involve some form of processing to help recognize when a given signal is present at the input of a system. Typically, noise is always present and a signal may or may not be there, or there is one of a set of several possible signals present in addition to noise. There may also be other signals we wish to discriminate against present at the input. The right type of processing should have a large output when the desired signal is, in fact, present, and a lower output when any other signal is applied at the input. Such processing, when restricted to be a linear operation, is called *matched filtering*. The linear filter with response $h(t)$ is said to be *matched* to $f(t)$, the waveform to be detected.

The University Library

The Andersonian Library

The University Library

Curran Building, 101 St. James' Road, Glasgow G4 0NS
READER SERVICES DIVISION
Tel: 0141-548 4625 Fax: 0141-552 3304

Derek G Law *University Librarian and*
Director of Information Strategy

UNIVERSITY OF STRATHCLYDE

RESERVATION REQUEST

BOOK No. **3 0 1 2 5**

Author _Pierre Lafrance_

Title _Fundamental concepts in communication_

Class No. _D 621.38 LAF_

	Reports
Library Use	
IN: -2 FEB 2000	

Name _Nishi Gill_

Address _36 BEACONSFIELD RD_

KELVINSIDE G-120NY

USER No.
2 0 1 2 5 0 0 4 1 3 8 0 3 5 T

GILL, N   21/2

Date _____

With reference to your request overleaf, please note the section marked.

☐ This book is recorded as not on loan. Please check the shelves.

☐ This book is available from the Short Loan Collection.

☐ This book is available for reference only. It cannot be borrowed.

☐ This book is now available and will be kept for you at the Borrowing and Return Desk until _____

☐

Derek G Law
University Librarian and Director of Information Strategy

2.4.1 Derivations of the Matched Filter

Matched filters are used in two conceptually different types of applications, both having to do with the detection of signals in additive noise. In the first application, the problem is to decide between the following two hypotheses:

$H_0 : y(t) = n(t)$, noise only is present;

$H_1 : y(t) = x(t) + n(t)$, both signal and noise are present.

This situation arises, for example, in radar detection, where the presence of a target would result in a reflected radar signal $x(t)$ being present at the receiver. If no target is present, only the noise $n(t)$ is measured. In this case, processing $y(t)$ with a filter matched to $x(t)$ will result in the largest possible filter output signal-to-noise ratio when $x(t)$ is applied to the input.

What characterizes this application is that a signal is not present at the input in one of the hypotheses. When a signal is present, as in the other hypothesis, its form is known a priori. The function of the matched filter in this case is to aid in the detection process by providing the largest possible signal indication to the detection circuitry, which is typically implemented as threshold crossing logic.

A similar situation arises in communication systems when a paging or synchronization preamble is transmitted at the beginning of a message. The purpose of this preamble may be to selectively address the specific receiving station(s) for which the message is intended or, perhaps, to supply the synchronization information necessary to properly process the message that follows. In this case, paging waveforms and their associated matched filters can be used to activate a receiver to process incoming signals as messages. This is illustrated in Fig. 2-8.

The other application for matched filters is processing for data decoding. Here the receiver is assumed to be synchronized to an incoming waveform that consists

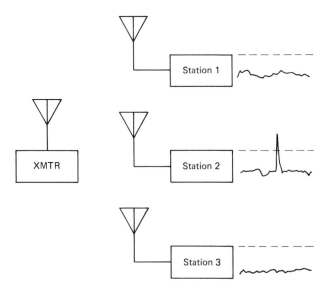

Figure 2-8. A paging system where each of the stations processes the incoming signals with a filter matched to its individual calling code. Only that code will cause the filter's output to be large enough to exceed a detection threshold. Other (unmatched) waveforms and noise will not cause detection to occur. In this example, the transmitter (XMTR) is sending the code to which station 2 is matched. Matched filter outputs as functions of time are shown to the right of each station. A dashed line represents the detection threshold level.

of symbols chosen from a finite alphabet. For example, binary transmissions would result in a sequence of "mark" or "space" signals. In this case, a separate matched filter is implemented for each one of the waveforms in the symbol alphabet. All of the matched filters have their inputs tied in parallel and presented with the same received waveform. The symbol corresponding to the received waveform is then identified as being associated with the matched filter having the largest output. During such information decoding, a signal is always present at the input of a matched filter bank. Decision logic at the outputs, usually implemented as amplitude comparisons, identifies the symbol most likely to have been transmitted as that associated with the largest matched-filter output. The subjects of detection and communication performance are addressed in more detail in Chapters 4 and 5.

In principle, symbol decoding is similar to a paging system, such as the one shown in Fig. 2-8, with each station representing a symbol and with all matched filters being included at a single station. Signaling then consists in "paging" the symbols sequentially by transmitting their associated waveforms. The corresponding matched filters at the receiving station can then be used to recognize which waveform was transmitted. This is usually implemented as a bank of matched filters, one for each symbol, and is shown in Fig. 2-9. We give two derivations for the matched filter. The traditional approach for complex functions uses the Schwarz inequality, and is presented first. This is followed by a derivation based on the calculus of variations.

The traditional derivation of the matched filter is based on the generalized Schwarz inequality, which states that

$$\left| \int_{-\infty}^{\infty} V(\nu) W^*(\nu) \, d\nu \right|^2 \leq \int_{-\infty}^{\infty} V^*(\nu) V(\nu) \, d\nu \cdot \int_{-\infty}^{\infty} W^*(\nu) W(\nu) \, d\nu \quad (2.87)$$

when the integrals exist, and that the equality holds when

$$V(\nu) = CW(\nu)$$

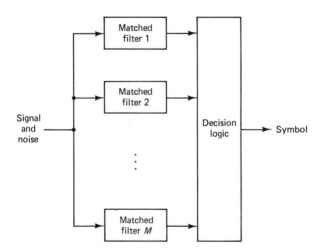

Figure 2-9. Symbol decoding using a bank of matched filters followed by decision logic implemented as amplitude comparators. The decision logic selects the largest matched-filter output.

for any constant C. The left-hand side of the Schwarz inequality assumes its maximum value when $V(\nu)$ is proportional to $W(\nu)$.

Now let $f(t)$ be a signal with Fourier transform $F(\nu)$, and let $G(\nu)$ be the energy spectral density of the additive noise process in which $f(t)$ is measured. We seek to find the linear filter with impulse response $h(t)$ that has the largest possible output signal-to-noise ratio t_0 seconds after the input $f(t)$ has been applied. Clearly, such a filter can be useful in processing signals for detection. Since the magnitude of its output is greatest when $f(t)$ is applied at the input, the filter's output can be taken as an indication of whether or not $f(t)$ is present at the input.

The output signal-to-noise ratio at time t_0 is

$$\frac{\left| \int_{-\infty}^{\infty} H(\nu) F(\nu) e^{2\pi j \nu t_0} \, d\nu \right|^2}{\int_{-\infty}^{\infty} H^*(\nu) H(\nu) G(\nu) \, d\nu}$$

where the filter's transform characteristics have been expressed in the frequency (ν) domain. The numerator is simply equivalent to the square of the convolution $f(t) * h(t)$ delayed by t_0 seconds. The denominator is the total noise energy at the filter output.

If we now let

$$V(\nu) = H(\nu)[G(\nu)]^{1/2}$$

and

$$W^*(\nu) = \frac{H(\nu) F(\nu)}{V(\nu)} e^{2\pi j \nu t_0} = \frac{F(\nu)}{[G(\nu)]^{1/2}} e^{2\pi j \nu t_0}$$

the generalized Schwarz inequality now reads

$$\left| \int_{-\infty}^{\infty} H(\nu) F(\nu) e^{2\pi j \nu t_0} \, d\nu \right|^2 \leq \int_{-\infty}^{\infty} H^*(\nu) H(\nu) G(\nu) \, d\nu \int_{-\infty}^{\infty} \frac{F^*(\nu) F(\nu)}{G(\nu)} \, d\nu$$

This can be rewritten as

$$\frac{\left| \int_{-\infty}^{\infty} H(\nu) F(\nu) e^{2\pi j \nu t_0} \, d\nu \right|^2}{\int_{-\infty}^{\infty} H^*(\nu) H(\nu) G(\nu) \, d\nu} \leq \int_{-\infty}^{\infty} \frac{F^*(\nu) F(\nu)}{G(\nu)} \, d\nu$$

where the left-hand side can be recognized as the output signal-to-noise ratio at time t_0. This quantity assumes its maximum value when

$$V(\nu) = CW(\nu)$$

or

$$H(\nu)[G(\nu)]^{1/2} = C \frac{F^*(\nu)}{[G(\nu)]^{1/2}} e^{-2\pi j \nu t_0}$$

giving for the matched-filter transfer function

$$H(\nu) = C \frac{F^*(\nu)}{G(\nu)} e^{-2\pi j \nu t_0} \qquad (2.88)$$

For noise with a constant spectral density, the corresponding time-domain function is

$$h(t) = f^*(t_0 - t) \tag{2.89}$$

When operating in noise with a specified energy spectral density, the useful property of matched filters can be summarized as follows. Of all possible input signals having the same total energy, the largest matched-filter output corresponds to the input signal to which the filter is matched.

We now use the calculus of variations to derive the form of the matched filter. Given a function $f(t)$, we wish to find the form of the linear filter that results in maximum output signal-to-noise ratio at time t_0. The filter output is given by the convolution

$$y(t) = h(t) * [f(t) + n(t)] \tag{2.90}$$

where $n(t)$ is a noise process with energy spectral density $G(v)$. We now go to the frequency domain by expressing the first term of the convolution as the inverse Fourier transform of the product of the transforms of $f(t)$ and $h(t)$, giving

$$h(t) * f(t) = \int_{-\infty}^{\infty} H(v)F(v)e^{2\pi j\, v t_0} \, dv \tag{2.91}$$

Maximizing this integral maximizes the output signal-to-noise ratio. The matched filter we seek is given by the function $H(v)$, which maximizes the last integral and which represents, in the frequency domain, the filter's desired response to the applied function $f(t)$. We also need to simultaneously minimize the integral

$$\int_{-\infty}^{\infty} H^*(v)H(v)G(v) \, dv$$

which represents the noise energy output process. These extremizations are to be carried subject to the constraint that

$$\int_{-\infty}^{\infty} H^*(v)H(v) \, dv = C_1$$

where C_1 is a constant. This constraint is a necessary condition in order for the function $h(t)$ to have the Fourier transform $H(v)$. This constrained variation problem can be solved by introducing a Lagrange multiplier λ and is equivalent to the unconstrained variation of

$$J = \int_{-\infty}^{\infty} H(v)F(v)e^{2\pi j\, v t_0} \, dv - \int_{-\infty}^{\infty} H^*(v)H(v)G(v) \, dv$$

$$- \lambda \left[\int_{-\infty}^{\infty} H^*(v)H(v) \, dv - C_1 \right] \tag{2.92}$$

The Euler-Lagrange equation corresponding to this problem is

$$(\partial/\partial H)[H(v)F(v)e^{2\pi j\, v t_0} - H^*(v)H(v)G(v) - \lambda H^*(v)H(v)] = 0 \tag{2.93}$$

and leads to the expression

$$F(\nu)e^{2\pi j \nu t_0} = [G(\nu) + \lambda]H^*(\nu)$$

Multiplying this by $H(\nu)$, integrating over ν, and making use of the constraint that the integral of $H^*(\nu)H(\nu)$ be finite gives

$$\lambda C_1 = \int_{-\infty}^{\infty} H(\nu)F(\nu)e^{2\pi j \nu t_0} \, d\nu + \int_{-\infty}^{\infty} H^*(\nu)H(\nu)G(\nu) \, d\nu = C_2$$

where C_2 is another constant. The Lagrange multiplier $\lambda = C_2/C_1$ is, therefore, also a constant. The solution to this problem can be formally written as

$$H(\nu) = \frac{F^*(\nu)}{G(\nu) + \lambda} e^{-2\pi j \nu t_0} \qquad (2.94)$$

Substituting this in the previous equation results in a condition that can only be satisfied by $\lambda = 0$, resulting in a matched-filter transfer function $H(\nu)$ that is identical with the expression obtained previously through the generalized Schwarz inequality.

Many of the applications of matched filtering involve detection in additive white noise, for which $G(\nu)$ is a constant. The output of the matched filter at time t_0 is then of the form

$$y(t_0) = \int_{-\infty}^{\infty} F^*(\nu)F(\nu)e^{2\pi j \nu t_0} \, d\nu \qquad (2.95)$$

The equivalent time-domain operation is

$$y(t_0) = \int_{-\infty}^{\infty} f^*(t)f(t + t_0) \, dt \qquad (2.96)$$

which is the autocorrelation function for $f(t)$. If some other function than $f(t)$ is present at the filter input, the filter output is still in the form of a correlation:

$$y(t_0) = \int_{-\infty}^{\infty} f^*(t)g(t + t_0) \, dt \qquad (2.97)$$

A matched filter can, therefore, be implemented as a correlator. By a simple change of integration variable, we can demonstrate that the matched filter can also be expressed as a convolution. Letting $\tau = t + t_0$, there results

$$y(t_0) = \int_{-\infty}^{\infty} f^*(\tau - t_0)g(\tau) \, d\tau = \int_{-\infty}^{\infty} h(t_0 - \tau)g(\tau) \, d\tau \qquad (2.98)$$

where $h(t) = f^*(-t)$ is the matched-filter impulse response. The correlation and convolution implementations of the matched filter are described in block diagram form in Fig. 2-10. Figure 2-10(a) shows the correlator implementation of the matched filter, which implements Eq. (2.97) for a function $g(t)$, $0 \le t \le T$, having a finite time duration T. This implementation is used in digital communication, where the received signal consists of a sequence of such time-limited waveforms, each

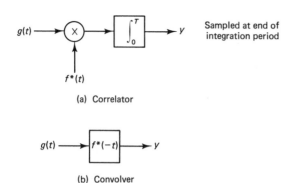

(a) Correlator

(b) Convolver

Figure 2-10. (*a*) Correlation and (*b*) convolution implementations of matched filtering.

representing a particular symbol. Assuming synchronization between the incoming waveform sequence and the integration interval, the integration will be performed precisely when $g(t)$ is applied at the correlator input.

The correlator form of matched filtering is used when it is possible to synchronize the reference waveform to the incoming signal. This is the case for symbol decoding in digital communication. The convolver is used when synchronization is not possible or when an estimate of the signal's time of arrival is desired, such as in radar. Both the correlator and the convolver forms are used in communication systems. For example, a synchronization preamble can be used in conjunction with the convolver implementation to establish synchronization. Here the detection strategy involves continuous processing by the matched filter and threshold detector. Just as in radar, performance is usually expressed in terms of the probabilities of detection and of false threshold crossing due to noise. The threshold is usually selected to keep the false-alarm probability constant. The convolver output must be interrogated sufficiently often to be able to accurately determine synchronization. Typically, synchronization timing errors should be small when compared to the duration of a symbol waveform.

Once synchronization has been established, a correlator bank may be used to decode incoming waveforms. If an alphabet consisting of M symbols is used for communication, then a set of M different signaling waveforms is used to uniquely represent these symbols. A bank of M synchronized correlators can be used to process the received signal. At the end of each integration period, the outputs of all M correlators are compared and the symbol corresponding to the largest output is decoded.

The statistical performance analysis of symbol decoding and constant false-alarm-rate processing will be covered in Chapters 5 and 6. There we shall also study how signal theoretic properties of waveforms, namely their norms and mutual metric distances, affect communication performance.

There is a subtle practical difference between the convolution and correlation forms of the matched filter. The convolution form implies that the received waveform $f(t)$ is continuously processed by a linear filter with impulse response $h(t) = f^*(-t)$. The filter output $y(t)$ is then fed to a threshold crossing detector. The presence of a matched waveform at the input is then inferred when the threshold is crossed. This implementation is used in radar detection, when it is desired to test the hypothesis of target presence as well as to measure the time at which such target is detected, so as to obtain range information. The convolver can also be used in communication applications if sampled at the time when the input waveform $g(t)$ is perfectly aligned with its reference $f^*(t)$. This assumes that synchronization has been established.

The correlation implementation is used in symbol decoding. Assuming waveform synchronization with the transmitter has been established, the received signal $g(t)$ in each waveform period of duration T seconds is processed by a bank of correlators. Each correlator (1) multiplies $g(t)$ with a conjugated reference waveform $f^*(t)$, and (2) integrates the product over the waveform duration.

The correlator implementation of a matched filter, therefore, takes the form

$$y_{\text{out}} = \int_0^T f^*(t)g(t)\, dt$$

where y_{out} is the correlator output, and where $t_0 = 0$ has been assumed without loss of generality. Note that y_{out} can be simply written as an inner product:

$$y_{\text{out}} = \langle f(t)|g(t)\rangle$$

By looking at matched filters as purely mathematical operations, both the convolution and the correlation implementations are functionals. They map the function into a scalar, which we have denoted as $y(t_0)$ or y_{out}.

It is important to distinguish matched filters, as they are used in detection, from the more general forms of convolution and correlation operations encountered in signal processing. In general, convolution and correlation are functions generated by functionals. They represent the entire output history of a filter or correlator. As such, an input waveform is continually transformed into an output waveform. In matched filtering through correlation, only the output at a particular instant is used. In the convolution implementation (e.g., in radar detection), the filter output is continuously sampled and the statistical hypotheses are tested anew with each sample. In the correlator implementation, the value y_{out} used in detection is the value of a definite integral. In both implementations, the matched filter acts as a functional that maps the received waveform into a single scalar, which is then used in detection.

2.4.2 Frequency-Domain Interpretation✳

In the time domain, the effect of the matched filter on the signal can be described by a convolution of the form

$$y(t) = h(t) * f(t)$$

evaluated at time t_0. This convolution represents filtering of the signal $f(t)$ with the function $h(t)$. A more intuitive feeling for the processing performed by a matched filter can be obtained by looking at this operation in the frequency domain, where the equivalent processing is

$$h(t) * f(t) \leftrightarrow \int_{-\infty}^{\infty} H(\nu)F(\nu)e^{2\pi j \nu t_0} d\nu$$

where $H(\nu)$ and $F(\nu)$ are the Fourier transforms of $h(t)$ and $f(t)$, respectively [La 87]. The proper form for $H(\nu)$ is given by Eq. (2.88):

$$H(\nu) = \frac{F^*(\nu)}{G(\nu)} e^{-2\pi j \nu t_0}$$

For white noise, term $G(\nu)$ is a constant. The matched-filter response $y(t)$ is a convolution of the waveform $f(t)$ with a filter with response $h(t)$, and can be represented by a product of Fourier transforms in the frequency domain:

$$Y(\nu) = H(\nu)F(\nu)$$

where $F(\nu)$, $Y(\nu)$, and $H(\nu)$ are the Fourier transforms of $f(t)$, $y(t)$, and $h(t)$, respectively. Expressed in the frequency domain, the matched-filter condition $h(t) = f^*(-t)$ becomes

$$H(\nu) = F^*(\nu)$$

and the matched-filter response is

$$Y(\nu) = F^*(\nu)F(\nu) = |F(\nu)|^2 \tag{2.99}$$

A few comments are in order here. First, $Y(\nu)$ is always real, and, therefore, $y(t)$ is always an even function. This is true regardless of waveform $f(t)$. The phase spectrum of $f(t)$ does not appear in the matched-filter response. This comes about because the matched filter $F^*(\nu)$ has precisely the phase spectrum that, when coherently combined with $F(\nu)$, produces in each Fourier component a resultant phase that aligns that component along the real axis. The phase spectra of $F(\nu)$ and $H(\nu)$ cancel exactly at all frequencies. All Fourier components, therefore, combine constructively to produce the maximum (real) matched-filter response. In the frequency domain, the matched filter aligns all of the complex phasors along the same direction for maximum output. With no loss in generality, we take $t_0 = 0$ as the time at which the matched-filter output is evaluated. This output is given by

$$y(t) = \int_{-\infty}^{\infty} F^*(\nu)F(\nu)e^{2\pi j \nu t} d\nu \tag{2.100}$$

from which it can be seen that the maximum filter output at $t = 0$ is equal to the total energy in the waveform.

The effect of the matched filter on the waveform to which it is matched is to coherently combine all of the spectral phasors, weighted by their complex conjugates, and expressing the result as a real scalar. The matched-filtering process collects the energy in all of the waveform degrees of freedom and outputs this total energy as one scalar, which is then used for detection purposes.

2.4.3 Matched Filtering and Detection

Matched filtering plays an important part as a signal-processing operation performed prior to detection. We have already seen that matched filtering is the linear operation that produces the maximum output signal-to-noise ratio. The matched-filter output has the largest possible norm when compared to the effect of other signals of equal energy presented at the filter input.

We now preview some results that will be covered in detail in Chapter 5. The emphasis in this section is to present the matched filter as a signal-processing operation for signal detection. Chapter 5 takes a close look at detection as a means of performing statistical inference to determine which of several competing statistical hypotheses is most compatible with observations.

Consider a detection problem in which the task is to infer whether or not a certain signal $s(t)$ has been received or not from a measurement $x(t)$ made in additive white Gaussian noise $n(t)$ having a one-sided power spectral density N_0. The signal present versus the signal absent conditions are represented by the two statistical hypotheses

$$H_0: \quad x(t) = n(t) \qquad \text{(signal absent)},$$
$$H_1: \quad x(t) = s(t) + n(t) \qquad \text{(signal present)}.$$

From a purely signal theoretic approach, the simplest way to decide between these two alternatives is to compare the measured signal $x(t)$ to each of the possibilities: $n(t)$ and $s(t) + n(t)$. Specifically, we compute the square of the metric distance between $x(t)$ and each of these two possibilities and decide in favor of the nearest of the two. We could use the metric distance by itself, but it turns out that the square of the metric is an easier quantity to handle and is totally equivalent to the metric for our purposes since squaring is a monotonic function and preserves any ordering of the magnitudes. The signal theoretic approach to detection involves the computation and thresholding of the difference Δ between the squares of these norms:

$$\Delta = \langle x - n | x - n \rangle - \langle x - (s + n) | x - (s + n) \rangle = -\mathcal{E} + 2\mathcal{R}e\langle x | s \rangle$$

where $\mathcal{E} = |s|^2$, and $\langle s | n \rangle$ vanishes since $s(t)$ and $n(t)$ are assumed uncorrelated. If both hypotheses are equally likely, then equal weight is assigned to each hypothesis and the proper threshold value for Δ is zero:

$$\text{declare } H_0 \text{ as true if } \Delta > 0,$$
$$\text{declare } H_1 \text{ as true if } \Delta \leq 0.$$

In the simplest detection problem, the task is to determine which of two probability density functions $p_0(x)$ or $p_1(x)$ is the most likely population distribution for a measured signal x. These densities for the measured signal correspond to the two statistical hypotheses. This leads to a statistical approach to detection, a subject covered in Chapter 5. The probability density for the norm $\|n\|$ of zero mean white Gaussian noise can be expressed as

$$p(n) = \alpha \exp \left[-N_0^{-1} \|n\|^2 \right]$$

where α is a constant of proportionality that may be determined through norm-alization. The probability densities $p_0(x)$ and $p_1(x)$ for the measurement x for the case of each statistical hypothesis can be determined from $p(n)$ by setting

$$p_0(x) = \text{Prob } \{x|H_0 \text{ is true}\} = p(x)$$

and

$$p_1(x) = \text{Prob } \{x|H_1 \text{ is true}\} = p(x - s)$$

We shall show in Chapter 5 that the proper statistical procedure to follow is to form the likelihood ratio

$$\lambda = \frac{p_0(x)}{p_1(x)}$$

evaluated at the measured value of x, and to attribute the measurement to $p_0(x)$ if $\lambda > 1$, and to $p_1(x)$ otherwise, provided the hypotheses are a priori equally likely. The likelihood ratio, or any monotonic function thereof, is the decision variable used in detection. We ask the reader to accept this fact at this time. A discussion will be presented in Chapter 5. For convenience, we adopt the logarithm of the likelihood ratio as the decision variable. This quantity is

$$N_0 \log \lambda = |x|^2 - |x - s|^2 = -\mathcal{E} + 2\mathcal{R}e\langle x|s\rangle$$

where the log likelihood has been premultiplied by N_0 for convenience. Apart from an inconsequential sign, this is the same decision variable obtained through metric considerations. Thresholding $-\mathcal{E} + 2\mathcal{R}e\langle x|s\rangle$ about zero is equivalent to thresholding λ about unity, as required by the statistical approach.

We also note that the signal energy $\mathcal{E}$ is a constant that can be incorporated in the threshold value itself. The only quantity that really need be computed and thresholded is the real part of the inner product $\mathcal{R}e\langle x|s\rangle$, which is of the form of a correlation between $x(t)$ and $s(t)$. Alternatively, we can interpret $\mathcal{R}e\langle x|s\rangle$ as the maximum value of the matched-filter output.

2.4.4 Matched-Filter Processing Gain

By setting $G(\nu) = N_0$ and using the results of Section 2.4.1, the signal-to-noise ratio (SNR) at the output of the matched filter is

$$\text{SNR}_{\text{out}} = \frac{\left|\int_{-\infty}^{\infty} H(\nu)F(\nu)e^{2\pi j \nu t_0} d\nu\right|^2}{\int_{-\infty}^{\infty} H^*(\nu)H(\nu)G(\nu) d\nu} = \frac{\mathcal{E}}{N_0}$$

since $H(\nu) = F^*(\nu)e^{-2\pi j \nu t_0}$.

The matched-filter input "sees" the waveform $f(t)$ having bandwidth W and duration T. The signal power at the filter input is, therefore, $S = \mathcal{E}/T$. The input noise power is simply the product of the noise spectral density N_0 times the full bandwidth $2W$ (i.e., the bandwidth including positive and negative frequencies). The input signal-to-noise ratio is, therefore,

$$\text{SNR}_{\text{in}} = (\mathcal{E}/N_0) \cdot 1/2TW \qquad (2.101)$$

The ratio of the output to the input SNR is, therefore, $2TW$, and represents the gain of the matched filter for noise having a uniform spectral density. The matched filter can thus be viewed as a device that enhances the SNR by a factor of $2TW$.

2.4.5 Signal Theoretic Considerations✳

From the relation $h(t) = f^*(-t)$, it is evident that the matched filter has the same bandwidth as the signal to which it is matched. In the frequency domain, this has the effect of passing as much signal energy as possible without passing too much noise. A wider bandwidth would result in additional noise energy at the filter output without significantly increasing signal energy. This would decrease the output signal-to-noise ratio. A narrower filter bandwidth would result in less output noise, but would also distort the desired signal. The matched filter is a compromise between these two extremes, and results in the maximum possible output signal-to-noise ratio.

Note that this is different than requiring the maximum possible filter output amplitude. The maximum filter output amplitude would be an impulse, which could in principle be produced by inverse filtering, i.e., with $H(\nu) = F^{-1}(\nu)$. This would have the additional desirable property of resulting in very high time resolution for waveform time-of-arrival measurements. However, since $F(\nu) \to 0$ as $|\nu| \to \infty$ for physically meaningful waveforms, the inverse filter gain $|F^{-1}(\nu)|$ becomes unbounded and such a filter would pass large quantities of noise. We must, therefore, settle for the matched filter.

An unavoidable consequence of this compromise is an inherent lack of sharpness in the time at which the filter output peaks. This is important in radar applications, where it is desired to accurately measure the time of arrival of pulses, and also in digital communication systems, where synchronization information is conveyed by special waveforms whose time of arrival must be accurately measured.

Consider, for example, the convolution implementation of the matched filter. The input waveform $x(t)$ is continually being processed by a filter with impulse response $h(t) = x^*(-t)$, producing a waveform $y(t)$ at the output. The temporal width of the filter response is the correlation width of the waveform $x(t)$, since the filter output is given by the autocorrelation of $x(t)$, which is the inverse Fourier transform of the waveform's spectral density

$$y(t) = \int_{-\infty}^{\infty} X^*(\nu)X(\nu)e^{2\pi j \nu t}\, d\nu \qquad (2.102)$$

The correlation duration of a waveform is the smallest amount of time during which the matched-filter output has appreciable magnitude. This duration is sometimes referred to as the filter's time resolution.

What is the maximum achievable matched-filter time resolution? A moment's reflection will suffice to realize that the time resolution can be made almost as small as one desires by letting the signal bandwidth get large. In that sense, there is no limit to the filter's temporal resolution. Since the bandwidth cannot be infinite, the matched-filter output peak cannot be made arbitrarily sharp. This is sometimes said to result in some uncertainty in the measurement of the time of the matched-filter peak.

The issue of uncertainty comes up in discussions of the ability of a waveform to be simultaneously localized in time and frequency. This is a generalization of the time resolution case discussed before. This generalization is perhaps best treated by introducing the waveform ambiguity function. The ambiguity function will simply turn out to be related to a generalization of the response of a matched filter to a signal that is both delayed in time and shifted in frequency.

Time and frequency measurements are more than of academic interest in communications. We already have mentioned the importance of the time-of-arrival measurement in the context of synchronization. There are also cases where frequency measurements are important. Consider the case of large Doppler shifts induced by rapidly moving platforms communicating by ultra-high-frequency radio. The a priori unknown receiving frequency may necessitate the acquisition of the waveform's carrier frequency as well as its time of arrival[†].

Consider a waveform having undergone a time delay τ and a frequency offset φ. Under ideal conditions, these offsets are zero and the matched-filter output is sampled at its maximum value, resulting in optimal detection. A subject of practical interest is to determine the matched-filter output under nonideal conditions when the filter is sampled at some time other than at maximum output or when the received waveform has suffered a Doppler shift not accounted for in the replica used by the filter. In general, we may be interested in the response of a matched filter to a radar pulse having undergone simultaneous time and Doppler shifts due to target range and range rate, respectively.

Consider some arbitrary complex waveform $f(t)$. In general, a waveform will suffer simultaneous displacements in both time and frequency. We can reasonably expect detection performance to depend on some measure of similarity between $f(t)$ and its shifted version. With no loss of generality, we can take the function $f(t)$ to be defined in a normed metric space. It is, therefore, natural to adopt the Euclidian metric, or any monotonic function thereof, as a proper measure of similarity, and calculate the square of the Euclidian metric between $f(t)$ and its time- and frequency-offset version.

Using the shift theorem of Fourier analysis [Br 65], we can write the frequency-shifted version of $f(t)$ as $f(t)e^{2\pi j \varphi t}$. This corresponds to $f(t)e^{2\pi j \varphi t} \leftrightarrow F(\nu - \varphi)$ when $f(t) \leftrightarrow F(\nu)$, where the doubleheaded arrow ($\leftrightarrow$) denotes a Fourier transform pair. If we now introduce a time delay of τ seconds in this expression, there results $f(t - \tau)e^{2\pi j \varphi(t - \tau)}$. The difference between the original and shifted functions, $f(t)$ and $f(t - \tau)e^{2\pi j \varphi(t-\tau)}$, respectively, can be symbolically written as

$$\Delta(\tau, \varphi; t) = f(t) - f(t - \tau)e^{2\pi j \varphi(t - \tau)} \tag{2.103}$$

The square of the Euclidian metric between $f(t)$ and its shifted version can easily be calculated, and is equal to the norm of $\Delta(\tau, \varphi; t)$:

$$\int_{-\infty}^{\infty} \Delta^*(\tau, \varphi; t)\Delta(\tau, \varphi; t)\, dt = 2\mathscr{E} - 2\mathscr{R}e\left[e^{2\pi j \varphi \tau} \int_{-\infty}^{\infty} f(t)f^*(t - \tau)e^{-2\pi j \varphi t}\, dt \right]$$

[†]To the best of my knowledge, this is not done in most communication systems. Intermediate-frequency bandwidths are made sufficiently large to accommodate the largest anticipated Doppler shifts. This, however, results in lower signal-to-noise ratios.

where $\mathcal{E}$ is the total waveform energy, defined by

$$\mathcal{E} = \int_{-\infty}^{\infty} f^*(t)f(t)\, dt \qquad (2.104)$$

and where the expression in square brackets is the *generalized time-frequency correlation function*, also called the *generalized response function*:

$$\psi(\tau,\ \varphi) = e^{2\pi j\,\varphi\tau} \int_{-\infty}^{\infty} f(t)f^*(t-\tau)e^{-2\pi j\,\varphi t}\, dt = e^{2\pi j\,\varphi\tau}\chi(\tau,\ \varphi) \qquad (2.105)$$

where

$$\chi(\tau,\ \varphi) = \int_{-\infty}^{\infty} f(t)f^*(t-\tau)e^{-2\pi j\,\varphi t}\, dt \qquad (2.106)$$

The function $\psi(\tau,\ \varphi)$ is called the generalized response function because it is the response of a matched filter to a waveform that is delayed in time by τ and shifted in frequency by φ.

The *ambiguity function* is defined as $\psi^*(\tau,\ \varphi)\psi(\tau,\ \varphi)$ or, equivalently, as $\chi^*(\tau,\ \varphi)\chi(\tau,\ \varphi)$. Note that $\psi(\tau,\ \varphi)$ reduces to the familiar matched-filter output when $\varphi = 0$:

$$\psi(\tau,\ 0) = \int_{-\infty}^{\infty} f(t)f^*(t-\tau)\, dt = \int_{-\infty}^{\infty} f(t)h(\tau - t)\, dt = f(t) * h(t) \qquad (2.107)$$

where $h(t) = f^*(-t)$.

The ambiguity function has very interesting mathematical properties, which we now proceed to explore. First, we show that the ambiguity function attains its maximum value at zero time and at frequency shifts: $|\chi(0,\ 0)|^2 = |\psi(0,\ 0)|^2$ is a maximum. To this end, we use the Schwarz inequality:

$$|\psi(\tau,\ \varphi)|^2 = \left|\int f(t)f^*(t-\tau)e^{-2\pi j\,\varphi t}\, dt\right|^2 \le \int |f(t)|^2\, dt \int |f(t-\tau)|^2\, dt = \mathcal{E}^2$$

where the integrals run from $-\infty$ to $+\infty$. The equality obtains when $\tau = \varphi = 0$. This is a simple generalization of the familiar result for matched filters that the maximum value is equal to the waveform energy. We, therefore, have the sought inequality

$$|\psi(\tau,\ \varphi)|^2 = |\chi(\tau,\ \varphi)|^2 \le \mathcal{E}^2 \qquad (2.108)$$

with equality when $\tau = \varphi = 0$.

Another important property of the ambiguity function is that its Euclidian norm is equal to its value at the origin:

$$\int_{-\infty}^{\infty}\int_{-\infty}^{\infty} \chi^*(\tau,\ \varphi)\chi(\tau,\ \varphi)\, d\tau\, d\varphi = |\chi(0,\ 0)|^2 \qquad (2.109)$$

Let us pause to reflect on the mathematical significance of the norm of an ambiguity function. The quantity $|\chi(0,\ 0)|^2$ is the square of the Euclidian norm of the generalized matched-filter response $\psi(\tau,\ \varphi)$. The last equation implies that

$$\int_{-\infty}^{\infty}\int_{-\infty}^{\infty}\psi^*(\tau,\ \varphi)\psi(\tau,\ \varphi)\ d\tau\ d\varphi = |\chi(0,\ 0)|^2 = \mathcal{E}^2 \qquad (2.110)$$

is a constant that depends only on signal energy. This is a conservation rule for the squared modulus $\psi^*(\tau,\ \varphi)\psi(\tau,\ \varphi)$ of the generalized time–frequency correlation function over the entire $(\tau,\ \varphi)$ plane. We want this response to be large. But it is necessary to distribute the waveform in time as well as frequency. This necessarily results in $\psi(\tau,\ \varphi)$ being distributed over both these domains. The last expression simply states that the total amount of generalized correlation $\psi(\tau,\ \varphi)$, as measured by its norm, is a constant equal to the waveform energy and independent of the temporal and spectral details of the waveform itself.

We now prove this important relationship. We have defined the function $\chi(\tau,\ \varphi)$ as follows:

$$\chi(\tau,\ \varphi) = \int_{-\infty}^{\infty} f(t)f^*(t-\tau)e^{-2\pi j\,\varphi t}\ dt$$

which can then be expressed in the equivalent form (see Prob. 2-17):

$$\chi(\tau,\ \varphi) = \int_{-\infty}^{\infty} F(\nu+\varphi)F^*(\nu)e^{2\pi j\,\varphi t}\ d\nu$$

We, therefore, have

$$\int\int |\chi(\tau,\ \varphi)|^2\ d\tau\ d\varphi$$

$$= \int\int\int\int f(t)f^*(t-\tau)e^{-2\pi j\,\varphi t}F^*(\nu+\varphi)F(\nu)e^{-2\pi j\,\nu\tau}\ dt\ d\nu\ d\tau\ d\varphi$$

$$= \int\int dt\,d\nu f(t)F(\nu)\int f^*(t-\tau)e^{-2\pi j\,\nu\tau}\ d\tau$$

$$\times \int F^*(\nu+\varphi)e^{-2\pi j\,\varphi t}\ d\varphi$$

But

$$\int_{-\infty}^{\infty} f^*(t-\tau)e^{-2\pi j\,\nu\tau}\ d\tau = e^{-2\pi j\,\nu t}\,F^*(\nu)$$

and

$$\int_{-\infty}^{\infty} F^*(\nu+\varphi)e^{-2\pi j\,\varphi t}\ d\varphi = e^{2\pi j\,\nu t}f^*(t)$$

so that

$$\int\int |\chi(\tau,\ \varphi)|^2\ d\tau\ d\varphi = \int f^*(t)f(t)\ dt \int F^*(\nu)F(\nu)\ d\nu = \mathcal{E}^2 \qquad (2.111)$$

A more subtle implication of the conservation law is that apart from total energy, the only distinguishing characteristic of a waveform used in detection is the manner in which $|\psi(\tau, \varphi)|^2$ is distributed over the (τ, φ) plane. In particular, attempting to achieve a large time resolution by making the ambiguity function narrow on the τ axis causes the frequency resolution to become poorer and vice versa.

This effect can be attributed to the well-known "uncertainty" principle for waveforms having a Fourier transform. The waveform uncertainty principle states that, under very general conditions, the product of the duration and the bandwidth of a function cannot be made less than a certain constant. For example, if the duration T and bandwidth W are defined by the expressions

$$T^2 = \mathscr{E}^{-1} \int_{-\infty}^{\infty} f^*(t)f(t)t^2\, dt \qquad \text{and} \qquad W^2 = \mathscr{E}^{-1} \int_{-\infty}^{\infty} F^*(\nu)F(\nu)\nu^2\, d\nu$$

$$(2.112)$$

where the centroids of $f^*(t)f(t)$ and of $F^*(\nu)F(\nu)$ have, without loss of generality, been taken to be zero, we have

$$T^2 W^2 = \mathscr{E}^{-2} \int_{-\infty}^{\infty} f^*(t)f(t)t^2\, dt \int_{-\infty}^{\infty} F^*(\nu)F(\nu)\nu^2\, d\nu$$

$$= (2\pi\mathscr{E})^{-2} \int_{-\infty}^{\infty} f^*(t)f(t)t^2\, dt \int_{-\infty}^{\infty} f_\lambda^*(\lambda)f_\lambda(\lambda)\, d\lambda$$

$$\geq (2\pi\mathscr{E})^{-2}\left| \int_{-\infty}^{\infty} f^*(t)f_t(t)t\, dt \right|^2$$

$$\geq (2\pi\mathscr{E})^{-2} \mathscr{R}e^2 \int_{-\infty}^{\infty} f^*(t)f_t(t)t\, dt$$

by the Schwarz inequality. Integration by parts yields

$$\mathscr{R}e \int_{-\infty}^{\infty} f^*(t)f_t(t)t\, dt = -\frac{1}{2}\mathscr{E}$$

so that we have

$$TW \geq (4\pi)^{-1} \qquad\qquad (2.113)$$

The fortuitous similarity of this expression with the Heisenberg uncertainty principle of quantum mechanics has encouraged the misinterpretation of the previous result as also being an uncertainty relation. The Heisenberg uncertainty principle states that there are certain conjugate variable pairs such as (position, momentum) and (energy, duration) for which simultaneous measurements result in variances whose products cannot be made smaller than a certain lower bound. This is a consequence of the statistical formulation of quantum physics and does represent a true uncertainty in the statistical-measurement sense.

The waveform "uncertainty" principle, on the other hand, has nothing to do with the accuracy of measurements, or with statistics. Indeed, the duration and the bandwidth of a waveform can both be measured as well as one desires in the absence of noise. In fact, one implies the other and this is precisely the nature of the previously derived constraint.

The expression $TW \geq (4\pi)^{-1}$ is a statement of the amount of freedom (or lack thereof) we have in specifying a function having certain temporal and spectral characteristics. By specifying a function $f(t)$ in one domain completely determines its Fourier transform $F(\nu)$, and vice versa. The two conjugate domains are intimately related by the functional mapping implied by Fourier transformation. A function and its Fourier transform may not be prescribed simultaneously, for one implies the other. In particular, we have the previous constraint on the product of the widths of a function and of its Fourier transform.

Note that the previous definitions of waveform and duration are in the form of second moments of the norms of $f(t)$ and $F(\nu)$, respectively. As defined here, T^2 and W^2 can be considered to be weighted averages of the square of the time t^2 and frequency ν^2 over regions where $f^*(t)f(t)$ and $F^*(\nu)F(\nu)$ are appreciable, respectively.

There are several definitions of waveform duration and bandwidth. The definitions used before are sometimes referred to as the *mean-square duration* and *mean-square bandwidth*. It is also possible to define these quantities as the time or frequency ranges over which $f^*(t)f(t)$ or $F^*(\nu)F(\nu)$ decrease by a specified amount (usually 3 dB) from maximum. In our discussion of band-limited signals, we interpreted the bandwidth in a much stricter sense as a measure of the entire frequency domain over which $F^*(\nu)F(\nu)$ is nonzero. Since a band-limited function cannot have a finite duration, we adopted a somewhat looser definition of waveform duration as being a measure of the time domain over which all but a small specified amount ϵ of the total waveform energy could be found. For band-limited functions with small ϵ (i.e., $\epsilon < 0.1$), these measures of bandwidth and duration tend to be larger than the mean-square versions.

Throughout this book, in discussing signals in the signal-space formalism introduced in this chapter, we consider a duration bandwidth product of unity as being an irreducible quantity for the representation of signals. Indeed, a signal for which $TW = 1$ needs only one signal coordinate for its representation, a quantity that cannot be decreased further. This does not contradict the uncertainty relation $TW \geq (4\pi)^{-1}$ because (1) the definitions of time and bandwidth are different in those two examples, with numerically larger T and W used in the signal-space formalism, and (2) the uncertainty relation is an inequality that is not a very tight bound.

Let us now examine the behavior of the ambiguity function near the origin. To this end, we expand the ambiguity function in a Maclaurin series. For notational simplicity, we define

$$\xi(\tau, \varphi) = \chi^*(\tau, \varphi)\chi(\tau, \varphi)$$

The Maclaurin series expansion for $\xi(\tau, \varphi)$ is

$$\xi(\tau, \varphi) = \xi(0, 0) + \tfrac{1}{2}\tau^2 \xi_{\tau\tau}(0, 0) + \tau\varphi \, \mathscr{Re}\{\xi_{\tau\varphi}\{(0, 0)\} + \tfrac{1}{2}\varphi^2 \xi_{\varphi\varphi}(0, 0) + \cdots$$

$$(2.114)$$

where higher-order terms have been neglected. The linear terms are absent in the expansion since $\xi(\tau, \varphi)$ achieves its maximum value at the origin. Also, the function $\psi(\tau, \varphi)$ has Hermitian symmetry (see Prob. 2.18), implying that $\xi(\tau, \varphi)$ is an even function. Let us investigate the various terms in the Maclaurin expansion for $\xi(\tau, \varphi)$. The first term is simply

$$\xi(0, 0) = \mathscr{E}^2$$

as discussed earlier. Consider now the quadratic terms in Eq. (2.114). The coefficient of τ^2 is simply the following expression evaluated at the origin:

$$\xi_{\tau\tau}(\tau, \varphi) = \chi(\tau, \varphi)\chi^*_{\tau\tau}(\tau, \varphi) + 2\chi^*_{\tau}(\tau, \varphi)\chi_{\tau}(\tau, \varphi) + \chi_{\tau\tau}(\tau, \varphi)\chi^*(\tau, \varphi) \quad (2.115)$$

From Prob. 2.19, we use the following representation for $\chi(\tau, \varphi)$:

$$\chi(\tau, \varphi) = \int_{-\infty}^{\infty} F(\nu + \varphi)F^*(\nu)e^{2\pi j \nu\tau}\, d\nu$$

and

$$\chi_{\tau}(\tau, \varphi) = 2\pi j \int_{-\infty}^{\infty} F^*(\nu)F(\nu + \varphi)\nu e^{2\pi j \nu\tau}\, d\nu$$

so that the second term in Eq. (2.114), evaluated at (0,0) becomes

$$2\chi^*_{\tau}(0,0)\chi_{\tau}(0,0) =$$

$$4\pi^2 \int_{-\infty}^{\infty} F^*(\nu)F(\nu)\nu\, d\nu \int_{-\infty}^{\infty} F^*(\nu')F(\nu')\nu'\, d\nu' = 4\pi^2\mathscr{E}^2\nu_0^2 \quad (2.116)$$

where ν_0 is the first moment of the energy spectral density $F^*(\nu)F(\nu)$, and is defined by

$$\nu_0 = \mathscr{E}^{-1}\int_{-\infty}^{\infty} F^*(\nu)F(\nu)\nu\, d\nu \quad (2.117)$$

Similarly,

$$\chi_{\tau\tau}(0,0) = \chi^*_{\tau\tau}(0,0) = -4\pi^2\int_{-\infty}^{\infty} F^*(\nu)F(\nu)\nu^2\, d\nu = -4\pi^2\mathscr{E}W_0^2$$

where W_0^2 is the second moment of the energy spectral density $F^*(\nu)F(\nu)$, and is defined by

$$W_0^2 = \mathscr{E}^{-1}\int_{-\infty}^{\infty} F^*(\nu)F(\nu)\nu^2\, d\nu \quad (2.118)$$

Combining these results, we get

$$\xi_{\tau\tau}(0,0) = -8\pi^2\mathscr{E}^2(W_0^2 - \nu_0^2) = -8\pi^2\mathscr{E}^2 W^2 \quad (2.119)$$

where W is the bandwidth defined by

$$W^2 = \mathscr{E}^{-1}\int_{-\infty}^{\infty} F^*(\nu)F(\nu)(\nu - \nu_0)^2\, d\nu \quad (2.120)$$

A few comments are in order at this point. First, the term $\xi_{\tau\tau}(0,0)$ is always negative, so that, being the coefficient of τ^2, it can only contribute to a decrease of $\xi(\tau, \varphi)$ away from its maximum value of $\mathscr{E}^2$ at the origin. Second, our definition of the spectral width W is a measure of the spread of spectral energy about the centroid of the distribution. This definition is analogous to the definition of the statistical standard deviation. It is, therefore, appropriate to call W the bandwidth of $f(t)$.

We now turn to the last term in Eq. (2.114):

$$\xi_{\varphi\varphi}(\tau, \varphi) = \chi(\tau, \varphi)\chi_{\varphi\varphi}^*(\tau, \varphi) + 2\chi_{\varphi}^*(\tau, \varphi)\chi_{\varphi}(\tau, \varphi) + \chi_{\varphi\varphi}(\tau, \varphi)\chi^*(\tau, \varphi)$$

But

$$\chi_{\varphi}(\tau, \varphi) = -2\pi j \int_{-\infty}^{\infty} f(t)f^*(t-\tau)e^{-2\pi j \varphi t}t\,dt$$

so that the second term in the expression for $\xi_{\varphi\varphi}(\tau, \varphi)$ becomes, at the origin,

$$2\chi_{\varphi}^*(0,0)\chi_{\varphi}(0,0) = 4\pi^2 \int_{-\infty}^{\infty} f^*(t)f(t)t\,dt \int_{-\infty}^{\infty} f^*(t')f(t')t'\,dt' = 4\pi^2\mathscr{E}^2 t_0^2$$

where t_0 denotes the first moment of the function $f^*(t)f(t)$, and is defined by

$$t_0 = \mathscr{E}^{-1} \int_{-\infty}^{\infty} f^*(t)f(t)t\,dt \tag{2.121}$$

Similarly,

$$\chi_{\varphi\varphi}(0,0) = \chi_{\varphi\varphi}^*(0,0) = -4\pi^2 \int_{-\infty}^{\infty} f^*(t)f(t)t^2\,dt = -4\pi^2\mathscr{E}T_0^2$$

where T_0^2 is the second moment of the function $f^*(t)f(t)$, and is defined by

$$T_0^2 = \mathscr{E}^{-1} \int_{-\infty}^{\infty} f^*(t)f(t)t^2\,dt \tag{2.122}$$

We, therefore, have

$$\xi_{\varphi\varphi}(0,0) = -8\pi^2\mathscr{E}^2(T_0^2 - t_0^2) = -8\pi^2\mathscr{E}^2 T^2 \tag{2.123}$$

where T is interpreted as the duration of the waveform $f(t)$, defined by

$$T^2 = \mathscr{E}^{-1} \int_{-\infty}^{\infty} f^*(t)f(t)(t-t_0)^2\,dt \tag{2.124}$$

Note that $\xi_{\varphi\varphi}(0,0)$ is negative. Turning our attention to the third term in the Maclaurin expansion of $\xi(\tau, \varphi)$, we have, for the coefficient of $\tau\varphi$, the quantity $\mathscr{R}e\,\xi_{\tau\varphi}(0,0)$. To evaluate this term, we note that

$$\xi_{\tau}(\tau, \varphi) = \chi^*(\tau, \varphi)\chi_{\tau}(\tau, \varphi) + \chi_{\tau}^*(\tau, \varphi)\chi(\tau, \varphi)$$

and, therefore,

$$\xi_{\tau\varphi}(\tau, \varphi) = \chi^*(\tau, \varphi)\chi_{\tau\varphi}(\tau, \varphi) + \chi_{\varphi}^*(\tau, \varphi)\chi_{\tau}(\tau, \varphi)$$
$$+ \chi_{\tau\varphi}^*(\tau, \varphi)\chi(\tau, \varphi) + \chi_{\tau}^*(\tau, \varphi)\chi_{\varphi}(\tau, \varphi) \tag{2.125}$$

Now

$$\chi_{\tau\varphi}(\tau,\,\varphi) = 2\pi j \int_{-\infty}^{\infty} F^*(\nu)F_\varphi(\nu + \varphi)e^{2\pi j\,\nu\tau}\nu\,d\nu$$

but

$$F_\varphi(\nu + \varphi) = (\partial/\partial\varphi)\int_{-\infty}^{\infty} f(t)e^{-2\pi j\,(\nu + \varphi)t}\,dt$$

$$= -2\pi j \int_{-\infty}^{\infty} f(t)e^{-2\pi j\,(\nu + \varphi)t}t\,dt$$

so that

$$\chi_{\tau\varphi}(\tau,\,\varphi) = 4\pi^2 \int_{-\infty}^{\infty}\int_{-\infty}^{\infty} F^*(\nu)f(t)e^{-2\pi j\,\nu(t - \tau)}e^{-2\pi j\,\varphi t}\nu t\,d\nu\,dt$$

$$= 4\pi^2 \int_{-\infty}^{\infty} f(t)e^{-2\pi j\,\varphi t}t\int_{-\infty}^{\infty} F^*(\nu)e^{-2\pi j\,\nu(t - \tau)}\nu\,d\nu\,dt$$

and

$$\chi_{\tau\varphi}(0,\,0) = 4\pi^2 \int_{-\infty}^{\infty} f(t)t\int_{-\infty}^{\infty} F^*(\nu)e^{-2\pi j\,\nu t}\nu\,d\nu\,dt$$

$$= 2\pi j \int_{-\infty}^{\infty} f(t)f_{\dot{t}}^*(t)t\,dt$$

The first and third terms of $\xi_{\tau\varphi}(\tau,\,\varphi)$ can be combined and evaluated at the origin, resulting in

$$4\pi\mathscr{E}\,\mathscr{R}e\,j \int_{-\infty}^{\infty} f(t)f_{\dot{t}}^*(t)t\,dt$$

The second and fourth terms can be combined to give, for arbitrary τ and φ,

$$2\,\mathscr{R}e\,\chi_\tau(\tau,\,\varphi)\chi_{\dot{\varphi}}^*(\tau,\,\varphi)$$

$$= 2\,\mathscr{R}e \int_{-\infty}^{\infty}(2\pi j\,)F^*(\nu)F(\nu + \varphi)e^{2\pi j\,\nu\tau}\nu\,d\nu\int_{-\infty}^{\infty}(2\pi j\,)f^*(t)f(t - \tau)e^{2\pi j\,\varphi t}t\,dt$$

$$= -8\pi^2\mathscr{E}^2\nu_0 t_0$$

We, therefore, have

$$\mathscr{R}e\,\xi_{\tau\varphi}(0,\,0) = 4\pi\mathscr{E}\,\mathscr{R}e\,j \int_{-\infty}^{\infty} f(t)f_{\dot{t}}^*(t)t\,dt - 8\pi^2\mathscr{E}^2\nu_0 t_0$$

But since $\mathscr{R}e(j\,z) = -\mathscr{I}m(z)$, this can be rewritten as

$$\mathscr{R}e\,\xi_{\tau\varphi}(0,\,0) = -4\pi\mathscr{E}\,\mathscr{I}m \int_{-\infty}^{\infty} f(t)f_{\dot{t}}^*(t)t\,dt - 8\pi^2\mathscr{E}^2\nu_0 t_0$$

$$= 2\pi j\,\mathscr{E} \int_{-\infty}^{\infty} f(t)f_{\dot{t}}^*(t)t\,dt - 2\pi j\,\mathscr{E} \int_{-\infty}^{\infty} f^*(t)f_{\dot{t}}(t)t\,dt - 8\pi^2\mathscr{E}^2\nu_0 t_0$$

$$\tag{2.126}$$

Let us temporarily put these results aside and consider the integral

$$I = \int_{-\infty}^{\infty} \int f^*(t)F(v)(t - t_0)(v + v_0)e^{2\pi j \, vt} \, dv \, dt \qquad (2.127)$$

Expanding the product $(t - t_0)(v - v_0)$ results in four terms. The first term is

$$\int_{-\infty}^{\infty} f^*(t)t \int_{-\infty}^{\infty} F(v)v e^{2\pi j \, vt} \, dv \, dt = (2\pi j)^{-1} \int_{-\infty}^{\infty} f^*(t)f_t(t)t \, dt$$

For the second term, we have

$$-v_0 t_0 \int_{-\infty}^{\infty} f^*(t) \int_{-\infty}^{\infty} F(v)e^{2\pi j \, vt} \, dv \, dt = -v_0 t_0 \int_{-\infty}^{\infty} f^*(t)f(t) \, dt = -v_0 t_0 \mathscr{E}$$

The third term is

$$-t_0 \int_{-\infty}^{\infty} F(v)v \int_{-\infty}^{\infty} f^*(t)e^{2\pi j \, vt} \, dv \, dt = -t_0 \int_{-\infty}^{\infty} F^*(v)F(v)v \, dv$$

$$= -(2\pi)^{-1}\mathscr{E}v_0 t_0$$

Finally, the fourth term is

$$v_0 \int_{-\infty}^{\infty} f^*(t)t \int_{-\infty}^{\infty} F(v)e^{2\pi j \, vt} \, dv \, dt = v_0 \int_{-\infty}^{\infty} f^*(t)f(t)t \, dt = (2\pi)^{-1}\mathscr{E}v_0 t_0$$

The integral I, therefore, becomes

$$I = (2\pi j)^{-1} \int_{-\infty}^{\infty} f^*(t)f_t(t)t \, dt - \mathscr{E}v_0 t_0$$

We, therefore, have

$$4\pi^2 \mathscr{E}I = -2\pi j \mathscr{E} \int_{-\infty}^{\infty} f^*(t)f_t(t)t \, dt - 4\pi^2 \mathscr{E}v_0 t_0$$

so that

$$\mathscr{Re}\,\xi_{\tau\varphi}(0, 0) = 4\pi^2\mathscr{E}(I + I^*) - 4\pi^2\mathscr{E}\,\mathscr{Re}I$$

which we rewrite in terms of a coupling coefficient ρ defined by the expression

$$\mathscr{Re}I = -\mathscr{E}TW\rho$$

This mathematical form is suggested by the squared modulus of I, which is equal to

$$\int_{-\infty}^{\infty}\int_{-\infty}^{\infty} f^*(t)f(t')(t - t_0)(t' - t_0) \int_{-\infty}^{\infty}\int_{-\infty}^{\infty} F^*(v)F(v')$$

$$\times (v + v_0)(v' + v_0)e^{2\pi j \, (vt' - v't)} \, dv \, dv' \, dt \, dt'$$

and can be expressed as

$$|I|^2 = \mathscr{E}^2 T^2 W^2 |\rho|^2 \qquad (2.128)$$

Equation (2.114) can, therefore, be written as

$$\xi(\tau, \varphi) = \mathcal{E}^2 - 4\pi^2\mathcal{E}^2[W^2\tau^2 + 2\rho T W \tau\varphi + T^2\varphi^2] \qquad (2.129)$$

This is a useful approximation to the ambiguity function when departures from perfect time synchronization (τ) and from perfect frequency alignment (φ) are small. The function $\xi(\tau, \varphi)$ provides a measure of the degradation suffered as a result of small errors in synchronization and frequency alignment. In the above approximate form, $\xi(\tau, \varphi)$ depends on waveform properties only through the bandwidth W, the duration T, and the coupling coefficient ρ. For more severe excursions away from perfect alignment, a more precise representation of $\xi(\tau, \varphi)$ is required.

One must be careful in interpreting the words "uncertainty" and "ambiguity" in the context of matched-filter processing. In the absence of noise, strictly speaking, there can be no ambiguity in the measurement of the time at which a waveform is processed by a matched filter. There is only one absolute maximum in the filter response, and this maximum unambiguously determines the time of arrival. A similar argument holds in the frequency domain.

What may happen, however, is that noise can introduce uncertainty, especially if the matched-filter output peak is broad. If, in addition to signal, noise is also present at the filter input, random fluctuations will appear at the output. However, fluctuations in the immediate neighborhood of a matched-filter peak can cause false maxima and lead the detection algorithm to declare detection at the wrong instant.

There is another context in which ambiguity plays a role. With several neighboring targets, there can be multiple closely spaced replicas of the waveforms at the filter input. A similar situation exists for communication systems in a multipath environment. In this case, broad matched-filter output peaks may make the simultaneous resolution of nearby signals difficult or even impossible.

In radar detection, and even in synchronization, one is interested in measuring precisely the time at which a detection is made. This timing information can be interpreted as range to the target. In synchronization, precise timing is essential to allow the alignment of a received waveform with stored replicas for accurate comparison. An important waveform property, therefore, is the precision with which timing information can be derived by matched filtering. This time resolution is related to the temporal characteristics of the matched-filter output when the proper waveform is applied at the input. The sharpness of the output is a measure of the available time resolution.

We bring this section to a close by exploring the concept of matched-filter resolution in a couple of examples.

EXAMPLE

It is interesting to examine the roles of spectral amplitude and phase in matched-filter temporal resolution. Both the matched filter and the function to which it is matched can be described in terms of spectral amplitude and phase as in

$$F(\nu) = |F(\nu)|e^{j\varphi(\nu)}$$

The phase term $\varphi(\nu)$ does not appear in the integral expression for $y(t)$ in Eq. (2.100), having already played its role in aligning the complex Fourier components along the real axis for coherent combining. This involves only the spectral magnitude.

The filter resolution is determined by the behavior of $y(t)$ for small values of t. The resolution depends entirely on the spectral magnitude, as can be seen from the Maclaurin expansion for $y(t)$:

$$y(t) = y(0) + y'(0)t + \tfrac{1}{2}y''(0)t^2 + \cdots$$

where

$$y(0) = \int_{-\infty}^{\infty} F^*(\nu)F(\nu)\, d\nu$$

$$y'(0) = 2\pi j \int_{-\infty}^{\infty} F^*(\nu)F(\nu)\nu\, d\nu$$

$$y''(0) = -4\pi^2 \int_{-\infty}^{\infty} F^*(\nu)F(\nu)\nu^2\, d\nu$$

and so on.

One can define the spectral width in terms of moments for $|F(\nu)|^2$:

$$(\delta\nu)^2 = \frac{\int_{-\infty}^{\infty} F^*(\nu)F(\nu)(\nu - \langle\nu\rangle)^2\, d\nu}{\int_{-\infty}^{\infty} F^*(\nu)F(\nu)\, d\nu}$$

where $\langle\nu\rangle = y'(0)/y(0)$ is the mean value of ν. The filter temporal resolution can be measured by the reciprocal of the spectral width, giving

$$\delta t \approx \left\{ \frac{1}{y(0)} \int_{-\infty}^{\infty} F^*(\nu)F(\nu)\nu^2\, d\nu - \left[\frac{1}{y(0)} \int_{-\infty}^{\infty} F^*(\nu)F(\nu)\nu\, d\nu \right]^2 \right\}^{-1/2}$$

which is a very general result.

EXAMPLE

A matter of practical consideration involves implementing an approximation to a matched filter. Consider now matched filtering involving a complex function $f(t)$, whose phase spectrum is known, but whose amplitude spectrum is not, except that most of the energy is known to reside within a finite bandwidth W. That being the case, the $F^*(\nu)F(\nu)$ kernel in the integrals of the previous example is now replaced by some arbitrary (but real) function $Q(\nu)$, which has appreciable magnitude only over a limited domain of bandwidth W. The details of $Q(\nu)$ are, in general, not known.

As a specific example, taking $Q(\nu) = 1$, the spectral phase-only filter response becomes

$$\delta t \approx \frac{(12)^{1/2}}{W}$$

Spreading $Q(\nu)$ uniformly over its bandwidth corresponds to making the fewest assumptions about the unknown magnitude spectrum. The interpretation given to this result is that the spectral phase-only matched filter produces an output whose duration is on the order of W^{-1}. The proportionality factor will vary slightly with different forms of $Q(\nu)$, but for band-limited functions, the results will be similar to those presented here. Alternatively, one could sum up all the terms in the Maclaurin series for $y(t)$ and solve for the time t_0 at which the filter response first vanishes, i.e., for $y(t_0) = 0$. This results in $t_0 = W^{-1}$.

PROBLEMS

2.1 (a) Show that the repeated application of the group composition operation between an element of a finite group and itself generates a cyclic sequence that has the group property.

(b) Show that the set of all integers (positive, negative, and zero) is not a group under the operation of arithmetic subtraction.

2.2 Find the multiplicative inverse of each element in the ring $\{0, 1, 2, 3, 4\}$ with arithmetic addition and multiplication modulo 5.

2.3 Construct the extension field GF(2^2) from the base field GF(2) using the primitive polynomial $x^2 + x + 1$.

2.4 (a) Construct the extension field GF(2^3) from the base field GF(2) using the primitive polynomial $x^3 + x + 1$.

(b) The field with four elements, GF(4), is given by the arithmetic tables

+	0	1	2	3		x	0	1	2	3
0	0	1	2	3		0	0	0	0	0
1	1	0	3	2		1	0	1	2	3
2	2	3	0	1		2	0	2	3	1
3	3	2	1	0		3	0	3	1	2

Solve the set of coupled linear equations in GF(4): $2x + y = 3$ and $x + y = 1$.

2.5 Show that for vectors defined as n-tuples over GF(2), the weight of the difference between any two vectors $w(\mathbf{x}, \mathbf{y})$ satisfies the properties of a metric.

2.6 Show that $\|f - g\|^2 \geq \|f\|^2 + \|g\|^2 - 2\|f\|\cdot\|g\| \geq 0$.

2.7 If $\mathbf{M}$ is a complete subspace of the Hilbert space $\mathbf{H}$, then the projection theorem asserts that the best representation $\tilde{f} \in \mathbf{M}$ of $f \in \mathbf{H}$ is given by the Fourier coefficients $\langle f | \varphi_k \rangle$, where the set $\{\varphi_k; k = 1, 2, \ldots; \varphi_k \in \mathbf{M}\}$ forms a basis in $\mathbf{M}$. Show that a change of basis mapping $\mathbf{M}$ into $\mathbf{M}$ preserves the optimality of $\tilde{f}$ as an approximation to f.

2.8 Evaluate the Euclidian metric between $x(t) = at$ and $y(t) = bt^2$, $t \in [-1, 1]$.

2.9 Show that $\sum_{k=1}^{n} |\langle \varphi_k | x \rangle|^2 \le \|x\|^2$ for any n, where the $\{\varphi_k\}$ form an orthonormal basis set. This is Bessel's inequality, and shows that $x_n = \sum_{k=1}^{n} \langle \varphi_k | x \rangle \varphi_k$ is a Cauchy sequence, and also that the Fourier coefficients $\langle \varphi_k | x \rangle$ are square summable. *Hint*: First show that

$$\|x - x_n\|^2 = \|x\|^2 - \sum_{k=1}^{n} |\langle \varphi_k | x \rangle|^2$$

2.10 Show that any two orthogonal vectors $\mathbf{x}$ and $\mathbf{y}$, with $\mathbf{x} \perp \mathbf{y}$ in Hilbert space, satisfy a generalization of the Pythagorean theorem: $\|\mathbf{x} + \mathbf{y}\|^2 = \|\mathbf{x}\|^2 + \|\mathbf{y}\|^2$.

2.11 Show that $\int_{-\tau}^{\tau} \varphi_k(t) \varphi_n(t) \, dt = \lambda_k \delta_{k,n}$, where λ_n is the eigenvalue associated with $\varphi_n(t)$, the nth prolate spheroidal function. *Hint*: Note that

$$\int_{-\infty}^{\infty} \varphi_k(t') \frac{\sin\,[2\pi W (t - t')]}{\pi(t - t')} \, dt' = \varphi_k(t)$$

with $\lambda_k = 1$ since all of the energy is contained in the time interval $(-\infty, \infty)$.

2.12 This problem explores a way of extrapolating a band-limited function $f(t)$ known only in the interval $t \in (-\tau, \tau)$. Writing $f(t)$ in terms of the basis $\{\varphi_k(t); k = 1, 2, \ldots\}$ of prolate spheroidal wave functions results in the unique expansion

$$f(t) = \sum_{k=1}^{\infty} a_k \varphi_k(t) \qquad \text{with} \qquad a_k = \int_{-\infty}^{\infty} f(t) \varphi_k(t) \, dt$$

since the $\{\varphi_k(t)\}$ form a complete set. The problem with this is that $f(t)$ is not known outside the interval $(-\tau, \tau)$ so that the a_k cannot be evaluated by means of the last integral. Find a way of relating the a_k to values of $f(t)$ inside $(-\tau, \tau)$.

2.13 Show that the solutions to the integral equation

$$\int_{-\infty}^{\infty} \xi(x) \frac{\sin\,[2\pi W (t - x)]}{\pi(t - x)} \, dx = \xi(t)$$

are of the form

$$\xi(t) = \frac{\sin\,(2\pi W t - k\pi)}{2\pi W t - k\pi}$$

2.14 Consider a continuous time signal $f(t)$ with finite energy and with a continuous Fourier transform $F(\nu)$. The transform $F(\nu)$ is uniformly sampled at the frequencies $\nu = k\nu_s$, thereby obtaining a sequence of transform samples $\{F(k\nu_s)\}$, where k is an integer in the infinite range $-\infty < k < \infty$, and ν_s is the frequency-sampling interval.
   (a) Show that if $f(t)$ is duration-limited so that it vanishes outside the interval defined by $|t| > T$, the signal is completely defined by specifying $F(\nu)$ at frequencies spaced $(2T)^{-1}$ apart.
   (b) Show how $F(\nu)$ can be reconstructed from its samples $\{F(k\nu_s)\}$.

2.15 Calculate and sketch as a function of ν the inner product over $(-\infty, \infty)$ between the complex exponential $e^{-2\pi j \nu t}$ and each of the following functions:
   (a) $\delta(t)$
   (b) $\cos \pi t$
   (c) $(\pi t)^{-1} \sin \pi t$

2.16 The construction of GF(2^3) from GF(2) uses a prime polynomial of degree 3 over GF(2), and results in the *polynomial* representation, because field elements are all expressed as polynomials. Two other useful representations are possible. In the *vector* representation, a field element of $GF(q^n)$ is represented as an n-tuple over $GF(q)$, with the entries of the n-tuple being scalars corresponding to the corresponding polynomial coefficients from $GF(q)$. Thus, the polynomial $x^2 + 1$ would be represented as $(1, 0, 1)$. Over $GF(2)$, this provides a neat binary labeling for all of the field elements. In the *power* representation, the nonzero field elements are represented as some element α raised to an integer power, i.e., α^k. By letting $\alpha = x$, and reducing modulo $p(x) = x^3 + x + 1$, all field elements are generated. Thus, the polynomial 1 becomes α^0, x becomes α^1, and so on.

(a) Construct a table of the power, polynomial, and vector representations of $GF(2^3)$. Indicate the order of each field element and whether that element is primitive.

(b) From the vectors you found in part (a), construct a set of vectors over $GF(2)$ such that the Hamming distance between any two vectors in the set is $d_H = 3$. Include the vector $(0, 0, 0)$ in the set. Repeat for $d_H = 2$, $d_H = 1$, and $d_H = 0$.

(c) Which of the four sets of vectors in part (b) form linear vector spaces?

2.17 A filter with impulse response $h(t)$ has an output

$$y(t) = \int_{-\infty}^{\infty} h(\tau) x(t - \tau) \, d\tau$$

where $x(t)$ is the signal applied to the filter's input. This filter can be viewed as performing a linear transformation on the signal $x(t)$ to produce the signal $y(t)$.

(a) What condition must $h(t)$ satisfy so that $x(t)$ is recoverable from $y(t)$?

(b) What condition must $h(t)$ satisfy so that the Euclidian norm is unchanged by the filtering operation? That is, $\|y\| = \|x\|$.

(c) As expressed by the above convolution, each point of $y(t)$ is a linear combination of all the points from $x(t)$. Find an orthogonal coordinate system for which each output-signal coordinate is simply equal to a scaled value of the corresponding input-signal coordinate, i.e., this coordinate system diagonalizes the transformation.

2.18 Since matched filtering is a functional of the signaling waveform, the matched-filter output, which determines detection performance, depends only on integral properties of the set of signaling waveforms and not on the details of these signals. Yet waveforms must be specified in terms of particular functions. This problem deals with the freedom with which such a set of functions may be specified.

Consider a set $\{s_1(t), s_2(t), \ldots, s_M(t)\}$ of signaling waveforms and a corresponding bank of matched filters $\{h_1(t), h_2(t), \ldots, h_M(t)\}$, where $h_k(t) = s_k^*(-t)$. All of the signaling waveforms have the same duration T and the same bandwidth W. The matched-filter bank is synchronized to the transmitted waveforms and one of the waveforms (plus white noise) is always present during any particular signaling interval, though not necessarily the same waveform in different intervals.

(a) What is implied about the signaling waveforms if we desire that the output of a particular matched filter at $t = 0$ vanish unless the waveform to which it is matched is present at the input?

(b) What is the maximum value of M under these conditions?

2.19 The signal reflected by a target and received by a synthetic-aperture radar has the quadratic phase history form

$$f(t) = \exp 2\pi j \left[(2r_0/\lambda) + \frac{1}{2} \kappa t^2 \right] \qquad -T/2 < t < T/2$$

where r_0, λ, and κ are constants.

(a) Calculate the response of the filter matched to this waveform.

(b) Now let us explore the case where only the in-phase signal is available. Express $f(t) = I(t) + jQ(t)$, where $I(t)$ and $Q(t)$ are the in-phase and quadrature signal components, respectively. Assume only $I(t)$ is available and calculate the response of a filter matched to $I(t)$. Express your answer in terms of Fresnel integrals.

2.20 The complex signal produced by a point target in a synthetic-aperture radar is of the form $f(t) = e^{j\pi\kappa t^2}$, $-T/2 < t < T/2$, where κ is the Doppler-induced chirp rate, and T is the time a target remains within view of the radar. Consider a processing filter matched to $f(t)$ but for which only the in-phase component of the return is available. Show that the filter output consists of two terms: the first term is the matched-filter response to the fully coherent waveform $f(t)$; the second term is attenuated by a factor proportional to the square root of the waveform time-duration product. Leave the second term expressed in terms of Fresnel integrals.

2.21 Show that if a time offset $(+\tau)$ instead of a time delay is introduced in the frequency-shifted version $f(t)e^{2\pi j\,\varphi t}$ of the function $f(t)$, then

$$\psi(\tau,\ \varphi) = e^{-2\pi j\,\varphi\tau} \int_{-\infty}^{\infty} f(t)f^*(t+\tau)e^{-2\pi j\,\varphi t}\,dt = e^{-2\pi j\,\varphi\tau}\chi_+(\tau,\ \varphi)$$

where

$$\chi_+(\tau,\ \varphi) = \int_{-\infty}^{\infty} f(t)f^*(t+\tau)e^{-2\pi j\,\varphi t}\,dt$$

and that this corresponds to the correlator implementation of a matched filter.

2.22 Show that $\chi(\tau,\ \varphi)$ may also be written as

$$\chi(\tau,\ \varphi) = \int_{-\infty}^{\infty} F^*(\nu)F(\nu+\varphi)e^{2\pi j\,\nu\tau}\,d\nu$$

2.23 Show that $\psi^*(-\tau,\ -\varphi) = \chi(\tau,\ \varphi)$.

2.24 Show that an ambiguity function is its own Fourier transform; i.e., if

$$\xi(\tau,\ \varphi) = \psi^*(\tau,\ \varphi)\psi(\tau,\ \varphi)$$

then

$$\xi(\tau,\ \varphi) = \int_{-\infty}^{\infty}\!\!\int \xi(\tau',\ \varphi')e^{-2\pi j\,(\tau'\varphi-\tau\varphi')}\,d\tau'\,d\varphi'$$

2.25 Consider a rectangular pulse with duration T:

$$s(t) = A\cos(2\pi\nu_c t) \qquad 0 \le t \le T$$
$$s(t) = 0 \qquad\qquad\qquad \text{otherwise}$$

(a) Find the value of A for which the pulse energy is unity.
(b) Find the impulse response for the filter matched to $s(t)$.

2.26 This problem examines several aspects of signal theory as it pertains to communication waveforms.
(a) What is the minimum time–bandwidth product for any of a set of binary waveforms to be used in communicating over a channel where the signal-to-noise power ratio at the receiver is -10 dB? Round your answer to the nearest integer. What is the approximate dimensionality of these signals?

(b) Determine the constant a_∞ that makes the two functions $\psi_1(t) = e^{-t}$ and $\psi_2(t) = 1 - ae^{-3t}$, for $t \geq 0$, and $\psi_1(t) = \psi_2(t) = 0$ otherwise orthogonal over the interval $[0, \infty)$.

(c) Determine the constant a_1 that makes $\psi_1(t)$ and $\psi_2(t)$ of part (b) orthogonal over the interval $[0, 1]$.

(d) The complex exponentials $\psi_k(t) = e^{-2\pi j kt}$ form a complete basis set over the interval $[0, 1]$. Find the representation of $\psi_1(t)$ and $\psi_2(t)$ of part (c) with respect to that basis. You need not evaluate the integrals.

(e) It is desired to use only the first N basis functions $\{\varphi_0, \varphi_1, \ldots, \varphi_{N-1}\}$, where N is twice the signal space dimensionality found in part (a). This is no longer a complete basis. Find the best representation of $\psi_1(t)$ and $\psi_2(t)$ of part (c) with respect to that basis.

NOISE

*Look for knowledge not in books
but in things themselves.*

William Gilbert

3

The process of communication consists of transforming messages into signals that are suitable for transmission or storage over a physical medium and the subsequent recovery of these messages from the medium. Sound, for example, consists of patterns of oscillations in air pressure. These oscillations can be captured by a microphone and converted to an equivalent set of electrical oscillations. Then these signals can be impressed on a radio carrier, which makes possible the use of radio-propagation channels for transmission over very large distances that would otherwise be out of reach to unaided sound. Alternatively, the electrical patterns can be mapped into corresponding spatial variations in the magnetization density on a thin film of iron oxide. Transmission consists in transforming or mapping signal variations associated with some message into recognizable variations in some physical medium. This mapping is generally called *modulation*. The common denominator in these and similar examples is an intimate association of the message-bearing signal with the medium or channel whose physical properties are being used to represent the message.

A necessary part of this process involves the recovery or *demodulation* of said signals from the medium and its eventual transformation back into the original message. To accomplish this transformation, we must place a measuring device in physical contact with the medium. In doing so, the measuring device is influenced not only by the modulation associated with the message, but also by fluctuations that are always present in physical systems. A common form of such fluctuations is thermal noise, generated by the random motion of electrons in electrical circuits. These random fluctuations are superimposed on the measured message signal and interfere with its recovery.

Noise is by definition a random process. It cannot be removed from the measured signal by deterministic means. The origin of this randomness can be traced to the overwhelmingly large number of degrees of freedom in noise-generating systems, such as electrons in motion in the components of a circuit. This is to be contrasted with the much smaller number of degrees of freedom associated with communication signals. The measurement of a single signal degree of freedom is thus influenced by the aggregate effect of a very large number of noise degrees of freedom, and results in random fluctuations in the measured quantity.

In severe cases, noise may make communication impossible. In most cases, it introduces a certain amount of degradation that is quantifiable if suitable statistical and spectral models exist. The design of communication systems must, therefore, proceed from a knowledge of not only messages and their representation as signals, but also from an understanding of noise and its effects.

The first two sections of this chapter discuss important results of probability theory that play a significant role in the development of a mathematical theory of communication. Chebyshev's theorem makes a very general statement about the distribution of probability in any random process. This theorem is subsequently used in the derivation of a number of other results. The Chernoff bound establishes a tight limit on the amount of probability contained in the tail of distributions and is used to establish important results of information theory. The law of large numbers is the gateway to the important theorems of information theory. It is introduced here as a theorem of probability theory and will be used extensively in Chapter 4 to develop coding theorems. Noise with Gaussian statistics is ubiquitous in communication systems. How Gaussian noise arises is described by the central limit theorem of probability theory. This theorem is derived and discussed in Section 3.2, which closes by cautioning the reader against possible abuse. Section 3.3 presents a discussion of the physical causes of certain sources of noise. Shot noise and thermal noise are introduced as the consequences of specific physical processes. Statistical and spectral characteristics for these types of noise are then developed.

3.1 FUNDAMENTAL CONCEPTS IN PROBABILITY

Before starting our study of communication, we must develop a few subjects that are necessary both for the appreciation as well as the use of probability theory in this discipline. A familiarity with the theory of probability is assumed, but a few basic concepts and tools need to be discussed in more detail than is usually done in introductory communication texts.

Although the reader is assumed to have been exposed to some elements of probability, there are a few topics we wish to develop in this chapter. Chebyshev's theorem is introduced because it makes a simple yet powerful example of a limit theorem of probability theory and is frequently used in the development of other important results. The Chernoff bound is discussed here because it is a useful tool for the study of communication systems. The law of large numbers can be stated in such a simple way as to make its status as a theorem seem questionable. Yet its consequences in the theory of communication are far from intuitive. This chapter introduces the law of large numbers as a mathematical theorem. Later in the book, we shall explore its implications in communication.

The concept of randomness appears in many guises in communications. In this chapter, we encounter randomness in the form of noise occurring over communication channels and introduce the statistical apparatus necessary for its description. In Chapter 4, communication signals are treated as stochastic processes. We develop mathematical techniques, implicitly relying on the reader's intuitive notion of randomness. Few communication texts address randomness as a concept in its own right. We, therefore, take time aside in this section to discuss some interesting aspects of randomness.

3.1.1 Philosophical Overview✳

Exactly what is randomness? How can randomness be measured? Randomness is a useful concept for which most of us have an intuitive feeling, but that at first glance may seem hard to define precisely. Randomness plays a central role in communication theory. But yet there appears to be something elusive about defining the attributes of something that purports to describe the unpredictable.

Consider the following two binary sequences:

$$0\ 0\ 1\ 1\ 0\ 1\ 0\ 1\ 1\ 0\ 0\ 0\ 1\ 1\ 0\ 1$$
$$1\ 0\ 0\ 0\ 1\ 0\ 0\ 0\ 1\ 0\ 0\ 0\ 1\ 0\ 0\ 0$$

The first sequence shows all appearances of being unpredictable and could be called random, whereas the second is clearly a repetition of the smaller sequence {**1 0 0 0**}. If one were asked to describe what the successive entries in each of these sequences would be, there might be some doubt initially as to how the first sequence might be extrapolated, but probably little hesitation in the second case. A pattern has been recognized in the second sequence. That pattern can be used to describe the sequence as well as infer what the probable following entries might be. No such pattern is apparent in the first sequence. It seems natural to call the first sequence random and the second sequence deterministic.

Now consider the following experiment: for different values of variable X, measure variable $Y(X)$; plot $Y(X)$ versus X and deduce the functional relationship between these two variables. After a curve is fit to the data, one notices that, even when the fit is "good", the data never fall exactly on the line, but scatter above and below a little. This is usually attributed to experimental error, the measure of which provides the accuracy of the measurement. When the experimental errors are small, one can claim to have found a pattern that explains or fits the data.

The experimental error is unpredictable and, to a large degree, outside the control of the experimentalist. What has been done, in fact, was to conceptually separate the measured data into two parts: the knowable model and the unpredictable random errors. The knowable model is given by the curve fit. We say that the curve provides a mathematical model (or a theory) about the data. If the measurements are repeatable, the same curve is obtained in each similar experiment, even though the details of the experimental-error fluctuations may differ from one experiment to the next. In this case, we should have no hesitation about using our model to predict what the measurement should be, within experimental error, whenever $Y(X)$ is measured again.

But what about the experimental error itself? This is usually considered a residual of the curve-fitting process. No physical significance is attached to these leftovers other than they were probably caused by noisy circuits, uncontrollable vibrations, etc. In this case, we say that these errors are "random" to signify that there is really no practical way to model these. They are usually dismissed as being outside our immediate ability to model, and, therefore, there is really nothing that can be known about them. Randomness, here, is used to describe our ignorance of the detailed mechanisms that are ultimately responsible for our measurements.

Usually, our state of knowledge improves with time as a consequence of being able to make better measurements of physical phenomena. Better instruments are devised, and the size of the experimental errors decreases, allowing us to probe into a finer level of physical structure. The bounds of knowledge can thus be pushed back. What usually happens is that yesterday's experimental noise level can be made to shrink to reveal measurements requiring a more elaborate theoretical model. The random-error level—an admission and measure of our ignorance—is replaced by a more complex theoretical model that reflects an increase in knowledge.

What one should notice here is that in this context, "randomness" is a very subjective concept. It is used to label what cannot be described in detail. What used to be random now can be, for the most part, explained, up to a smaller and smaller uncertainty that will hopefully yield to tomorrow's improved measuring instruments.

If a pattern or a certain order can be discerned in data, then these data can be modeled, leaving a random process as the remaining unexplainable part. Creating order out of initial chaos reduces the size of uncertainty and also reduces subjective randomness. As an example, let us return to the two sequences introduced earlier. As it turns out, the first sequence will be recognized as being the fourth through seventh Fibonacci numbers, each expressed as four-digit binary numbers. Fibonacci numbers are generated by the simple recursion

$$x_1 = 1, x_2 = 1 \qquad x_n = x_{n-1} + x_{n-2} \qquad n = 3, 4, 5, \ldots \qquad (3.1)$$

Having removed the mystery out of the first sequence, we can no longer claim it is random, at least in the subjective sense. Yet we cannot deny the need for the concept of randomness. There is always something that remains unexplainable, the details of which cannot, in principle or in practice, be modeled. What is needed is an objective definition of randomness.

Many books on probability [Cr 46, Fe 68, Ho 62, Pa 84] introduce the concept of a random variable as one having a real numerical value assigned to it from the outcome of some random experiment that may be repeated a large number of times under uniform conditions. Most of the elementary examples of such experiments (viz., flipping a coin, throwing dice, drawing colored balls from urns) introduce the element of unpredictability by having a simple system such as a coin or a pair of dice interact with its surroundings, and where these surroundings are endowed with an extremely large number of degrees of freedom. Thus, the ballistics of the coin or dice are said to be influenced by unpredictable muscular tremors in the launch phase, by air turbulence, as well as complicated multiple bouncings of the object as it lands. The details of these interactions are too complicated to be described, and the sole remaining regularity lies in the statistics of the process being studied.

The theory of probability provides us with useful tools. We forego the need to describe the details of a process and settle for the ability to describe certain regularities, in the average. This situation is well known to students and practitioners of statistical mechanics. According to the tenets of classical mechanics, the detailed dynamics of a large system of interacting objects, such as the air molecules filling a room, can, in principle, be predicted. The equations of motion for the components of this system are known. Their trajectories are fully determined by known equations and a set of initial conditions provided by the simultaneous specifications of their positions and velocities at some fixed time instant. The only thing standing before the realization of this task is the immense complexity implied in the specification of these conditions, not to mention the mathematical computation of the resulting trajectories. It is, however, extremely impractical to calculate them. We are, therefore, forced to forego the specifics for the general and to adopt statistical approaches in our study of systems with a very large number of degrees of freedom.

Day-to-day manifestations of randomness can be explained by the fact that our experiments are in some way coupled with the rest of the universe, a system with a very large number of degrees of freedom. This provides a very convenient starting point for probability texts to introduce the concept of randomness as arising from interactions with this unpredictable system. This subjective interpretation of randomness has its roots in the implied impracticality or impossibility of fully specifying the dynamics of a system. Randomness—an objective definition of which will be provided later—is a consequence of our limited knowledge of the complicated interactions between the large number of degrees of freedom in systems.

The student and practitioner of communication quickly realize the importance of probability theory to this and other parts of engineering. The motivation for using probability is usually introduced by pointing out that messages can be modeled as random events and that interfering noise is also a random process. Good mathematical models exist for these, and it would be quite possible to go through our study of communication without a second look at the fundamental importance of randomness. The subject of randomness cannot be treated in detail in this book. We shall, however, discuss enough of it to hopefully arouse the reader's interest and to provide a justification for using probabilistic methods that is far more satisfying than considering probability as a necessary approximation to an otherwise unmanageable situation.

Communication deals with two types of random signals: messages and noise. Messages are random in the sense that they are not predictable at the receiver. Noise is random since it is ultimately the result of the interaction of a very large number of particles, as in the case of thermal noise.

The theory of algorithmic complexity provides a useful definition of randomness [Ch 75, Fo 83] that can loosely be paraphrased as follows. A sequence of symbols is random if the smallest algorithm required to specify it is on the same order of complexity as the sequence itself. As used here, *complexity* is measured in bits, a unit of information to be introduced in the next chapter. For the present purpose, it suffices to mention that complexity can be measured by the number of statistically independent symbols, chosen from a fixed alphabet, required to represent sequences or algorithms. This definition of randomness essentially says that a sequence can be considered random if, to specify it, another sequence of the same length must be used. By implication, a sequence that is not random can, in principle, be compressed (mapped one to one and onto) into a shorter sequence from which it can be reconstituted. The shortest such sequence is known as the *minimal algorithm* for the sequence.

The question of how randomness arises is perhaps best investigated by pursuing the logic advanced by classical physics. A delightfully inspiring discussion on that subject is given by Katz [Ka 67]. We shall elaborate on that discussion.

Classical physics maintains that a detailed description of events we would call random, such as the individual motions of gas particles, can, in principle, be obtained by supplementing the known differential equations of motion with initial conditions for all of the relevant interacting particles involved. For example, the detailed trajectory of a flipped coin could be determined by specifying its exact shape, material density distribution, the translational and rotational position and velocity at the time of launch, the ambient air flow, and the elastic properties of the table on which it will bounce, etc. A much more difficult problem, but one of fundamental importance in physics, is the derivation of the macroscopic properties of matter (such as heat capacities) from the properties of the microscopic particles themselves and their interactions. In both cases, a purely classical approach is deemed impractical (but, in principle, feasible) because of the large number of interacting elements. This view holds that macroscopic observables can, in principle, be derived from the microscopic interactions of the constituent particles.

The difficulty with this approach is not only computational. There is a fundamental reason for objecting to such a program as a way of building macroscopic physical theory from the complex interactions of constituent particles. Simply stated, a system of N particles requires a set of N initial conditions to supplement their equations of motion. By initial condition, we include position and velocity for each particle degree of freedom. For macroscopic systems of interest, a conservative estimate for the number N can easily be on the order of 10^{20} or more. All of the information about such highly complex systems resides almost entirely in the initial conditions. Thus, to predict the course of a system of a given complexity requires a computer having at least as large a complexity, as measured, for example, by the number of storage elements required for the specification of the initial conditions. Katz points out that such an approach can be used only for exceedingly small systems that do not interact with their surroundings. Such couplings would only serve to increase the number N of participating elements. In particular, it is, in principle, impossible to describe the development of the universe in this way, since there is no system large enough to contain all of the necessary information, other than the universe itself, which can be considered its own algorithmic representation [Ka 67].

Katz' argument can be strengthened considerably by noting that even for a finite system having relatively few elements, it is not possible to infer a system's evolution from imprecisely known initial conditions. The unavoidable uncertainties that attend the measurement of initial conditions propagate exponentially in the computed system's evolution, resulting in a predicted motion that becomes increasingly at variance with observation [Fo 83]. Measurements having infinite accuracy, even if possible, would require infinitely large systems to store and process the information. Hence, even small interactions are important, which makes it very difficult to justify that a system is closed, i.e., completely isolated from the rest of the universe, one that increases the number of elements that must be considered, possibly with infinite accuracy.

The alert reader will be perhaps intrigued with this discussion, and with possible implications to determinism as well as to exactly how much is knowable about a system. Ford [Fo 83] and the references cited therein provide additional discussion. For the purpose of this book, we simply mention that the randomness we experience cannot be explained by our lack of detailed knowledge about the environment, or by poor physical models. Randomness is a fundamental part of the way the universe works.

3.1.2 Chaitin's Measure of Randomness※

If we are going to use the concept of randomness, it stands to reason that we need a solid definition that does not rely on subjective expectations. A rigorous definition should use only the intrinsic characteristics of the random signal itself and should not rely on arguments based on its physical origins.

An interesting article by Gregory J. Chaitin [Ch 75] on this subject dealt with the definition of randomness and with areas of mathematics related to the proving of theorems in formal mathematical systems. However, the ideas that emerge from Chaitin's definition of randomness also shed light on coding techniques.

Chaitin correctly maintains that the method of origin of a probabilistic event cannot be considered a valid criterion of randomness. As an example, he produces the following two sequences:

0 1 0 1 0 1 0 1 0 1 0 1 0 1 0 1 0 1 0 1
0 1 1 0 1 1 0 0 1 1 0 1 1 1 1 0 0 0 1 0

The first sequence is clearly the tenfold repetition of the subsequence {0 1}, which hardly seems random, and the second one was actually generated by flipping a coin 20 times. However, it is true that both sequences are equally likely to have been produced by flipping a coin, with the same probability, assuming independent events. With a fair coin, the probability for obtaining each of these sequences is 2^{-20}. Yet, the same is true for any other binary sequence of 20 digits. We are, therefore, not justified in considering one sequence as being randomer than the other on the sole basis of the mechanism that generated them. On purely probabilistic grounds, we are not justified in showing surprise when, say, 20 coin flips all result in heads.

Chaitin presents a definition of randomness that depends only on the characteristics of the sequences themselves. He approaches randomness from the algorithmic complexity point of view. The first sequence could be reproduced by a simple algorithm: "Print **0 1** ten times". Had the original sequence been much longer, say, a millionfold repetition of {**0 1**}, the corresponding algorithm would only require a minor change to reproduce the entire sequence. In this case, the complexity of the algorithm, as measured by the number of bits required to represent it, grows at a much slower rate than the original sequence. The complexity of the algorithm "Print **0 1** M times" is approximately $\frac{1}{2} \log_2 M$.

In the case of the second sequence, however, there is no obvious way to boil it down to a simple algorithm. The simplest algorithm required to reproduce it has approximately the same complexity as the sequence itself: "Print **0 1 1 0 1 1 0 0 1 1 0 1 1 1 1 0 0 0 1 0**". This algorithm grows at the same rate as the sequence it models. The complexity of the algorithm required to reproduce a random sequence of M binary digits is approximately M, for equiprobable digits **0** and **1**.

A measure of the randomness of a sequence can be defined as being the complexity of the smallest, or *minimal*, algorithm required to reproduce the sequence. These minimal algorithms play an important role in measuring randomness as well as in certain information source-coding applications to be discussed later.

Chaitin defines randomness as follows: "A series of numbers is random if the smallest algorithm capable of specifying it . . . has about the same number of bits of information as the series itself." The bit unit of information will be formally introduced in Chapter 4. For the purposes of understanding the concepts presented here, the number of bits is a measure of the number of statistically independent symbols required to describe a sequence or algorithm. By measuring the complexity of a minimal algorithm by its size, one arrives at the equivalent definition: "A random series of digits is one whose complexity is approximately equal to its size." This implies that a random sequence cannot be modeled by any simpler sequence. This agrees well with our intuitive sense of randomness. Any sequence possessing obvious symmetries, patterns, and correlations can be described by a shorter algorithm that exploits these symmetries, patterns, and correlations. A consequence of this definition is that a minimal algorithm must be random.

The size of this minimal algorithm is a measure of the complexity of the process it models. Note that although the introductory example consisted of a binary sequence, the results are clearly extendable to any stochastic process.

EXAMPLE

What has been said of the modeling of physical measurements also applies to source coding. The purpose of source coding is essentially to find the minimal algorithm for a given information stream. The complexity of such a minimal algorithm can be no greater than that of the original signal from the information source. A savings in transmission resources can, therefore, be enjoyed by transmitting the minimal algorithm itself rather than the original signal.

This approach is well exemplified by some techniques used for the coding of speech signals. Certain speech-waveform coding algorithms exploit the correlations, and, hence, partial predictability, in speech signals. Consider the speech signal-processing system shown in Fig. 3-1. The input $x(n)$ is a sequence of samples from a band-limited speech signal. The minimum bandwidth required to maintain speech intelligibility is roughly 3 kHz, the approximate bandwidth of telephone lines. This requires a sampling rate of at least 6000 samples per second. At this sampling rate, there is a substantial amount of correlation from sample to sample. One can express the value of the current speech sample as a linear combination of the past m samples:

$$x(n) = \sum_{k=1}^{m} a(k)x(n-k) + \epsilon(n) \tag{3.2}$$

This can be recognized as an autoregressive, or linear, prediction model for speech,

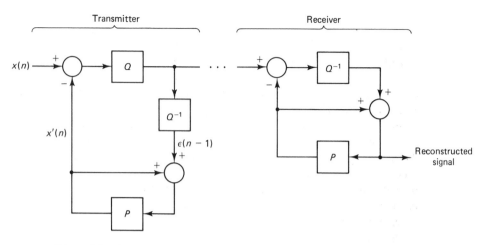

Figure 3-1. Source coder using linear prediction to remove waveform correlations. Q is a quantizer, Q^{-1} its inverse, and P is a linear predictor of order m.

where m is the order of the model, $a(k)$ are the prediction coefficients, and $\epsilon(n)$ is the residual prediction error process [Ra 78].

The model order and the coefficients $a(k)$ are fixed quantities chosen to minimize the square of the error norm $\|\epsilon\|^2$ over a large set of speech signals believed to be representative. In Fig. 3-1, the quantities $a(k)$ are constants. Current predicted values $\tilde{x}(n)$ are generated from past predictions using the linear predictive model:

$$\tilde{x}(n) = \sum_{k=1}^{m} a(k)\tilde{x}(n-k) \tag{3.3}$$

and subtracted from the input $x(n)$, resulting in the smaller and uncorrelated error signal $\epsilon(n)$

$$\epsilon(n) = x(n) - \tilde{x}(n)$$

which, in turn, is presented to the quantizer. In the previous equations, the tilde ($\tilde{}$) denotes a linear prediction. In this way, a priori information about speech is incorporated in the prediction coefficients $a(k)$. Since it is available to the receiver as well as to the transmitter, the $a(k)$ information need not be explicitly transmitted over the channel. Only the unpredictable residuals $\epsilon(n)$ need be transmitted.

The accumulation of quantization error is avoided by basing the prediction on the quantized residuals of past samples [Ja 74]. Letting a prime denote the reconstructed signal, the sample error is

$$\mathscr{E}(n) = x(n) - x'(n)$$

We now seek the prediction coefficients $a(k)$ that minimize the mean-square error energy:

$$E[\mathscr{E}^2] = E[(x - x')^2]$$

We must, therefore, minimize

$$E\{[x(n) - \sum_k a(k)x'(n - k)]^2\}$$

where the summation index k is understood to run from 1 to m. But since $x'(n) = x(n) - \mathscr{E}(n)$, the quantity to be minimized is

$$E\{[x(n) - \sum_k a(k)x(n - k) + \sum_k a(k)\mathscr{E}(n - k)]^2\}$$

Minimization is accomplished in a straightforward manner by requiring that the m derivatives of the last expression with respect to each of the $a(k)$ individually vanish. This leads to the expression

$$E[x(n)x(n - j)] = \sum_k a(k)E[x(n - k)x(n - j)]$$

$$+ \sum_k a(k)E[\mathscr{E}(n - j)\mathscr{E}(n - k)]$$

The term on the left-hand side is simply equal to the autocorrelation $R_x(-j) = R_x(j)$ by virtue of the autocorrelation of a real waveform having even symmetry. By a simple change of index variable, the first term on the right-hand side can also be related to R_x. An approximate solution for the optimal set of prediction coefficients can be found by neglecting the second term on the right-hand side, since it is on the order of the square of the error energy, a small quantity compared to the other terms for an effective coder. The resulting expression is

$$R_x(j) = \sum_{k=0}^{m-1} a(k)R_x(j - k) \tag{3.4}$$

which are recognized as the Yule–Walker equations. Note that the index k now runs from 0 to $m - 1$, with the stipulation that $a(0) = 1$. The prediction properties of R_x are identical to those of the autoregressive process x itself. The optimal set of predictor coefficients $a(k)$ can be found by solving the last set of linear equations when the correlation properties of the waveform $x(n)$ are known.

The Yule–Walker equations are a set of m simultaneous linear equations for the coefficients $a(k)$. They may be expressed in the more compact matrix notation

$$\mathbf{Ra} = \mathbf{b} \tag{3.5}$$

where $\mathbf{R}$ is the circulant matrix:

$$\begin{vmatrix} R_x(0) & R_x(1) & \cdots & R_x(m - 1) \\ R_x(-1) & R_x(0) & \cdots & R_x(m - 2) \\ \vdots & \vdots & \ddots & \vdots \\ R_x(-m + 1) & R_x(-m + 2) & \cdots & R_x(0) \end{vmatrix} \tag{3.6}$$

and where $\mathbf{a} = [a(0), a(1), \ldots, a(m - 1)]^T$ is the solution vector of prediction coefficients, and $\mathbf{b} = [R_x(1), R_x(2), \ldots, R_x(m)]^T$ is the vector of correlations.

The solution of this equation is

$$\mathbf{a} = \mathbf{R}^{-1}\mathbf{b} \tag{3.7}$$

Correlation matrices of the form such as $\mathbf{R}$ just given are Hermitian and Toeplitz. A Toeplitz matrix is one with the property that all of the elements of a given diagonal are equal.

Exploitation of the speech-correlation information contained in the $a(k)$ coefficients results in a residual signal having a smaller variance than that of the original speech signal $x(n)$. This, in turn, results in a smaller coding error, and, therefore, a closer approximation to the speech signal. Thus, one way to view coding is as a process that separates the predictable from the random in a signal. Only the random component need be transmitted, as it contains all of the information about a waveform that is not known to the receiver.

3.1.3 Chebyshev's Theorem

There are many occasions in the application of probability theory to communication where it is important to characterize the outcomes of random events by general features of their probability distribution functions. In several instances, we shall be dealing with a very large number M of possible random events $\{x_k; k = 1, \ldots, M\}$, whose probabilities $\{P_k; k = 1, \ldots, M\}$ sum up to unity, but with an arbitrary probability distribution. One intuitively expects the probability to be concentrated about the mean μ of the distribution, with a spread that is measured by the standard deviation σ. These statistics are defined in the usual way:

$$\mu = \sum_{k=1}^{M} x_k P_k \quad \text{and} \quad \sigma^2 = \sum_{k=1}^{M} (x_k - \mu)^2 P_k$$

Similar expressions exist for continuous random variables. For a random variable x with probability density function $p(x)$, we have

$$\mu = \int_{-\infty}^{\infty} x p(x)\, dx \quad \text{and} \quad \sigma^2 = \int_{-\infty}^{\infty} (x - \mu)^2 p(x)\, dx$$

One problem that comes up frequently in this situation is to determine just how tightly the total probability is concentrated about the mean of the distribution. While this problem could be approached numerically with each individual distribution, there is a very general theorem that provides much insight and requires few computations. Chebyshev's theorem follows.

Theorem. For a random variable x with mean μ and standard deviation σ and for any $\epsilon > 0$, the total amount of probability contained in an interval within $\epsilon\sigma$ units away from the mean is lower bounded by the quantity $1 - 1/\epsilon^2$. Stated mathematically, this becomes

$$\text{Prob } \{|x - \mu| \le \epsilon\sigma\} \ge 1 - \frac{1}{\epsilon^2} \tag{3.8}$$

This situation is illustrated in Fig. 3-2.

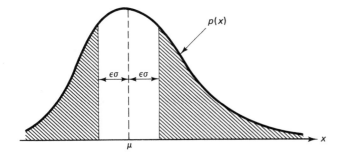

Figure 3-2. The probabilities in Chebyshev's theorem. The combined probabilities under both tail (total shaded area) is upper bounded by $1/\epsilon^2$.

The clear area represents the probability located within $\epsilon\sigma$ units away from the mean. Chebyshev's theorem states that no matter what the probability density is, the shaded area represents an amount of total probability that is at most equal to $1/\epsilon^2$.

Chebyshev's theorem can be restated in an equivalent way that suggests practical applications:

$$\text{Prob } \{|x - \mu| \geq \epsilon\sigma\} \leq \frac{1}{\epsilon^2} \tag{3.9}$$

This form of the theorem is interpreted as a bounding of the tails of the probability density function. This type of result is particularly useful in finding bounds in cases where an analytical evaluation would be impractical.

The proof of Chebyshev's theorem is very simple. Letting $\mathcal{R}$ denote the region for which the random variable x satisfies the inequality $|x - \mu| \geq \epsilon\sigma$, we have

$$\sigma^2 = \int_{-\infty}^{\infty} (x - \mu)^2 p(x)dx \geq \int_{\mathcal{R}} (x - \mu)^2 p(x)dx$$

$$\geq \epsilon^2\sigma^2 \int_{\mathcal{R}} p(x)dx = \epsilon^2\sigma^2 \text{ Prob } \{|x - \mu| \geq \epsilon\sigma\}$$

As presented here, Chebyshev's theorem applies to both tails of a distribution. There are cases where one's interest is restricted to the upper tail. In this case, the following generalization of the theorem applies:

$$\text{Prob } \{x \geq \delta\} \leq \frac{\mu}{\delta} \tag{3.10}$$

since

$$\mu = \int_{-\infty}^{\infty} xp(x)dx \geq \int_{\delta}^{\infty} xp(x)dx \geq \delta \int_{\delta}^{\infty} p(x)dx = \delta \text{ Prob } \{x \geq \delta\}$$

EXAMPLE

To illustrate Chebyshev's theorem, consider an experiment where some outcome A occurs with probability P. In a series of n such experiments, the probability of getting exactly k occurrences of the outcome A is binomially distributed:

$$\text{Prob } \{k\} = \binom{n}{k} P^k (1 - P)^{n-k}$$

where all realizations of any k occurrences of the variable A are considered equivalent. For the binomial probability distribution, the mean and variance are given by $\mu = nP$ and $\sigma^2 = nP(1 - P)$, respectively. Chebyshev's theorem states that the probability of realizing a number of occurrences of A that is further away from the mean than $\epsilon\sigma$ is

$$\text{Prob } \{|x - nP| \geq \epsilon[nP(1 - P)]^{1/2}\} \leq \frac{1}{\epsilon^2}$$

and, therefore,

$$\text{Prob } \{x \leq nP - \epsilon[nP(1 - P)]^{1/2}\} + \text{Prob } \{x \geq nP + \epsilon[nP(1 - P)]^{1/2}\} \leq \frac{1}{\epsilon^2}$$

For example, flipping a fair coin results in a head (event A) with probability $\frac{1}{2}$. By flipping a coin 10 times, the total number of heads is a random variable with a mean value $\mu = 5$ and standard deviation $\sigma = (2.5)^{1/2}$, so that for this experiment, the probability of realizing a number of heads more than one ($\epsilon = 1$) standard deviation away from the mean is upper bounded by 1. An exact calculation using the binomial distribution shows that the actual value is given by

$$2 \times 2^{-10} \times \left[\binom{10}{0} + \binom{10}{1} + \binom{10}{2} + \binom{10}{3} \right] = 0.344$$

If we now choose $\epsilon = 2$, the probability of realizing a number of heads more than two standard deviations away from the mean is upper bounded by 0.25; an exact calculation gives

$$2 \times 2^{-10} \times \left[\binom{10}{0} + \binom{10}{1} \right] = 0.021$$

These results are summarized in Table 3-1.

If we are interested only in the upper tail of the distribution, then the second form of the theorem must be used. For $\delta = \mu + \sigma = 6.581$, we have an upper bound given by Prob $\{x \geq 6.581\} \leq 0.760$, and the exact value is 0.172. For $\delta = \mu + 2\sigma = 8.162$, we have Prob $\{x \geq 8.162\} \leq 0.613$, and the exact value is 0.011. For $\delta = \mu + 3\sigma = 9.743$, we have Prob $\{x \geq 9.743\} \leq 0.513$, and the exact value is 0.001. These results are summarized in Table 3-2.

TABLE 3-1. COMPARISON OF CHEBYSHEV'S BOUND FOR BOTH TAILS, EQ. (3.9), PROB $\{|x - \mu| \geq \epsilon\sigma\}$, WITH EXACT CALCULATION

ϵ	Chebyshev	Exact
1	1.0	0.344
2	0.25	0.021

TABLE 3-2. COMPARISON OF CHEBYSHEV'S
BOUND FOR A SINGLE TAIL, EQ. (3.10),
PROB $\{x \mid \geq \delta\}$, WITH EXACT CALCULATION

ϵ	Chebyshev	Exact
$\mu + \sigma$	0.760	0.072
$\mu + 2\sigma$	0.613	0.011
$\mu + 3\sigma$	0.513	0.001

Chebyshev's theorem is too conservative for practical numerical estimates. Examples of probability tails estimates will be given in the following section since the Chernoff bound is much tighter. The importance of Chebyshev's theorem lies in the ease with which such a general statement can be used in theoretical calculations.

3.1.4 The Chernoff Bound

The Chernoff bound for the tail of a probability density function is much tighter than that provided by Chebyshev's theorem. We now derive the Chernoff bound, which, incidentally, provides a good example of how Chebyshev's theorem is used in a theoretical context. Consider a random variable x with probability density function $p(x)$ defined over the domain $x \geq 0$. Since the exponential function is monotonic, we can write

$$\text{Prob } \{x \geq \delta\} = \text{Prob } \{e^{\nu x} \geq e^{\nu \delta}\}$$

for any $\nu \geq 0$. Letting $y = e^{\nu x}$, the probability density function $q(y)$ for the continuous random variable y is given by

$$q(y) = p(x)\frac{dx}{dy} = \nu^{-1}e^{-\nu x}p(x)$$

so that

$$\text{Prob } \{e^{\nu x} \geq e^{\nu \delta}\} \leq E[y]e^{-\nu \delta}$$

by Chebyshev's theorem, Eq. (3.10), where $E[y] = E[e^{\nu x}]$ is the statistical expectation value of the variable y. We, therefore, have the bound

$$\text{Prob } \{x \geq \delta\} \leq e^{-\nu \delta}E[e^{\nu x}] \tag{3.11}$$

The term $E[e^{\nu x}]$ is simply the statistical expectation value of $e^{\nu x}$, also known as the moment-generating function of the density $p(x)$ defined by

$$\Phi(\nu) = \int_{-\infty}^{\infty} e^{\nu x}p(x)dx$$

This integral exists for many densities of practical interest, and is well tabulated. See, for example, Hastings and Peacock's excellent monograph [Ha 75] or Oberhettinger's book [Ob 73]. The important term in the Chernoff bound is the negative exponential $e^{-\nu\delta}$. This term guarantees that the bound can be made arbitrarily small by properly choosing δ.

The only restriction imposed thus far on the parameter ν is that it be nonnegative. The next step in the derivation is to select that value of ν, denoted by $\hat{\nu}$, that yields the tightest bound. This is easily found by differentiation by solving for the value of ν that satisfies the following equation:

$$\frac{d}{d\nu}\{e^{-\nu\delta}E[e^{\nu x}]\} = 0$$

which results in the following equation for $\hat{\nu}$:

$$E[xe^{\nu x}] - \delta E[e^{\nu x}] = 0$$

In actual calculations, the moment-generating function $E[e^{\nu x}]$ for a given case can usually be obtained without too much difficulty from the probability literature. The term $E[xe^{\nu x}]$ is simply the derivative of $E[e^{\nu x}]$ with respect to ν.

EXAMPLE

In the previous example for 10 coin tosses, we have $n = 10$ and $p = 1/2$. For the binomial distribution, the moment-generating function is

$$\Phi(\nu) = (1 - p + pe^{\nu})^n = E[e^{\nu x}]$$

The value of $\hat{\nu}$ that minimizes the upper bound is given by

$$\hat{\nu} = \ln\left(\frac{\delta}{n - \delta}\frac{1 - p}{p}\right)$$

For $\delta = \mu + \sigma = 6.581$, $\hat{\nu} = 0.655$, and the upper-tail probability is bounded by 0.601. For $\delta = \mu + 2\sigma = 8.162$, $\hat{\nu} = 1.491$, and the upper-tail probability is bounded by 0.115. For $\delta = \mu + 3\sigma = 9.743$, $\hat{\nu} = 3.637$, and the upper-tail probability is bounded by 0.003.

These results are summarized in Table 3-3. Comparing these results with those of Chebyshev's theorem, we see that the further out we go on the tail of the distribution, the better the Chernoff bound becomes as an approximation to the actual tail probability.

Another example of an application of the Chernoff bound will be given in Section 3.2.3; in addition, this bound is used in Chapter 4 to introduce important concepts in information theory.

TABLE 3-3. COMPARISON OF PROB $\{|x| x \geq \mu + m\sigma\}$ AS OBTAINED FROM CHEBYSHEV'S THEOREM, THE CHERNOFF BOUND, AND EXACT CALCULATION

m	Chebyshev	Chernoff	Exact
1	0.760	0.601	0.072
2	0.613	0.115	0.011
3	0.513	0.003	0.001

3.1.5 The Law of Large Numbers

The evidence for many chance events in our surroundings has motivated scientists and mathematicians to develop models for the description and study of random processes. Probability can be said to be the discipline that studies the regularities found in irregular events. Indeed, the random processes encountered in communication have regularities that can be exploited. The modern theory of communication, as formulated by Shannon, clearly exposes these regularities and identifies their practical applications. A fundamental result necessary to understand the mathematical theory of communication is the law of large numbers.

Just like Chebyshev's theorem and the Chernoff bound, the law of large numbers makes a general statement about the concentration of probability in a certain portion of the domain of a random variable. The regularity alluded to earlier refers to the behavior of this concentration of probability as the number of random variables considered increases.

We present a special case of the law of large numbers, in which the random variables in question are the outcomes of Bernoulli trials. A *Bernoulli trial* is one in which there are only two outcomes with probabilities P (for successes) and $1 - P$ (for failures). The outcomes of Bernoulli trials are statistically independent. Flipping a coin is a good example of a Bernoulli trial, in which the independent outcomes are the realization of heads or tails.

Consider a sequence of n Bernoulli trials. The number k of successes in a run of n Bernoulli trials is a random variable that follows the binomial distribution

$$\text{Prob } \{k\} = \binom{n}{k} P^k (1 - P)^{n-k}$$

having a mean $\mu = nP$ and a variance $\sigma^2 = nP(1 - P)$. Applying Chebyshev's theorem to the probability contained within ϵ standard deviations from the mean, we obtain

$$\text{Prob } \{|k - nP| \leq \epsilon[nP(1 - P)]^{1/2}\} \geq 1 - \frac{1}{\epsilon^2}$$

The parameter ϵ is entirely at our disposal. We choose the value $\epsilon = \alpha(n)^{1/2}$, where α is a free parameter. Chebyshev's theorem then becomes

$$\text{Prob } \{|k/n - P| \leq \alpha[P(1 - P)]^{1/2}\} \geq 1 - \frac{1}{n\alpha^2}$$

Now choose a particular value of α, which we denote by α_0, such that $\alpha_0[P(1 - P)]^{1/2} \leq \delta$, where δ is a quantity that is as small as we desire. Any δ however small can be chosen, provided n is made sufficiently large. At this point, both δ and α_0 are constants. In terms of these parameters, Chebyshev's theorem reads

$$\text{Prob } \{|k/n - P| \leq \delta\} \geq 1 - \frac{1}{n\alpha^2} \tag{3.12}$$

It now remains to take the limit of this expression as n becomes arbitrarily large, resulting in the following special case of the law of large numbers:

Theorem.   The relative frequency k/n of k successes in n Bernoulli trials for events having probability P obeys the following limit for arbitrarily small δ:

$$\lim_{n \to \infty} \text{Prob} \{|k/n - P| \leq \delta\} = 1$$

This version of the law of large numbers states that the ratio of successes to the total number of independent trials can be made to approach the probability P arbitrarily closely by considering sufficiently large numbers of trials. This agrees well with how intuition tells us probabilities should behave. Although the outcomes themselves are random, their aggregate behavior in terms of the relative frequency of successes exhibits a certain regularity by converging to a quantity that we call the probability.

It is important to note that the law of large numbers is a statement about the frequency of successes k/n and not about the number k of successes. The regularity implied by the law of large numbers is a statement about the convergence in probability of k/n to the quantity P. The behavior of the number k of successes becomes more and more erratic as n grows large. This is immediately seen in the standard deviation for k, which grows as $n^{1/2}$.

We can also interpret P as being the average value of k/n. In this case, the law of large numbers tells us that as n becomes large, all of the probability for the total number of successes tends to be confined to a neighborhood of size 2δ centered about P, with δ being an arbitrarily small quantity. Another way of stating this is as follows. The outcomes of sets of n trials can be divided into two disjoint groups as $n \to \infty$. In the first group are found those whose frequency of successes lies arbitrarily close to P. The other group consists of events whose total probability measure approaches zero.

As presented, we have introduced the law of large numbers as a statement about the sum of n independent random variables having values 1 or 0, depending on whether the realized event is a success (1) or a failure (0). The law of large numbers can be generalized to apply to any random variable, not just to those that follow the binomial distribution. In this form, the theorem reads as follows:

Theorem.   If $\{x_k\}$ is a sequence of independent random variables having a common probability distribution, then

$$\lim_{n \to \infty} \text{Prob} \left\{ \left| n^{-1} \sum_{k=1}^{n} x_k - \mu \right| \leq \delta \right\} = 1 \tag{3.13}$$

where μ is the mean value of the $\{x_k\}$ and δ is an arbitrarily small quantity.

To prove this theorem, we again use the versatile theorem by Chebyshev. If the $\{x_k\}$ have a mean μ and standard deviation σ, then the sum of n such independent variables has a mean $n\mu$ and a standard deviation $\sigma(n)^{1/2}$. Chebyshev's theorem states that for such a sum,

$$\text{Prob} \left\{ \left| \sum_{k=1}^{n} x_k - n\mu \right| \leq \epsilon\sigma(n)^{1/2} \right\} \geq 1 - \frac{1}{\epsilon^2}$$

for any $\epsilon > 0$. This may be rewritten as

$$\text{Prob}\left\{\left|n^{-1}\sum_{k=1}^{n}x_k - \mu\right| \le \frac{\epsilon\sigma}{n^{1/2}}\right\} \ge 1 - \frac{1}{\epsilon^2}$$

Letting $\delta = \epsilon\sigma/n^{1/2}$, we have

$$\text{Prob}\left\{\left|n^{-1}\sum_{k=1}^{n}x_k - \mu\right| \le \delta\right\} \ge 1 - \frac{\sigma^2}{n\delta^2}$$

for any $\delta > 0$. Passing to the limit for very large n and fixed δ (which may be arbitrarily small), there results

$$\lim_{n\to\infty}\text{Prob}\left\{\left|n^{-1}\sum_{k=1}^{n}x_k - \mu\right| \le \delta\right\} = 1$$

and the theorem is proved.

3.2 THE CENTRAL LIMIT THEOREM

Of all the limit theorems of probability theory, the most widely used in communication is the central limit theorem. The central limit theorem asserts that under very nonrestrictive conditions, the distribution of the sum of a large number of independent random variables approaches the normal distribution as the number of terms in the sum increases without bound, provided all of the terms contribute more or less equally to the sum.

There are many examples in communication systems where sums of independent random variables occur. Consequently, Gaussian processes are found with predictable and welcome regularity. This is a pleasing result since the resulting probability problems are, in general, solvable, often in closed form.

In this section, we present a derivation for a simple form of the central limit theorem and point the reader in the direction of more general results not proven here. We then show how the validity conditions for the central limit theorem arise in practical situations, thus justifying the use of Gaussian processes in a large number of applications. We close the section by emphasizing that the theorem should never be used blindly and that a certain amount of caution is to be exercised in certain cases.

3.2.1 Derivation of the Central Limit Theorem

The central limit theorem of probability theory deals with the asymptotic behavior of the statistics of the sum of a large number of independent random variables. There are really several central limit theorems, differing mainly in their generality and in conditions that must be satisfied.

The central limit theorem addresses the asymptotic statistical behavior of a sum of n independent random variables as n becomes large. The simplest case of the central limit theorem is that for which all members of the sum are identically distributed. In this form, the theorem is usually referred to as the Lindeberg–Lévy form of the central limit theorem.

Theorem. Given a set $\{\xi_1, \xi_2, \xi_3, \ldots\}$ of independent random variables having the same arbitrary probability distribution with a mean μ_0 and a standard deviation σ_0 for each ξ_k, their sum

$$\xi = \sum_{k=1}^{n} \xi_k \tag{3.14}$$

is asymptotically (as $n \rightarrow \infty$) normal with mean $\mu = n\mu_0$ and variance $\sigma^2 = n\sigma_0^2$.

Note that to use the theorem, we do not need to know the common distribution for the ξ_k, but only their mean and standard deviation, quantities that are usually easily obtained. We can consider μ_0 and σ_0 to be partial information about the distribution for the ξ_k. It is pleasing to see that it is possible to infer something about the distribution of the sum ξ based on so little information.

Before proving this theorem, we recall from the elementary theory of probability that the probability density $p(\xi)$ for the sum $\xi_1 + \xi_2 + \xi_3 + \ldots$ of independent random variables having probability densities $p_1(\xi), p_2(\xi), p_3(\xi), \ldots$, respectively, can be obtained with the use of characteristic functions. The *characteristic function* $\psi_k(\nu)$ associated with the density $p_k(\xi)$ is simply the Fourier transform of $p_k(\xi)$:

$$\psi_k(\nu) = \int_{-\infty}^{\infty} P_k(\xi)e^{-2\pi j \nu \xi}d\xi \quad \text{and} \quad p_k(\xi) = \int_{-\infty}^{\infty} \psi_k(\nu)e^{2\pi j \nu \xi}d\nu \tag{3.15}$$

The existence of such a Fourier transform pair is assured if

1. $\int_{-\infty}^{\infty} |P_k(\xi)|d\xi < \infty$, and

2. function $p_k(\xi)$ has at most a finite number of discontinuities.

These conditions are easily satisfied by probability densities. The characteristic function $\psi(\nu)$ of the sum of independent random variables is simply the product of the individual characteristic functions:

$$\psi(\nu) = \psi_1(\nu)\psi_2(\nu)\psi_3(\nu) \cdots \tag{3.16}$$

Equivalently, the density of the sum itself is the multiple convolution of the constituent densities:

$$p(\xi) = p_1(\xi)*p_2(\xi)*p_3(\xi)* \cdots \tag{3.17}$$

where $f(\xi)*g(\xi)$ denotes the convolution:

$$f(\xi)*g(\xi) = \int_{-\infty}^{\infty} f(u)g(\xi - u)du = \int_{-\infty}^{\infty} g(u)f(\xi - u)du \tag{3.18}$$

This method for finding the probability density of the sum of independent random variables is general and exact in the sense that it involves no approximations and is valid for any finite number of summed variables.

EXAMPLE

Let $\xi = \xi_1 + \xi_2$ be the sum of two independent random variables ξ_1 and ξ_2 with densities $p_1(x)$ and $p_2(x)$, respectively. The probability density function $p(x)$ corresponding to their sum ξ is defined by

$$\text{Prob }\{x < \xi \leq x + dx\} = p(x)dx \approx \text{Prob }\{\xi \approx x\}$$

But this can be written as

$$\text{Prob }\{\xi \approx x\} = \left(\text{Prob }\{\xi_1 = y,\ \xi_2 = x - y\}\right)_{\text{averaged over}}$$
$$\text{all values of } y$$

$$= dx \times \int p_1(y)p_2(x - y)dy$$

$$= dx \times p_1(x)*p_2(x) = p(x)dx$$

and, therefore,

$$p(x) = p_1(x)*p_2(x)$$

where the asterisk denotes a convolution. In general, the sum of n independent random variables result in an n-dimensional convolution.

A probability density function $p(\xi)$ and its characteristic function $\psi(\nu)$ form a Fourier transform pair. The characteristic function $\psi(\nu)$ may be expanded in a Maclaurin series:

$$\psi(\nu) = \psi(0) + \nu\psi_\nu(0) + \tfrac{1}{2}\nu^2\psi_{\nu\nu}(0) + \cdots \tag{3.19}$$

where the coefficients $\psi(0)$, $\psi_\nu(0)$, $\psi_{\nu\nu}(0)$, etc., can be related to the moments of $p(\xi)$. Thus,

$$\psi(0) = \int_{-\infty}^{\infty} p(\xi)d\xi = 1 \tag{3.20}$$

$$\psi_\nu(0) = -2\pi j \int_{-\infty}^{\infty} p(\xi)\xi d\xi = -2\pi j\,\mu_0 \tag{3.21}$$

$$\psi_{\nu\nu}(0) = -4\pi^2 \int_{-\infty}^{\infty} p(\xi)\xi^2 d\xi = -4\pi^2(\sigma_0^2 + \mu_0^2) \tag{3.22}$$

and so on. We can, therefore, write the Maclaurin series expansion of any characteristic function in the form

$$\psi(\nu) = 1 - 2\pi j\,\mu_0\nu - 2\pi^2(\sigma_0^2 + \mu_0^2)\nu^2 - \cdots \tag{3.23}$$

The characteristic function of a zero-mean random variable has a maximum at $\nu = 0$ since zero mean implies the presence of an extremum at the origin because $\psi_\nu(0) = 0$.

That this extremum must be a maximum is guaranteed by the sign of the second derivative, which is always negative since $\psi_{\nu\nu}(0) = -4\pi^2(\sigma_0^2 + \mu_0^2) < 0$.

Another important property of the characteristic function is that its magnitude is upper bounded by unity: $|\psi(\nu)| \leq 1$. This is easily proven using the Schwarz inequality:

$$|\psi(\nu)|^2 = \left| \int_{-\infty}^{\infty} p(\xi) e^{-2\pi j \nu \xi} d\xi \right|^2 = \left| \int_{-\infty}^{\infty} [p(\xi)]^{1/2} e^{-\pi j \nu \xi} [p(\xi)]^{1/2} e^{-\pi j \nu \xi} d\xi \right|^2$$

$$\leq \int_{-\infty}^{\infty} p(\xi) d\xi \cdot \int_{-\infty}^{\infty} p(\xi) d\xi = 1 \tag{3.24}$$

Figure 3-3 shows the general shape of the characteristic function $\psi(\nu)$ for a zero-mean random variable. The function $\psi(\nu)$ reaches its maximum value of unity at $\nu = 0$. The maximum value of a characteristic function is always unity. For a nonzero-mean random variable, this maximum value is reached at some other value of ν, as is obvious from Eq. (3.23). The shape of $\psi(\nu)$ in the neighborhood of its maximum value can be approximated by a parabola. Away from its maximum value, $\psi(\nu)$ assumes a shape that depends on the details of its associated probability density function $p(x)$. However, $\psi(\nu)$ must be symmetrical about $\nu = 0$, since $p(x)$ is always real.

We now turn to the proof of the Lindeberg–Lévy form of the central limit theorem. All of the ξ_k are identically distributed with an arbitrary probability density function having mean μ_0 and standard deviation σ_0. Consider the sum

$$\xi(n) = \sum_{k=1}^{n} \xi_k$$

of n of the ξ_k. The mean and variance of the sum $\xi(n)$ are, therefore, given by $\mu = n\mu_0$ and $\sigma^2 = n\sigma_0^2$, respectively. It remains to be shown that $\xi(n)$ is asymptotically normally distributed.

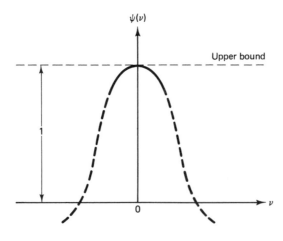

Figure 3-3. General shape for the characteristic function $\psi(\nu)$ of a zero-mean random variable. The function $\psi(\nu)$ is everywhere upper bounded by 1, always assumes a parabolic shape near $\nu = 0$, and is always symmetrical about $\nu = 0$. Away from $\nu = 0$, $\psi(\nu)$ may assume any value consistent with the upper-bound and symmetry constraints.

Our approach is to show that a sum equivalent to the previous one becomes asymptotically normally distributed as $n \to \infty$. We cannot, however, use the previous sum directly because its mean and variance increase at least as fast as n and that this will introduce complications when we pass to the limit as $n \to \infty$. We must first rescale the variables ξ_k in such a way as to end up with a sum $\xi(n)$ whose statistics remain bounded as $n \to \infty$.

To this end, we introduce the variables ς_k defined by

$$\varsigma_k = \frac{\xi_k - \mu_0}{\sigma_0 n^{1/2}} \tag{3.25}$$

All of the ς_k are independent and identically distributed with zero mean and a standard deviation equal to $1/n^{1/2}$. Summing these variables results in the sum $\varsigma(n) = [\xi(n) - \mu]/\sigma_0 n^{1/2}$. The variable $\varsigma(n)$ is distributed with zero mean and unit standard deviation. We must show that the sum $\varsigma(n)$ is asymptotically normal as $n \to \infty$.

Let the characteristic function for the probability density $p_0(\varsigma_k)$ be denoted by $\psi_0(\nu)$. Similarly, we denote the characteristic function for the probability density of the sum $\varsigma(n)$ by $\psi(\nu)$. Since the ς_k are identically distributed, we have

$$\psi(\nu) = [\psi_0(\nu)]^n$$

We also know that $|\psi_0(\nu)| \le 1$. Also, we conclude from Eq. (3.23) that the $\psi_0(\nu)$ attain their maximum value of unity at $\nu = 0$. These properties are inherited by $\psi(\nu)$. Raising $\psi_0(\nu)$ to a very large power results in a function that is appreciable only near the origin. The part of $\psi_0(\nu)$ that contributes significantly to $\psi(\nu)$ is, therefore, confined to a small neighborhood about the origin. We may, therefore, expand $\psi(\nu)$ in a Maclaurin series and write

$$\psi(\nu) \approx [1 - 2\pi^2 \nu^2/n - \cdots]^n$$

where higher-order terms have been neglected. It remains to take the limit of $\psi(\nu)$ as $n \to \infty$. This results in

$$\psi_{\lim}(\nu) = \lim_{n \to \infty} \psi(\nu) = \lim_{n \to \infty} (1 - 2\pi^2 \nu^2/n)^n = e^{-2\pi^2 \nu^2}$$

The corresponding probability density function can be found by evaluating the inverse Fourier transform of $\psi_{\lim}(\nu)$, giving

$$p_{\lim}(\xi) = \int_{-\infty}^{\infty} \psi_{\lim}(\nu) e^{2\pi j \nu \xi} d\nu = \frac{1}{(2\pi)^{1/2}} e^{-\xi^2/2} \tag{3.26}$$

which is immediately recognized as a normal density, thereby proving the theorem. There are more general forms of the central limit theorem. A slightly less restrictive form is stated without proof:

Theorem.   Given a set $\{\xi_k\}$ of independent random variables having corresponding means $\{\mu_k\}$ and standard deviations $\{\sigma_k\}$, their sum

$$\xi = \sum_{k=1}^{n} \xi_k$$

is asymptotically (as $n \to \infty$) normal with mean μ and variance σ^2 given by

$$\mu = \sum_{k=1}^{n} \mu_k \quad \text{and} \quad \sigma^2 = \sum_{k=1}^{n} \sigma_k^2$$

provided that the following conditions are met:

1. there exist constants $\lambda_k < \infty$ such that $\eta_k = E[|\xi_k - \mu_k|^3] \le \lambda_k$ for every k, and

2. $\displaystyle \lim_{n \to \infty} \sigma^{-1} \sum_{k=1}^{n} \eta_k = 0$

For further discussions of the central limit theorem, the interested reader is referred to the works of Cramér [Cr 46], Feller [Fe 68, Fe 71], and Khinchin [Kh 49].

3.2.2 Justification for the Use of Gaussian Processes

There are several instances where a random process is caused by the superposition of a large number of independent fluctuations. For example, the aggregate of free electrons undergoing thermal agitation produces a time-varying electric field that, at every point in space, is the vector sum of the fields due to each electron's random position. Each component of the resultant electric field, as well as the potential difference between two points, is, therefore, a fluctuating quantity having its origin in the summation of a very large number of independent random variables. The validity conditions for the central limit theorem are satisfied and the statistics of such sum are, for practical purposes, indistinguishable from those of Gaussian variables. Noise caused by the thermal motion of charged particles is called *thermal noise* and will be discussed in Section 3.3.

Another example is provided by white noise of arbitrary statistics applied at the input of an ideal narrow-band filter having constant magnitude response over its passband. The conditions of constant noise spectral density and flat filter response ensure that no single spectral component dominates the filter output. The time-domain response of this filter to a noisy input is a convolution (i.e., a weighted sum) of the random input function, and, therefore, has, to a good degree of approximation, Gaussian statistics.

EXAMPLE

Zero-mean white noise with constant spectral density is applied to the input of an ideal low-pass filter of bandwidth W. The autocorrelation of the filter output is, therefore, of the form

$$R(\tau) = \int_{-W}^{W} e^{2\pi j \, \nu \tau} d\nu = 2W \frac{\sin 2\pi \tau W}{2\pi \tau W}$$

Samples from the filter output have, within the approximation of the central limit theorem, Gaussian statistics, but, in general, are correlated. Note, however, that

$$R(\tau) = 0 \quad \text{for} \quad \tau = \frac{k}{2W}, \quad k = 1, 2, 3, \ldots$$

so that an uncorrelated Gaussian output process may be obtained by spacing the samples by an integral multiple of $\frac{1}{2}W$. Such samples are also statistically independent.

Assuming Gaussian statistics for the noise process appearing in most communication systems is often justifiable on the basis of the central limit theorem, all communication systems are subject to thermal noise and involve some filtering or other operation whose effect is to sum up random quantities. A common model used in many communication analyses assumes that the noise process is spectrally white and has Gaussian statistics. This special process is called *additive white Gaussian noise* (AWGN). In addition to being well justified by the central limit theorem, AWGN turns out to be analytically tractable. This may be one of the few instances where nature makes things easier for the engineer. Chapter 6 is entirely devoted to the performance of communication in AWGN.

3.2.3 Caveat for Small Tail Probabilities

The central limit theorem makes a remarkable statement about the sum of independent random variables. Under very general conditions, as the number of variables in the sum becomes large, the distribution of the sum asymptotically approaches the normal. What makes this statement remarkable is that it is true regardless of the distribution from which the individual random variables are drawn. Furthermore, it turns out that in many applications, the statistical distribution of the sum approximates a Gaussian distribution reasonably well when only a few (say, 20) random variables are added. This theorem finds countless applications in physics and engineering by providing an analytically tractable approximation to what would otherwise be a computational burden.

While it is true that the distribution of a sum rapidly approaches "Gaussianity", there are important cases where the validity of that approximation should be verified. This is particularly true of problems involving a constant false-alarm rate (CFAR) approach to detection. CFAR detection will be discussed in Chapter 5. We will discuss here a mathematical model for detection based on a thresholded sum of individual radar pulses, where a very low false-alarm rate (tail probability) is desired.

Specifically, we consider the validity of the central limit theorem when applied to the tail of the distribution, where the probability under the tail is required to be a very small quantity. For a statistical distribution with probability density function $f(x)$, we establish a correspondence between the area under the tail and the probability that the random variable x exceeds a certain threshold λ_0,

$$\text{Prob}\{x \geq \lambda_0\} = \int_{\lambda_0}^{\infty} f(x)\,dx = P_0$$

and associate the threshold λ_0 with the probability P_0.

In many cases, $f(x)$ is not available or is analytically untractable. If, however, the process giving rise to $f(x)$ involves a sum of independent random variables with known mean and variance, the central limit theorem can be invoked and $f(x)$ is then approximated by the normal distribution. It is then a simple matter to determine the CFAR threshold corresponding to a given probability P_0.

Should P_0 be a very small quantity, however, the previous integral will involve a portion of $f(x)$, which is very small in magnitude and, in fact, may be on the same order of or even smaller than the error in the central-limit-theorem approximation. Stated differently, the number of independent summed random variables that correspond to the small tail area must itself be a small quantity. For very small P_0, this number may be too small to justify the asymptotic normal form. The tails of $f(x)$ retain more of the characteristics of the statistics of the constituent members of the sum, whereas the region near the mean has "forgotten" about the original statistics. Detection problems involving false-alarm probabilities of 10^{-6} or smaller are not uncommon. It would, therefore, seem prudent in these cases to examine the validity of results derived under the central-limit-theorem Gaussian assumption.

This section examines a typical detection problem involving the sum of M samples with statistics following the chi-square probability density. The problem is to determine a threshold corresponding to a given tail probability P_0. This problem is solved in three ways. First, since a closed-form solution exists for this case, the exact value of the threshold, denoted by λ_0, is known. Then the central limit theorem is used to obtain a Gaussian approximation for the distribution of the decision variable used in detection. From this approximation, an estimate for the threshold, denoted by λ_{CLT}, is calculated. Finally, the Chernoff bound is used to provide an upper λ_C bound to the threshold. The relationship between these variables are shown in Fig. 3-4. The consequence of using either of these threshold approximations is then investigated.

Consider two identical, statistically independent, zero-mean, unit-variance, Gaussian random processes y_1 and y_2. Two such samples are squared and added. The result is a strictly positive random variable that is chi-square distributed with 2 degrees of freedom with a probability density function given by

$$f(z) = \frac{1}{2\sigma^2} e^{-z/2\sigma^2} \tag{3.27}$$

This is a special case of the chi-square distribution with n degrees of freedom:

$$f(z) = \frac{1}{\sigma^n 2^{n/2} \Gamma(n/2)} z^{n/2-1} e^{-z/2\sigma^2} \tag{3.28}$$

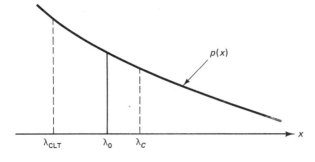

Figure 3-4. Relative locations of the true (λ_0), central-limit-theorem (λ_{CLT}), and Chernoff (λ_C) thresholds corresponding to a given tail probability P_0.

For $n = 2$, this reduces to Eq. (3.27), with a mean of $n\sigma^2 = 2\sigma^2 = 2$ and a variance of $2n\sigma^4 = 4$. Let a sequence of such measurements be denoted by $\{z_k\}$. The mean of a member z_k of this sequence is 2 and its variance is 4.

Next, form the sum of M such variables

$$x = \sum_{k=1}^{M} z_k$$

resulting in a random variable x that is chi-square distributed with $2M$ degrees of freedom; see Fig. 3-5. The tail probability for $f(x)$ can be expressed in closed form:

$$P_0 = e^{-\lambda_0/2} \sum_{k=0}^{M-1} \frac{1}{k!}\left(\frac{\lambda_0}{2}\right)^k \tag{3.29}$$

The central limit theorem gives the following relation between P_0 and λ_{CLT}:

$$P_0 = \tfrac{1}{2}\mathrm{erfc}\left[(2M\,\lambda_{\mathrm{CLT}} - 1)\left(\frac{M}{2}\right)\right]^{1/2} \tag{3.30}$$

where erfc ($\cdot$) is the complementary error function defined by

$$\mathrm{erfc}\,(z) = \frac{2}{(\pi)^{1/2}} \int_z^{\infty} e^{-t^2}dt \tag{3.31}$$

The Chernoff bound provides an upper limit to the tail probability and can be expressed as

$$\mathrm{Prob}\,\{x \ge \delta\} \le e^{-\nu\delta} E\,[e^{\nu x}]$$

where E[$\cdot$] denotes the statistical expectation operation, and ν is the solution to the equation

$$E\,[x\,e^{\nu x}] - \delta E\,[e^{\nu x}] = 0 \tag{3.32}$$

The Chernoff bound was used to establish a one-to-one correspondence between P_0 and λ_C by setting $\mathrm{Prob}\,\{x \ge \lambda_C\} = P_0$ in the previous expressions and to solve for the λ_C that satisfies the resulting bound. The thresholds λ_0, λ_{CLT}, and λ_C were calculated for a given probability P_0. Figures 3-6 through 3-9 compare the ratios $\lambda_{\mathrm{CLT}}/\lambda_0$ and λ_C/λ_0 as functions of M for several values of P_0. For the chi-square

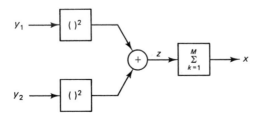

Figure 3-5.   Formation of central chi-square random variable x with $2M$ degrees of freedom.

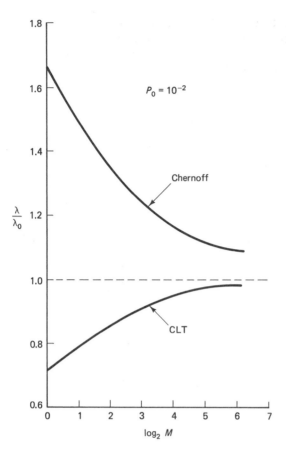

Figure 3-6. Threshold ratios λ_{CLT}/λ_0 and λ_C/λ_0 as a function of M for $P_0 = 10^{-2}$.

example considered here, λ_{CLT} always underestimates λ_0, although the estimate converges to the true value as M increases, λ_{CLT} is, therefore, a consistent estimator for λ_0. The Chernoff estimate λ_C is also consistent, but always overestimates λ_0.

An interesting behavior emerges from these examples. For values of P_0 larger than 10^{-4}, λ_{CLT} provides a better estimate to λ_0 than λ_C. For smaller values of P_0, the Chernoff estimate provides a smaller error in estimating λ_0.

A better measure of the consequence of these estimation errors can be obtained by evaluating the exact tail probabilities Prob $\{x \geq \lambda_{CLT}\}$ and Prob $\{x \geq \lambda_C\}$ by using the known closed-form expression. The deviation of these quantities from P_0, for example, as measured by the fractional error is

$$\epsilon = \frac{\text{Prob } \{x \geq \lambda_C\} - P_0}{P_0} \tag{3.33}$$

with a similar expression for the probability error induced by λ_{CLT}. The absolute value of this error is shown in Figure 3-10. For the cases calculated, the errors due to the Chernoff bound do not vary significantly with either M or P_0. The Chernoff

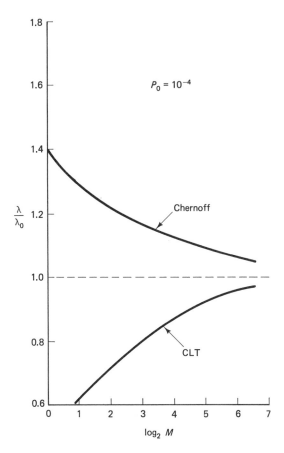

Figure 3-7. Threshold ratios λ_{CLT}/λ_0 and λ_C/λ_0 as a function of M for $P_0 = 10^{-4}$.

fractional error is in the vicinity of unity, which can be shown to be an upper bound for that error.

The central limit theorem approximations to the CFAR thresholds result in very large fractional errors, typically orders of magnitude greater than P_0. These errors decrease with increasing M.

Warned by the example presented here, it would appear prudent to include the Chernoff bound in calculations that involve the central limit theorem and very small tail probabilities. Although this example says nothing about variables that are not chi-square distributed, the results suggest caution in using part of the probability density function, which may not be well modeled by the central limit theorem.

3.3 THE PHYSICS AND MATHEMATICS OF NOISE

Although it is not possible to describe every source of noise in this section, we attempt to introduce, through a few simple examples, important properties that are shared by many noise processes. We begin with a definition of noise and follow

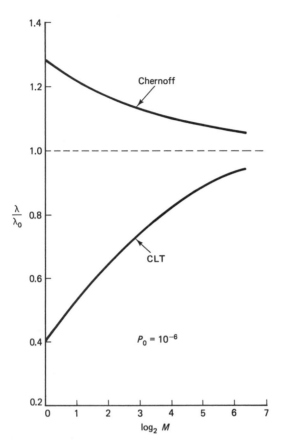

Figure 3-8. Threshold ratios λ_{CLT}/λ_0 and λ_C/λ_0 as a function of M for $P_0 = 10^{-6}$

with a few examples. We then present a discussion of noisy signals using some of the linear signal-space concepts introduced in Chapter 2. "Signal" in this section refers to any random waveform.

3.3.1 Sources of Noise

By *noise*, we mean a random signal obtained as the result of measuring some physical quantity. Characteristic of physical measurements is that in addition to the physical quantity of interest, other effects can influence the outcome. These effects are due to the unpredictable and uncontrollable interactions of the measuring instrument with its environment. This definition is very general, includes noise generated from a variety of processes, and considers communication as a special case of making a physical measurement.

Noise is not the physical process itself, but rather the incomplete representation of a complex process by a signal having few degrees of freedom. Noise comes about because we operate measuring equipment in an environment that is subject to unavoidable interactions with a large number of particles in random motion. These interactions are too complex to be accurately represented by the measurement.

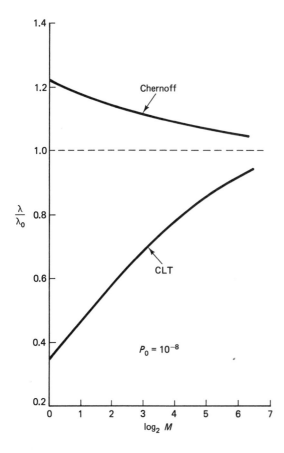

Figure 3-9. Threshold ratios λ_{CLT}/λ_0 and λ_C/λ_0 as a function of M for $P_0 = 10^{-5}$.

EXAMPLE

The most common form of noise in communication is *thermal noise*. Because of its ubiquity, thermal noise is important enough to warrant a full section (Section 3.3.3) for its description and an entire chapter (Chapter 6) for a discussion of its consequences on communication performance, where it appears as an additive Gaussian process.

Thermal noise originates in the random thermal agitation of charged particles. Thermal motion occurs at any temperature above absolute zero, with the agitation becoming increasingly severe as temperature increases. Temperature is a measure of the average kinetic energy of the particles. These charged particles remain bound to the medium but are free to move within its boundaries. Frequent collisions with the fixed atoms and with each other cause these particles to constantly scatter in various directions, resulting in a state of overall chaos.

The potential difference across such a medium, or the current through it, is the cumulative result of the effect of these charged particles. Although the net average voltage or current may be zero or perhaps some constant value, there are always rapid fluctuations about the mean value that reflect the constant

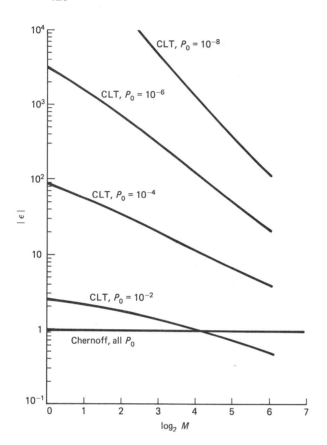

Figure 3-10. Magnitudes of the error incurred by using the central-limit-theorem and Chernoff approximations to the detection threshold for a given tail probability.

geometrical reorganization of a large number of interacting charged particles. Since, in particular, this process occurs in communication equipment, the random signals that result are superimposed on the communication signals, resulting in additive noise. Thermal noise is of fundamental importance in communication because it occurs everywhere. The only way to reduce it is to cool the equipment to temperatures close to absolute zero, a costly approach that is used only where essential.

Noise involves the interaction of the measuring instrument with a system having a very large number of degrees of freedom. In the previous example, this system is the electron gas present in a resistive medium. Other examples include pressure fluctuations due to molecular collisions in an ordinary gas. Noise need not be generated by microscopic processes (although these often turn out to be the easiest processes to describe statistically). Interactions with macroscopic systems having a large number of degrees of freedom can also cause random fluctuations. Examples affecting communication are the weather, ionospheric propagation fluctuations, and human error. There is no clear separation between microscopic and macroscopic systems. Interactions occur across dissimilar scales, reinforcing our view of randomness as chaos that results from the dynamics of systems having a very large number of degrees of freedom viewed through instruments having much fewer degrees of freedom. We are looking at the physical world through very small windows.

All examples of noise have a common characteristic. Noise manifests itself in measuring equipment that interacts, however weakly, with a complex environment it cannot measure exactly. The environment itself has a large complexity, as measured by its number of degrees of freedom. Such an environment exhibits a behavior that cannot be described exactly, even in principle. On the other hand, the signals used in measurements and communication have relatively few degrees of freedom. Each of the signal's degrees of freedom reflects the average influence of a very large number of environmental degrees of freedom. To a very good approximation, the result is noise with Gaussian statistics by virtue of the central limit theorem.

We shall concentrate in this section on types of noise for which there are simple statistical models. In particular, we place special importance on additive noise with Gaussian statistics. There are many types of noise that cannot be represented in this manner, for example, noise caused by lightning crashes or propagation fluctuations. There is no comprehensive theory that covers all types of noise. However, there are cases that are both important in engineering applications and are amenable to theoretical analysis.

3.3.2 Shot Noise

Shot noise is caused by electrical current not being a continuous quantity, but rather a flow of discrete charge-bearing particles. The result is that the current flowing past a point in a circuit can, under certain conditions, exhibit a granularity owing to the quantization of electrical charge. The fundamental unit of electrical charge is 1.602×10^{-19} coulomb. This charge is positive when carried by a proton, or a hole in a semiconductor, and negative when carried by an electron. The simplest example of shot noise involves current flowing through a vacuum tube. Vacuum tubes may appear out of place in the silicon age. To be sure, shot noise can be found in semiconductors, but the simplicity of the vacuum tube example warrants its use as it exposes the fundamental nature of shot noise with a minimum of confusion.

Let us first take a look at the physics of shot noise. Shot noise in vacuum-tube diodes, the simplest form of a vacuum tube, is caused by the random number of electrons leaving the cathode and arriving at the anode, also called the plate. Figure 3-11 shows an experimental setup that could be used to generate shot noise. The cathode of a vacuum tube is made of a conducting material, usually tungsten. In a metal, the atoms themselves are fixed, whereas their outer valence electrons are shared by the entire material. These electrons are free to move about and are only loosely bound to the bulk of the metal. These free electrons do not normally leave the metal and are retained by a certain amount of binding energy.

If the metal is heated to such an extent that the free electrons acquire sufficient energy to overcome the binding energy, then these electrons can leave the metal. This boiling off of the free electrons is a statistical process. Only those electrons having sufficient kinetic energy leave the metal. The cathode of a vacuum tube is a conductor that is heated to such temperatures to encourage large numbers of electrons to leave. This process is called *thermionic emission*.

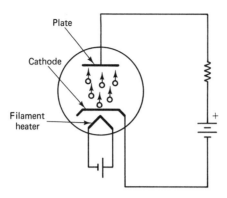

Figure 3-11. A vacuum-tube-diode circuit. Individual electrons traveling from cathode to plate give rise to shot noise.

Current in a vacuum tube is produced by maintaining the plate at a positive potential with respect to the heated cathode. Electrons from the cathode experience a force caused by the electrical field maintained between the cathode and the plate and are attracted toward the plate, giving rise to a current. This current is composed of individual electrons, and a detailed description of this current must involve the arrival at the plate of discrete charges, causing the current to fluctuate in discrete increments of 1.602×10^{-19} coulomb. These fluctuations are the basis of shot noise.

It is clear from the physics of thermionic emission that these electrons must arrive at the plate at random times and that their arrivals are statistically independent events. Let us consider at first very small currents, for which the granularity is pronounced. By this we mean that the ratio of the fluctuations to the mean current is large. The probability p that an electron reaches the plate in the time interval between t and $t + \Delta t$, where Δt is a small quantity, is proportional to Δt, is

$$p = \lambda \Delta t$$

where λ is a constant. For sufficiently small Δt, the probability of simultaneous arrivals at the plate can be made arbitrarily small. The random arrival of an electron at the plate can, therefore, be modeled by a Bernoulli trial. Now consider a larger time interval $T = n \Delta t$. The probability that exactly k electrons reach the plate during this interval is given by the binomial distribution:

$$P(k) = \binom{n}{k} p^k (1 - p)^{n-k} \tag{3.34}$$

Expressing this in terms of λ and Δt, we have

$$P(k) = \frac{n!}{k!(n-k)!} (\lambda \Delta t)^k (1 - \lambda \Delta t)^{n-k}$$

This can be rewritten as

$$P(k) = \frac{n(n-1)(n-2) \cdots (n-k+1)(n-k)!}{k!(n-k)!} n^{-k} (\lambda n \Delta t)^k (1 - \lambda \Delta t)^{n-k} \tag{3.35}$$

We now take the limit of Eq. (3.35) as $n \to \infty$ and $\Delta t \to 0$ in such a way as to keep λ constant. The first k terms in the numerator of Eq. (3.35) become

$$n(n-1)(n-2) \cdots (n-k+1) \approx n^k$$

and cancel the n^{-k} term appearing to the immediate right of the fraction. For $n \gg k$, we have

$$(1 - \lambda \Delta t)^{n-k} \approx (1 - \lambda \Delta t)^n \approx 1 - n \lambda \Delta t + \tfrac{1}{2}(n \lambda \Delta t)^2 - \cdots \approx e^{-\lambda n \Delta t}$$

with the approximation becoming an equality in the stated limits. Now letting $\mu = \lambda n \Delta t$ represent the average number of electrons reaching the plate during the time interval $T = n \Delta t$, there results the Poisson distribution

$$P(k) = e^{-\mu} \frac{\mu^k}{k!} \qquad k = 0, 1, 2, 3, \ldots \tag{3.36}$$

for the arrival statistics. The parameter λ is the number of electrons reaching the plate per unit time. Note that λ is proportional to the current since it is a measure of the amount of charge per unit time flowing through the tube. As the current increases, λ becomes larger and the probability distribution for the number of electrons reaching the plate becomes Gaussian. This may be shown with the help of the DeMoivre–Laplace theorem. For a complete proof of this theorem, the reader is referred to [Fe 68].

Theorem. If $\xi(n)$ is the total number of successes in a sequence of n Bernoulli trials, each having probability p, then the variable

$$\zeta = \frac{\xi - \mu}{\sigma} \tag{3.37}$$

becomes asymptotically normally distributed with zero mean and unit standard deviation as $n \to \infty$, where $\mu = np$ and $\sigma = [np(1-p)]^{1/2}$.

This is not a surprising result. As the plate current increases, the number of electrons arriving per unit time also increases. The total number of arrivals is the sum of a large number of independent quantities. The central limit theorem guarantees an asymptotic normal distribution for such a variable.

We have thus far attributed three probability distributions to shot noise: the binomial, the Poisson, and the normal. Let us put these three probabilistic models in perspective. The binomial distribution was used to show that the electron arrivals at the plate obey Poisson statistics. The derivation is based on the observation that if Δt is made sufficiently small, then only two outcomes are possible: either a single electron arrives at the plate during that time interval or no electron arrives. Multiple applications of a large number of such Bernoulli trials each over a time interval of vanishingly small duration were then used to derive the generally valid result that the total number of electrons arriving at the plate in any finite time interval is a Poisson-distributed random variable.

On the other hand, when many electrons are involved, the contribution of an individual electron to the sum becomes relatively unimportant and the normal distribution may be used. How good this approximation is in actual cases depends on the particular application. The caveat discussed in Section 3.2.3 should be heeded.

EXAMPLE

A measurement of duration T seconds is made on a plate current of I_p amperes results in a total electrical charge

$$Q = I_p T = \mu e$$

composed of a number of electrons that is Poisson-distributed with mean and variance μ. A measure of the fluctuations in the number of electrons collected is given by the ratio of the standard deviation to the mean, which is

$$\mu^{-1/2} = \left(\frac{e}{I_p T} \right)^{1/2}$$

To appreciate just how small such a quantity can be, consider a 1 μs measurement of a plate current of 1 μA. Even with such small quantities, the fluctuations are only on the order of 40 parts per million.

A simple argument shows that the power spectral density of shot noise must be very close to white. Assuming that electrons are point charges, the tube current is due to a random superposition of point charges reaching the plate. Each point charge contributes impulsively to the current and has a corresponding power spectral density that is flat. The cumulative effects of a number of electrons arriving at random at the plate, therefore, is a flat power spectral density.

3.3.3 Thermal Noise

Thermal noise is the result of thermal agitation of charge carriers. Electrons in a resistive medium constantly collide with the fixed atoms and interchange energy with them. This results in a random motion of the electrons, similar to Brownian motion. When this system is in thermal equilibrium, the electron "gas" imparts as much energy to its surroundings as it receives from it. This condition is one of constant chaotic motion. Each electron moves independently from the rest and interacts with its surroundings through random scattering.

A study of thermal noise brings us in contact with some of the most interesting yet simple aspects of theoretical physics. We shall discuss two related physical mechanisms that share a common energy spectrum: thermal noise and blackbody radiation.

Consider a medium in which charged particles are in thermal motion. If the material is held at constant temperature, then thermal equilibrium prevails and the spectral distribution of energy follows a certain law, which we proceed to derive on very general grounds.

Our approach is to consider a cavity within the body of the material. The boundaries of this cavity consist of surface charges in random motion. These charges are constantly being accelerated and consequently emit electromagnetic radiation within the cavity. The charged particles exchange energy with each other as well as with the radiation fields. At thermal equilibrium, each part of the system (particles and radiation) gives up as much energy as it receives, on the average. No significant increase or decrease of energy occurs anywhere.

It therefore follows that the energy spectrum of the radiation field must be identical to that of the charged particles. If this were not the case, the system would not be in thermal equilibrium, contrary to our assumption. We are about to derive Planck's law for the spectral distribution of energy within the cavity. The results are independent of the detailed physical properties of the charged particles that give rise to this radiation; the only significant physical property is that they carry a unit of charge. Since these particles are in thermal equilibrium with the radiation field, Planck's law will apply to them as well. Thus, our analysis will apply to the spectral properties of noise signals measured from such a material.

We need to say a few words of guidance before proceeding with the derivation. Planck's law is an early result of quantum mechanics. The historical significance of Planck's result is that it demonstrated the necessity of quantizing the energy levels of an electromagnetic radiation field to bring its spectrum in agreement with experimental measurements. Thus, Planck paved the way for the development of modern quantum theory. This feat earned Max Planck the Nobel Prize for physics in 1918.

Planck's spectrum correctly predicts the energy distribution over all frequencies. From this result, we shall show that in the range of frequencies of interest to engineers, the energy spectral density can, to a very good approximation, be considered a constant that depends only on the absolute temperature. This justifies the use of flat noise power spectral densities in many analyses. This limiting result at "low" frequencies can also be demonstrated within the framework of classical physics, but at the price of serious disagreement at higher frequencies. We therefore prefer to follow the quantum mechanical approach, which turns out to be mathematically very simple.

We must first establish some important results of classical physics. This will provide a limiting form to which the quantum mechanical description must reduce. The systems we shall consider consist of a very large number of weakly interacting particles in thermal equilibrium with an external heat reservoir. For definiteness, we can think of these particles as being electrons, but the development that follows is quite general. The restriction to weak interactions simply means that we allow exchanges of energy between the particles themselves and between the particles and the heat reservoir, but the interaction energy itself is a negligibly small fraction of the system's total energy. The heat reservoir is an outside agent used to maintain the system's total average energy constant.

The system's total energy $\mathscr{E}$ is the sum of the energies of all of its constituent particles. The energy of one such particle can range from zero to infinity, and undergoes constant fluctuations because of Brownian motion. For the purpose of discussing the statistical behavior of systems in a state of thermal equilibrium, it suffices to distinguish (i.e., label) systems according to their total energy.

It is useful at this point to introduce the notions of microstate and macrostate. A *microstate* refers to the detailed configuration of the individual particles comprising the entire system in question. For example, the microstate of a system at a given instant is specified by a listing of the energies of all of its constituent particles. By contrast, a system's *macrostate* is defined by its total average energy alone. The microstate of a system constantly changes because the particles' energies are constantly changing owing to random motion. However, we can view the microstates of a system at a given temperature as forming a statistical ensemble for a particular macrostate. A macrostate corresponds to a very large number of microstates. The microstate/macrostate concept is a useful theoretical construct used to provide a description at the particle level and relate this description to the macroscopic level. Macrostates provide a system's representation in terms of macroscopically observable features such as total energy, pressure, voltage, etc.

We begin by labeling each microstate i by its corresponding energy ϵ_i and calculate the probability P_i of finding the system in a representative microstate. Specifically, we say that the system is in the microstate i if its total energy ϵ lies within the interval

$$\epsilon_i \leq \epsilon \leq \epsilon_i + \delta\epsilon$$

The form of the probability P_i is readily obtained by variational methods. See, for example, [Ja 57a, Ja57b]. The probability P_i must satisfy two conditions. The first is the usual normalization condition that must be satisfied by any probability function:

$$\sum_i P_i = 1 \tag{3.38}$$

where $P_i = \text{Prob}\{\epsilon_i \leq \epsilon \leq \epsilon_i + \delta\epsilon\}$. The second condition is the conservation of energy, and requires that the mean value of ϵ be a constant:

$$\sum_i \epsilon_i P_i = A \tag{3.39}$$

Note that these sums are sums over states, so that the constant A represents the average energy per state and not the total system energy.

Within the restrictions imposed by the previous two constraints, our system is allowed to assume any configuration over microstates and will do so in a random manner from instant to instant. Our system is, therefore, described by a statistical ensemble of systems distributed over microstates according to some probability distribution P_i. A criterion for finding P_i is that it must correspond to the most random (i.e., disorderly) distribution over microstates consistent with the previous two constraints. Stated differently, we are seeking the P_i that maximizes the entropy of statistical mechanics:[†]

$$S = -\sum_i P_i \ln P_i \tag{3.40}$$

[†]The concept of entropy appears in statistical physics as well as in information theory. In both disciplines, entropy serves as a measure of the number of different realizations of a system. The entropy of information theory measures the information content of an ensemble and will be discussed fully in Chapter 4. The entropy of statistical mechanics measures the amount of disorder in a physical system. Not surprisingly, the two concepts are related and share a common mathematical expression. The calculation shown here follows the usual statistical physics approach [Ja 57a, Ja 57b].

subject to the two constraints previously introduced. This approach is the only unbiased way of making a statistical inference about P_i on the basis of partial information (viz., the constraints). This is a standard problem in constrained extremization, and can be solved for the P_i that maximizes the expression

$$J = -\sum_i P_i \ln P_i - \alpha\left(\sum_i P_i - 1\right) - \beta\left(\sum_i \epsilon_i P_i - A\right) \tag{3.41}$$

where α and β are Lagrange multipliers. Again we remind the reader that these sums are over microstates and not particles. The Euler–Lagrange equation corresponding to this variational problem is simply

$$\frac{\partial J}{\partial P_i} = 0$$

which leads to

$$1 + \ln P_i + \alpha + \beta\epsilon_i = 0 \tag{3.42}$$

The probabilities P_i are, therefore, given by

$$P_i = e^{-(1+\alpha)}e^{-\beta\epsilon_i}$$

The first term is a constant that can be determined through normalization. The parameter β turns out to be given by

$$\beta = \frac{1}{k_B T}$$

where $k_B = 1.38054 \times 10^{-23}$ J/K is Boltzmann's constant, and T is the absolute temperature.[†] The resulting probability distribution is

$$P_i = Ce^{-\epsilon_i/k_B T} \tag{3.43}$$

where

$$C^{-1} = \sum_i e^{-\epsilon_i/k_B T}$$

This important result is known as the *canonical distribution* of statistical mechanics. The canonical distribution describes the probability of finding a system in thermal equilibrium in a state with total energy ϵ_i.

The next result we wish to establish is the equipartition of energy theorem, which states that under certain very general conditions, the available energy in a system in thermal equilibrium distributes itself so that the average energy corresponding to each independent degree of freedom is $\frac{1}{2} k_B T$. This is strictly a classical (i.e., not quantum) result and leads directly to the well-known result that the two-sided power spectral density of thermal noise is given by $\frac{1}{2} k_B T$.

[†] The symbol T here denotes absolute temperature. There should be no confusion with the same symbol used elsewhere in the book to denote waveform duration.

In classical mechanics, the dynamics of a system can be described in terms of the system's generalized coordinates [Go 50]. For example, the behavior of a gas modeled as a collection of point particles is totally specified by the position and momentum of each particle. Since position and momentum are three-dimensional vectors, six scalars are needed to describe each particle. These scalars are *generalized coordinates* of the system. There is a perfect analogy between the generalized coordinates of a dynamical system and the signal-space coordinates introduced in Chapter 2. In both cases, the coordinates are scalars that completely describe the system or signal. Just as there are several possible choices for signal-space coordinates corresponding to different bases in linear signal space, the generalized coordinates of a physical system are not unique and need not correspond to positions and momenta.

In general, the total energy of a system is a function of the generalized coordinates

$$\mathscr{E} = \mathscr{E}(x_1, x_2, \ldots, x_m)$$

We now restrict our attention to systems for which the total energy is a quadratic function of these coordinates. This is not a very severe restriction. For example, kinetic energy is a quadratic function of the momenta. We can represent the total energy of the system as a quadratic function of the generalized coordinates. Since energy is additive, we must have

$$\mathscr{E}(x_1, x_2, \ldots, x_m) = \sum_{i=1}^{m} a_i x_i^2$$

where the $\{a_i\}$ are constants. Since the system in question is in thermal equilibrium, the probability of finding it in a state corresponding to a total energy $\mathscr{E}$ is given by the canonical distribution

$$\frac{e^{-\beta \mathscr{E}(x_1, x_2, \ldots, x_m)} dx_1, dx_2, \ldots, dx_m}{\int_{-\infty}^{\infty} \cdots \int_{-\infty}^{\infty} e^{-\beta \mathscr{E}(x_1, x_2, \ldots, x_m)} dx_1, dx_2, \cdots dx_m}$$

where the probability has been written in terms of a joint probability density that depends on all of the m generalized coordinates through which the total energy depends in a quadratic manner. This form reminds us that the state of a system is defined by the configuration of all of its constituent particles.

Now consider one of the generalized coordinates x_j. The average value of the energy associated with this coordinate is

$$\overline{\epsilon_j} = \frac{\int_{-\infty}^{\infty} \epsilon_j \, e^{-\epsilon_j / k_B T} dx_j \int_{-\infty}^{\infty} \cdots \int_{-\infty}^{\infty} e^{-(\mathscr{E} - \epsilon_j)/k_B T} dx_1 \cdots dx_m}{\int_{-\infty}^{\infty} e^{-\epsilon_j / k_B T} dx_j \int_{-\infty}^{\infty} \cdots \int_{-\infty}^{\infty} e^{-(\mathscr{E} - \epsilon_j)/k_B T} dx_1 \cdots dx_m}$$

In both numerator and denominator, the first integral is over the coordinate x_j and the multiple integrals are over all other coordinates. The multiple integrals are identical and therefore cancel. Evaluation of the remaining integrals results in

$$\overline{\epsilon_j} = \tfrac{1}{2} k_B T \tag{3.44}$$

This result was obtained by substituting $\epsilon_j = a_j x_j^2$ in the remaining integrals. The actual value of a_j is irrelevant. The result depends solely on the quadratic dependence of the energy upon system coordinates. This is known as the *equipartition of energy theorem* and states that for classical systems for which the functional dependence of the total energy on generalized coordinates is quadratic, the total energy is distributed in such a way as to contribute an equal amount $\frac{1}{2} k_B T$ to each system degree of freedom. The simplicity of this result belies its importance in practical situations.

EXAMPLE

In electrical engineering, the most direct use of the equipartition theorem is in the derivation of the power spectral density N_0 for thermal noise. An expression for N_0 is easily obtained by combining the equipartition theorem with the concept of signal degrees of freedom introduced in Chapter 2.

Consider a waveform of duration D and bandwidth W measured at the output of a resistor held at temperature T. We use D instead of the usual symbol T to denote waveform duration here because, in this example, T denotes absolute temperature. This waveform is a typical realization of a thermal-noise process. Such a waveform has $2DW$ independent coordinates and, therefore, possesses $2DW$ independent degrees of freedom through which the energy depends quadratically. According to the equipartition theorem, the average total energy in the waveform is given by

$$\mathscr{E} = 2DW \cdot \tfrac{1}{2}k_B T = DW\, k_B T$$

The noise power N produced by the resistor is simply the ratio of the average signal energy $\mathscr{E}$ divided by the signal duration D:

$$N = \frac{\mathscr{E}}{D} = k_B T W = (\tfrac{1}{2}k_B T)\cdot(2W)$$

a familiar result in electrical engineering. The thermal-noise power is proportional to the absolute temperature and to the bandwidth. The constant of proportionality is Boltzmann's constant. Finally, the thermal-noise power spectral density N_0 is given by

$$N_0 = \frac{N}{2W} = \tfrac{1}{2}k_B T \tag{3.45}$$

Note that a constant thermal-noise output level in time does not violate conservation of energy. Since the resistor is held at constant temperature, it receives as much heat energy as it releases as electrical noise. In a state of thermal equilibrium, the inflow and outflow of energy are in balance.

The classical result just derived implies a flat thermal-noise power spectral density, i.e., white noise. For most applications, the frequency dependence of thermal noise is so slight that, to a good approximation, the process may be considered white. At sufficiently high frequencies, however, that approximation must break down and the power spectral density must eventually vanish.

The reason for this behavior is to be found in the quantum nature of electromagnetic radiation. Again, we use a variational approach to evaluate the probability distribution P_n over states by maximizing the entropy of the distribution subject to appropriate constraints. This problem reduces to the unconstrained maximization of

$$J = -\sum_n P_n \ln P_n - \alpha \left(\sum_n P_n - 1 \right) - \beta \left(\sum_n \epsilon_n P_n - \mathscr{E} \right)$$

The Euler–Lagrange equation corresponds to a probability distribution of the form

$$P_n = e^{\alpha - 1} e^{\beta \epsilon_n} = C e^{\beta n h \nu}$$

where $\epsilon_n = nh\nu$ has been used in accordance with Planck's quantization rule for electromagnetic radiation, which we now view as quantized packets (photons). A photon of frequency ν carries with it an amount $h\nu$ joules of energy, where $h = 6.62559 \times 10^{-34}$ joule-second is Planck's constant. The constant C can be determined through normalization:

$$\sum_{n=0}^{\infty} P_n = \frac{A}{1 - e^{\beta h \nu}} = 1$$

so that $A = 1 - e^{\beta h \nu}$. The constraint of constant average energy yields

$$\sum_{n=0}^{\infty} \epsilon_n P_n = \mathscr{E}$$

Substituting $\epsilon_n = nh\nu$ and the expression for P_n results in

$$\mathscr{E} = \mathscr{E}(\nu) = \frac{h\nu}{e^{n\nu/k_B T} - 1} \tag{3.46}$$

which is Planck's law for the distribution of energy over the frequency spectrum. At low frequencies, i.e., for $h\nu \ll k_B T$, we have $\mathscr{E}(\nu) \approx k_B T$, the white-noise spectral density. Note that quantum effects become appreciable only when the quantum energy is on the same order as the thermal energy. The threshold condition for this is $h\nu \approx k_B T$. At room temperature ($T \approx 300$ K), the frequency would have to be above 6000 GHz for quantum effects to be noticeable.

3.3.4 Statistics of Noise Signals✳

In Section 3.ⅎ 3, we took a detailed look at the physical origin of thermal noise, and our attention turned to the statistical behavior of charged particles in random motion and the resulting electromagnetic fields. We now describe measurements of such noise processes. A measurement consists in recording some macroscopic features of a system. For the present discussion, we might consider measuring, for example, the thermal-noise voltage appearing at the terminals of a resistor held at constant temperature.

As was mentioned in Section 3.3.3, the distinction between microstate and macrostate is a very fuzzy one. A resistance held at constant temperature has associated with it a very large number of degrees of freedom. However, in principle, an instrument with sufficient bandwidth and a sufficiently long measuring interval could measure these. In practice, the number of physical degrees of freedom associated with a physical system and the number of degrees of freedom in a measuring instrument (as measured by the bandwidth-duration product of the measured waveform) are separated by many orders of magnitude. Thus, each measured signal coordinate represents the averaged effect of an overwhelmingly large number of physical degrees of freedom. Under very general conditions, the central limit theorem may be applied and the measured noise process can be considered Gaussian.

In the present section, we approach the subject of noise waveform from a purely mathematical point of view. We assume that the measured noise process is normally distributed over a finite number of signal coordinates. Without loss of generality, such processes are assumed to have zero mean. Although the language of mathematics—rather than physics—is used, it should soon become apparent that there is considerable similarity between this section and Section 3.3.3. In particular, Section 3.3.3 was developed around the concept of signal states corresponding to the same energy. In the present section, a similar role is played by the norm of a signal. The square of the norm is a measure of the energy content of a signal. The signal "size" as measured by the Euclidian norm and signal energy are thus two ways of referring to the same quantity. We, therefore, use energy and the square of the Euclidian norm interchangeably.

A physical measurement of a signal of duration T seconds made with an instrument of bandwidth W provides a "snapshot" of the physical process responsible for generating the signal. This snapshot consists of $N = 2TW$ scalars representing the signal in N-dimensional space. If the measured signal is from a stochastic process, then the values of the N coordinates are random variables, and the measurement statistics should reflect the statistical properties of the generating physical process.

A signal can be represented by an N-dimensional system, i.e., a system with N independent coordinates. The process of measuring can be viewed as bringing this measuring system in temporary contact with a stochastic process (e.g., thermal noise). For most processes of interest, the exact value for the total waveform energy thus measured is random, but its average value is a known constant. When the number of degrees of freedom N is sufficiently large that the central limit theorem applies, this approach leads to the canonical ensemble. Not surprisingly, a similar result arises in signal theory when measurements made on systems that correspond to the canonical ensemble.

Consider a very large statistical ensemble of random signals. A representative member of this ensemble corresponds to N independent measurements $\{x_i\}$ from a limited-duration band-limited zero-mean Gaussian stochastic process. We can associate with each of the N signal coordinates an energy corresponding to the expectation of the square of the value of the signal at that coordinate. The energy at each coordinate is a random variable. In a signal space with Euclidian metric, the square root of the energy is simply the norm of the signal.

We now introduce the function $\Omega(\epsilon)$, which is the number of distinguishable signals having energy ϵ. More precisely, we say that the number of distinguishable signals $\delta\Omega(\epsilon)$ in the energy range between ϵ and $\epsilon + \delta\epsilon$ is given by

$$\delta\Omega(\epsilon) = \rho(\epsilon)\,\delta\epsilon \tag{3.47}$$

Equivalently, we have the density of signal states

$$\rho(\epsilon) = \frac{d\Omega(\epsilon)}{d\epsilon} \tag{3.48}$$

Since signals having the same energy belong to the same state, we also refer to $\rho(\epsilon)$ as the density of states.

Although there is an infinite number of signals having a specified energy, not all of these signals are necessarily physically distinguishable. Signals can be characterized by the values of their coordinates in signal space. A signal measurement is equivalent to measuring these coordinates. However, all physical measuring devices are subject to limitations in accuracy. Signals that are sufficiently close (in the Euclidian metric sense) to one another cannot be resolved as separate (and, hence, are not distinguishable) if the metric distance between them is less than what the instrument can distinguish. The result is that an infinite number of signals are partitioned into a finite number of equivalence classes by the limitations of the measuring apparatus. This subject is fundamental to communication and is covered in greater detail elsewhere in this book. For the moment, it suffices to accept on these very general grounds that $\rho(\epsilon)$ and $\Omega(\epsilon)$ are bounded functions.

The density of signals $\rho(\epsilon)$ corresponding to energy ϵ is equal to the number of signals per energy increment located at a distance $\epsilon^{1/2}$ from the origin in a space with N dimensions. The density $\rho(\epsilon)$ is the density of distinguishable signals having an energy between ϵ and $\epsilon + \delta\epsilon$.

The picture that forms is one of concentric spherical hypershells in N-dimensional signal space, the surface of each shell being the locus of coordinate points corresponding to signals having a norm $\epsilon^{1/2}$, as shown in Fig. 3-12. Mathematically, ϵ is just a constant. However, we have already observed that it is equal to the signal energy. The number of signal states corresponding to a particular energy is a rapidly increasing function of ϵ. To be distinguishable, signals must be spaced apart by some minimum distance that is independent of ϵ, but is a function of the resolving power of the measuring device. Since the surface area of a hyper-

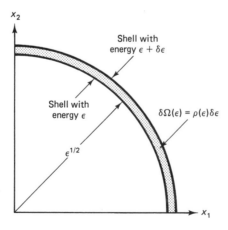

Figure 3-12. Two-dimensional drawing of a signal space with coordinates x_1, and x_2. The density of states $\rho(\epsilon)$ is a function of the "radial" coordinate $\epsilon^{1/2}$. The number of signal states $\delta\Omega(\epsilon)$ contained within the spherical shells of radii $\epsilon^{1/2}$ and $(\epsilon + \delta\epsilon)^{1/2}$ is given by Eq. (3.52). For clarity, only the signal states having energy between ϵ and $\epsilon + \delta\epsilon$ are shown as dots within the shells.

sphere increases rapidly with the radius, the total number of states $\Omega(\epsilon)$ that can be accommodated increases very rapidly with ϵ. The same is true for the density of states $\rho(\epsilon)$.

The density of signals by itself is not sufficient to describe the signal statistics. We also need the probability that the signal has a total energy ϵ. The measurement corresponding to the kth coordinate is x_k, and the corresponding energy is x_k^2. If the x_k are zero-mean independent Gaussian variables, the joint probability density function for the N measurements is of the form $e^{-\beta\epsilon}$, where ϵ is the sum of all the statistically independent x_k^2, and β is a constant. This is a weak restriction. Band-limited signals occurring in communication and radar systems are the result of filtering wide-band stochastic processes. These filtered signals are well approximated by Gaussian statistics by virtue of the central limit theorem. This very general result is of fundamental importance in statistical mechanics as well as in information theory.

The exponential factor $e^{-\beta\epsilon}$ is known as the Boltzmann factor to physicists; to engineers, it is the familiar exponential distribution of energy that results when the envelope of a Gaussian process is squared. The corresponding probability distribution function is the canonical distribution.

The canonical distribution arises whenever a measuring apparatus or system is made to interact with a system with a large number of degrees of freedom with a constant average energy, such as measurements of thermal noise. The mean system energy is known, but the actual total system energy is a random variable that fluctuates about the mean, owing to the random energies x_k^2 in each of the degrees of freedom. This is precisely what happens when a signal-measuring instrument with N degrees of freedom interacts with a stochastic process with a constant power spectral density or sample variance.

We now introduce the partition function $Z(\beta)$, which is defined by the integral

$$Z(\beta) = \int_0^\infty e^{-\beta\epsilon}d\Omega(\epsilon) = \int_0^\infty \rho(\epsilon)e^{-\beta\epsilon}d\epsilon \qquad (3.49)$$

where β is an as-of-yet unspecified constant. The partition function is, to within an additive constant, a measure of the total number of available states actually occupied by a signal. The integrand of the partition function is proportional to the probability that the signal energy is between ϵ and $\epsilon + \delta\epsilon$. The density of states increases rapidly with ϵ; the exponential term decreases rapidly with that variable.

The partition function has several interesting properties. The mean energy is given by

$$\mathscr{E} = -\frac{1}{Z}\frac{\partial Z}{\partial \beta} = -\frac{\partial \ln Z}{\partial \beta} \qquad (3.50)$$

The fluctuations in the total energy are given by

$$\sigma_{\mathscr{E}}^2 = \frac{\partial^2 \ln Z}{\partial \beta^2} \qquad (3.51)$$

We can also derive the statistical entropy of the ensemble from the partition function. To this end, we note that the integrand of the partition function is composed of a term that increases rapidly with energy (the density of states) and a term that decreases rapidly with energy (the Boltzmann factor). This means that the integrand itself is highly peaked in the vicinity of the average energy $\mathscr{E}$. The overwhelming majority of states have nearly the same energy, equal to the mean energy. This approximation is strictly valid only for systems with a very large number of degrees of freedom. An alternative way of looking at this is that a very large portion of the volume of an N-dimensional sphere is located within a very small distance of its surface. Most of the states are located near the surface and share the energy corresponding to the square of the metric distance of the surface to the origin. The higher the number of dimensions, the better this approximation.

The partition function can be approximated by

$$Z = [\rho(\mathscr{E})\,\delta\epsilon]e^{-\beta\mathscr{E}} = \delta\Omega(\mathscr{E})e^{-\beta\mathscr{E}}$$

where $\delta\epsilon$ is the narrow energy range near $\epsilon = \mathscr{E}$, where the integrand is maximized. The entropy of this system is, therefore, given by

$$H = \log\delta\Omega(\mathscr{E}) = \log Z(\beta) + \beta\mathscr{E}$$

The partition function, as previously noted, is a measure of the number of available states. All of the important statistical quantities can be expressed in terms of the partition function.

Consider making a finite-duration measurement on band-limited Gaussian noise. Specifically, consider measurements made on a stochastic process modeled by zero-mean Gaussian noise of thermal origin with constant two-sided power spectral density $N_0 = \frac{1}{2}k_B\theta$. There are $N = 2TW$ real samples, which constitute an approximate description of the signal in a space of N dimensions. The samples are taken from a zero-mean Gaussian process with standard deviation σ. The total noise power in bandwidth W is then

$$P = 2N_0W = k_B\theta W \tag{3.52}$$

giving, for the total energy,

$$\mathscr{E} = k_B\theta W T = \tfrac{1}{2}N\,k_B\theta \tag{3.53}$$

The average energy per coordinate (degree of freedom) is, therefore, given by $\frac{1}{2}k_B\theta$. This is the equipartition theorem for energy, which states that, on the average, each degree of freedom receives an equal share of the total energy. An alternative interpretation is that the (white) noise-energy distribution in N-dimensional space is spherically symmetric, or isotropic, about all of the coordinates. No one coordinate is favored with more or less energy.

The noise measurements can be represented by the sequence $\{x_k\}$, with the index k running from 1 to N. The members of that sequence are distributed with zero mean and standard deviation σ. The total energy in the signal is given by

$$\mathscr{E} = \sum_k x_k^2$$

where the summation index runs over all of the space dimensions. Therefore, $\mathscr{E}$ follows a central chi-square distribution with N degrees of freedom. The probability density function for $\mathscr{E}$ is

$$P(\mathscr{E}) = \frac{1}{\sigma^N 2^{N/2}\Gamma(N/2)}\mathscr{E}^{N/2-1}e^{-\mathscr{E}/2\sigma^2} \tag{3.54}$$

where Γ denotes the gamma function. $P(\mathscr{E})$ has a mean $N\sigma^2$ and a variance $2N\sigma^4$.

The density of states can easily be calculated by counting the number of hyperspheres of radius equal to the square root of the noise sample energy ($\frac{1}{2}k_B\theta)^{1/2}$ that will fit in the N-dimensional volume enclosed between hyperspheres corresponding to energies between ϵ and $\epsilon + \delta\epsilon$, and then dividing by $\delta\epsilon$, and passing to the limit $\delta\epsilon \to 0$. This gives

$$\rho(\epsilon) = \frac{1}{2}(\frac{1}{2}k_B\theta)^{-N/2}N\epsilon^{N/2-1} \tag{3.55}$$

The probability of the signal having energy ϵ is proportional to $e^{-\beta\epsilon}$. The number of signal states with energy ϵ is, therefore, proportional to $\rho(\epsilon)e^{-\beta\epsilon}$. For large N, $\rho(\epsilon)$ increases rapidly and $e^{-\beta\epsilon}$ decreases rapidly. The function $\rho(\epsilon)e^{-\beta\epsilon}$ is, therefore, a highly peaked function, as shown in Fig. 3-13. The mean signal energy is, therefore, tightly distributed about a quantity that can be estimated as the value of $\epsilon = \mathscr{E}$ that maximizes $\rho(\epsilon)e^{-\beta\epsilon}$. For very large N, the mean energy turns out to be $N/2\beta$. Comparing this with the known mean energy $\frac{1}{2}Nk_B\theta$ identifies the constant $\beta = (k_B\theta)^{-1}$ as being the reciprocal of the noise power spectral density. Alternatively, the same result for $\mathscr{E}$ can be found directly from the partition function

$$\mathscr{E} = \frac{1}{2}Nk_B\theta \tag{3.56}$$

The variance of $\mathscr{E}$, $\sigma_{\mathscr{E}}^2$, can also be found, as stated earlier, by differentiating the logarithm of Z twice with respect to β, giving

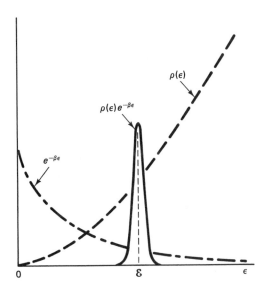

Figure 3-13. The function $\rho(\epsilon)e^{-\beta\epsilon}$ is sharply peaked at $\epsilon = \mathscr{E} = \frac{1}{2}Nk_B\theta$.

$$\sigma_{\mathscr{E}}^2 = 2N(\tfrac{1}{2}k_B\theta)^2 \tag{3.57}$$

By identifying the measurement sample variance σ^2 with $\frac{1}{2}k_B\theta$, these results are identical to the moments of the central chi-square distribution of energy presented earlier.

A very common form of noise model used in the study of communication and detection systems is white Gaussian noise. By probing a little into the nature of noise, the reason for the uniquity of white Gaussian noise now becomes apparent. First, the randomness itself is caused by the interaction between an overwhelmingly large number of particles such as charge carriers. These cannot be individually measured, but their aggregate effect is impressed on any measuring instrument that comes in contact with them. Second, the Gaussian statistics are a direct consequence of the central limit theorem. Noise is typically the cumulative effect of a very large number of random causes, all adding to produce a quantity that, to a very good approximation, is normally distributed. Last, thermal noise is usually spectrally flat, at least over most of the frequency range of interest in electrical engineering. That is a consequence of equipartition of energy for systems having a very large number of degrees of freedom and for which the total energy is a quadratic function of the system coordinates.

The important point to remember about this discussion is not so much that many instances of noise is white and Gaussian, but, however, to be able to determine where these approximations break down. Rather than complacently falling in the comfortable routine of assuming white Gaussian noise for every application, the careful engineer, especially when confronted with a new application, should question the validity of these assumptions. The material in this chapter provides the quantitative tools to do this. These tools are based on an understanding of the physical and mathematical causes of events.

We summarize the main results with a few rules of thumb. In general, summing a few tens of random quantities produces a variable that is, for all practical purposes, normally distributed. Some applications are sensitive to this approximation, however, and a verification should always be made. The alert engineer, aware of the physical nature of noise production, should realize that certain processes do not give rise to Gaussian noise.

EXAMPLE

There are communication systems in which information is transmitted in discrete units. For example, the number of telephone calls handled by a telephone switching exchange during any given time period, say, a minute, is Poisson-distributed. The same can be said for the arrival of digital radio "packets" in any fixed time interval. The probability of receiving k telephone messages on your telephone answering machine in a period of τ hours is given by

$$\text{Prob \{exactly } k \text{ messages in } \tau \text{ hours\}} = \frac{1}{k!}(\lambda\tau)^k e^{-\lambda\tau}$$

where λ is the average message arrival rate, measured in messages per hour. Another example of Poisson processes occurring in communication systems is the statistics for photon arrival at a photodetector.

Thermal noise can be considered white as long as thermal energy is much larger than quantum energy-level spacing, i.e., below a frequency of order $k_B T/h$. For this case, the quantum nature of matter is unimportant and charge carriers behave as a cloud or "gas" of interacting classical particles.

PROBLEMS

3.1 A message consists of n independently transmitted symbols. Each symbol is received in error with probability α. Using Chebyshev's inequality, find the least value of n for which the probability of exceeding m symbol errors per message is at most β.

3.2 Use the Chernoff bound in Problem 3.1 instead of Chebyshev's inequality and obtain an algebraic expression that can be solved for n.

3.3 Consider a binary communication system, i.e., one that uses two symbols, x_0, and x_1, to represent information. These symbols can be grouped as segments; each segment contains m binary symbols. Let the probabilities for the occurrence of x_0 and x_1 be P_0 and P_1, respectively.
  (a) Calculate the total number Ω of m-ary segments containing all possible combinations of x_0 and x_1.
  (b) Transmitting messages one symbol at a time requires two waveforms: one for x_0 and another for x_1. If the unit of transmission is the m-ary segment rather than the binary symbol, then we need Ω different waveforms if $P_0 = P_1$. Now consider the case where $P_1 \neq \frac{1}{2}$, that is, one of the binary symbols occurs more frequently than the other. What is the probability that an m-ary segment will contain exactly n occurrences of the symbol x_0?
  (c) In general, what is the probability of exactly n occurrences of x_0, for $n \neq mP_0$? Assume that n is an integer.
  (d) What can you infer about the ratio n/m as $m \to \infty$?

3.4 Consider messages consisting of m binary digits. The effect of noise is to cause each binary digit to be received in error independently and with probability α.
  (a) What is the total number of distinct error patterns?
  (b) What is the probability of a message containing exactly n binary digits received in error?
  (c) What can be said about the ratio n/m calculated in part (b) as $m \to \infty$?

3.5 The sum of any number of independent normally distributed random variables is a normally distributed variable. The converse of this theorem is also true, namely, that if the sum $x = x_1 + x_2 + \cdots, x_n$ of n independent random variables is normally distributed, then each of the variables x_k, $k = 1, 2, \ldots, n$, itself is normally distributed. Why does this not contradict the central limit theorem?

3.6 An industrial processing plant uses several temperature sensors to determine the average temperature in a process. All of the sensor outputs x_i are added and fed to a computer. In the industrial environment, all sensor outputs have uniform probability density functions with possible values ranging from T_1 to T_2.

(a) If a total of four sensors are used, how would you determine the probability density function $p(y)$ of the adder's output?

(b) If 500 sensors were used, how would you determine $p(y)$? Give an approximate expression for $p(y)$.

3.7 Consider statistically independent uncorrelated samples $\{x(k)\}$ from a real zero-mean wide-sense stationary stochastic process with probability density function

$$p(x) = \frac{e^{x/\alpha}}{\alpha(1 + e^{x/\alpha})^2} \qquad -\infty \le x \le \infty$$

This distribution is called the "logistic" probability density function, and the variance of x is given by

$$\langle x^2 \rangle = \sigma^2 = \pi^2 \alpha^2/3$$

where α is a constant. These signal samples are processed with a finite impulse-response digital filter whose output is defined by

$$y(k) = \sum_{i=1}^{N} b(i)x(k - i)$$

where the N filter coefficients $b(i)$ are given real constants.

(a) Find the mean and variance of y for arbitrary N.

(b) For very large N (say, $N > 200$), find a good approximation for the probability density function of y.

(c) For small values of N (say, $N < 6$), describe how you would calculate the exact probability density function of y.

(d) Discuss the validity of your answer in part (c) as N increases.

3.8 Sketch the Planck energy distribution $\mathscr{E}(\nu)$ in the low-temperature regime. This is the energy spectrum that would be measured at these temperatures. Determine the 3-dB bandwidth and the implied temporal correlation scale. Discuss the origin and significance of these correlations and the implication vis-à-vis statistical independence.

INFORMATION THEORY AND CODING

*Thus, we may have knowledge of
the past but cannot control it; we
may control the future but not
have knowledge of it.[†]*

Claude E. Shannon

4

A goal of coding theory is the parsimonious representation of information. Parsimonious source coding refers to the ability to reversibly represent a given information source by as few distinguishable system states as possible. The practical consequences are that information storage or transmission channel resources (the capacity) can be used more efficiently. A typical communication task involves an information source whose output must be given some intermediate representation for storage or transmission. An important problem is the conversion of one representation into another in a reversible manner and the reliable communication of this information over a noisy channel. The details of the physical systems used to represent information are irrelevant. What matters is their capacity for representing information. One can, therefore, speak about these systems in the abstract, without having to describe their intimate workings. The single mathematical quantity necessary for describing physical systems is their information capacity.

Information theory is concerned with two important applications: the storage and transmission of information. A physical system's capacity is a measure of the total number of distinguishable states it can assume. Channel capacity is related to the complexity of the signals it can support. This chapter introduces the notion and measure of information, and discusses important theorems of information theory that specify limits on coding and transmission of information.

[†]Reprinted by permission from reference [Sh 59]. © 1959 IRE (now IEEE).

4.1 MEASURING INFORMATION

Two of the central tasks of information theory are the systematic representation of information with a suitable set of symbols and the reversible conversion from one specific representation to another. This section introduces the notion of information and quantitative measures for the information capacity of a system or channel, and also for the information content of a message.

4.1.1 Hartley's Measure of Information Capacity

In order to formulate a quantitative measure of information, we need to define what is meant by information. Information is a measure of the number of equiprobable choices between several possible alternatives. More precisely, information is measured by the logarithm of the number of such alternatives. We must at the outset distinguish between the amount of information and the value of information. For example, your stockbroker's recommendation to either buy or sell a stock resolves a decision on your part between two different actions, namely, to buy or to sell. If these outcomes are equally probable, this corresponds to one bit of information. The unit of information, the bit, is a contraction of binary digit, and measures the information implied by two equally likely alternatives. Although, in this case, the amount of information is one bit, its value may mean several thousands of dollars to your portfolio. Now consider a weatherman's abbreviated report of rain or shine, to which you listen so as to decide whether to carry an umbrella or not. This also carries one bit of information if the probabilities of rain and sunshine are equal, but its value may be quite different than the stockbroker's message. Information theory concerns itself exclusively with the amount of information and not its value.

It is possible to recognize the value of information in communication systems. For example, in the electronic transfer of funds between financial institutions, the consequence of a transmission error in one of the digits is very different, depending on just what the digit is. The consequence of mistaking a cents digit is radically different than if the digit had specified the number of millions of dollars. In many cases, a cost can be assigned to the various outcomes of information transmission and communication reliability can be apportioned accordingly. This, however, is more closely related to the theory of mathematical expectation than it is to information theory.

Communication engineering concerns itself with the reliability with which information is transmitted from one point to another via a specified channel. Questions concerning the value of the information are left to the user, whose responsibility it is to specify to the communication engineer the reliability of a communication system, for example, in terms of maximum acceptable transmission-error probabilities.

Information implies the ability to resolve uncertainty, or a choice between several possible alternatives. The simplest uncertainty is that which is completely resolved by an answer to a YES or NO question. This corresponds to one bit of information when the prior anticipation of either answer is equally likely.

A system's capacity for storing information is fully described by a count of its distinguishable states. Each *state* of a physical system is a different configuration of the system. Thus, an ON/OFF switch has two states and can be used to label any two different conditions. A digital watch showing hours, minutes, and seconds has $12 \times 60 \times 60 = 43,200$ states that are used to label each of the seconds in a half day. The addition of an AM/PM indicator doubles the total number of states, which now provide unique labels for all the seconds in a day. The more states a system has, the more information it can store. For a system consisting of switches, the number of states is equal to the total number of switch-position combinations. If n binary (i.e., ON/OFF) switches are used, there are 2^n combinations or states. Each one of these combinations corresponds to a certain amount of information. The number of bits of information capacity in such a system can be arrived at by counting the number of independent equally probable YES/NO questions required to fully specify any of the system states. It is easy to see that one has only to inquire about the position of each binary switch to do so. Since there are n such (binary) switches, n such questions are required, and the information capacity is n bits.

What are the desirable properties of an information capacity measure? Three such properties come to mind:

1. a measure of information capacity should increase monotonically with the number of system states;
2. information should be additive: the aggregate information capacity of two separate systems should be the sum of each system's capacity;
3. the amount of information associated with a system having only one state should be zero.

It is not difficult to see that the logarithm of the total number of system states satisfies all three conditions. If Ω is the total number of distinguishable states in a system, then the system's information capacity is given by

$$C = \log \Omega \qquad (4.1)$$

Unless otherwise specified, we shall take the base to be 2 and express information in bits. For switches having M positions, there are 2^M possible positions. One might (correctly) expect that larger numbers of switch positions correspond to a larger capacity for information storage. Systems having the same number of states are informationally equivalent, since a correspondence can be established between each state of the one with a state of the other. It, therefore, does not matter how these systems are implemented, as long as a one-to-one and onto mapping can be established between pairs of corresponding states.

An important corollary is that any information may be represented by a sequence or strings of symbols.

EXAMPLE

The sequence of YES/NO answers to a set of questions aimed at determining the settings of a set of switches completely characterizes that switch system. The number of such questions ultimately determines the number of bits required to describe the system. The symbols in this case are simply the binary digits into which the YES/NO answers are coded.

EXAMPLE

The use of writing to represent information is an excellent example of a sequence or string of symbols, namely letters, numbers, and other typographical symbols, to represent information. This is merely a generalization of the binary-coded YES/NO answers described in the previous example.

The information capacity of a 450-page book, assuming 500 words per page, each word containing five symbols chosen at random from a 37-ary alphabet (26 letters, 10 digits, and a blank space) is

$$C = 450 \times 500 \times 5 \times \log_2 37 = 5.9 \times 10^6 \text{ bits}$$

This is the capacity needed to store the information contained in a representative book of that size. This sort of calculation could be used, for example, in sizing up the data-storage requirement for a word processing system to be used in the production of such a book. More refined estimates can be obtained by taking into account typographical symbols, graphics, etc. The previous numbers are, of course, a "back of the envelope" calculation. Statistical correlations exist between letters, and the letters themselves do not all occur with equal probabilities. The calculation shown here represents an upper bound for the information capacity. This subject will be taken up in more detail in this chapter.

EXAMPLE

Deoxyribonucleic acid (DNA) is a beautiful example of a biomolecular string used to carry the information necessary for the replication of life. The informationally functional part of DNA consists of a very long string of four nucleotides: adenine (A), thymine (T), guanine (G), and cytosine (C). These molecules form the four symbols in a 4-ary alphabet. Each nucleotide represents $\log_2 4 = 2$ bits of information storage capacity. The order in which these symbols are arranged along the linear DNA molecule determines the information content of a gene. The variety of life we see around us is determined to a large extent by the information contained in DNA, a biomolecular message that is passed from one generation to the next.

4.1.2 Shannon's Measure of Information Content

The previous section establishes a correspondence between a system's number of distinguishable states and its ability to store information. A system's capacity for information storage depends on its number of states and not on the physical details of its composition. The study of information capacity is thus reduced to a purely mathematical problem. In particular, we can find no fundamental difference between a system and its mathematical representation in terms of symbols provided there is a sufficient number of symbols to uniquely label all system states. The information capacity of a system reduces to the logarithm of the number of different system states.

Having discussed a system's capacity to store information and having described that capacity purely in terms of a single property of the system, namely, its number of states, we now turn to the problem of measuring the information content of a message. Equivalently, we can address the task of measuring the average information content of typical messages issuing from some information source. An information source is some device or system that produces a sequence of symbols chosen from a finite alphabet according to some set of statistical rules. This is essentially the problem of determining the information rate of the source, and the two problems, although sometimes mentioned separately, are identical.

Our goal is to arrive at a method for measuring the information content of a message consisting of a string of symbols. Equivalently, we wish to measure the average information per symbol associated with an information source producing these symbols.

The logarithmic measure of information capacity is the fundamental starting point in our study of information theory. Implicit in the use of $\log \Omega$ for Ω equiprobable states as a measure of information capacity is a complete freedom in specifying which of the Ω states the system is in. Any restriction in this freedom must necessarily decrease the total number of system specifications (i.e., decrease Ω) and, consequently, decrease the system capacity. For example, an obvious way to decrease capacity is to make some of the states inaccessible or even infrequently accessible.

The information content of a message is a function of the number of message states and of the probability of the states actually being occupied. The message states and their probabilities are governed by the information source, which may be viewed as an ergodic stochastic process. The number of different messages of fixed length issuing from such a source is a measure of the information content of such messages. This number can be calculated from the statistical properties of the information source and, in general, is smaller than the number corresponding to complete freedom in selecting among the possible symbols composing the message.

The transition from discussing the information capacity of a system to that of the information content of a message is not an abrupt one, and merely involves a new use for the concept of information capacity. The simplest example of an information source is a discrete memoryless source (DMS) that produces statistically independent symbols from a finite alphabet $\{x_1, x_2, \ldots, x_M\}$ with corresponding symbol probabilities $\{P(x_1), P(x_2), \ldots, P(x_M)\}$. It is tempting to liken a message of n such symbols to a system with M^n states and conclude that the information content of the message is $n \log M$. This would be true only for the very special case of equiprobable symbols. As an extreme counterexample, consider an information source that is constantly outputting the same symbol with unit probability. Such a source is a discrete memoryless source with, for example, $P(x_1) = 1$ and $P(x_2) = \ldots = P(x_M) = 0$. This corresponds to a system with a single state. In other words, the smallest system required to contain this information is a system with only one state. Such messages are completely predictable and, therefore, contain no information. Clearly then, the statistical properties of the symbols must be featured in a measure of information content.

Consider, for the sake of definiteness, a message of n statistically independent symbols from a discrete memoryless source. The size of the message (n) and the statistical rules [statistical independence, symbol probabilities $P(\mathbf{x}_1), P(\mathbf{x}_2), \ldots, P(\mathbf{x}_M)$] define the composition of such messages. The ensemble of possible messages consistent with these rules can be associated with distinct realizations of a system whose states are labeled by the messages themselves. In other words, we are considering a system whose physical composition is immaterial, but with as many states as there are messages in the ensemble. Through this artifice, we are able to use a single logarithmic measure for the information capacity of a system and the information content of a message.

This is where the mathematical aspect of information theory departs from the technological applications of communication engineering. Technologists are engaged in the development of systems that can pack as much information in as little volume, bandwidth, or time as possible. To an information theorist, all of these systems share a similarity that stops at the count of distinguishable system states.

The capacity of such a system is the logarithm of the total possible number of messages, and corresponds to the information content of such messages. The task of measuring the information content of a message composed according to specified probabilistic rules reduces to the problem of counting the total number of such messages.

We now present a way of counting these messages. This will serve to introduce Shannon's entropy measure of information content of messages. If n is very large, then a typical message will contain, with high probability, $n_k = nP(\mathbf{x}_k), k = 1, 2, \ldots, M$ occurrences of the symbol $\mathbf{x}_k$, where $\sum_k n_k = n$. In fact, this can be taken to be a definition of $P(\mathbf{x}_k) = n_k/n$ as $n \to \infty$. What we are about to do is to count the number of very long (large n) messages and then "discover" that the result can be expressed in terms of the fractions n_k/n. Letting $n \to \infty$ (and, therefore, $n_k \to \infty \ \forall \ k$) will allow us to express the final result in terms of the probabilities $p_k = P(\mathbf{x}_k)$.

The number Ω of messages consisting of n_1 occurrences of the symbol x_1, n_2 occurrences of the symbol $\mathbf{x}_2$, etc. is given by the combinatorial multinomial coefficient

$$\Omega = \begin{pmatrix} n \\ n_1, n_2, \ldots, n_M \end{pmatrix} = \frac{n!}{n_1! n_2! \ldots n_M!} \tag{4.2}$$

where $\sum_k n_k = n$. If we now let n be very large, so that each of the n_k is also very large, then we can use Stirling's approximation for the factorials:

$$n! \approx (2\pi)^{1/2} n^{n+1/2} e^{-n} \tag{4.3}$$

for n and also for each of the n_k appearing in the multinomial coefficient. The expression for Ω then becomes

$$\Omega = \frac{(2\pi)^{1/2} e^{-n} n^{n+1/2}}{(2\pi)^{M/2} \prod_{k=1}^{M} e^{-n_k} \prod_{k=1}^{M} n_k^{n_k+1/2}} \tag{4.4}$$

The product of exponential terms in the denominator is simply e^{-n} and cancels the like term appearing in the numerator. For $n_k \gg 1$, the exponents $n_k + 1/2$ and, therefore, also $n + 1/2$ can be approximated by n_k and n, respectively. Furthermore, writing $n^n = n^{n_1 + n_2 + \cdots + n_M}$ in the numerator in Eq. (4.4), we have

$$\Omega \approx (2\pi)^{-(M-1)/2} \prod_{k=1}^{M} (n/n_k)^{n_k}$$

with the approximation getting progressively better as the n_k become larger. The term n/n_k is simply the reciprocal of the probability $p_k = P(\mathbf{x}_k)$. Strictly speaking, we are implicitly invoking the law of large numbers. As both n_k and n become very large, the ratio n_k/n converges to a number we call the probability p_k. The n_k in the exponent can then be written as $n_k = nP(\mathbf{x}_k)$, giving

$$\log \Omega = \tfrac{1}{2}(M-1) \log(2\pi) + \sum_{k=1}^{M} \log p_k^{-np_k}$$

$$= \tfrac{1}{2}(M-1) \log(2\pi) - n \sum_{k=1}^{M} p_k \log p_k$$

For sufficiently large n, the second term dominates, so that we have

$$\log \Omega = -n \sum_{k=1}^{M} p_k \log p_k \tag{4.5}$$

This expression, $-\sum_k p_k \log p_k$, is called the *entropy* associated with the symbol probability distribution $\{p_1, p_2, \ldots, p_M\}$. The entropy is a measure of the average information content associated with one symbol. Our expression for $\log \Omega$, the information content of a message consisting of n statistically independent symbols, is simply n times the entropy per symbol. This is an intuitively pleasing result.

Note that the entropy per symbol is in the form of a statistical average of the quantity $-\log p_k$. Interpreting the entropy as average information (averaged over the symbol probabilities), we are naturally led to interpret the quantity $-\log p_k$ as the amount of information associated with the uncertainty of an event whose probability is p_k. This is the interpretation taken in information theory. The preceding discussion shows how this measure can be associated with the counting of possible messages.

EXAMPLE

In written English, the individual letters (including the blank space) occur with the probability distribution shown in Table 4-1. The source alphabet for this example consists of 27 symbols: the 26 letters plus a blank space. We ignore numerals for the time being. If we assume that the letters in written English are statistically independent (which they are not), then the source entropy for this model is

$$H = -\sum_{k=1}^{27} P(\mathbf{x}_k) \log P(\mathbf{x}_k) = 4.08 \text{ bits/symbol} \tag{4.6}$$

TABLE 4-1. PROBABILITY DISTRIBUTION FOR THE LETTERS OCCURRING IN WRITTEN ENGLISH

k	$\mathbf{x}_k$	$P(\mathbf{x}_k)$	k	$\mathbf{x}_k$	$P(\mathbf{x}_k)$
1	space	0.186	15	F	0.021
2	E	0.103	16	M	0.020
3	T	0.080	17	W	0.018
4	A	0.064	18	Y	0.016
5	O	0.063	19	P	0.015
6	N	0.057	20	G	0.015
7	I	0.057	21	B	0.013
8	S	0.051	22	V	0.008
9	R	0.048	23	K	0.005
10	H	0.047	24	X	0.001
11	D	0.032	25	J	0.001
12	L	0.032	26	Q	0.001
13	U	0.023	27	Z	0.001
14	C	0.022			

Adapted by permission from [RE 61].

The actual entropy, of course, is somewhat smaller than this because the symbols are not independent, but are statistically correlated. Nonetheless, the assumption of statistical independence leads to a useful upper bound for the actual entropy.

The statistical rules that describe the functioning of an information source act as constraints that limit the composition of messages to those symbol sequences that are consistent with the statistical properties of the source. The least constraining rule allows all symbols to be statistically independent and to occur with equal probability. The information content of a message of n equiprobable symbols chosen from an M-ary alphabet is simply $n \log M$, which is the capacity of a system with M^n states. The other extreme case is the one for which only one of the messages (it does not matter which) is produced by the source. Intuition suggests that equiprobable messages contain the largest amount of information, whereas the single message source produces no information at all. We shall show that intuition is correct in both cases.

Consider a discrete memoryless source with symbols $\{\mathbf{x}_1, \mathbf{x}_2, \ldots, \mathbf{x}_M\}$ and corresponding symbol probabilities $\{P(\mathbf{x}_1), P(\mathbf{x}_2), \ldots, P(\mathbf{x}_M)\}$. These probabilities represent an a priori uncertainty of finding the corresponding symbols at the output of the DMS. The information rate of the DMS (or of any source for that matter) must be related in some way to this uncertainty. The larger the uncertainty resolved by the realization of these symbols, the larger the information content of the message.

We can approach a quantitative measure of information content by requiring that the measure be larger for the less frequent symbols, i.e., those corresponding to small $P(\mathbf{x}_j)$, and smaller for the more frequent ones. The justification for this choice is that symbols occurring more frequently are more predictable. In fact, a symbol for which $P(\mathbf{x}_M) = 1$ is entirely predictable and hence has no uncertainty, and carries no information. Guided by our discussion of the number of possible messages composed of independent symbols having specified probabilities, a possible choice for an information content measure is the logarithmic function. Other choices may come to mind, but it will turn out that these will be eliminated as we impose more requirements on such a measure.

By convention, information is a positive quantity, so that we use the negative of the logarithm of a probability to measure it. For statistically independent symbols, the information associated with the symbol $\mathbf{x}_i$ is, therefore,

$$I(\mathbf{x}_i) = -\log P(\mathbf{x}_i) \tag{4.7}$$

The average information per symbol is obtained by statistically averaging $I(\mathbf{x}_i)$ over all symbols. This results in the following expectation value for the average of $I(\mathbf{x}_i)$:

$$H(\mathbf{x}) = -\sum_{i=1}^{M} P(\mathbf{x}_i) \log P(\mathbf{x}_i) \tag{4.8}$$

which is the entropy associated with the probabilities $\{P(\mathbf{x}_i); i = 1, \ldots, M\}$. The logarithmic base determines the units in which information is measured. In the previous expression for entropy, we shall take $P(\mathbf{x}_i) \log P(\mathbf{x}_i) = 0$ if $P(\mathbf{x}_i) = 0$.

The entropy function, as defined in Eq. (4.8), has a number of reasonable properties we intuitively associate with information. For example, if one of the $P(\mathbf{x}_i) = 1$ [and consequently $P(\mathbf{x}_j) = 0 \; \forall j \neq i$, since we require $\sum_k P(\mathbf{x}_k) = 1$], then $H(\mathbf{x}) = 0$. This corresponds to the case of total certainty and is, therefore, devoid of information.

Let us now explore another property of entropy by determining the particular values of $P(\mathbf{x}_k)$, for $k = 1, 2, \ldots, M$, that results in the largest possible value for $H(\mathbf{x})$ for statistically independent symbols. This is a constrained maximization problem, with the constraint being the usual normalization $\sum_k P(\mathbf{x}_k) = 1$ for probabilities. This extremization problem is easily solved by using a Lagrange multiplier, by determining the $P(\mathbf{x}_j)$ that maximizes the expression

$$J = -\sum_{k=1}^{M} p_k \log p_k - \lambda \left(\sum_{k=1}^{M} p_k - 1\right)$$

where we have used $p_k = P(\mathbf{x}_k)$, and λ is a Lagrange constant multiplier. Differentiating J with respect to p_j and setting the result to zero, we obtain M relations of the following form, one for each value of j:

$$\partial J / \partial p_j = -\log p_j - 1/\ln 2 - \lambda = 0$$

from which p_j must be a constant. From the normalization condition, the constant must be M^{-1}. Hence, the probability distribution that results in the largest entropy is the uniform distribution, in which all outcomes are equally probable, in agreement with intuition.

$$p_j = 1/M \tag{4.9}$$

Now consider two independent sets A and B of outcomes with symbols $A:\{\mathbf{x}_1, \mathbf{x}_2, \ldots, \mathbf{x}_r\}, B:\{\mathbf{y}_1, \mathbf{y}_2, \ldots, \mathbf{y}_s\}$ and associated probabilities $A:\{p_1, p_2, \ldots, p_r\}$ and $B:\{q_1, q_2, \ldots, q_s\}$, respectively, with $\sum_k p_k = 1$ and $\sum_k q_k = 1$.

From previous considerations, we have

$$H(\mathbf{x}) = -\sum_k p_k \log p_k \qquad \text{and} \qquad H(\mathbf{y}) = -\sum_k q_k \log q_k$$

Now consider these two systems to be part of a single larger system that corresponds to an information source producing pairs of symbols $\mathbf{x}_i \mathbf{x}_j$. If A and B are independent, then a typical pair of symbols appears with probability $p_i q_j$, and can be considered to be a symbol from the extended product alphabet $AB : \{\mathbf{z}_k : \mathbf{x}_i \mathbf{y}_j ; i = 1, 2, \ldots, r ; j = 1, 2, \ldots, s\}$. Note that the subdivision of the extended product alphabet AB into the separate alphabets A and B is purely conceptual and should, therefore, have no effect whatsoever on the information content of either alphabet. The entropy associated with the extended alphabet is (remembering that A and B are statistically independent)

$$H(\mathbf{z}) = -\sum_{i,j} p_i q_j \log p_i q_j$$

$$= -\sum_{i,j} p_i q_j (\log p_i + \log q_j)$$

$$= -\sum_i p_i \log p_i \sum_j q_j - \sum_j q_j \log q_j \sum_i p_i$$

$$= -\sum_i p_i \log p_i - \sum_j q_j \log q_j$$

$$= H(\mathbf{x}) + H(\mathbf{y}) \tag{4.10}$$

as expected. The case of A and B being statistically dependent will be taken later.

Consider now the discrete set of probabilities p_k and q_k, with $k = 1, \ldots, N$, and with the usual normalization

$$\sum_{k=1}^{N} p_k = 1 \qquad \text{and} \qquad \sum_{k=1}^{N} q_k = 1$$

We shall henceforth understand summation indices to run from 1 to N. Now consider the function

$$\sum_k p_k \log(q_k/p_k) = \sum_k p_k \log q_k - \sum_k p_k \log p_k$$

We now assume that the p_k are given, and we are to find the values for the q_k that maximize the last expression. This is a straightforward problem in constrained extremization. We, therefore, set the following derivatives with respect to q_j equal to zero:

$$(\partial / \partial q_j) \left[\sum_k p_k \log q_k - \sum_k p_k \log p_k - \lambda \left(\sum_k q_k - 1 \right) \right] = 0$$

from which

$$p_j - \lambda q_j = 0$$

Solving for the Lagrange multiplier λ, we use the normalization of probabilities:

$$p_j = \lambda q_j$$

$$\sum_j p_j = \lambda \sum_j q_j$$

implying that $\lambda = 1$ and, therefore, $p_j = q_j$. That this indeed maximizes the expression in square brackets is easily verified. The second derivative of the expression in square brackets is simply $(\partial^2/\partial q_j^2)\{\cdot\} = -p_j/q_j^2 \leq 0$, since $p_j \geq 0$ and $q_j \geq 0$, so we really have a maximum. The maximum value occurs when $p_j = q_j$. Furthermore, the maximum value is simply

$$\sum_k p_k \log(p_k/p_k) = \sum_k p_k \log(1) = 0$$

We summarize this result, which is sometimes known as the *fundamental inequality*:

$$\sum_k p_k \log(q_k/p_k) \leq 0 \qquad (4.11)$$

with the equality holding when $p_k = q_k$. The fundamental inequality is used in proving other results of information theory.

There is an interesting parallelism between Chaitin's measure of algorithmic complexity for randomness and Shannon's entropy measure for the information content of a sequence. Chaitin measures the randomness of a sequence with the size of the minimal algorithm needed to exactly reproduce that sequence. One way to arrive at the minimal algorithm is to remove all predictable components and to boil down the sequence to its irreducible core of unpredictable symbols. It is almost paradoxical that what remains is a totally unpredictable sequence, but yet it is precisely that minimal sequence that contains the information needed to represent the original data. Chaitin arrives at information through randomness.

The entropy measure of information introduced by Shannon

$$H = -\sum_k p(k) \log p(k) \qquad (4.12)$$

brings about a similar interpretation. This is so in the sense that a completely deterministic signal corresponds to $H = 0$, whereas the largest value of H attaches to a set of symbol probabilities corresponding to maximum unpredictability. The expression for H is maximized over a finite ensemble (say, consisting of M members), subject to the usual normalization constraint for $p(k)$, by the distribution $p(k) = 1/M$. This corresponds to the most unpredictable set of occurrences for the symbols.

An information source producing a large amount of information is characterized by large values of H and corresponds to a symbol sequence that has the least predictable structure. We are justified in calling messages issuing from such information sources random. Not surprisingly, we find that the best source codes are those that form a minimal algorithm from an information source or, at least, an approximation to the minimal algorithm associated with the stream of information symbols. The best code, according to Shannon, is one whose information rate approaches the source entropy H. Shannon arrives at randomness through information.

Chaitin does not use probabilistic concepts in his definition and measure of randomness, and Shannon does not discuss randomness other than through the specification of symbol probabilities $p(k)$. Yet randomness and information seem to be inseparable companions.

4.1.3 Conditional and Mutual Information

The concept of entropy can be extended to joint ensembles. We shall consider only pairs of ensembles and eventually will establish a correspondence between these two ensembles and the transmitted and received symbol strings. In general, however, the entropy concept can be extended to any number of ensembles.

Consider two ensembles of symbols $\{\mathbf{x}_i; i = 1, \ldots, M\}$ and $\{\mathbf{y}_j; j = 1, \ldots, N\}$ and also their joint probability distribution $P(\mathbf{x}_i, \mathbf{y}_j)$. The *joint entropy* between the ensembles $\mathbf{x}$ and $\mathbf{y}$ is defined as

$$H(\mathbf{x}, \mathbf{y}) = -\sum_{i,j} P(\mathbf{x}_i, \mathbf{y}_j) \log P(\mathbf{x}_i, \mathbf{y}_j) \tag{4.13}$$

The simplest thing to consider at this point is the amount of information provided about the event $\mathbf{x}_i$ by the occurrence of the event $\mathbf{y}_j$. In this case, the initial uncertainty (i.e., before knowing $\mathbf{y}_j$) is $-\log P(\mathbf{x}_i)$ and the final uncertainty, once $\mathbf{y}_j$ becomes known, is $-\log P(\mathbf{x}_i|\mathbf{y}_j)$. The amount of information gained in this process is given by subtracting the final uncertainty from the initial uncertainty, giving

$$I(\mathbf{x}_i, \mathbf{y}_j) = \log P(\mathbf{x}_i|\mathbf{y}_j) - \log P(\mathbf{x}_i)$$

This can also be written as

$$I(\mathbf{x}_i, \mathbf{y}_j) = \log \left[\frac{P(\mathbf{x}_i|\mathbf{y}_j)}{P(\mathbf{x}_i)} \right]$$

By a similar reasoning, we can write the expression for the information about the event $\mathbf{y}_j$ provided by the occurrence of the event $\mathbf{x}_i$. This is simply

$$I(\mathbf{y}_j, \mathbf{x}_i) = \log \left[\frac{P(\mathbf{y}_j|\mathbf{x}_i)}{P(\mathbf{y}_j)} \right]$$

However, we know from conditional probabilities that the following expression always holds:

$$\frac{P(\mathbf{x}_i|\mathbf{y}_j)}{P(\mathbf{x}_i)} = \frac{P(\mathbf{y}_j|\mathbf{x}_i)}{P(\mathbf{y}_j)}$$

We, therefore, must have equality between the above two measures of information:

$$I(\mathbf{x}_i, \mathbf{y}_j) = I(\mathbf{y}_j, \mathbf{x}_i) \tag{4.14}$$

Because of this symmetrical relationship, the quantity $I(\mathbf{x}_i, \mathbf{y}_j)$ is called the *mutual information* between events $\mathbf{x}_i$ and $\mathbf{y}_j$. The symmetry between the two ensembles can be made even more explicit in the expression for the *average mutual information* between $\mathbf{x}_i$ and $\mathbf{y}_j$. This is obtained by evaluating the statistical average of $I(\mathbf{x}_i, \mathbf{y}_j)$ over the probabilities $P(\mathbf{x}_i, \mathbf{y}_j)$:

$$I(\mathbf{x}, \mathbf{y}) = \sum_{i,j} I(\mathbf{x}_i, \mathbf{y}_j) P(\mathbf{x}_i, \mathbf{y}_j) \tag{4.15}$$

and using the identity

$$\frac{P(\mathbf{x}_i|\mathbf{y}_j)}{P(\mathbf{x}_i)} = \frac{P(\mathbf{x}_i, \mathbf{y}_j)}{P(\mathbf{x}_i)P(\mathbf{y}_j)}$$

leading to the following symmetrical form for the average mutual information between the ensembles $\mathbf{x}$ and $\mathbf{y}$:

$$I(\mathbf{x}, \mathbf{y}) = \sum_{i,j} P(\mathbf{x}_i, \mathbf{y}_j) \log \left[\frac{P(\mathbf{x}_i, \mathbf{y}_j)}{P(\mathbf{x}_i)P(\mathbf{y}_j)} \right] \tag{4.16}$$

The interpretation given to the average mutual information $I(\mathbf{x}, \mathbf{y})$ is that it is the average information about the ensemble $\mathbf{y}$ provided by the ensemble $\mathbf{x}$, and vice versa. We shall have occasion to use the average mutual information later in defining the information-carrying capacity of a channel as being the largest possible value that $I(\mathbf{x}, \mathbf{y})$ can assume. Note also that the average mutual information is always nonnegative: $I(\mathbf{x}, \mathbf{y}) \geq 0$.

In considering the joint ensembles $\{\mathbf{x}_i; i = 1, \ldots, M\}$ and $\{\mathbf{y}_j; j = 1, \ldots, N\}$ related by the joint probabilities $P(x_i, y_j)$, the occurrence of y_j provides only partial information about the occurrence of x_i. The remaining information required to fully specify x_i once y_j is known is measured by the *conditional self-information* of the event x_i given the occurrence of the event y_j. The conditional self-information is given by

$$I(\mathbf{x}_i|\mathbf{y}_j) = -\log P(\mathbf{x}_i|\mathbf{y}_j) \tag{4.17}$$

The conditional self-information can be averaged over the probabilities $P(\mathbf{x}_i, \mathbf{y}_j)$ to give a quantity called the *conditional entropy*. The conditional entropy is interpreted as the average amount of information needed to specify $\mathbf{x}$ once $\mathbf{y}$ has been specified. The expression for conditional entropy is

$$H(\mathbf{x}|\mathbf{y}) = -\sum_{i,j} P(\mathbf{x}_i, \mathbf{y}_j) \log P(\mathbf{x}_i|\mathbf{y}_j) \tag{4.18}$$

We now provide identities relating the three forms of average information that have been presented: average self-information, average mutual information, and conditional entropy:

$$I(\mathbf{x}, \mathbf{y}) = H(\mathbf{x}) - H(\mathbf{x}|\mathbf{y}) = H(\mathbf{y}) - H(\mathbf{y}|\mathbf{x}) \tag{4.19}$$

This identity follows directly from the symmetrical form for $I(\mathbf{x},\mathbf{y})$. We can also derive a following useful pair of identities that include the joint entropy.

$$H(\mathbf{y}|\mathbf{x}) = -\sum_{i,j} P(\mathbf{x}_i, \mathbf{y}_j) \log P(\mathbf{y}_j|\mathbf{x}_i)$$

$$= -\sum_{i,j} P(\mathbf{x}_i, \mathbf{y}_j)[\log P(\mathbf{x}_i, \mathbf{y}_j) - \log P(\mathbf{x}_i)] \tag{4.20}$$

$$= -\sum_{i,j} P(\mathbf{x}_i, \mathbf{y}_j) \log P(\mathbf{x}_i, \mathbf{y}_j) + \sum_{i,j} P(\mathbf{x}_i, \mathbf{y}_j) \log P(\mathbf{x}_i)$$

$$= H(\mathbf{x}, \mathbf{y}) - H(\mathbf{x})$$

and, therefore,

$$H(\mathbf{x}, \mathbf{y}) = H(\mathbf{x}) + H(\mathbf{y}|\mathbf{x}) \tag{4.21}$$

Similarly, owing to the symmetry between $\mathbf{x}$ and $\mathbf{y}$, we also have

$$H(\mathbf{x}, \mathbf{y}) = H(\mathbf{y}) + H(\mathbf{x}|\mathbf{y}) \tag{4.22}$$

We now justify the functional form of the entropy with a theorem due to Shannon. A proof of this theorem is given by Shannon [Sh 48a] and Khinchin [Kh 57] and will not be repeated here.

Theorem. Let $H(p_1, p_2, \ldots, p_n)$ be a continuous function of its positive definite arguments $p_k \geq 0, k = 1, 2, \ldots, n$, satisfying the normalization condition $\sum_k p_k = 1$. In addition, let the function H satisfy the following properties:

1. The function $H(p_1, p_2, \ldots, p_n)$ assumes its largest value when $p_k = 1/n$, $k = 1, 2, \ldots, n$.

2. For the two schemes $\mathbf{x}:\{\mathbf{x}_1, \mathbf{x}_2, \ldots, x_M\}$ and $\mathbf{y}:\{\mathbf{y}_1, \mathbf{y}_2, \ldots, \mathbf{y}_N\}$ with joint probabilities $P(\mathbf{x}_i, \mathbf{y}_j)$, we have $H(\mathbf{x}, \mathbf{y}) = H(\mathbf{x}) - H(\mathbf{x}|\mathbf{y})$.

3. $H(p_1, p_2, \ldots, p_n, 0) = H(p_1, p_2, \ldots, p_n)$. In other words, the addition of an event having zero probability does not change the entropy.

Then, the function

$$H(p_1, p_2, \ldots, p_n) = -\beta \sum_{k=1}^{n} p_k \log p_k \tag{4.23}$$

where β is a positive constant and is the only function that satisfies the previous conditions.

4.1.4 The Entropy of the Discrete Memoryless Source

One of the simplest models for a random event is a Bernoulli trial. A Bernoulli trial is a random experiment in which (1) there are only two possible outcomes associated with probabilities p and $1 - p$, respectively, and (2) the outcomes of separate trials are statistically independent. Bernoulli events are convenient for modeling a binary (0, 1) information source.

A Bernoulli trial is a mathematical model for what an information theorist calls a zero-memory binary information source, i.e., a source for which the present binary symbol is not related to the string of symbols that preceded it. This information source consists of statistically independent binary symbols and is characterized by a single parameter, namely p.

The outcomes of strings of Bernoulli trials are binomially distributed. We can think of the outcomes of a single trial to be, for example, the production of the binary symbol 0 or 1 by the information source. The probabilities for these outcomes are

$$\text{Prob } \{0\} = p \quad \text{and} \quad \text{Prob } \{1\} = q = 1 - p \tag{4.24}$$

Now consider a message consisting of N such binary symbols. The probability that this message contains exactly t of the symbol 0 in any order is $\binom{N}{t} p^t (1-p)^{N-t}$, where

$$\binom{N}{t} = \frac{N!}{t!(N-t)!} \tag{4.25}$$

is the number of combinations of N objects taken t at a time.

The messages in this ensemble consist of all the possible binary N-tuples. If all these complexions were equally probable, then the entropy per message would simply be the logarithm to the base 2 of the total number of states:

$$I = \log_2 2^N = N \text{ bits per message} \tag{4.26}$$

However, the entropy is actually less than this, in general, since some of the messages are more probable than others. $I = N$ bits/message is valid only if $p = \frac{1}{2}$. The actual entropy of a sequence of Bernoulli trials depends on the parameter p. To pursue things further, we must introduce a very interesting property of sequences of Bernoulli trials.

In a message of N binary symbols generated by Bernoulli trials where $P\{0\} = p$, there are on the average pN occurrences of the symbol 0. The standard deviation about this average is $(p(1-p)N)^{1/2}$. As N grows large for fixed p, both the mean and the standard deviation increase, but the mean increases at a faster rate. The net effect is that the relative spread (relative to N) about the mean decreases. Another way of saying this is that as N increases, more and more of the probability clusters tightly about the mean.

The example that follows is a typical exercise in the application of probability to information theory. The goal is to determine where the fixed total amount of probability clusters as one or more parameters are varied. This sort of approach is often used, and the example to be presented will resurface in slightly different guise several times throughout this book.

EXAMPLE

Tossing a coin provides a good illustration of this. For a fair coin,

$$\text{Prob } \{heads\} = \text{Prob } \{tails\} = 1/2$$

We now construct the following table of probabilities of getting exactly $0.2N, 0.4N, 0.5N, 0.6N$, and $0.8N$ heads for various values of N. These probabilities are given by

$$\text{Prob \{exactly } t \text{ heads\}} = 2^{-N} \binom{N}{t}$$

Alternatively, we can say we are calculating the probability of getting a fraction $\alpha - t/N$ of heads:

$$\text{Prob \{}\alpha\} = 2^{-N} \binom{N}{\alpha N} \qquad (4.27)$$

Table 4-2 lists values of Prob $\{\alpha\}$ for various choices of N.

TABLE 4-2. BINOMIAL PROBABILITIES FROM EQ. (4.27).

N	$\alpha = 0.2$	0.4	0.5	0.6	0.8
10	4.39×10^{-2}	0.205	0.246	0.205	4.39×10^{-2}
40	6.99×10^{-5}	5.72×10^{-2}	0.125	5.72×10^{-2}	6.99×10^{-5}
100	4.23×10^{-10}	1.08×10^{-2}	7.96×10^{-2}	1.08×10^{-2}	4.23×10^{-10}

What this simple example shows is that as N becomes large, an increasing fraction of the probability clusters tightly about the mean. This agrees well with intuition. In a series of 1000 coin tosses, we would hardly expect to get a total number of heads that deviates significantly from 500. Note that in the above table, the probability entries are symmetrical about $\alpha = 0.5$. When $p \neq 1/2$, the values still cluster about $\alpha = p$, albeit in an unsymmetrical manner.

This calculation illustrates a fairly obvious example of the law of large numbers of probability theory. For simplicity, a sequence of Bernoulli (i.e., binary) events has been used. We found that the total probability shows a tendency of clustering about the mean. This result agrees well with intuition. The generalizations of this example, however, do not.

We can state this important result in more mathematical terms and prove that the probability of finding values that differ from the mean $\mu = pN$ by an arbitrarily small amount can be made as small as we like. The proof involves two separate uses of the Chernoff bound. First, we show that the number of values exceeding μ by an arbitrarily small amount can be made arbitrarily small by making N sufficiently large. Then we prove that the number of values that are smaller than the mean by an arbitrarily small quantity can also be made arbitrarily small in the same way. Together, these results show that deviations from the mean, however small, can be made as unlikely as one wishes by choosing a sufficiently large N.

Consider messages of N symbols generated by Bernoulli trials with Prob $\{0\} = p$ and Prob $\{1\} = q = 1 - p$. The total number of occurrences t of the symbol 0 is a discrete random variable that follows a binomial distribution:

$$P(t) = \binom{N}{t} p^t (1 - p)^{N-t} \qquad (4.28)$$

An upper limit on the probability of t exceeding a given quantity is provided by the Chernoff bound:

$$\text{Prob } \{t \geq \delta\} \leq e^{-\hat{\nu}\delta} E\,[e^{\hat{\nu}t}]$$

where $\hat{\nu}$ is the positive solution to

$$E\,[t\,e^{\nu t}] = \delta E\,[e^{\nu t}] \tag{4.29}$$

For the binomial distribution,

$$E\,[e^{\nu t}] = \psi(\nu) = [1 - p + p e^{\nu}]^{N} \tag{4.30}$$

is the moment-generating function $\psi(\nu)$. The probability of t exceeding $\mu = pN$ by an arbitrarily small quantity ϵ is bounded by

$$\text{Prob } \{t \geq \mu + \epsilon\} \leq e^{-\hat{\nu}(\mu + \epsilon)} \psi(\hat{\nu}) = e^{-\hat{\nu}(pN + \epsilon)} \psi(\hat{\nu}) \tag{4.31}$$

From Eq. (4.30), we have

$$E\,[t\,e^{\nu t}] = \frac{d\psi}{d\nu} = \nu N\,p e^{\nu}[1 - p + p e^{\nu}]^{N-1}$$

The condition of Eq. (4.29) becomes

$$1 - p + p e^{\nu} = \nu N\,\delta^{-1} p e^{\nu}$$

from which

$$p e^{\nu} = \frac{\delta(1 - p)}{N\nu - \delta}$$

so that

$$\psi(\nu) = \left[1 - p + \frac{\delta(1 - p)}{N\nu - \delta}\right]^{N} \tag{4.32}$$

Note that $\psi(\nu)$ approaches 0 as N becomes large. The negative exponential term in Eq. (4.31) guarantees that Prob $\{t \geq \mu + \epsilon\}$ can be made as small as one wishes by choosing N to be sufficiently large, no matter how small ϵ is. We, therefore, have

$$\lim_{N \to \infty} \text{Prob } \{t \geq \mu + \epsilon\} = 0 \tag{4.33}$$

An identical line of reasoning can be used to show that the same exponential bound also applies to Prob $\{t \leq \mu - \epsilon\}$. To this end, we first note that this is equal to the probability Prob $\{t' \geq \mu + \epsilon\}$, where $t' = N - t$ is the number of times the symbol **1** appears in the message. The probability distribution for t' is

$$P(t') = \binom{N}{t'}(1 - p)^{t'} p^{N - t'}$$

$$= \binom{N}{t} p^{t}(1 - p)^{N - t}$$

$$= P(t)$$

since $\binom{N}{t'} = \binom{N}{t}$.

We have just proven a special case of the law of large numbers involving a binomially distributed random variable. As the number N of Bernoulli trials increases, the total number of possible different messages increases exponentially as 2^N. However, the ratio t/N approaches the mean $\mu = pN$, and most of the probability is concentrated tightly about μ. This means that although there are 2^N possible messages, only those for which $t \approx \mu = pN$ are likely to occur. All other messages occur with vanishingly small probability as $N \to \infty$.

Let us now return to the message consisting of N binary symbols selected by Bernoulli trials, each one determining whether a **0** or a **1** appears. If N is large, then by reason of the considerations just discussed, there are, on the average, approximately $M = \binom{N}{pN}$ equally probable combinations of pN symbol **0** and $N - pN = N(1 - p)$ symbol **1** occurring in some permuted order. The approximation gets better as N becomes larger. The total number of distinguishable messages is, therefore, $M = \binom{N}{pN}$. These messages all tend to have the same weight (i.e., the same number of occurrences for a given symbol), and to occur with the same probability

$$P = \binom{N}{pN} p^{pN} (1 - p)^{N(1-p)} \tag{4.34}$$

All other messages occur with vanishingly small probability as N becomes large. This result is not so intuitive, and is of fundamental importance in information theory.

Since these messages are equiprobable, the information content of any one of these messages is simply given by $\log_2 M$:

$$H = \log M = \log N! - \log(pN)! - \log(qN)! \tag{4.35}$$

where $q = 1 - p$. For large x, we can use Stirling's approximation for the factorial

$$x! \approx (2\pi x)^{1/2} x^x e^{-x} \tag{4.36}$$

Using Stirling's approximation for the factorials appearing in Eq. (4.35), there results, after some simple algebra,

$$H \approx N(-p \log p - q \log q) \tag{4.37}$$

Note that this is precisely N times the entropy associated with a single Bernoulli trial. This simple calculation points to the additive nature of the entropy measure of information: if the information contained in a single binary symbol is $h = -p \log p - q \log q$, then the information contained in N statistically independent such symbols is Nh.

There is yet another way of arriving at Eq. (4.37). The law of large numbers states that

$$\lim_{N \to \infty} \text{Prob} \{|\frac{t}{N} - p| \geq \epsilon\} = 0 \tag{4.38}$$

for any $\epsilon \geq 0$. As $N \to \infty$, the likely messages are found in a neighborhood of size 2ϵ about p. We denote by M the number of such likely messages, and find an approximate asymptotic expression for M.

Since the occurrence of the symbols **0** and **1** are Bernoulli events with Prob $\{\mathbf{0}\} = p$, the number t occurrences of the symbol **0** is binomially distributed. There are $\binom{N}{t}$ messages with t occurrences of the symbol **0**, the probability of which is given by Eq. (4.34). When N is large, this probability tends to cluster about $t = pN$, with most of the probability being contained in a neighborhood of size $2\epsilon N$ about $t = pN$. Figure 4-1(a) shows the entire probability distribution. In Fig. 4-1(b), we have enlarged that portion of the distribution in the immediate vicinity of $t = pN$.

It is now a simple matter to count (approximately) the number M of likely messages by summing the binomial coefficients $\binom{N}{t}$ corresponding to the likely interval

$$(p - \epsilon)N \;\leq\; t \;\leq\; (p + \epsilon)N$$

We, therefore, have

$$M \approx \sum_{t=(p-\epsilon)N}^{(p+\epsilon)N} \binom{N}{t} \tag{4.39}$$

with the approximation getting better as N becomes larger. Now note that $P(t)$ is a slowly varying function of t near $t = pN$. We can, therefore, approximate the sum M in Eq. (4.39) by the value of $\binom{N}{t}$ evaluated at $t = pN$ multiplied by the number $2\epsilon N$ of discrete probabilities in the interval of interest. That is, we write

$$M \approx \sum_{t=(p-\epsilon)N}^{(p+\epsilon)N} \binom{N}{t} \approx 2\epsilon N \binom{N}{pN} \tag{4.40}$$

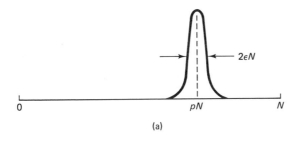

(a)

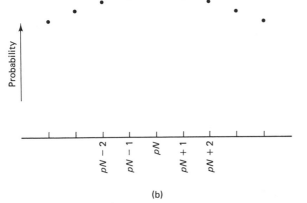

(b)

Figure 4-1. (*a*) Binomial probability distribution for large N. (*b*) Closeup of the distribution near pN.

Taking $\binom{N}{pN}$ as the representative value of $\binom{N}{t}$ by which to multiply $2\epsilon N$ overestimates M. However, attempting to get a better approximation by multiplying the right-hand side of Eq. (4.39) by any factor that grows at a lesser rate than N is, as we soon shall see, inconsequential in this approximation.

Since $P(t)$ is approximately constant in the interval, the likely messages occur with approximately the same probability. The information in the set of M equally likely messages is, therefore, obtained by evaluating the logarithm of M. By using the right-hand side of Eq. (4.40), this gives the result

$$H = \log M = \log 2\epsilon N + \log\binom{N}{pN} \tag{4.41}$$

The first term on the right-hand side of Eq. (4.41) is of order $\log N$. We have already shown that $\log \binom{N}{pN}$ is of order N, and, therefore, much larger than $\log 2\epsilon N$ for large N. We can, therefore, safely neglect $\log 2\epsilon N$ and write, for large N,

$$H = \log\binom{N}{pN} \tag{4.42}$$

where Eq. (4.37) follows through the use of Stirling's approximation.

The previous calculation, though simple, is approximate. We had to rely on the fact that N is large. Such approaches to asymptotic properties of information theoretic quantities are very useful. We followed that approach to introduce an example of such an asymptotic technique as well as to introduce the concentration of probability about the mean as N becomes large. It turns out, however, that the additivity property of entropy is an exact result and can be proved on more rigorous grounds. For this, however, we must introduce the concept of the nth extension of a zero-memory information source.

The nth extension is a simple mathematical construct by means of which systematically more complex coding alphabets can be generated in terms of simpler ones. The idea is to consider as our new symbols blocks (n-tuples) of n consecutive old symbols.

EXAMPLE

Consider a binary information source with statistically independent symbol probabilities given by Prob $\{0\} = p$ and Prob $\{1\} = q = 1 - p$. If we look at pairs ($n = 2$) of consecutive symbols, we now have four symbols in our new alphabet, with the following associated probabilities:

$$\text{Prob }\{00\} = q^2$$
$$\text{Prob }\{01\} = qp$$
$$\text{Prob }\{10\} = pq$$
$$\text{Prob }\{11\} = p^2$$

We can easily generalize this example to the case of n-tuples. This leads to the following definition.

Definition. If S is a zero-memory information source with symbols from the alphabet $\{s_1, s_2, \ldots, s_q\}$ with the corresponding probabilities $\{p_1, p_2, \ldots, p_q\}$, then the nth extension $S^{(n)}$ of S is a zero-memory source with the q^n symbols $\sigma_k = (\mathbf{s}_{k_1}, \mathbf{s}_{k_2}, \ldots, \mathbf{s}_{k_n})$, $k = 1, 2, \ldots \mathbf{s}, q^n$. Each of the σ_k corresponds to a permuted concatenation of the $\mathbf{s}_i$. The probability associated with σ_k is $P(\sigma_k) = P(\mathbf{s}_{k_1}) \cdot P(\mathbf{s}_{k_2}) \cdots P(\mathbf{s}_{k_n})$.

EXAMPLE

Anticipating the subject of source coding, we now consider the problem of encoding the symbols of an extended alphabet of statistically independent symbols. Specifically, we are dealing with an alphabet of 37 equiprobable symbols consisting of the 26 letters, a blank space, and ten digits. The symbols are assumed to be equiprobable to simplify the calculations. In actuality, they follow a nonuniform probability distribution that results in a lower value for the entropy. However, that is irrelevant for what we want to show here.

Assume that the symbols available for coding are binary digits. We are going to calculate the average number of such binary digits required to encode (i.e., label) a typical symbol from the 37-ary alphabet. In fact, we are ultimately interested in using the fewest number of the shortest labels possible, a topic to be fully addressed in a subsequent section. If we encode one symbol at a time, we need at least six bits per symbol, since $2^5 < 37 < 2^6$. We need at least six bits to represent the 37 possibilities. Note, however, that this is wasteful. Had there been exactly 32 symbols, we would have needed five bits. As things stand, we are forced to use six bits, corresponding to 64 possibilities. This results in $64 - 37 = 27$ unused possibilities, which must, nevertheless, be assigned coding labels. Another way of looking at this is that the source entropy is simply $H = \log_2 37 = 5.21$ bits per symbol. Using binary digits for coding, we must, therefore, go to the next higher integer, which is 6.

This serves to introduce one problem of coding. We are given a source alphabet, with associated probabilities, and the task is to design a coding technique that is as efficient as possible. In this case, "efficient" means with as little waste as possible. We are not free to reduce the source alphabet, since this would exclude information from being transmitted. We are, on the other hand, reluctant to use six bits, as this uses up transmission resources (namely, channel capacity, to be discussed in the following section) without increasing the information throughput.

Let us now consider coding pairs of symbols, i.e., the second extension of the original alphabet. Each symbol from this extended alphabet contains $\log_2 (37 \cdot 37) = 10.42$ bits. This requires 11 binary digits per extended alphabet symbol, or 5.50 binary digits per original symbol. Note that by going from encoding individual symbols to encoding them in pairs, the average number of binary digits required for encoding has decreased from 6.0 to 5.5 digits per original symbol. This motivates us to consider encoding in triplets, groups of four, five, etc. Table 4-3 summarizes the results. The entropy of a group of n symbols from the nth extension is simply $\log_2 37^n$ bits per extension symbol. The next higher integer gives the total number of binary digits required, and the last column expresses this result in terms of binary digits per original symbol, a quantity that can be compared for different values of n.

Note that as n increases and progressively higher-order extensions of the original alphabet are being encoded, the number of binary digits per original alphabet symbol decreases, although not uniformly. If Table 4-3 were to be continued, much of the same behavior would be manifested. In particular, the number of binary digits per original alphabet symbol appears to approach some limit in the vicinity of 5.21 bits, the entropy of the original alphabet. Values that are close to this are indicated in the table with arrows. It does not appear possible to obtain values that are lower than 5.21 binary digits per source symbol.

Although this example is experimental in nature and, therefore, does not prove anything in a strict mathematical sense, it does prepare us for some important results of information theory to be introduced later. It does turn out that 5.21 bits per character is a lower limit and that we are guaranteed the existence of codes that approach this efficient limit as close as one desires. This example argues for the plausibility of such coding and introduces a brute-force way of finding such a code.

Efficient codes are associated with higher-order extensions of the original alphabet. Of course, we may be lucky and hit the limit exactly on the nose, as with the case of an equiprobable alphabet consisting of a number of symbols equal to an integral power of 2. In the general case, however, we must resort to more complex coding techniques. Higher-order extensions are one way of approaching this limit, but at the price of coding delays and complexity.

The symbols of the discrete memoryless source can be described as an extension of the symbols produced by a Bernoulli trial. This is done by letting the Bernoulli trials generate binary $\log_2 M$ bit labels for the M symbols of the DMS.

One would expect that the entropy per symbol in $S^{(n)}$ be exactly n times the entropy per symbol in S. We now proceed to prove that this is true.

The entropy for the nth extension of a zero-memory information source is clearly

$$H[S^{(n)}] = - \sum_{k \in S^{(n)}} P(\sigma_k) \log P(\sigma_k) \tag{4.43}$$

TABLE 4-3. BINARY CODING OF SUCCESSIVE EXTENSIONS OF A 37-ARY ALPHABET OF EQUIPROBABLE SYMBOLS

n	$\log_2 37^n$	Total Binary Digits	Binary Digits/Symbol
1	5.21	6	6.00
2	10.42	11	5.50
3	15.63	16	5.33
4	20.84	21	→5.25
5	26.05	27	5.40
6	31.26	32	5.33
7	36.47	37	5.29
8	41.68	42	→5.25
9	46.89	47	→5.22
10	52.09	53	5.30

where the index k ranges over all of the elements in $S^{(n)}$. Now, since

$$P(\sigma_k) = P(\mathbf{s}_{k_1}) \cdot P(\mathbf{s}_{k_2}) \cdots P(\mathbf{s}_{k_n}) \qquad (4.44)$$

we can express the logarithm $\log P(\sigma_k)$ in terms of a sum of logarithms

$$H[S^{(n)}] = - \sum_{k \in S^{(n)}} P(\sigma_k)[\log P(\mathbf{s}_{k_1}) + \ldots + \log P(\mathbf{s}_{k_n})] \qquad (4.45)$$

The sum over $k \in S^{(n)}$ is equivalent to n independent sums, each ranging over the q elements of S. We, therefore, have

$$H[S^{(n)}] = - \sum_{k_1=1}^{q} \cdots \sum_{k_n=1}^{q} P(\mathbf{s}_{k_1}) \cdots P(\mathbf{s}_{k_n})[\log P(\mathbf{s}_{k_1}) + \ldots + \log P(\mathbf{s}_{k_n})]$$

$$= \sum_{j=1}^{n} \sum_{k_1=1}^{q} \cdots \sum_{k_n=1}^{q} P(\mathbf{s}_{k_1}) \cdots P(\mathbf{s}_{k_n}) \log P(\mathbf{s}_{k_j})$$

$$= \sum_{j=1}^{n} - \sum_{k_1=1}^{q} P(\mathbf{s}_{k_j}) \log P(\mathbf{s}_{k_j}) \left[\sum_{k_i \neq k_j = 1}^{q} P(\mathbf{s}_{k_i}) \right]^{n-1}$$

$$= nH(S)$$

$$(4.46)$$

4.1.5 The Entropy of the Discrete Markov Source

We now generalize our concept of information sources, and consider sources for which the generation of a particular symbol depends on the past source output history. Specifically, we consider a q-ary alphabet $\{\mathbf{x}_1, \mathbf{x}_2, \ldots, \mathbf{x}_q\}$. The information source selects the current symbol from this alphabet with probabilities that depend on the m symbols that precede it. Such an information source is called an mth-*order Markov source.*

Markov sources are mathematical models for sources such as written English, where the letters that occur in normal text are not statistically independent, but are in some way related. For example, a Q is always followed by a U, and an L is never followed by an X. In fact, the intersymbol correlations are a measure of the level of redundancy in a written language. The functional significance of redundancy is that it imparts a certain robustness against transmission errors and accidental symbol deletions.

Markov processes form an important part of the study of probability theory and encompass a range of behavior that is much wider than what is needed for modeling information sources. Excellent treatments of Markov processes can be found in Feller [Fe 68], Kemeny and Snell [Ke 76], and Papoulis [Pa 84].

The identifying charatheristic of an mth-order Markov source is that the probability that the current symbol $\mathbf{s}_k$ is equal to one of the $\mathbf{x}_j$ is determined by the set $\{\mathbf{s}_{k-1}, \mathbf{s}_{k-2}, \ldots, \mathbf{s}_{k-m}\}$ of m symbols that immediately precede $\mathbf{s}_k$. Such a source can be thought of as having a memory that spans the m preceding symbols, the occurrence of each of which was, in turn, determined by probabilities conditioned on still earlier symbols. The probability for $\mathbf{s}_k$ being one of the $\mathbf{x}_j$ is thus determined by the conditional probabilities that previous symbols $\mathbf{s}_{k-j}$ are equal to each of the $\mathbf{x}_i$. For each of the $\mathbf{s}_{k-j}$, $j = 1, 2, \ldots, m$, there are q possibilities for $\mathbf{x}_i$. The probability of the current source symbol $\mathbf{s}_k$ is, therefore, conditioned on q^m events, namely the possible occurrence of each of the $\mathbf{x}_i$ for each of the m symbols preceding s_k. We call these q^m events the *states* of the Markov source, and the source is said to undergo transitions from one state to another according to conditional probabilities that govern these transitions.

The study of Markov processes as a subfield of mathematical stochastic processes is not necessarily tied to sets of symbols, but rather with probabilities. It is not necessary to associate Markov processes with the production of symbols. Our study could be confined to the dynamics of state transitions. This is the approach usually followed in the mathematical literature. A Markov process initially in one of its q^m states will jump from state to state according to probabilistic transition rules, so that an initial distribution of probability over the states will gradually diffuse over other states at a rate that is determined by the transition probabilities linking them.

One useful way to visualize Markov processes is to imagine a finite amount of probability (summing up to unity) being distributed over a set of initial states. Each new step in the Markov process involves a redistribution of this total probability over states that are "connected" to the initial ones by transition probabilities. Thus, the probability of finding the system in various states after the first step involves the transition probabilities conditioned on the initial probability distribution over the states. This process can be continued step by step and involves the gradual diffusion of that same amount of total probability over some or all of the states.

As we mentioned earlier, the general properties of Markov processes include behavior that is not necessarily characteristic of information sources. Thus, there are Markov processes for which all of the probability eventually accumulates, with probability 1, in one of the states, and remains there. Such a state is called an *absorbing state*. It is also possible for the general diffusion behavior to exhibit periodicity, where the probability oscillates between sets of states. There is also the uninteresting case of a Markov process remaining in its initial state; this would happen if the initial state happened to be an absorbing state. Obviously, these Markov processes find limited use in communication theory.

We shall selectively borrow from the study of Markov processes to create a mathematical model for an information source for which symbols are statistically correlated. The motivation for this is that symbols from information sources often tend to be correlated. We shall then adopt the Markov formalism, but will restrict our applications to processes for which, if we wait a sufficiently large number of steps, any given state will eventually occur. Furthermore, over a sufficiently large number of steps, the Markov states occur with some definite probabilities π_k, $k = 1, 2, \ldots, q^m$. We, therefore, specifically exclude absorbing states. Implicit in our restriction is the requirement that the Markov process be stationary, and that after a sufficiently long time has elapsed, the system tends toward an equilibrium probability distribution π_k, $k = 1, 2, \ldots, q^m$, that is independent of the initial distribution. Such processes are called *ergodic processes*.

Our association with Markov processes will be strictly limited to ergodic processes. For these processes, the time-averaged statistical properties are equal to the corresponding ensemble averages. In particular, ergodicity implies stationariness so that the statistical properties of ergodic information sources are time-invariant. The particular consequences of considering ergodic Markov sources is that over suitably long observation periods, all of the possible symbol sequences have a nonvanishing probability of being realized, these probabilities being $\pi_k, k = 1, 2, \ldots, q^m$.

The transition from the mathematical theory of Markov processes to their application in communications is most easily accomplished as follows:

1. We restrict ourselves to ergodic processes.

2. The meaning we attach to communication symbols is that they are simply labels for the states of a Markov process. Each state can be specified by the m-tuple formed by the concatenation of m symbols from a q-ary alphabet. A typical state label consists in the specification of m consecutive symbols, each one of which could be an element from the set of symbols from a q-ary alphabet.

The information conveyed by the last symbol s_k from a Markov source is the same as the information provided by the kth state transition. Considerable simplification in notation and clarity results by considering the states and associated probabilities of a Markov source rather than the symbols themselves. Calculations involve averages over all q^m members of the ensemble, and it turns out to be easier to recognize this at the outset rather than having to force a symbol-oriented notation to eventually fit within this formalism.

To this end, we adopt the following notation. We shall label the q^m states of a Markov information source with $c_k, k = 1, 2, \ldots, q^m$. Note that c is not in boldface, to distinguish it from a symbol. This is a compact notation for every possible concatenation of m symbols from a q-ary alphabet:

$$c_k = (s_{k-m+1}, s_{k-m+2}, \ldots, s_k) \qquad k = 1, 2, \ldots, q^m \qquad (4.47)$$

Viewed in this manner, the probability $p_k(n)$ of state $c_k, k = 1, 2, \ldots, q^m$, being realized at step n depends only on the transition probabilities $a_{kj}, j = 1, 2, \ldots, q^m$, tying state k to all other states, including itself, and conditioned on $p_j(n), j = 1, 2, \ldots, q^m$, the probabilities of the various states having been realized on the previous step. What we, in fact, have succeeded in doing is to replace an mth-order Markov process over a q-ary alphabet by a first-order process over q^m states. We note in passing that c_k, as defined, is simply the label for an element of the mth extension of the q-ary alphabet $\{x_1, x_2, \ldots, x_q\}$.

We now have to relate probabilities for symbols to corresponding probabilities over states, following which we have only to work with state probabilities. The motivation for considering Markov processes as models for information sources is that for many sources, the probability that a particular symbol is produced by the source is influenced by past source outputs. For an mth-order Markov source drawing from a q-ary alphabet, the probability that the kth symbol is x_j given that the preceding m symbols are $s_{k-1}, s_{k-2}, \ldots, s_{k-m}$ can be expressed as a conditional probability Prob $\{s_k = x_j | s_{k-1}, \ldots, s_{k-m}\}$. To transform this to an unconditional probability, we must multiply this expression by the joint probability $P(s_{k-1}, s_{k-2}, \ldots, s_{k-m})$, where the variables s_{k-j} are considered random variables, taking values over the set defined by the q-ary alphabet. We, therefore, have

$$\text{Prob } \{s_k = x_j\} = \text{Prob } \{s_k = x_j | s_{k-1}, \ldots, s_{k-m}\} \cdot P(s_{k-1}, \ldots, s_{k-m}) \quad (4.48)$$

The joint probability $P(s_{k-1}, \ldots, s_{k-m})$ is simply the probability associated with the previous Markov state, whereas the conditional probabilities $\text{Prob } \{s_k = x_j | s_{k-1}, \ldots, s_{k-m}\}$ represent the transition probabilities from the previous state to each of the q accessible current states.

The current Markov state shares the last $m - 1$ symbols in common with the previous state, but ends with the current symbol, s_k, which takes values from the set $\{x_j ; j = 1, 2, \ldots, q\}$ with corresponding probabilities $\text{Prob } \{s_k = x_j | s_{k-1}, \ldots, s_{k-m}\}$. This, in turn, provides the joint probability for the symbols in the current Markov state, for we can write Eq. (4.48) as

$$P(s_k, s_{k-1}, \ldots, s_{k-m+1}) =$$
$$\text{Prob } \{s_k | s_{k-1}, \ldots, s_{k-m}\} \cdot P(s_{k-1}, s_{k-2}, \ldots, s_{k-m}) \quad (4.49)$$

Although the concepts involved are simple, the notational difficulty of explicitly working with the symbols of a Markov source becomes evident. This difficulty arises from the necessity of keeping track of the m previous symbols. We choose, instead, to deal directly with the states of a Markov source with the following interpretation: we shall use as labels for these states the q^m symbols from the mth extension of a q-ary alphabet. The immediate consequence is that we are now dealing with a first-order Markov process over the states labeled by symbols drawn from the extension alphabet.

The resulting first-order process probabilities can be written as

$$p_k(n) = \alpha_{kj} p_j(n - 1) \quad (4.50)$$

with the interpretation that the source was in state j at step $n - 1$, and that the probability of finding the source in state k at step n is given by $p_k(n)$. The (extended) source memory spans only one step. However, by the use of the extension alphabet, this simple first-order model can be made to represent Markov sources of any order. In other words, we enjoy the mathematical simplicity of working with a first-order model, but by defining this model to be over an extended alphabet, our representation is valid for a Markov process of any order. We can, therefore, work with a first-order Markov process in the abstract, since it embodies the fundamental idea of step-to-step statistical correlation, and be assured that the results can be extended to Markov sources of any order. This "trick" can be used to simplify mathematical derivations and proofs involving mth-order Markov processes.

The introduction of a new symbol by the source causes the Markov state to change. As mentioned earlier, the net gain in information due to the new symbol is equal to the information gain due to the realization of a new state. Following the approach presented in Section 4.1.3, the net information gain at step n is

$$I(k, j) = - \log p_k(n) + \log p_j(n - 1) = - \log \alpha_{kj} \quad (4.51)$$

The average information, or entropy, is obtained by averaging $I(k,j)$ over the joint probability $P(c_k, c_j)$:

$$H(M) = \sum_{k,j} I(k,j) P(c_k, c_j)$$

$$= -\sum_{k,j} P(c_k, c_j) \log \alpha_{kj} \tag{4.52}$$

where $H(M)$ denotes that the entropy is calculated for a Markov process.

Since the Markov transition probabilities represent constraints on the information source, we expect the entropy of a Markov source to be upper bounded by the entropy of the discrete memoryless source, for which there are no such constraints. The following discussion confirms our intuition in this regard.

Consider the expression

$$-\sum_{k,j} P(k,j) \log\left[\frac{P(k,j)}{P(k)P(j)}\right] \tag{4.53}$$

where we have written $P(k,j)$ for $P(c_k, c_j)$ and $P(k)$ for $P(c_k)$ to simplify the notation. By the fundamental inequality, the last expression must be upper bounded by zero. Furthermore, since $P(k,j) = \alpha_{kj} P(j)$, we have

$$-\sum_{k,j} P(k,j) \log\left[\frac{\alpha_{k,j}}{P(k)}\right] \le 0$$

and, therefore,

$$-\sum_{k,j} P(k,j) \log \alpha_{kj} \le -\sum_{k,j} P(k,j) \log P(k) \tag{4.54}$$

The left-hand side of this inequality is simply $H(M)$. By summing the right-hand side over j, we obtain an expression that is identical to the entropy $H(D)$ for a discrete memoryless source with symbol probabilities $\{P(k); k = 1, 2, \ldots, q^m\}$. We, therefore, have

$$H(M) \le H(D) \tag{4.55}$$

with the equality holding if $P(k,j) = P(k)P(j)$, i.e., if the Markov process reduces to a discrete memoryless process.

Let us step back and examine this important result. The inequality we have just derived compares the entropies of two different information sources. One is a Markov source with transition probabilities α_{kj} and state probability distribution $P(k)$. The other is a discrete memoryless source having the same state probability distribution $P(k)$ as the Markov process. The only difference between these two sources is that the Markov outputs are statistically correlated, whereas the DMS outputs are not. In all other respects, and most importantly in the first order probabilities $P(k)$, the sources are identical.

Our result, as stated in the inequality $H(M) \le H(D)$, indicates that, *coeteris paribus*, a Markov source always provides less information than a discrete memoryless source having the same symbol probabilities. Since the symbols of the DMS are statistically uncorrelated, these symbols contain the most information, on the average.

The average amount of information per symbol is measured by the source entropy, which is defined in terms of the statistical properties of the source. An interesting picture emerges from the analysis presented in this section. If we were to rank information sources on the basis of entropy, we would find that the source associated with the highest entropy is the discrete memoryless source having equiprobable symbols. This is the freest source possible, as there are no constraints (other than normalization) on the probabilities.

When symbol probabilities are specified, but the symbols are statistically independent, the source with the next highest entropy is still the discrete memoryless source, for which freedom in selecting symbols is constrained by the specified symbol probability distribution.

Finally, the Markov source imposes the additional restriction of statistical correlations between symbols. This has the effect of further reducing the source entropy. These quantitative remarks supplement our initial notion that information measures the amount of freedom of choice between possible alternatives.

EXAMPLE

Returning to the entropy of written English, as described by 27 symbols consisting of the 26 letters plus a blank, we recall that considering all symbols to be statistically independent leads to an entropy of $\log_2 27 = 4.75$ bits per symbol, which we know to be an upper limit to the entropy since the symbols are not independent, but are selected according to specific grammatical and linguistic rules.

The next level of sophistication in calculating the entropy of written English is to use the first-order symbol probabilities given in an earlier example. This led to a value of 4.08 bits per symbol for the entropy, or a decrease of 0.67 bits per symbol from the assumption of equiprobability.

Calculations have been made of the entropy using correlations between pairs of symbols (≈ 3.3 bits per symbol) and triplets (≈ 3.1 bits per symbol). Shannon [Sh 51] estimates that the actual entropy of written English is somewhere in the vicinity of one bit per symbol.

4.1.6 The Continuous Information Source

The information sources studied thus far have all been discrete. They are probabilistic models for realizations of strings of discrete symbols taken from a finite alphabet. We now briefly consider continuous information sources, where the information "string" appears as samples assuming a continuous range of random values. The relation between discrete and continuous information sources is the same as exists between discrete and continuous random variables.

A continuous information source is a stochastic process whose samples can assume a continuous range of values. These samples could be the sampled values of a random function or the signal-space coordinates of a such a function. For communication signals, such functions are restricted to those that can be represented in finite-dimensional linear function spaces. We can, therefore, replace the problem of dealing with continuous functions with the equivalent one of dealing with its projections onto the finite number of coordinates. As we discussed in Chapter 2, these projections are calculated as the inner products of the original function with the basis functions that span the finite-dimensional linear function space. For continuous information sources, these projections are random variables and, in general, may assume values over the range $-\infty < \mathbf{x} < \infty$, with a probability density $p(\mathbf{x})$ with the interpretation that the probability of realizing the variable $\mathbf{x}$ with values between $\mathbf{x}$ and $\mathbf{x} + d\mathbf{x}$ is $p(\mathbf{x})d\mathbf{x}$.

Examples of continuous information signals include speech, music, and analog signals from measuring instruments for such physical parameters as temperature, pressure, displacement, angle, etc. The development of information theory for continuous information sources has many similarities with what was developed for discrete sources. There are, however, important differences. This section explores some of these similarities and differences.

Just as was done for a discrete set of probabilities, we can define the entropy of a continuous random variable having probability density $p(x)$ to be

$$H(\mathbf{x}) = -\int p(\mathbf{x}) \log p(\mathbf{x})d\mathbf{x} \qquad (4.56)$$

In the case of a function described by several coordinates $\{\mathbf{x}_1, \mathbf{x}_2, \ldots, \mathbf{x}_n\}$, we can generalize this definition by introducing the multidimensional probability density function $p(\mathbf{x}_1, \mathbf{x}_2, \ldots, \mathbf{x}_n)$, and write

$$H(\mathbf{x}) = -\int \cdots \int p(\mathbf{x}_1, \mathbf{x}_2, \ldots, \mathbf{x}_n) \log p(\mathbf{x}_1, \mathbf{x}_2, \ldots, \mathbf{x}_n)d\mathbf{x}_1 d\mathbf{x}_2 \cdots d\mathbf{x}_n$$
$$(4.57)$$

which we abbreviate by writing

$$H(\mathbf{x}) = -\int p(\mathbf{x}) \log p(\mathbf{x})d\mathbf{x} \qquad (4.58)$$

The "argument" $\mathbf{x}$ in $H(\mathbf{x})$ is not an independent variable, but simply a label to remind us that $H(\mathbf{x})$ is calculated for the ensemble $\mathbf{x}$. Just as with discrete information sources, we can define the joint entropy between two continuous ensembles $\mathbf{x}$ and $\mathbf{y}$ as

$$H(\mathbf{x}, \mathbf{y}) = -\int \int p(\mathbf{x}, \mathbf{y}) \log p(\mathbf{x}, \mathbf{y})d\mathbf{x}d\mathbf{y} \qquad (4.59)$$

Similarly, conditional entropies can also be defined as

$$H(\mathbf{x}|\mathbf{y}) = -\int \int p(\mathbf{x}, \mathbf{y}) \log p(\mathbf{x}|\mathbf{y})d\mathbf{x}d\mathbf{y} \qquad (4.60)$$

$$H(\mathbf{y}|\mathbf{x}) = -\int \int p(\mathbf{x}, \mathbf{y}) \log p(\mathbf{y}|\mathbf{x})d\mathbf{x}d\mathbf{y} \qquad (4.61)$$

and the average mutual information is

$$I(\mathbf{x}, \mathbf{y}) = \int \int p(\mathbf{x}, \mathbf{y}) \log \left[\frac{p(\mathbf{x}, \mathbf{y})}{p(\mathbf{x})p(\mathbf{y})} \right] d\mathbf{x} d\mathbf{y} \qquad (4.62)$$

In particular, we have the following useful identities:

$$I(\mathbf{x}, \mathbf{y}) = H(\mathbf{x}) - H(\mathbf{x}|\mathbf{y}) = H(\mathbf{y}) - H(\mathbf{y}|\mathbf{x}) \qquad (4.63)$$

$$H(\mathbf{x}, \mathbf{y}) = H(\mathbf{x}) + H(\mathbf{y}|\mathbf{x}) = H(\mathbf{y}) + H(\mathbf{x}|\mathbf{y}) \qquad (4.64)$$

So far, there seems to be a direct correspondence between entropies calculated for discrete and continuous processes. There are some important differences, however. Consider, for instance, a uniformly distributed random variable:

$$p(\mathbf{x}) = a^{-1} \qquad 0 \le \mathbf{x} \le a$$

The entropy corresponding to this probability density is $\log a$, which is negative for $a < 1$ and singular as $a \to 0$. The various entropies associated with continuous variables are not necessarily positive or finite. This does not preclude entropy from being a useful concept for continuous ensembles.

As another illustrative example of singular behavior, consider the self-information for continuous ensembles as obtained by approaching the continuous case with a limiting operation. Consider, for example, the discrete random variable X taking values on the set $\{\mathbf{x}_1, \mathbf{x}_2, \ldots, \mathbf{x}_N\}$, where $\mathbf{x}_k = \mathbf{x}_{k-1} + \Delta$. Corresponding to these values of $\mathbf{x}$ are the probabilities $\{P_k; k = 1, \ldots, N\}$. The entropy for this set of probabilities is

$$H = -\sum_{k=1}^{N} P_k \log P_k \qquad (4.65)$$

and is also the average self-information.

By letting the size of Δ of the $\mathbf{x}$ intervals decrease and N increase in such a way as to leave the total length $L = N \Delta$ of the interval constant, the total probability becomes continuously distributed over the interval $[0, L]$, with density $p(\mathbf{x}) = P_k/\Delta$, where $\mathbf{x} = k\Delta$. With this limiting process, the entropy becomes

$$H = \lim_{\Delta \to 0, N \to \infty} -\sum_{k=1}^{N} p(k\Delta) \Delta \log[p(k\Delta)\Delta]$$

$$= \lim_{\Delta \to 0, N \to \infty} \sum_{k=1}^{N} p(k\Delta) \Delta \log p(k\Delta) - \lim_{\Delta \to 0, N \to \infty} \sum_{k=1}^{N} p(k\Delta) \Delta \log \Delta$$

$$= -\int p(\mathbf{x}) \log p(\mathbf{x}) d\mathbf{x} - \lim_{\Delta \to 0, N \to \infty} \sum_{k=1}^{N} p(k\Delta) \Delta \log \Delta \qquad (4.66)$$

The first term is simply the entropy of the continuous ensemble. The second term approaches the sum of an infinite number of terms, each of order $\Delta \log \Delta$. Such a sum must diverge from the following consideration. Consider the limit

$$\lim_{\Delta \to 0, N \to \infty} \sum_{k=1}^{N} p(k\Delta)\Delta = -\int_0^L p(x)\,dx = 1$$

For $\Delta < 1$, we have

$$|p(k\Delta)\Delta| < |p(k\Delta)\Delta \log \Delta|$$

For $\Delta \to 0$, the ratio of the right-hand side (RHS) term to the left-hand side (LHS) term approaches infinity. But the sum of an infinite number of terms like the LHS is known to converge to unity. Since each of the RHS terms becomes infinitely larger than the corresponding LHS term, the sum of an infinite number of terms like $p(k\Delta)\Delta \log \Delta$ is unbounded.

The reason for the singular behavior exhibited in the previous two examples is that the specification of an arbitrary number on the real line requires an infinite amount of information. The number of points on the line is an infinity of order $\aleph_1$ and implies that an infinite number of states is required to specify any point. One can approach the entropy of a continuous ensemble as the amount of information relative to the precision or resolution with which quantities are specified on the real line. In any case, singularities do not appear in calculations of channel capacities as these involve differences of entropies, where like singularities cancel out.

It is, of course, impossible to encode continuous sources exactly. Some approximation must be made to represent infinite information sources with a finite alphabet. This very interesting and practical problem is the subject of rate-distortion theory, which is discussed in Chapter 8.

4.2 CHANNEL CAPACITY

We have encountered several models for discrete information sources in Section 4.1. There information sources were viewed as ergodic stochastic processes that generate symbols according to some statistical rules. The information source was considered a closed system having no inputs and producing a stream of information symbols. Information is communicated by transmitting it over a communication channel. Being physical systems, communication channels impose certain limitations on the rate at which information can be transmitted. This section looks at communication channels and their capacity for carrying or storing information.

4.2.1 Characteristics of Channels

Communication channels are physical systems used to record or transmit information. Examples of communication channels abound. The air around us serves as a medium that supports the passage of sound waves, which we use for speech communication with people in our immediate vicinity. On a larger scale, the Earth and the ionosphere surrounding it form a waveguide for some radio waves. Light has been used for communications. A modern use of light employs fiber optics as a transmission channel. Communication is not an exercise limited to humans. Computers and other devices also exchange information. Information has been stored on a large number of media such as stone, wood, paper, punched holes in cards, etched grooves on vinyl disks, the magnetization of a thin layer of iron compounds, semiconductor devices, etc. The list is hardly complete, and probably gives no hint at what future technological advances will bring.

In view of this diversity, the study of communication would at first appear to require an intimate knowledge of a vast amount of technology. Furthermore, keeping abreast of modern developments in the field of communication technology itself seems to promise to occupy all of one's time. While it is true that the communication technologist can make an interesting career in developing devices for the storage and transmission of information, life is made simpler by recognizing that all communication channels share a fundamental property that is sufficient for understanding all that is necessary about them: *capacity*. Despite differences in their physical makeup, all communication channels are systems with a limited number of distinguishable physical states that can be used to label information. Different channels differ only in their information capacities.

This is the basic difference between the technologist's and the theorist's approaches to communication. The technologist is concerned with the physical properties of systems. One chief concern is to develop devices that store more information in a smaller volume (e.g., semiconductor chips) or that provide larger bandwidths for transmission (e.g., fiber optics). The theorist indiscriminately combines all of these systems as various physical manifestations of systems possessing a finite number of distinguishable states that provide capacity for information.

In this section, we shall encounter several models of communication channels. In each case, the relevant characteristic will be the information capacity, which is the amount of information that can be stored or transmitted for each use of the channel.

The very notion of a communication channel acknowledges the constraint that exists between the sender and the intended recipient of information. If the information source and destination were co-located in time and/or in space, information could (in principle) be handed from one to the other and that would complete the process. However, in all cases involving information transmission, an intermediate medium or channel is always present, and the physical limitations of that medium impose a fundamental limitation on the rate at which information can be transmitted without distortion.

Since communication channels are physical systems, they cannot react infinitely fast to stimuli. Because of inertia, physical systems have a finite reaction time to inputs and, consequently, have a finite bandwidth. All physical systems have a finite number of distinguishable states, and this imposes a limitation on their information storage capacity. Also, channels introduce transmission errors, which restrict the rate at which signals may be transmitted.

Two types of channels will be studied: discrete and continuous. For each channel use, the discrete channels are characterized by their number of distinguishable states as well as by the probability of transmission errors through the channel (state transition probabilities). Our study of continuous channels will be limited to the additive white Gaussian noise (AWGN) channel, which is a channel of finite bandwidth over which white noise with Gaussian statistics and with a specified power spectral density is added to the signal.

Quantities like the number of channel states, the state-transition probabilities, bandwidth, and noise level can be related to channel physical characteristics, although this is usually considered the province of the technologist. The communication theorist need only be concerned with the final channel mathematical specifications, as discussed here, and not with the physics behind it. Certain elements of physics, however, should be kept in mind, such as the role played by thermal noise, its statistics in signal space, and its relation to system bandwidth, as was presented in Chapter 3.

4.2.2 Discrete Memoryless Channel Capacity

The communication channel can be viewed as a restriction to the flow of information between a source and a destination. This limitation takes the form of a restriction in the rate at which information can be reliably transmitted on the channel. Although we can assume the properties of a channel to be known, its effect on the information stream is probabilistic in nature and, therefore, cannot be accounted for in a deterministic manner.

Consider a communication channel with input symbols chosen from the M-ary alphabet $\mathbf{x}:\{\mathbf{x}_1, \mathbf{x}_2, \ldots, \mathbf{x}_M\}$ and output symbols from the N-ary alphabet $\mathbf{y}:\{\mathbf{y}_1, \mathbf{y}_2, \ldots, \mathbf{y}_N\}$. We must, at this point, make two important notes. First, the input alphabet is not necessarily identical with the information source alphabet. The user-supplied information symbols are, in general, not in the same format as the symbols that are transmitted over the channel. We must, therefore, make an important distinction between information source symbols and channel symbols. Channel symbols can be derived from information source symbols by a process called coding, to be discussed later. For the purpose of the present section, we assume the channel input symbols $\mathbf{x}: \{\mathbf{x}_1, \mathbf{x}_2, \ldots, \mathbf{x}_M\}$ to be given.

The second important note is that, in general, $M \neq N$. The numbers of input and output symbols need not be the same, nor need they be chosen over the same alphabet. What characterizes a channel is the set of $M \cdot N$ conditional probabilities $P(\mathbf{y}_j | \mathbf{x}_i)$ of symbol $\mathbf{y}_j$ being received, given that $\mathbf{x}_i$ was transmitted. The $\mathbf{y}_j$ and $\mathbf{x}_i$ are, therefore, statistically correlated. According to Section 4.1.3, the average mutual information between $\mathbf{x}$ and $\mathbf{y}$ is given by

$$I(\mathbf{x}, \mathbf{y}) = \sum_{i,j} P(\mathbf{x}_i, \mathbf{y}_j) \log\left[\frac{P(\mathbf{x}_i, \mathbf{y}_j)}{P(\mathbf{x}_i)P(\mathbf{y}_j)}\right] \qquad (4.67)$$

Recall that the interpretation attached to $I(\mathbf{x}, \mathbf{y})$ is that it is the average information about the ensemble $\mathbf{x}$ provided by the ensemble $\mathbf{y}$, and vice versa. In other words, $I(\mathbf{x}, \mathbf{y})$ measures the average amount of information about the channel input symbols $\mathbf{x}$ provided by the output symbols $\mathbf{y}$.

Recall that the joint probability distribution $P(\mathbf{x}_i, \mathbf{y}_j)$ can be expressed in terms of the conditional probabilities, since

$$P(\mathbf{x}_i, \mathbf{y}_j) = P(\mathbf{y}_j | \mathbf{x}_i)P(\mathbf{x}_i) = P(\mathbf{x}_i | \mathbf{y}_j)P(\mathbf{y}_j)$$

The conditional probabilities characterizing the channel are assumed known, as are the input and output symbol probabilities $P(\mathbf{x}_i)$ and $P(\mathbf{y}_j)$, respectively. We note in particular that the first-order output symbol probabilities $P(\mathbf{y}_j)$ are completely determined by the first-order input probabilities $P(\mathbf{x}_i)$ and by the channel transition probabilities $P(\mathbf{y}_j|\mathbf{x}_i)$, since summing over the last equation gives

$$P(\mathbf{y}_j) = \sum_i P(\mathbf{x}_i, \mathbf{y}_j) = \sum_i P(\mathbf{y}_j|\mathbf{x}_i)P(\mathbf{x}_i)$$

The channel characteristics are usually not within the communication engineer's control, so that the conditional probabilities $P(\mathbf{y}_j|\mathbf{x}_i)$ are considered given properties of the channel around which the engineer must work. The last equation can be loosely likened to a statistical transfer function relating the first-order probabilities at either end of the channel in terms of channel probabilistic transfer characteristics. We can, therefore, view the input-symbol probabilities $P(\mathbf{x}_i)$ as free parameters that determine the output probabilities $P(\mathbf{y}_j)$ through the action of the transitions described by the conditional probabilities $P(\mathbf{y}_j|\mathbf{x}_i)$.

A channel consisting of M input symbols $\{\mathbf{x}_1, \mathbf{x}_2, \ldots \mathbf{x}_M\}$, N output symbols $\{\mathbf{y}_1, \mathbf{y}_2, \ldots, \mathbf{y}_N\}$, and with input-output transition probabilities completely specified by the first-order conditional probabilities $\{P(\mathbf{y}_j|\mathbf{x}_i); i = 1, 2, \ldots, M; j = 1, 2, \ldots, N\}$ is called a *discrete memoryless channel*.

$I(\mathbf{x}, \mathbf{y})$ is a functional of the input probabilities $P(\mathbf{x}_i)$. Different choices for $P(\mathbf{x}_i)$ result in different values for $I(\mathbf{x}, \mathbf{y})$. In particular, there must be at least one choice for $\{P(\mathbf{x}_i); i = 1, 2, \ldots, M\}$ for which $I(\mathbf{x}, \mathbf{y})$ is a maximum. This corresponds to a condition for which the $\{\mathbf{y}_j; j = 1, 2, \ldots, N\}$ provide as much information as is possible about the $\{\mathbf{x}_i; i = 1, 2, \ldots, M\}$ over the channel. The maximum value of $I(\mathbf{x}, \mathbf{y})$ is the information capacity of the channel and represents the maximum amount of information that can be accommodated by the channel.

The channel capacity C can be defined in terms of the variational problem of finding the input probabilities $\{P(\mathbf{x}_i); i = 1, 2, \ldots, M\}$ that maximize $I(\mathbf{x}, \mathbf{y})$ subject to the usual normalization constraints $\sum_i P(\mathbf{x}_i) = 1$ and $\sum_j P(\mathbf{y}_j) = 1$. Thus,

$$C = \max_{P(\mathbf{X})} I(\mathbf{x}, \mathbf{y}) \tag{4.68}$$

The following calculation of capacity is due to Shannon [Sh 49a]. Recall from Section 4.1.3 that

$$I(\mathbf{x}, \mathbf{y}) = H(\mathbf{y}) - H(\mathbf{y}|\mathbf{x})$$

$$= -\sum_j P(\mathbf{y}_j) \log P(\mathbf{y}_j) + \sum_{i,j} P(\mathbf{x}_i, \mathbf{y}_j) \log P(\mathbf{y}_j|\mathbf{x}_i)$$

but $P(\mathbf{y}_j) = \sum_k P(\mathbf{y}_j|\mathbf{x}_k)P(\mathbf{x}_k)$, so that

$$\begin{aligned} I(\mathbf{x}, \mathbf{y}) = &-\sum_{i,j} P(\mathbf{y}_j|\mathbf{x}_i)P(\mathbf{x}_i) \log \sum_k P(\mathbf{y}_j|\mathbf{x}_k)P(\mathbf{x}_k) \\ &+ \sum_{i,j} P(\mathbf{y}_j|\mathbf{x}_i)P(\mathbf{x}_i) \log P(y_j|\mathbf{x}_i) \end{aligned} \tag{4.69}$$

Note that Eq. (4.69) expresses $I(\mathbf{x}, \mathbf{y})$ entirely in terms of the transition probabilities $P(\mathbf{y}_j|\mathbf{x}_i)$ and the channel input-symbol probability distribution $P(\mathbf{x}_i)$. Looking for the probability distribution $P(\mathbf{x}_i)$ that maximizes $I(\mathbf{x}, \mathbf{y})$ subject to the normalization condition $\sum_i P(\mathbf{x}_i) = 1$ is a problem in the calculus of variations. The solution is easily found by using a Lagrange multiplier λ and considering the equivalent unconstrained variation of

$$J = -\sum_{i,j} P(\mathbf{y}_j|\mathbf{x}_i)P(\mathbf{x}_i) \log \sum_k P(\mathbf{y}_j|\mathbf{x}_k)P(\mathbf{x}_k)$$

$$+ \sum_{i,j} P(\mathbf{y}_j|\mathbf{x}_i)P(\mathbf{x}_i) \log P(\mathbf{y}_j|\mathbf{x}_i) - \lambda \sum_i P(\mathbf{x}_i) - \lambda$$

which leads to expressions of the form

$$\sum_j P(\mathbf{y}_j|\mathbf{x}_k)\left[\log P(\mathbf{y}_j|\mathbf{x}_k) - \log \sum_i P(\mathbf{y}_j|\mathbf{x}_i)P(\mathbf{x}_i)\right] = \lambda + 1$$

Multiplying through by $P(\mathbf{x}_k)$ and summing over k, there results

$$\lambda + 1 = -H(\mathbf{y}|\mathbf{x}) + H(\mathbf{y}) = I_{\max}(\mathbf{x}, \mathbf{y}) = C \qquad (4.70)$$

where C is the channel capacity, since $P(\mathbf{x}_k)$ is precisely the probability distribution that maximizes $I(\mathbf{x}, \mathbf{y})$. If the conditional probability $P(\mathbf{y}_j|\mathbf{x}_i)$ has an inverse $Q(\mathbf{x}_i|\mathbf{y}_j)$ defined by the relation

$$\sum_k P(\mathbf{y}_j|\mathbf{x}_k)Q(\mathbf{x}_k|\mathbf{y}_m) = \delta_{j,m} \qquad (4.71)$$

then we can solve for the prior probabilities $P(\mathbf{y}_j|\mathbf{x}_i)$ that achieve channel capacity. Multiplying Eq. (4.70) by $Q(\mathbf{x}_k|\mathbf{y}_m)$ and summing over k, we obtain

$$\sum_{j,k} P(\mathbf{y}_j|\mathbf{x}_k)Q(\mathbf{x}_k|\mathbf{y}_m) \log P(\mathbf{y}_j|\mathbf{x}_k) - \sum_{j,k} P(\mathbf{y}_j|\mathbf{x}_k)Q(\mathbf{x}_k|\mathbf{y}_m) \log \sum_i P(\mathbf{y}_j|\mathbf{x}_i)P(\mathbf{x}_i)$$

$$= C\sum_k Q(\mathbf{x}_k|\mathbf{y}_m)$$

and

$$\sum_{j,k} P(\mathbf{y}_j|\mathbf{x}_k)Q(\mathbf{x}_k|\mathbf{y}_m) \log P(\mathbf{y}_j|\mathbf{x}_k) - \log \sum_i P(\mathbf{y}_m|\mathbf{x}_i)P(\mathbf{x}_i) = C\sum_k Q(\mathbf{x}_k|\mathbf{y}_m)$$

We, therefore, have

$$\sum_i P(\mathbf{y}_m|\mathbf{x}_i)P(\mathbf{x}_i) = e^{\phi(m)^{\ln 2}}$$

where

$$\phi(m) = \sum_{j,k} P(\mathbf{y}_j|\mathbf{x}_k)Q(\mathbf{x}_k|\mathbf{y}_m) \log P(\mathbf{y}_j|\mathbf{x}_k) - C\sum_k Q(\mathbf{x}_k|\mathbf{y}_m) \qquad (4.72)$$

The factor of $\ln 2$ appears because "log" is the logarithm with respect to base 2. By multiplying through by $Q(\mathbf{x}_i|\mathbf{y}_m)$ and summing over m, there results

$$P(\mathbf{x}_i) = \sum_m Q(\mathbf{x}_i|\mathbf{y}_m)e^{\phi(m)\ln 2} \tag{4.73}$$

This is the input probability distribution that maximizes $H(\mathbf{x},\mathbf{y})$ and, therefore, that achieves channel capacity.

4.2.3 The Binary Symmetric Channel

The simplest model for a discrete channel is the binary symmetric channel (BSC). The BSC has identical input and output symbol alphabets, namely, the binary alphabet $\mathbf{x}$: $\{0, 1\}$ and $\mathbf{y}$: $\{0, 1\}$. The BSC is characterized by symmetrical transition probabilities for the probability that the symbol that is received is the same as the symbol that was transmitted. If the transition probability ($0 \rightarrow 1$ or, since the channel is symmetric, $1 \rightarrow 0$) is p, then

$$\text{Prob } \{\mathbf{y} = 0|\mathbf{x} = 0\} = q$$
$$\text{Prob } \{\mathbf{y} = 0|\mathbf{x} = 1\} = p$$
$$\text{Prob } \{\mathbf{y} = 1|\mathbf{x} = 0\} = p \tag{4.74}$$
$$\text{Prob } \{\mathbf{y} = 1|\mathbf{x} = 1\} = q$$

with $q = 1 - p$. A convenient graphical representation of the BSC channel transition properties is shown in Fig. 4-2.

We now derive the capacity for the binary symmetric channel. To do this, we could apply the general method presented in the previous section. Instead, we exploit the symmetry of the BSC and introduce a simpler way of calculating the capacity of discrete channels for which the crossover probabilities are equal, independent of channel symbol labels.

For the BSC, the probability of decoding the correct channel symbol is $q = 1 - p$ and the probability of making a decoding error is given by the crossover probability p. This is true for either of the channel symbols. We arbitrarily label the channel symbols with 0 and 1. We are looking for the input probabilities $P(0) = \text{Prob } (\mathbf{x}=0)$ and $P(1) = \text{Prob } (\mathbf{x} = 1) = 1 - P(0)$ that achieve channel capacity by maximizing $I(\mathbf{x},\mathbf{y})$.

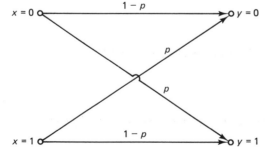

Figure 4-2. The binary symmetric channel.

We shall approach this task with a simple thought experiment. If we were to proceed by trial and error, we could select possible candidates for $P(0)$ and $P(1)$ and calculate the resulting $I(\mathbf{x}, \mathbf{y})$. Actually, the search space is single-dimensional since $P(1) = 1 - P(0)$. With each trial, we obtain a new value for $I(\mathbf{x}, \mathbf{y})$. Capacity is defined as the value for which $I(\mathbf{x}, \mathbf{y})$ is a maximum. This value is unique and corresponds to a unique input probability $P(0)$.

Now choose a particular value ξ for $P(0)$, and, consequently, $P(1) = 1 - \xi$. Label the resulting value of mutual information by $I(p, \xi)$; this reminds us that mutual information is a property of the input probabilities as well as of the channel crossover probabilities. Now consider the symmetrical situation obtained by setting $P(0) = 1 - \xi$ and $P(1) = \xi$. This results in a mutual information value of $I(p, 1 - \xi)$. If $I(p, \xi) \neq I(p, 1 - \xi)$, then either $I(p, \xi) > I(p, 1 - \xi)$ or $I(p, \xi) < I(p, 1 - \xi)$. But since the channel probabilities have not changed, all that was done was to interchange the labels 0 and 1, and this cannot result in a change of mutual information. We must, therefore, have the situation that $I(p, \xi) = I(p, 1 - \xi)$. The function $I(p, \xi)$ must, therefore, be an even function in ξ, with even symmetry about the value for which $\xi = 1 - \xi$, that value being $\xi = 1/2$.

It follows, therefore, that $I(p, \xi)$ either has a maximum or a minimum at $I(p, \xi = 1/2)$, and that this must be so for any value of p. In particular, it must be true for $p = 1$. For this case, the channel is transparent and the output probabilities are equal to the input probabilities, and we already know that equal probabilities $P(0) = P(1) = 1/2$ results in a maximum amount of information. We conclude, therefore, that $I(p, \xi)$ has a maximum at $\xi = 1/2$. For a symmetrical channel, capacity is achieved with equal input-symbol probabilities.

By substituting $P(0) = P(1) = 1/2$ and the appropriate channel transition probabilities in the expression for mutual information $I(\mathbf{x}, \mathbf{y})$, we obtain the following expression for the capacity of the binary symmetric channel:

$$C(p) = 1 + p \log p + (1 - p) \log (1 - p) \tag{4.75}$$

Note that this expression depends only on p. This is sometimes written as $C(p) = 1 - h(p)$, where $h(p) = -p \log p - (1 - p) \log(1 - p)$ is the binary entropy function for the probability pair $(p, 1 - p)$. The function $C(p)$ is plotted against p in Fig. 4-3. Note that $C(p)$ is an even function in p, with a minimum at $p = 1/2$.

4.2.4 The Discrete Memoryless Channel

The discrete memoryless channel (DMC) is one for which a number of output symbols are related to a (generally different) number of input symbols through channel symbol crossover probabilities. Figure 4-4 illustrates the configuration for the discrete memoryless channel. The channel crossover probabilities in the DMC are constants and do not depend on previous channel uses, hence, the qualifier "memoryless." The DMC is a generalization of the BSC, but without the symmetry of the latter.

The variational calculation of discrete channel capacity presented in Section 4.2.2 can be used to calculate the capacity of the discrete memoryless channel. There is a special case, however, for which the calculation is particularly simplified. Just as with the BSC, we can consider a special case of the DMC for which (1) there

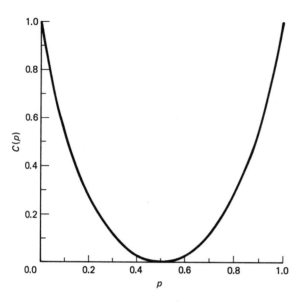

Figure 4-3. The capacity of the binary symmetric channel as a function of the channel parameter p. $C(p) = 1 + p \log p + (1 - p) \log(1 - p)$.

are equal numbers of input and output channel symbols, and (2) all of the probabilities of decoding the wrong channel symbols are equal. We call this channel the *symmetric DMC*.

By using arguments based on symmetry, just as we did for the binary symmetric channel, the input probability distribution that results in the highest value of the mutual information is the uniform distribution over input symbols. The symmetry imparted by the equal decoding error (crossover probabilities) is reflected in $I(\mathbf{x}, \mathbf{y})$ being an even function of the input probabilities under a permutation of the input symbols. The situation associated with equal input-symbol probabilities then corresponds to the maximum value of $I(\mathbf{x}, \mathbf{y})$. We emphasize that this is true only if the channel crossover probabilities are equal.

To calculate the capacity of the symmetric DMC with M channels, we write

$$I(\mathbf{x}, \mathbf{y}) = H(\mathbf{y}) - H(\mathbf{y}|\mathbf{x})$$

$$= -\sum_{j=1}^{m} P(\mathbf{y}_j) \log P(\mathbf{y}_j) + \sum_{i,j}^{m} P(\mathbf{y}_j|\mathbf{x}_i) P(\mathbf{x}_i) \log P(\mathbf{y}_j|\mathbf{x}_i)$$

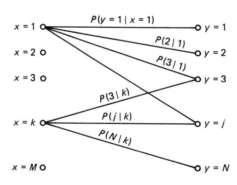

Figure 4-4. The discrete memoryless channel.

The first term is upper bounded by $\log m$ and achieves that bound when all input probabilities are equal, the condition required to achieve channel capacity. For the symmetric DMC, the conditional probabilities in the second term are independent of the index i, and so the double sum may be rewritten as two separate sums:

$$I(\mathbf{x}, \mathbf{y}) = \log m + \sum_i P(\mathbf{x}_i) \sum_j P(\mathbf{y}_j|\mathbf{x}_i) \log P(\mathbf{y}_j|\mathbf{x}_i)$$

$$= \log m + (1-p)\log(1-p) + p\log[p/(m-1)] \qquad (4.76)$$

$$= \log m - h(p) - p\log(m-1)$$

which is the capacity of the symmetric DMC.

4.2.5 The Additive White Gaussian Noise Channel

The additive white Gaussian noise (AWGN) channel is a very important model for the discussion of communication systems. The BSC and DMC, which have already been discussed, are discrete channels in that the input and output signals are members of finite alphabets of symbols. The additive white Gaussian noise channel, on the other hand, is associated with input and output signals that can assume a continuous range of values. In general, these values can be complex, although in this case, we can simply view the complex channel as two real channels in parallel. For each real channel, the input signal x ranges over $-\infty < x < \infty$ and the output variable y is defined by the additive relation

$$y = x + n \qquad (4.77)$$

where n is a zero-mean normal variable defined over the range $-\infty < x < \infty$.

Pierce [Pi 80] presents a very lucid, yet extremely simple, derivation of the AWGN channel capacity. The discussion centers around geometrical arguments. We shall present a similar approach here, but couched in the language of signal theory, as introduced in Chapters 2 and 3.

We consider signals that can be represented in a finite (m-) dimensional linear signal space. Such signals can be represented by their m projections onto the basis functions that span the space. The effect of the channel is to add a like amount of zero-mean noise at each of the coordinates, thus limiting the accuracy with which each signal projection can be measured. Quantities that differ by an amount that is (approximately) smaller than the noise standard deviation are indistinguishable. In this way, noise limits the number of signals that can be unambiguously discriminated.

Let us now discuss this quantitatively with signal-space concepts. We shall consider $m = 2TW$ dimensions in a linear signal space, where the effect of the channel is to

1. band limit all signals to a bandwidth W, and

2. add zero-mean noise with variance $\sigma_0^2 = N_0$ to each of the coordinates.

Let us first consider random signals from an ergodic source. These signals can be represented by their coordinates $\{x_k; k = 1, 2, \ldots, m = 2TW\}$. These signals have norms that measure the distance from the signal coordinates to the origin. The distance measure is the Euclidian metric. The total signal energy is simply the square of the Euclidian norm:

$$\mathscr{E} = \sum_{k=1}^{m} \epsilon_k = \sum_{k=1}^{m} x_k^2 \tag{4.78}$$

where $\epsilon_k = x_k^2$ is the energy in the kth coordinate.

For an ergodic signal source, the average energy ϵ_k per coordinate fluctuates, and the total energy $\mathscr{E} \approx m\epsilon$ to a good approximation, where ϵ is the average energy per signal coordinate. For large m, the total energy $\mathscr{E}$ exhibits very small fluctuations about a constant value.

For large m, most signals have the same total energy $\mathscr{E}$. Of all possible signals from an ergodic source, we can define two classes:

1. a class of probable signals having total energy very close to $\mathscr{E}$, and

2. a class of improbable signals whose total energy differs significantly from $\mathscr{E}$.

The law of large numbers ensures that the distinction between these two classes is more pronounced for large m. For such signals, we need only concentrate on the probable class whose total energy is $\mathscr{E} = m\epsilon$. In signal space, these signals lie very close to the surface of a hypersphere of radius $(m\epsilon)^{1/2}$. Note that in m-dimensional space, most of the volume of a hypersphere is concentrated near the surface.

The total energy of the signal-plus-noise combination is $m(\epsilon + N_0)$ and corresponds to points on the hypersphere of radius $[m(\epsilon + N_0)]^{1/2}$. The coordinates of signals in signal space are uncertain by an amount $(mN_0)^{1/2}$, the radius of the noise hypersphere corresponding to total noise energy mN_0. Signals differing by a Euclidian metric distance less than $(mN_0)^{1/2}$ are, therefore, indistinguishable. The total number of distinguishable signals having total energy $\mathscr{E}$ can, therefore, be found by partitioning signal-space volume in units of noise hypersphere volumes and by counting how many such noise hyperspheres completely fill the signal-plus-noise hypersphere corresponding to total energy $m(\epsilon + N_0)$. The total number Ω of distinguishable signal-plus-noise states is equal to the number of noise hyperspheres of radius $mN_0^{1/2}$ that completely fill the signal-plus-noise hypersphere of radius $[m(\epsilon + N_0)]^{1/2}$. This number is

$$\Omega = \left\{ \frac{[m(\epsilon + N_0)]^{1/2}}{(mN_0)^{1/2}} \right\}^m$$

$$= \left(\frac{\epsilon + N_0}{N_0} \right)^{m/2} = (1 + \epsilon/N_0)^{m/2} \tag{4.79}$$

The information content of the system is, therefore,

$$I = \log \Omega = \tfrac{1}{2} m \log(1 + \epsilon/N_0) \tag{4.80}$$

Since $\mathscr{E} = m\epsilon$, this can be written as

$$I = \tfrac{1}{2} m \log(1 + \mathscr{E}/mN_0) = \tfrac{1}{2} m \log(1 + 2\gamma/m) \tag{4.81}$$

where $\gamma = \frac{1}{2}\mathscr{E}/N_0$ is the energy-contrast ratio, a fundamental performance parameter for communication in AWGN that we shall encounter again in Chapter 6. Note that the discussion thus far has been very general. The only requirement has been that the noise spectrum must be white. The preceding discussion does not require Gaussian noise statistics.

Let us now study the behavior of I. As γ increases, the effect of the noise becomes less important and more signals of dimension n can be distinguished. This corresponds to being able to measure each coordinate component with increased precision. As $\gamma \to 0, I \to 0$ and no information can be conveyed through such waveforms over the AWGN channel.

The most interesting property of I is arrived at by letting m grow very large for a fixed γ.

$$I_\infty = \lim_{m \to \infty} 1/2m \log(1 + 2\gamma/m) = \gamma/\ln 2 \qquad (4.82)$$

This corresponds to considering the information content (or the capacity) of signals in infinite-dimensional space or signals represented by systems of infinite complexity in the presence of additive white noise. Note that the limiting process converges to some finite value of information content. If we now let I_∞ be one bit, then $\gamma_b = \ln 2$ is interpreted as being the smallest energy-contrast ratio required to convey one bit of information over the infinite-complexity additive white-noise channel.

This is a fundamental limit of information theory. The capacity of the additive white-noise channel increases as more degrees of freedom are made available for the representation of information, as long as the energy contrast ratio exceeds $\ln 2$. The best that can be done is to allocate an infinite number of degrees of freedom, for example, by allocating infinite bandwidth. However, even then, we must have $\gamma > \ln 2$ in order for capacity to be nonzero. The quantity $\gamma = \ln 2$ represents a fundamental signal-to-noise energy-contrast ratio limit for communication systems.

Let us now reinterpret the result just obtained for the capacity of the additive white-noise channel. Letting

$$n = 2TW \qquad (4.83)$$

$$S = \text{signal power} = \mathscr{E}/T \qquad (4.84)$$

$$N = \text{noise power} = 2N_0W \qquad (4.85)$$

we have, for the information content in bits for a T-second segment of signal,

$$I = TW \log(1 + S/N) \qquad (4.86)$$

Dividing through by T, we obtain the capacity of the additive white-noise channel in bits per second in terms of the channel bandwidth and signal-to-noise power ratio:

$$C = W \log(1 + S/N) \qquad (4.87)$$

It should be noted that the channel capacity represents an upper bound to the rate at which information can be transmitted. Practically realizable information rates usually fall below channel capacity.

Note from Eq. (4.87) that the channel capacity increases without bound as S/N (or, equivalently, γ) becomes larger. This corresponds to increased precision in measuring a signal in noise. The number of distinguishable signals increases without bound as the ratio of signal-to-noise norms increases.

Equation (4.87) also includes dependence on bandwidth. This is a special case of Eq. (4.81), where information capacity is shown to be a function of the number m of available signal coordinates. How does channel capacity increase with bandwidth? Letting $N = 2N_0 W$ in Eq. (4.87), we obtain

$$C = W \log\left(1 + \frac{S}{2N_0 W}\right) \tag{4.88}$$

Taking the limit of Eq. (4.116) as $W \to \infty$, we obtain

$$C_\infty = \frac{S}{2N_0 \ln 2} \tag{4.89}$$

bits per second. This is called the *infinite-bandwidth channel capacity*. As the bandwidth increases without bound, the channel capacity approaches the finite limit C_∞ given by Eq. (4.89). This result represents a fundamental limit for signaling over the channel and corresponds to using waveforms of infinite complexity for signaling. Any finite signaling scheme achieves a smaller capacity than C_∞ by using a limited number of available signaling degrees of freedom.

Note that with $S = \mathscr{E}/T$, Eq. (4.89) becomes

$$C_\infty = \frac{\gamma}{T \ln 2} \tag{4.90}$$

bits per second or, equivalently,

$$\gamma = (T C_\infty) \ln 2 = I_\infty \ln 2 \tag{4.91}$$

where

$$\gamma = \gamma_b = \ln 2 \tag{4.92}$$

for $I_\infty = 1$ bit, as previously discussed.

Note that Eqs. (4.82) and (4.89) are really similar in result, with Eq. (4.82) being the more general of the two. Similarly, Eq. (4.81) is a more general statement of Eq. (4.87). The number of signal coordinates is a function of both signal duration and bandwidth. However, Eqs. (4.87) and (4.89) are encountered more often in the engineering literature.

We now turn to a more formal derivation of the AWGN channel capacity. Shannon [Sh 49a] elegantly introduces the capacity of the AWGN channel by directly considering the channel information-rate limitation due to the addition of noise that is statistically independent of the signal.

One of the fundamental conceptual breakthroughs introduced by Shannon is the realization that communication involves situations where both the message and the noise are members of separate statistical ensembles. We shall consider a channel output ensemble $\mathbf{y}$ as being produced by the sum of the statistically independent channel input $\mathbf{x}$ and noise $\mathbf{n}$ ensembles:

$$\mathbf{y} = \mathbf{x} + \mathbf{n} \tag{4.93}$$

Let the channel input-probability density be $p_x(x)$ and the noise probability density be $p_n(n)$. Since $\mathbf{y} = \mathbf{x} + \mathbf{n}$, the conditional probability density of the variable $\mathbf{y}$ assuming a value y at the channel output given that $\mathbf{x}$ assumes the value x at the input is given by

$$p_{y|x}(y|x) = p_n(n) = p_n(y - x) \tag{4.94}$$

The corresponding conditional entropy is given by

$$
\begin{aligned}
H(\mathbf{y}|\mathbf{x}) &= -\int\int p_{x,y}(x,y) \log p_{y|x}(y|x) \, dx \, dy \\
&= -\int\int p_{y|x}(y|x) p_x(x) \log p_{y|x}(y|x) \, dx \, dy \\
&= -\int p_x(x) \, dx \int p_{y|x}(y|x) \log p_{y|x}(y|x) \, dy \\
&= H(\mathbf{n})
\end{aligned}
\tag{4.95}
$$

The average mutual information between channel input and output is, therefore,

$$I(\mathbf{x}, \mathbf{y}) = H(\mathbf{y}) - H(\mathbf{y}|\mathbf{x}) = H(\mathbf{y}) - H(\mathbf{n}) \tag{4.96}$$

and is equal to the rate of information flow through the channel. The information rate through the channel is simply the difference between two entropies: the entropy of the output ensemble minus the entropy of the noise ensemble. The capacity of the channel is the maximum value of $I(\mathbf{x}, \mathbf{y})$. We have, therefore,

$$C = \max_{p(\mathbf{x})} H(\mathbf{y}) - H(\mathbf{n}) \tag{4.97}$$

No difficulty results from integrating over continuous densities because we eventually use the difference between such integrals. This result presents us with a particularly simple way of calculating the capacity of the AWGN channel. We first note that since the processes $\mathbf{y}$ and $\mathbf{n}$ are statistically independent, we merely need to maximize $H(\mathbf{y})$ over the possible input signal ensembles, subject to a constant average-energy constraint. For a received (i.e., channel output) signal with average power $S + N$, where S is the information-bearing signal, and N is the noise power, we need to find the largest entropy $H(\mathbf{y})$ consistent with the average power $S + N$. The required signal ensemble is a Gaussian ensemble of average power S (see Probs. 4.7 and 4.8). The corresponding entropy for the channel output, in bits per second, is

$$H(\mathbf{y}) = W \log[2\pi e(S + N)] \tag{4.98}$$

Similarly, the noise ensemble entropy is

$$H(\mathbf{n}) = W \log(2\pi e N) \tag{4.99}$$

The channel capacity becomes, therefore,

$$C = H(\mathbf{y}) - H(\mathbf{n}) = W \log(1 + S/N) \tag{4.100}$$

This equation is known as the *Shannon-Hartley capacity formula*.

EXAMPLE

Telephones have a bandwidth of roughly 3 kHz and a signal-to-noise ratio of approximately 30 dB. The maximum data rate that such a signal can support is, therefore,

$$C = 3000 \log (1 + 1000) = 29.9 \text{ kbps}$$

Several comments are in order. First, the bandwidth and signal-to-noise ratio are approximate. There are several ways of defining bandwidth, and these different definitions result in different numbers for channel capacity. The Shannon-Hartley capacity formula applies to a fully utilized channel bandwidth, implying a spectrally flat signal.

If the signal spectrum or system spectral response is not flat, the equivalent noise bandwidth can be used. The *equivalent noise bandwidth* is the bandwidth of a hypothetical system that (1) passes as much white-noise power and (2) has the same zero-frequency (DC) response as the system under study. Thus, a linear system with impulse response $h(t)$ having a Fourier transform (transfer function) $H(\nu)$ and spectral power-transfer characteristic $G(\nu) = H^*(\nu)H(\nu)$ has a noise equivalent bandwidth given by

$$W_{eq} = \frac{1}{G(0)} \int_{-\infty}^{\infty} G(\nu)d\nu$$

The signal-to-noise ratio in the previous example was also an approximation. In real systems, it can vary from one telephone to another and can be nonstationary. One should be aware of these effects in using the Shannon-Hartley formula to bound the capacity of a system. In many cases, the result will be approximate because of the approximate nature of the data used in the formula.

We now consider an example involving deep-space communication and the associated channel capacity.

EXAMPLE

The use of deep-space probes to explore our solar system involves a radio communication link from the probe back to Earth. The amount of data that can be sent back is limited by channel capacity. It is, therefore, very important to be able to estimate this capacity. To do so, we must first discuss some relevant aspects of deep-space communication, namely, those related to noise level and bandwidth.

The noise encountered in deep-space communication applications is thermal in origin and has Gaussian statistics. There are several sources for this noise: the 3 K background radiation level left over from the "Big Bang," thermal noise in the receiving circuitry, and receiving antenna side-lobe contamination from undesired sources. Careful design and cryogenic receiver front ends can reduce much of this noise, but some always remains, and it is customary to lump all residual input noise into a *system* or *antenna temperature*.

The concept of system or antenna temperature involves a fictitious source of noise applied at the receiver input. All of the noise applied to the input is assumed to be produced by a resistor whose resistance is equal to the receiver input impedance and whose temperature is of such a magnitude as to account for the observed noise level. Through careful design and the use of cryogenic front-end receivers, the antenna temperature can be considerably lower than the ambient temperature.

The bandwidth available for deep-space communication is typically much greater than that used by systems that have been launched. The deep, space channel is not band-limited. We are, therefore, justified in using the infinite-bandwidth capacity

$$C_\infty = \lim_{W \to \infty} W \log(1 + S/N) = \frac{S}{k_B \theta \ln 2}$$

where S is the received power, $k_B = 1.23 \times 10^{-23}$ J/K is Boltzmann's constant, and θ is the receiving antenna temperature.

The received power is simply the transmitted power, augmented by the transmitting- and receiving-antenna gains and attenuated by the inverse square space losses. These effects are succinctly expressed in Friis' formula:

$$\text{received power} = \text{transmitted power} \times \frac{A_R A_T}{(\lambda L)^2}$$

where A_T and A_R are the transmitting- and receiving- antenna areas, respectively, λ is the wavelength, and L is the distance separating the transmitter from the receiver.

The deep-space communication problem we consider here is the Voyager probe, which was launched in 1977 on a journey through the solar system and scheduled to make encounters with several of the outer planets. Voyager's transmitter outputs 18.2 watts at X band ($\lambda = 0.036$ m) into a directional antenna 3.6 m in diameter. The earthbound receiving link consists of a directional antenna 64 m in diameter (the Parkes radio astronomy antenna operated by CSIRO in Australia) and a receiving system for which the antenna temperature is 30 K. At the occasion of its encounter with the planet Uranus, Voyager was 3.2×10^{12} m away from home.

Several factors conspire to reduce a system's capacity below that given by this primitive analysis. Antenna efficiency, pointing accuracy losses (which can be significant for higher-gain antennas at small wavelengths), and factors adversely affecting the system temperature, such as the presence of the sun or other radiators in antenna side lobes, all contribute to a reduction of system capacity. When these can be calculated or measured, a refined estimate of capacity can result. We presently estimate these losses to amount to 5 dB, so we shall consider the received power to be reduced to 32 percent of the figure calculated from Friis' formula.

With these considerations, the channel capacity turns out to be about 56 kbps.

4.3 SOURCE CODING

In this section, we address the problem of representing the information issuing from a source with the symbols from a signaling alphabet. We shall consider the problem of encoding so as to use the shortest possible average symbol length. The motivation for this is to use as little of the transmission channel resources (time, bandwidth, energy) as possible.

4.3.1 Source Entropy and Coding

In the preceding sections of this chapter, we have been studying information and its measure in the abstract sense. We must now face the task of representing this information with a set of signaling symbols. Coding an information source consists in assigning labels for the messages issuing from that source. Efficient coding results in using, on the average, the shortest possible labels. The study of the problem of coding begins with the study of the statistical properties of messages from an ergodic information source.

In Section 4.1.2, we calculated the information content of a typical message composed from the symbols $\{\mathbf{x}_1, \mathbf{x}_2, \ldots, \mathbf{x}_M\}$, with corresponding probabilities $\{p_k = P(\mathbf{x}_k); k = 1, 2, \ldots, M\}$. These messages were composed of n_1 symbols $\mathbf{x}_1$, n_2 symbols $\mathbf{x}_2$, and so on, and in any order such that the total number of symbols was $n = n_1 + n_2 + \ldots + n_M$. The information content was calculated by evaluating the logarithm of the total number Ω of such messages, where it was found that

$$\log \Omega = -n \sum_{k=1}^{M} p_k \log p_k = nH \tag{4.101}$$

where H is the entropy per symbol. Let us now consider the same situation, but from a slightly different approach. If the messages are very long, then there will be, with high probability, very close to $n_k = np_k$ occurrences of the symbol $\mathbf{x}_k$ in the message. The message itself will occur with probability

$$p = \prod_{k=1}^{M} p_k^{n_k} = \prod_{k=1}^{M} p_k^{p_k n}$$

where

$$\log p = n \sum_{k=1}^{M} p_k \log p_k$$

These results suggest that

$$-\log p = nH$$

Since the logarithmic base is 2, this expression is equivalent to

$$p = 2^{-nH} \tag{4.102}$$

which is the constant probability for the majority of messages. Therefore, there are approximately

$$\Omega = 2^{nH} \tag{4.103}$$

such equiprobable messages. We shall prove these results more rigorously in a moment. Let us first comment on what has just been said. First, we note that the entropy H is bounded by

$$H \leq \log M \tag{4.104}$$

which corresponds to the case of all M symbols being equiprobable. The maximum total number of messages is then simply the sum of multinomial coefficients:

$$\Omega_{\text{max}} = \sum_{n_1=1}^{M} \sum_{n_2=1}^{M} \cdots \sum_{n_M=1}^{M} \binom{n}{n_1 \, n_2 \ldots n_M} = M^n$$

We have, therefore,

$$\Omega = 2^{nH} \leq 2^{n \log M} = \Omega_{\text{max}} \tag{4.105}$$

The implication of these results is that $\Omega = \Omega_{\text{max}}$ only if the symbols themselves are equiprobable. In all other cases, there will be fewer probable messages, even though all symbols are randomly used in their composition. Because these symbols occur with unequal probabilities, we can partition the set of Ω_{max} total possible messages into two distinct categories. In one category, we have $\Omega = 2^{nH}$ probable messages, occurring with equal probability $p = 2^{-nH}$. In the other category are the remaining $\Omega_{\text{max}} - \Omega$ improbable messages, which occur with vanishingly small probability as n becomes large. As the length n of these messages becomes very long, the category of $\Omega = 2^{nH}$ probable messages includes practically all the messages that ever occur and messages from the improbable category are almost never produced by the source. We, therefore, need only encode these $\Omega = 2^{nH}$ probable messages and can safely ignore the rest. That is, we assign labels only to the most probable messages, each of which occurs with the same probability. There will, of course, be $\Omega_{\text{max}} - \Omega$ messages for which no labels are assigned, and failure to transmit these will cause a communication error. But the probability of such an event can be made as small as desired by encoding over long ($n \gg 1$) sequences of source symbols.

Let us now justify these statements. We limit our discussion to ergodic information sources. At this point, we must use the law of large numbers. There are actually two statements of this law, known as the "weak" law of large numbers and the "strong" law of large numbers. We present a statement of both and refer the interested reader to Chapter 3 and [Fe 68] for proofs and more detailed mathematical discussions.

The weak law of large numbers states that if we consider a sequence $\{X_1, X_2, \ldots, X_q\}$ of independent random variables having a common probability distribution, then the probability that the arithmetic average of a large number of such random variables differs from the expectation value calculated from the distribution can be made as small as one desires by including more terms in the average.

This can be stated more compactly as

$$\lim_{q \to \infty} \text{Prob } \{|q^{-1}(X_1 + X_2 + \cdots + X_q) - \mu| > \epsilon\} = 0$$

where $\mu = E(X)$ is the expectation value of the random variable X, and ϵ is any positive quantity, however small. As q becomes very large, not only does the average approach μ, but the probability distribution of the average becomes more and more concentrated about μ in such a way that the probability that the average differs from μ by an arbitrarily small amount (viz., ϵ) approaches zero. When these conditions are satisfied, we say that the random variables X_k obey the weak law of large numbers.

The weak law of large numbers makes a global statement about $q^{-1}(X_1 + X_2 + \cdots + X_q)$ converging to μ in probability as $q \to \infty$, but allows for the possibility that the convergence may not be uniform. The only thing the weak law of large numbers guarantees is that $q^{-1}(X_1 + X_2 + \cdots + X_q)$ equals μ only when an infinite number of terms are included in the average.

A more restrictive result is made by the strong law of large numbers. We say that the random variables X_k obey the strong law of large numbers if for every pair of positive quantities $\epsilon > 0$ and $\delta > 0$, there exists a number s such that for every $s > 0$, we have

$$\text{Prob } \{|q^{-1}(X_1 + X_2 + \cdots + X_q)| - \mu > \epsilon\} < \delta$$

for $q = r, r + 1, r + 2, \ldots, r + s$. Convergence is, therefore, assured for any run of s averages, however large s may be and however small ϵ and δ.

We now examine one of the fundamental theorems of information theory. We have already seen examples of this so that the theorem should not be a surprise at this time.

Theorem. [Sh 49a] For any $\epsilon > 0$ and $\delta > 0$, there exists a number n_0 for which sequences of any length $n \geq n_0$ fall into two classes:

1. a set all of whose members have probabilities satisfying the inequality

$$|n^{-1} \log p^{-1} - H| < \delta$$

where

$$H = -\sum_k p_k \log p_k \tag{4.106}$$

and

2. the remaining sequences, whose total probability is less than ϵ.

What this theorem implies is that as n becomes very large, all of the likely messages have nearly the same probability, given by $p = 2^{-nH}$ and that all messages for which this is not true are members of a set of total probability ϵ, which can be made as small as one desires by taking n_0 to be sufficiently large.

Consider a discrete ergodic Markov (for generality) information source with state probabilities p_k and state-transition probabilities $P(j|k)$. For a very large number n of state transitions, the number n_j of occurrences of the jth state lies with high probability $(1 - \epsilon)$, according to the law of large numbers, within $\pm \delta n$ of the quantity $n \sum_k P(j|k)p_k$. That is,

$$\text{Prob } \{|n_j - n \sum_k P(j|k)p_k| > \delta n\} < \epsilon$$

so that probable sequences occur with probability

$$p = \prod_{j,k} [P(j|k)]^{[P(j|k)p_k \pm \delta]n}$$

Taking the logarithm of this expression, we obtain

$$\log p = \sum_{j,k} [P(j|k)p_k \pm \delta]n \log P(j|k)$$

$$= n \sum_{j,k} P(j,k) \log P(j|k) \pm \delta n \sum_{j,k} \log P(j|k)$$

The first term is recognized as $-n$ times the entropy of the Markov source. The second term is a quantity n that can be made as small as desired by making δ small. We have, therefore,

$$|n^{-1} \log p^{-1} - H| < \eta$$

and the theorem is proved.

What we have shown is that out of the set of all possible messages, there is a smaller set of probable messages and a set of improbable messages with a probability measure that can be made as small as one desires. The probable message set contains all of the information that has to be coded, the information content being given by the logarithm of the total number of probable messages 2^{nH}. We are now ready to consider the task of encoding these messages.

4.3.2 The Average Code Length

The encoding of messages consists in assigning unique labels (code words) to each of the possible messages. In the present context, the word "message" is used in its most general sense and can be taken to mean individual source symbols or any extension of the source alphabet. If encoding is to be done in a practical way, then there are additional constraints that must be considered. Practical encoding means parsimony, economically motivated by the lowest utilization rate for transmission resources such as time, bandwidth, and energy. This will be reflected in our endeavors as favoring coding schemes requiring code words of the smallest average length.

The process of encoding is one of assigning labels, or symbols, to the outputs of an information source. We must, therefore, distinguish between the source symbols taking values over the set S of the source symbol alphabet $\{s_1, s_2, \ldots, s_q\}$ and the coding symbols taking values over the set C of the code alphabet $\{\alpha_1, \alpha_2, \ldots, \alpha_r\}$. We shall deal extensively with block codes, which are codes that map each of the source alphabet symbols into a sequence of the code symbols. In general, we shall speak of coding as assigning to each of the source symbols s_k a code word consisting of a sequence of symbols from the coding alphabet. Thus, in general, a code word is an n-tuple of the form $c_k = \alpha_{k1}\alpha_{k2} \ldots \alpha_{kn}$, where each of the α is from the code alphabet $\{\alpha_1, \alpha_2, \ldots, \alpha_r\}$.

An important concept is that of uniquely decodable codes. This follows naturally from the necessity of such mappings being one to one and onto. A code is said to be *uniquely decodable* if the code words corresponding to each of its extensions are distinct. If code words were all of the same length, unique decodability would be the only required property of codes. However, we also want to consider code words of unequal length, since we suspect that their use will lead to efficient coding, for example, by assigning the shortest code words to the most frequently occurring source symbols.

Consideration of code words having unequal lengths forces an additional restriction on their structure. If the code words have unequal lengths, there has to be a system to delineate code-word boundaries, a problem that does not arise with code words of equal lengths. That system has to be part of the code itself. In other words, the code must supply labels for the source symbols and also contain within its structure the property of unambiguously indicating when one code word ends and another starts. This serves to introduce the concept of an *instantaneous code*.

EXAMPLE

Consider the following two codes, from the binary coding alphabet, for the source symbols s_1, s_2, s_3, and s_4:

Source	First Code	Second Code
s_1	00	0
s_2	01	01
s_3	10	010
s_4	11	110

Each of these codes has distinct code words. If code words of equal length were desired, the first code, which is a simple binary coding of the source alphabet, would suffice. That code would be uniquely decodable since the code-word boundaries are fixed and the code words are distinct.

If, however, $P(s_1) > P(s_2) > P(s_3) > P(s_4)$ and we wished to exploit this property, then it would make sense to use code words of unequal lengths and to assign the shortest code words to the most frequent source symbols. On the average, this results in shorter messages. The second code shown in this example is an attempt at this. Note, however, that this does not result in a uniquely decodable sequence. For example, the coded sequence **010** could either be decoded as s_3 or as s_2s_1.

A moment's reflection reveals where the problem is: the first two symbols of s_3 are identical with the code word for s_2. In other words, symbol s_2 is a prefix for another symbol, namely, s_3. Similarly, the code word assigned to $s_1(\mathbf{0})$ is a prefix for the code words **01** and **010**.

It is clear that we must avoid the situation of a code word being a prefix for another code word in order to avoid the sort of decoding ambiguity discussed in the example. Codes with the property that no code word is a prefix to another code word are called *instantaneous codes*. The reason for this name is that an instantaneous code word can be uniquely decoded as soon as all of its symbols have been received.

A useful device for visualizing the decoding of instantaneous codes is a decoding tree, where the path through the tree is determined by the successively received code-word symbols. Each path ultimately leads to a unique code word, at which point the decoding of the current symbol is complete. Since no code word is the prefix to another, the path to any code word is unique.

EXAMPLE

Consider the following instantaneous code, from the binary coding alphabet, for the source symbols s_1, s_2, s_3, and s_4:

Source	Code Words
s_1	**0**
s_2	**10**
s_3	**110**
s_4	**111**

Note that no code word in this code is a prefix for another. These code words, therefore, describe an instantaneous code. The symbol **0** terminating the first three code words serves as a marker for the end of these code words. The last code word needs no marker since it is the only one consisting of a succession of three consecutive **1** symbols. Such codes are called *comma codes*, since the special character **0** serves as a delimiter between code words. This code consists of one symbol (**0**) of length 1, one symbol (**10**) of length 2, and two symbols (**110**, **111**) of length 3. This code may be decoded with the help of the decoding tree shown in Fig. 4-5. In fact, the existence of such a decoding tree is a necessary and sufficient condition for the code to be instantaneously decodable.

The essential requirement of unique decodability for code words of unequal lengths imposes constraints on the structures of these codes. Specifically, the number of code words in a code and the code-word lengths must satisfy a constraining relation known as Kraft's inequality in order for an instantaneous code with those code-word lengths to exist. Kraft's inequality states that a necessary and sufficient condition for the existence of an instantaneous code having code words of lengths $\lambda_1, \lambda_2, \ldots, \lambda_q$ is that

$$\xi = \sum_{k=1}^{q} r^{-\lambda_k} \leq 1 \tag{4.107}$$

where r is the number (radix) of symbols comprising the code alphabet.

EXAMPLE

In the previous example, the coding alphabet was binary, so that $r = 2$ and $q = 4$. Furthermore, the code-word lengths were $\lambda_1 = 1$, $\lambda_2 = 3$, $\lambda_3 = 3$, and $\lambda_4 = 3$.

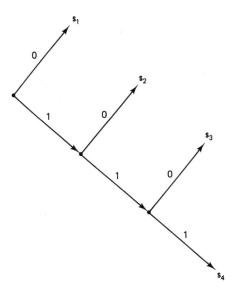

Figure 4-5.   Decoding tree for an
instantaneous code.

This leads to

$$\xi = \sum_{k=1}^{4} r^{-\lambda_k} = 2^{-1} + 2^{-2} + 2^{-3} + 2^{-3} = 1$$

Kraft's inequality guarantees that there is an instantaneously decodable code with radix 2 having this code-word length distribution.

Note that Kraft's inequality says nothing about a particular code being instantaneous or not. It only makes a statement about the possibility of the existence of some instantaneous code with a given radix and code-word length distribution.

Hamming [Ha 83a] gives an elegant proof of Kraft's inequality based on the decoding tree. The proof is based on mathematical induction. For simplicity, consider a radix $r = 2$. The inequality is trivially true for code words of length 1 since $2^{-1} = \frac{1}{2} < 1$ for one symbol and $2^{-1} + 2^{-1} = \frac{1}{2} + \frac{1}{2} = 1$ for two symbols. Next, assume that the theorem is true for code words of length less than n. This means that by hypothesis, the inequality is true for trees of length less than n. We must prove that this is also true for trees of length n.

The relevant situation is depicted in Fig. 4-6. The first bifurcation in the tree of length n leads to two subtrees with respective Kraft sums ξ_1 and ξ_2. By hypothesis, these subtrees satisfy Kraft's inequality, so that we have $\xi_1 \le 1$ and $\xi_2 \le 1$. The Kraft sum ξ associated with the tree of length n is simply the sum of ξ_1 and ξ_2, each multiplied by $\frac{1}{2}$, since all code-word lengths λ_k in a subtree must be increased by one unit when they are joined to form the tree of length n. We have, therefore,

$$\xi = \tfrac{1}{2}\xi_1 + \tfrac{1}{2}\xi_2 \le 1$$

and the theorem is proved. This theorem is easily generalized to arbitrary radix r by considering r branches at each tree node.

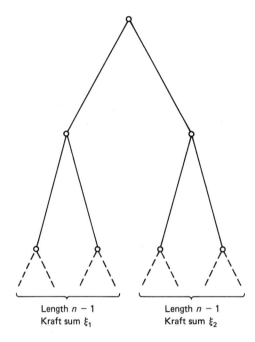

Length $n - 1$ Length $n - 1$ **Figure 4-6.**   Decoding tree of length n
Kraft sum ξ_1 Kraft sum ξ_2 used in the proof of Kraft's inequality.

The Kraft inequality is a theorem that applies to instantaneous codes. Recall that these codes are a special case of uniquely decodable codes. It turns out that the same inequality also generally applies to uniquely decodable codes. This more general theorem is called McMillan's inequality. Since we can construct a uniquely decodable code (namely, an instantaneous code) of radix r and code-word lengths $\lambda_1, \lambda_2, \ldots, \lambda_q$, the sufficiency part of McMillan's theorem is proven. For the necessity part, consider the expression ξ^n, where ξ is the Kraft sum. When raised to the nth power, the Kraft sum becomes a sum of various powers of r^{-1}.

The lowest possible power is simply n and corresponds to $\lambda_1 = 1$. The highest power is $n\lambda_{\max}$, where $\lambda_{\max}$ is the largest code-word length. We can, therefore, write ξ^n in the form

$$\xi^n = \sum_{k=n}^{n\lambda_{max}} N_k r^{-k}$$

where N_k is the number of code words of length k. For the code to be uniquely decodable, there can be at most r^k code words of length r, and, therefore, $N_k \leq r^k$. Consequently,

$$\xi^n \leq \sum_{k=n}^{n\lambda_{max}} 1 = 1 + n(\lambda_{max} - 1) < n\lambda_{max}$$

Since this must be true for any n however large, we must have $\xi < 1$, and the theorem is proved.

With the help of the Kraft inequality, we can find a relationship between the average code length and the entropy of an information source. Consider an instantaneous code for which the Kraft inequality must necessarily hold:

$$\xi = \sum_{k=1}^{q} r^{-\lambda_k} \leq 1$$

Now consider the set of quantities $Q_i = \xi^{-1} r^{-\lambda_i}, i = 1, 2, \ldots, q$. These quantities behave just like probabilities, since $0 \leq Q_i \leq 1$ and $\sum_i Q_i = 1$. We now associate each of the q code words with an information-source symbol, these symbols having probabilities $\{p_k; k = 1, 2, \ldots, q\}$. The quantities Q_i and p_k must satisfy the fundamental inequality

$$\sum_{k=1}^{q} p_k \log (Q_k/p_k) \leq 0$$

Expanding the logarithm, we have

$$\sum_{k=1}^{q} p_k \log Q_k - \sum_{k=1}^{q} p_k \log p_k \leq 0$$

The second term is simply the source entropy H. The first term can be computed as follows:

$$\sum_{k=1}^{q} p_k \log Q_k = -\sum_{k=1}^{q} p_k \log \xi - \sum_{k=1}^{q} p_k \log r^{\lambda_k}$$

$$= -\log \xi - \log r \sum_{k=1}^{q} p_k \lambda_k$$

$$= -\log \xi - L \log r$$

where $L = \sum_k p_k \lambda_k$ is the average code length. The fundamental inequality, therefore, becomes

$$-\log \xi - L \log r + H \leq 0$$

or $H \leq L \log r$, since $\xi \leq 1$. For an instantaneous code, the source entropy, therefore, provides a lower bound on the average code length.

4.3.3 Shannon's Source-Coding Theorem

Let us first consider encoding a zero-memory source with symbol $S : \{x_1, x_2, \ldots, x_M\}$ having probabilities $\{p_k = P(x_k); k = 1, 2, \ldots, M\}$. Let symbol x_k have a length λ_k, which we take to be some integer. Since $-\log_r p_k$ is the information in symbol x_k, we can consider assigning coding symbols on the basis of their lengths such that

$$-\log_r p_k \leq \lambda \leq -\log_r p_k + 1$$

This approach has the advantage of pairing infrequent symbols with long code words, thus favoring shorter code lengths, on the average. Note that we emphasize that the logarithmic base is the code radix. It is easy to show that this approach is consistent with instantaneous codes. Raising r to powers given by both sides of the inequality $-\log_r p_k \leq \lambda_k$ leads to

$$p_k \geq r^{-\lambda_k}$$

which can be summed over all k to give Kraft's inequality. If we now multiply each term in the inequality $-\log_r p_k \leq \lambda_k - \log_r p_k + 1$ by p_k and sum over all k, we obtain

$$H(S) \leq H(S) + 1 \qquad (4.108)$$

where L is the average code-word length:

$$L = \sum_{k=1}^{M} \lambda_k p_k \qquad (4.109)$$

The implication of this result is that there exists an instantaneous code whose average code word length is bounded by $H(S)$ and $H(S) + 1$. In other words, there is a code whose average length is at most equal to one unit more than the source entropy. This in itself is an interesting result, but we soon shall derive an even stronger statement.

Consider now the nth extension $S^{(n)}$ of S. Going through the previous steps and recalling the result from Section 4.1.4 that $H[S^{(n)}] = nH(S)$, there results

$$H[S^{(n)}] \leq L_n \leq H[S^{(n)}] + 1$$

and, therefore,

$$H(S) \leq n^{-1}L_n \leq H(S) + n^{-1} \qquad (4.110)$$

As $n \to \infty$, L_n becomes large and n^{-1} becomes small such that their product $n^{-1}L_n$ remains finite. L_n is the average code length for the nth extension of S, any member of which is composed of one of the concatenations of n symbols from S. The quantity $n^{-1}L_n$, therefore, represents an average code-word length measured in the units of symbols from S. The previous inequalities imply that there exists an instantaneous code with average code length $n^{-1}L_n$ arbitrarily close to the source entropy $H(S)$. To see this, note that the additive term n^{-1} on the right-hand side can be made arbitrarily small by taking n to be sufficiently large.

The implication of this result is that there exists at least one instantaneous code with a rate as close as one desires to the source entropy. Such a code is efficient in the sense that its representation requires, on the average, the same number of bits per symbol as the source. Note that the theorem fails to specify just what such a code is. However, from the derivation, we can get an inkling at what is involved. Coding efficiency is achieved only by encoding every large block of symbols. It is only by considering successively higher-order extensions of S that efficiency is obtained. The implication is that coding efficiency is achieved at the price of coding complexity.

We formally state this as a theorem:

Theorem. It is possible to encode a discrete memoryless source having an entropy of H bits per source symbol with an instantaneous code having an average code-word length of L bits per source symbol, where $L = H + \epsilon$ for any $\epsilon > 0$. It is not possible to encode such a source with fewer than H bits per source symbol.

It is understood that we are referring to codes that allow a perfect representation of the source. The previous result, known as Shannon's first theorem, was derived for a discrete memoryless source. It is easy to generalize to include Markov sources. Recall from Section 4.1.5 that the entropy $H(M)$ of a Markov source is always less than or equal to $H(D)$, the entropy of the discrete memoryless source having the same symbol probabilities. This result is valid for Markov sources of any order. Since there exists an instantaneous code of length L for which $H(D) \leq L$, we have

$$H(M) \leq H(D) \leq L \leq H(D) + 1$$

Extending our consideration to the nth extension of such a source, we have

$$H[D^{(n)}] \leq L_n \leq H[D^{(n)}] + 1$$

For a Markov source, we have (see Prob. 4.3)

$$H[D^{(n)}] = (n - 1)H(M) + H(D)$$

and, therefore,

$$(1 - n^{-1})H(M) + n^{-1}H(D) \leq n^{-1}L_n \leq (1 - n^{-1})H(M) + n^{-1}H(D) + n^{-1}$$

Taking the limit $n \to \infty$ proves the theorem.

While we are guaranteed the existence of arbitrarily efficient codes, such efficiency seems to be achievable only through great complexity. It must be remembered, however, that the theorem is a very general one. It is a very beautiful result of the general mathematical theory of communication. One of its many uses is in establishing a measure of how efficient a code can be. This can be a useful benchmark with which to gauge actual codes. Efficient coding is not necessarily difficult to achieve. For example, equiprobable source symbols from an alphabet whose size q is a power of 2 can be exactly represented with finite-length code words of $\log_2 q$ bits each. There are other cases, such as with Huffman coding [Ha 83a] where high efficiency can be realized with relative ease.

4.3.4 Coding for a Continuous Information Source

The results obtained thus far apply to discrete information sources. These sources have a finite entropy and, consequently, a finite average amount of information rate (bits per symbol, or bits per second when the number of symbols per second is given). There is a large number of applications where it is necessary to encode a continuous source of information. It will be recalled that a continuous information source corresponds to an infinite information rate. It is, therefore, impossible to encode these with any sort of finite scheme. Since we are restricted to finite communication systems, some distortion is clearly unavoidable.

A continuous information source generates an ergodic stochastic process $f(t)$ that represents the information to be transmitted. The process $f(t)$ plays the same role as the q-ary information symbols $s_k, k = 1, 2, \ldots, q$, from the discrete sources already studied. We generalize this case to include functions $f(t)$ whose independent and dependent variables may vary continuously over defined ranges. We restrict our attention to band-limited functions so that $f(t)$ can be completely specified, for example, by uniform sampling. Any communication signal is band-limited and can, therefore, always be represented by a sequence of its samples. Samples are not the only possible representation. In general, a signal $f(t)$ in N-dimensional signal space can be represented with respect to any suitable basis, and the N projections of this function onto any set of basis functions contain all of the information about $f(t)$. These coordinates, in general, can assume any values over the range $(-\infty, \infty)$. It is, therefore, not possible to represent them perfectly with any finite coding scheme.

The main thrust of this chapter is encoding at rates at least as large as the source information rate (i.e., coding from which perfect reconstruction is possible). This condition can be succinctly stated as $R \geq H(S)$, where R is the coding rate, and $H(S)$ is the source entropy. The branch of information theory dealing with $R < H(S)$ is called *rate-distortion theory* and deals with the minimum amount of unavoidable distortion incurred for a given coding rate R below source entropy. Rate-distortion theory will be covered in more detail in Chapter 8. We merely wish to alert the reader at this point that a significant portion of information theory has not been covered in this chapter, and will be covered later.

4.4 CHANNEL CODING

We now discuss a fundamental result concerning the possibility of error-free communication over a discrete noisy channel. The important result in this section is that it is possible to transmit messages at a rate as close to channel capacity as one desires and yet enjoy arbitrarily small decoding error rates. Conversely, it is impossible to transmit information above channel capacity without some degradation in the form of decoding errors. This surprising result is a fundamental theme of information theory.

4.4.1 Signaling Speed and Error Rates

Let us use the tools already developed to measure the information flow through a channel. In Section 4.1.3, we introduced the concept of average mutual information and presented the identity

$$I(\mathbf{x}, \mathbf{y}) = H(\mathbf{x}) - H(\mathbf{x}|\mathbf{y}) \tag{4.111}$$

The average mutual information, it will be recalled, is a measure of the information gained about the ensemble $\mathbf{x}$ as a result of measurements on the ensemble $\mathbf{y}$. This relationship was derived generally for any pair $\mathbf{x}$ and $\mathbf{y}$ of statistical ensembles. $I(\mathbf{x}, \mathbf{y})$ represents the information gain that results when the final uncertainty $H(\mathbf{x}|\mathbf{y})$ in $\mathbf{x}$ remaining after measuring $\mathbf{y}$ is subtracted from the initial uncertainty $H(\mathbf{x})$ in $\mathbf{x}$. We now apply this mathematical result to the situation where $\mathbf{x}$ is the ensemble of symbols applied at the input of a channel, and $\mathbf{y}$ is the corresponding ensemble of symbols decoded at the output. These ensembles need not have an equal number of elements, but are entirely characterized by sets of symbol probabilities and are, in general, correlated, since for useful communication systems, the output symbols are in some way related to the input symbols.

Following common usage [Ab 63, Ha 83a, Sh 48a, Sh 48b, Sh 49a], we shall refer to the average conditional entropy $H(\mathbf{x}|\mathbf{y})$ as the *equivocation* and attach the following interpretation to the last equation. The average mutual information $I(\mathbf{x}, \mathbf{y})$ is the rate at which information flows through the channel such that, measuring the output ensemble $\mathbf{y}$, we gain $I(\mathbf{x}, \mathbf{y})$ bits of information about ensemble $\mathbf{x}$ per channel use.

The equivocation is bounded by zero and $H(\mathbf{x})$. If the channel is noiseless, then the equivocation vanishes and $I(\mathbf{x}, \mathbf{y}) = H(\mathbf{x})$, implying that all of the source information appears at the channel output (see Prob. 4.9). If, on the other hand, the channel is so noisy that the input and output ensembles are statistically independent (i.e., the worst possible case for communication), then the equivocation is equal to $H(\mathbf{x})$, causing the average mutual information (or, equivalently, the average channel information rate) to vanish. All other cases fall between these two extremes.

Equivocation has the same interpretation as conditional entropy: $H(\mathbf{x}|\mathbf{y})$ is the average amount of information needed to specify $\mathbf{x}$ once $\mathbf{y}$ has been determined. Equivocation is nonzero when the channel is noisy and is the measure of the ambiguity about $\mathbf{x}$ introduced by the noisy channel. Were it not for channel-induced errors, all of the information $H(\mathbf{x})$ about $\mathbf{x}$ would appear at output $\mathbf{y}$, and there would result $I(\mathbf{x}, \mathbf{y}) = H(\mathbf{x})$ bits of information about $\mathbf{x}$ at the channel output. For a noisy channel, the average mutual information and, consequently, the channel information rate is less than $H(\mathbf{x})$ by an amount equal to the equivocation. We can, therefore, regard equivocation as a measure of information loss or degradation introduced by the channel.

The effect of the channel is to introduce symbol decoding errors that limit the amount of information about $\mathbf{x}$ appearing at the channel output. We have already met this concept in Section 4.2, where BSC and DMC channel capacities were expressed in terms of transition rates.

EXAMPLE

We can improve the reliability of communication by repeating a message several times. Consider a BSC with transition probability $p < \frac{1}{2}$. For $p \geq \frac{1}{2}$, we simply interchange symbols **0** and **1**. The probability of an error at the channel output is p. If each input symbol is repeated m times, then the new input symbols are the m-tuples $\mathbf{00} \cdots (m \text{ times}) \cdots \mathbf{0}$ and $\mathbf{11} \cdots (m \text{ times}) \cdots \mathbf{1}$. This is equivalent to using only two symbols out of the mth extension of the original coding alphabet. All of the other symbols are not used in coding the input, but are legitimate output symbols. The probability of any k-bit error pattern in such m-ary code words is given by the expression $P(k) = \binom{m}{k} p^k (1 - p)^{m-k}$. As m becomes large, an overwhelming majority of the output m-tuples have error-pattern weights that are very close to the mean mp. Since $p < \frac{1}{2}$ for a BSC with usable capacity, fewer than $m/2$ binary digits can be received in error if m is made sufficiently large. Majority logic decoding will, therefore, result in a probability of decoding error that can be made arbitrarily small by increasing m.

This example argues that arbitrarily large reliability can be achieved through redundancy. By using an m-ary repetition code (with m being odd), the probability of making a decoding error by selecting the decoded symbol corresponding to the most preponderant occurrence of **0** or **1** in the received string can be made arbitrarily small by choosing m to be as large as necessary. This technique is predicated on the fact that unless p is very close to $\frac{1}{2}$, no more than half of the symbols comprising a code word will be altered by the channel. In fact, the law of large numbers leads us to expect that the fraction of received strings in which the number of symbols received in error deviates significantly from mp approaches zero as m is made sufficiently large.

The price paid for such reliability is redundancy. The message must be repeated many times to achieve a given reliability. However, this example shows that it is possible to transmit information over a channel with arbitrarily high reliability. Furthermore, the example hints at the fact that such reliability is achieved by encoding using a more complex alphabet than the original information string.

This simple example introduces a somewhat surprising result. We have shown that it is possible to transmit information over a noisy channel with arbitrarily good reliability. Our result is valid for BSC transition rates as close to the worst case (i.e., $p = \frac{1}{2}$) as desired, where capacity approaches zero. Yet, for sufficiently long code-word length m, simple majority decoding logic yields an average decoding error probability that can be made vanishingly small. The occurrence of channel symbol errors does not necessarily imply a degradation in communication. We have shown the existence of a simple code that can effectively combat the effects of channel errors.

It is clear from this example that reliability and redundancy can be traded one for the other. We will show that as long as the information rate remains below channel capacity, no such trade-off need be made, however. There are codes (albeit complex ones) that can be used to transmit information with arbitrarily high reliability over a channel at a rate equal to channel capacity. This is perhaps the most surprising result of information theory.

4.4.2 The Hamming Metric and Decoding

Let us consider encoding with code words composed of m binary digits. This will facilitate the presentation. More general results are applicable for the case of arbitrary symbols making up the code words, but the general proof adds little more to the elucidation of the fundamental principles at the price of a substantial increase in mathematical complexity.

For this discussion, the waveforms of interest are all of the form of a concatenation of m members of the binary alphabet $\{\mathbf{0}, \mathbf{1}\}$. A useful property of a collection of such waveforms is the Hamming metric between any two such waveforms, which is defined as the number of places in which two such waveforms differ.

EXAMPLE

If $\mathbf{c}_1 = (\mathbf{1\ 1\ 0\ 0\ 1\ 0})$ and $\mathbf{c}_2 = (\mathbf{0\ 1\ 0\ 1\ 1\ 1})$, then the Hamming metric can be found by calculating the weight of the difference pattern:

$$d(\mathbf{c}_1, \mathbf{c}_2) = w(\mathbf{c}_1 - \mathbf{c}_2) = 3$$

where the difference $\mathbf{c}_1 - \mathbf{c}_2$ is calculated modulo 2 (exclusive-OR) between the corresponding binary symbols of $\mathbf{c}_1$ and $\mathbf{c}_2$. The Hamming metric satisfies all of the usual properties of a metric introduced in Chapter 2. It is, therefore, a valid measure of the distance between $\mathbf{c}_1$ and $\mathbf{c}_2$ in that it specifies the number of binary digits that must be changed in one symbol to transform it into the other.

Let $\mathbf{c}_1$ be a symbol applied to the input of a BSC. By that we understand that each of the binary digits comprising $\mathbf{c}_1$ is separately applied at the input and that m channel uses are required to transmit $\mathbf{c}_1$. Alternatively, $\mathbf{c}_1$ can be considered to be one of the 2^m inputs to the symmetric DMC. Let $\mathbf{c}_2$ be the corresponding output symbol. Note again that the input symbols can be constrained to a subset (the code words) of all possible binary m-tuples, but that the output symbols can be any one of the 2^m m-tuples.

Let us define the error pattern to be the binary-digit difference between $\mathbf{c}_1$ and $\mathbf{c}_2$. Thus, in the last example, the error pattern is $\mathbf{e} = \mathbf{c}_1 - \mathbf{c}_2 = (\mathbf{1\ 0\ 0\ 1\ 0\ 1})$. We note in passing that the order in which $\mathbf{c}_1$ and $\mathbf{c}_2$ appear in this operation is irrelevant. The weight of the error pattern is simply the Hamming metric between $\mathbf{c}_1$ and $\mathbf{c}_2$:

$$d(\mathbf{c}_1, \mathbf{c}_2) = w(\mathbf{e}) \tag{4.112}$$

which is numerically equal to 3 in the example given. For the BSC, the probability of any error pattern of weight $w(\mathbf{e})$ is simply

$$P[w(\mathbf{e})] = p^{w(\mathbf{e})}(1 - p)^{m - w(\mathbf{e})} \tag{4.113}$$

For large m, given that code word $\mathbf{c}_1$ was transmitted, the effect of the channel on the transmission is more likely to result in received m-tuples that are at a Hamming distance $w(\mathbf{e})$ away from $\mathbf{c}_1$. The law of large numbers tells us that as m becomes very large, the probability that the Hamming distance between transmitted and received m-tuples differs from $w(\mathbf{e})$ by an arbitrarily small amount can be made as small as desired. We can visualize this by imagining "spheres" of radius $w(\mathbf{e})$ centered about each transmitted code word. The m-tuples located on the surfaces of such "spheres" are those likely to be received. Very few of the received m-tuples will correspond to points not on those surfaces.

This suggests an approach to coding and decoding such waveforms. If we choose code words that are at least $2w(\mathbf{e})$ apart from one another, then the closest code word to a received m-tuple must have been, with high probability, the transmitted code word. Given a received m-tuple $\mathbf{r}$, the receiver calculates the m Hamming metrics $\{d(\mathbf{r}, \mathbf{c}_k); k = 1, 2, \ldots, m\}$ and decodes the symbol corresponding to the smallest $d(\mathbf{r}, \mathbf{c}_k)$. This is called *minimum-distance decoding*. It is desirable, therefore, to select as signaling code words m-tuples that exhibit a large intercode-word Hamming metric. Those code words will be less likely to be mapped into each other through the effect of the channel transmission errors. Specifically, the effects of errors can be made small, for large code-word length m, if the minimum Hamming distance between any two code words satisfies the inequality

$$d_{\min} \geq 2w(\mathbf{e}) + 1 \tag{4.114}$$

We must use, therefore, a sufficiently high extension of a coding alphabet to provide a sufficient number of such code words to encode the source while maintaining an appropriate Hamming distance between them.

The need for reliability dictates the use of large Hamming distances. Obtaining a sufficient number of such code words requires using large coding alphabet extensions. That is indeed one way of obtaining reliable communication, by trading reliability for redundancy, as was the case with the simple repetition code. The significance of Shannon's second theorem, to be introduced in the following section, is that there are codes that allow arbitrarily reliable communication, up to a rate equal to the channel capacity. In other words, the channel capacity can be fully used for information transmission, with arbitrarily small redundancy and arbitrarily small equivocation.

4.4.3 Shannon's Second Theorem for the BSC

We now present a heuristic proof of Shannon's second theorem. Consider a channel whose input $\mathbf{x}_i$ and output $\mathbf{y}_j$ symbols are mth extensions of the binary alphabet $\{0, 1\}$. These symbols could be transmitted, for example, one binary digit at a time over a BSC with crossover probability p. Coding consists in selecting some subset of the input symbols as code words. We might expect that code words that are "far" apart from one another in the Hamming metric sense might perform well. Although the proof that follows does not prescribe any specific selection rule, the point is brought up to emphasize that, in general, some code selections are better than others for reliable communication. Shannon's second theorem proves the existence of a set of code words that allows transmission of information at the channel capacity rate with a probability of decoding error that can be made arbitrarily small. That is a remarkable result.

The proof itself is remarkable in that it uses a very clever technique, due to Shannon, where the decoding-error probability is averaged over all possible codes, good and bad. The average probability of error turns out to be an arbitrarily small quantity, implying that there are codes in the averaged ensemble that must perform at least as well.

First, consider the behavior of the mth extension of the BSC. Let $\{\mathbf{x}\}$ be the ensemble of input symbols, together with the associated probabilities, that maximize the average mutual information $I(\mathbf{x}, \mathbf{y})$, where $\{\mathbf{y}\}$ is the corresponding output ensemble. In other words, $\{\mathbf{x}\}$ is the input ensemble that achieves channel capacity. For large m, out of all possible input 2^m binary m-tuples, there will be $2^{mH(\mathbf{x})}$ of these that occur with large probability; the remaining occur with a probability that can be made small by increasing m. Similarly, out of all 2^m possible output binary m-tuples, only $2^{mH(\mathbf{y})}$ will occur with appreciable probability in a large number m of BSC channel uses involving the transmission of a large random selection of code words. Corresponding to the transmission of any one particular code word, the number of output binary m-tuples that can be reasonably expected is $2^{mH(\mathbf{y}|\mathbf{x})}$. Decoding consists in selecting the closest code word, in the Hamming metric sense, to one of these $2^{mH(\mathbf{y}|\mathbf{x})}$ likely received output binary m-tuples.

Let us now calculate the probability of decoding error. The process of decoding consists in examining the closest $2^{mH(\mathbf{y}|\mathbf{x})}$ binary m-tuples in the immediate vicinity of a received m-tuple. These are all equally likely, occurring with probability $2^{mH(\mathbf{y}|\mathbf{x})}$. Furthermore, for large m, these m-tuples all have the same error-pattern weight. This is easily proved by recalling the first example in Section 4.1.4, which can now be interpreted as a study of the statistics of Bernoulli trials describing the bit-transmission errors in code words. As the code-word length m becomes very large, the fraction of the bits received in error approaches p with high probability. The number of code words for which the fraction of bit errors differs from p by an arbitrarily small amount can be made arbitrarily small by choosing an appropriately large m. For large code-word length m, we expect, therefore, to receive almost exclusively binary m-tuples corresponding to an error-pattern weight equal to pm, and little else. A useful trick in visualizing what is happening is to assume that the all-zero code word was transmitted. In this case, the received binary m-tuples are the error patterns themselves.

Let us denote by ρ the Hamming distance from the transmitted code word to any of the received binary m-tuples. By the previous argument, we have $\rho = pm$. There are $\binom{m}{pm}$ binary m-tuples situated at a distance pm away from any given code word. The number of patterns with Hamming distance pm away from a specific code word is $2^{mH(\mathbf{y}|\mathbf{x})}$.

Since the binary m-tuples corresponding to a given transmitted code word all have the same error-pattern weight, minimum metric decoding cannot differentiate between them. If one and only one of the code words is found among these $2^{mH(\mathbf{y}|\mathbf{x})}$ binary m-tuples, then that code word is decoded. If either no code word is found or if there is more than one, then there is no basis for choosing and a decoding error is declared. We shall show that there are codes for which this strategy can result in an arbitrarily small probability of decoding error at information rates arbitrarily close to channel capacity.

There are two mechanisms by which a decoding error can occur: either no code word is found among the closest $2^{mH(\mathbf{y}|\mathbf{x})}$ binary m-tuples or more than one code word is found. Let us denote by $S(\rho)$ the set of closest $2^{mH(\mathbf{y}|\mathbf{x})}$ binary m-tuples to a received sequence. $S(\rho)$ can be thought as a "sphere" radius ρ in the m-dimensional space of binary m-tuples. We can restate these conditions in a way that is more useful for proving the theorem. A decoding error occurs when either of the following two conditions is met:

1. no code word is in $S(\rho)$,
2. more than one code word is in $S(\rho)$.

The probability P_e for this event can be expressed as

$$P_e = \text{Prob}\{\text{no code word in } S(\rho)\} + \text{Prob}\{\text{ more than one code word in } S(\rho)\}$$

This, of course, is equivalent to

$$P_e = 1 - \text{Prob}\{\text{exactly one code word in } S(\rho)\}$$

and we shall show that this can be made as small as desired. We show this first by proving that the occurrence of no code word in $S(\rho)$ can be made extremely improbable and then by showing that more than one code word can also be made very improbable.

The probability that no code word is found in $S(\rho)$ is simply the probability that the channel transforms the transmitted code word into an m-tuple whose Hamming distance from the code word is more than ρ. An identical situation was examined in Section 4.1.4, where the Chernoff bound was used to prove that in a very long sequence m of Bernoulli trials, where the occurence of an event is p, the total probability found outside a small neighborhood about the mean pm could be made as small as desired by choosing m sufficiently large. This result is directly applicable to the case at hand, for the probability that no code word is in the neighborhood $S(\rho)$ about a transmitted code word can also be made arbitrarily small by choosing sufficiently large code-word lengths.

The second term in the equation for P_e requires a little more finesse. We must calculate the probability that two or more code words fall within a neighborhood containing $2^{mH(\mathbf{y}|\mathbf{x})}$ m-tuples. To make the results independent of the particular choice of a code, Shannon introduced the clever artifice of selecting R code words randomly (and with replacement) from the set of all possible m-tuples. This choice allows all possible codes to be considered. Since the result is that arbitrarily good coding performance can be achieved below channel capacity, there must be one code among all possible choices that at least achieves that performance. That is the essence of the proof of Shannon's second theorem.

Choosing R code words at random from a set of 2^m m-tuples results in $M = 2^{mR}$ possible code words. The error probability we seek is the probability that two or more code words from a given randomly selected code fall within a region containing $2^{mH(\mathbf{y}|\mathbf{x})}$ likely output m-tuples, when the code selection is averaged over all possible choices.

The probability α that an m-tuple chosen at random falls within that region is, owing to the random selection method for code words, simply the ratio of the number $2^{mH(\mathbf{y}|\mathbf{x})}$ of m-tuples in that region to the total number $2^{mH(\mathbf{y})}$ of likely output m-tuples:

$$\alpha = 2^{mH(\mathbf{y}|\mathbf{x})} \cdot 2^{-mH(\mathbf{y})} = 2^{m[H(\mathbf{y}|\mathbf{x})-H(\mathbf{y})]}$$

Next, we use the union bound to bound the error probability. The probability of two or more code words from a randomly selected code falling within the region is equal to the probability of one or more of the wrong (i.e., not transmitted) code words falling in that region. This probability must be bounded by the sum of the probabilities of all of the $M-1$ wrong code words falling in the region. But because of the way the codes were selected, this is simply $(M-1)\alpha$. We have, therefore,

$$P_e \le (M-1)\alpha < M\alpha$$

But we have

$$M\alpha = 2^{mR} \cdot 2^{m[H(\mathbf{y}|\mathbf{x})-H(\mathbf{y})]} = 2^{-m[I(\mathbf{x},\mathbf{y})-R]}$$

We have, therefore, since the channel capacity C is equal to $I(\mathbf{x},\mathbf{y})$,

$$P_e \le 2^{-m[I(\mathbf{x},\mathbf{y})-R]} \tag{4.115}$$

The implication of this result is that as long as $R = C - \epsilon$, where ϵ is an arbitrarily small quantity, the probability of error P_e can always be made as small as desired by choosing m sufficiently large. We have, therefore, proven Shannon's second theorem:

Theorem. Given a channel with capacity C and an information source with information rate R, it is possible to encode the output of the information source for transmission over the channel with an arbitrarily small probability of decoding error if $R = C - \epsilon$, where ϵ is an arbitrarily small positive quantity. It is not possible to transmit without error over the channel if $R > C$.

4.4.4 Remarks on Shannon's Theorems

In Section 4.4.3, Shannon's second theorem was derived under restrictions: the channel in question was assumed to be the BSC. This was done to present a particularly simple form of the proof using a channel and examples that have been previously discussed in this book. The approach has been to use intuitive examples to lead to a counterintuitive result. Shannon's second theorem, however, has a much wider validity, as it also applies to the discrete memoryless channel, for which the numbers of input and output symbols are finite. This is significant because many practical communication channels can be modeled by the DMC. Chapter 6 is essentially a discussion of the properties of communication waveforms for the symmetrical DMC.

Although Shannon's theorems form a landmark in the development of information theory, they offer little help to the designer of communication systems. Shannon's theorems guarantee the existence of efficient codes for source and channel coding. They are not constructive theorems in the sense of providing a deterministic method for generating such codes.

For example, random coding is generally not a practical way of generating channel-encoding procedures. This is particularly true if the code words are very long. It is desirable to introduce some mathematical structure in codes. This makes coding a mathematically tractable discipline based on understandable fundamental principles that have general validity. Also, a mathematically structured code is more likely to have algorithmically definable encoding and decoding procedures that are more efficient than the table look-up methods implied by random coding. For very long codes, this again can have practical significance.

Guided by the material presented in this chapter, we can deduce some of the characteristics of channel codes that may be derived by constructive means. A large number of communication systems employ the DMC, in which a q-ary alphabet is used to communicate over the channel. Given that a particular symbol is transmitted, the probability of it being correctly decoded is given by $1 - p$ and the probability of decoding in error is $p/(q - 1)$.

We learned in Section 4.2.4 that capacity is achieved over the symmetric DMC by equiprobable input symbols. It is, therefore, natural to consider, for such channels, a set of code words with equal lengths. Considering, for simplicity, the binary $\{0, 1\}$ alphabet for the code-word symbol, we are led to the choosing of code words from a set of binary m-tuples. We also know that the Hamming distance between code words plays an important part in defining performance. In particular, the minimum distance $d_{\min}$ between any two code words defines a lower bound on the decoding-error probability. This forces us to select our code words from a subset of all possible 2^m binary m-tuples. This subset is characterized by the desired metric distance properties of the code words. If q code words are selected, we necessarily have $q < 2^m$ and the code words contain a certain amount of redundancy since, being equiprobable, they convey $\log_2 q$ bits of information, which is less than the $m = \log_2 2^m$ binary digits required by the code. A certain amount of redundancy is, therefore, unavoidable and is to be traded for performance. The practical implementation of channel-coding procedures will be covered in more detail in Chapter 7.

PROBLEMS

4.1 Show that $I(\mathbf{x}, \mathbf{y}) = H(\mathbf{x}) - H(\mathbf{x}|\mathbf{y}) = H(\mathbf{y}) - H(\mathbf{y}|\mathbf{x})$.

4.2 An inventor claims to have built a device that can store arbitrary English text in a computer memory using one bit of memory for every 10 Latin letters. You, as a patent examiner, must decide whether to accept or reject the claim. You may assume that English text is composed of 26 equiprobable Latin letters [Wy 81].

4.3 Let S be a first-order Markov source with a q-ary alphabet. Show that

$$H[S'^{(n)}] = (n - 1)H(S) + H(S')$$

where the prime denotes the corresponding discrete memoryless source having the same symbol probabilities as the Markov source. Hint: Express $H[S'^{(n)}]$ in terms of the q^n symbol probabilities of the nth extension of the Markov source.

4.4 Show that if $p(x) = 0$ for $x \leq 0$, then the probability density having the greatest entropy subject to the constraints

$$\int_0^\infty p(x)\,dx = 1, \qquad \text{and} \qquad \int_0^\infty xp(x)\,dx = \alpha$$

is the exponential distribution $p(x) = \alpha^{-1}e^{-x/\alpha}$.

4.5 Show that the probability density having the greatest entropy subject to the constraints

$$\int_{-\infty}^\infty p(x)\,dx = 1 \qquad \int_{-\infty}^\infty xp(x)\,dx = \mu, \text{and} \qquad \int_{-\infty}^\infty x^2 p(x)\,dx = \sigma^2$$

is the normal density with mean μ and variance σ^2.

4.6 Show that the entropy of a normally distributed variable with mean μ and variance σ^2 is given by $H(x) = \log \sigma(2\pi e)^{1/2}$.

4.7 Comment on the result of Problem 4.6 when $\sigma < (2\pi e)^{-1/2}$.

4.8 Comment on the fact that $H(\mathbf{x})$ does not depend on μ in Problem 4.6.

4.9 (a) Show that the equivocation $H(\mathbf{x}|\mathbf{y})$ is equal to the input-symbol entropy $H(\mathbf{x})$ when the ensembles $\mathbf{x}$ and $\mathbf{y}$ are statistically independent.

(b) Show that $H(\mathbf{x}|\mathbf{y}) = 0$ when the channel is noiseless.

4.10 Consider a binary symmetric channel with $P\{1|0\} = P\{0|1\} = 1/32$. The input to the channel consists of the four equiprobable code words:

$\mathbf{x}_1$	1 1 1
$\mathbf{x}_2$	1 0 0
$\mathbf{x}_3$	0 1 0
$\mathbf{x}_4$	0 0 1

(a) Calculate $P\{0\}$ and $P\{1\}$ at the input.

(b) Code efficiency is defined as the ratio of the source entropy to the number of binary digits per code word. Calculate the efficiency for this code.

(c) Calculate the channel capacity.

(d) Comment on the possibility of distortion-free communication for this situation.

4.11 An engineer claims to have invented a coding scheme for reliable information transmission at 50 kilobits per second over a telephone line. As his manager, you must evaluate his work and decide whether or not company development funds should be allocated to this project. State and explain your recommendation. You may assume a telephone line to be modeled by an additive white Gaussian noise channel with a bandwidth of 3 khz and a signal-to-noise ratio of 26 dB.

4.12 Pluto (the <u>planet</u>, not the dog!) is about 6×10^{12} m from Earth. Ideally, how fast could data be sent back from a space probe near Pluto for error-free reception? Assume the only source of noise is from space, where the average background temperature is 3.5 K. The antennas have areas of 10 m^2 (transmitter) and 1000 m^2 (receiver). The wavelength is 1 cm and the transmitter power is 10 W. Boltzmann's constant is 1.37×10^{-23} J/K. A good approximation for the ratio of received to transmitted powers is given by Friis' formula:

$$\frac{P_R}{P_T} = \frac{A_R A_T}{\lambda^2 L^2}$$

where A_R and A_T are the receiving- and transmitting-antenna areas, respectively; λ is the wavelength; and L is the distance from transmitter to receiver.

4.13 There have been several attempts to search for radio messages from extraterrestrial sources. With your knowledge of information theory, determine if it is practical to transmit information over intragalactic distances.

(a) Calculate the minimum amount of energy per bit required to transmit information against the 3.5 K noise background of space over a distance of 30,000 light years, the distance to the center of our galaxy.

The ratio of received-to-transmitted powers is given by Friis' formula

$$(P_R/P_T) = A_R A_T/(\lambda L)^2$$

which takes into account the gains from receiving and transmitting antennas of areas A_R and A_T, respectively, at wavelength λ, and the inverse square propagation losses at distance L. Assume that the antennas used are of the same size as the radiotelescope at Arecibo, PR, which has a diameter of 305 m. The wavelength is 21 cm, corresponding to the hydrogen spin flip transition.

(b) Convert your answer to kilowatt-hours and calculate the minimum cost per bit of sending a message to the center of the galaxy if the cost of electrical energy is 6.3 cents per kilowatt-hour.

4.14 A discrete memoryless source produces the following code words with the associated probabilities:

Code Word	Probability
00	1/4
01	3/8
10	1/8
11	1/4

These code words are transmitted over a binary symmetric channel with a crossover probability of 1/10.

(a) Determine the source entropy per code word.

(b) Determine the channel capacity and comment on the quality of the communication for the given source.

(c) How could the source be modified to allow the channel to provide distortion-free communication?

4.15 A particular keyboard consists of the following characters: 26 letters, 10 digits, 25 punctuation marks, and 15 assorted control characters. Assume all of these are equiprobable. This keyboard is used to administer typing tests to candidates applying for a secretarial position. The keyboard is connected to a display device, located in another room, with twisted pair conductors having a bandwidth of 10 Hz and a signal-to-noise ratio of 15 dB.

One of the applicants is suing the company administering the typing tests, and claims to be able to type 100 words per minute (at five characters per word), but consistently failed the typing test. The applicant claims that the testing equipment is defective.

You, as an information theorist, are to appear in court as an expert. Is there sufficient reason to believe the plaintiff's claim to be true? Explain.

4.16 If the words in a language are ranked from most frequent to least frequent, the probability of occurrence for the mth most common word is approximately given by Zipf's law:

$$P(m) \approx 0.1/m$$

This turns out to be a fairly good approximation for many languages. However, $\sum_k P(m)$ is not finite when k ranges from 1 to infinity, so that this model implies a maximum vocabulary size M.

(a) Find M.

(b) Find the corresponding number of bits per word, assuming statistical independence.

(c) Your boss decides at the last minute to send you on a business trip to the Republic of Vulgaria, where no English is spoken. You do not speak Vulgarian, nor have sufficient time to become fluent. You suddenly remember Zipf's law from an old homework problem and decide on a compromise: you will learn the minimum number of words to enable you to convey an average of at least one bit of information per word. How many words must you learn?

(d) Your travel companion adopts a different approach. Noting that the Vulgarian word for "zygomorphic" is used with very low probability (≈ 0.001), he decides to learn that single word, which conveys $\log_2 0.001 = 9.97$ bits of information. Comment.

4.17 Find the entropy of the source alphabet having the following probability distribution: 1/4, 1/8, 1/8, 3/16 and 5/16.

4.18 A telephone channel has a bandwidth of approximately 3.2 kHz. What is the minimum signal-to-noise ratio required to support a data rate of 9.6 kilobits per second?

4.19 The Morse code is one of the earliest examples of a digital code used to represent information symbols. A table of the Morse code is supplied, together with the timing rules for generating Morse symbols. Simply stated, the Morse symbols can be described in terms of an ON/OFF keyed waveform with a "dot" lasting one unit of time, and a "dash" lasting three. The chart also shows that the delay between the elements (i.e., a "dot" or a "dash") of a symbol is one unit, and the delay between symbols is three units. From this chart, it is possible to convert any Morse symbol into an equivalent string of "zeros" and "ones" indicating the sequence in which the carrier is keyed.

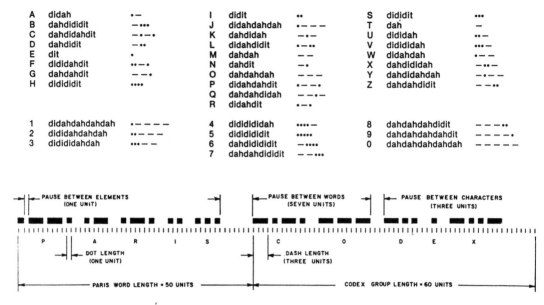

A	didah	· —	I	didit	· ·	S	dididit	· · ·
B	dahdididit	— · · ·	J	didahdahdah	· — — —	T	dah	—
C	dahdidahdit	— · — ·	K	dahdidah	— · —	U	dididah	· · —
D	dahdidit	— · ·	L	didahdidit	· — · ·	V	didididah	· · · —
E	dit	·	M	dahdah	— —	W	didahdah	· — —
F	dididahdit	· · — ·	N	dahdit	— ·	X	dahdididah	— · · —
G	dahdahdit	— — ·	O	dahdahdah	— — —	Y	dahdidahdah	— · — —
H	didididit	· · · ·	P	didahdahdit	· — — ·	Z	dahdahdidit	— — · ·
			Q	dahdahdidah	— — · —			
			R	didahdit	· — ·			
1	didahdahdahdah	· — — — —	4	didididah	· · · · —	8	dahdahdahdidit	— — — · ·
2	dididahdahdah	· · — — —	5	dididididit	· · · · ·	9	dahdahdahdahdit	— — — — ·
3	didididahdah	· · · — —	6	dahdidididit	— · · · ·	0	dahdahdahdahdah	— — — — —
			7	dahdahdidididit	— — · · ·			

Figure P-4-19   The International Morse Code. Adapted by permission from *ARRL*, Newington, CT.

(a) What is the average code-word length for Morse code if it is used to encode English text consisting of a space plus 26 letters? Assume that the information symbols are statistically independent and have probabilities as given by Table 4-1.

(b) Is the Morse code an instantaneous code? Provide a mathematical justification for your answer.

(c) Compare the average code-word length from part (a) with the entropy per letter for written English. Comment on the possibility of encoding English with the Morse code.

(d) The comparison in part (c) is valid for English only because the probabilities in Table 4-1 are for English text. What, if anything, can be said about the possibility of using Morse code to represent other languages that use any other alphabet having 27 (possibly correlated) symbols? Note that both the average code length L and the source entropy change with a different assignment of source symbol probabilities.

(e) Show that a code with equal codeword lengths can be an instantaneous code.

4.20 Consider the following simplified model for DNA replication. A gene is a sequence of nucleotides (complex molecules). There are four kinds of nucleotides, which we shall label A, C, T and G. Thus, a typical gene with 7 nucleotides might look something like this:

$$C\text{–}A\text{–}A\text{–}G\text{–}T\text{–}G\text{–}G$$

During cell division, a gene should replicate itself exactly, proceeding sequentially, one nucleotide at a time. Occasionally however, a mutation will occur and the daughter gene will differ from the parent gene, and pass this trait to its own daughters. The occurrences of mutations are independent from nucleotide to nucleotide. The simplest model is one in which the probability of any incorrect nucleotide replication is p, regardless of the nucleotide, and in which each of the four nucleotides are equally represented in a gene.

(a) What is the information content of a hypothetical gene consisting of a sequence of N nucleotides?

(b) How much information is passed from one generation to the next?

(c) In how many generations will half of the original information be destroyed by mutations if $N = 10,000$ and $p = 10^{-4}$?

STATISTICAL DETECTION THEORY

*La théorie des probabilités n'est
que le bon sens confirmé par le
calcul.*

Pierre Simon de Laplace

5

The process of communication, in many cases, consists of estimating random signals contaminated by additive random noise. In previous chapters, we have studied random noise and the probabilistic nature of communication signals as separate topics. The present chapter brings these two concepts together and considers the problem of providing the best possible estimate of the transmitted signal when all that is available is a single realization of the received waveform consisting of a signal plus additive noise.

Section 5.2 describes statistical hypothesis testing in its simplest form, preparing the way for the methodical development of a statistical approach for detection. The process of detection is conceptually divided into two parts, consisting of a processing step that produces a decision variable, followed by a decision step that compares the decision variables on the basis of which a symbol is decoded.

When studied with the tools of signal analysis in linear vector spaces, detection can be formulated as the process of choosing a vector whose metric distance to the nearest reference symbol or code word is smallest. This approach has the advantages of not requiring a statistical description of the noise process, is related to least-squares estimation, elegantly reduces to matched filtering, and has a simple geometrical interpretation.

The likelihood ratio is introduced as a consequence of Bayesian statistics and provides a basic building block in the statistical inference process found in detection. The simplest problem of dealing with multiple hypotheses given a single measured sample is described first, so as to show clearly the role of the likelihood ratio in detection. The development is then easily extended to the more general case of arbitrary waveforms.

The section closes with the development of coherent and noncoherent detection of arbitrary waveforms in additive Gaussian noise. This leads to the familiar matched filter forms for coherent and noncoherent processing. Here, again, signal-space concepts are used to shorten and clarify the derivations.

The last section covers the Neyman–Pearson approach to detection, used when prior symbol probabilities cannot be assigned. This leads to the constant false-alarm-rate (CFAR) detection, used in communication preamble detection for synchronization, as well as in radar and sonar detection problems. In addition to the traditional presentation of CFAR detection, this section takes a second look at the subject from the point of view of information theory and addresses the issue of how much information is gained through a CFAR detection measurement.

5.1 STATISTICAL INFERENCE

A communication receiver is a statistical inference engine. With a knowledge of the alphabet of permissible communication symbols, their prior probabilities, and the properties of the channel over which they are transmitted, the receiver must convert the information contained in the measurement of a signal into the best possible statistical inference as to which symbol was most likely transmitted. Detection, therefore, reduces to a problem of statistical inference.

Figure 5-1 presents an overall simplified view of the communication problem. An information source, viewed mathematically as a system producing a stochastic process, outputs an analog or digital signal that is then coded for transmission over the channel. The coder performs a mapping from the information source set of waveforms to a set of discrete symbols. Conceptually, the coding process can be broken into two steps: source coding and channel coding. The purpose of source coding is to remove redundancy from the incoming information stream so as to use the fewest number of symbols per unit time for its representation. The motivation for this is economy: transmitting these symbols over a real channel will use up resources such as energy, time, and bandwidth. The channel coder may use some error-protection code (to be discussed in Chapter 7) to protect against noise introduced by the channel. The decoder reverses this process as best it can by doing a many-to-one mapping from the set of all possible received waveforms onto the set of allowed signaling symbols. This process involves statistical inference, which is the subject of this chapter.

5.1.1 Hypothesis Testing

Consider an alphabet of symbols, which we label with the symbol **k**. Let us further assume that there is a finite number of such symbols and that their prior probabilities

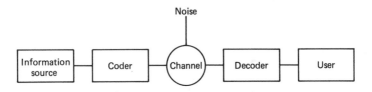

Figure 5-1.   A simplified view of communication.

$P(\mathbf{k})$ are known. From a knowledge of the effects of the channel on transmissions, it is then possible to calculate the posterior probabilities $P(r \mid \mathbf{k})$ that a waveform r is received given that $\mathbf{k}$ was in fact transmitted. One could regard $P(r \mid \mathbf{k})$ as the statistical equivalent of a transfer characteristic for the channel.

When nothing is known about which symbol was actually transmitted (for there is no need to transmit an otherwise predictable symbol), the posterior probabilities $P(r \mid \mathbf{k})$ represent all the information that is available about the likelihood of a particular symbol $\mathbf{k}$ having been transmitted. The receiver is thus faced with having to decide among several competing statistical hypotheses as to the most likely cause for the received waveform r. There are as many such statistical hypotheses as there are possible symbols. The kth such hypothesis is

H_k: symbol $\mathbf{k}$ was transmitted

The waveform r was drawn from a statistical process described by the posterior probability $P(r \mid \mathbf{k})$.

It is, therefore, natural to consider a receiver that first calculates all possible such posterior probabilities and then compares them pairwise to select as the decoded symbol that which corresponds to the largest $P(r \mid \mathbf{k})$. This is the *maximum-likelihood* decoder.

5.1.2 Minimum Metric Formulation

The previous discussion represents the statistical side of decoding. The process of detection that implements the statistical inference process can be described as consisting of two parts. First, a decision variable is extracted from the measured waveform. This decision variable is then subjected to certain tests. The calculation of the posterior probabilities $P(r \mid \mathbf{k})$ from the received waveform r involves signal-processing operations that precede the actual comparisons and decoding decisions. The details of this information processing prior to actual detection will turn out to be one of the by-products of calculating the likelihood ratio in a later section. At this point, we remark that the processing depends on the statistics involved as well as the way in which the noise is combined with the symbols by the communication channel. Figure 5-2 shows the various signal-processing steps involved.

A number of important applications involve a noise process n that is additively combined with the symbol signal s, resulting in a received waveform

$$r = s + n$$

The traditional discussions of detection of signals measured in an additive stochastic noise usually proceed along statistical lines of reasoning, lead to the maximization of the likelihood ratio, and prescribe correlation processing or, equivalently, matched filtering as the optimal processing for detection. While this standard approach is developed in this chapter, we also wish to call the reader's attention to a slightly different way of looking at processing for detection.

The signal-space formalism can also be used to specify the type of linear processing to be used for detection. Matched filtering is the optimum type of linear transformation to be applied to a signal corrupted by an additive stochastic process.

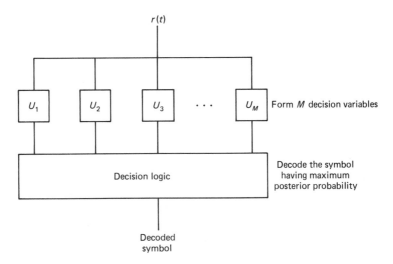

Figure 5-2.   Signal processing for detection involving an M-ary signaling alphabet.

Of fundamental importance is that matched filtering and correlation processing can be shown to be consequences of metric minimization between received signal and reference waveforms.

Consider the general problem of binary detection in the presence of an additive stochastic process. The objective of binary detection is to statistically infer the validity of two competing hypotheses regarding the presence or identity of a given signal $s(t)$ measured in additive noise $n(t)$. In general, we may assume the attributes of the signal to be given. The noise can be modeled as having been generated by a stochastic process whose statistical and spectral characteristics are known.

A waveform $r(t)$ is received and, in the simplest case, two statistical hypotheses are formed:

$$H_1: \quad r(t) = s_1(t) + n(t)$$
$$H_2: \quad r(t) = s_2(t) + n(t)$$

(5.1)

Assuming that these quantities can be represented in N-dimensional signal space, signals $s_1(t)$ and $s_2(t)$ are each uniquely represented by N deterministic scalars, namely, their projections onto N basis functions. Similarly, noise $n(t)$ can be represented by a set of N random variables. The "time" argument (t) is superfluous, as a given waveform is represented by a set of N coordinates that fully specify the signal distribution over the time–frequency plane. We can, therefore, describe the received waveform $r(t)$ in terms of the set of N constants $\{r_k; \ k = 1, \ldots, N\}$, and, similarly, for $s_1(t)$, $s_2(t)$, and $n(t)$.

Equation (5.1) can be written explicitly in terms of the N signal-space coordinates:

$$H_1: \quad r_k = s_{1k} + n_k$$
$$H_2: \quad r_k = s_{2k} + n_k$$

(5.2)

Detection involves a process of statistical inference that bases a decision on the relative likelihoods of the measured waveform $\{r_k\}$ being attributable to specified statistical hypotheses. These likelihoods are the posterior probabilities. If there were no stochastic process to confuse the issue, the decision would be unambiguous. In the presence of an additive noise process, one can expect the outcome of the detection process to be affected by the relative magnitudes of the signal and the noise.

Let us now be more careful by what is meant by the term "relative magnitudes." A detection error will occur only insofar as a noise waveform will, owing to its random nature, come close to approximating a signal waveform. This degree of approximation can be measured by any monotonic function of the metric for that signal space. This is tantamount to declaring detection whenever a measured waveform is sufficiently close (in the metric sense) to a reference signal waveform. The process of measurement thus implies a continuum of outcomes associated with all possible distances from the reference waveform. When the statistics of the random noise process are known, probabilities can be associated with these distances.

Consider the case where the noise components n_k in Eq. (5.2) are independent. The signals are all represented with respect to the N signal-space coordinates $\{x_1, x_2, \ldots, x_N\}$. The probability of finding the received waveform r with components $\{r_k\}$ between x_k and $x_k + dx_k$, given that $s_1(t)$ was transmitted, is

$$dP(r_k|1) = p(r_k|1)\,dx_k$$

Similarly, we can form posterior probabilities conditioned on $s_2(t)$ having been transmitted:

$$dP(r_k|2) = p(r_k|2)\,dx_k$$

where $p(r_k|1)$ and $p(r_k|2)$ are the conditional probability density functions for the component r_k of the received waveform. Given the probabilities $dP(r_k|1)$ and $dP(r_k|2)$, a maximum-likelihood statistical decision favoring hypothesis H_1 is made if

$$dP(r_k|1) > dP(r_k|2)$$

and favoring hypothesis H_2 if

$$dP(r_k|2) > dP(r_k|1)$$

The maximum-likelihood statistical decision rule can also be expressed in terms of probability densities. We simply form the *likelihood ratio*

$$\lambda_k = \frac{p(r_k|1)}{p(r_k|2)} \tag{5.3}$$

and choose hypothesis H_1 if $\lambda_k > 1$ and hypothesis H_2 if $\lambda_k < 1$. We can generalize this approach to include all of the signal coordinates. For binary signaling, the likelihood ratio becomes

$$\lambda = \frac{p(r_1, r_2, \ldots, r_N|1)}{p(r_1, r_2, \ldots, r_N|2)} = \frac{p(r|1)}{p(r|2)} \tag{5.4}$$

where λ is the ratio of the joint conditional probability-density functions corresponding to the two hypotheses. The maximum-likelihood statistical decision favors hypothesis

H_1 if $\lambda > 1$ and favors hypothesis H_2 otherwise. A graphical description of maximum-likelihood statistical detection for two hypotheses is shown in Fig. 5-3.

Consider now the special, but often occurring case of additive Gaussian noise, where the noise components n_k are statistically independent and are zero-mean variables with constant variance σ_0^2. For this case, the joint conditional probability densities that appear in Eq. (5.4) can be expressed as products of the individual densities for each of the r_k:

$$p(r_1, r_2, \ldots, r_N | j) = p(r_1 | s_{j_1}) p(r_2 | s_{j_2}) \cdots p(r_N | s_{j_N}) \tag{5.5}$$

where $j = 1, 2$, and the $\{s_{j_k}; k = 1, \ldots, N\}$ are the signal components of $s_j(t)$. The likelihood ratio becomes

$$\lambda = \frac{\displaystyle\prod_{k=1}^{N} p(r_k | s_{1_k})}{\displaystyle\prod_{k=1}^{N} p(r_k | s_{2_k})} \tag{5.6}$$

For Gaussian noise with equal energy in each of the noise coordinates, we have

$$p(r_k | s_{jk}) = \frac{1}{\sigma_0 (2\pi)^{1/2}} \exp\left[-\frac{1}{2}\left(\frac{r_k - s_{j_k}}{\sigma_0}\right)^2\right] \tag{5.7}$$

Upon substituting Eq. (5.7) into Eq. (5.6) and evaluating the natural logarithm of λ, there results the *log likelihood ratio*:

$$\ln \lambda = \frac{1}{2\sigma_0^2} \sum_{k=1}^{N} (r_k - s_{2_k})^2 - \frac{1}{2\sigma_0^2} \sum_{k=1}^{N} (r_k - s_{1_k})^2$$

$$= \frac{1}{2\sigma_0^2}\left(\|r - s_2\|^2 - \|r - s_1\|^2\right) \tag{5.8}$$

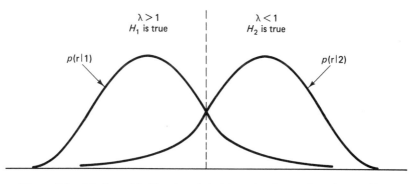

Figure 5-3. Maximum-likelihood statistical detection for two hypotheses with λ given by Eq. (5.4).

A very important result emerges from Eq. (5.8). Making a maximum-likelihood statistical decision based on whether the likelihood ratio λ is greater or less than unity is equivalent to making a decision based on which of the two norms $\|r - s_1\|$ or $\|r - s_2\|$ is the largest. Since the norm can be used to define a metric distance—in this case, the Euclidian metric—we have reduced the statistical inference problem to that of finding which of the two signaling waveforms, $s_1(t)$ or $s_2(t)$, is closest, in the metric sense, to the received waveform $r(t)$.

The reason for using the natural logarithm of λ instead of λ is a simplification of the calculations. Actually, any monotonic function of λ could as well be used for maximum-likelihood detection. By using the natural logarithm, the quantities to be compared turn out to be the squares of the Euclidian distances between waveforms. Using other monotonic functions of λ would result in comparing more complicated functions of these distances, and with the same result.

Processing for detection consists in obtaining from the received signal a measure of its metric distance from the various waveforms contained in the signaling alphabet. This viewpoint is illustrated in Fig. 5-4. We shall show in subsequent sections that detection can be done by determining which of the signaling waveforms is closest, in the metric sense, to the received waveform.

Consider a detection decision variable of the form of the square of the Euclidian metric between the measurement and a reference signal:

$$d^2(s, r) = \langle s - r | s - r \rangle = \|s\|^2 + \|r\|^2 - 2\mathcal{R}e \langle s|r \rangle \qquad (5.9)$$

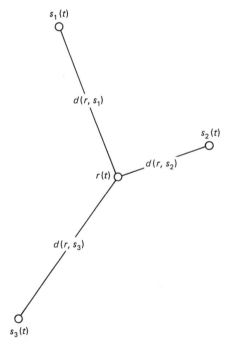

Figure 5-4. Detection viewed as a selection of the least metric distance between the received signal $r(t)$ and each of the signaling waveforms $s_k(t)$. In the example shown, the symbol corresponding to $s_2(t)$ would be decoded.

For constant $\|s\|^2$ and $\|n\|^2$, the square of the metric $d^2(s,r)$ is minimized by the function r that maximizes the real part of the correlation $\mathcal{R}e\,\langle s|r\rangle$. This operation is usually performed by matched filtering or by direct correlation with a reference waveform.

Maximum-likelihood detection in additive white Gaussian noise seeks the signaling waveform that is closest to the received waveform r. The matched filter can be used in this process. Finding the signal s that minimizes $d(s, r)$ is equivalent to finding the s that maximizes

$$2\mathcal{R}e\,\langle s|r\rangle - \|s\|^2 - \|r\|^2$$

Since $r = s + n$, we have

$$\|r\|^2 = \|s + n\|^2 = \|s\|^2 + \|n\|^2$$

for the case of no correlation between s and n. In this case, maximum-likelihood detection seeks the s that maximizes

$$2\mathcal{R}e\,\langle s|r\rangle - 2\|s\|^2 - \|n\|^2 \tag{5.10}$$

The quantities $\|s\|^2$ and $\|n\|^2$ are usually known a priori.

5.1.3 The Karhunen–Loève Transformation

In applying the techniques of probability theory to communications, it often occurs that one has to calculate probabilities associated with a random function. For example, the received signal $r(t)$ may consist of one of M signal waveforms $s_m(t)$ plus zero-mean additive Gaussian noise $z(t)$:

$$r(t) = s_m(t) + z(t) \tag{5.11}$$

A typical example is the need to compute the conditional probability $P(r|\mathbf{k})$ that $r(t)$ was received given that a specific waveform $s_k(t)$ was transmitted. It is important to realize that $r(t)$ represents a stochastic process rather than a random variable. More precisely, $r(t)$ is a time-limited segment from a random process consisting of the finite-duration deterministic signal $s_m(t)$ plus some additive noise process $z(t)$. The probabilities must be expressed in terms of random variables. What is needed is a way to represent $r(t)$, or any continuous stochastic process, in terms of a countable set of random variables.

The solution to this problem is to use signal-space concepts and express $r(t)$ in terms of its projections onto a set of coordinates. This provides a set of scalars, each one of which is a random variable. There are as many such scalars as there are dimensions in the linear signal space required to express $r(t)$. For example, for the case of a strictly time-limited function $r(t)$, Fourier series coefficients could be used in the representation.

The analysis of such problems can be greatly simplified if these scalars happen to be uncorrelated. For example, in the case where $z(t)$ is from a Gaussian process, uncorrelatedness implies statistical independence, and the joint probability density function for the scalars can then be expressed as a product of the individual densities for each scalar.

What is needed for this is a particular complete set of basis functions $\{\varphi_i(t)\}$ with the property that a stochastic process $x(t)$ expressed in terms of that basis set yields a set of uncorrelated scalars. We also require that these basis functions be orthogonal:

$$\langle \varphi_i(t) | \varphi_j(t) \rangle = \lambda_j \, \delta_{i,j} \tag{5.12}$$

The expansion of a stochastic process in terms of these basis functions is called a Karhunen–Loève expansion, and results in uncorrelated expansion coefficients.

We start by expressing a stochastic process $x(t)$ in terms of the as-of-yet unspecified but complete orthogonal basis set:

$$x(t) = \sum_i x_i \varphi_i(t) \tag{5.13}$$

where the index i runs over all of the signal-space coordinates. The expansion coefficients x_i are given by

$$x_i = \lambda_i^{-1} \langle \varphi_i(t) | x(t) \rangle \tag{5.14}$$

We now calculate the correlation between two arbitrary such coefficients and require that the resulting expression vanishes unless the two coefficients are identical. The resulting expression can then be solved for the appropriate basis functions $\varphi_i(t)$. In this way, we impose the constraint that the expansion yield uncorrelated coefficients. The statistical correlation between x_i and x_j is given by the expectation value:

$$E[x_i^* x_j] = \lambda_i^{-1} \lambda_j^{-1} E[\langle x(t) | \varphi_i(t) \rangle \langle \varphi_j(t') | x(t') \rangle] = \sigma_j^2 \delta_{i,j} \tag{5.15}$$

where the second set of angular brackets has been rendered in boldface to indicate that the inner product operation is carried with respect to the primed variable t' and has no effect on the unprimed variable t. The constant σ_j^2 is the variance of the jth component of the stochastic process. Statistical expectation and the inner-product operation represented by the angular brackets are linear and not related; these operations, therefore, commute. Equation (5.15) can then be rewritten as follows, with the statistical expectation operation now appearing inside the angular brackets

$$\langle\langle \varphi_j(t') | E[x^*(t) x(t')] | \varphi_i(t) \rangle\rangle = \lambda_i \lambda_j \sigma_j^2 \delta_{i,j} \tag{5.16}$$

but the indicated expectation can be recognized as the autocorrelation of the process $x(t)$:

$$E[x^*(t) x(t')] = R_x(t, t')$$

so that we have

$$\langle\langle \varphi_j(t') | R_x(t, t') \varphi_i(t) \rangle\rangle = \langle \varphi_j(t') | \langle R_x(t, t') \varphi_i(t) \rangle\rangle = \lambda_i \lambda_j \sigma_j^2 \delta_{i,j}$$

and for $i = j$, there follows

$$\langle \varphi_i(t') | \langle R_x(t, t') \varphi_i(t) \rangle\rangle = \lambda_i^2 \sigma_i^2$$

Recalling that $R_x(t, t') = R_x^*(t', t)$, we now invoke the orthogonality properties of the basis functions to identify the term within light brackets with $\lambda_i \sigma_i^2 \varphi_i(t')$:

$$\langle R_x(t, t') | \varphi_i(t') \rangle = \lambda_i \sigma_i^2 \varphi_i(t) \tag{5.17}$$

This is an integral equation for the *Karhunen–Loève* basis functions $\varphi_i(t)$. Note that these basis functions are determined by the correlation properties of the stochastic process. Different processes result in different sets of basis functions.

EXAMPLE

If the stochastic process in question is white noise, $\sigma_i = \sigma_0 = $ constant, and

$$R_x(t, t') = \sigma_0^2 \delta(t - t')$$

and the integral equation for the Karhunen–Loève basis functions becomes

$$\sigma_0^2 \langle \delta(t - t') | \varphi_i(t') \rangle = \lambda_i \sigma_0^2 \varphi_i(t)$$

which is satisfied by any set of orthogonal functions with $\lambda_i = 1$.

EXAMPLE

Now consider a band-limited process over the interval $[-\tau, \tau]$, whose power spectral density is constant with value N_0 in the frequency range $-W \leq \nu \leq W$ and vanishes everywhere else. The autocorrelation for such a process is given by

$$R(t - t') = N_0 \frac{\sin[2\pi W (t - t')]}{\pi(t - t')}$$

and the integral equation for the Karhunen–Loève basis functions is

$$\int_{-\tau}^{\tau} \frac{\sin[2\pi W (t - t')]}{\pi(t - t')} \varphi_k(t') dt' = \lambda_k \varphi_k(t)$$

The solutions to this integral equation are the prolate spheroidal wave functions.

For large τ, i.e., for large time-bandwidth products, the $\varphi_i(t)$ are well approximated by the Whittaker interpolating functions. The implication is that for such waveforms with large time-bandwidth products, samples spaced $0.5/W$ apart in time are uncorrelated.

Transformations where the basis set $\{\varphi_k(t)\}$ satisfies the eigenvalue problem of the form

$$\langle R_x(t, t') | \varphi_i(t') \rangle = \lambda_i \varphi_i(t) \tag{5.18}$$

can find many useful applications in communication. The examples we have just discussed concern themselves primarily with the restatement of a statistical problem into a form that is more amenable to analysis. The Karhunen–Loève transformation can also be used in practical applications where it is desired to obtain an efficient basis set for signal representation.

An interesting application of the Karhunen–Loève transform involves the construction of a small set of basis functions with which to represent musical tones [St 88a]. Although Fourier techniques can be used in the analysis/synthesis of musical tones, a large number (≈ 30) of Fourier components are required for satisfactory reproduction. The resulting computational load turns out to be impractical for real-time synthesis in applications such as home electronic organs. This problem can be alleviated if a smaller set of basis functions is used.

The problem with Fourier series is their slow rate of convergence. Mathematically, any complete set can be used to represent an arbitrary function. Those representations that turn out to have practical value converge more rapidly, i.e., contain most of the represented waveform's energy in the smallest number of terms. Stapleton and Bass set out to find such a preferred set of basis functions for the representation of musical tones.

Their approach is of interest for three different reasons. First, it describes the solution of a very practical problem by means of statistical signal processing techniques presented in this book. Second, their analysis is couched in matrix notation, which introduces us with yet another way of applying our analysis techniques. Third, the problem they treat can be interpreted as an information theory problem in that they have really developed a minimal algorithm for the representation of musical tones. Moreover, it paves the way for the study of rate-distortion theory in Chapter 8, where we tackle the problem of coding continuous signals whose information rate exceeds the coding rate and results in unavoidable distortion that must then be minimized.

EXAMPLE

Consider the problem of finding an economical way to represent a set of musical tones. We start with an ensemble of discrete time functions, which we write as vectors

$$\mathbf{x}_i = [x_i(1), x_i(2), \ldots, x_i(m), \ldots, x_i(M)]^T$$

where the superscript T denotes the vector transpose conjugate, and the subscript i runs over all the members of the ensemble. The ensemble of vectors $\{\mathbf{x}_i\}$ represents the data to be used for generating the basis set. Each member of this ensemble consists of M equispaced samples of a band-limited signal, which, in this case, consists of a musical tone. For $M = 2TW$, where $T \gg 1/W$, $\mathbf{x}_i$ can be approximately represented in an M-dimensional linear vector space.

The ensemble $\{\mathbf{x}_i\}$ can be generated experimentally by recording an actual musical instrument. The different members of the ensemble correspond to different pitch periods during the sustained portion of a musical tone. These pitch periods are generally similar, save for differences that give the tone a natural sound. These differences account for the variations among the members of the ensemble.

For large TW, the vector $\mathbf{x}_i$ can be approximately represented in an M-dimensional linear vector space with respect to some set $\{\varphi_k : \varphi_k(m); \, k, \, m = 1, 2, \ldots, M\}$ of basis vectors:

$$x_i(m) = \sum_{k=1}^{M} a_{ik} \varphi_k(m)$$

To represent musical tones with sufficient fidelity, and for the M-dimensionality approximation to hold, the number of space dimensions turns out to be impractically large. We, therefore, seek to represent $\mathbf{x}_i$ with fewer basis functions:

$$x_i(m) \approx \sum_{k=1}^{N} a_{ik}\varphi_k(m)$$

where $N < M$. In vector notation, this becomes

$$\mathbf{x}_i \approx \sum_{k=1}^{N} a_{ik}\varphi_k \tag{5.19}$$

with the $\{\varphi_k\}$ chosen to be orthonormal in the sense that the inner product between φ_k and φ_n, with $k \neq n$, vanishes:

$$\varphi_k^T \varphi_n = \delta_{k,n} \tag{5.20}$$

Written explicitly in terms of the M scalar components of φ_k and φ_n, the orthonormality condition takes the more familiar form of an inner product:

$$\sum_{m=1}^{M} \varphi_k^*(m)\varphi_n(m) = \delta_{k,n}$$

It might appear that the solution to this problem is simply to select the first N prolate spheroidal wave functions as the $\varphi_k(m)$. According to the projection theorem, this would give us the best approximation. This would be true if the ensemble $\{\mathbf{x}_i\}$ were allowed to cover all possible band-limited functions, each sampled M times. Stapleton and Bass [St 88a] considered this problem and limited their ensemble to a set of measured musical tones. The $\{\varphi_k\}$ that result in an optimal representation over this restricted ensemble is not necessarily the set of prolate spheroidal wave functions. Indeed, we expect the form of the $\{\varphi_k\}$ to be determined by the particular statistical nature of the $\{\mathbf{x}_i\}$. We also note that the prolate spheroidal wave functions form an orthogonal—and not orthonormal—basis on a finite time interval. Whether the basis used by Stapleton and Bass is orthogonal or orthonormal is irrelevant since the difference will, in any case, be incorporated in the functions for which they solve.

According to the projection theorem, the coefficients a_{ik} are given by

$$a_{ik} = \varphi_k^T \mathbf{x}_i = \langle \varphi_k | x_i \rangle \tag{5.21}$$

The error in the fit is given by

$$\Delta x_i = \sum_{k=1}^{M} a_{ik}\varphi_k - \sum_{k=1}^{N} a_{ik}\varphi_k = \sum_{k=N+1}^{M} a_{ik}\varphi_k$$

With $a_{ik} = \langle \varphi_k | x_i \rangle$, this can be written as

$$\Delta x_i = \sum_{k=N+1}^{M} \langle \varphi_k | x_i \rangle \varphi_k$$

We wish to find the φ_k that minimize the expected error:

$$E_{ij}\{\langle \Delta x_i | \Delta x_j \rangle\} = \sum_{k,n} \langle \varphi_k | \varphi_n \rangle E_{ij}\{\langle x_i | \varphi_k \rangle \langle \varphi_n | x_j \rangle\} \tag{5.22}$$

where the statistical expectation is over i and j. The orthonormality condition results in $\langle \varphi_k | \varphi_n \rangle = \delta_{k,n}$, so that we have

$$E_{ij}\{\Delta x_i | \Delta x_j\} = \sum_{k=N+1}^{M} E_{ij}\{\langle x_i | \varphi_k \rangle \langle \varphi_k | x_j \rangle\}$$

$$= \sum_{k=N+1}^{M} E_{ij}\{\langle \varphi_k | x_j \rangle \langle x_i | \varphi_k \rangle\}$$

$$= \sum_{k=N+1}^{M} \langle \varphi_k | E_{ij}\{|x_j \rangle \langle x_i|\} | \varphi_k \rangle$$

$$= \sum_{k=N+1}^{M} \langle \varphi_k | R_\mathbf{x}(i, j) | \varphi_k \rangle = \sum_{k=N+1}^{M} \varphi_k^\mathrm{T} R_\mathbf{x} \varphi_k \qquad (5.23)$$

where $R_\mathbf{x}$ is the covariance matrix associated with the process $\{\mathbf{x}_i\}$. It can be shown (Prob. 5.4) that the set $\{\varphi_k\}$ that minimizes ϵ subject to the orthonormality constraint satisfies the eigenvalue problem

$$R_\mathbf{x} \varphi_k = \lambda_k \varphi_k \qquad (5.24)$$

Using this approach, Stapleton and Bass were able to represent each of several musical tones using only a few basis functions for each tone. To standardize the processing, tone periods were normalized to correspond to 128 samples. Signal phases were aligned to force related features of the sample functions to occur at about the same time. This reduces the number of basis functions required for representation. Table 5-1 lists musical instruments considered by Stapleton and Bass, with the number of basis functions required to represent each instrument according to perceptual criteria. The number of basis functions shown in Table 5-1 results in a reproduction quality considered to be as desirable as that of the original tone.

TABLE 5-1. BASIS FUNCTION
REQUIREMENTS FOR SEVERAL
MUSICAL INSTRUMENTS

Diapason	2
French Horn	2
Trombone	2
Tenor saxophone	2
Alto saxophone	2
Guitar	3
Trumpet	3
Clarinet	3
Flute	4
Marimba	4
Violin	4

Adapted by permission from
[St 88a]. ©1988 IEEE.

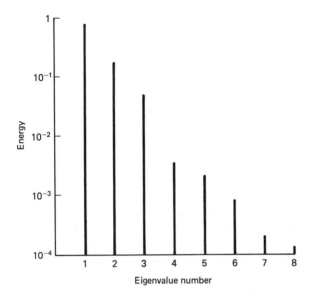

Figure 5-5. Eigenvalue distribution for trumpet, French horn, and trombone. (Adapted by permission from [St 88a]. © 1988 IEEE.)

The eigenvalue distribution for instruments such as the trumpet, French horn, and trombone are shown in Fig. 5-5. Approximately 99.3 percent of the total energy is contained in the first three eigenmodes. This is typical of the results obtained with this approach. Figure 5-6 compares the original and synthesized waveforms for a trombone.

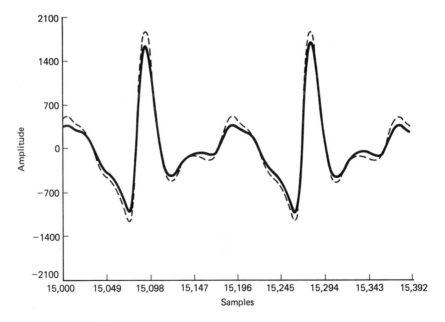

Figure 5-6. Comparison of synthetic (dashed line) and original trombone. (Adapted by permission from [St 88a]. © 1988 IEEE.)

The representation of musical tones by sets of the fewest possible signal-space coordinates (here, K–L functions) is an example of an attempt to produce a minimal algorithm for encoding information. In this context, Stapleton and Bass have developed an efficient source coding algorithm for a particular type of information source.

5.1.4 Bayesian Statistics and the Likelihood Ratio

Consider a transmission consisting of a sequence of symbol waveforms $s_m(t)$ selected from a finite alphabet of M symbols. For each such waveform transmitted, the receiver measures a waveform $r(t)$ and attempts to associate with it one of the M possible transmitted symbols. Were it not for noise, this task would be unambiguous. However, channel noise alters the transmitted waveform in an unpredictable manner, but with a process whose statistical properties can be measured and taken into account in the design of a communication system. Detection is a process of statistical inference, whereby one of the M possible symbols is decoded based on the information contained in a single realization of $r(t)$.

The receiver's task is to make the best possible estimate of what symbol was transmitted, given that it has measured the waveform $r(t)$. This is a problem of statistical inference using conditional probabilities. Bayes' rule states that the probability that symbol $\mathbf{m}$ was sent, given that waveform r was received, is

$$P(\mathbf{m}|r) = \frac{P(r|\mathbf{m})P(\mathbf{m})}{P(r)} \tag{5.25}$$

where $P(\mathbf{m})$ is the prior probability of symbol $\mathbf{m}$ having been transmitted, and $P(r)$ is the probability of receiving the waveform $r(t)$. The denominator in the last expression can be rewritten by using the identity

$$P(r) = \sum_{\mathbf{k}} P(r|\mathbf{k})P(\mathbf{k}) \tag{5.26}$$

so that Bayes' rule can be expressed as

$$P(\mathbf{m}|r) = \frac{P(r|\mathbf{m})P(\mathbf{m})}{\sum_{\mathbf{k}} P(r|\mathbf{k})P(\mathbf{k})}$$

The sum is over all M alphabet symbols. Dividing both the numerator and denominator of the right-hand side by $P(r|\mathbf{m})$ results in

$$P(\mathbf{m}|r) = \frac{P(\mathbf{m})}{\sum_{\mathbf{k}} \frac{P(r|\mathbf{k})}{P(r|\mathbf{m})}P(\mathbf{k})} \tag{5.27}$$

Two types of quantities appear in the expression for the conditional probability $P(\mathbf{m}|r)$. The prior probabilities $P(\mathbf{m})$ and $P(\mathbf{k})$ relate to the a priori probabilities of symbol transmission and can be assumed to be known in advance. The other quantities are conditional posterior probabilities $P(r|\mathbf{m})$. These conditional probabilities appear as ratios of the form

$$\Lambda_{km} = \frac{P(r|\mathbf{k})}{P(r|\mathbf{m})} \tag{5.28}$$

The ratio Λ_{km} is called the *likelihood ratio* and measures the relative probabilistic balance between two competing statistical hypotheses. In this case, waveform $r(t)$ has been received and Λ_{km} weighs the probability that symbol $\mathbf{k}$ was sent versus the probability that symbol $\mathbf{m}$ was sent.

We note two properties of the likelihood ratio. Because of the symmetry in the way Λ_{km} depends on $\mathbf{k}$ and $\mathbf{m}$, the following identities hold:

$$\Lambda_{km}\Lambda_{mk} = 1$$
$$\Lambda_{kk} = 1 \tag{5.29}$$

The conditional probabilities appearing in the likelihood ratio can be related to the signal measured by the receiver. The problem of statistical inference for the receiver can be expressed, therefore, as one of determining which symbol $\mathbf{m}$ maximizes the probability $P(\mathbf{m}|r)$. This in turn can be reinterpreted as an extremizing problem for Λ_{km} and leads directly to the maximum-likelihood formalism of statistical inference and detection.

Figure 5-7 shows conceptually how statistical inference is used to define the processing architecture for a maximum-likelihood M-ary receiver. When all the prior probabilities $\{P(\mathbf{k})(\mathbf{k} = 1, 2, \ldots, M\}$ are equal, it can be shown that $P(\mathbf{m}|r) = P(r|\mathbf{m})$ for any $\mathbf{m}$ (see Prob. 5.3). For this commonly encountered case in communication, maximizing $P(\mathbf{m}|r)$ is equivalent to maximizing $P(r|\mathbf{m})$.

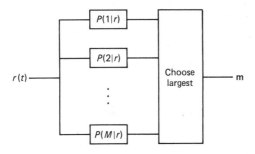

Figure 5-7. Conceptual-processing architecture for a M-ary maximum-likelihood receiver.

5.2 MAXIMUM-LIKELIHOOD ESTIMATION

This section introduces the statistical formalism for decoding communication messages. The likelihood ratio approach introduced in the last section is developed further and applied to statistical inference situations involving multiple hypothesis testing for single samples as well as for waveforms with several degrees of freedom.

5.2.1 General Formalism

Before starting with the development of the statistical formalism itself, it is instructive to pause and explain where we are heading and where this section fits in the greater scheme of decoding performance, a topic pursued in the following chapter.

The basis for choosing among various competing statistical hypotheses, given the available information, revolves around the maximization of the likelihood ratio. This scheme is appropriately named maximum-likelihood estimation, or decoding. The likelihood ratio was introduced in the last section as a way of comparing two competing statistical hypotheses through the relative magnitudes of their posterior probabilities. With multiple pairwise comparisons, this approach can be extended to apply to multiple hypotheses and, therefore, to the decoding of communication symbols.

For clarity, we will first apply the maximum-likelihood approach to the simple case where the measured waveform consists of a single scalar. This is done to expose the important points of multiple hypothesis statistical inference, without the additional notational complications of measurements having several degrees of freedom.

The development of maximum-likelihood decoding with waveform measurements having many degrees of freedom then proceeds along similar lines. The chief difference is that the waveform is represented as a set of N scalars in an N-dimensional signal space. These scalars are chosen to be Karhunen–Loève coordinates, corresponding to uncorrelated samples in general and statistically independent samples for additive Gaussian noise in particular.

The important case of additive Gaussian noise is treated separately. Here the formalism takes off in two separate directions corresponding to coherent and noncoherent processing. In coherent processing, the received symbols correspond exactly, apart from the noise, to a set of symbol replicas in the receiver. This leads to information processing consisting of correlation of the received waveform with a set of symbol replicas. The outputs of these correlators are then used directly in a comparison that selects which symbol is to be decoded.

In the noncoherent case, the received waveforms are assumed to have undergone a phase shift of unknown magnitude. Information processing for detection still consists of correlations, but the outputs of these correlators must now have their envelope extracted prior to detection.

5.2.2 Multiple Hypothesis Inference with a Single Sample

We illustrate maximum-likelihood detection by first considering the simplest example: distinguishing between alternative statistical hypotheses based on a measurement of one sample. The single measurement multiple hypothesis problem is a simple yet informative way of getting acquainted with the use of the maximum-likelihood approach in statistical inference. Later this approach will be generalized to the detection of coherent and noncoherent waveforms.

We are allowed a single measurement, denoted by x, with which we are to infer which one out of several possible population probability density functions is most likely to have generated it. We are, therefore, dealing with a set of mutually exclusive hypotheses, each one corresponding to a particular probability density function:

$$H_1: \quad p_1(x)$$

$$H_2: \quad p_2(x)$$

$$H_3: \quad p_3(x)$$

$$\cdot$$
$$\cdot$$
$$\cdot$$

$$H_M: \quad p_M(x)$$

The posterior conditional probability that the mth hypothesis is the correct one, given that a measurement of x is available, is given in terms of the likelihood ratios as

$$P(m|x) = \frac{P(m)}{\sum_k \Lambda_{km} P(k)} \tag{5.30}$$

where $P(k)$ is the prior probability that x was drawn from distribution $p_k(x)$. The likelihood ratios can be expressed in terms of the probability density functions corresponding to the competing statistical hypotheses:

$$\Lambda_{km} = \frac{\text{Prob}\,(x|H_k)}{\text{Prob}\,(x|H_m)} = \frac{p_k(x)}{p_m(x)} \tag{5.31}$$

From a statistical point of view, the best possible inference is to choose that hypothesis corresponding to the maximum posterior probability $P(m|x)$. In principle, one could compute all M posterior probabilities, compare them to one another, and then select the largest. For example, one could start by picking a pair of posterior probabilities, compare them, select the largest of the two and discard the smallest. This largest probability is then compared with another probability chosen from the M-2 remaining, and so on until all cases are exhausted. In all, M-1 comparisons are made and the final selection is the result of M-1 elementary decisions. One such elementary decision, the comparison of $P(m|x)$ and $P(n|x)$, can be expressed mathematically by thresholding the ratio:

$$\frac{P(m|x)}{P(n|x)} = \frac{P(x|m)}{P(x\,n)} \cdot \frac{P(m)}{P(n)} = \Lambda_{mn} \frac{P(m)}{P(n)} \overset{m}{\underset{n}{\overset{>}{<}}} 1 \tag{5.32}$$

Since the quantities $P(m)$ and $P(n)$ can be considered to be known in advance, the elementary decisions of statistical inference involve only the likelihood ratios, which may be thresholded according to the decision rule:

$$\Lambda_{mn} \underset{\underset{n}{<}}{\overset{\overset{m}{>}}{}} \frac{P(n)}{P(m)} \tag{5.33}$$

EXAMPLE

Consider the simplest case of only two hypotheses: H_0 corresponding to $p_0(x)$ and H_1 corresponding to $p_1(x)$. The posterior probabilities are given by

$$P(0|x) = \frac{P(0)}{\Lambda_{00} P(0) + \Lambda_{10} P(1)}$$

$$P(1|x) = \frac{P(1)}{\Lambda_{01} P(0) + \Lambda_{11} P(1)}$$

Noting that $\Lambda_{01} = (\Lambda_{10})^{-1} \equiv \Lambda$ and that $\Lambda_{00} = \Lambda_{11} = 1$, and further denoting the ratio of prior probabilities $P(0)/P(1)$ by α, the ratio of posterior probabilities takes the form

$$\frac{P(0|x)}{P(1|x)} = \frac{\Lambda\alpha + 1}{(\Lambda\alpha)^{-1} + 1} \underset{<}{\overset{>}{}} 1$$

This corresponds to Λ being thresholded at the critical value $\Lambda_{\text{crit}} = \alpha^{-1}$. Values of Λ greater than α^{-1} result in H_0 being declared true; values of Λ smaller than α^{-1} result in H_1 being declared true.

If the prior probabilities are equal, $P(0) = P(1)$ and $\alpha = 1$. For this special case, $\Lambda_{\text{crit}} = 1$ and, therefore, since

$$\Lambda_{\text{crit}} = \frac{P(0|x_{\text{crit}})}{P(1|x_{\text{crit}})} = \frac{p_0(x_{\text{crit}})}{p_1(x_{\text{crit}})}$$

the proper threshold for x is where the probability density functions $p_0(x)$ and $p_1(x)$ intersect, i.e., x_{crit} is the solution to

$$p_0(x) = p_1(x)$$

The likelihood ratios contain all of the information necessary for statistical inference and detection.

5.2.3 Multiple Hypothesis Inference with a Waveform

In general, more than one sample is usually available for detection. Communication is often accomplished by means of signals of finite duration. Detection for communication waveforms, therefore, involves statistical inference using probabilities associated with these waveforms.

The formalism needed is a simple extension of the single sample discussion given before, which can be viewed as a problem of statistical inference with one degree of freedom, namely, the single sample available. This approach can be generalized to waveforms having several degrees of freedom through the representation of these waveforms by a set of scalars given by their signal-space coordinates.

Just as before, we are dealing with M distinct statistical hypotheses. These hypotheses now correspond to the M possible waveforms $\{s_1(t), s_2(t), s_3(t), \ldots, s_M(t)\}$. With these M symbols are associated a set of M corresponding prior probabilities $\{P(1), P(2), P(3), \ldots, P(M)\}$ assumed to be known quantities. The difference is that now we have available a measured waveform $r(t)$. Furthermore, let us assume that waveform $r(t)$ can be represented in a signal space. The statistical hypotheses can be enumerated as follows:

$$H_1: \quad p_1(r)$$

$$H_2: \quad p_2(r)$$

$$H_3: \quad p_3(r)$$

$$\cdot$$

$$\cdot$$

$$\cdot$$

$$H_M: \quad p_M(r)$$

The posterior probabilities are now ranked by means of M-1 elementary decisions based on comparing pairs of posterior probabilities:

$$\frac{P(m|r)}{P(n|r)} = \frac{P(r|m)}{P(r|n)} \cdot \frac{P(m)}{P(n)} = \Lambda_{mn} \frac{P(m)}{P(n)} \underset{n}{\overset{m}{\underset{<}{>}}} 1 \qquad (5.34)$$

The indices m and n run over all possible M alphabet symbols. This is equivalent to thresholding the likelihood ratios:

$$\Lambda_{mn} \underset{n}{\overset{m}{\underset{<}{>}}} \frac{P(n)}{P(m)} \qquad (5.35)$$

We now express Λ_{mn} in terms of the waveform $r(t)$. To this end, we write the likelihood ratio in terms of probability density functions associated with the corresponding statistical hypotheses:

$$\Lambda_{mn} = \frac{P(r|m)}{P(r|n)} = \frac{\text{Prob } \{r(t)|H_m \text{ is true}\}}{\text{Prob } \{r(t)|H_n \text{ is true}\}} = \frac{p_m(r)}{p_n(r)} \qquad (5.36)$$

Now the probability densities $p_k(r)$ appearing in the last equation can each be expressed as a joint probability density in terms of the N coordinates of $r(t)$ in some signal space:

$$p_k(r) = p_k(r_1, r_2, r_3, \ldots, r_N) \quad \text{where } r_j = \langle \varphi_j(t) | r(t) \rangle \tag{5.37}$$

The functions $\varphi_j(t)$ are basis functions in an N-dimensional signal space. Considerable simplification results when the r_j are statistically independent, for then the joint probability density can be expressed in terms of the product of individual densities for each of the r_j:

$$p_k(r_1, r_2, r_3, \ldots, r_N) = p_{k_1}(r_1) p_{k_2}(r_2) p_{k_3}(r_3) \ldots p_{k_N}(r_N) \tag{5.38}$$

This happy circumstance fortunately occurs often in communication systems. If the signals are transmitted in additive Gaussian noise, then the joint probability density function is a joint Gaussian density function. Choosing the $\varphi_j(t)$ to be the Karhunen–Loève basis functions results in uncorrelated r_j coefficients that, by virtue of being Gaussian, are also statistically independent.

5.2.4 Coherent Waveform Detection in Gaussian Noise

We now apply the results of the foregoing discussions of hypothesis testing to the specific problem of detecting a waveform in additive Gaussian noise. This is done for both coherent and envelope detection. First, we examine the case of coherent detection.

The received signal is

$$r(t) = s_m(t) + z(t) \tag{5.39}$$

where $s_m(t)$ is one of M possible waveforms from a signaling alphabet. The noise process $z(t)$ is Gaussian with zero mean, with variance σ_k^2 in the kth degree of freedom and with the autocorrelation function $E[z^*(t)z(t')] = R_z(t, t')$.

A Karhunen–Loève expansion of the last equation results in N expressions describing the uncorrelated (and, therefore, statistically independent) components of the measured waveform, the kth one of which is

$$r_k = s_{mk} + z_k \tag{5.40}$$

where

$$r_k = \langle \varphi_k(t) | r(t) \rangle \qquad s_{mk} = \langle \varphi_k(t) | s_m(t) \rangle \qquad z_k = \langle \varphi_k(t) | z(t) \rangle \tag{5.41}$$

and where the Karhunen–Loève basis functions $\varphi_k(t)$ are orthonormal solutions to the equation

$$\langle R_z(t, t') | \varphi_k(t') \rangle = \sigma_k^2 \varphi_k(t) \tag{5.42}$$

Since the expansion coefficients r_k are normally distributed, a typical probability density function $p_{mk}(r_k)$ is fully described in terms of the mean and variance of r_k for the mth statistical hypothesis. These quantities are

$$E[r_k] = s_{mk} \tag{5.43a}$$

$$E[(r_k - s_{mk})^2] = \sigma_k^2 \tag{5.43b}$$

The probability density function $p_{mk}(r_k)$ can then be written as

$$p_{mk}(r_k) = \frac{1}{\sigma_k (2\pi)^{1/2}} \exp\left[-\frac{(r_k - s_{mk})^2}{2\sigma_k^2} \right] \tag{5.44}$$

The joint density for the posterior probability of receiving $r(t)$ corresponding to the mth hypothesis can be written as a product of probability densities, since the r_k are statistically independent:

$$p_m(r) = \prod_k p_{mk}(r_k) \tag{5.45}$$

The likelihood ratio is given by the ratio of two such posterior probability densities, each density corresponding to one of the competing statistical hypotheses:

$$\Lambda_{mn} = \frac{p_m(r)}{p_n(r)} \tag{5.46}$$

With Gaussian statistics, the likelihood ratio becomes

$$\Lambda_{mn} = \exp\left[\sum_{k=1}^{N} \frac{|r_k - s_{nk}|^2 - |r_k - s_{mk}|^2}{2\sigma_k^2}\right] \tag{5.47}$$

Noting that r_k and s_{nk} are, in general, complex, the last equation for Λ_{mn} can be expanded and written in the form

$$\Lambda_{mn} = \exp\left\{-\mathscr{Re}\left[\sum_{k=1}^{N} \frac{r_k^*(s_{nk} - s_{mk})}{\sigma_k^2} + \sum_{k=1}^{N} \frac{s_{mk}^* s_{mk} - s_{nk}^* s_{nk}}{2\sigma_k^2}\right]\right\}$$

Next we introduce the quantities

$$\psi_{nk} = s_{nk}/\sigma_k^2 \tag{5.48}$$

which are the Karhunen–Loève expansion coefficients for the time functions

$$\psi_n(t) = \sum_k \psi_{nk}\varphi_k(t) \tag{5.49}$$

where $\psi_{nk} = \langle\varphi_k(t)|\psi_n(t)\rangle$. The likelihood ratio can now be written as

$$\Lambda_{mn} = \exp\left\{-\mathscr{Re}\left[\sum_k r_k^*(\psi_{nk} - \psi_{mk}) + \frac{1}{2}\sum_k s_{mk}^*\psi_{mk} - \frac{1}{2}\sum_k s_{nk}^*\psi_{nk}\right]\right\}$$

$$\tag{5.50}$$

where the indicated sums are over the space-coordinate index k. Next we use a theorem of linear signal-space theory, introduced in Chapter 2, that guarantees the equality of the inner product between two functions and the inner product of their representations with respect to an orthonormal basis set. More precisely, if S is an arbitrary N-dimensional space spanned by an orthonormal basis set, then, for any function $x \in S$, there is a one-to-one correspondence between x and its representation in the space of complex N-tuples. Furthermore, there is an equality of inner products in both spaces. This theorem allows us to make the following associations:

$$\sum_k r_k^* \psi_{nk} = \langle r(t) | \psi_n(t) \rangle \tag{5.51a}$$

$$\sum_k r_k^* \psi_{mk} = \langle r(t) | \psi_m(t) \rangle \tag{5.51b}$$

$$\sum_k s_{mk}^* \psi_{mk} = \langle s_m(t) | \psi_m(t) \rangle \tag{5.51c}$$

$$\sum_k s_{nk}^* \psi_{nk} = \langle s_n(t) | \psi_n(t) \rangle \tag{5.51d}$$

Let us determine the form of the functions $\psi_n(t)$ defined in Eqs. (5.48) and (5.49). We have

$$\psi_n(t') = \sum_k \frac{1}{\sigma_k^2} s_{nk} \varphi_k(t')$$

Multiplying both sides by $R_z(t,t')$, integrating over t', and using the inner product notation for the integral, we have

$$\langle R_z(t,t') | \psi_n(t') \rangle = \sum_k \frac{1}{\sigma_k^2} s_{nk} \langle R_z(t,t') | \varphi_k(t') \rangle$$

But the inner products on the right-hand side are simply

$$\langle R_z(t,t') | \varphi_k(t') \rangle = \sigma_k^2 \varphi_k(t)$$

so that we have

$$\langle R_z(t,t') | \psi_n(t') \rangle = \sum_k s_{nk} \varphi_k(t) = s_n(t)$$

The functions $\psi_n(t)$ are, therefore, solutions to the integral equations

$$\langle R_z(t,t') | \psi_n(t') \rangle = \varphi_n(t) \tag{5.52}$$

We can now offer an interesting interpretation for our expression for Λ_{mn}. The quantity within square brackets in Eq. (5.50) is simply

$$\mathscr{R}e\left[\langle r | \psi_n \rangle - \langle r | \psi_m \rangle - \tfrac{1}{2}\langle s_m | \psi_m \rangle + \tfrac{1}{2}\langle s_n | \psi_n \rangle \right] = U_n - U_m \tag{5.53}$$

where

$$U_k = \mathscr{R}e \langle r | \psi_k \rangle + \tfrac{1}{2}\langle s_k | \psi_k \rangle \tag{5.54}$$

Processing for detection in additive colored Gaussian noise, therefore, consists in evaluating the quantities U_k and then decoding in favor of the largest U_k. Note that the first term in the expression for U_k simply describes passing the received waveform $r(t)$ through a correlation filter having the impulse response $\psi_k(t)$. Equivalently, a matched filter may be used. The $\psi_k(t)$ are related to the signaling waveforms $s_k(t)$ and to the noise covariance $R_z(t,t')$ by the integral equation $\langle R_z(t,t')|\psi_n(t')\rangle = s_n(t)$. The second term in the expression for U_k is a known bias term. For equal energy signals in white noise, this term is a constant for all k and can be omitted from the calculation.

For the important case of white Gaussian noise, the noise variance is a constant for all degrees of freedom

$$\sigma_k^2 = \sigma_0^2 = \text{constant} \tag{5.55}$$

and we have

$$\psi_m(t) = s_m(t)/\sigma_0 \qquad \text{and} \qquad \psi_n(t) = s_n(t)/\sigma_0$$

$$\langle s_m(t)|\psi_m(t)\rangle = \mathcal{E}_m/\sigma_0^2 \qquad \text{and} \qquad \langle s_n(t)|\psi_n(t)\rangle = \mathcal{E}_n/\sigma_0^2$$

where $\mathcal{E}_m$ and $\mathcal{E}_n$ are the energies in the mth and in the nth waveforms, respectively. The likelihood ratio can finally be reduced to the simpler form

$$\Lambda_{mn} = \exp\left\{-\mathcal{R}e\left[\langle r(t)|s_n(t)\rangle - \langle r(t)|s_m(t)\rangle + \frac{1}{2}(\mathcal{E}_m - \mathcal{E}_n)\right]\Big/\sigma_0^2\right\}$$

For detection, the likelihood ratio is thresholded as follows:

$$\Lambda_{mn} \mathop{\substack{m \\ > \\ < \\ n}} \frac{P(n)}{P(m)}$$

The exponential function is monotonic in its argument. It may be more practical, both analytically as well as in implementations, to threshold a quantity proportional to the argument of the exponential function. To this end, we rewrite the likelihood ratio as

$$\Lambda_{mn} = \exp(U_m - U_n) \tag{5.56}$$

where

$$U_m\sigma_0^2 = \mathcal{R}e\,\langle r(t)|s_m(t)\rangle - \tfrac{1}{2}\mathcal{E}_m \tag{5.57a}$$

$$U_n\sigma_0^2 = \mathcal{R}e\,\langle r(t)|s_n(t)\rangle - \tfrac{1}{2}\mathcal{E}_n \tag{5.57b}$$

The threshold condition then becomes

$$\mathcal{R}e\,\langle r(t)|s_m(t)\rangle - \mathcal{R}e\,\langle r(t)|s_n(t)\rangle \mathop{\substack{m \\ > \\ < \\ n}} \tfrac{1}{2}(\mathcal{E}_m - \mathcal{E}_n) + \sigma_0^2[\ln P(n) - \ln P(m)] \tag{5.58}$$

Further obvious simplifications are possible if, as is in fact the case with many communication waveforms, all signals $s_n(t)$ have the same energy. In this case, the terms $\mathcal{E}_m$ and $\mathcal{E}_n$ are all equal and signal energy need not enter in the threshold equation. In addition, if all symbols are equally probable a priori, prior symbol probabilities need not be considered. When both these simplifications hold, the right-hand side of the threshold equation vanishes. This is usually the case with communication systems. The resulting decoding rule selects the symbol corresponding to the largest value of $\Re e\langle r(t)|s_m(t)\rangle$, the correlator output.

Let us pause and take note of where our analysis has taken us. We started with a very general likelihood-ratio approach to hypothesis testing and applied it to the problem of detecting waveforms in additive white Gaussian noise. The result, it turned out, involved a threshold operation on quantities of the form $\Re e\langle r(t)|s_m(t)\rangle$. The maximum likelihood formulation, therefore, prescribes a particular approach to processing and detection. First, one calculates the real part of the inner product of the received waveform $r(t)$ with each of the possible symbol waveforms $s_m(t)$ from the M-ary alphabet. The symbol corresponding to the largest value of the decision variable $\Re e\langle r(t)|s_m(t)\rangle$ is then decoded.

5.2.5 Noncoherent Waveform Detection in Gaussian Noise

We now turn to the case of noncoherent detection, where only the waveform's envelope is available for statistical inference. The approach is very similar to what was done with coherent detection.

The received signal is

$$r(t) = s_m(t) \exp[-j\,\theta_m(t)] + z(t) \tag{5.59}$$

where $j = (-1)^{1/2}$, and $s_m(t)$ is one of M possible waveforms from a signaling alphabet. Here we have explicitly expressed the received waveform (exclusive of the noise term) in terms of its real amplitude $s_m(t)$ and of a random phase term $\theta_m(t)$. The noise process $z(t)$ is Gaussian with zero mean, with variance σ_k^2 in the kth degree of freedom, and with the autocorrelation function given by the expectation $E[z^*(t)z(t')] = R_z(t,t')$. The received waveform can be decomposed in terms of Karhunen–Loève expansion coefficients, the kth one of which is

$$r_k = s_{mk} \exp(-j\,\theta_{mk}) + z_k \tag{5.60}$$

where the phases θ_{mk} are uniformly distributed from 0 to 2π. The uniform distribution is the most random. Uniform distribution of the phases corresponds to maximum uncertainty. Statistical inference starts with the calculation of the likelihood ratio, which is a ratio of posterior probabilities with densities of the form

$$p_m(r) = \prod_k p_{mk}(r_k)$$

This form implicitly assumes that the received waveform $r(t)$ has been expressed in terms of its uncorrelated Karhunen–Loève expansion coefficients, so that the joint probability density for a Gaussian process can be written as a product of individual coefficient probability densities.

The variable r_k is normally distributed with a mean and variance given by

$$E[r_k] = \mu_k = E[s_{mk} \exp(-j\,\theta_{mk})] \tag{5.61a}$$

$$E[(r_k - \mu_k)^2] = \sigma_k^2 \tag{5.61b}$$

The posterior probability densities can now be written explicitly in terms of joint probability densities for the amplitude and phase in each of the Karhunen–Loève components:

$$p_m(r, \theta_m) = \left(\frac{1}{2\pi}\right)^{N/2} \prod_{k=1}^{N} \frac{1}{\sigma_k} \exp\left[-\frac{|r_k - s_{mk}\exp(-j\theta_{mk})|^2}{2\sigma_k^2}\right] \tag{5.62}$$

The corresponding marginal densities in terms of the amplitudes only may be obtained from the last expression by averaging over the uniformly distributed phase θ_{mk}. That is, we multiply each side of Eq. (5.62) by $(2\pi)^{-N} d\theta_{m1} d\theta_{m2} \ldots d\theta_{mN}$ and integrate each integral from 0 to 2π. The left-hand side integrates to $p_m(r)$. The resulting expression becomes

$$p_m(r) = \left(\frac{1}{2\pi}\right)^{N/2-N} \prod_{k=1}^{N} \frac{1}{\sigma_k} \int_0^{2\pi} \exp\left[-\frac{|r_k - s_{mk}\exp(-j\theta_{mk})|^2}{2\sigma_k^2}\right] d\theta_{mk}$$

$$= \left(\frac{1}{2\pi}\right)^{N/2-N} \left(\prod_{k=1}^{N} \frac{1}{\sigma_k}\right) \int_0^{2\pi} \exp \sum_{k=1}^{N} \left[-\frac{|r_k - s_{mk}\exp(-j\theta_{mk})|^2}{2\sigma_k^2}\right] d\theta_{mk} \tag{5.63}$$

The numerator in the square brackets can be expanded to become

$$-|r_k|^2 - |s_{mk}|^2 + r_k^* s_{mk}\exp(-j\theta_{mk}) + r_k s_{mk}^* \exp(j\theta_{mk})$$

so that the integral in Eq. (5.63) can be rewritten as

$$\exp\left(-\sum_{k=1}^{N} \frac{|r_k|^2 + |s_{mk}|^2}{2\sigma_k^2}\right) \int_0^{2\pi} \exp\left(\sum_{k=1}^{N} \frac{r_k^* s_{mk} e^{-j\theta_{mk}} + r_k s_{mk}^* e^{j\theta_{mk}}}{2\sigma_k^2}\right) d\theta_{mk}$$

The integral may be written as

$$\int_0^{2\pi} \beta^*(\theta)\beta(\theta)\, d\theta = 2\int_0^{\pi} \beta^*(\theta)\beta(\theta)\, d\theta$$

where $\beta(\theta) = \exp(\alpha_m e^{-j\theta})$, and α_m is the complex quantity

$$\alpha_m = \sum_{k=1}^{N} \frac{r_k^* s_{mk}}{2\sigma_k^2}$$

Expressing the complex exponential in the argument of $\beta(\theta)$ in terms of trigonometric functions and using Euler's identity

$$e^{jx} = \cos x + j\sin x$$

gives

$$\beta(\theta) = e^{\alpha_m \cos \theta}[\cos(\alpha_m \sin \theta) - j \sin(\alpha_m \sin \theta)]$$

so that

$$\beta^*(\theta)\beta(\theta) = e^{2\alpha_m \cos \theta}$$

and the integral reduces to

$$2\int_0^\pi \beta^*(\theta)\beta(\theta)\, d\theta = 2\int_0^\pi e^{2\alpha_m \cos \theta}\, d\theta = 2\pi I_0(\alpha_m)$$

where $I_0(\alpha_m)$ is a modified Bessel function of order zero. The posterior probability for the mth hypothesis may be written, therefore, as

$$p_m(r) = \left(\frac{1}{2\pi}\right)^{\frac{N}{2}}\left(\prod_{k=1}^N \frac{1}{\sigma_k}\right)\exp\left(-\sum_{k=1}^N \frac{|r_k|^2 + |s_{mk}|^2}{2\sigma_k^2}\right)I_0\left(\left|\sum_{k=1}^N \frac{r_k^* s_{mk}}{2\sigma_k^2}\right|\right)$$

The argument of the Bessel function appears as an absolute value since $I_0(\alpha)$ is an even function of α, i.e., $I_0(\alpha_m)$ depends on α only through the combination $\alpha_m^* \alpha_m$. The likelihood ratio becomes

$$\Lambda_{mn} = \exp\left(-\sum_{k=1}^N \frac{|s_{mk}|^2 - |s_{nk}|^2}{2\sigma_k^2}\right)\frac{I_0(\alpha_m)}{I_0(\alpha_n)}$$

For signals having equal energy, the argument of the exponential vanishes and there remains

$$\Lambda_{mn} = \frac{I_0(\alpha_m)}{I_0(\alpha_n)} \underset{n}{\overset{m}{\underset{<}{>}}} 1$$

where the corresponding decoding decision rule is indicated. For additive white Gaussian noise, $\sigma_k^2 = \sigma_0^2$, and there results

$$\left|\sum_{k=1}^N \frac{r_k^* s_{mk}}{2\sigma_0^2}\right| = \frac{1}{2\sigma_0^2}|\langle r|s_m\rangle| \tag{5.64}$$

If all of the waveforms have the same energy, then the decision variable is given by the absolute value of the inner product $|\langle r|s\rangle|$, since $I_0(\cdot)$ is a monotonic function of its argument.

Optimal noncoherent detection in additive white Gaussian noise with equally probable equal-energy signals consists in forming the M decision variables $U_k = |\langle r(t)|s_k(t)\rangle|$, $k = 1, \ldots, M$, and then decoding in favor of the symbol corresponding to the largest U_k. Note that U_k is the absolute value of the inner product of $r(t)$ with $s_k(t)$, which can be computed with a correlator or a matched filter. The implementation of this processing system consists of a matched filter followed by an envelope detector.

EXAMPLE

As an important example of noncoherent detection, we consider the processing of a continuous wave radar pulse with amplitude A, duration T, and angular frequency ω. The noise is Gaussian with zero mean and variance σ^2. The two statistical hypotheses correspond to the signal-absent and signal-present cases:

$$H_0: \quad r(t) = n(t) \qquad\qquad \text{noise-only hypothesis}$$

$$H_1: \quad r(t) = Ae^{j(\omega t - \theta)} + n(t) \qquad \text{signal plus noise hypothesis}$$

The formalism of this section is applicable with $s_0(t) = 0$ and $s_1(t) = Ae^{j\omega t}$. We have, therefore

$$\sum_{k=1}^{N} \frac{r_k^* s_{0k}}{2\sigma_k^2} = 0 \quad \text{and} \quad \prod_{k=1}^{N} \frac{r_k^* s_{1k}}{2\sigma_k^2} = \frac{Aq}{2\sigma^2}$$

and there follows

$$\alpha_0 = 0 \qquad I_0(\alpha_0) = 1 \qquad \text{and} \qquad \alpha_0 = \frac{Aq}{2\sigma^2}, \text{ where } q = |\langle r(t)|e^{j\omega t}\rangle|$$

The likelihood ratio is

$$\Lambda_{10} = \exp\left(-\frac{A^2 T}{2\sigma^2}\right) I_0\left(\frac{A}{2\sigma^2} |\langle r(t)|e^{j\omega t}\rangle|\right)$$

The Bessel function $I_0(x)$ has the following power series expansion

$$I_0(x) = \sum_{k=0}^{\infty} \frac{[(\tfrac{1}{2}x)^2]^k}{(k!)^2}$$

so that $I_0(x)$ depends on x only in a quadratic manner. Furthermore, $I_0(x)$ is a monotonic increasing function of x. Instead of thresholding the likelihood ratio Λ_{10}, we can equivalently threshold q or q^2. Choosing the latter, we have

$$q^2 = |\langle r(t)|e^{j\omega t}\rangle|^2 = |\langle r(t)|\cos\omega t\rangle|^2 + |\langle r(t)|\sin\omega t\rangle|^2 \qquad (5.65)$$

The calculation of q^2 from the received waveform $r(t)$ can easily be implemented with a processing structure called a *quadrature demodulator*, which is shown in Fig. 5-8. In a quadrature demodulator, the received waveform $r(t)$ is split equally into two arms. In one arm, it is mixed with the signal $\cos\omega t$, integrated from 0 to T, squared and sampled at the instant $t = T$ when the integration is complete. The other arm undergoes similar steps, but with mixing with the signal $\sin\omega t$. The results of both arms are then added to produce the output q^2.

In addition to introducing the quadrature demodulator, this example serves to show that the maximum likelihood approach actually specifies the processing structure of the receiver. What began as a statistical approach for choosing between several alternative hypotheses eventually led us to a rational method for designing an optimum receiver structure.

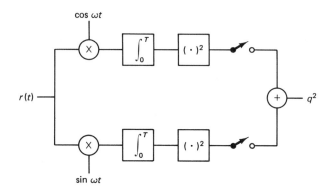

cos ωt

$r(t)$

q^2

sin ωt

Figure 5-8. Quadrature receiver for noncoherent detection.

In order to better appreciate the functioning of the quadrature demodulator, consider the simple example of receiving the signal $r(t) = A\cos(\omega t + \theta)$, where θ is an unknown phase. The output of the mixer in the top arm is

$$x(t) = A\cos(\omega t + \theta)\cos \omega t = A(\cos \omega t \cos \theta - \sin \omega t \sin \theta)\cos \omega t$$

$$= A\cos^2 \omega t \cos \theta - A\sin \omega t \cos \omega t \sin \theta$$

Similarly, for the lower arm, we have

$$y(t) = A\cos(\omega t + \theta)\sin \omega t = A(\cos \omega t \cos \theta - \sin \omega t \sin \theta)\sin \omega t$$

$$= A\cos \omega t \sin \omega t \cos \theta - A\sin^2 \omega t \sin \theta$$

We take T to be an integral number of periods. In actuality, this is not necessarily the case, but the frequency is usually so high, $\omega \gg 2\pi/T$, that the difference is negligibly small. The corresponding integrator outputs are then

$$\int_0^T x(t)\, dt = \frac{AT}{2}\cos \theta \qquad \int_0^T y(t)\, dt = \frac{AT}{2}\sin \theta$$

Squaring and summing, there results

$$q^2 = \frac{A^2 T^2}{4}(\cos^2 \theta + \sin^2 \theta) = \frac{A^2 T^2}{4} \tag{5.66}$$

so that $q = \frac{1}{2}AT$. Note that the dependence on the unknown phase θ has disappeared. Had the phase been known, only the top arm of the quadrature demodulator would have been sufficient, for then the phase in the reference signal could have been adjusted to correspond to the phase in the received signal. This, of course, is the matched filter for a perfectly known waveform. By viewing the received sinusoid as a phasor, the reference signal is an identical (in frequency and phase) phasor that tracks the received signal. The operations of multiplying $r(t)$ by the reference signal and integrating is an inner product whose effect is to project $r(t)$ onto a reference real axis that exactly tracks $r(t)$ in frequency and phase. The projection is always maximum and is equal to the norm of $r(t)$.

When the phase θ is not known, a single demodulator arm can no longer be used without degradation. In general, phasor $r(t)$ will no longer be aligned exactly along one of the axes, but will have a projection on both. Using the signal from only one of the arms leads to a loss of part of the signal. The quadrature demodulator computes both projections: one corresponding to a $\cos \theta$ term and another to a $\sin \theta$ term. The entire signal is recovered by squaring and adding, which gets rid of the unknown phase dependence.

The argument of the Bessel function to be thresholded is

$$\frac{Aq}{2\sigma^2} = \frac{\mathscr{E}}{2\sigma^2} = \gamma \tag{5.67}$$

where the signal energy $\mathscr{E} = \frac{1}{2}A^2T$, and γ is the ratio of signal energy to the noise energy per waveform degree of freedom.

Since the quadrature demodulator appears to recapture all of the signal energy without requiring a knowledge of the phase, it is not immediately obvious why one should go through the trouble of demodulating coherently (i.e., with a matched filter) when possible. There is, in fact, some degradation associated with quadrature demodulation when compared with coherent demodulation. This is so because coherent processing uses only one of the arms in the demodulator. The noncoherent quadrature processor uses two arms and, therefore, passes twice the amount of noise through. This results in poorer performance than for coherent processing.

5.3 NEYMAN–PEARSON STATISTICS

We have seen that the maximum likelihood approach to detection is a statistical inference method consisting of elementary decisions based on thresholding the likelihood ratio in accordance with the ratio of prior probabilities corresponding to the statistical hypotheses. This thresholding rule was derived as

$$\Lambda_{mn} \underset{\underset{n}{<}}{\overset{\overset{m}{>}}{}} \frac{P(n)}{P(m)} \tag{5.68}$$

Sometimes the prior probabilities $P(m)$ and $P(n)$ are not known or cannot be defined. The arrival of a synchronization packet is such an example. Another is the familiar example of radar or sonar detection. In both these examples, the two statistical hypotheses are

$$H_0: \quad \text{signal present}$$

$$H_1: \quad \text{signal absent}$$

In neither case can a prior probability be defined. Yet, clearly, there is the need for a rational detection strategy. This section explores the Neyman–Pearson approach to detection, which results in constant false-alarm-rate (CFAR) detection.

5.3.1 Neyman–Pearson Detection

The problem with extending the likelihood ratio approach to the type of detection problems considered in this section is that a threshold cannot be computed from the prior probabilities. Yet, one is still left with much of the usual formalism of statistical inference. Let us explore this with the simple example of a single measurement x and two competing statistical hypotheses. This will eventually lead us to binary CFAR processing.

One can still assign posterior probability densities with each of the two statistical hypotheses:

$$H_0: \quad p_0(x)$$

$$H_1: \quad p_1(x)$$

The consequences of thresholding measurement x are shown in Figure 5-9. The threshold value is denoted by δ, leading to the threshold condition

$$x \begin{array}{c} H_0 \\ < \\ > \\ H_1 \end{array} \delta$$

Two types of detection errors will happen as a result of this. First, there is the possibility of missing a detection when H_1 is true but $x < \delta$. This type of detection error occurs with probability

$$1 - P_d = \int_{-\infty}^{\delta} p_1(x)\, dx \tag{5.69}$$

where P_d is the probability of detection. Second, H_0 might be true but $x > \delta$. For example, no signal is present but the noise happens to be strong enough to exceed threshold. A detection will be wrongly declared. This is known as a false alarm and occurs with probability

$$P_{fa} = \int_{\delta}^{\infty} p_0(x)\, dx \tag{5.70}$$

Neither type of detection error can be completely avoided, but the balance of one relative to the other is controlled by the choice of the threshold δ. One possible strategy for choosing δ is to minimize the overall cost or risk associated with both types of detection errors. For example, if the cost of missing a detection is C_0 and that of a false alarm is C_1, then the expected value of the cost associated with this strategy is

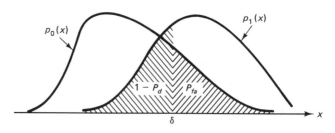

Figure 5-9. Thresholded binary detection. The shaded areas correspond to the two types of error that may occur.

$$C(\delta) = C_0(1 - P_d) + C_1 P_{fa}$$

This expression is minimized by the value of δ that causes the derivative of $C(\delta)$ with respect to δ to vanish

$$\frac{dC(\delta)}{d\delta} = C_0 p_1(\delta) - C_1 p_0(\delta) = 0 \quad \text{at } \delta = \delta'$$

where δ' is the value of δ that is a solution to the last equation. This results in the following condition:

$$\frac{p_0(\delta')}{p_1(\delta')} = \frac{C_0}{C_1} = \lambda(\delta') \tag{5.71}$$

where $\lambda(\delta')$ is a constant that depends only on the threshold δ'. If decision costs can be assigned, the last expression can then be solved for the threshold δ'. Note that $\lambda(\delta')$ is a ratio of posterior probability densities and, therefore, is a likelihood ratio.

This formalism is easily extended to the case of binary detection, where the measurement is a waveform r with N independent degrees of freedom. The measurement r can always be expressed in terms of uncorrelated coordinates $\{r_1, r_2, r_3, \dots, r_N\}$, for example, the Karhunen–Loève expansion coefficients. If these variables are also statistically independent (such would be the case for Gaussian noise), then the two hypotheses are

$$H_0: \quad p_{01}(r_1)p_{02}(r_2) \dots p_{0N}(r_N)$$
$$H_1: \quad p_{11}(r_1)p_{12}(r_2) \dots p_{1N}(r_N)$$

The expression for the probability of a missed detection is

$$1 - P_d = \int_{-\infty}^{\delta_1} p_{01}(r_1) \, dr_1 \int_{-\infty}^{\delta_2} p_{02}(r_2) \, dr_2 \dots \int_{-\infty}^{\delta_N} p_{0N}(r_N) \, dr_N \tag{5.72}$$

and the probability of a false alarm is

$$P_{fa} = \int_{\delta_1}^{\infty} p_{11}(r_1) \, dr_1 \int_{\delta_2}^{\infty} p_{12}(r_2) \, dr_2 \dots \int_{\delta_N}^{\infty} p_{1N}(r_N) \, dr_N \tag{5.73}$$

The cost is now a function of all of the δ_k:

$$C(\boldsymbol{\delta}) = C_0(1 - P_d) + C_1 P_{fa} \tag{5.74}$$

where $\boldsymbol{\delta} = \{\delta_1, \delta_2, \delta_3, \dots, \delta_N\}$ has been explicitly denoted as an N-dimensional vector. The thresholds are the solutions to the vector equation

$$\nabla_{\boldsymbol{\delta}} C(\boldsymbol{\delta}) = 0 \tag{5.75}$$

where $\nabla_{\boldsymbol{\delta}}$ is the gradient operator in terms of the partial derivatives with respect to the variables $\{\delta_1, \delta_2, \delta_3, \dots, \delta_N\}$. This results in a set of coupled equations that may be solved for the thresholds $\{\delta_1', \delta_2', \delta_3', \dots, \delta_N'\}$.

5.3.2 Binary Constant False-Alarm-Rate Detection

Returning to the simple case of single-sample binary detection, recall that the ratio of probability densities for the two hypotheses evaluated at the threshold was given by Eq. (5.71). The selection of a threshold is determined by the costs for making each of the two types of detection errors. We have already explored a strategy for determining the threshold δ' that minimizes the total expected value of the cost.

Another possibility exists for determining a threshold. In some applications, the threshold may be fixed to result in a specified constant false-alarm probability or rate (CFAR):

$$P_{fa} = \int_{\delta}^{\infty} p_0(x)\, dx \tag{5.76}$$

This expression can be solved for the appropriate CFAR threshold δ'. The resulting probability of detection is

$$P_d = \int_{\delta'}^{\infty} p_1(x)\, dx \tag{5.77}$$

The interested reader can consult [Wh 71] for more details.

5.3.3 Information-Theoretic Considerations

Consider again the simplest case of binary detection. The output of a matched filter is compared to a specified detection threshold. The detection threshold is usually adjusted to result in a constant false-alarm probability. A measurement consists in determining whether the detection threshold has been exceeded or not. If it has, a detection is declared. The result is a simple Bernoulli event. Its two possible outcomes, labeled y and taking values on the set $\{0, 1\}$, correspond to no detection ($y = 0$) and detection ($y = 1$). Associated with this measurement are the usual probabilities of detection (P_d) and false alarm (P_{fa}).

A useful heuristic approach consists in viewing detection as a measurement of some underlying process made through a binary asymmetric channel with transition probabilities related to the probabilities of detection and false alarm. The underlying process is the presence or absence of a target. A typical measurement consists of a binary thresholded decision that provides information about the underlying process. The detection channel is shown in Figure 5-10.

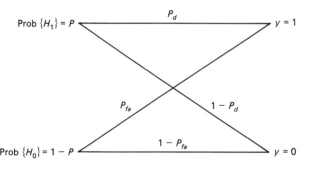

Figure 5-10. The CFAR detection channel.

The underlying process consists of the mutually exclusive statistical hypotheses H_0 and H_1, which are associated with probabilities $1 - P$ and P, respectively. This can be symbolically represented by a channel input variable x that can assume values over the set $\{0, 1\}$ with respective probabilities $1 - P$ and P. The measurement variable y is a random variable over the set $\{0, 1\}$ with associated probabilities defined by

$$\text{Prob}\{y = 1\} = p(y)$$
$$\text{Prob}\{y = 0\} = 1 - p(y) \tag{5.78}$$

The information provided about a particular x event by a particular measurement y is

$$I(x, y) = \log \frac{P(x|y)}{P(x)} \tag{5.79}$$

and the average mutual information between $\mathbf{x}$ and $\mathbf{y}$ is

$$H(\mathbf{x}, \mathbf{y}) = \sum_x \sum_y P(x, y) \log \frac{P(x|y)}{P(x)} \tag{5.80}$$

For the detection channel described before, the average mutual information between $\mathbf{x}$ and $\mathbf{y}$ is

$$H(\mathbf{x}, \mathbf{y}) = H_m - P H_d - (1 - P) H_{fa} \tag{5.81}$$

where H_m is the measurement binary entropy associated with $p(y)$, H_d is the binary entropy associated with the probability of detection P_d, and H_{fa} is the binary entropy associated with the probability of false alarm P_{fa}.

In a communication channel, the channel capacity (i.e., the amount of information that can be carried with arbitrarily good fidelity) is defined as the maximum value of $H(\mathbf{x}, \mathbf{y})$ and corresponds to a particular set of symbol prior probabilities $P(x)$ that maximizes the average mutual information. In the present application, maximizing $H(\mathbf{x}, \mathbf{y})$ is meaningless, since the prior probabilities are fixed. However, the unique value of the average mutual information that results can still be regarded as a fundamental measurement limitation of the detection channel.

Now consider two mutually exclusive hypotheses H_1 and H_0 with respective prior probabilities P and $1 - P$:

$$\text{Prob}\{H_1\} = P$$
$$\text{Prob}\{H_0\} = 1 - P \tag{5.82}$$

The likelihood ratio λ is the ratio of the conditional probabilities

$$\lambda = \frac{\text{Prob}\{y|H_1\}}{\text{Prob}\{y|H_0\}}$$

With the help of Bayes' theorem, this can be rewritten as

$$\lambda = \frac{\text{Prob}\{H_1|y\}}{P} \cdot \frac{1 - P}{\text{Prob}\{H_0|y\}}$$

and leads to the following expression for the log likelihood:

$$\log \lambda = \log\left(\frac{\text{Prob }\{H_1|y\}}{P}\right) - \log\left(\frac{\text{Prob }\{H_0|y\}}{1 - P}\right)$$

Each of the two terms on the right-hand side can be recognized as expressions for mutual information:

$$\log \lambda = I(H_1, y) - I(H_0, y) \tag{5.83}$$

The logarithm of the likelihood ratio can now be interpreted as a difference between two mutual informations. $I(H_0, y)$ represents the information gained about H_0 through a measurement of the variable y. Similarly, $I(H_1, y)$ represents the information gained about H_1 through a measurement of the variable y. These two mutual informations appear with opposing signs in the expression for the log likelihood, indicating that the measurement attempts to discriminate between two competing hypotheses. In fact, the detection process consists in thresholding $\log \lambda$ to determine toward which hypothesis the measurement is being driven by the net mutual information.

It may help at this point to briefly review what has been done and where this is leading. In this chapter, we have treated detection as a statistical inference process. This must be so because each symbol sent by the transmitter may correspond to several received signals due to the effect of noise on the channel. The receiver must produce the best estimate of the transmitted symbol. This led to the maximum-likelihood formalism, which was developed from Bayesian statistics. This, in turn, described the optimum receiver structure that, with additive Gaussian channel noise, turned out to be the matched filter. In the next chapter, we will apply this formalism to determining the performance of various signaling waveforms. We shall look at binary and M-ary signaling with coherent and nonconherent demodulation.

PROBLEMS

5.1 Show that the maximum value of the correlation between two signals is numerically equal to the signal energy and results only when the signals are equal.

5.2 Three equiprobable symbols $\{s_1, s_2, s_3\}$ are encoded using the following code words:

$$s_1 \rightarrow c_1 = 0\ 0\ 0\ 0\ 0\ 0\ 0$$

$$s_2 \rightarrow c_2 = 1\ 1\ 0\ 1\ 0\ 1\ 0$$

$$s_3 \rightarrow c_3 = 0\ 1\ 0\ 1\ 1\ 0\ 1$$

(a) Calculate the Hamming distances $d_H(c_1 - c_2), d_H(c_1 - c_3)$, and $d_H(c_2 - c_3)$.

(b) These code words are transmitted one binary digit at a time over a BSC with crossover probability p. What is the probability of a code-word decoding error? Use approximations where appropriate.

(c) Which symbol is decoded if the received binary sequence is $0\ 1\ 0\ 1\ 0\ 0\ 1$?

(d) What is the probability that c_1 was transmitted given that $0\ 1\ 0\ 1\ 0\ 0\ 1$ is received? Use approximations where appropriate.

5.3 Show that for any $\mathbf{m}$, $P(r \mid \mathbf{m}) = P(\mathbf{m} \mid r)$ when all $P(\mathbf{k})$ are equal.

5.4 Show that the set $\{\varphi_k\}$ that minimizes

$$\epsilon = \sum_{k=N+1}^{M} \varphi_k^{\mathbf{T}} R_{\mathbf{x}} \varphi_k$$

subject to the orthonormality constraint $\varphi_k^{\mathbf{T}} \varphi_n = \delta_{k,n}$ and where the covariance $R_{\mathbf{x}} = E[\mathbf{x}_i \mathbf{x}_j^{\mathbf{T}}]$ satisfies the eigenvalue problem $R_{\mathbf{x}} \varphi_k = \lambda_k \varphi_k$.

5.5 Show that if the costs of missing a detection and incurring a false alarm are identical, then the optimum binary threshold lies where the $p_0(x)$ and $p_1(x)$ curves intersect.

COMMUNICATION PERFORMANCE IN AWGN

Whenever you can, count.

Sir Francis Galton

6

In Chapter 5, we developed the best statistical strategy for inferring which communication symbol was most likely to have been transmitted given the information contained in the received waveform. The maximum-likelihood formalism suggested the form of the optimal processor for both coherent and noncoherent signaling in additive noise.

The present chapter is a natural extension of the maximum-likelihood formalism already introduced. We shall consider the performance of coherent and noncoherent communication in the presence of additive white Gaussian noise. We will describe the performance of coherent and noncoherent M-ary communication and compare efficiencies for different types of signaling. For the most part, we will restrict our attention to the case where all symbol waveforms contain an equal amount of energy. This restriction both simplifies the arithmetic and corresponds to a large number of communication systems. We shall also assume that the receiver is perfectly synchronized to the transmitted waveform.

Coherent and noncoherent performances are presented in separate sections. For clarity, each section begins with a description of the binary signaling case so as to present the essential mathematics of the problem at an early stage. Calculating the decoding performance of a communication system consists in calculating the probabilities that decoding errors are made. This is then followed by a generalization to the M-ary case. This introduces the concept of coding gain for energy-efficient waveforms. Lastly, we infer the performance behavior as M grows without bounds, approximating a signal of large complexity. Here we find that $\gamma_b = \ln 2$ is the minimum energy contrast ratio per bit required for orthogonal signaling in AWGN. We also introduce a powerful result of information theory that states that arbitrarily small decoding errors are achievable over the AWGN channel provided coding complexity is made sufficiently large and provided $\gamma_b > \ln 2$.

This chapter also covers the subject of resource utilization. Waveforms fall into two broad categories, depending on whether they are energy efficient or bandwidth efficient.

6.1 COHERENT COMMUNICATION IN AWGN

Recall from Chapter 5 that the optimal coherent decoding of communication symbols $s_m(t)$ in additive white Gaussian noise consists in computing M decision variables of the form

$$U_m = \mathscr{R}e\langle r(t)|s_m(t)\rangle \qquad (6.1)$$

and in decoding the symbol corresponding to the largest U_m. The probability that maximum-likelihood decoding results in the correct symbol is a function of the relative balance between signal and noise energies present in the received waveform $r(t)$. This performance also depends on the statistics of the noise. We shall adopt as measures of performance the probability of decoding error and relate this probability to the ratio of symbol energy to the noise power spectral density.

Figure 6-1 presents the principal components of a digital communication system. The information source generates a stream of information, here represented as a sequence of binary digits. The coder, discussed in Chapter 4, associates symbols c_k, $k = 1, 2, \ldots, M$, with the states of the information source. These states can be the binary digits themselves or blocks of such digits. A good source coder eliminates much of the redundancy in the information source so that the entropy rate of the $\{c_k\}$ is not much greater than the information source's entropy rate.

The modulator associates a unique waveform $s_k(t)$ with each symbol c_k. Usually, the $\{s_k(t)\}$ describe the voltage or current of an electrical waveform. Whereas the $\{c_k\}$ are simply labels to describe information states, the $\{s_k(t)\}$ are physical signals chosen for their propagation characteristics over the intended channel medium. The AWGN channel adds white Gaussian noise with zero mean and constant variance to the signal, but otherwise leaves it undistorted. This is represented as a channel output of $s_k(t) + n(t)$, where $n(t)$ is a zero-mean Gaussian-noise process. The purpose of the demodulator is to recover $s_k(t)$ from the channel output. In Chapter 5, we studied maximum-likelihood detection and found that it

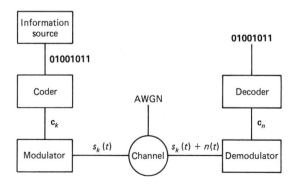

Figure 6-1.   The major building blocks of a digital communication system.

naturally led to matched-filter processing for the case of additive Gaussian noise. We also found that detection is a statistical inference process and, as such, is prone to decoding errors.

This chapter looks at the performance of various signal sets $\{s_k(t)\}$ as well as at the properties of these signals responsible for the stated performance. The measure of performance we use is the probability of a random decoding error and is a function of the signal structure as well as the decoding technique. We shall look at several signals and at two general approaches to decoding: coherent and noncoherent decoding. In *coherent* decoding, the carrier phase of the incoming signal is assumed known. In practice, this means that the local matched-filter waveform reference is synchronized to the received signal phase. In *noncoherent* decoding, the signal phase is not known. Noncoherent decoding is easier to implement than coherent decoding, but has poorer performance.

6.1.1 Coherent Signaling

Signaling for communication consists of several techniques for generating and using signals to convey information over a noisy channel. Since the communication engineer has wide latitude in the selection of waveform characteristics, these characteristics can be chosen to optimize detection performance.

One of the simplest detection problems involves detecting known signals in AWGN. In communications, this is generally referred to as coherent (or phase-coherent) signaling to emphasize that the receiver is in carrier phase synchrony with the received waveform. This is the best possible situation from the point of view of performance in that it results in the lowest rate of decoding errors for a given signal-to-noise ratio. For this reason, coherent signaling is a convenient performance benchmark against which other signaling techniques can be measured.

The superior performance of coherent signaling is obtained at the cost of having to implement the necessary hardware to track the carrier phase. It often happens, however, that satisfactory performance can be achieved without requiring a knowledge of the phase. The resulting class of signaling methods is called noncoherent and involves more simply implemented envelope detection.

The detection performance of both coherent and noncoherent signaling is addressed in this chapter, with this section being devoted to the coherent case. Within each category, subclasses of signaling can be defined, depending on the signal properties of the communication waveforms.

Although the mathematical analysis that follows provides a complete description of communication performance, it is instructive to provide, in addition to these calculations, a qualitative comparison of coherent and noncoherent signaling. We now present such a comparison from a signal-space point of view.

With coherent signaling, everything about the allowed symbol waveforms is known a priori to the receiver. In the case of coherent M-ary signaling, the possible received waveform signals can be represented by M points in signal space. We refer to these M points as code words. In the absence of noise, decoding would consist in identifying which of these M points corresponds to the received signal. With noise present, thresholding is used to associate a neighborhood of points around each of the M code words with a decoded symbol. The process of detection consists in determining which of the M code words is closest (in the metric-distance sense) to the received waveform.

With noncoherent signaling, signals are identical in all respects to the code words except for their phases, all values of which are considered equivalent. This means that there are more points (or volume) in signal space associated with each code word. Each code-word neighborhood consists of the signal-space volume used in coherent signaling and the additional volume associated with all possible values of the signal phases. Thus, each noncoherent code word consists of several signals that differ in their phases, but that are considered informationally equivalent since phase is not used to distinguish between them. Since a larger signal-space volume is allocated to each code word, the capacity of noncoherent signaling, coeteris paribus, is less than for coherent signaling over the AWGN channel. This is manifested as a higher signal-to-noise ratio requirement for a given decoding error probability.

6.1.2 Binary Signaling

In the binary case, we have two symbols $s_0(t)$ and $s_1(t)$. It is customary to assume that one of the waveforms was actually transmitted. From this, the probability of error is defined as the probability of the other (i.e., wrong) symbol being decoded. Let us assume $s_0(t)$ was transmitted. We, therefore, form the two statistical hypotheses:

$$H_0: \quad r(t) = s_0(t) + n(t)$$

$$H_1: \quad r(t) = s_1(t) + n(t)$$

where $n(t)$ is a zero-mean stationary Gaussian process with variance σ_0^2 per degree of freedom. We now form the two decision variables:

$$U_0 = \mathcal{R}e\langle r(t)|s_0(t)\rangle = \mathcal{R}e\langle s_0(t)|s_0(t)\rangle + \mathcal{R}e\langle n(t)|s_0(t)\rangle$$

$$= \mathscr{E} + \mathcal{R}e\langle n(t)|s_0(t)\rangle \tag{6.2}$$

$$U_1 = \mathcal{R}e\langle r(t)|s_1(t)\rangle = \mathcal{R}e\langle s_0(t)|s_1(t)\rangle + \mathcal{R}e\langle n(t)|s_1(t)\rangle$$

$$= \mathscr{E}\mathcal{R}e(\rho_{01}) + \mathcal{R}e\langle n(t)|s_1(t)\rangle \tag{6.3}$$

where ρ is the normalized complex intersymbol correlation given by

$$\rho_{01} = \mathscr{E}^{-1}\langle s_0(t)|s_1(t)\rangle \tag{6.4}$$

which is a special case of the more general definition

$$\rho_{km} = (\mathscr{E}_k\mathscr{E}_m)^{-1/2}\langle s_k(t)|s_m(t)\rangle \tag{6.5}$$

Since $s_0(t)$ is assumed to have been transmitted, the only way for a decoding error to occur is for $s_1(t)$ to be decoded. This will happen with probability

$$P_e = \text{Prob}\{U_0 < U_1\} = \text{Prob}\{U_0 - U_1 < 0\} \tag{6.6}$$

Our goal is to calculate the decoding bit error P_e as a function of the ratio of signal and noise energies. In the example chosen, a symbol corresponds to one bit of information since there are two symbols in the alphabet. The resulting error, therefore, corresponds to the bit error rate.

Calculating P_e requires a knowledge of the statistics of U_0 and U_1 or, equivalently, of the variable $U = U_0 - U_1$. Since $n(t)$ is a zero-mean process, the mean value of U is simply

$$\mu = \mathcal{R}e\langle s_0(t)|s_0(t)\rangle - \mathcal{E}\mathcal{R}e(\rho_{01}) = \mathcal{E}(1 - \rho_r) \tag{6.7}$$

where ρ_r denotes the real part of ρ_{01}. The variance of U is given by

$$\sigma^2 = E[(U - \mu)^2] = E\{[\mathcal{R}e\langle n(t)|s_0(t)\rangle - \mathcal{R}e\langle n(t)|s_1(t)\rangle]^2\}$$

$$= E\{\mathcal{R}e\,z\} \tag{6.8}$$

where $z = z(t) = \langle n(t)|s_0(t) - s_1(t)\rangle$ to simplify the notation. The variance σ^2 then becomes

$$\sigma^2 = \tfrac{1}{2}E[(z + z*)^2] = \tfrac{1}{2}E[(z + z*) \cdot (z* + z)]$$

$$= \tfrac{1}{2}E(2z*z + z^2 + z*^2) = E(z*z) + \tfrac{1}{2}E(z^2 + z*^2) \tag{6.9}$$

We shall show later that $E(z^2 + z*^2)$ in Eq. (6.9) vanishes. Presently, there results

$$E(z*z) = E(\langle s_0 - s_1|n\rangle \cdot \langle n|s_0 - s_1\rangle)$$

$$= E(\langle s_0|n\rangle \cdot \langle n|s_0\rangle + \langle s_1|n\rangle \cdot \langle n|s_1\rangle$$

$$-\langle s_0|n\rangle \cdot \langle n|s_1\rangle - \langle s_1|n\rangle \cdot \langle n|s_0\rangle) \tag{6.10}$$

The first term of this expression reduces to

$$\langle s_0|E(|n\rangle\langle n|)|s_0\rangle = \langle s_0|\sigma_0^2|s_0\rangle = \sigma_0^2\mathcal{E}$$

and, similarly, for the second term:

$$\langle s_1|E(|n\rangle\langle n|)|s_1\rangle = \langle s_1|\sigma_0^2|s_1\rangle = \sigma_0^2\mathcal{E}$$

where $\mathcal{E}$ is the energy in either of the waveforms $s_0(t)$ or $s_1(t)$. This follows from the expansions

$$\langle n| = \sum_k n_k^*\langle k| \qquad \text{and} \qquad |n\rangle = \sum_m n_m|m\rangle$$

The expectation value of the operator $|n\rangle\langle n|$ now can be written as

$$E(|n\rangle\langle n|) = \sum_{k,m} E(n_k^* n_m)|k\rangle\langle m|$$

$$= \sum_k E(n_k^* n_k)|k\rangle\langle k|$$

$$= \sum_k \sigma_k^2|k\rangle\langle k| = \sigma_0^2 \mathbf{1} \tag{6.11}$$

where $|k\rangle\langle m|$ is the projection operator $\mathbf{P}_{km}$ from coordinate m to coordinate k, and vanishes except when $m = k$ since these coordinates are orthogonal. This results in the closure relation

$$\sum_k |k\rangle\langle k| \equiv \mathbf{1} \tag{6.12}$$

where $\mathbf{1}$ is the identity operator. The remaining term in Eq. (6.10) is

$$-2E\,\mathcal{R}e\{\langle s_0|n\rangle \cdot \langle n|s_1\rangle\} = -2\mathcal{R}e\langle s_0|E\,\{|n\rangle \cdot \langle n|\}|s_1\rangle$$

$$= -2\mathcal{E}\rho_r\,\sigma_0^2 \tag{6.13}$$

where $\rho_r = \mathcal{R}e\rho_{01}$. The expression for the variance of the decision variable U, therefore, becomes

$$\sigma^2 = 2\mathcal{E}\sigma_0^2(1 - \rho_r) \tag{6.14}$$

We must now show that the term $E\,(z^2 + z^{*2})$ vanishes. Equivalently, we must show that the quantity $E\,(\mathcal{R}e z^2)$ vanishes. For any complex quantity $z = x + jy$, we have

$$z^2 = (x + jy) \cdot (x + jy) = x^2 - y^2 + 2jxy$$

so that

$$\mathcal{R}e z^2 = x^2 - y^2$$

Now $z = \langle n|s_0 - s_1\rangle$ is a zero-mean Gaussian random variable for which $\sigma_z^2 = \sigma_x^2 + \sigma_y^2$ with $\sigma_x^2 = E\{x^2\} = \sigma_y^2 = E\{y^2\}$. Therefore,

$$E\{\mathcal{R}e z^2\} = E\{x^2\} - E\{y^2\} = 0$$

as claimed.

The variable U is normally distributed with mean μ and variance σ^2. The probability of a decoding error is, therefore,

$$P_e = \text{Prob}\,\{U < 0\} = \int_{-\infty}^0 p(U)\,dU \tag{6.15}$$

where $p(U)$ is the Gaussian probability density function having mean μ and variance σ^2. The integral can be expressed in terms of the complementary error function

$$P_e(\gamma) = \tfrac{1}{2}\,\text{erfc}\,[\mu/\sigma(2)^{1/2}] = \tfrac{1}{2}\,\text{erfc}\,[\tfrac{1}{2}(1 - \rho_r)\gamma]^{1/2} \tag{6.16}$$

where $\gamma = \tfrac{1}{2}\mathcal{E}/\sigma_0^2$ is the *energy contrast ratio*. The complementary error function $\text{erfc}\,z = 1 - \text{erf}\,z$ is defined in terms of the error function $\text{erf}\,z$, which is in turn defined as [Ab 72]:

$$\text{erf}\,z = \frac{2}{\pi^{1/2}} \int_0^z e^{-x^2}\,dx \tag{6.17}$$

If both $s_0(t)$ and $s_1(t)$ are transmitted with equal probability (i.e., $\tfrac{1}{2}$), then the probability that a transmitted waveform $s_1(t)$ is decoded into $s_0(t)$ is also given by the previous expression for P_e, and the average bit error rate is equal to P_e.

Note that as defined, $2\gamma = \mathscr{E}/\sigma_0^2$. At the matched-filter output, the signal energy is $\mathscr{E}$ and the noise energy is σ_0^2; the signal-to-noise ratio at the matched-filter output is, therefore, also $\mathscr{E}/\sigma_0^2$. The energy contrast ratio is usually written as $\gamma = \mathscr{E}/N_0$, where $N_0 = \sigma_0^2$ is the two-sided noise power spectral density. The equivalence between the two forms of γ follows from the fact that the total noise energy is simply σ_0^2 multiplied by $2TW$, the total number of waveform degrees of freedom, where T is the waveform duration, and W is the system bandwidth. The factor of $\frac{1}{2}$ in the definition of the energy contrast ratio is adopted for convenience, as this parameter is usually defined in terms of the one-sided noise power spectral density in the literature. The energy contrast ratio measures the relative strength of two competing forces in detection: signal energy and noise energy.

The energy contrast ratio is a fundamental performance parameter for communication in AWGN. Another performance parameter, the signal-to-noise ratio, is also commonly used. The two are simply related. The waveform energy $\mathscr{E}$ is simply the average signal power S multiplied by the waveform duration T. The noise power N is the two-sided noise power spectral density N_0 multiplied by twice the bandwidth W. This results in the expression

$$2\gamma = (SNR)_{\text{mfo}} = 2TW \times (SNR)_{\text{mfi}} \tag{6.18}$$

where SNR stands for the signal-to-noise ratio, subscript mfo is an abbreviation for matched-filter output, and mfi for matched-filter input. Then twice the energy contrast ratio can, therefore, be considered to be a signal-to-noise ratio measured at the output of a matched filter with gain $2TW$. Recall that $2TW$ is also the signal-space dimension of the waveform to which the filter is matched.

Detection performance depends solely on γ. As was found in Chapter 3, γ is equal to the signal-to-noise ratio at the matched-filter input times $2TW$, the matched-filter gain. Thus, regardless of waveform details, signals having the same value of $2TW$ have the same matched-filter gain. Also, waveforms having the same γ have the same detection performance in AWGN.

This interpretation may be useful when matched filtering is used to process a waveform for detection. Here $(SNR)_{\text{mfi}}$ is the "ambient" signal-to-noise ratio, as measured, for example, at the receiver antenna. The energy contrast ratio γ is one-half the signal-to-noise ratio on which detection performance directly depends. Except for the matched filter, all of the linear components of a receiver (amplifiers, filters, etc.) leave the signal-to-noise ratio unchanged since they affect both the signal and the noise equally. Only the matched filter can alter the signal-to-noise ratio. Thus, with a knowledge of the ambient SNR and of the waveform duration and bandwidth characteristics, one can accurately predict system performance in AWGN, assuming that a matched filter is used. Furthermore, this estimate corresponds to the best possible performance using a linear processor, since the matched filter is the best linear processor for detection in an additive noise process.

6.1.3 Antipodal Signaling

The real part of the waveform cross-correlation ρ_r may assume any value over the closed interval $-1 \leq \rho_r \leq 1$. The choice of ρ_r corresponds to different classes of signaling. Clearly, the best choice for ρ_r is that which minimizes P_e, namely, $\rho_r = -1$. This optimal choice results in $s_0(t) = -s_1(t)$ and is called antipodal signaling. Binary phase-shift keying (PSK) is an example of antipodal signaling. The resulting bit error rate is

$$P_e(\gamma) = \tfrac{1}{2} \operatorname{erfc} \gamma^{1/2} \tag{6.19}$$

This is an important result in that it represents the best binary error rate performance achievable. In addition, this performance is easily calculated. For these reasons, the performance for antipodal signaling represents an important benchmark against which other signaling methods can be compared.

6.1.4 Orthogonal *M*-ary Signaling

From the definition of ρ_{km}, a vanishing correlation between symbol waveforms corresponds to an orthogonality condition between these signals. Communication using waveforms for which $\rho_{km} = 0$ is said to use orthogonal signaling. The simplest example of orthogonal signaling is when there are only two waveforms. By using the result derived in Section 6.1.2, the bit error rate for binary orthogonal signaling is obtained by setting $\rho_r = 0$, giving

$$P_e(\gamma) = \tfrac{1}{2} \operatorname{erfc} (\gamma/2)^{1/2} \tag{6.20}$$

A comparison of the bit error probabilities for binary antipodal and orthogonal signaling immediately shows that for the same bit error rate, binary orthogonal is poorer than binary antipodal by exactly a factor of 2 in γ. This comparison is shown in Fig. 6-2.

Generalizing to *M*-ary signaling alphabets introduces more choices for implementing communication systems and also a wider range of possible performance. One possibility for the intersymbol correlation is to require that the symbols be uncorrelated. That is, we require that the correlations vanish for all possible symbol pairs: $\rho_{km} = 0$ for all $k \neq m$. This is called orthogonal signaling since the interpretation of $\rho_{km} = 0$ in signal space is that $s_k(t)$ and $s_m(t)$ share no common projections and are, therefore, orthogonal.

Orthogonal signaling uses symbol waveforms that form a basis function set in signal space. There can be, therefore, only a finite number of orthogonal signaling waveforms in a finite-dimensional space. In particular, there are only $2TW$ orthogonal waveforms of approximate duration T and bandwidth W.

To calculate the probability of a decoding error, we assume that symbol $s_1(t)$ was transmitted. The M decision variables are, therefore,

$$\begin{aligned}
U_1 &= \mathscr{R}e\langle s_1(t) + n(t) | s_1(t) \rangle \\
&= \mathscr{R}e\langle s_1(t) | s_1(t) \rangle + \mathscr{R}e\langle n(t) | s_1(t) \rangle \\
&= \mathscr{E} + \mathscr{R}e\langle n(t) | s_1(t) \rangle \tag{6.21}
\end{aligned}$$

Note that U_1 is a Gaussian random variable with mean $\mathscr{E}$ and ranges over the interval $(-\infty, \infty)$. Similarly, we have for U_m, $m = 2, \ldots, M$:

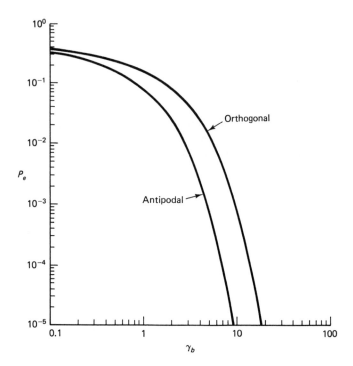

Figure 6-2. Comparison of binary antipodal and orthogonal signaling.

$$U_m = \mathcal{R}e\langle s_1(t) + n(t)|s_m(t)\rangle$$

$$= \mathcal{R}e\langle s_1(t)|s_m(t)\rangle + \mathcal{R}e\langle n(t)|s_m(t)\rangle$$

$$= \mathcal{R}e\langle n(t)|s_m(t)\rangle \qquad (6.22)$$

since $\rho_{1m} = 0$. Now U_1 is a Gaussian random variable with mean $\mathcal{E}$ and variance $\sigma^2 = \mathcal{E}\sigma_0^2$. Similarly, U_m is a Gaussian random variable with zero mean and variance $\sigma^2 = \mathcal{E}\sigma_0^2$. The corresponding probability density functions are, therefore,

$$p(U_1) = \frac{1}{\sigma(2\pi)^{1/2}} \exp\left[-\frac{(U_1 - \mathcal{E})^2}{2\sigma^2}\right]$$

and

$$p(U_m) = \frac{1}{\sigma(2\pi)^{1/2}} \exp\left(-\frac{U_m^2}{2\sigma^2}\right)$$

In this case, the probability of a decoding error is more easily calculated as the complement of the probability of a correct decoding:

$$P_e(M, \gamma) = 1 - P_C(M, \gamma) \qquad (6.23)$$

and $P_C(M, \gamma)$ can be expressed as the probability that U_1 exceeds U_m for all possible values of U_1. We write this as

$$P_C(M, \gamma) = \int \text{Prob} \{U_1 > U_2, U_1 > U_3, \cdots, U_1 > U_M | U_1\} p(U_1) dU_1 \quad (6.24)$$

where the limits of integration are understood to include the entire range of U_1. In terms of the probability density functions, this expression becomes

$$\text{Prob} \{U_1 > U_k | U_1\} = \int_{-\infty}^{U_1} p(U_k) dU_k = \tfrac{1}{2} + \tfrac{1}{2} \text{erf} (U_1 / \sigma 2^{1/2}) \quad (6.25)$$

Since the U_k are uncorrelated and Gaussian, they are statistically independent. The probability function Prob $\{U_1 > U_2, U_1 > U_3, \cdots, U_1 > U_M | U_1\}$, therefore, can be written as the $(M - 1)$-fold product of individual probabilities of the form Prob $\{U_1 > U_k | U_1\}$, each of which is identical and equal to the expression computed before. Then Prob $\{U_1 > U_2, U_1 > U_3, \cdots, U_1 > U_M | U_1\}$ is, therefore, equal to $\tfrac{1}{2} + \tfrac{1}{2} \text{erf} (U_1 / \sigma 2^{1/2})$ raised to the $M - 1$ power, and Eq. (6.24) becomes, since $-\infty < U_1 < \infty$,

$$P_C(M, \gamma) = 2^{1-M} \int_{-\infty}^{\infty} [1 + \text{erf} (U_1 / \sigma 2^{1/2})]^{M-1} p(U_1) dU_1 \quad (6.26)$$

By changing the variable of integration, this expression can be further simplified to

$$P_C(M, \gamma) = \frac{2^{1-M}}{\pi^{1/2}} \int_{-\infty}^{\infty} [1 + \text{erf} (x + \gamma^{1/2})]^{M-1} e^{-x^2} dx \quad (6.27)$$

The previous argument is true for the assumption of any one of the symbols having been transmitted. The probability of a particular symbol being received in error is $1 - P_C(M, \gamma)$. If these symbols are equiprobable, then the M-ary probability of symbol error is simply given by $P_e(M, \gamma) = 1 - P_C(M, \gamma)$. Figure 6-3 shows the behavior of the M-ary symbol error probability $P_e(M, \gamma)$ as a function of $k = \log_2 M$ and γ_b, the energy contrast ratio per bit. It is a simple matter to express γ_b as a function of γ. In M-ary signaling, there are M distinguishable waveforms and, therefore, $k = \log_2 M$ bits per symbol waveform. Conservation of energy, therefore, requires that $\gamma = \gamma_b \log_2 M$.

The decoding performance shown in Fig. 6-2 compares various M-ary coherent orthogonal symbol error probabilities, all plotted as functions of γ_b. This is a useful format for comparing performance on the basis of available signal energy per bit, one of the limited resources available for communications. The effect of another resource, namely, signal-space dimensionality (e.g., signal duration, available channel bandwidth, or a combination of the two) also affects performance and will be discussed later.

In Fig. 6-3, we observe that as $k = \log_2 M$ increases, the decoding error rate decreases for a given value of γ_b. Code words with large M correspond to waveforms with large complexity. With increasing values of k, the energy contrast ratio required to achieve a given symbol decoding error probability decreases. This result suggests that larger values of k correspond to more efficient use of energy with M-ary orthogonal signaling. This coding energy efficiency is achieved at the cost of generating and processing waveforms with a large number of degrees of freedom. In addition, the communication channel must be capable of accommodating these waveforms of large complexity.

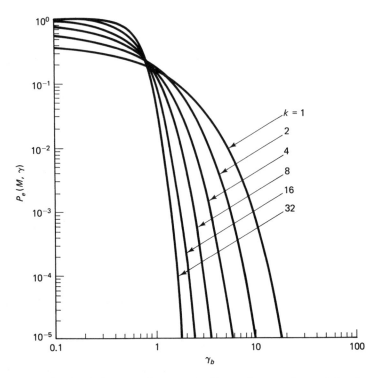

Figure 6-3. Symbol error performance for M-ary coherent orthogonal signaling.

We are now in a position to make an interesting comparison between coded and uncoded communications. Given a message of fixed length (i.e., a fixed number of bits) to be transmitted and a fixed amount of energy to do so, information could be, in principle, communicated through any one of the M-ary orthogonal signaling formats. Are some choices of M better than others? What are the consequences of selecting a particular value of M? The answers to these questions provide insight into the fundamental performance limits of coded signaling.

Let us first look into the performance brought about by M-ary coding. Given a message represented as a sequence of bits, one could send each bit individually, incurring a bit error probability of

$$P_b(\gamma_b) = \tfrac{1}{2}\,\mathrm{erfc}\,(\gamma_b/2)^{1/2} \tag{6.28}$$

for each bit transmission. In transmitting the $k = \log_2 M$ bits of an M-ary symbol, the symbol itself can be considered to have been received in error if any one or more of the k bits are incorrectly decoded. The uncoded M-ary symbol probability of error is, therefore,

$$P_u(\gamma_b) = 1 - [1 - P_b(\gamma_b)]^k \tag{6.29}$$

A comparison of uncoded $P_u(\gamma_b)$ and coded $P_e(M, k\gamma_b)$ symbol error probabilities is shown for $k = 5$ in Fig. 6-4. Again, all performance comparisons can be made in terms of γ_b so that we can have a direct way of evaluating the relative merits of coded versus uncoded signaling. Clearly, coded signaling is superior to uncoded communication. For example, at a symbol error rate of 10^{-3}, coding a signal into 32-ary symbols ($k = 5$) requires a factor of 4.2 (6.2 dB) less energy than if the bits had been transmitted individually. Similar results obtain for other values of k, with better γ_b advantage being associated with the larger values of k.

The energy contrast ratio advantage of coded communications over uncoded signaling is called *coding gain*, and is commonly expressed in decibels, with the uncoded value of γ_b providing the reference level for a given value of k. Coding gain is very real in the sense that it represents performance that would be achieved without coding by actually increasing the energy per uncoded bit by a corresponding factor. For that reason, M-ary orthogonal signaling is useful in applications where energy resources are limited.

In order to meaningfully compare various M-ary orthogonal signaling techniques, it is necessary to take into account the fact that different values of M correspond to different amounts of information. It would be useful to be able to compare these techniques on the basis of a common measure, for example, the equivalent probability of a bit error as a function of the energy contrast ratio per bit. We must, therefore, replace $P_e(M, \gamma)$ by an equivalent coded bit error probability $P_{be}(M, \gamma_b)$, for M-ary coding, as a function of the bit energy contrast ratio γ_b.

To calculate the coded bit error probability $P_{be}(M, \gamma_b)$, we note from conditional probabilities that

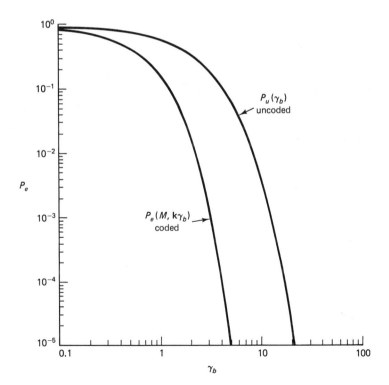

Figure 6-4.   Uncoded $P_u(\gamma_b)$ and coded $P_e(M, k\gamma_b)$ symbol error probabilities for coherent orthogonal signaling with $k = 5$.

$$\text{Prob } \{B|S\} \text{ Prob } \{S\} = \text{ Prob } \{S|B\} \text{ Prob } \{B\}$$

where we used the shortened notation B for bit error, and S for M-ary symbol error.

We now make the identification Prob $\{B\} = P_{be}(M, \gamma_b)$ and Prob $\{S\} = P_e(M, \gamma)$, recalling that $\gamma = \gamma_b \log_2 M$. We can, therefore, solve the previous equation for $P_{be}(M, \gamma_b)$ if we can find expressions for Prob $\{B|S\}$ and Prob $\{S|B\}$.

We note that there are 2^k symbols in all. One of these corresponds to the correct decoding, leaving $2^k - 1$ equiprobable possibilities for a symbol error. Bringing our attention on the bit occupying the nth position in the symbol, we note that since the 2^k symbols exhaust all binary representation possibilities, this bit is **0** in half of the symbols and **1** in the other half.

This argument is true only if M is an integer power of 2. This means that there are 2^{k-1} symbols that differ from the correct one in the nth bit position. Given that a symbol is in error, there results

$$\text{Prob } \{B|S\} = 2^{k-1}/(2^k - 1) \tag{6.30}$$

where the term $2^k - 1$ in the denominator accounts for all of the possible bit combinations resulting in a symbol error. Next we realize that Prob $\{S|B\} = 1$, since a symbol must be in error if any of its bits is in error. The coded bit error rate is, therefore, given by

$$P_{be}(M, \gamma_b) = P_e(M, \gamma_b \log_2 M) \cdot 2^{k-1}/(2^k - 1) \tag{6.31}$$

Figure 6-5 is a plot of the decoded bit error probabilities for various values of k, the number of bits per code word. These probabilities are all given as functions of γ_b. The figure, therefore, provides a direct way of comparing one M-ary coherent orthogonal signaling scheme with another.

It is evident from Fig. 6-5 that the larger values of k result in a more efficient use of the energy available for communication. It is also clear that the benefits of coding result in a lesser incremental gain as k increases. The bit energy contrast ratio γ_b seems to be approaching a limiting value as $k \to \infty$. This interesting behavior can be investigated analytically. The following approach is due to Viterbi [Vi 66].

We first consider the limit of $P_C(M, \gamma)$ as $M \to \infty$. This is equivalent to letting k approach infinity. We, therefore, consider the expression

$$\lim_{M \to \infty} P_C(M, \gamma) = \lim_{M \to \infty} \frac{1}{\pi^{1/2}} \int_{-\infty}^{\infty} \{\tfrac{1}{2} + \tfrac{1}{2} \operatorname{erf} [x + (\gamma_b \log_2 M)^{1/2}]\}^{M-1} e^{-x^2} dx$$

$$= \frac{1}{\pi^{1/2}} \int_{-\infty}^{\infty} \lim_{M \to \infty} \{\tfrac{1}{2} + \tfrac{1}{2} \operatorname{erf} [x + (\gamma_b \log_2 M)]\}^{M-1} e^{-x^2} dx$$

Consider now the limit of the natural logarithm of the expression within braces:

$$\lim_{M \to \infty} \ln \{\tfrac{1}{2} + \tfrac{1}{2} \operatorname{erf} [x + (\gamma_b \log_2 M)^{1/2}]\}^{M-1}$$

$$= \lim_{M \to \infty} \frac{\ln \{\tfrac{1}{2} + \tfrac{1}{2} \operatorname{erf} [x + (\gamma_b \log_2 M)^{1/2}]\}}{\frac{1}{M-1}}$$

Treating M as a continuous variable and using l'Hôpital's rule, we obtain the following after some algebraic manipulation:

$$\frac{-1}{2\pi^{1/2}} \lim_{M\to\infty} \frac{(M-1)^2}{M^{1+\gamma_b/\ln 2}} \left(\frac{\gamma_b}{\ln 2 \ln M}\right)^{1/2} \frac{\exp[-x^2 - 2x(\gamma_b \log_2 M)^{1/2}]}{1 + \mathrm{erf}[x + (\gamma_b \log_2 M)^{1/2}]}$$

$$= \begin{cases} -\infty & \text{if } \gamma_b < \ln 2 \\ 0 & \text{if } \gamma_b > \ln 2 \end{cases}$$

The consequences on $P_C(M, \gamma)$ are

$$\lim_{M\to\infty} P_C(M, \gamma) = \begin{cases} 0 & \text{if } \gamma_b < \ln 2 \\ 1 & \text{if } \gamma_b > \ln 2 \end{cases}$$

In this limit, the M-ary probability of bit error becomes

$$\lim_{M\to\infty} P_{be}(M, \gamma_b) = \begin{cases} \frac{1}{2} & \text{if } \gamma_b < \ln 2 \\ 0 & \text{if } \gamma_b > \ln 2 \end{cases} \tag{6.32}$$

The interpretation we give to this result is that error-free decoding is not possible unless the energy contrast ratio per bit achives at least the minimum value of $\ln 2$. More precisely, an arbitrarily small probability of decoding error is possible only

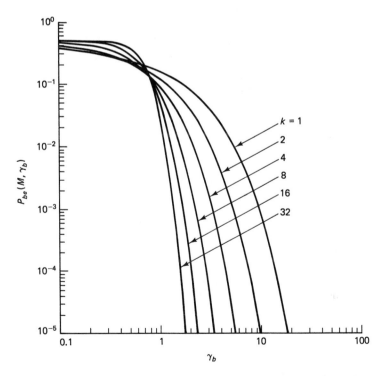

Figure 6-5.   Probability of bit error for M-ary coherent orthogonal signaling.

if the complexity (M) of the signaling waveforms is made very large and provided $\gamma_b \geq \ln 2$. There is an interesting connection with what was said in Section 4.2 about the AWGN channel capacity. Recall that as the number of degrees of freedom of a waveform over the AWGN is increased without bound, the amount of information it can convey approaches a constant value

$$I_\infty = \gamma/\ln 2 \qquad (6.33)$$

The minimum energy contrast ratio per bit is found by setting $I_\infty = 1$ bit and $\gamma = \gamma_b$, again yielding the limiting value of $\ln 2$ for the ratio of waveform energy to noise energy per degree of freedom. This is the minimum signal energy required in order to make a one bit (i.e., a detection) in an AWGN environment.

The information theoretic implications of this result are significant. The error rate calculations provide a link between the energy contrast ratio per bit and the channel information throughput. The effect of the channel is to induce decoding errors, which in turn limit the rate at which information may be conveyed. One way to increase the information rate is to increase the energy contrast ratio. The amount of energy per bit may be considered to be the price paid for extracting information in an AWGN environment.

6.1.5 Biorthogonal *M*-ary Signaling

A simple extension of orthogonal signaling consists in forming a set of M biorthogonal waveforms from any $M/2$ orthogonal signals $\{s_m(t)\}$ and their negatives $\{-s_m(t)\}$. Decoding proceeds as with orthogonal signaling, but with only $M/2$ matched filters or correlators. Decoding is based not only on selecting the maximum processor output, but also on the polarity of that output.

Assuming, as before, that waveform $s_1(t)$ was transmitted, the $M/2$ decision variables are

$$U_1 = \mathscr{E} + \mathscr{R}e\langle n(t)|s_1(t)\rangle \qquad (6.34)$$

and

$$U_m = \mathscr{R}e\langle n(t)|s_m(t)\rangle \qquad m = 2, \ldots, M/2 \qquad (6.35)$$

As before, all decision variables are normally distributed with variance $\mathscr{E}\sigma_0^2$. U_1 has a mean value of $\mathscr{E}$ and all the other U_m are zero-mean variables. The probability of correct decoding is

$$P_C = \int_0^\infty \text{Prob}\{|U_2| < U_1, |U_3| < U_1, \ldots, |U_{M/2}| < U_1|U_1\}p(U_1)dU_1$$

$$= \int_0^\infty \left[\frac{1}{\sigma(2\pi)^{1/2}} \int_{-U_1}^{U_1} e^{-U_2^2/2\sigma^2}dU_2\right]^{M/2-1} p(U_1)dU_1 \qquad (6.36)$$

with $p(U_1)$ being a normal distribution with mean $\mathscr{E}$ and variance $\mathscr{E}\sigma_0^2$. The inner integral can be expressed in terms of the error function, resulting in

$$P_C(M, \gamma) = \frac{1}{\pi^{1/2}} \int_{-\gamma^{1/2}}^{\infty} \left[\operatorname{erf} \left(x + \gamma^{1/2} \right) \right]^{M/2-1} e^{-x^2} dx \qquad (6.37)$$

for coherent M-ary biorthogonal signaling, where $\gamma = k\gamma_b$. The decoded symbol error probability can be calculated as before with the expression

$$P_s(M, \gamma_b) = 1 - P_C(M, \gamma_b \log_2 M) \qquad (6.38)$$

This result is plotted in Fig. 6-6 for various values of k as a function of γ_b.

6.1.6 Equicorrelated *M*-ary Signaling

Let us now explore the more general case of M-ary coherent signaling with non-vanishing correlation ρ_{km} between symbol waveforms. Assuming that waveform $q_k(t)$ was transmitted, we have the decision variables

$$U_k = \mathcal{R}e\langle q_k(t) + n(t) | q_k(t) \rangle = \mathcal{E}_k + \mathcal{R}e\langle n(t) | q_k(t) \rangle \qquad (6.39)$$

and

$$U_m = \mathcal{R}e\langle q_k(t) + n(t) | q_m(t) \rangle$$

$$= (\mathcal{E}_k \mathcal{E}_m)^{1/2} \mathcal{R}e\rho_{km} + \mathcal{R}e\langle n(t) | q_m(t) \rangle \qquad (6.40)$$

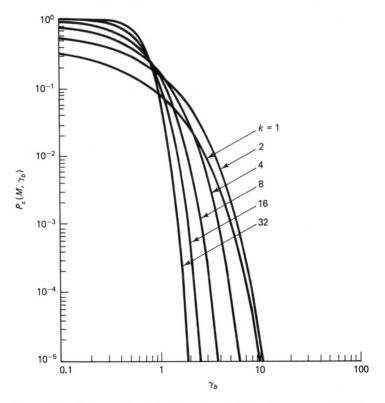

Figure 6-6.   Coherent M-ary biorthogonal symbol-decoding-error probabilities.

where $\mathscr{E}_k$ is the energy in the kth waveform. U_k is normally distributed with mean $\mathscr{E}_k$ and with variance $\sigma^2 = \mathscr{E}\sigma_0^2$; U_m is normally distributed with mean $\mu_m = (\mathscr{E}_k\mathscr{E}_m)^{1/2}\mathscr{R}e\rho_{km}$ and with variance $\sigma^2 = \mathscr{E}\sigma_0^2$. The probability of correct decoding is given by

$$P_C(M, \gamma) = \int \text{Prob}\{U_k > U_2, U_k > U_3, \cdots, U_k > U_M\}p(U_k)dU_k \quad (6.41)$$

However, care must be exercised in evaluating this expression, as the decision variables are statistically correlated. We shall return to this problem later.

In general, decoding performance depends on the waveform energies $\mathscr{E}_k$ as well as on the symbol intercorrelations ρ_{km}. We have already shown that for binary waveforms having equal energies, a correlation of -1 resulted in the best possible performance, but antipodal signaling is possible only for binary signals. In dealing with M-ary signaling, we can use a symmetry argument to help us choose values for the waveform energies as well as for the correlations. We shall require that performance be unchanged by a permutation of the symbol labels. To justify this approach, note that M-ary signaling is equivalent to communicating over a discrete memoryless channel. If the prior probabilities of the symbols being transmitted are equal, then invariance under the symbol label permutation group implies that the channel crossover probabilities are all equal, resulting in equal symbol error probabilities. This can only happen if all symbol waveforms have the same energy and cross-correlations.

Let the signaling waveforms $s_k(t)$ and $s_m(t)$ be represented by the indices k and m, respectively. The square of the metric distance between these two waveforms is

$$d^2(k, m) = \langle k - m | k - m \rangle$$

$$= \langle k|k \rangle + \langle m|m \rangle - \langle k|m \rangle - \langle m|k \rangle$$

$$= \mathscr{E}_k + \mathscr{E}_m - 2(\mathscr{E}_k\mathscr{E}_m)^{1/2}\mathscr{R}e\rho_{km} \quad (6.42)$$

Good performance corresponds to large differences between U_k and U_m. This difference has a mean of

$$E(U_k - U_m) = \mathscr{E}_k - (\mathscr{E}_k\mathscr{E}_m)^{1/2}\mathscr{R}e\rho_{km}$$

If we now require that performance be unchanged by a permutation of the coding symbols, the result is equal waveform energies

$$\mathscr{E}_k = \mathscr{E}_m = \mathscr{E} \quad (6.43)$$

and equal correlation between symbol waveforms

$$\rho_{km} = \rho \quad (6.44)$$

We, therefore, have

$$E(U_k - U_m) = \mathscr{E}(1 - \mathscr{R}e\rho) \quad (6.45)$$

showing that the lowest possible correlation will yield the largest difference between decision variables and, therefore, the best detection performance. This class of equal energy, equicorrelated signaling, is characterized by waveforms that are equidistant from one another in signal space, since

$$d^2(k,m) = 2\mathscr{E}(1 - \mathscr{R}_e\rho) \tag{6.46}$$

is a constant. The probability of decoding error, therefore, is the same for any one of the M symbols being transmitted. That is, the resulting decoding errors do not depend on the details of the sequence of transmitted symbol waveforms. Note that the square of the distance between symbols is a measure of the amount of noise energy required to transform a received waveform from one symbol to another. We, therefore, conclude that the intersymbol metric distance is a fundamental signaling performance parameter and that large intersymbol distances are associated with good decoding performance.

The appropriate dimensionless performance parameter for this case is the metric distance between any two symbol waveforms, normalized by the norm of the noise. This parameter, denoted β, is given by

$$\beta^2 = \frac{d^2(k,m)}{\langle n(t)|n(t)\rangle} = \frac{2\mathscr{E}(1 - \mathscr{R}_e\rho)}{\sigma_0^2}$$

This dimensionless parameter provides a rough indication of decoding performance. Note that β can be expressed in terms of the symbol energy contrast ratio:

$$\beta^2 = 4\gamma(1 - \mathscr{R}_e\rho)$$

If we view symbols as equidistant code words in signal space, then noise introduces a waveform measurement uncertainty that can be pictured as a hypersphere of radius σ_0. This implies that the metric distance between code words is an important factor contributing to decoding performance. Code words should be spaced at least $4\sigma_0$ apart in order to be distinguishable in noise. This yields $\gamma = 4/(1 - \mathscr{R}_e\rho)$. We find that a borderline value for γ_b is 2 for antipodal signaling ($\rho = -1$) and $\gamma_b = 4$ for binary orthogonal ($\rho = 0$) signaling. From Fig. 6-2, we find that these correspond to bit error probabilities on the order of 10^{-2}, marginal performance for most applications.

We conclude from the previous discussions that lower values of ρ correspond to better decoding performance. Since ρ is bounded from below by -1, the best decoding performance is achieved by antipodal signaling, for which this bound is achieved. For any other type of M-ary signaling, a larger intersymbol correlation is unavoidable. For orthogonal signaling, $\rho = 0$. In order to achieve better M-ary decoding performance than with orthogonal signaling, we must use equicorrelated (i.e., equidistant) signaling waveforms for which $-1 < \rho < 0$.

We now explore the possibility of communication via a set of equal energy, equicorrelated signaling waveforms. We first show how to construct such a set so that the intersymbol correlation is as negative as possible. We then explore the decoding error performance of such a set. We shall find it useful to express any one of a set $\{q_k(t); k = 1, \ldots, M\}$ of equal energy ($\mathscr{E}$) equicorrelated (ρ) waveforms as a linear combination of elements from a set $\{s_m(t); m = 1, \ldots, M\}$ of equal energy ($\mathscr{E}_0$) orthogonal waveforms:

$$q_k(t) = \sum_m \alpha_{km} s_m(t) \qquad \text{where } \alpha_{km} = \langle s_m(t)|q_k(t)\rangle \tag{6.47}$$

Note that completeness of the set $\{s_m(t)\}$ is not implied. Only the orthogonality property of the $s_m(t)$ is required. The energy in waveform $q_k(t)$ is

$$\mathscr{E} = \langle q_k | q_k \rangle = \sum_{m,n} \alpha_{km}^* \alpha_{kn} \langle s_n | s_m \rangle$$

$$= \mathscr{E}_0 \sum_m \alpha_{km}^* \alpha_{km} \tag{6.48}$$

The correlation ρ_{kl} between waveforms $q_k(t)$ and $q_l(t)$ is a constant ρ for all $k \neq l$

$$\rho = \mathscr{E}^{-1} \langle q_k | q_l \rangle = \mathscr{E}^{-1} \langle q_l | q_k \rangle \tag{6.49}$$

implying that ρ must be real. We now show that all of the M expansion coefficients α_{km} themselves must be real and equal. This is proven by mathematical induction by (1) showing that it is true for $M = 1$ (notwithstanding the fact that $M = 1$ is not informationally useful) and (2) by showing that if it is true for $M = Q$, then it is also true for $M = Q + 1$. The correlation between q_k and q_l is

$$\rho = \mathscr{E}^{-1} \langle q_k | q_l \rangle$$

$$= \mathscr{E}^{-1} \langle \sum_m \alpha_{km} s_m | \sum_n \alpha_{ln} s_n \rangle$$

$$= \mathscr{E}^{-1} \sum_{m,n} \alpha_{km}^* \alpha_{ln} \langle s_m | s_n \rangle$$

$$= \mathscr{E}_0 \mathscr{E}^{-1} \sum_m \alpha_{km}^* \alpha_{lm} \tag{6.50}$$

Note that when $k = l$, we have

$$\rho = \mathscr{E}_0 \mathscr{E}^{-1} \sum_m \alpha_{km}^* \alpha_{km} = 1 \tag{6.51}$$

For $k \neq l$, we have

$$\rho_{kl} = \rho_{lk} = \rho \qquad \text{a real constant } \forall \, k, l \ni \cdot k \neq l$$

$$\mathscr{E}_0 \mathscr{E}^{-1} \sum_{m=1}^{M} \alpha_{km}^* \alpha_{lm} = \mathscr{E}_0 \mathscr{E}^{-1} \sum_{m=1}^{M} \alpha_{lm}^* \alpha_{km} = \text{real constant} \tag{6.52}$$

When $M = 1$, we have

$$\alpha_{k1}^* \alpha_{l1} = \alpha_{l1}^* \alpha_{k1} = (\alpha_{k1}^* \alpha_{l1})^* \tag{6.53}$$

so that $\alpha_{k1}^* \alpha_{l1}$ must be real. Then we either must have α_{k1} and α_{l1} both real or else we must have $\alpha_{k1} = \alpha_{l1}^*$. If both α_{k1} and α_{l1} are real, then they must also be equal in order that their product give the same real constant for all k and l. The other possibility, namely, $\alpha_{k1} = \alpha_{l1}^*$, can only be true for all $k \neq l$ if and only if the α's are real and equal. For $M = 1$ we, therefore, have

$$\alpha_{k1} = \alpha \qquad \text{a real constant for } k \neq l$$

When $M = Q$, we have

$$\sum_{m=1}^{Q} \alpha_{km}^* \alpha_{lm} = \sum_{m=1}^{Q} \alpha_{lm}^* \alpha_{km} = \text{a real constant}$$

and where all α's up to order Q are real and equal. When $M = Q + 1$, we have

$$\sum_{m=1}^{Q} \alpha_{km}^* \alpha_{lm} + \alpha_{k,Q+1}^* \alpha_{l,Q+1} = \sum_{m=1}^{Q} \alpha_{lm}^* \alpha_{km} + \alpha_{l,Q+1}^* \alpha_{k,Q+1} = \text{a real constant}$$

But the summations are equal to each other and to a real constant by assumption. All real constants can be incorporated on the right-hand side, yielding

$$\alpha_{k,Q+1}^* \alpha_{l,Q+1} = \alpha_{l,Q+1}^* \alpha_{k,Q+1} = \text{a real constant}$$

We have already shown that this implies the equality and reality of the α's. The proof is complete.

For $k \neq m$, we simplify the notation by setting $\alpha_{km} = \alpha$. Without loss of generality, we set α_{kk} to unity and choose α to determine the value of ρ. The equicorrelated waveform energy is

$$\mathcal{E} = \mathcal{E}_0[1 + (M - 1)\alpha^2] \tag{6.54}$$

and the correlation becomes

$$\rho = \mathcal{E}_0 \mathcal{E}^{-1}[2\alpha + (M - 2)\alpha^2] \tag{6.55}$$

Eliminating $\mathcal{E}$ between these two relations gives

$$\rho = \frac{2\alpha + (M - 2)\alpha^2}{1 + (M - 1)\alpha^2}$$

The value of α that minimizes ρ can be found by setting the derivative of ρ with respect to α equal to zero, and that leads to the following expression that may be solved for α:

$$(M - 1)\alpha^2 - (M - 2)\alpha - 1 = 0$$

which has the two solutions

$$\alpha = \frac{M - 2 \pm M}{2(M - 1)}$$

We choose the lower value of α, namely, $\alpha = -1/(M - 1)$, as this results in the lowest value for ρ, which is

$$\rho_{\min} = \frac{-1}{M - 1} \tag{6.56}$$

Note that $\rho_{\min} \to 0_-$ as M becomes large, implying that the decoding performance of equicorrelated signaling approaches that of orthogonal signaling in this limit.

We now return to the task of calculating the probability of decoding errors for equicorrelated signaling. Assuming that waveform $q_k(t)$ was transmitted, the probability of correct decoding is given by

$$P_C(M, \gamma) = \int \text{Prob} \{U_k > U_2, \ U_k > U_3, \ \cdots, \ U_k > U_M | U_k\} p(U_k) dU_k$$

$$(6.57)$$

The decision variables U_k and U_m, $m = 1, \ldots, M$, with $k \neq m$ are given by

$$U_k = \mathcal{E} + \mathcal{R}e\langle n | q_k \rangle$$

and

$$U_m = \rho\mathcal{E} + \mathcal{R}e\langle n | q_m \rangle$$

but

$$q_k = s_k + \alpha \sum_{l \neq k} s_l$$

where the s_l are orthogonal waveforms with energy $\mathcal{E}_0$. A similar expression holds for q_m. Substitution of these orthogonal expansions in Eqs. (6.39) and (6.40) gives

$$U_k = \mathcal{E} + \mathcal{R}e\langle n | s_k \rangle + \alpha \sum_{l \neq k} \mathcal{R}e\langle n | s_l \rangle$$

$$U_m = \rho\mathcal{E} + \mathcal{R}e\langle n | s_m \rangle + \alpha \sum_{l \neq m} \mathcal{R}e\langle n | s_l \rangle$$

We rewrite these decision variables as

$$U_k = \mathcal{E} + \zeta_k + \alpha \sum_{l \neq k} \zeta_l \qquad (6.58)$$

$$U_m = \rho\mathcal{E} + \zeta_m + \alpha \sum_{l \neq m} \zeta_l \qquad (6.59)$$

where $\zeta_j = \mathcal{R}e\langle n | s_j \rangle$, $j = 1, \ldots, M$, are uncorrelated Gaussian random variables with zero mean and variance $\sigma_\zeta^2 = \mathcal{E}_0 \sigma_0^2$.

We can now express probabilities of the form Prob $\{U_k > U_m\}$ in terms of these statistically independent variables. To that end, note that

$$U_k - U_m = \mathcal{E}(1 - \rho) + (1 - \alpha)(\zeta_k - \zeta_m)$$

so that

$$\text{Prob} \{U_k > U_m\} = \text{Prob} \{\mathcal{E}(1 - \rho) + (1 - \alpha)(\zeta_k - \zeta_m) > 0\}$$

$$= \text{Prob} \{\zeta_m < \zeta_k + \mathcal{E}\} \qquad (6.60)$$

since $\pi = \alpha$. The average probability of correct M-ary symbol decoding is, therefore,

$$P_C(M, \gamma) = \int_{-\infty}^{\infty} \left[\text{Prob} \left\{ \zeta_m < \zeta_k + \mathscr{E} \right\} \right]^{M-1} p(\zeta_k) d\zeta_k \tag{6.61}$$

where $p(\zeta_k)$ is the Gaussian probability distribution function for the variable ζ_k. Writing the expression within square brackets explicitly as a Gaussian probability, the equation for $P_C(M, \gamma)$ reduces to

$$P_C(M, \gamma) = \frac{1}{\pi^{1/2}} \int_{-\infty}^{\infty} \left(\frac{1}{\pi^{1/2}} \int_{-\infty}^{x + [\gamma M / (M-1)]^{1/2}} e^{-y^2} dy \right)^{M-1} e^{-x^2} dx$$

where $\gamma = \mathscr{E}/2\sigma_0^2$ is the M-ary symbol energy contrast ratio. This expression can be further simplified by expressing the inner integral in terms of the error function:

$$P_C(M, \gamma) = \pi^{-1/2} \int_{-\infty}^{\infty} \left(\tfrac{1}{2} + \tfrac{1}{2} \,\text{erf} \left\{ x + [\gamma M / (M-1)]^{1/2} \right\} \right)^{M-1} e^{-x^2} dx \tag{6.62}$$

The M-ary symbol error probability is given as before by

$$P_e(M, \gamma) = 1 - P_C(M, \gamma) \tag{6.63}$$

and plotted in Fig. 6-7.

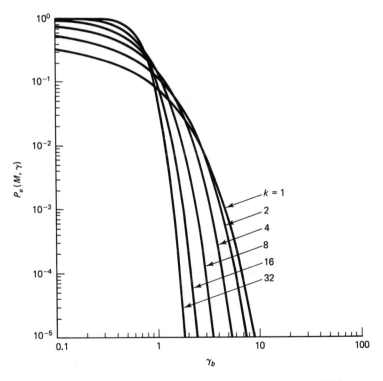

Figure 6-7.   Coherent M-ary equicorrelated symbol error probabilities.

6.2 NONCOHERENT COMMUNICATION IN AWGN

We continue with a discussion of noncoherent communication performance over the AWGN channel. Because of the relative ease with which envelope detection can be implemented, noncoherent communication systems offer an attractive alternative to coherent systems, especially when the signal-to-noise ratio is good.

We develop a statistical performance analysis for noncoherent orthogonal signaling, much in the same way as was done for the coherent case. Bit error probabilities are calculated as a function of the energy contrast ratio per bit. As with coherent orthogonal signaling, noncoherent orthogonal signaling exhibits properties such as coding gain and a minimum value for γ_b.

6.2.1 Noncoherent Signaling

For noncoherent signaling over the AWGN channel with equal energy waveforms $\{s_m(t)\}$, we found in Chapter 5 that the optimal receiver computes the decision variables $|\langle r(t)|s_m(t)\rangle|$ from the received waveform $r(t)$ and then decodes the symbol corresponding to the largest such variable. Equivalently, we can use any monotonic function of $|\langle r(t)|s_m(t)\rangle|$ as a decision variable. The expression $|\langle r(t)|s_m(t)\rangle|$ corresponds to the envelope of the matched-filter output. Detection based on this decision variable is known as envelope detection for noncoherent signaling. Note that all information about the signal phase is lost. We, therefore, expect noncoherent signaling to have a poorer detection performance than coherent signaling. In practical terms, the detection performance difference is only a few dBs for moderate energy contrast ratios and decreases with increasing γ. The principal appeal of noncoherent signaling is that envelope detection is easier to implement (and, therefore, less expensive) than a coherent system.

An M-ary noncoherent receiver can be implemented as a bank of M matched filters, with the output of each being passed through an envelope detector. For definiteness, we shall restrict our attention to orthogonal waveforms having equal energies. As with the coherent case, decoding is done by selecting the largest of the M outputs. The only salient difference is that in the noncoherent case, the probability density functions for the decision variables are not Gaussian.

There are two types of decision variables. The output of a filter, when subjected to an orthogonal waveform to which it is not matched, contains only noise. When the matched waveform is present at the filter input, the filter output contains signal plus noise. If the noise is additive, white, and Gaussian, then the M matched-filter outputs consist of $M - 1$ "noise-only" values and one "signal-plus-noise" value. As these are then passed through envelope detectors, we must then calculate the probability density functions for the envelopes of Gaussian noise and for a constant signal plus Gaussian noise. Furthermore, we shall consider the Gaussian noise process to have zero mean and variance σ_0^2 at the matched-filter output.

The output of each matched filter can be expressed in terms of uncorrelated in-phase and quadrature components. When noise is present at the input, these form two statistically independent Gaussian variables with zero mean and variance σ_0^2. When a constant signal is present in addition to the noise, the mean of the in-phase component becomes A and all of the other statistics remain unchanged.

Letting x and y be the in-phase and quadrature components, respectively, we have, for the signal-present case,

x: Gaussian with mean A and variance σ_0^2

y: Gaussian with mean 0 and variance σ_0^2

Since x and y are statistically independent, their joint probability density function is given by

$$p(x,y) = \frac{1}{2\pi\sigma_0^2} \exp\left[-\frac{(x-A)^2 + y^2}{2\sigma_0^2}\right]$$

$$= \frac{1}{2\pi\sigma_0^2} \exp\left[-\frac{x^2 + y^2 - 2Ax + A^2}{2\sigma_0^2}\right] \tag{6.64}$$

We now do a transformation of random variables from cartesian (x,y) to polar (r,θ). Physically, the variable r represents the envelope of the statistical process and θ is the phase. The transformation is defined by

$$p(x,y)\, dx\, dy = p(r,\theta) r\, dr\, d\theta$$

where

$$r^2 = x^2 + y^2 \qquad \text{and} \qquad \theta = \tan^{-1}(y/x)$$

The joint probability density function for the envelope and the phase then is

$$p(r,\theta) = \frac{r}{2\pi\sigma^2} \exp\left(-\frac{r^2 - 2Ar\cos\theta + A^2}{2\sigma_0^2}\right) \tag{6.65}$$

The probability density function for the envelope alone can be found by integrating $p(r,\theta)$ over all values of θ:

$$p(r) = \int_0^{2\pi} p(r,\theta)\, d\theta = \frac{r}{\sigma_0^2} e^{-(r^2+A^2)/2\sigma_0^2} I_0\left(\frac{rA}{\sigma_0^2}\right) \tag{6.66}$$

where $I_0(\cdot)$ is a modified Bessel function of the first kind and order zero. This density is known as the *Rician* probability density function for the envelope of the sum of a constant signal and zero-mean Gaussian noise.

When no signal is present, we set $A = 0$ and there results

$$p(r) = \frac{r}{\sigma_0^2} e^{-r^2/2\sigma_0^2} \tag{6.67}$$

This is the *Rayleigh* probability density function for the envelope of a zero-mean Gaussian process.

6.2.2 Binary Signaling

This is the simplest case of noncoherent signaling with equiprobable orthogonal waveforms of equal energy $\mathscr{E} = A^2$. Assuming that waveform $s_1(t)$ was transmitted, then we identify hypothesis H_0 with the Rayleigh density $p_0(r)$ and hypothesis H_1 with the Rician density $p_1(r)$ for the measured envelope r:

$$H_0: r \text{ is Rayleigh} : p_0(r) = \frac{r}{\sigma_0^2} e^{-r^2/2\sigma_0^2}$$

$$H_1: r \text{ is Rician} \quad : p_1(r) = \frac{r}{\sigma_0^2} e^{-(r^2+A^2)/2\sigma_0^2} I_0\left(\frac{rA}{\sigma_0^2}\right)$$

The probability of a decoding error is given by the probability that noise alone exceeds the signal plus noise:

$$P_e = \int_0^\infty p_1(r) \int_r^\infty p_0(x) \, dx \, dr \tag{6.68}$$

The inner integral simply becomes

$$\frac{1}{\sigma_0^2} \int_r^\infty e^{-r^2/2\sigma_0^2} r \, dr = e^{-r^2/2\sigma_0^2}$$

With the energy contrast ratio defined in the usual way as $\gamma = \frac{1}{2} A^2 / \sigma_0^2$, the probability of a decoding error becomes

$$P_e = e^{-\gamma} \int_0^\infty e^{-x^2} I_0\left[x(2\gamma)^{1/2}\right] x \, dx$$

which simply reduces [Gr 65] to

$$P_e = \tfrac{1}{2} e^{-\gamma/2} \tag{6.69}$$

6.2.3 Orthogonal *M*-ary Signaling

We now generalize the results of the preceding section to an *M*-ary orthogonal alphabet of equiprobable equal-energy waveforms. Again, it is easier to approach the probability of a decoding error via a calculation of the probability of correct decoding. A symbol is properly decoded only if its corresponding decision variable is larger than all of the other $M - 1$ decision variables. The decision variable U_1 corresponding to the correct symbol is Rician-distributed with probability density $p_1(r)$. All other $M - 1$ variables U_n, $n = 2, \ldots, M$, are Rayleigh-distributed with probability density $p_0(r)$. The probability of correct decoding is, therefore, given by

$$P_C(M, \gamma) = \int_0^\infty \text{Prob}\{U_2 < U_1, U_3 < U_1, \cdots, U_M < U_1 | U_1\} p_1(U_1) \, dU_1$$

$$= \int_0^\infty (\text{Prob}\{U_n < U_1 | U_1\})^{M-1} p_1(U_1) \, dU_1 \tag{6.70}$$

The probability inside the parentheses is given by

$$\text{Prob}\{U_n < U_1 | U_1\} = \int_0^{U_1} p_0(r)\, dr$$

$$= 1 - e^{-U_1^2/2\sigma_0^2}$$

The probability of correct decoding can, therefore, be written as

$$P_C(M, \gamma) = \frac{1}{\sigma_0^2} \int_0^\infty \left[1 - e^{-r^2/2\sigma_0^2} \right]^{M-1} e^{-(r^2 + A^2)/2\sigma_0^2} I_0\left(\frac{rA}{\sigma_0^2} \right) r\, dr$$

Letting $x = r^2/2\sigma_0^2$ and $\gamma = A^2/2\sigma_0^2$, this expression can be simplified to

$$P_C(M, \gamma) = e^{-\gamma} \int_0^\infty \left(1 - e^{-x} \right)^{M-1} e^{-x} I_0\left[2(\gamma x)^{1/2} \right] dx$$

To evaluate this integral in closed form, we expand $(1 - e^{-x})^{M-1}$ using the binomial theorem:

$$\left(1 - e^{-x} \right)^{M-1} = \sum_{m=0}^{M-1} (-)^m \binom{M-1}{m} e^{-mx}$$

This leads to

$$P_C(M, \gamma) = e^{-\gamma} \sum_{m=0}^{M-1} (-)^m \binom{M-1}{m} \int_0^\infty e^{-(m+1)x} I_0\left[2(\gamma x)^{1/2} \right] dx$$

$$= \sum_{m=0}^{M-1} \frac{(-)^m}{m+1} \binom{M-1}{m} e^{-m\gamma/(m+1)} \tag{6.71}$$

The equivalent bit error probability can be found in the usual way:

$$P_{be}(M, \gamma_b) = P_e(M, k\gamma_b) \cdot 2^{k-1}/(2^k - 1) \tag{6.72}$$

where $P_e(M, k\gamma_b) = 1 - P_C(M, \gamma)$, $k = \log_2 M$, and $\gamma = k\gamma_b$. The decoding performance of noncoherent M-ary orthogonal signaling is shown in Fig. 6-8.

Noncoherent orthogonal signaling exhibits coding gain. An example of this is shown in Fig. 6-9, where the uncoded M-ary symbol error probability is given by

$$P_u(\gamma_b) = 1 - \left[1 - P_b(\gamma_b) \right]^k \tag{6.73}$$

where

$$P_b(\gamma_b) = \tfrac{1}{2} e^{-1/2\gamma_b} \tag{6.74}$$

$P_u(\gamma_b)$ is plotted with $P_e(M, k\gamma_b)$ for $k = 5$. At a symbol error rate of 10^{-3}, the coding gain is 6.2 dB.

We now compare the performance of coherent versus noncoherent signaling. Figure 6-10 shows both coherent and noncoherent M-ary orthogonal bit error probabilities for $k = 1$ and 4 as a function of γ_b. Three interesting effects may be observed

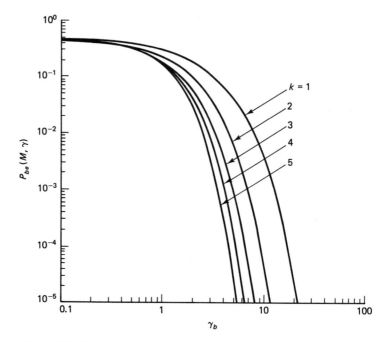

Figure 6-8.   Noncoherent M-ary orthogonal signaling bit error probabilities.

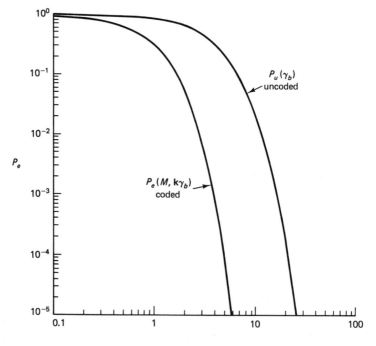

Figure 6-9.   Coded versus uncoded noncoherent M-ary orthogonal signaling; $k = 5$.

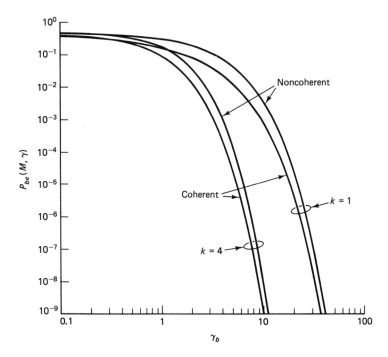

Figure 6-10.   Performance comparison between coherent and noncoherent M-ary orthogonal signaling.

in the figure. First, we note that for moderate to large γ_b, the $k = 4$ curves are all to the left of the $k = 1$ curves. This indicates the effect of coding gain, which is evident here for both coherent and noncoherent signaling. Second, for a fixed value of k and a fixed bit error probability, coherent signaling is slightly but consistently more energy efficient than noncoherent signaling. Third, the energy-efficiency advantage of coherent over noncoherent signaling decreases as γ_b becomes large. In Fig. 6-10, the bit error probability scale has been greatly compressed to show this effect clearly.

Lastly, we explore the performance behavior of noncoherent orthogonal signaling as M becomes large. We present the following derivation due to Lindsey [Li 65]. Recall that probability of correct decoding for M-ary noncoherent orthogonal signaling is

$$P_C(M, \gamma) = \int_0^\infty g(x) e^{-(x+\gamma)} I_0\big[2(\gamma x)^{1/2}\big] dx \qquad (6.75)$$

where $g(x) = (1 - e^{-x})^{M-1}$. As M becomes large, function $g(x)$ can be approximated by

$$g(x) \approx \begin{cases} 0 & x < \ln(M-1) \\ 1 & x > \ln(M-1) \end{cases}$$

which is a unit step located at $\ln(M-1)$, the point of inflection of $g(x)$. Substituting this in the expression for $P_C(M,\gamma)$ gives

$$P_C(M,\gamma) \approx \int_{\ln(M-1)}^{\infty} g(x)e^{-(x+\gamma)}I_0\left[2(\gamma x)^{1/2}\right]dx = \int_{\ln(M-1)}^{\infty} e^{-(x+\gamma)}I_0\left[2(\gamma x)^{1/2}\right]dx$$

(6.76)

This integral is the Marcum Q function of detection theory [He 68, Ma 60a, Wh 71]. Letting $x = \frac{1}{2}z^2$, the integral can be transformed to

$$P_C(M,\gamma) = \int_{\beta}^{\infty} e^{-1/2(z^2+\alpha^2)}I_0(\alpha z)dz = Q(\alpha,\beta)$$

(6.77)

where $\alpha = (2\gamma)^{1/2}$ and $\beta = [2\ln(M-1)]^{1/2}$. Marcum's Q function admits the following two power series expansions [He 68]:

$$Q(\alpha,\beta) = \begin{cases} e^{\frac{1}{2}(\alpha^2+\beta^2)} \displaystyle\sum_{n=0}^{\infty} \left(\frac{\alpha}{\beta}\right)^n I_n(\alpha\beta) & \alpha < \beta \\[4mm] 1 - e^{\frac{1}{2}(\alpha^2+\beta^2)} \displaystyle\sum_{n=1}^{\infty} \left(\frac{\beta}{\alpha}\right)^n I_n(\alpha\beta) & \alpha > \beta \end{cases}$$

(6.78)

We consider, therefore, the following two cases:

$$\alpha < \beta: \qquad \frac{\gamma_b}{\ln 2}\ln M < \ln(M+1)$$

$$\alpha > \beta: \qquad \frac{\gamma_b}{\ln 2}\ln M > \ln(M+1)$$

as M tends to infinity in $P_C(M,\gamma)$. For $\alpha < \beta$, we have

$$\lim_{M\to\infty} P_C(M,\gamma)$$

$$= \lim_{M\to\infty} \exp\left(-\frac{\gamma_b}{\ln 2}\ln M - \ln(M-1)\right) \sum_{n=0}^{\infty} \left(\frac{\gamma_b}{\ln 2}\right)^{n/2} I_n\left[2\ln M(\gamma_b/\ln 2)^{1/2}\right]$$

This expression converges only if $\gamma_b < \ln 2$, in which case it converges to zero. For $\alpha > \beta$, we have

$$\lim_{M\to\infty} P_C(M,\gamma)$$

$$= 1 - \lim_{M\to\infty} \exp\left(-\frac{\gamma_b}{\ln 2}\ln M - \ln(M-1)\right) \sum_{n=0}^{\infty} \left(\frac{\gamma_b}{\ln 2}\right)^{-n/2} I_n\left[2\ln M(\gamma_b/\ln 2)^{1/2}\right]$$

which converges to 1 provided $\gamma_b > \ln 2$.

Summarizing these results and using $P_e(M,\gamma) = 1 - P_C(M,\gamma)$, we have

$$\lim_{M\to\infty} P_e(M,\gamma) = \begin{cases} 0 & \text{if } \gamma_b > \ln 2 \\ 1 & \text{if } \gamma_b < \ln 2 \end{cases}$$

(6.79)

These are identical to the corresponding results for the performance of coherent orthogonal signaling. We conclude that as the signaling complexity increases without bound, the performance of noncoherent orthogonal signaling approaches ideal performance in that an arbitrarily small decoding error probability can be enjoyed as M is made sufficiently large, provided $\gamma_b > \ln 2$.

6.3 RESOURCE UTILIZATION EFFICIENCY

Signaling with waveforms utilizes two types of communication resource: signal degrees of freedom (i.e., bandwidth and time) and signal energy. This section introduces the time–bandwidth expansion factor as a way of comparing different signaling techniques on the basis of their information rate per signal degree of freedom. We shall introduce the time–bandwidth expansion factor to measure the efficiency with which a modulation technique utilizes signal-space coordinates. We shall also compare the performance of various waveforms on that basis.

6.3.1 The Time–Bandwidth Expansion Factor

The information-carrying capacity of the AWGN channel was given in Section 4.2 as

$$C = W \log_2(1 + S/N) \tag{6.80}$$

bits per second, where W is the channel bandwidth, and S/N is the signal-to-noise power ratio. A waveform with $2TW$ degrees of freedom in an AWGN environment can convey, therefore, no more than

$$I = TW \log_2(1 + S/N) \tag{6.81}$$

bits of information. We can express the signal-to-noise power ratio in terms of more elementary quantities. If $\mathcal{E}$ is the waveform energy, then $\mathcal{E} = ST$. If N_0 is the two-sided noise power spectral density, then $N = 2N_0W$. We have, therefore,

$$I = TW \log_2(1 + \gamma/TW) \tag{6.82}$$

bits. The size of I is a measure of the waveform's information-carrying capacity. This simple equation suggests two different approaches to signaling in AWGN.

Let us define the *time–bandwidth expansion factor* η as the ratio of waveform information (in bits) to the number of signal degrees of freedom:

$$\eta = \frac{I}{2TW} = \frac{1}{2\ln 2}\ln\left(1 + \frac{\gamma_0 \log_2 2TW}{TW}\right) \tag{6.83}$$

where γ_0 is the energy contrast ratio normalized by the logarithm (base 2) of the number of signal degrees of freedom. The bandwidth expansion factor η measures the amount of signaling information that can be accommodated by a given number of signaling waveform degrees of freedom $2TW$. For communication employing signaling waveforms of duration T seconds and bandwidth W hertz, the quantity 2η has the following interpretation: it is the number of bits per second per hertz that can be accommodated by the signaling technique. As such, η is a useful measure of channel resource utilization.

Signaling efficiency is sometimes measured by the bandwidth expansion factor $R/W = 2\eta$, where R is the data rate in bits per second. The bandwidth expansion factor is a measure of how bandwidth is being utilized to provide channel capacity for a given modulation scheme. We now explore two separate cases, depending on whether $2TW$ is large or small.

6.3.2 Energy-Efficient Communication

When the number of waveform degrees of freedom is very large, η becomes

$$\eta \approx \frac{\gamma_0}{\ln 2} \frac{\log_2 2TW}{2TW} \tag{6.84}$$

This situation corresponds to the coded signaling techniques studied in the previous sections. With coherent M-ary orthogonal or equicorrelated signaling, the waveforms are based on a set of M orthogonal signals. These signals form a basis in an M-dimensional linear signal space. We can, therefore, identify M with the number of coordinates in that space:

$$M = 2TW \tag{6.85}$$

so that for orthogonal or equicorrelated waveforms, we have $\gamma_0 = \gamma_b$, and there follows

$$\eta = \frac{\log_2 M}{M} \tag{6.86}$$

since $\gamma_b = \ln 2$ in the limit of large M. With biorthogonal signaling, we use only $M/2$ waveforms of dimension $2TW$, so that $M = TW$ and

$$\eta = 2\frac{\log_2 M}{M} \tag{6.87}$$

which implies that biorthogonal signaling is twice as efficient in time–bandwidth utilization as either orthogonal or equicorrelated signaling.

These signaling techniques are sometimes called energy efficient. They are characterized by coding gain as M increases and, therefore, by an efficient utilization of signaling energy. Recall, however, that the fundamental limit of $\gamma_b = \ln 2$ applies in this case. The trade-off with energy-efficient signaling is that the number of bits per waveform (i.e., the signaling rate) increases only logarithmically with the number of degrees of freedom. Thus, a large amount of bandwidth is required to support energy-efficient signaling.

The advantage of energy-efficient signaling is that as long as $\gamma_b \geq \ln 2$, error-free communication is theoretically possible, albeit at the cost of very complex signaling. This is the essence of the coding theorem for the AWGN channel.

Energy-efficient signaling is characterized by decoding error probability curves such as shown in Figs. 6-5, 6-6, and 6-8. As the waveform complexity (k) increases, the amount of energy per bit required to achieve a given error rate decreases. We have already conveniently referred to this effect as *coding gain*, which associates with a given modulation an effective gain in signal-to-noise ratio.

EXAMPLE

There are many ways to construct such energy-efficient signals. We have already considered orthogonal and equicorrelated signals. A good example of orthogonal signaling is frequency-shift keying (FSK). In FSK, each one of M possible signaling waveforms is implemented as a sinusoid

$$s_k(t) = (2\mathcal{E})^{1/2} \cos(2\pi \nu_k t)$$

To each signal $s_k(t)$ there corresponds a distinct frequency ν_k. Typically, these frequencies are contiguous, so that the entire FSK signal occupies a single block of the frequency spectrum. The frequencies ν_k are determined by the requirement of orthogonality between dissimilar waveforms. For signals with duration of T seconds, we have

$$\langle s_k | s_m \rangle = 2\mathcal{E} \int_0^T \cos(2\pi \nu_k t) \cos(2\pi \nu_m t)\, dt$$

$$= \frac{\sin[2\pi(\nu_k - \nu_m)T]}{2(\nu_k - \nu_m)} + \frac{\sin[2\pi(\nu_k + \nu_m)T]}{2(\nu_k + \nu_m)}$$

$$= 0 \text{ when } 2\pi(\nu_k - \nu_m) = K\pi \quad K = 1, 2, 3, \ldots$$

Assuming signaling frequencies separated by an integer multiple of some common spacing $\Delta\nu$, this condition reduces to $\Delta\nu \cdot T = \frac{1}{2}K$, $K = 1, 2, 3, \ldots$. The minimum frequency spacing is obtained by setting $K = 1$, resulting in $\Delta\nu = 0.5/T$.

Although any integer multiple of $0.5/T$ would work just as well, the minimum frequency separation results in the least total signaling bandwidth required when all signaling frequencies are contiguous. The quantity $\Delta\nu$ is called the *frequency shift*. The coding level M and the frequency shift are selected to match the data rate to the available bandwidth.

FSK can be demodulated both coherently and noncoherently. Figure 6-11 shows both types of demodulators. The signaling frequencies used in this binary example are ν_1 and ν_2 Hz. The general structure of FSK demodulation is a bank of band-pass filters tuned to the signaling frequencies and followed by magnitude comparators.

6.3.3 Time–Bandwidth-Efficient Communication

The expression

$$I = TW \log_2(1 + \gamma/TW) \tag{6.88}$$

suggests that for any fixed TW, arbitrarily large amounts of information can be conveyed on the AWGN channel if the energy contrast ratio is sufficiently large. In other words, the precision with which one can make a measurement (such as on a communication signal) can be made arbitrarily fine provided the energy contrast ratio is sufficiently large. Here the complexity of the signaling alphabet does not matter. One can use, in fact, a single waveform $f(t)$ and generate an M-ary signaling alphabet suitable for large γ by varying its amplitude, phase, or both. This has the

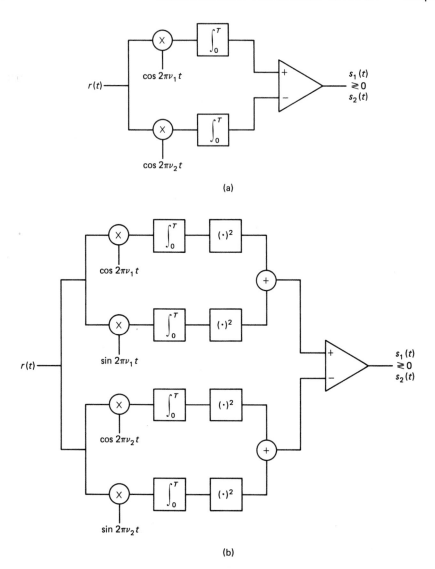

Figure 6-11. Demodulators for (a) coherent and (b) noncoherent FSK. The generalization to M-ary is straightforward and involves an M-ary replication of the matched filters, one for each signaling frequency, followed by a greatest-out-of-M decision box.

obvious advantage of requiring only one matched filter $f*(\tau - t)$, but the energy contrast ratio has to be large enough to allow the distinction between M different levels or phases at the matched-filter output.

With $\gamma = M \gamma_b$ and since the decoding decision is made at the output of a single matched filter where $2TW = 1$, the time–bandwidth expansion factor can be as low as

$$\eta = \tfrac{1}{2} \log_2 (1 + 2M\gamma_b) \qquad (6.89)$$

This type of signaling is called time–bandwidth-efficient. These techniques are characterized by a requirement for increasing γ_b as M increases to maintain a fixed decoding error probability.

The simplest example of time–bandwidth-efficient signaling is pulse-amplitude modulation (PAM). In PAM, information is transmitted via any one of M equally probable constant signal levels. If we consider M bipolar signals, the possible amplitudes corresponding to a constant spacing A between amplitude levels are

$$\alpha_k = \pm A/2, \; \pm 3A/2, \; \pm 5A/2, \; \ldots, \; \pm(M-1)A/2$$

These signals are indicated in Fig. 6-12, along with the corresponding probability density functions at the receiver. In AWGN, these probability densities are all Gaussian with mean a_k and variance σ_0^2. In M-ary PAM, the detection thresholds are located at the intersections of the probability density curves: $0, \; \pm A, \; \pm 2A, \; \ldots$. The shaded areas in Fig. 6-12 correspond to regions of decoding errors. Calculating the overall probability of decoding error, therefore, reduces to a calculation of the probabilities associated with the tails of these Gaussians. The probability corresponding to any one tail is

$$Q = \int_0^\infty p(\mu = -\tfrac{1}{2}A, \; \sigma_0; \; x) \, dx = \tfrac{1}{2} \, \text{erfc} \left(\frac{A}{2\sigma_0 2^{1/2}} \right)$$

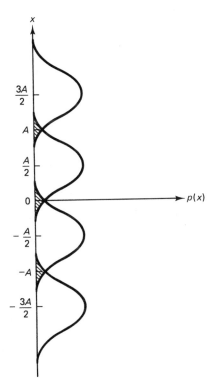

Figure 6-12. PAM signal levels and associated probability densities for the $M = 4$ case. Regions of overlap correspond to decoding errors.

where $p(\mu, \sigma_0^2; x)$ is the Gaussian probability density with mean μ and variance σ_0^2.

Each of the signaling waveforms occurs with probability $1/M$. Each of the inner amplitude levels is associated with a conditional probability of error equal to $2Q$, since each of the corresponding probability density functions has two error tails (i.e., overlaps with two other densities). Each of the outer levels has an error probability of Q. The average probability of error is, therefore,

$$P_e = \frac{1}{M}[2Q + (M - 2)2Q] = 2\left(\frac{M - 1}{M}\right)Q = \left(\frac{M - 1}{M}\right) \text{erfc}\left(\frac{A}{2\sigma_0 2^{1/2}}\right)$$

It remains to express the argument of the complementary error function in terms of the average energy contrast ratio. To this end, we note that the signal energy corresponding to the signal amplitude level a_k is

$$\mathscr{E}_k = a_k^2 = \left[\tfrac{1}{2}(2k - 1)A\right]^2 \qquad k = \pm 1, \pm 2, \ldots, \pm M/2$$

and the average symbol energy is

$$\mathscr{E} = \frac{2}{M} \sum_{k=1}^{M/2} \mathscr{E}_k = \frac{2}{M}(\tfrac{1}{2}A)^2 \sum_{k=1}^{M/2} (2k - 1)^2 = \left(\frac{M^2 - 1}{12}\right)A^2$$

The argument of the complementary error function can be written, therefore, as

$$\frac{A}{2\sigma_0 2^{1/2}} = \left(\frac{3\gamma}{M^2 - 1}\right)^{1/2}$$

where $\gamma = \tfrac{1}{2}\mathscr{E}/\sigma_0^2$. The probability of a symbol decoding error is, therefore,

$$P_e(\gamma) = \left(\frac{M - 1}{M}\right) \text{erfc}\left(\frac{3\gamma}{M^2 - 1}\right)^{1/2} \qquad (6.90)$$

and is plotted as a function of γ_b in Fig. 6-13, where $\gamma = \gamma_b \log M$.

The various signals in PAM all have different amplitudes and are decoded assuming a constant-amplitude spacing between signal levels. This places a strong requirement for linearity on PAM-processing systems. In particular, transmitting hardware must have linear characteristics. For example, power amplifiers must be operated in class A or AB and, therefore, at or below 60-percent efficiency. To increase the efficiency of radio power amplification requires operation in class C, where the amplifier is biased near cutoff and operated in the nonlinear regime. It would be desirable, therefore, to consider constant-envelope signaling waveforms, which do not suffer distortion by nonlinear amplifiers.

Another disadvantage of PAM is that intersymbol envelope discontinuities generate out-of-band interference. This would also be mitigated by the use of constant-envelope signaling. We are thus led to consider M-ary phase-shift keying (PSK), where signals consist of equal-amplitude sinusoids having different phases. PSK must, of course, be demodulated coherently.

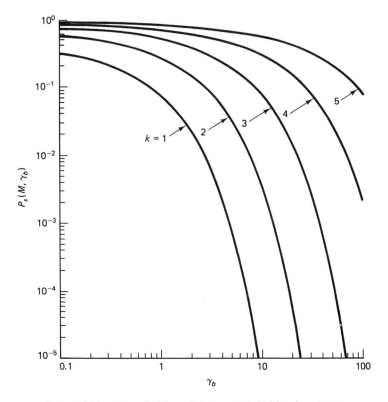

Figure 6-13.   *M*-ary PAM symbol-error probabilities; $k = \log M$.

As an example of bandwidth-efficient signaling, let us look at *M*-ary phase-shift keying (MPSK). Consider a set of *M* signaling waveforms:

$$s_m(t) = (2\mathscr{E})^{1/2} \cos(2\pi \nu_c t + \theta_m) \tag{6.91}$$

where ν_c is the carrier frequency, and

$$\theta_m = 2\pi(m-1)/M \qquad m = 1, \ldots, M \tag{6.92}$$

are the *M* signaling phases. The cosine of the sum of two arguments can be written as

$$s_m(t) = i_m \cos(2\pi \nu_c t) - q_m \sin(2\pi \nu_c t) \tag{6.93}$$

where

$$i_m = (2\mathscr{E})^{1/2} \cos(\theta_m) \qquad \text{and} \qquad q_m = (2\mathscr{E})^{1/2} \sin(\theta_m) \tag{6.94}$$

are the in-phase and quadrature signal amplitudes, respectively. These correspond to a constant energy $\mathscr{E}$ and a phase given by $\theta_m = \tan^{-1}(q_m/i_m)$. The received waveform is of the form

$$r(t) = s_k(t) + n(t) \tag{6.95}$$

where $s_k(t)$ may be any one of the signaling waveforms, and $n(t)$ is a zero-mean Gaussian noise process with variance σ_0^2. We can express $r(t)$ in terms of in-phase and quadrature components, ensuring that the normalization yields a mean value of $\mathscr{E}$:

$$r(t) = r_i \cos(2\pi\nu_c t) - r_q \sin(2\pi\nu_c t) \tag{6.96}$$

where

$$
\begin{aligned}
r_i &= \langle r(t)|(2\mathscr{E})^{1/2} \cos(2\pi\nu_c t)\rangle \\
&= \langle s_k(t)|(2\mathscr{E})^{1/2} \cos(2\pi\nu_c t)\rangle + \langle n(t)|(2\mathscr{E})^{1/2} \cos(2\pi\nu_c t)\rangle \\
&= (2\mathscr{E})^{1/2} i_k + n_i \tag{6.97}
\end{aligned}
$$

where

$$n_i = \langle n(t)|(2\mathscr{E})^{1/2} \cos(2\pi\nu_c t)\rangle \tag{6.98}$$

is a Gaussian variable with zero mean and variance σ_0^2. Similarly,

$$
\begin{aligned}
r_q &= \langle r(t)|(2\mathscr{E})^{1/2} \sin(2\pi\nu_c t)\rangle \\
&= \langle s_k(t)|(2\mathscr{E})^{1/2} \sin(2\pi\nu_c t)\rangle + \langle n(t)|(2\mathscr{E})^{1/2} \sin(2\pi\nu_c t)\rangle \\
&= n_q \tag{6.99}
\end{aligned}
$$

where

$$n_q = \langle n(t)|(2\mathscr{E})^{1/2} \sin(2\pi\nu_c t)\rangle \tag{6.100}$$

is a Gaussian variable with zero mean and variance σ_0^2. Recall from Chapter 5 that the optimum coherent processor for equal energy $\mathscr{E}$ signals on the AWGN channel is given by thresholding decision variables of the form

$$U_m = \mathscr{R}e \langle r(t)|s_m(t)\rangle \tag{6.101}$$

Since r_i and r_q are not functions of time, they are constants that can be factored out of the inner product. Detection consists in computing the in-phase (r_i) and quadrature (r_q) components of the received signal $r(t)$, and in determining its phase through the relation

$$\theta = \tan^{-1}(r_q/r_i) \tag{6.102}$$

A detection error occurs whenever the phase estimate differs by more than $\Delta\theta = \pm\pi/M$ from the phase of the transmitted waveform. To calculate the probability of a decoding error, we must first calculate the probability density function for the received phase. The in-phase $x = r_i$ component is normally distributed with mean $2\mathscr{E}$ and variance $\mathscr{E}\sigma_0^2$. The quadrature $y = r_q$ component is normally distributed with zero mean and variance $\sigma^2 = \mathscr{E}\sigma_0^2$. The in-phase and quadrature components are uncorrelated and, therefore, statistically independent. The joint probability density function for x and y is

$$p(x, y) = \frac{1}{2\pi\sigma^2} \exp\left(\frac{x^2 + 4\mathscr{E}^2 - 4x\mathscr{E} + y^2}{2\sigma^2}\right) \tag{6.103}$$

We now do a change of variables, $(x, y) \rightarrow (r, \theta)$, such that $x = r \cos \theta$ and $y = r \sin \theta$. The joint probability density function becomes

$$p(r, \theta) = \frac{r}{2\pi\sigma^2} \exp\left(\frac{r^2 - 4\mathscr{E}r \cos \theta + 4\mathscr{E}^2}{2\sigma^2}\right) \qquad (6.104)$$

The marginal probability density for the phase θ can now be found by integrating $p(r, \theta)$ over all values of r, resulting in the following expression:

$$p(\theta) = \int_0^\infty p(r, \theta)dr =$$

$$(2\pi)^{-1}e^{-\gamma}\left\{1 + (\pi\gamma)^{1/2} \cos \theta e^{\gamma \cos^2 \theta}[1 + \text{erf}(\gamma^{1/2} \cos \theta)]\right\} \qquad (6.105)$$

The M-ary symbol error probability can now be calculated as

$$P_e(M, \lambda) = 1 - \int_{-\pi/M}^{\pi/M} p(\theta) \, d\theta \qquad (6.106)$$

The symbol error probability $P_e(M, \gamma)$ for MPSK is shown in Fig. 6-14 as a function of the energy contrast ratio per bit $\gamma_b = \gamma \log_2 M$.

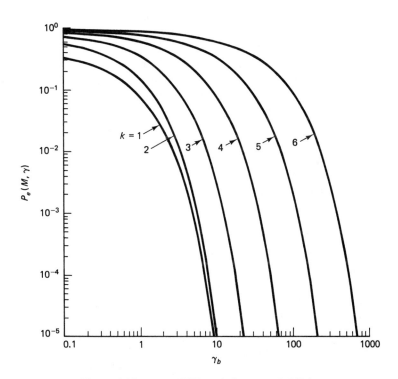

Figure 6-14. M-ary PSK symbol-error probabilities.

Note in Fig. 6-14 that for M-ary PSK, a bandwidth-efficient signaling technique, the energy contrast ratio per bit requirement increases rapidly with each additional bit per signaling waveform. The bandwidth requirement does not change with increasing k, but a larger energy contrast ratio is needed to maintain the ability to distinguish between more waveforms of like complexity in a constant-AWGN environment.

6.3.4 Quadrature Modulation Techniques

When spectral efficiency is required, there are attractive modulation techniques that can be used. These techniques are variations on the same theme that the in-phase and quadrature components of a signal can be independently modulated. We have already encountered the quadrature demodulator in Section 5.3.5, where it was used to detect noncoherent signals. The basic idea is to project the received waveform $r(t)$ that has been impressed on a carrier with frequency ω onto the two orthogonal signals cos ωt and sin ωt. A signal with unknown phase is guaranteed to have a nonzero projection on at least one of these sinusoids. Squaring and adding the in-phase (cos ωt) and quadrature (sin ωt) channels yields a signal that is independent of the unknown phase.

If, however, the phase is known so that coherent demodulation is possible, then we already remarked that only one arm of the quadrature demodulator (without the square-law device) is needed. That is because the phase can be tracked exactly and the received signal can be projected entirely in one or the other arm of the demodulator. The result is complex demodulation, and the received signal is translated to baseband.

By using both arms, however, spectral efficiency can result. Let us discuss at first only the modulation/demodulation aspect of processing, as opposed to information detection. A baseband signal $a(t)$ can be mixed with (i.e., modulate) the carrier cos ωt to produce the band-pass signal $a(t)$ cos ωt. This is represented graphically in Fig. 6-15(a), where the power spectral density of the resulting signal is plotted. The same power spectral density (and, hence, spectral occupancy) would have been obtained had $a(t)$ been used to modulate the carrier term sin ωt. However, since cos ωt and sin ωt are orthogonal, they can be demodulated separately. The implication is that we can use $a(t)$ to modulate the in-phase carrier term cos ωt and some *other* signal $b(t)$ having similar spectral characteristics to modulate the quadrature carrier sin ωt.

The two resulting modulated signals share the same spectrum, i.e., their power spectral densities overlap. These two signals do not interfere with each other, however, because they are imposed on separate orthogonal carriers that happen to share the same carrier frequency. Figure 6-15(b) shows the modulator and demodulator for this modulation technique. Here the integration time T should be long compared to the duration of a carrier cycle, i.e., $T \gg 2\pi/\omega$.

It is possible to combine the performance of antipodal signals with the spectral efficiency of quadrature modulation. Each of the in-phase and quadrature signals can be used to carry a separate antipodal signal: binary phase-shift keying (BPSK). The performance for each channel will be the same as for BPSK. Spectral efficiency

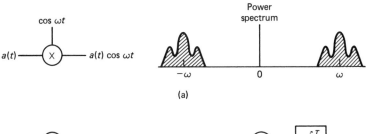

(a)

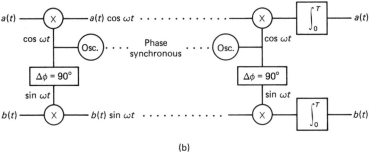

(b)

Figure 6-15. Quadrature modulation as a generalization of coherent carrier signaling. (*a*) Single-channel in-phase modulation. (*b*) Coherent quadrature modulator and demodulator.

is achieved by having the two separate signals share the same bandwidth. It is actually irrelevant whether the two modulating signals are independent or whether they are the deinterleaved odd- and even-numbered bits from a single data source. This modulation technique is called *quadrature phase-shift keying* (QPSK). In what follows, we shall assume that a single bit stream is demultiplexed into its odd and even bits and that these substreams are used to modulate the in-phase and quadrature channels, respectively. The modulator and demodulator for QPSK are shown in Fig. 6-16.

The in-phase and quadrature components of a QPSK signal having energy $\mathscr{E}$ are

in-phase signal: $i(t) = (2\mathscr{E})^{1/2} \cos(\omega t + a_k \pi)$

quadrature signal: $q(t) = (2\mathscr{E})^{1/2} \sin(\omega t + b_k \pi)$ (6.107)

where a_k and b_k are chosen from the set $\{0, 1\}$. The total signal is the sum of two orthogonal antipodal signals:

$$s(t) = i(t) + q(t) = (2\mathscr{E})^{1/2} \cos(\omega t + a_k \pi) + (2\mathscr{E})^{1/2} \sin(\omega t + b_k \pi)$$
(6.108)

Consider the four separate cases corresponding to the different values assumed by (a_k, b_k).

Case 1: $a_k = b_k = 0$, and we have $s(t) = (2\mathscr{E})^{1/2} \cos(\omega t - \pi/4)$
Case 2: $a_k = 0$, $b_k = 1$, and we have $s(t) = (2\mathscr{E})^{1/2} \cos(\omega t + \pi/4)$
Case 3: $a_k = 1$, $b_k = 0$, and we have $s(t) = (2\mathscr{E})^{1/2} \cos(\omega t - 3\pi/4)$
Case 4: $a_k = 1$, $b_k = 1$, and we have $s(t) = (2\mathscr{E})^{1/2} \cos(\omega t + 3\pi/4)$

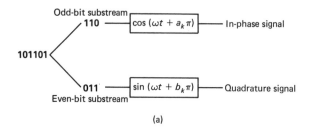

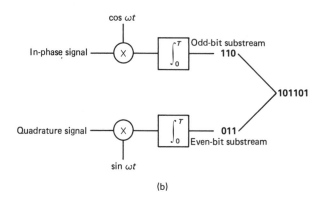

Figure 6-16. (*a*) Modulator and (*b*) demodulator for QPSK. Carriers in both the modulator and the demodulator must be phase-synchronized.

We can summarize all these cases with the single four-phase waveform:

$$s(t) = (2\mathcal{E})^{1/2} \cos\left[\omega t + (2m - 1)\pi/4\right] \tag{6.109}$$

where the values of m correspond to the values of (a_k, b_k) in the manner shown in Table 6-1. A useful way to represent digital communication waveforms is by means of signal constellations such as is shown in Fig. 6-17. QPSK is identical with 4-ary PSK and shares the same detection performance. In a signal constellation, signal amplitude and phase are represented by polar coordinates. In the simple example shown in Fig. 6-17, all amplitudes are identical; this is expressed graphically by situating all four signal points at an equal distance from the origin. These points are separated by $\pi/2$ radians, indicating that the least phase shift between any two waveforms is $\pi/2$ radians.

Note in Fig. 6-17 that the QPSK signal phase

- remains constant when neither a_k nor b_k changes,
- changes by $\pi/2$ radians when either a_k or b_k changes, and
- changes by π radians when both a_k and b_k change.

TABLE 6-1. PARAMETERS FOR QPSK WAVEFORM

m	$(2m - 1)\pi/4$	a_k	b_k
1	$\pi/4$	0	1
2	$3\pi/4$	1	1
3	$5\pi/4$	1	0
4	$7\pi/4$	0	0

These phase changes result in out-of-band interference that could be reduced by eliminating the discontinuities in the signaling waveforms that occur at the instants of bit changes. One way to accomplish this is to weigh the in-phase and quadrature signals by a function that smoothly passes through zero at the instant of bit changes. This results in a signal of the form

$$s(t) = i_k \cos\left(\tfrac{1}{2}\pi t/T\right)\cos \omega t + q_k \sin\left(\tfrac{1}{2}\pi t/T\right)\sin \omega t \qquad (6.110)$$

where T is the bit duration, and

$$i_k = (2\mathscr{E})^{1/2}(\cos a_k \pi + \sin b_k \pi) \qquad \text{and} \qquad q_k = -(2\mathscr{E})^{1/2}(\sin a_k \pi - \cos b_k \pi) \qquad (6.111)$$

Note that without the $\cos\left(\tfrac{1}{2}\pi t/T\right)$ and $\sin\left(\tfrac{1}{2}\pi t/T\right)$ envelope terms, $s(t)$ is simply the QPSK signal. The period of these envelope terms maintains orthogonality between in-phase and quadrature components provided that the integration period is $2T$. During this time interval, the waveform can assume four different states according to the values of a_k and b_k, so that one bit of information is conveyed every T seconds.

The resulting signal can be written in the form

$$s(t) = \tfrac{1}{2}(i_k + q_k) \cos\left[2\pi(\nu_c - \Delta\nu)\tau\right] + \tfrac{1}{2}(i_k - q_k) \cos\left[2\pi(\nu_c + \Delta\nu)\tau\right] \qquad (6.112)$$

where $\nu_c = \omega/2\pi$ is the carrier frequency. This signal can be recognized as an FSK signal with frequency shift $2\Delta\nu = (2T)^{-1}$. This modulation is called *minimum-shift keying* (MSK) because it uses the minimum frequency shift that still preserves orthogonality between in-phase and quadrature channels. Because MSK has no discontinuities, its bandwidth is less than that of QPSK.

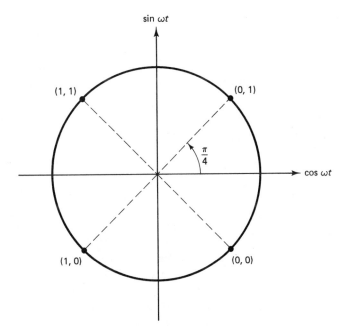

Figure 6-17. Signal constellation for QPSK. (a_k, b_k) pairs are indicated.

6.3.5 Performance and Trade-Offs

We shall now attempt to provide a unified view of modulation and discuss some of the trade-offs that are involved in the selection of a modulation scheme. In Chapter 4, we derived the Shannon–Hartley capacity formula for the AWGN channel:

$$R = W \log (1 + S/N) \tag{6.113}$$

This fundamental result of information theory sets an upper bound R on the information rate through an AWGN channel of bandwidth W. We can express the signal power S as

$$S = \frac{\mathscr{E}}{T} = \frac{n}{T}\mathscr{E}_b = R\mathscr{E}_b \tag{6.114}$$

and the noise power as $N = 2N_0 W$. The signal-to-noise ratio, therefore, becomes

$$\frac{S}{N} = \frac{R}{W}\frac{\mathscr{E}_b}{2N_0} = \frac{R}{W}\gamma_b \tag{6.115}$$

The Shannon–Hartley capacity formula can, therefore, be rewritten as

$$2\eta = \log_2 (1 + 2\eta\gamma_b) \tag{6.116}$$

where $2\eta = R/W$. The quantity 2η represents the maximum possible information rate on the AWGN channel. The quantity γ_b represents the energy cost per bit that must be paid to achieve this information rate. This equation is expressed in terms of natural parameters that can be used to cross-compare any modulation and coding schemes. Such a comparison is shown in Fig. 6-18, where there is a plot of $R/W = 2\eta$ as a function of γ_b. The units of R/W are bits per second per hertz. Note that the γ_b axis is in decibels. The solid line represents the maximum achievable information rate given by $\log_2 (1 + 2\eta\gamma_b)$ as per the Shannon–Hartley formula. Achievable information rates all lie below and to the right of that limiting curve.

This figure summarizes the performance of different signaling methods on the basis of time–bandwidth efficiency and the γ_b required for a bit error probability of 10^{-5}. The figure is a concise way of showing how closely the Shannon–Hartley limit is approached by actual modulation techniques. As such, the data shown must be interpreted in terms of the Shannon–Hartley capacity formula.

A very general way of understanding these results in terms of the Shannon–Hartley formula is to note that there are two fundamentally different ways of transmitting information with signals. One way is to use signals having very few—possibly only one—degrees of freedom and distinguishing between different signals on the basis of their distinct amplitudes or phases. This approach leads to PAM, PSK, and other similar waveforms, where both amplitude and phase may be varied. The motivation for using this approach is that the transmission channel may be limited in the number of available signal degrees of freedom. For example, certain channels such as telephone are severely bandwidth-limited. The resulting time–bandwidth-efficient signaling techniques can be associated with the signal-to-noise ratio (S/N) term in the Shannon–Hartley capacity formula. Capacity can be bought with sufficient S/N, even for time–bandwidth limited channels.

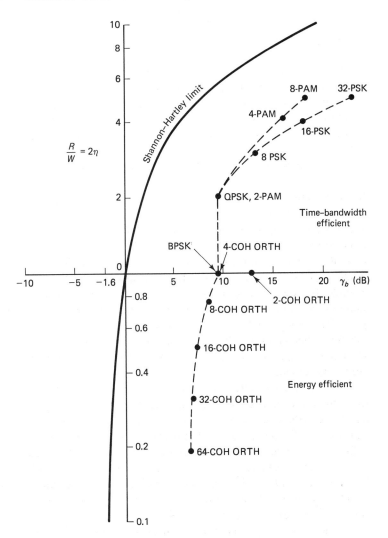

Figure 6-18.   *M*-ary waveform efficiency for a bit-error probability of 10^{-5}.

The other extreme is a channel that is signal-to-noise limited. This is equivalent to a limitation on the energy available to transmit a bit of information. This is typical of deep-space applications, where there is plenty of bandwidth, but where spacecraft power is severely rationed. For such applications, energy-efficient signaling is called for, and signals with many degrees of freedom (large bandwidth) are used to provide coding gain. This is associated with the bandwidth (*W*) term in the Shannon–Hartley formula. Orthogonal and equicorrelated signals are good examples of energy-efficient waveforms.

No waveform is entirely time–bandwidth efficient or entirely energy efficient. These two broad categories are used to describe general properties of signals and to relate them to mathematical features of information theory. Figure 6-18 is as close as we can come to describing the relative efficiencies of different signaling techniques, as well as to comparing different members of the same signaling family. The ordinate is the bandwidth-expansion factor $R/W = 2\eta$, expressed on a logarithmic scale. Higher values of R/W correspond to time–bandwidth-efficient signaling that, for a given bit error probability, requires progressively more γ_b. Improvements in signaling efficiency are possible up to the information-theoretic limit imposed by the Shannon–Hartley law. The abscissa is γ_b, also on a logarithmic scale, and arbitrarily divides the plabe into two regimes: time–bandwidth efficient above $R/W = 1$ and energy efficient below $R/W = 1$.

The Shannon–Hartley capacity limit is approached, albeit very slowly, by energy-efficient signaling by increasing M, the number of symbols in the signaling alphabet. This is shown in Fig. 6-18 by the series of points representing the performance of 2-, 4-, 8-, 16-, 32-, and 64-ary coherent orthogonal signaling. The orthogonality may be expressed either in time, frequency, or both domains. It is clear from the behavior of these points that higher-level orthogonal coding yields very little improvement for a large price paid in time–bandwidth product. Still when signal dimensionality is an inexpensive commodity, attractive gains can be realized. It should be noted that gains in excess of those shown on Fig. 6-18 can be achieved by adding other layers of coding through error-control techniques, the subject of Chapter 7. Time–bandwidth-efficient signaling can be used to approach the theoretical channel capacity limit when sufficient signal-to-noise ratio is available. Increasing M increases signaling capacity, but only at the expense of a higher signal-to-noise ratio requirement.

Not discussed here are the economics of system design. In addition to physical limitations that may force the designer to choose among different signaling techniques, there are cost factors to be considered. With both energy- and time–bandwidth-efficient signaling, hardware complexity increases approximately linearly with M. For example, M-ary orthogonal signaling requires M separate matched filters. M-ary PAM requires $M - 1$ threshold comparisons. It often happens that for one reason or another, binary signaling is very attractive. But note that QPSK doubles the information rate for no increase in γ_b and we have seen that MSK offers better spectral efficiency than QPSK.

The waveforms whose performance is summarized in Fig. 6-18 are a small subset of available signaling techniques. The goal here has been to discuss the factors leading to the performance rather than to provide an exhaustive catalog of waveforms. For a more complete survey of waveform performance, the reader should consult [Ha 83b, Pr 83, Ta 86].

We may be sometimes forced by physical or economic constraints to adopt some modulation scheme that may not provide all the gain we need, e.g., with bandwidth-efficient schemes or with $M = 2$ (easy to implement, but with not much gain). It is always possible to increase the complexity of a waveform by increasing its time–bandwidth product. The easiest way to approach this is to consider whatever set of signaling waveforms is thrust upon us by physical or economic constraints as addresses in a look-up table, where the entries are code words with increased complexity and coding gain. These code words are then transmitted instead of the original waveforms. In more precise terms, we realize the possibility of a one-to-one and onto mapping between two sets of waveforms, one having more coding gain than the other.

The additional coding gain can be viewed in any of several ways: increased resistance to decoding errors, detection and/or correction of channel decoding errors, or an attempt to approach the Shannon limit. At this point in the book, we have visited all of the fundamentally important topics in communication theory. We have by no means covered the ground in depth. There are countless variants and improvements on the coding and signaling techniques that have been introduced in these chapters. Having read thus far, the reader should be able to study these refinements, if so desired.

PROBLEMS

6.1 Calculate the energy contrast ratio per bit (γ_b) at which the information throughput through a BPSK system is reduced to 0.5, 0.2, and 0.1 bit per transmitted binary digit. Repeat the calculation for coherent and noncoherent FSK.

6.2 Calculate the approximate bit error probability for a binary noncoherent 170-Hz shift FSK signal bounced off the moon and with the following characteristics: 1 kilowatt output power fed into a directional antenna with 23-dB gain. The same type of antenna is used for transmitting and receiving. The receiver operates at an effective temperature of 300 K. Assume 7 dB of overall system losses. The data rate is 50 bits per second. Assume the moon isotropically reflects 0.1 percent of the power incident upon it. What is the bit error rate if BPSK is used?

6.3 What is the capacity of the channel described in Prob. 6.2?

6.4 A telephone channel has a bandwidth of approximately 3 kHz. Estimate the maximum data rates for modems utilizing BFSK, BPSK, and QPSK.

6.5 QPSK is used to transmit eight-bit packets two bits at a time. What is the average length of a run of consecutive error-free packets? Repeat the calculations for noncoherent BFSK transmission of the individual bits in a packet. Assume $\gamma_b = 10$.

6.6 It is not necessary that FSK use orthogonal waveforms. For coherent binary FSK, find the frequency shift that minimizes the bit error rate. What is the resulting bit error rate as a function of γ_b? What is the intersymbol correlation for this choice of $\Delta\nu$?

6.7 What is the minimum frequency shift compatible with noncoherent orthogonal FSK?

6.8 Binary noncoherent FSK with a frequency shift of 170 Hz is commonly used on the high-frequency bands in the amateur radio service. What is the maximum data rate this method can support? Repeat your calculation for the 425- and 850-Hz shifts used by the news, commercial, and private services.

6.9 Let $p(t)$ be a strictly band-limited pulse shape with no frequency components outside the range $|\nu| > W$. Band-limitation is a necessity since transmission channels are band-limited and radio receivers have finite intermediate frequency bandwidths. A baseband transmission waveform is made by modulating $p(t)$ with a sequence of amplitudes a_k, where the a_k are chosen from the binary alphabet $\{0, 1\}$; thus, the baseband signal is of the form

$$x(t) = \sum_{k=0}^{\infty} a_k p(t - kT) = a_0 p(t) + \sum_{k=1}^{\infty} a_k p(t - kT)$$

where T is the symbol duration. Since $p(t)$ is band-limited, its duration exceeds any finite quantity. In particular, the baseband signal contains not only the desired $a_0 p(t)$, but also the delayed responses from past signaling intervals, represented by the second term. This effect is called *intersymbol interference*, a consequence of the impossibility of having a signal that is both strictly band-limited and time-limited. Find the band-limited (W) pulse shape that is free of intersymbol interference. Comment.

6.10 The output of a digital receiver in the presence of noise only consists of a succession of randomly decoded characters. Digital squelch can be used to keep the receiver's output turned off when no message is being received. This can be accomplished by the use of a special squelch-breaking preamble consisting of a specific sequence of symbols. Consider a receiver that uses *M*-ary noncoherent orthogonal signaling and a squelch-breaking preamble consisting of m symbols. Assume each symbol is individually processed by matched filtering and that all preamble symbols must be received correctly to break squelch. Find expressions for the probability of correctly breaking squelch when a synchronization symbol is received and also for the probability of falsely breaking squelch when only noise is present at the input.

6.11 When it is not practical or possible to decode a squelch symbol with matched filtering, postdetection logic must be used. Consider a squelch symbol consisting of M bits transmitted via noncoherent BFSK.

   (a) What is the probability of correctly decoding an individual bit when $\gamma_b = 5$, 10, and 15 dB?

   (b) What is the probability of falsely decoding an individual bit when, in fact, no signal is present?

   To break squelch, we require that at least L out of the M consecutive received bits match the M-bit preamble.

   (c) What is the probability of missing breaking squelch if $M = 64$, $L = 60$ for the γ_b given in part (a)?

   (d) What is the probability of breaking squelch when no signal is present?

ERROR-CONTROL CODING

"Did you say 'pig,' or 'fig'?"
said the Cat.†

Lewis Carroll
Alice's Adventures in Wonderland

7

Chapter 4 introduced Shannon's second theorem, which guarantees the existence of codes that allow communication approaching the channel capacity rate with arbitrarily good fidelity. We remarked that the theorem is not constructive in the sense that it does not provide a way of deriving such codes.

The present chapter picks up where Chapter 4 left off. We study codes that attempt to approach the happy state of affairs Shannon proved is achievable. We shall first spend some time reflecting on the meaning and implications of such codes. Section 7.1 reexamines Shannon's channel coding result and introduces important and general properties of codes.

There are two ways of thinking about error-control codes and to each corresponds a way of measuring performance. We approach error-control codes from the point of view that they are mathematical structures that allow us to achieve more reliable, and sometimes more efficient, channel coding. Ideally, we would like to reach the Shannon limit: error-free communication at the channel capacity rate. In practice, we must be satisfied with a reduced capacity and a residual bit error rate. The appropriate measure of performance corresponding to this view is the achievable information rate through the channel at a specified error rate. This is a user-centered view and looks at the final bit error rate as a measure of the reliability that can be achieved in practice. We can also look at the energy contrast ratio per bit required to achieve a given decoding error rate. Some error-control codes allow for a lower γ_b than uncoded signaling. This may result in coding gain. This topic was introduced in Chapter 6 and some of the results of the present chapter can be interpreted in terms of coding gain. This is an engineer-centered view and places a premium on the efficient use of transmission energy.

---

†From *Alice's Adventures in Wonderland* by Lewis Carroll. Reprinted by permission from Crown Publishers, Inc.

Sections 7.2 and 7.3 show how the general properties of codes can be implemented in various ways. Section 7.2 continues the development begun in Section 7.1. Here the connection between a code's algebraic linearity and its minimum distance is pointed out. The linearity of a code guarantees a certain minimum distance. In addition, linear codes that are also cyclic have efficient encoding and decoding algorithms that can be conveniently implemented in digital hardware. Block codes that process fixed-length blocks of data symbols are discussed in Sections 7.1 and 7.2.

We make an important distinction between the mathematical structure and performance properties of these codes, and the algorithms used to generate and process them. With few exceptions, we shall limit our discussion mostly to a description of these codes and to the performance implied by their mathematical structures. A satisfactory discussion of algorithms used to implement coding and decoding procedures involves a sizeable amount of mathematics and cannot be adequately covered even in a few chapters. Although this is a fascinating subject, it really belongs to the field of digital signal processing over discrete algebraic structures and is not covered in this book. The algebraic theory of coding is the subject of several very good texts [Bl 83, Ca 86, Li 83, Pe 72, Pr 83], and the reader is referred to them. Those wishing to supplement what is treated in this chapter may also consult [Mi 85, Vi 79, Wo 65].

This chapter deals strictly with the general mathematical properties of codes. For the most part, we shall not be concerned where these codes came from, how they are generated, or the details of how they are processed. We shall concentrate instead on their metric properties and look at minimum-distance decoding as a general approach at decoding. This will enable us to use what has already been discussed about the relation between signaling waveform performance and metric properties.

7.1 GENERAL PRINCIPLES

In this section, we explore general properties of codes. Transmission over the BSC is considered, one binary digit at a time, and with a constant probability of receiving any binary digit in error equal to p. The theory of error-control codes can be developed for more general signaling alphabets, but the binary case is a much easier example to study and can be used to demonstrate the most important properties of codes.

7.1.1 Channel Coding Revisited

In Section 4.4, we studied channel coding. The principal result of that section is Shannon's second theorem, which states that it is possible to signal as closely as desired to the channel capacity rate with an arbitrarily small probability of decoding error. This theorem was presented in its simplest form for the BSC, but it was remarked that it also holds for more general discrete channels.

We shall further explore this theorem through the easily conceptualized set of signals consisting of vectors with n components. Each component is a scalar from some field. We shall refer to these signals as n-tuples. The most useful such n-tuples for demonstrating the properties of codes are those that form a linear vector space over $GF(2)$.

A very important special case, both for practical and pedagogical purposes, consists of the set of codes over $GF(2)$. These codes can be described as subsets of the nth extension of the binary alphabet $\{0, 1\}$. Each of the n binary digits of the n-tuple is independently communicated via a BSC with transition probability p. Recall that with each use of the BSC (i.e., for each binary digit transmitted) the maximum amount of information transmitted can at most be equal to the channel capacity, which is

$$C(p) = n[1 - h(p)] = n[1 + p \log p + (1 - p) \log (1 - p)] \qquad (7.1)$$

For each bit transmitted, we get less than one bit of information at the receiving end because of the degrading effect of the channel. This assumes, of course, that $p \neq 0$ or 1. The signaling rate, which is one binary digit per channel use, is always greater than the information rate, measured in received bits per channel use.

With the BSC driven by equally probable and statistically independent bits at the transmitter end, the maximum amount of information that can be transmitted is equal to the capacity given by Eq. (7.1). The actual information throughput is less than this because of decoding errors. What we are aiming to do is to transmit these bits with higher reliability. What this means is that without coding, the bits are received in error with probability p. If p exceeds the maximum tolerable error rate for the particular application in mind, then the channel can be considered useless. Coding, however, allows for the recovery of the original message, with a bit error probability p' that is less than p.

This implies a certain unavoidable amount of redundancy. Since $C(p) = n[1 - h(p)] \leq n$, an n-tuple consists of at most $n[1 - h(p)]$ information bits and at least $n h(p)$ redundant bits, adding up to a total of n bits. Thus, a BSC with nonzero transition probability requires signaling with nonzero redundancy in order to effect channel coding in the Shannon sense. It is not clear at this point in the discussion just how these redundant bits are determined or how they are to be combined with the data bits. However, the general channel-coder structure must be as shown in Fig. 7-1.

In general, the coder maps k information symbols into the n symbols of an n-tuple we call a *code word*. The code words are a subset of all possible q^n n-tuples; this subset is used for signaling purposes. The set of all q^k code words forms a *code*. A *linear code* is one where any linear combination of code words is also a code word. If $\mathbf{c}_j$ and $\mathbf{c}_k$ are any two code words from a linear code over $GF(q)$, then $\alpha\mathbf{c}_j + \beta\mathbf{c}_k$ is also a code word for any scalars α and β from $GF(q)$. A linear code is a subspace of $GF(q)^n$. The codes we shall concentrate on in this chapter are subspaces of $GF(2)^n$.

What can we say about how these redundant symbols are to be used? Let us quickly look ahead at some of the results we shall encounter. In the ideal case,

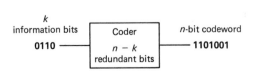

Figure 7-1. Channel-coding scheme. The coder computes $n - k$ redundant bits from the k information bits. All bits are then combined to form an n-bit code word, or n-tuple. In this example, $k = 4$ and $n = 7$.

Shannon says that communication can be made error-free. Recall from Section 4.4 that the ideal case was arrived at by letting n grow very large (i.e., this is an asymptotic result). For now, we note that for every n-bit transmitted code word, the unprocessed (i.e., undecoded) output of the detector is another n-tuple, with bits occasionally differing from the corresponding bits at the transmitter. This is so because these bits are obtained by decoding signals received over a noisy channel. Some or all of these errors must be corrected if communication reliability is to be improved. The redundant symbols must then provide the necessary information for error correction. As will be seen in later sections, code words can correct errors, but not necessarily all of the errors appearing at the receiver. For any given code, there is an upper bound on the number of random symbol errors that can be corrected. If the number of symbol errors in a received n-tuple is within the correctable limit for the particular code used, decoding results in an exact replica of the transmitted code word, from which the information bits can be deduced through the inverse procedure of the coding mapping.

Coding that realizes efficient use of the channel is *error-control coding*. The structure of the decoder corresponding to the coder in Fig. 7-1 is shown in Fig. 7-2. As an illustration, the received bit sequence differs from the transmitted code word of Fig. 7-1 in the fourth bit. The received 7-tuple contains one error.

In the simple example shown in Figs. 7-1 and 7-2, $k = 4$ information symbols (here, bits) are input to the coder, which in turn outputs a code word of seven bits. For this code, there are $2^k = 16$ possible code words, and each one is a binary 7-tuple. The code word is then presented to a modulator, which maps it into a unique signaling waveform. Each code word bit is transmitted serially, for example, by using any binary modulation scheme studied in Chapter 6.

EXAMPLE

A linear code containing sixteen 7-tuples over $GF(2)$ was introduced in an example presented in Section 2.1.4. This code can be used to transmit $k = \log_2 16 = 4$ information bits per code word. The remaining $7 - 4 = 3$ bits are used for parity checks. This is a *Hamming* code with $n = 7$ and $k = 4$. The Hamming $(7, 4)$ code words are given in Table 7-1.

Note that the k information bits could have been transmitted in parallel. This can be accomplished by having the modulator map them directly into some 16-ary signaling scheme with the attendant economy in transmitting power or bandwidth, depending on the scheme chosen. There are times, however, when design constraints dictate the use of either bandwidth-efficient modulation or, when the simplest binary scheme must be used and coding gain must be obtained, by some other means than by selecting an M-ary waveform enjoying inherent coding gain, such as with orthogonal signaling. That other means may be provided

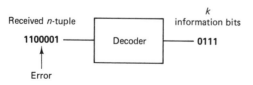

Figure 7-2. Decoder corresponding to the coder shown in Fig. 7-1.

TABLE 7-1. CODE WORDS FOR
THE BINARY HAMMING (7,4)
CODE

0000000	1010001
1101000	0111001
0110100	1100101
1011100	0001101
1110010	0100011
0011010	1001011
1000110	0010111
0101110	1111111

by error-control coding, which can be viewed as an additional structure imposed on the waveform.

In Figs. 7-1 and 7-2, the received bit sequence (**1 1 0 0 0 0 1**) corresponding to the transmitted code word differs in the fourth bit. The received sequence is, in general, not a code word, but can be expressed as the transmitted code word plus an n-tuple that we call the *error pattern*, denoted by the vector **e**. In this example, the error pattern is **0 0 0 1 0 0 0**, so that we have

received n-tuple = transmitted code word + error pattern **e**

1 1 0 0 0 0 1 = 1 1 0 1 0 0 1 + 0 0 0 1 0 0 0

In this case, the channel can be modeled as adding a particular error pattern to the transmitted code word. The details of the error pattern are, of course, statistical in nature. In this example, the BSC is used so that the probability of incurring any error pattern of weight $w(\mathbf{e})$ is simply

$$p^{w(\mathbf{e})}(1-p)^{n-w(\mathbf{e})} \tag{7.2}$$

where p is the BSC channel bit transition probability.

The redundant symbols should provide sufficient information to indicate which of the received symbols (here, binary digits) have been received in error. We shall not be concerned about the algorithmic details of the processing. From an information-theoretic point of view, however, we must insist that the number of redundant symbols be sufficient to label all the correctable error patterns. Specifically, there are $n-k$ redundant bits that can point to 2^{n-k} distinct correctable error patterns.

7.1.2 The Distribution of Error Weights

The signals considered in this section are binary n-tuples, that is, strings of n binary symbols. These n-tuples form a linear vector space where addition is bit by bit modulo 2 (exclusive-OR). The Hamming metric is used to measure distance between different n-tuples. Out of all 2^n possible n-tuples, we choose 2^k signaling waveforms, called code words, and use these to convey k bits of information.

In Section 4.4.2, we introduced the minimum-distance decoding of such waveforms. Transmission errors can be corrected if the minimum distance between signaling code words satisfies the inequality

$$d_{\min} \geq 2w(\mathbf{e}) + 1 \tag{7.3}$$

where $w(\mathbf{e})$ is the weight of the error pattern incurred during reception. It is possible to correct all error patterns of weight up to and including $w(\mathbf{e})$ with a code where the minimum distance between code words is $d_{\min}$. This is shown graphically in Fig. 7-3. The figure shows three spheres in signal space, each with radius $w(\mathbf{e})$. The reader is reminded that the word "sphere" is used figuratively, for ease of visualization through an analogy with familiar three-dimensional Euclidian space. In reality, we are referring to regions of a metric space where the metric is the Hamming distance. By a sphere of radius t centered about a point in signal space, we mean the set of all n-tuples with a Hamming distance less than or equal to t from that point.

The center of each sphere is located at a code word in signal space. The surface of a sphere includes all n-tuples that are at a distance $w(\mathbf{e})$ from the central code word: they are obtained by adding to the code word all error patterns with weight $w(\mathbf{e})$. The interior of the sphere contains points that correspond to the addition of error patterns of weight less than $w(\mathbf{e})$. The code word itself can be considered as being added to the all-zero error pattern.

The inequality $d_{\min} \geq 2w(\mathbf{e}) + 1$ simply means that the code words must be placed sufficiently far apart from each other so that any error pattern of weight $w(\mathbf{e})$ added to a code word results in an n-tuple that is still closer to the transmitted code word than to any other code word. In this sense, although the received n-tuple is not a code word, it can still be unambiguously associated with the correct transmitted code word. This is minimum metric decoding. In that sense, the code corrects errors. This gives a clue as to how to select good code words out of all 2^n possible n-tuples. The code words should be sufficiently apart so that the most likely error patterns can be corrected.

Of course, as is the actual error pattern, its weight is a random quantity from one received n-tuple to the next. Note that, in general, the same error pattern, when added to different code words, results in a different n-tuple. The problem of analyzing code performance, therefore, is a statistical one. However, it still makes sense to maintain some minimum distance between code words, for this guarantees that all error patterns of weight up to and including $w(\mathbf{e})$ can be corrected; we call the

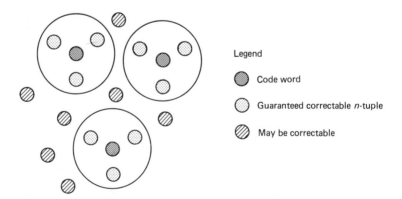

Figure 7-3. Code-word geometry. The circles indicate the guaranteed t-error correcting capability of the code. Received n-tuples outside this range may be correctable, depending on the code. For perfect codes, there are no n-tuples outside the correcting radius.

corresponding error patterns *correctable*. In this book, we will be mainly concerned with random symbol errors.

The number of random symbol errors in a code word is the weight $w(\mathbf{e})$ of the error pattern $\mathbf{e}$. This weight is binomially distributed with parameter p, the probability of a single symbol error. In Chapter 3, when we studied the law of large numbers, we found that a certain statistical regularity set in as n, the code-word size, grew large. We interpreted the law of large numbers as saying that as n, the total number of Bernoulli trials, grew large, we could classify the outcomes into two distinct categories. One category includes a set of equiprobable code-word weights $w(\mathbf{e}) = pn$. The other set includes all other error patterns and occurs with vanishingly small probability.

This statistical regularity was exploited in Chapter 4 in formulating the source-coding theorem. There it was realized that only those information patterns that occur frequently have to be coded. The error resulting from not assigning coding labels to sequences having vanishingly small probability itself has a vanishingly small probability.

A similar line of reasoning will be followed here in our discussion of error-control coding. This should illustrate the importance of the law of large numbers to information theory. The sequences we deal with are error patterns instead of information symbols, but the idea is very much the same. The errors occur randomly, but this randomness possesses an exploitable asymptotic regularity. In source coding, we had to assign a label to each of the information sequences that had nonvanishing probability. In error-control coding, we require that the overhead check symbols correspond to enough information to label all error sequences having nonvanishing probability.

Just as was the case with information sequences, error patterns can be understood in terms of the law of large numbers. As the code-word length n increases, the binomially distributed error weights tend to become concentrated near $w(\mathbf{e}) = pn$. In the limit of very large n, error patterns can be lumped into two distinct groups, one of which corresponds to weight $w(\mathbf{e}) = pn$ and the other having vanishingly small probability and containing all other weights. The most efficient error-control codes will correct only those error patterns that occur with nonvanishing probability.

In the following section, we pursue this line of reasoning mathematically to arrive at a new appreciation for Shannon's channel-coding theorem.

7.1.3 Shannon and the Law of Large Numbers

Let us look at some of the general mathematical properties of codes. We start with a hypothetical code consisting of code words that are binary n-tuples and gain some familiarity with the implications of Shannon's second theorem. If n is allowed to become very large (and this is precisely the limit in which Shannon tells us codes become good), then we expect that the overwhelming majority of error patterns will have a weight $w(\mathbf{e}) \approx pn$. This is a consequence of the law of large numbers. As the code-word length n becomes large, the probability that the ratio $w(\mathbf{e})/n$ differs from p becomes negligibly small. This means that as n becomes very large, virtually all of the error patterns are those with weight $w(\mathbf{e}) \approx pn$. It is this statistical regularity that is exploited by error-control codes.

How many such error patterns are there? Counting them is a straightforward problem in combinatorial analysis. The law of large numbers states that for arbitrarily small δ,

$$\lim_{n \to \infty} \text{Prob} \{|w(\mathbf{e}) - pn| \leq \delta n\} = 1$$

This can be interpreted as saying that for sufficiently large n, most of the error-pattern weights are within δn of pn. The error weights converge to pn in probability as n increases without bound. The most likely patterns are those with weight within δn of the mean pn. To count these patterns, we form the sum

$$\Omega = \binom{n}{(p - \delta)n} + \binom{n}{(p - \delta)n + 1} + \cdots + \binom{n}{(p + \delta)n}$$

and note that for small δ, the combinatorial coefficients change very slowly and are all approximately equal to $\binom{n}{pn}$. To this degree of approximation, we have

$$\Omega \approx 2 \delta n \binom{n}{pn} \tag{7.4}$$

In the limit of infinitely large n, this accounts for virtually all of the error patterns. A good code should be able to correct all such error patterns. Although we will not look at the algorithmic details of actual decoding and correcting, we can say something about the properties of such codes. The added redundant binary digits must provide information to point to any one of the Ω error patterns. That is, the $n - k$ redundant digits must at least total up to log Ω. This logarithm is

$$\log \Omega = \log \binom{n}{pn} + \log(2\delta n) \tag{7.5}$$

Now it can be shown that (see Prob. 7.1)

$$\lim_{n \to \infty} \log \binom{n}{pn} = n h(p) \tag{7.6}$$

where $h(p) = -p \log p - (1 - p) \log(1 - p)$. In the limit of large n, we therefore have

$$\lim_{n \to \infty} \log \Omega = n h(p) + \log n + \log 2\delta \approx n h(p) = n - k$$

so that

$$k = n[1 - h(p)] \tag{7.7}$$

since n increases much more rapidly than log n. The redundancy ratio, the ratio of the number of redundant bits to the total number of bits, is therefore,

$$\rho = \frac{n - k}{n} = h(p) \tag{7.8}$$

so that the *coding rate* (the ratio of information bits to the total number of bits) becomes

$$R = k/n = 1 - h(p) = C(p) \tag{7.9}$$

This is precisely the channel capacity per channel use. There are k/n information bits communicated for every BSC channel use. Furthermore, there is sufficient redundancy to unambiguously label every one of the error patterns that can occur. This is what Shannon's second theorem promises.

Just as the source-coding theorem promises coding efficiency in the limit of very long source symbol sequences, the channel-coding theorem promises transmission efficiency in the same limit. In both cases, efficiency means that the coding alphabet information rate arbitrarily approaches the rate of the symbols being encoded. With source coding, this means that the average number of coding bits per source symbol approaches (from above) the source information entropy. With channel coding, information may be passed over the channel with arbitrarily high fidelity at information rates approaching (from below) the channel capacity. In both cases, this efficiency is the result of the statistical regularity found in very long sequences of Bernoulli trials.

Viewed from this perspective, it is now difficult to justify differences (if any), on purely mathematical ground, between source and channel coding. Both cases deal with essentially the same application of the law of large numbers to count and classify sequences of random events. The separation of source and channel coding seemed natural until now and allowed us to study these processes individually. However, it is not clear at this point that we are, in fact, dealing with two different things. We will return to this interesting philosophical point in Chapter 8.

These coding results have been discussed in terms of a simple binary alphabet, but can be generalized for arbitrary alphabets. We do not present a mathematical proof, but advance the following intuitive justification. Any alphabet can be represented in terms of binary symbols, for which the coding theorems have been proven. The results should be independent of the symbol labeling scheme and therefore should apply to any alphabet.

7.1.4 Error Detection and Correction

We can partition signal space into regions, each consisting of a code word surrounded by a set of error patterns. Large distances between code words result in a large error-correcting capability. We would therefore like to choose code words that are maximally distant from one another. It is natural to ask, what is the maximum number of code words having a specified minimum distance between them? For codes over $GF(2)$, the "volume" of the entire signal space is given by 2^n, the total number of n-tuples. There are $\binom{n}{1}$ n-tuples at a Hamming distance of 1 from any given code word. Similarly, there are $\binom{n}{2}$ n-tuples two units away and, in general, there are $\binom{n}{m}$ n-tuples m units away. The total amount of volume included within a distance t from a code word is therefore given by

$$V(t) = \sum_{m=0}^{t} \binom{n}{m} \tag{7.10}$$

The total signal-space volume is given by the identity

$$2^n = \sum_{m=0}^{\infty} \binom{n}{m}$$

The ratio $2^n/V(t)$ is thus an upper bound on the number of spheres of radius t that can fit in the space. That is also an upper bound for the number of code words. In general, this ratio will not be a whole number, but when it is, we say that the code is a *perfect code*. A perfect code has the following two properties:

1. all spheres of Hamming radius $t = [\frac{1}{2}(d_{\min} - 1)]$ centered about the 2^k code words are disjoint, and
2. every n-tuple falls in one of these spheres.

The expression [x] with boldface square brackets denotes the largest integer contained in x; this operation truncates x to the nearest integer.

For a perfect code, all 2^{n-k} error patterns are correctable. These 2^{n-k} error patterns, when added to each of the 2^k code words, cover all of the signal space. A perfect code thus leaves no gaps between the code words. There are 2^k code words and, since the total number of n-tuples cannot exceed 2^n, we have

$$2^k \sum_{m=0}^{t} \binom{n}{m} \le 2^n$$

or, equivalently,

$$2^{n-k} \ge \sum_{m=0}^{t} \binom{n}{m}$$

with the equality holding for perfect codes. This inequality gives an upper bound, called the *Hamming bound*, for the error-correcting capability t of a linear code.

An upper bound on the number of code words is $[2^n/V(t)]$, and the corresponding whole number of information bits per code word is $k = [\log [2^n/V(t)]]$. Table 7-2 presents several possibilities for code parameters; in this table, $t = w(\mathbf{e})$ specifies the Hamming weight of guaranteed correctable error patterns. From this table, we find that there are at most 2^k n-tuples $d_{\min}$ apart from one another in the space of all possible 2^n n-tuples. These 2^k code words guarantee the correction of all error patterns of weight less than or equal to $t = w(\mathbf{e}) = [\frac{1}{2}(d_{\min} - 1)]$. We shall denote such codes as $(n, k; d_{\min})$ codes to emphasize that code performance depends in a fundamental way on metric properties. The parameters in Table 7-2 represent necessary but not sufficient conditions for these codes to exist.

Table 7-2 may give the erroneous impression that perfect codes are common. In fact, very few perfect codes exist. There are only three general classes of perfect codes. The first class includes Hamming codes, a binary example of which was presented earlier. Hamming codes over $GF(q)$ have the parameters

$$n = \frac{q^m - 1}{q - 1} \qquad k = n - m \qquad d_{\min} = 3 \qquad t = 1 \qquad (7.11)$$

for any positive integer $m \ge 3$. The second class of perfect codes includes the binary Golay $(23, 12; 7)$ and the ternary Golay $(11, 6; 5)$ codes [Ma 77].

TABLE 7-2. PARAMETERS FOR SOME $(n, k; d_{\min})$ CODES

n	(d_{min})	$t = w(\mathbf{e})$	k	Perfect?	Maximum?
3	3	1	1	Yes	Yes
4	3	1	1	No	No
5	3	1	2	No	No
5	5	2	1	Yes	Yes
7	3	1	4	Yes	No
7	5	2	2	No	No
7	7	3	1	Yes	Yes
8	3	1	4	No	No
8	5	2	2	No	No
8	7	3	1	No	No
15	7	3	5	No	No
15	5	2	8	No	No
15	3	1	11	Yes	No
23	7	3	12	Yes	No

EXAMPLE

We have already encountered a simple example of a code in Section 4.4.1. Using the present notation, we call it an $(n, 1; n)$ code. These are called *repetition codes* and can be decoded by *majority logic*. For example, if the n-tuples $(0, 0, \ldots, 0)$ and $(1, 1, \ldots, 1)$ with n odd are code words, then a received n-tuple is decoded to $(0, 0, \ldots, 0)$ if it contains more zeros than ones, and vice versa. The odd value of n precludes a tie on the decoding vote. The last class of perfect codes includes all repetition codes of odd length. A repetition code has two code words that consist of n repetitions of the information bit. These codes can be decoded by majority logic.

Several repetition codes are listed in Table 7-1. The eight possible received 3-tuples corresponding to a $(3, 1; 3)$ code are listed below, with the code words in boldface.

$$
\begin{array}{cc}
\mathbf{0\,0\,0} & 0\,1\,1 \\
0\,0\,1 & 1\,0\,1 \\
0\,1\,0 & 1\,1\,0 \\
1\,0\,0 & \mathbf{1\,1\,1}
\end{array}
$$

The selection of a pair of n-tuples as code words is entirely arbitrary. Any pair of complementary 3-tuples could have been selected as code words. The 3-tuples appearing in lightface all correspond to one of the code words and an error pattern. Any of the 3-tuples appearing in the first column have weight 1 and are decoded as **0 0 0**. Any of the 3-tuples appearing in the second column have weight 2 and are decoded as **1 1 1**. Note that **1 1 1** is an undetectable error pattern when 0 0 0 is transmitted, and vice versa.

We note that the $(n, 1; n)$ repetition codes over $GF(2)$ carry only one bit of information and use a large portion of their redundancy to correct errors. These signal pairs consist of any n-tuple and its binary complement. Only one bit of information is conveyed per code word, but these codes have a high resistance to channel errors. These are the discrete signal equivalents to the antipodal signals encountered in Chapter 6. Like their antipodal cousins, they enjoy the best performance on noisy channels.

Another important concept is that of a maximum-distance code. A *maximum-distance code* is one for which, for a given k, has the greatest distance between code words. This distance is bounded by the *Singleton bound*: $d_{min} \leq n - k + 1$. Codes for which this bound is an equality are called maximum-distance codes, or, simply, maximum codes. If the minimum distance of a code is d_{min}, then at least one of the code words must be changed in at least d_{min} places to result in another code word.

In general, a code word (i.e., an n-tuple) over $GF(q)$ consists of k scalars from $GF(q)$ to represent information (*information scalars* or *information places*) and $n - k$ scalars for redundancy (also called *check scalars* or *check places*). If k scalars are reserved for information and at least d_{min} scalars must be changed to change one code word to another, then there must be at least $d_{min} - 1$ check scalars so that $k + (d_{min} - 1) \leq n$, which is the Singleton bound. Maximum codes are those that have the maximum number of information scalars for a given minimum distance. Table 7-1 does not exhaust all code possibilities, but does exhibit examples of the interrelations between the parameters for various $(n, k; d_{min})$ codes.

In general, code words are not equidistant from one another. This results from the limited freedom in choosing code words in a discrete signal space of n-tuples. However, code words can be selected to satisfy a minimum-distance criterion. The number of code-word selections decreases as the minimum intercode-word distance increases for a fixed set of n-tuples. In other words, the number of information bits per code word can be traded for robustness against channel errors.

An important property of the code is its minimum distance d_{min}. It can be used to provide an upper bound for the decoding error probability. This is so because all of the code words of a code are at least d_{min} apart from one another and the decoding is at least as good as if they were all exactly d_{min} apart.

A useful measure of code performance is the probability that a received n-tuple is incorrectly decoded. The Hamming bound gives an upper limit to the number t of symbol errors that can be corrected by a code. All n-tuples with t or fewer symbol errors are always correctable. When the number of symbol errors exceeds t, the error pattern may or may not be correctable, depending on the error pattern and on the details of the particular code used. An exact calculation of the decoding error probability would be difficult and restricted to special cases. We can, however, bound the decoding error probability by assuming that exceeding t symbol errors per code word always results in a decoding error. This is a conservative approach since there are usually correctable error patterns with more than t symbol errors. By choosing to ignore this, we arrive at an upper bound for the decoding error probability. This probability is bounded by the expression

$$P_e \leq \sum_{k=t+1}^{n} \binom{n}{k} p^k (1 - p)^{n-k} \qquad (7.12)$$

where p is the independent symbol error probability.

For linear codes, the minimum distance is simply the minimum nonzero code word weight. That this must be so is easy to prove. Consider a code where the minimum distance occurs between code words $\mathbf{c}_i$ and $\mathbf{c}_j$. The Hamming metric distance is $d_{\min} = w(\mathbf{c}_i - \mathbf{c}_j)$. But, in a linear code, $\mathbf{c}_i - \mathbf{c}_j$ is also a code word, and since $\mathbf{c}_i$ and $\mathbf{c}_j$ form the closest code-word pair, the code word $\mathbf{c}_i - \mathbf{c}_j$ must have the least weight of all nonzero code words in the code. This makes it easy to determine the minimum distance for a linear code: it suffices to inspect the code words and pick that one having the least weight, excluding the all-zero code word. For a nonlinear code, the distance between all possible code word pairs must be calculated.

Code weight distributions are not known for every linear code. When known, they can be used to exactly calculate the code's error-correcting performance. In most cases, however, bounds are easier to use. We now give examples of code word weight distributions for a few codes. Letting $\alpha(w)$ denote the number of code words with weight w, we always have

$$\sum_{w=0}^{n} \alpha(w) = 2^k \tag{7.13}$$

For the binary repetition code $(n, 1; n)$, we have $\alpha(0) = \alpha(n) = 1$, and $\alpha(w) = 0$ for all other choices of w. For the binary Hamming $(7, 4; 3)$ code introduced earlier, we have, from inspection of the code words, the weight distribution shown in Table 7-3.

TABLE 7-3. WEIGHT
DISTRIBUTION FOR THE
BINARY HAMMING
$(7, 4; 3)$ CODE

w	$\alpha(w)$
0	1
3	7
4	7
7	1

The binary Golay $(23, 12; 7)$ code has the code-word weight distribution given in Table 7-4.

TABLE 7-4. WEIGHT DISTRIBUTION
FOR THE BINARY GOLAY
$(23, 12; 7)$ CODE

w	$\alpha(w)$
0	1
7	253
8	506
11	1288
12	1288
15	506
16	253
23	1

With $t = [\frac{1}{2}(d_{\min} - 1)]$, the decoding error probability for a code word is bounded by

$$P_e \leq \sum_{k=t+1}^{n} \binom{n}{k} p^k (1-p)^{n-k} = 1 - \sum_{k=0}^{t} \binom{n}{k} p^k (1-p)^{n-k} \qquad (7.14)$$

where p is the BSC symbol-error probability. This bound is more easily calculated than the actual decoding error probability, which is a function of all code distances (i.e., of the code word weight distribution). In addition, this upper bound for the decoding error probability is a conservative figure, an important design consideration. For perfect codes, Eq. (7.14) is an exact result when $t = [\frac{1}{2}(d_{\min}-1)]$.

The second expression in Eq. (7.14) is often easier to calculate than the first. This is because the combinatorial coefficient grows very fast, even for very moderate values of k. For moderate to large values of the summation index, a typical term in the sum is the product of a very large and a very small quantity. This in itself can cause computational difficulties, even on high-precision machines. Calculations of probabilities should always be done with the highest available precision on a computer. Whenever possible, the quantity to be calculated should be expressed in a way that avoids the very large and very small terms that can come about. The quantity t in the sum typically remains much smaller than n in most applications, so that fewer terms of the summation have to be calculated when the second expression is used.

The performance of a code depends entirely on its mathematical structure and, in particular, its metric structure. With a linear code, this metric structure is entirely specified by the code's weight distribution. This follows since the distance between any two code words is another code word, so that any code word weight measures the distance between two code words. The selection of a particular code for some application requires an understanding of how a code's metric structure affects performance.

Consider a code over $GF(2)$ (i.e., a set of 2^k code words selected from the 2^n n-tuples). We denote these code words by the set $\{c_1, c_2, \ldots, c_M\}$ and the corresponding M nonzero code-word weights $\{\alpha_1, \alpha_2, \ldots, \alpha_M\}$, where $\alpha_j = w(c_j)$, $j = 1, 2, \ldots, M$. There are 2^k code words and a larger number 2^n of possible received n-tuples. The code words are known a priori by the receiver. Thus, any received n-tuple that is not a code word immediately implies the presence of one or more bits received in error. Not all error patterns, however, are detectable. For example, it could happen that the error pattern exactly transforms one code word into another. In this case, the received n-tuple is another code word, and there is no way the error can be detected by the receiver.

EXAMPLE

Consider an $(n, n-1; 2)$ code over $GF(2)$. Half of the 2^n n-tuples are used as code words and the minimum distance for this code is 2. This code can detect all error patterns of weight 1. It can also detect some of the other error patterns. An error pattern of weight 1 changes the parity (i.e., the oddness or evenness of the weight) of any n-tuple. This can be used as the basis of an error-detection algorithm. We simply need to know the parity a priori and check for it at the receiver. The parity check bit added to the $n - 1$ information bit can be selected to make the parity of all n code word bits of the same agreed-upon parity. This is the *single-parity check code*, the simplest example of an error-detecting code.

Note, however, that two simultaneous bit errors restore the original parity; this results in an undetected code word error. In general, this code can detect any error pattern of odd weight and fails to detect any of the even-weight error patterns.

How many error patterns are undetectable? In general, there can be as many undetectable error patterns as there are distinct code-word pairs:

$$\binom{M}{2} = \frac{M!}{2!(M-2)!} = \frac{M(M-1)}{2} \tag{7.15}$$

where $M = 2^k$ is the number of code words. To each code word, there correspond $n - 1$ error patterns that map it into any one of the other $n - 1$ code words. The factor of 2 in the denominator prevents counting the same error pattern twice when the other code word of a pair is considered.

The situation is much simpler for a linear code. Recall that a linear vector space must contain the zero element. Since the sum of any two code words is also a code word, the undetectable error patterns correspond precisely to the nonzero code words, and there are exactly $2^k - 1$ such undetectable patterns, leaving $2^n - 2^k$ detectable error patterns. For a linear code with minimum distance $d_{\min}$, the minimum error pattern weight required to change one code word into another is $d_{\min}$. Therefore, any error pattern with weight less than or equal to $d_{\min} - 1$ is guaranteed to be detectable. We can now summarize the situation for a linear code. Any error pattern with weight $d_{\min} - 1$ or less can always be detected. In addition, many more patterns (up to a maximum of $2^n - 2^k$) are detectable. For each transmitted code word, we have the following situation:

1 transmitted code word,
$2^k - 1$ undetectable error patterns, and
$2^n - 2^k$ detectable error patterns,

adding up to a total of 2^n possible n-tuples.

The probability of undetected error is easy to calculate for a linear code. Since the error patterns responsible for undetected errors correspond to the code words themselves, the probability that an undetected error patterns occurs is equal to the probability that a pattern identical to one of the code words occurs. Since the code words have weight distribution $\{\alpha_1, \alpha_2, \ldots, \alpha_M\}$ and binary digits errors occur with probability p, we can express the probability of an undetected code word error P_{uc} as

$$P_{uc} = \sum_{j=1}^{M} \alpha_j p^j (1-p)^{n-j} \tag{7.16}$$

We can also make a general statement about error correction. There are error patterns that are always correctable and others that will also be corrected. We have already seen that a code with minimum distance $d_{\min}$ guarantees correcting all error patterns of weight no greater than $t = [\frac{1}{2}(d_{\min} - 1)]$. The code-word error probability is therefore upper bounded by

$$P_e \leq \sum_{k=t+1}^{n} \binom{n}{k} p^k (1 - p)^{n-k} \tag{7.17}$$

To appreciate the implications of this measure, consider that all code words have length n and that the number of bits received in error in any code word is a random number t that is binomially distributed and depends on p (and, therefore, on the energy contrast ratio, as per Chapter 6). At the decoder input, the bit error statistics are described by a Bernoulli process.

Now, let us examine the situation at the decoder output. Two outcomes are possible for each decoded n-tuple. If $t \leq [\frac{1}{2}(d_{\min} - 1)]$, then the number of bit errors is within the correcting capability of the code and the decoder will output the correct code word (i.e., the code word that was, in fact, transmitted). All of the bits in the code word will be received correctly. If $t > [\frac{1}{2}(d_{\min} - 1)]$, then the decoder may output one of the $2^k - 1$ wrong code words, resulting in a code word decoding error. Which wrong code word is output depends on the details of the decoding algorithm.

The decoder output, therefore, consists of a string of correct code words, with some code words having been incorrectly decoded. If code word errors are statistically independent, then the occurrence of code word errors is a Bernoulli process with well-defined statistics. In passing through a coder, we go from binomially distributed bit errors to binomially distributed code-word errors. The input bit errors are binomially distributed with parameter p, and the output code word errors are binomially distributed with parameter P_e, the code word error probability.

If we want to describe the output bit error statistics, things become more complicated because the details of the decoding mechanism are involved. The input bit errors are randomly distributed, but the output bit errors occur in bursts of length equal to a multiple of the code word length. After decoding, some of the code word binary digits correspond to information bits, and others to redundant bits. It is possible that a code word decoded in error still yields some of the information bits correctly. A conservative estimate of the effect of decoding errors on the output information bit stream can be obtained by assuming the worst-case situation of an output bit error rate of 0.5 for those code words in error. More refined estimates are still the subject of research. For example, Torrieri reported on a simple approximation that depends neither on the code weight structure nor on the details of the decoder algorithm [To 84]. The subject of quantifying the decoded bit error probability is one that lends itself to few generalizations. Approximations are often used.

More error patterns can be detected than can be corrected. Error detection gives partial information about a received signal: it indicates whether there are one or more errors somewhere among the n binary digits. Error correction requires more information: we must know precisely which bits are in error; these can then be corrected by complementing. For more general codes, where the symbols are not necessarily binary digits but elements from some Galois field $GF(q)$, pointing to the symbol in error is not sufficient; there must be enough information to decide how correction is to be accomplished (i.e., which of the other $q - 1$ field elements should be substituted in place of the incorrect symbol).

For a fixed number of information bits per code word, increasing the error-detection or error-correction capability necessarily increases the size of the n-tuple. This means increasing the intercode word distance. The distance requirement increases faster (approximately twice) with error correction than with error detection.

In summary, a code with minimum distance d_{min} can be used to detect all error patterns with weight $w(\mathbf{e}) \leq [d_{min} - 1]$. There are

$$\sum_{t=1}^{[d_{min}-1]} \binom{n}{t} \tag{7.18}$$

error patterns that are guaranteed to be detectable. Such a code is also guaranteed to correct up to

$$\sum_{t=1}^{[\frac{1}{2}(d_{min}-1)]} \binom{n}{t} \tag{7.19}$$

error patterns with weight $w(\mathbf{e}) \leq [\frac{1}{2}(d_{min} - 1)]$. Thus, more error patterns can be detected than corrected, and all correctable patterns are also detectable. Therefore, there are uncorrectable patterns that are detectable. It is possible to simultaneously detect and correct errors. This is a very useful way of using the redundancy of coding. Instead of using all of the redundancy to correct errors, we may require that some errors be corrected (presumably, the most likely error patterns).

7.1.5 Approaching the Shannon Limit

Shannon's channel-coding theorem guarantees perfect communication reliability when infinitely long code words are used. Realizable systems are restricted to finite-length code words and, therefore, have less than ideal performance. We are interested in codes that make efficient use of signal space. We would also like to maximize the benefit for the price paid in redundancy. A measure of effectiveness for comparing various codes is needed. This measure should be independent of the coding and decoding algorithms and should involve only the general metric properties of the code. We shall compare these codes on the basis of their performance. We shall leave aside the important issue of implementation complexity, as this would take us into the realm of signal processing and away from the fundamental nature of communication.

It would be philosophically satisfying to develop a performance comparison that is directly based on the Shannon channel-coding theorem. Shannon defines a channel capacity C and proves the existence of codes that allow error-free communication at a rate R that approaches C as closely as one desires. This, as we have seen, requires codes of infinite complexity. Codes that can be implemented have a finite complexity and always result in a residual decoding probability of error. It is, therefore, not possible to directly compare a particular code (that results in a finite error rate) with the ideal performance of codes that achieve the Shannon bound.

Codes can be compared on the basis of a specified decoded bit error rate. For example, consider the use of $(n, k; d_{\min})$ codes over the BSC, as shown in Fig. 7-4. Information bits are grouped in blocks of k bits. To these, the code assigns $n - k$ check bits to form code words from an alphabet of $M = 2^k$ code words. These code words are transmitted one binary digit at a time over the BSC, but are decoded as M-ary signals after n binary digits have been received.

Since the bit errors on the BSC are statistically independent events, then so are the M-ary symbol decoding errors. Letting p be the BSC transition probability and P_e be the decoded M-ary code word error probability, the output (i.e., decoded) information bit probability of error for equiprobable orthogonal signaling is given by

$$p' = \frac{2^{k-1}}{2^k - 1} P_e$$

a result first encountered in Chapter 6. In general, the use of codes does not result in orthogonal waveforms. The decoded bit error probability depends in a complicated way on the weight structure of the code. Very few exact results if any are available for codes in general. It is, however, possible to bound the decoded bit error probability. Using conditional probabilities, we can write the decoded bit error probability as

$$p' = \text{Prob \{bit error | code word error\}} \cdot P_e \tag{7.20}$$

where Prob {bit error | code word error} is the probability of a bit error conditioned on the event that a code word error occurs. The probability that an M-ary code word error occurs is upper bounded by

$$P_e = P_e(p) \leq \sum_{k=t+1}^{n} \binom{n}{k} p^k (1 - p)^{n-k} \tag{7.21}$$

For the worst possible case, Prob {bit error |code word error} $= \frac{1}{2}$, where half of the bits are in error, on the average. The decoded bit error probability must therefore be upper bounded by

$$p' \leq \frac{1}{2} \sum_{k=t+1}^{n} \binom{n}{k} p^k (1 - p)^{n-k} \tag{7.22}$$

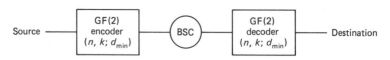

Figure 7-4.   Coder and decoder for the BSC.

Except where noted, this bound is used in all subsequent calculations of the decoded bit error probability. Note that there are two distinct bit error probabilities. There is the BSC transition probability p for binary digits transmitted on the channel. There is the information bit error probability p' at the output of the decoder. The latter is the bit error rate of concern to the user.

Different codes can now be compared on the basis of their information rates. The information rate of a code can be defined as

$$R(p) = [1 - P_e(p)]k/n \qquad (7.23)$$

The interpretation given this equation is that the decoded code words fall into two categories: those that are decoded correctly and, with probability $P_e(p)$, those that are not. A correct decoding occurs with probability $1 - P_e(p)$, which by the law of large numbers, is the fraction of decoded code words that corresponds to error-free information bits. This, when multiplied by the code rate k/n, results in the effective error-free information rate.

The code-word error probability $P_e(p)$ can be upper-bounded by the probability of exceeding the t-error correcting capability of the code, as in Eq. (7.21). Note that only for perfect codes is this bound actually reached. Comparing codes, therefore, consists in selecting a common characteristic output bit error probability p' and then calculating the $R(p)$ corresponding to that p' for each code. Note that in practical applications, p' is quite small, on the order of 10^{-3} or less, and that $P_e(p)$ is so small that to a good approximation, we have $1 - P_e(p) \approx 1$ and $R(p) \approx k/n$. This approach is motivated by a paper by Gilbert [Gi 52] that approximated the information rate by k/n, keeping constant the code word error probability $P_e(p)$. Since different code words carry different numbers of information bits, our approach compares different codes with respect to the same measure: the probability of information bit error.

Figure 7-5 plots $R(p)$ versus p for four codes. On this plot, several values of p' (from left to right, we have $p' = 10^{-6}$, 10^{-5}, 10^{-4}, 10^{-3}, 10^{-2}, and 10^{-1}) are indicated by dots on the curves. The dots corresponding to $p' = 10^{-4}$ are joined by a dashed line. Each of the codes has a rate $R(p)$ that remains approximately constant ($\approx k/n$) for $p < 10^{-2}$ and then decreases at higher channel transition probabilities. Note that each curve has a knee where p is approximately equal to the ratio t/n, i.e., where the correction capability of the code is exceeded.

In a typical design problem, we are given a channel with some fixed transition probability p for which a coding scheme must be chosen. The general features of the performance trade-off for this problem can be studied on Fig. 7-5. For each code, the $R(p)$ versus p curve can be interpreted as a parametric curve for p' as a function of p. For a code to be useful, it is reasonable to expect that $p' \ll p$, so that the portion of the curve to the left of the knee for each code represents a potentially practical application. For these cases, we note that codes having higher rates also correspond to higher p' and vice versa. This is an example of the trade-off between information rate and the ability to perform in a noisy environment.

In practical applications of coding, information rate is traded for noise immunity. This is a practical difference from the Shannon coding theorem, which says that no information rate has to be traded provided $R < C$. The important caveat, of course, is that impractically long code words would have to be used for the ideal

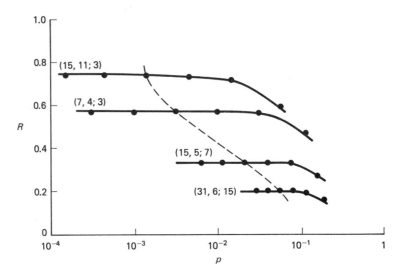

Figure 7-5. Performance comparison for various (n, k; d_{min}) codes.

situation described by Shannon. A reasonable practical trade-off can be achieved by choosing a code that provides the highest rate $R(p)$ for the given channel transition probability p and which still provides an output information bit error probability p' below the critical value specified by the user.

Alternatively, a code can be chosen to meet the required information rate exactly, but with the smallest possible p' for a given p such that p' is below the user-specified bit error rate. Such a conservative design provides the desired data capacity at or below the maximum tolerable error rate. This safety margin allows for possible increases in channel transition rate. Channel and system parameters may fluctuate. Robustness can sometimes be introduced in a system design by exceeding performance specifications.

The communication engineer must reconcile the user's requirements for some reliable information rate R at an information-bit error not to exceed some specified figure p' over a channel with transition rate p. A plot such as that shown in Fig. 7-5 can be generated for any number of codes and can be used to select a code that meets all of the requirements, if such a code exists.

EXAMPLE

A user requires 2.4 kbps at $p' = 10^{-4}$ or better over a BSC with transition rate 10^{-3} and a signaling rate fixed at 4800 binary digits per second. Which of the codes shown in Fig. 7-5 are appropriate? The coding rate $R \approx k/n$ must be at least one-half, and the user-specified error rate performance eliminates all operating points to the right of the dashed line. The remaining codes are the (15, 11; 3) and (7, 4; 3) codes. Either would meet user requirements, but the (7, 4; 3) will do so at a slightly better information bit error rate.

Figure 7-5 is an approximate performance comparison that must be used with caution. By similar reasoning, the uncoded BSC at $p = \frac{1}{2}$ has an effective bit rate of $\frac{1}{2}$ since one-half of the bits are correctly decoded. There is no information throughput, however, since the BSC capacity vanishes there. The curves in Fig. 7-5 should be used only where they flatten out, in the region where $R \approx k/n$. In this region, few decoding errors occur and the information rate is well approximated by the ratio k/n. For a given p, codes can then be compared on the basis of the trade-off between p' and k/n.

Note in Fig. 7-5 that as p decreases, R asymptotically approaches k/n, a quantity that is always less than one information bit per BSC use and that measures the maximum information rate achievable with an $(n, k; d_{min})$ code. This suggests another way to look at the performance of error-control codes. As shown in Fig. 7-4, we have effectively replaced a BSC with capacity $C(p)$ and a low reliability (i.e., high p) with a DMC of lower capacity ($\approx k/n$) and higher reliability ($p' < p$).

The simple communication system model considered here consists of a binary source of information fed to a channel coder with symbols from $GF(2)$. We are not concerned here with the effects of a source encoder, which can, in any case, be considered part of the information source. The binary information symbols are assumed to be equiprobable, and the channel is the binary symmetric channel with capacity

$$C_{BSC}(p) = 1 - h(p) = 1 + p \log p + (1 - p) \log (1 - p) \qquad (7.24)$$

where p is the BSC channel transition probability. This is the system shown in Fig. 7-4.

The interpretation of the BSC channel capacity $C_{BSC}(p)$ is that it is the highest rate at which information can be transmitted with arbitrarily high reliability over the channel. For $p \neq 0$, this requires the use of some coding, and Shannon's work guarantees the existence of such codes. The task is, therefore, possible in principle. In practice, many codes are available to the engineer, who must then choose a particular coding scheme to fit the situation. These codes, however, all introduce some redundancy and therefore use up some of the available channel capacity.

The view we now take is to consider the encoder, channel, and decoder as comprising an M-ary symmetric channel, where $M = 2^k$. This channel is a discrete memoryless channel (DMC) with an alphabet of M symbols.

Without coding, the channel capacity is simply $C_{BSC}(p) = 1 - h(p)$. With coding, communication is done via a signaling alphabet of $M = 2^k$ symbols transmitted as code words over $GF(2)$. An $(n, k; d_{min})$ code is capable of correcting any error patterns with weight

$$t = w(\mathbf{e}) \leq [\tfrac{1}{2}(d_{min} - 1)] \qquad (7.25)$$

The probability of a code-word error is therefore upper bounded by the probability P_e of incurring more than t bit errors in any code word.

Equipped with this bound for the code-word error rate, we can calculate the corresponding symmetric DMC capacity

$$C_{\mathrm{DMC}}(P_e) = k - h(P_e) - P_e \log(2^k - 1) \tag{7.26}$$

with P_e given by Eq. (7.21).

We now define an *effective information rate* as

$$R(p) = n^{-1}C_{\mathrm{DMC}}[P_e(p)] \tag{7.27}$$

for an $(n, k; d_{\min})$ code. The effective information rate measures the DMC channel capacity per transmitted binary digit and is, therefore, directly comparable with the BSC capacity $C_{\mathrm{BSC}}(p)$. For a given BSC transition rate p, Shannon theory tells us we can achieve a maximum rate of $C_{\mathrm{BSC}}(p) = 1 - h(p)$. In practice with an $(n, k; d_{\min})$ code, we achieve a rate $R(p) < C_{\mathrm{BSC}}(p)$. The best code for a given p is that which has the highest $R(p)$. Comparing two codes for a given BSC with transition rate p reduces to a calculation of their respective effective information rates.

Note that Eq. (7.26) for $C_{\mathrm{DMC}}(P_e)$ assumes a symmetric channel, i.e., one for which the symbol error probability is not a function of the particular code word transmitted. This is not true for most codes. By assuming symmetry, Eq. (7.26) overbounds the capacity provided by a code. However, the approximation is good for small p, where the capacity asymptotically approaches k/n. This is the useful regime for codes. For an exact calculation, the actual metric distance between code words must be used to calculate the actual channel capacity. That capacity is reached by some a priori symbol probability distribution that is peculiar to the code's specific metric structure. Although feasible in principle, these calculations would be cumbersome and applicable only to one particular code.

The approximate capacities corresponding to a (5, 1; 5), a (7, 4; 3), and a (23, 12; 7) code are compared to the BSC capacity in Fig. 7-6. These curves represent

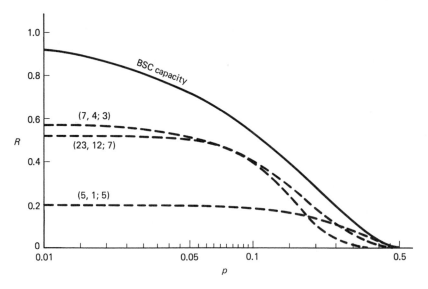

Figure 7-6. Capacity performance of perfect codes compared with the uncoded BSC.

information rates for small values of p. Figure 7-6 shows upper bounds for the capacities achieved by various error-control codes. These capacities are all below the BSC capacity. However, the output bit error probability is less than that for the uncoded BSC. Output bit error probabilities for some codes are shown in Fig. 7-5. Thus, by giving up some channel capacity (used up by the redundancy symbols), a higher communication reliability is achieved.

7.1.6 Coding Gain

A practical comparison of codes for communication system design with the analysis illustrated by Fig. 7-5 has the advantage of providing a measure of performance based on user requirements: a given data rate at a stated reliability. There is another basis for comparing coding performance. To complete our general discussion of coding, we now look at the signaling efficiency of codes, as measured by the γ_b required to achieve a stated decoded error probability.

It is possible to compare codes with a measure of performance of concern to the engineer: coding gain. The ability to resist decoding errors implies the ability to perform in noisier environments. This is equivalent to increasing the transmitted power (or, more generally, the received signal-to-noise ratio) by a certain amount equal to the coding gain. The use of some error-control codes allows signaling with a smaller γ_b than with uncoded signaling for the same information bit error probability.

Communication waveforms exhibiting coding gain were studied in Chapter 6. There we learned that M-ary orthogonal, biorthogonal, and equicorrelated signals have a signal-to-noise ratio advantage over uncoded signals. We called the resulting waveforms energy- (or power-) efficient. There is really nothing fundamentally new with the coding gain obtained from error-control coding. Error-control coding is a method for giving additional algebraic structure to an existing waveform. Error-control coding is basically a mapping of 2^k signals onto another set of 2^k signals having a larger signal-space dimensionality. Coded signals are defined in a linear signal space with more coordinates. In principle, the entire mapping could have been done at once with a suitable modulator and processed at the receiver with the corresponding matched filter. No fundamental distinction can be made between modulation and coding.

A practical distinction can be made, however, based on the approach to decoding such signals. The approach implied in the last section is shown in Fig. 7-7 (a). Here coding and modulation are shown as two distinct processes. An $(n, k; d_{\min})$ code is used to transform an information stream, represented by bits, i.e., symbols from $GF(2)$, into code words over $GF(2)$. These code words are then transmitted one binary digit at a time over the BSC. This is a common and practical approach to error-control coding. The decoding process is also accomplished in two separate steps. First, binary digits from the BSC are individually decoded and formed into n-tuples. Then, the n-tuples themselves are separately decoded into code words.

This approach is called *hard-decision* decoding because a separate irrevocable decision is made for each incoming binary digit. The M-ary symbol decision is delayed until all of the code word binary digits resulting from hard-decision decoding are collected and processed. This is equivalent to hard limiting the binary demod-

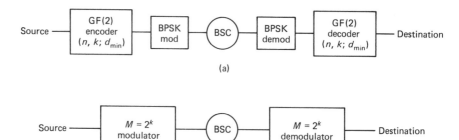

Figure **7-7.** Communication system model for evaluating the coding gain. S: source, D: destination (*a*) Separate coder and modulator sections. Hard-decision decoding. (*b*) Equivalent *M*-ary modulator and matched filter. Soft-decision decoding.

ulator output, keeping at most one bit of information, which is then passed along to the $(n, k; d_{min})$ decoder. The additional demodulator information thrown away involves the actual demodulator levels and, thus, could have provided information about the reliability of the hard decisions.

Contrast this with what we already know is the best possible approach (in AWGN). We can conceptually lump the modulation and $(n, k; d_{min})$ coding processes into a single modulator that outputs the same waveforms given input blocks of k information bits. A matched filter for the entire waveform can be used at the receiver that provides the best possible performance in AWGN. This approach, called *soft-decision* decoding, is shown in Fig. 7-7(b).

Consider a pair of waveforms $s_0(t)$ and $s_1(t)$, which are the two outputs of a binary modulator. For the system shown in Fig. 7-7(a), binary phase-shift keying (antipodal signaling) is used, so that we have $s_1(t) = -s_0(t)$. In general, the signals need not be antipodal and are related by the correlation $\rho_{01} = \mathscr{E}^{-1}\langle s_0(t)|s_1(t)\rangle$, where $\mathscr{E}$ is the signal energy per transmitted binary digit. Coding gain need not necessarily be evaluated relative to antipodal signaling. In practice, one would use whatever channel signaling scheme is to be used or considered for a system. Coding gain measures the relative signal-to-noise ratio merit of using versus not using an error-control coding scheme.

If an $(n, k; d_{min})$ code is used over the channel, then $M = 2^k$ signaling waveforms can be transmitted, a typical one being of the form

$$x_i(t) = \sum_{j=1}^{n} c_{ij} s_0(t - j T_b) + \bar{c}_{ij} s_1(t - j T_b) \qquad i = 1, 2, 3, \ldots, M \quad (7.28)$$

where T_b is the duration corresponding to one binary digit, and the code is over $GF(2)$ and can be represented by the M n-tuples

$$(c_{i1}, c_{i2}, \ldots, c_{in}) \qquad c_{ij} \in \{0, 1\}$$

and $\bar{c}_{ij}$ is the binary complement of c_{ij}. Without loss of generality, we can assume that the all-zero code word is sent. The resulting composite transmitted waveform is denoted $x_1(t)$, where

$$x_1(t) = \sum_{j=1}^{n} s_1(t - j T_b) \tag{7.29}$$

i.e., a concatenation of n replicas of the signal $s_1(t)$.

The correlation between signaling waveforms is an important determinant of performance. As was found in Chapter 6, the less the correlation, the better the performance in terms of decoding error probabilities. If we now let $x_m(t)$ represent the mth signaling waveform, corresponding to a code word having Hamming weight w_m, we can write

$$x_m(t) = \sum_{j=1}^{n} c_{mj} s_0(t - j T_b) + \bar{c}_{mj} s_1(t - j T_b) \qquad i = 1, 2, 3, \ldots, M \tag{7.30}$$

The inner product between $x_m(t)$ and $x_1(t)$ is

$$\langle x_m(t) | x_1(t) \rangle = \sum_{j=1}^{n} c_{mj} \langle s_0 | s_1 \rangle + \bar{c}_{mj} \langle s_1 | s_1 \rangle$$

$$= \mathscr{E} \sum_{j=1}^{n} [c_{mj} \rho_{01} + \bar{c}_{mj}]$$

$$= \mathscr{E}[w_m \rho_{01} + (n - w_m)]$$

$$= \mathscr{E}[n - w_m(1 - \rho_{01})] \tag{7.31}$$

The normalized correlation ρ_m between $x_m(t)$ and $x_1(t)$ is found by dividing this inner product by the total waveform energy $n\mathscr{E}$, giving

$$\rho_m = \frac{1}{n\mathscr{E}} \langle x_m(t) | x_1(t) \rangle = 1 - \frac{w_m}{n}(1 - \rho_{01}) \tag{7.32}$$

For antipodal signals $s_0(t)$ and $s_1(t) = -s_0(t)$, this reduces to $\rho_m = 1 - 2w_m/n$. Large code-word weights correspond to small correlations. Performance depends on the weight distribution of a code.

In a linear code, the weight distribution corresponds to distance distributions and the smallest nonzero weight is the minimum distance for the code. For a linear code, the largest correlation is given, therefore, by

$$\rho_{\max} = 1 - \frac{d_{\min}}{n}(1 - \rho_{01}) \tag{7.33}$$

Throughout the remainder of this section, we compare the performance of hard- versus soft-decision decoding. This performance comparison will be made on the basis of coding gain. The method followed is to generate curves of the decoded bit error probability versus γ_b with and without the use of a code, for a given channel signaling scheme. In our discussion, we use perfect codes, for which the error probability can be calculated exactly, to point out the differences between hard- and soft-decision decoding.

A coding gain calculation is always made assuming a certain channel signaling scheme. Simple examples include antipodal and binary orthogonal signaling. These schemes provide practical signals over $GF(2)$ and have analytically tractable decoding error probabilities. Antipodal signaling is often used because it is the best binary scheme for the AWGN. For this case, the uncoded bit error probability is given by

$$P_{uc} = \tfrac{1}{2} \text{ erfc } (\gamma_b)^{1/2}$$

For equiprobable symbols having the same error probability P_{uc}, the coded output bit-error probability can be bounded by

$$p' \leq \tfrac{1}{2} \sum_{k=t+1}^{n} \binom{n}{k} P_{uc}^k (1 - P_{uc})^{n-k} \qquad (7.34)$$

These expressions allow the calculation of $p'(\gamma_b)$ for any code for which n, k, and t are known.

Figure 7-8 shows plots of $p'(\gamma_b)$ for four examples of transmissions using antipodal signaling over the BSC: uncoded, and coded with a Hamming (7, 4; 3), a Golay (23, 12; 7) and a (5, 1; 5) repetition code. The gain characteristics are relative

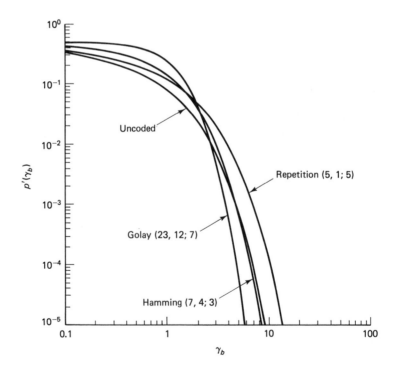

Figure 7-8. $p'(\gamma_b)$ for a few perfect codes using antipodal signaling and hard decoding.

TABLE 7-5. CODING GAINS FOR HARD-DECISION DECODING
OF PERFECT CODES

Code	γ_b	Gain (dB) at $p' = 10^{-5}$
Uncoded	9.1 (9.6 dB)	0
(5, 1; 5)	13.5 (11.3 dB)	-1.7
(7, 4; 3)	8.3 (9.2 dB)	0.4
(23, 12; 7)	5.8 (7.6 dB)	2.0

not only to the channel modulation technique, but also to a reference output bit error rate, which in this case we take to be $p' = 10^{-5}$, with p' given by Eq. (7.34). The gains for the codes shown in Fig. 7-8 relative to uncoded antipodal signaling are summarized in Table 7-5. These gains are relative to antipodal signaling at a bit error rate of 10^{-5}, which requires $\gamma_b = 9.1$ (9.6 dB). The efficiency of signaling with error-control coding is measured by the resulting gain. It is immediately apparent from Fig. 7-8 as well as from Table 7-5 that error-control coding does not always result in a net gain. The gains corresponding to the Golay (23, 12; 7) and Hamming (7, 4; 3) codes are modest, whereas the (5, 1; 5) binary repetition code actually exhibits a loss.

Figure 7-9 graphically shows the evolution of signaling efficiency of hard-decision decoded repetition codes. As the length of the repetition code word increases, the coding gain rapidly approaches an asymptotic value. All of the repetition

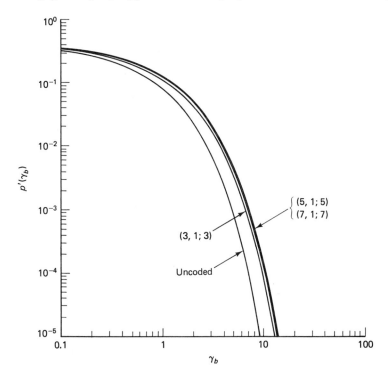

Figure 7-9.   Hard decoding of binary repetition code.

codes have approximately the same signaling efficiency. All exhibit approximately 1.7 dB of coding loss with respect to uncoded antipodal signaling. The use of these codes is justified solely on the basis of the improvement in bit error rate. Figure 7-10 follows the evolution of the signaling efficiency of hard-decoded binary Hamming codes. The codes shown are (7, 4; 3), (31, 26; 3), and (127, 129; 3). At sufficiently high γ_b, these codes exhibit a small gain.

We now turn to measuring the signaling efficiency of codes with soft-decision decoding. Let us assume, without loss of generality, that the code word corresponding to the decision variable U_1 is transmitted and that this code word is the all-zero code word. The elements of transmitted code words are from $GF(2)$ and are transmitted using antipodal signals. Optimal (soft-decision) processing in AWGN corresponds to an implementation consisting of M matched filters, one for each of the code words. The outputs of these M filters are compared and decoding is made in favor of the code word corresponding to the largest matched filter output. The matched filter bank corresponding to this implementation is shown in Fig. 5-7. Let us denote by U_j the output of the jth matched filter. The filter output U_1 therefore corresponds to signal plus noise, and all other outputs contain noise only.

The probability of making an error in comparing the signal-plus-noise variable U_1 to any other noise-only U_j is given by

$$P_e = \tfrac{1}{2} \operatorname{erfc} \left[\tfrac{1}{2}(1 - \rho_j)\gamma \right]^{1/2} \tag{7.35}$$

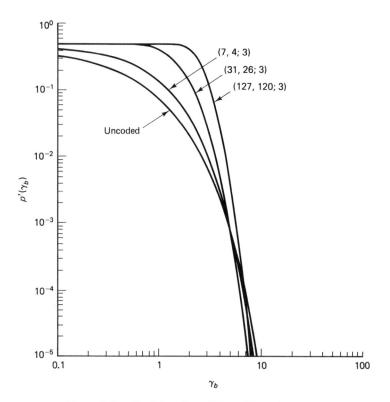

Figure 7-10.   Hard decoding of binary Hamming codes.

where ρ is the correlation between coded signaling waveforms, which we have already determined to be $\rho_j = 1 - 2w_j/n$ when antipodal signaling is used, and where $\gamma = k\gamma_b$ is the energy contrast ratio for the k-bit coded waveform. P_e can now be expressed in terms of γ_b and w_j, giving

$$\text{Prob } \{U_1 \leq U_j\} = P_{e,j}(\gamma_b) = \tfrac{1}{2} \text{ erfc } (R_c w_j \gamma_b)^{1/2} \qquad (7.36)$$

where $R_c = k/n$ is the code rate.

We do not yet have an expression for the code-word decoding error probability, but the last expression already suggests a general result concerning coding gain. The term $R_c w_j$ acts as a multiplier on γ_b. Larger $R_c w_j$ correspond to smaller decoding error rates. Large code rates, large code-word weights, and, in particular, large code minimum distances contribute to good performance. Note, however, that R_c and w_j are not independent and that, in particular, w_j must decrease if R_c is to increase.

The probability P_M of an M-ary code-word soft decoding error is given by

$$P_M = 1 - \int_{-\infty}^{\infty} \text{Prob } \{U_1 > U_2,\ U_1 > U_3,\ \cdots,\ U_1 > U_M\} \zeta(U_1)\, dU_1$$

where Prob $\{U_1 > U_2,\ U_1 > U_3,\ \cdots,\ U_1 > U_M\}$ is the joint probability of U_1 exceeding each of the noise-only decision variables, and $\zeta(U_1)$ is the probability density function for the signal-plus-noise variable U_1. In general, the code-word weight distribution causes the $M - 1$ events $\{U_1 > U_j\}, j = 2, 3, \ldots, M$, to be statistically correlated. Consequently, the joint probability Prob $\{U_1 > U_2,\ U_1 > U_3,\ \cdots,\ U_1 > U_M\}$ cannot easily be expressed in an analytically convenient form. We can, however, bound the code-word soft decoding error probability with the union bound.

If A_1 and A_2 are two events, then the probability of their union $A_1 \cup A_2$ is

$$\text{Prob } \{A_1 \cup A_2\} = \text{ Prob } \{A_1\} + \text{ Prob } \{A_2\} - \text{ Prob } \{A_1 \cap A_2\}$$

The probability Prob $\{A_1 \cup A_2\}$ of the union of A_1 and A_2 is the sum of the individual event probabilities less the probability of the intersection between them. For statistically independent events A_1 and A_2, the probability of their intersection Prob $\{A_1 \cap A_2\}$ vanishes and we have Prob $\{A_1 \cup A_2\} = $ Prob $\{A_1\} + $ Prob $\{A_2\}$. From this special case, we see that

$$\text{Prob } \{A_1 \cup A_2\} \leq \text{ Prob } \{A_1\} + \text{ Prob } \{A_2\}$$

with equality holding when the events are statistically independent (and, therefore, uncorrelated). This is easily illustrated with the help of Venn diagrams, as is done in Fig. 7-11.

This can be generalized to N events [Fe 68]. If $A_1, A_2, \ldots, A_N$ are probabilistic, possibly correlated events, then the probability of the union of these events is always upper bounded by the sum of the probabilities of individual events.

$$\text{Prob } \{A_1 \cup A_2 \cup \cdots \cup A_N\} \leq \sum_{j=1}^{N} \text{ Prob } \{A_j\}$$

The bound is actually reached only if the events are statistically independent. This

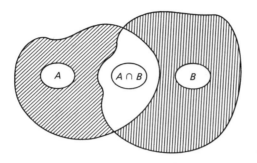

Figure 7-11. The probability of the union is upper bounded by the sum of the probabilities of individual events: Prob $\{A_1 \cup A_2\} \leq$ Prob $\{A_1\}$ + Prob $\{A_2\}$.

is the *union bound* and can be used to bound the probability of a set of statistically dependent events.

The probability of an M-ary code-word error is bounded by the union of the $M - 1$ events $\{U_1 \leq U_j\}$, $j = 2, 3, \ldots, M$. This is because a decoding error occurs if any one of the events $\{U_1 \leq U_j\}$ occurs. We now apply the union bound to the $M - 1$ events $\{U_1 \leq U_j\}$, $j = 2, 3, \ldots, M$. The M-ary code-word error probability is, therefore, bounded by

$$P_M \leq \tfrac{1}{2} \sum_{j=2}^{M} \text{erfc } (R_c w_j \gamma_b)^{1/2} \tag{7.37}$$

where the summation is over all code words with nonzero weight.

EXAMPLE

The soft-decoding performance of the Hamming (7, 4; 3) can be bounded by Eq. (7.37) and with the code-word weight distribution given in Table 7-2. For this code, the rate is $R_c = k/n = 4/7$. The resulting decoded bit error probability can be approximated as $p'(\gamma_b) \approx \tfrac{1}{2} P_M$ and has been plotted in Fig. 7-12. This figure also shows the code's hard-decoding performance for comparison. At an output bit error probability of 10^{-5}, soft decoding always performs better than hard decoding. We have already seen that the hard-decoded Hamming (7, 4; 3) code has a 0.4-dB gain over uncoded transmission. Soft decoding achieves an additional 1.5-dB gain over the hard-decoded case. This additional gain is obtained at the cost of increased implementation complexity.

Hard decoding for this case requires only two matched filters and a table look-up for decoding the $2^7 = 128$ possible received 7-tuples. By contrast, soft-decision decoding requires $2^4 = 16$ matched filters and the comparison circuitry required to select the maximum filter output. The complexity, as measured by the number of matched filters required, increases exponentially with k for soft-decision decoding.

These calculations have been repeated for the Golay (23, 12; 7) code whose weight structure is shown in Table 7-3. The results are shown in Fig. 7-13. The hard-decoded gain over uncoded transmissions is 2 dB, and soft decoding provides an additional 1.8 dB of gain. Here the trade-off between additional gain and implementation complexity is even more pronounced. Soft decoding the Golay (23, 12; 7) code requires $2^{12} = 4096$ matched filters and the associated comparison circuitry. Problem 7-15 discusses a way to simplify this implementation.

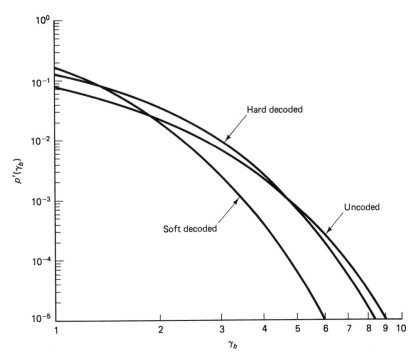

Figure 7-12. Hard- and soft-decoding performance comparison for the Hamming (7, 4; 3) code.

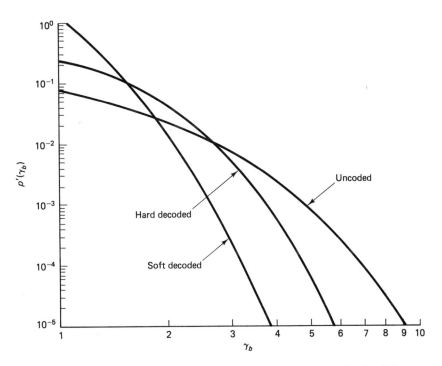

Figure 7-13. Hard and soft-decoding performance comparison for the Golay (23, 12; 7) code.

7.1.7 Trellis-Coded Modulation

Chapter 6 introduced modulation schemes that have various degrees of bandwidth efficiency and robustness on the AWGN channel. Energy-efficient signals trade bandwidth for good performance in noise. With bandwidth-efficient signals, capacity is achieved at the cost of higher signal-to-noise ratios. To further improve the performance of these signaling schemes over noisy channels, error-control coding was introduced as a means of supplementing the algebraic structure of signaling waveforms. To maintain the same information rate, using an error-control code means that the signaling bandwidth must be increased to accommodate the additional redundant symbols.

The additional bandwidth, however, may not be available. This is often the case for telephone channels, whose bandwidth is about 3.2 kHz, and also for satellite channels. The design of high-data-rate digital modems for these and other applications can be a very challenging problem.

Trellis-coded modulation is a recent breakthrough in communication engineering. The pioneering work in that area appeared in 1982 and has already left a mark on communication engineering. Trellis-coded modulation achieves large coding gains over uncoded modulation without sacrificing bandwidth. This does not represent a violation of allowable trade-offs, but rather a sizeable step toward developing codes that more closely approximate what Shannon found to be possible. Trellis-coded modulation, therefore, represents a significant advance in the state of the art. In addition, trellis-coded modulation serves as an excellent example that brings together many of the important points of this book. This section is based mainly on the articles by Ungerboeck. References [Be 88, Sk 88, Un 82, Un 87, Un 87b] should be consulted for additional details.

Figure 6-18 and the accompanying discussion in Chapter 6 show that we are still short of the Shannon ideal of achieving reliable communication at channel capacity. The possibility of more efficient signaling schemes is not ruled out by information theory. The search for such schemes has for the most part been limited either to looking for spectrally efficient modulations or for better error-control codes.

In Section 6.3.4, we discussed a spectrally efficient quadrature modulation technique. There the idea was simply to use two BSPK signals in quadrature having the same spectral occupancy, but being independently modulated. Other spectrally efficient modulation schemes exist, and it is not possible to describe all of them here. We may briefly mention minimum-shift keying [Pa 79], which has found many applications, and quadrature–quadrature-shift keying [Sa 83, Sa 86].

In the area of error-control coding, we must digress a little from the main discussion and at least mention *convolutional coding* and the Viterbi algorithm, which makes possible an efficient implementation of convolutional decoders. The error-control codes we consider in this chapter are block codes. With block codes, the information stream is broken into blocks of k information symbols, which are then mapped into blocks of $n > k$ channel symbols. Decoding similarly proceeds one block at a time. The idea behind convolutional coding is that it is also possible to encode the information stream without breaking it into blocks. A convolutional encoder associates an output stream of channel symbols with the input information stream. Of course, the output stream has a higher rate than the input stream, just as the coded block length n for a k/n rate block code is larger than the corresponding uncoded information block length k. Convolutional encoding proceeds sequentially, with n output symbols produced for every k information symbol presented to it. However, the coding scheme depends on the *history* of a certain number of input symbols. In other words, a convolutional encoder has memory and is able to effectively map long strings of information symbols into even longer encoded strings. This coding operation over long strings of symbols makes it possible to exploit the statistical regularities in the received error sequence, just as long block code words do. A convolutional encoder enjoys the coding advantages that result from encoding long strings of symbols, but the encoding mechanism itself proceeds a few symbols at a time. The rules for choosing the next coded symbol depends on the recent information symbol history.

It is not necessary at this time to go into the details of convolutional encoding. This would necessitate looking into the coding rules and even into the actual signal-processing structure of encoders and decoders. However, we can gain an appreciation for the basic principles by transforming the problem of convolutional encoding into that of block encoding. In other words, we will attempt to explain the end product of convolutional encoding (rather than the processing details) in terms of what we know about block coding. This approach will be used to explain the broad features of convolutional codes, but will leave unexplained some of the details.

A convolutional code transforms, a few symbols at a time, an input string of information symbols into an output string of coded channel symbols. Let us now step back and consider a long string of K information symbols that has been convolutionally encoded into a longer string of N channel symbols. The K information symbols could, for example, be the entire message to be transmitted. For simplicity, let us take the symbols to be binary. Extending this argument to higher-level alphabets is a simple matter.

While the encoding and decoding is actually done a few ($\ll K$) symbols at a time, nothing prevents us from viewing the entire coding process globally, as mapping the entire information message of K bits into a coded symbol of N bits. Viewed this way, the information message is but one out of a possible 2^K meta-alphabet of information symbols, each such K-bit symbol representing a possible message. Similarly, the output alphabet contains 2^N channel symbols. Obviously, an (N, K) block code could have been used to do the encoding. In fact, if the coding were done in a "black box" whose contents are not known, it would not be possible to tell without opening the box whether it contained a block or a convolutional encoder if only the K input and N output symbols were known. Either way, a block of K symbols is mapped into a block of N symbols. Decoding could simply be accomplished by determining which of the 2^K code words (i.e., possible messages) has the least Hamming distance to the received N-tuple, since that would be the most likely message transmitted.

A convolutional encoder is a finite-state algorithm with memory spanning a number of past states and whose state transitions determine the next symbol to be added to the coded string. The allowed transitions are chosen to maximize the Hamming distance between the allowed output symbol strings. By examining the received symbols, the decoder identifies the input symbol string that, when encoded, results in an output symbol string that is closest in Hamming distance to the observed string. Put another way, the decoder selects the most likely sequence of state transitions leading to the received sequence.

This selection proceeds sequentially as new symbols are available to the decoder. An efficient algorithm for convolutional decoding was found by Viterbi [Vi 67]. The efficiency of the Viterbi algorithm results from keeping as part of the decision process only the most likely state-transition sequences. The reader in need of more details on convolutional codes and the Viterbi algorithm will find the literature rich in that area. Of the many references, we may cite [Be 88, Bl 83, Li 83, Mi 85, Pe 72, Pr 83, Sk 88, St 88b, Vi 67, Vi 79].

The basic ideas behind block and convolutional encoding are much the same. Redundant symbols are added to the source symbols, and decoding is based on minimizing a Hamming distance. In either case, modulation and coding are performed as separate operations. Ungerboeck realized that this may lead to inefficiencies, identified the nature of these inefficiencies, and suggested an elegant solution, namely, trellis-coded modulation [Un 82, Un 87a, Un 87b].

As an illustration, Ungerboeck compares uncoded 4-ary PSK with coded 8-ary PSK [Un 87a]. In both cases, there are two information bits per symbol. 8-ary modulation allows the use of a rate 2/3 error-control code. If the 4-ary PSK system performs at a symbol error rate of 10^{-5}, the same signal-to-noise ratio results in a symbol error rate of 10^{-2} for the demodulated (but not decoded) 8-ary PSK system. You will recall that M-ary PSK is a bandwidth-efficient signaling scheme and that going from 4-ary to 8-ary PSK at the same symbol error rate requires an increase in signal-to-noise ratio. Conversely, the same signal-to-noise ratio results in a higher symbol error rate when M is increased. A rate 2/3 binary convolutional code could be used to decrease the error rate of the 8-ary system, at the cost of higher complexity. However, this results in an error performance that breaks even with the uncoded 4-ary PSK.

Ungerboeck recognized that there are two difficulties with this approach. One of the inefficiencies with signaling schemes that separate modulation and coding is that the signals must first be demodulated with hard decisions prior to decoding. We have already seen that a better approach is soft-decision decoding, where the decoder processes the unquantized demodulator output directly. With soft-decision decoding, it is not possible to speak of separate modulation and coding performance. Indeed, the notion of error correction is no longer appropriate since there are no hard demodulation decoding errors to be corrected [Un 87a].

The other problem with conventional modulation-cum-decoding is that when nonbinary alphabets are used, maximizing the Hamming distance is not equivalent to maximizing the Euclidian distance on which communication performance ultimately depends. This is a serious problem. The Euclidian distance (or any monotonic function of it) is the proper measure to use in decoding in AWGN. Optimal performance in AWGN results from decoding on the basis of minimum Euclidian distance between the received waveform and the members of a signaling alphabet. Conversely, good signaling alphabets are those having maximum Euclidian distance between signals.

Recall that the definition of Hamming distance involves only the equality between corresponding symbols of an n-tuple. In particular, it does not measure the degree of dissimilarity if these symbols are not alike. For nonbinary alphabets, the Hamming metric is only a crude measure of distance. Other than for the binary case, there is no monotonic relation between Hamming and Euclidian distances. Decoding on the basis of Hamming distance does not necessarily result in optimal performance in the Euclidian distance sense.

The problem faced in developing reliable bandwidth-efficient communications is now clear. Some form of channel coding must be used. If the bandwidth is restricted, the redundancy required for coding must be obtained by increasing the alphabet size of a bandwidth-efficient signaling scheme. This forces us to use nonbinary alphabets, for which good codes are hard to come by because conventional codes are hard decoded on the basis of Hamming distances.

Ungerboeck proposed a very elegant solution to this dilemma. Rather than trying to compose coded signals by appending an error-control code onto existing modulations, he accomplished both functions simultaneously by soft-decision decoding augmented signaling alphabets based on Euclidian distance. This approach did away with Hamming distance altogether, and a more efficient coding is achieved. The redundancy needed for coding is achieved by enlarging the signaling alphabet, the members of which are chosen to maximize the Euclidian distance between allowed transmitted sequences.

Before describing how trellis-coded modulation accomplishes this, let us follow Ungerboeck's early steps in the analysis of the expected performance gains [Un 82]. Communication performance can be measured in terms of the capacity provided by various signaling schemes. Consider an alphabet of M discrete symbols. These symbols are to be soft-decoded. The proper channel model for this situation is one having discrete inputs and continuous outputs.

One- and two-dimensional modulations are considered. The prototype for one-dimensional modulation is M-ary PAM, where the amplitude along a single signal-space coordinate is divided into multiple levels for signaling. Two-dimensional modulation includes M-ary PSK and also simultaneous modulation of amplitude and phase, called *quadrature amplitude-shift keying* (QASK). These modulation types are represented graphically as signal constellations in Fig. 7.14. In these constellations, the radial dimension represents the amplitude and the angle measured from the horizontal axis is the phase. Equivalently, the horizontal (vertical) axis denotes the real (imaginary) part of the signal.

Let the **x** ensemble denote the symbol alphabet $\{x_1, x_2, \ldots, x_M\}$ having the corresponding prior symbol probabilities $\{P_1, P_2, \ldots, P_M\}$. By letting the continuous random variable z denote the demodulator output, Eq. (4.16) for the average mutual information between two ensembles **x** and **y** can be rewritten as

$$I = \sum_{k=1}^{N} P_k \int_{-\infty}^{\infty} p(z|x_k)\{\log p(z|x_k) - \log \sum_{m=1}^{N} P_m p(z|x_M)\}\, dz \qquad (7.38)$$

In zero-mean additive white Gaussian noise having variance σ^2, the probability density function $p(z|x_k)$ is simply the Gaussian density given by

$$p(z|x_k) = A^{-1} \exp\left[-\|z - x_k\|^2/2\sigma^2\right] \qquad (7.39)$$

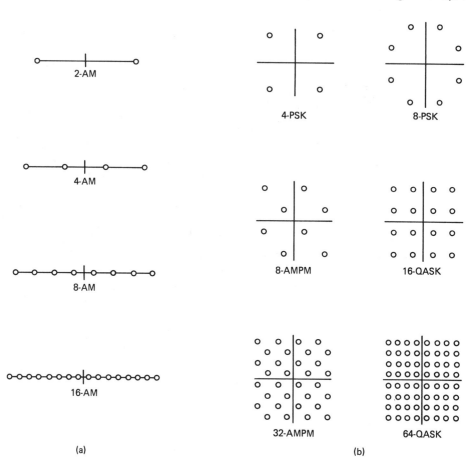

Figure 7-14. Signal-modulation constellations: (*a*) one-dimensional modulation and (*b*) two-dimensional modulation. (Reproduced by permission from [Un 82]. ©1982 IEEE.)

where $A = \sigma(2\pi)^{1/2}$ for one-dimensional modulation, and $A = 2\pi\sigma^2$ for two-dimensional modulation. The demodulator output itself when x_k is transmitted is

$$z = x_k + n$$

where n is the additive noise process.

The information capacity of this channel could be found by maximizing Eq. (7.38) through a variation of the $\{P_k\}$. This tedious problem is circumvented by limiting our attention to equiprobable symbols, so that $P_k = 1/M$. Subject to this constraint, the channel capacity becomes

$$C = \log M - \frac{1}{M}\sum_{k=1}^{M} E\{\log \sum_{m=1}^{M} \exp\left[-(\|x_k - x_m + n\|^2 - \|n\|^2)/2\pi\sigma^2\right]\}$$

$$(7.40)$$

where $E\{\cdot\}$ represents a Gaussian expectation value. This expression for C was estimated using Monte Carlo simulations producing random numbers $\{n\}$ having zero mean and variance $\|n\|^2$. The signal-to-noise ratio is defined as

$$\text{SNR} = E\{\|x_k\|^2\}/E\{\|n\|^2\}$$

These signal-to-noise ratios are measured at the output of a soft-decision demodulator (i.e., of a matched filter) and, therefore, are equal to twice the energy contrast ratio γ defined in Chapter 6. Stated in decibels, the signal-to-noise ratios given here are 3 dB over γ. The results of these simulations are shown in Fig. 7.15. This figure shows two plots corresponding to one- and two-dimensional modulations. Each plot shows the capacity, in bits per modulation interval (the time required to transmit one symbol over the channel) as a function of the signal-to-noise ratio in decibels, for several values of the multiplicity parameter M. These curves also show the maximum capacity achievable over the AWGN channel. At low signal-to-noise ratios, the capacity increases with SNR and then tapers out at a value $C = \log M$, beyond which increasing the signal-to-noise does not affect the capacity. In the high signal-to-noise regime, noise has a negligible probability of causing a symbol to be received in error.

The small circles appearing on the curves indicate the points at which the probability of uncoded hard-decoded symbol error is 10^{-5}. For uncoded hard-decoded 4-ary PSK (two bits per symbol), a signal-to-noise ratio of 12.9 dB is required to achieve a probability of symbol error of 10^{-5}. This may be verified from Fig. 6-14, remembering that the signal-to-noise ratio is twice the energy contrast ratio.

By doubling the number of available signals (i.e., by using 8-ary PSK) two bits per symbol may be conveyed with to a signal-to-noise ratio of 5.9 dB ($\gamma = 2$), provided some form of coding is used. This would result in signaling that is only 1.2 dB away from the Shannon limit. Similar results hold for other values of M. The point of this exercise is that most of the available gain may be achieved by simply doubling the signaling alphabet and using an appropriate code. A reasonably efficient code, therefore, need not be very complex. This is a pleasing result that makes efficient signaling within the reach of engineering. The remaining problem is to find a good code.

An exhaustive computer search for these codes is possible. The simplest of these can be found by hand and provides excellent models for illustrating how trellis-coded modulation works. The codes we are seeking are rate $k/(k + 1)$ codes and are to be soft-decoded. For example, a rate 2/3 code could be implemented by using 8-ary PSK to convert two bits of information per symbol. The eight symbols in the alphabet represent a twofold choice in selecting a waveform for transmission. The rules for this selection are chosen to maximize the Euclidian distance between allowed transmitted sequences.

Figure 7-16(a) presents uncoded 4-ary PSK and introduces elementary notions of trellis coding. At the upper left of the figure is the signaling constellation for 4-ary PSK. The four possible signals are arbitrarily labeled $\{0, 1, 2, 3\}$. These signals have been normalized to unit energy. Some of the Euclidian distances between these

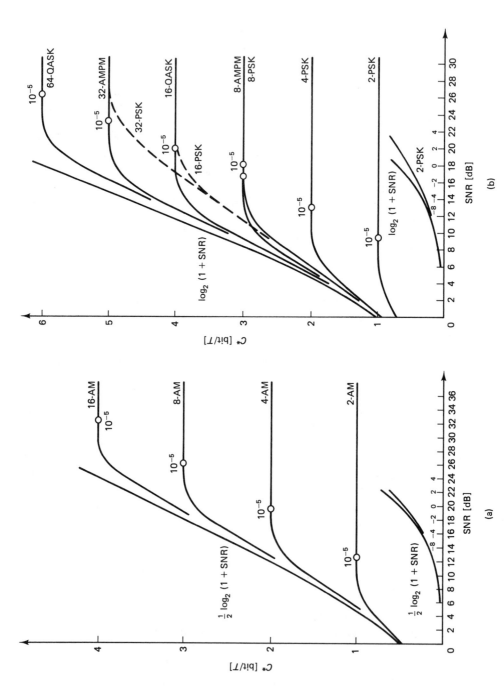

Figure 7-15. Channel capacity Eq. (7.40) for an AWGN channel with discrete input symbols and continuous output. (*a*) One-dimensional modulation and (*b*) two-dimensional modulation. (Reproduced by permission from [Un 82], © 1982 IEEE.)

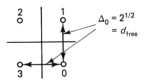

4-PSK signal set

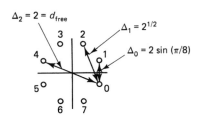

One-state trellis

(a)

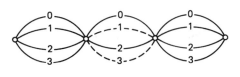

Redundant 8-PSK signal set

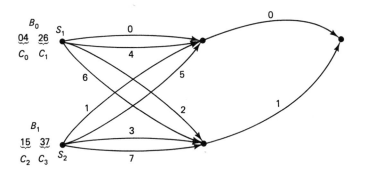

Two-state trellis

(b)

Figure 7-16. (a) Uncoded 4-ary PSK and (b) two-state trellis-coded 8-ary PSK. (Adapted by permission from [Un 82]. ©1982 IEEE.)

signals are also shown. For this constellation, we have $d(0, 2) = d(1, 3) = 2$; we also have $d(0, 1) = d(0, 3) = 2^{1/2}$, corresponding to the least intersymbol distance. We call this least distance the *free distance* for the signal set. The free distance sets a bound on achievable performance, just as the minimum distance of linear block codes does. For this 4-ary PSK signal set, $d_{\text{free}} = 2^{1/2}$.

In the lower left corner of Fig. 7-16, a trellis representation of uncoded 4-ary PSK is shown to introduce the concept of a trellis. Each circle represents a node in the trellis. Successive nodes are separated in time by one signaling interval. The path from one state to another represents the symbol transmitted and carries the same label $\{0, 1, 2, 3\}$ as the four symbols. For the uncoded 4-ary PSK case, there are four possible transitions between consecutive nodes, and these correspond to the four possible symbols.

There is no redundancy in transmission and, consequently, one of these four transitions must occur between any two nodes. These four paths correspond to the two bits per signaling interval. These paths are entirely described by the sequence of symbols that form messages. A message, which is a sequence of symbols, can be described by a particular path through the trellis. All of the paths through the trellis correspond to possible messages.

The paths joining any two nodes correspond to the choice of symbols transmitted between these nodes. The shortest path between nodes in Fig. 7-16(a) involves the transmission of one of the symbols $\{0, 1, 2, 3\}$. The performance associated with this transmission is determined by the Euclidian metric between the corresponding waveforms and is bounded by the shortest such distance, the minimum free distance d_{free}. In this example, $d_{\text{free}} = 2^{1/2}$. If only one bit per interval were to be transmitted, choosing an antipodal pair such as $\{0, 2\}$ or $\{1, 3\}$ would result in $d_{\text{free}} = 2$. In terms of a trellis, this amounts to selecting the path leading to a maximum Euclidian distance.

Now consider Fig. 7-16(b). The signal set has been doubled, resulting in 8-ary PSK. The minimum Euclidian distance between these waveforms is $\Delta_0 = 2 \sin(\pi/8)$. However, we shall use this 8-ary set to convey only two bits of information. We shall do so in a way that realizes a free distance that is greater than what was obtained with uncoded 4-ary PSK.

The top of Fig. 7-16(b) shows the 8-ary PSK signal constellation with some of the intersymbol distances. The bottom of Fig. 7-16(b) shows a two-state trellis using all eight PSK waveforms to convey two bits of information per signaling interval. State S_1 corresponds to transmissions from the subset $\{0, 2, 4, 6\}$ and state S_2 corresponds to transmissions from the subset $\{1, 3, 5, 7\}$. The coder is always in one of the two states, from which four transitions are possible. Thus, a choice between four possible alternatives is always possible, and two information bits are transmitted with each transition from one node to the next. There are now two "parallel" families of nodes, corresponding to the two coder states. The four possible transitions from a trellis state convey the two bits of information. The particular state from which these transitions originate provides the redundancy required for robustness.

In the uncoded 4-ary PSK trellis of Fig. 7-16(a), some of the transitions between two successive nodes correspond to a distance of 2, whereas others involve only the minimum distance $2^{1/2}$. We would like to build a two-state trellis to avoid using small distances as much as possible. At the top of the two-state trellis, we have kept one of the antipodal sets $\{0, 4\}$ between successive nodes of state S_1. The other antipodal set $\{2, 6\}$ causes the trellis to transition to a node of state S_2. This intentional detour forces the coder to take a longer path before returning to a node of state S_1 and increases the distance between the correponding coded sequences.

There are now two possible paths between nodes of state S_1. The first path corresponds to using the antipodal set $\{0, 4\}$ and realizing a distance 2 between nodes. The second path is from the first to the third node of state S_1 via a node of state S_2. This second path must be traversed in two consecutive transitions. The first transition involves a distance difference $\Delta_1 = 2^{1/2}$ between the waveforms of antipodal sets $\{0, 4\}$ and $\{2, 6\}$. The second transition involves a distance difference $\Delta_0 = 2 \sin (\pi/8)$ between the waveforms of antipodal sets $\{1, 5\}$ and $\{0, 4\}$. This corresponds to a total distance Δ between the initial and final node, where

$$\Delta^2 = \Delta_1^2 + \Delta_0^2$$

Since $\Delta_0 = 2 \sin (\pi/8)$ and $\Delta_1 = 2^{1/2}$, we have $\Delta = 1.608$, which is less than 2, the distance between consecutive nodes of state S_1. Since the transitions are defined symmetrically with respect to the states, the minimum free distance for this trellis is, therefore, 1.608, which represents a slight increase over the uncoded 4-ary PSK distance of $2^{1/2} = 1.414$.

It is important to point out that an increase in the minimum free distance, and, therefore, a better performance in AWGN, has been achieved without having to increase the system bandwidth. Two bits are transmitted during each signaling interval, but the decoder must now suffer a processing delay of two intervals. This increased distance was obtained by doubling the alphabet size from 4 to 8, and by defining a multistate trellis whose paths are chosen precisely in such a way as to achieve this large distance. The freedom to choose among possible paths is a consequence of the larger alphabet size. This is the basis for trellis-coded modulation. In principle, optimal paths through a trellis could be found by exhaustive search by a computer. The simpler trellises, however, can be arrived at without mechanical assistance. Figure 7-17 shows the possible trellises for 8-ary PSK. Whereas the two-state trellis achieves a modest increase in minimum free distance over the uncoded 4-ary case, trellises with a larger number of states can force longer paths and achieve substantial gains.

The large Euclidian distances between waveforms is accomplished by partitioning the original signal set into successive sets having larger and larger intersymbol distances. Figure 7-18 shows how this is done for 8-ary PSK. The original signal set is depicted as a constellation with minimum distance $\Delta_0 = 2 \sin (\pi/8)$. From these eight signals, two sets (B_0 and B_1) of four signals having minimum distance $\Delta_1 = 2^{1/2}$ can be formed. These, in turn, can be subdivided into signal sets $B_0 \rightarrow \{C_0$ and $C_1\}$ and $B_1 \rightarrow \{C_2$ and $C_3\}$, which are made of antipodal pairs for which the minimum distance is $\Delta_2 = 2$.

2 trellis states

C_0 C_2
0 4   2 6

C_1 C_3
1 5   3 7

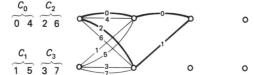

$d_{free} = (\Delta_1^2 + \Delta_0^2)^{1/2} = 1.608$
(1.1-dB gain over 4-PSK)

4 trellis states

C_0 C_2
0 4   2 6
C_1 C_3
1 5   3 7

2 6   0 4

3 7   1 5

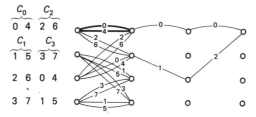

$d_{free} = \Delta_2 = 2.000$
(3.0-dB gain over 4-PSK)

8 trellis states

0 4 2 6
1 5 3 7
4 0 6 2
5 1 7 3
2 6 0 4
3 7 1 5
6 2 4 0
7 3 5 1

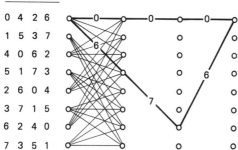

$d_{free} = (\Delta_1^2 + \Delta_0^2 + \Delta_1^2)^{1/2} = 2.141$
(3.6-dB gain over 4-PSK)

16 trellis states

0 4 2 6
1 5 3 7
4 0 6 2
5 1 7 3
2 6 0 4
3 7 1 5
6 2 4 0
7 3 5 1
4 0 6 2
5 1 7 3
0 4 2 6
1 5 3 7
6 2 4 0
7 3 5 1
2 6 0 4
3 7 1 5

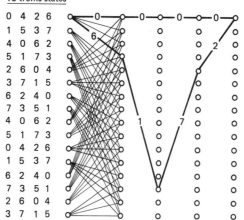

$d_{free} = (\Delta_1^2 + \Delta_0^2 + \Delta_0^2 + \Delta_1^2)^{1/2} = 2.274$
(4.1-dB gain over 4-PSK)

Figure 7-17. Trellis-coded 8-ary PSK modulation. (Adapted by permission from [Un 82]. ©1982 IEEE.)

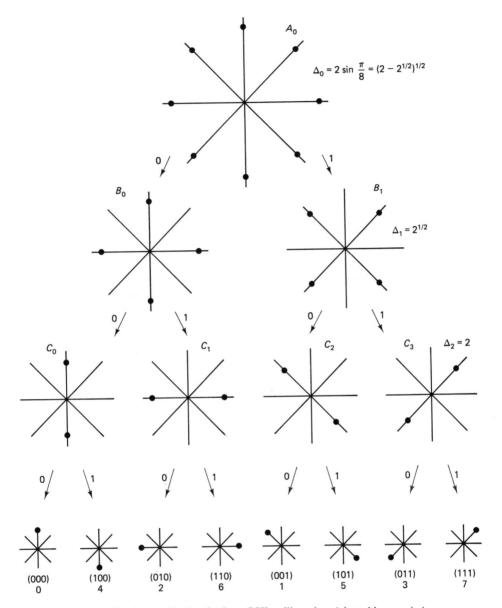

Figure 7-18.   Set partitioning for 8-ary PSK trellis codes. Adapted by permission from [Be88]

Paths through the trellis are selected according to the following three rules [Un 87a]:

1. **Parallel transitions from any trellis state are associated with the largest minimum distance. For 8-ary PSK, this is $\Delta_2 = 2$ and corresponds to the signal sets $\{0, 4\}$, $\{1, 5\}$, $\{2, 6\}$, and $\{3, 7\}$.**

2. **Transitions originating from or terminating into one state are associated with signals with the smallest distance (e.g., $\Delta_1 = 2^{1/2}$ for 8-ary PSK) between them. This corresponds to $\{0, 2, 4, 6\}$ and $\{1, 3, 5, 7\}$.**

3. **All of the signals have equal probabilities.**

The free distances associated with 8-ary PSK using trellises having 2, 4, 8, and 16 states are indicated in Fig. 7-17. As more states are used, the free distance increases and, therefore, so does the communication performance. This performance improvement can be measured by the gain over uncoded communication. It is easy to convert Euclidian distances to gains since the average waveform energy is simply the square of the signal's norm.

Using PSK as an example, the minimum free distance for the uncoded 4-ary case is $\Delta_1 = 2^{1/2}$. This represents an average energy of 2 for the waveforms of that set. Since PSK is a constant-envelope signaling scheme, every waveform has the same energy, which is equal to the average energy. This is not true for PAM or QASK. The gain of coded communications over uncoded signaling is simply

$$G = \frac{\text{average coded waveform norm}}{\text{average uncoded waveform norm}} = \frac{\text{square of coded free distance}}{\text{square of uncoded minimum distance}}$$

By using a trellis with four states, the coded free distance is $d_{\text{free}} = 2$. The gain over uncoded 4-ary PSK is, therefore,

$$G = \frac{d_{\text{free}}^2}{\Delta_1^2} = 2 \quad (3 \text{ dB})$$

Table 7-6 summarizes the gain performance for rate 2/3 trellis-coded modulation using PAM, QASK, and PSK. Ungerboeck notes that one- and two-dimensional modulations exhibit roughly the same gain characteristics Gains on the order of 3 to 4 dB are easily obtained with simple trellises having four to eight states. This represents most of the gain achievable with trellis-coded modulation. As the number of trellis states increases, the gain also increases, albeit at a progressively slower rate. Thus, gains of 6 dB or more using PAM or PSK require over a thousand states, a substantial increase in complexity.

TABLE 7-6. GAINS IN dB OVER UNCODED SIGNALING FOR TRELLIS-CODED MODULATION
USING 8-ARY PAM, PSK, AND 16-ARY QASK[a]

States	Rate 2/3 8-ary PAM	Rate 3/4 16-ary PAM	Rate 2/3 8-ary PSK	Rate 3/4 16-ary PSK	Rate 3/4 16-ary QASK
4	3.3	3.5	3.0	3.5	4.4
8	3.8	3.9	3.6	4.0	5.3
16	4.2	4.3	4.1	4.4	6.1
32	5.0	5.1	4.6	5.1	6.1
64	5.2	5.4	4.8	5.3	6.8
128	5.8	6.0	5.0	5.3	7.4
256	—	—	5.4	5.5	7.4
512	—	—	5.7	—	—
1,024	—	—	5.7	—	—

[a]The gain of 16-ary QASK is relative to uncoded 8-ary PSK.
Source: Adapted by permission from [Un 82, Un 87b]. © 1982 IEEE.

7.2 LINEAR BLOCK CODES

Section 7.1 introduced the concept of error-control coding, exhibited simple examples of such codes, and presented methods for assessing their performance. Emphasis was given to basic principles rather than to implementation.

In this section, we continue the discussion of block codes started in Section 7.1. We also introduce examples of error-control codes and describe their performance. We will not get involved in the mechanical details of coding and decoding. However, many important codes have been developed around an algebraic structure that allows an efficient implementation. For this reason, we provide a brief introduction to the algebraic structure of cyclic codes. The reader is referred to a number of very good texts [e.g., Bl 83, Li 83, Ma 77, Mi 85, Pe 72] devoted to error-control coding for additional details on the implementation of coding and decoding algorithms for these codes.

7.2.1 Algebraic Structure

The study of error-control coding can be greatly simplified if a few elementary statements are made to put some subjects in their proper perspective. Section 7.1 provided a general introduction to codes. With a block code, the information symbol stream is divided into blocks of k symbols, which are then processed, one block at a time, to form code words of n symbols each. This is not the only way to encode, but it is a convenient way to introduce the subject.

Until now, we have not paid too much attention to the question of whether a code is linear or not. Much of Section 7.1 applies to both linear and nonlinear codes and emphasizes the metric structure of codes. We did mention that for linear codes, this metric structure can be directly obtained from the code-word weights. Linear codes are easy to work with.

There are two fundamental reasons why the development of coding theory has concentrated heavily on linear codes. The first is that the development of coding theory into a science requires a unifying mathematical structure other than an exhaustive search for codes. Brute-force searches can be used, but they are neither elegant nor particularly illuminating when an understanding of the subject is required. Linear vector-space theory provides a simple yet effective tool for describing codes. Most important, the linearity of a code guarantees a minimum distance that can be used for error control. We shall have more to say about this in the following paragraphs. The second reason is that the development of coding theory into a science that can be applied to practical engineering problems requires algorithms for encoding and decoding other than table look-up. This is especially true when very large codes containing many long code words are desired. Linear codes lend themselves to efficient algorithms for encoding and decoding.

The previous section introduced the concept of code words as vectors in some signal space. Since large metric distances between code words lead to good performance, it is desirable to generate codes in which the code words are more or less uniformly distributed over the space, leaving as much distance between them as possible. There is little use for code words that are bunched in some small region of the space. We will begin with a heuristic argument for the use of linear codes.

Let us try do develop a code over $GF(2)$. We can start with an arbitrary code word. Without loss of generality, we start with the all-zero $c_1 = (0, 0, 0, 0, 0, 0, 0)$ code word. We methodically search for other code words, with the only restriction that the code be linear. In $GF(2^n)$, linearity simply means that the sum of two code words is also a code word. For the next code word, we could choose $c_2 = (1, 0, 0, 0, 0, 0, 0)$. The two code words c_1 and c_2 certainly form a linear code over $GF(2)$. However, the last six binary digits of each code word are identical and, therefore, serve no useful purpose in this code. For all practical purposes, c_1 and c_2 form a (1, 1; 1) linear code over $GF(2)$. Although this code is formally expressed in a seven-dimensional linear vector space, six of the coordinates are unused. This code has no capability for error detection or correction. We briefly consider the possibility of unit-weight code words. For example,

$$c_1 = (1, 0, 0, 0, 0, 0, 0)$$

$$c_2 = (0, 1, 0, 0, 0, 0, 0)$$

$$c_3 = (0, 0, 1, 0, 0, 0, 0)$$

$$c_4 = (0, 0, 0, 1, 0, 0, 0)$$

$$c_5 = (0, 0, 0, 0, 1, 0, 0)$$

$$c_6 = (0, 0, 0, 0, 0, 1, 0)$$

$$c_7 = (0, 0, 0, 0, 0, 0, 1)$$

Now, all of the space coordinates are used. In fact, c_1 through c_7 form a basis in a seven-dimensional space over $GF(2)$. These vectors, however, do not form a linear code because they are linearly independent. No code word can be expressed as a linear combination of any of the others. In fact, c_1 through c_7 form a basis for the space $GF(2)^7$. Linear independence forces us to dismiss this choice of unit-weight code words.

There are two constraints that determine the composition of a linear code. The first is that the code must use all available dimensions, i.e., places in the n-tuple representation. This prevents the code from having unused dimensions. Each of the code's dimension must be used somewhere in at least one of the code words. This restriction applies to both linear as well as to nonlinear codes. The other requirement is that the code be linear and further restricts the choice of code words.

In considering code words of weight 2, we again can eliminate many candidates with the linearity criterion. A moment's consideration will suffice to see that by the same token, their binary complements can also be eliminated. This leaves possible code words of weight 3 and 4. In fact, we have already seen that the Hamming (7, 4; 3) code over $GF(2)$ consists of $c_1 = (0, 0, 0, 0, 0, 0, 0)$, $c_{16} = (1, 1, 1, 1, 1, 1, 1)$, seven code words of weight 3 and their binary complements: seven code words of weight 4. A second look at Table 7-3 for the weight distribution of the binary Hamming (7, 4; 3) code shows that most of the code word weights are chosen from the center of the weight distribution, i.e., around $w(c_j) \approx \frac{1}{2}n$. This is also true for the Golay (23, 12; 7) code, whose weight distribution is given in Table 7-4. For a linear code, it makes sense to start selecting code words from the middle of the weight distribution. These codes exhibit a symmetry about $w(c_j) \approx \frac{1}{2}n$ in their weight distribution. With the exception of the maximally distant all-zeros and all-ones code words, the code-word weight table fills from the middle out, reducing the minimum available code distance as more and more code words are introduced to fill the linear code space.

Although the preceding discussion does not constitute a mathematical proof, a case is made for the use of linear codes. The fact that the sum of two code words must also be a code word ensures that the linear space is filled more or less uniformly with code words spaced apart by a distance that is at least equal to the weight of the minimum-weight code word. In fact, the minimum-weight code word serves as a natural unit of length that determines the spacing between code words.

The minimum code-word weight in a linear code again emerges as the important element. Upper and lower bounds can be found for the minimum distance of a linear code. These bounds are plotted in Fig. 7-19 and are discussed in [Ma 77] and [Pe 72]. Only the principal results are reviewed and presented here without proof. For a more detailed discussion, the reader is referred to these references.

The minimum distance of a linear $(n, k; d_{\min})$ code over $GF(q)$ is upper bounded by the code's average code-word weight:

$$d_{\min} \leq n q^{k-1}(q - 1)/(q^k - 1) \tag{7.41}$$

This is the *Plotkin bound*, a loose upper bound on the minimum distance. The Plotkin bound places an upper limit on the error-detecting and -correcting capability of a linear code with a given rate. This and other bounds appear in asymptotic form for very large n in Fig 7-19. The code rate k/n varies from $1/n$ to 1 corresponding to minimum distances ranging from n to 0.

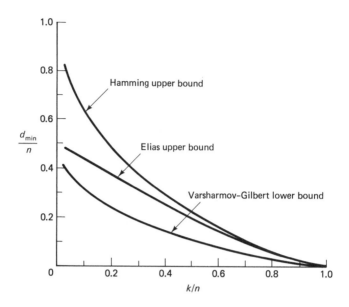

Figure 7-19.   Bounds on the minimum distance for binary block codes.

The Hamming bound of Section 7.1.4 is

$$2^{n-k} \geq \sum_{m=0}^{t} \binom{n}{m} \tag{7.42}$$

where t is the maximum number of correctable errors can also be used to upper bound a code's minimum distance. This inequality can easily be generalized for codes over $GF(q)$:

$$n - k \geq \log_q \sum_{m=0}^{t} \binom{n}{m} (q-1)^m \tag{7.43}$$

The discussion of Section 7.1.4 introducing the Hamming bound is quite general, and this bound is also valid for nonlinear codes. This bound is equivalent to a bound on the minimum distance by setting $t = [\frac{1}{2}(d_{\min} - 1)]$. It can be shown [Pe 72] that asymptotically (as $n \to \infty$), the ratio t/n for a linear block code is upper bounded by a quantity α that satisfies the equation

$$n - k = nh(\alpha)$$

where $h(\alpha) = -\alpha \log \alpha - (1 - \alpha) \log (1 - \alpha)$.

A tighter upper bound is provided by the *Elias bound*:

$$d_{\min} \leq 2t(1 - t/n)\left(\frac{\beta}{\beta - 1}\right) \tag{7.44}$$

where t satisfies

$$\sum_{m=0}^{t} \binom{n}{m} > 2^{n-k}$$

and where β is the smallest integer satisfying

$$\sum_{m=0}^{t} \binom{n}{m} \leq \beta 2^{n-k}$$

For large n, the asymptotic form of the Elias bound is

$$d_{\min} \leq 2n\alpha(1-\alpha) \qquad (7.45)$$

where α satisfies the relation $n - k = nh(\alpha)$ [Pe 72].

The minimum distance of a linear code can also be lower bounded. An important lower bound for the minimum distance is the *Varsharmov–Gilbert* bound, which maintains that there exists a linear code over $GF(q)$ with minimum distance $d_{\min}$ for which the following inequality is satisfied:

$$\sum_{m=0}^{d_{\min}-2} \binom{n}{m}(q-1)^{m} \geq q^{n-k} \qquad (7.46)$$

For large n, the following asymptotic formula may be obtained [Pe 72]:

$$n - k \leq nh[(d_{\min} - 2)/n] \qquad (7.47)$$

The minimum-distance bounds shown in Fig. 7-19 all apply to linear codes. Many, however, also apply to nonlinear codes. As a class, linear codes have minimum distances lower bounded by the Varsharmov–Gilbert bound and upper bounded by the Elias bound. In particular, the Varsharmov–Gilbert lower bound guarantees a nonzero minimum distance for a linear code.

EXAMPLE

Let us apply the Varsharmov–Gilbert bound to linear block codes over $GF(2)$. For $n = 7$ and $k = 4$, we have $2^{n-k} = 2^{3} = 8$ and the smallest value of d satisfying the inequality

$$\sum_{m=0}^{d-2} \binom{n}{m} \geq 8$$

is $d = 3$. An example of such a code is the binary Hamming (7, 4; 3) code.

With $n = 23$ and $k = 12$, we have $2^{n-k} = 2^{11} = 2048$ and the smallest value of d satisfying the inequality is 5 since

$$\binom{23}{0} + \binom{23}{1} + \binom{23}{2} + \binom{23}{3} = 2048$$

The algebraic structure of linear codes, namely, their linearity, is a rich source of codes with useful minimum distances. A general theory of linear codes can be built on the mathematical foundation of linear vector spaces over $GF(q)$.

7.2.2 Polynomial Description of Codes

The traditional approach to algebraic coding theory starts with a discussion of algebraic field and linear vector-space properties, and eventually arrives at a description of cyclic codes, which are then shown to have error-control properties. This approach is attractive from a purely mathematical point of view, but gives the strange impression that codes are born fully grown from the algebraic structure, and leaves little in the way of motivating the reader along the way as to why the mathematical development is proceeding in this particular direction. The result is a description of cyclic error-control codes, but a lot of mathematics has to be digested before the end product can be appreciated. This may leave the totally erroneous impression that algebraic coding theory is an esoteric or difficult subject.

The fundamental idea behind linear codes is extremely simple. We start with a simple but somewhat rough analogy using integers that will serve to illustrate our approach. This analogy will point out the properties required of a code. It will then be a simple matter to look for these properties in algebraic structures to arrive at the properties of a code.

The development of the guiding analogy starts with the need for an $(n, k; d_{min})$ code for error control. Implied in this statement is the need for redundancy: a code over $GF(q)$ consists of q^k symbol code words chosen among q^n vectors in an n-dimensional linear vector space. A typical n-tuple $\mathbf{x}$ may be expressed as the sum of the nearest code-word vector $\mathbf{c}$ and an error vector $\mathbf{r}$:

$$\mathbf{x} = \mathbf{c} + \mathbf{r}$$

This is suggestive of a linear vector space in which every vector $\mathbf{x}$ is in the neighborhood of some code word $\mathbf{c}$. We can partition the space into neighborhoods of error patterns about each of the code words. The receiver decodes an n-tuple by selecting the nearest code word. If an error pattern is within the error-correcting radius of a code word, i.e., within less than half the code's minimum distance from the transmitted code word, then correct decoding will occur. Any means of determining $\mathbf{r}$ is equivalent to decoding since $\mathbf{c} = \mathbf{x} - \mathbf{r}$.

There is a suggestive similarity between this and the following problem: given an integer a, find the closest multiple of another integer g. The analogy we are trying to make is that "code words" are the multiples $c = d \cdot g$ of g and that a received signal is a number a that may differ from c by some quantity e, which represents the magnitude of the error: $a = c + e$. For example, if "code words" are the multiples of $g = 5$, then the number $a = 19$ is decoded into the "code word" 20 since 20 is the closest "code word" to 19, corresponding to the smallest error magnitude of 1. Note that code word 15 could have been transmitted and received with an error $e = 4$. This and similar cases, however, result in ambiguities that cannot be resolved from a measurement of a alone. Minimum-distance decoding always gives the right answer as long as the error pattern is within the decoding radius of the code, which in this case is 2.

This arithmetic analogy with remaindering can be recast in the language of vectors used as communication waveforms. From what we know of communication signals as vectors in a linear signal space, we would like to distribute code words more or less uniformly over the space, with as much distance between them as possible. One way to do this is to use a particular vector g as a starting point and generate from it all other code words. We require each code word c to be a "multiple" $d \cdot g$ of the generating code word g, with the full meaning of the word "multiple" to be explained in the following paragraph. To see if a received signal a is a code word, it suffices to determine if it is a multiple of the generating vector. If it is not, the remainder, or *residue* after division by g, can be uniquely related to the nearest code word if the error pattern is within the correcting radius of the code.

We now relate this coding problem to the residue algebra over a finite field. Our simple analogy relies on addition, subtraction, multiplication, and division of quantities. However, multiplication and division between two vectors is not defined. This is where the concepts of base and extension fields come into play. There is a one-to-one correspondence between vectors over the base field $GF(q)$ in an n-dimensional linear vector space and the q^n elements of the extension field $GF(q^n)$. The code words are a subset of the n-dimensional vectors over $GF(q)$. We saw in Chapter 2 that these vectors can be represented as n-tuples over $GF(q)$. Equivalently, they can be represented as polynomials of degree $n - 1$ with coefficients from $GF(q)$.

We can express vectors over $GF(q)$ as polynomials of degree $n - 1$ with coefficients from $GF(q)$. Addition is done term by term with addition over $GF(q)$. Multiplication is polynomial multiplication, where closure is established by remaindering modulo a polynomial $m(x)$ of degree n. This allows us to view coded communication waveforms either as vectors over $GF(q)$ or as a set of some of the field elements from $GF(q^n)$. The latter view is more computationally convenient since we can apply the concept of multiplication, division, and remaindering.

The procedure of generating an extension field $GF(q^n)$ from the base field $GF(q)$ assigns a one-to-one equivalence between vectors over $GF(q)$ and the scalars from $GF(q^n)$. This allows us to perform any desired algebraic operation (addition, subtraction, multiplication, and division) in the field $GF(q^n)$, keeping in mind that the elements of $GF(q^n)$ are really labels for vectors over $GF(q)$. If $m(x)$ is irreducible over $GF(q)$, then polynomial reduction modulo $m(x)$ produces the entire extension field $GF(q^n)$, the largest extension that can be produced in this manner from $GF(q)$. In general, $m(x)$ can be composite, and each of its irreducible factors can generate an extension field of its own, whose elements can be labeled with a subset of the elements of $GF(q^n)$.

We now have enough material to start building codes over $GF(q)$. We shall express field elements of $GF(q^n)$ as polynomials of degree $n - 1$ over $GF(q)$. A typical code word may thus be expressed as

$$c(x) = c_{n-1}x^{n-1} + c_{n-2}x^{n-2} + \cdots + c_1 x + c_0 \tag{7.48}$$

We refer to this as a *code word polynomial*. The coefficients $c_{n-1}, c_{n-2}, \ldots, c_0$ are elements from the base field $GF(q)$. Addition in the polynomial field is simply addition over $GF(q)$ of coefficients of like powers of x. Multiplication is done modulo some polynomial $m(x)$ of degree n. Code words are multiples of a *generating polynomial* $g(x)$

$$g(x) = g_{n-k-1}x^{n-k-1} + g_{n-k-2}x^{n-k-2} + \cdots + g_1 x + g_0 \tag{7.49}$$

Since we require that the code words form a field, the product of any two code words, expressed as polynomials modulo $m(x)$, must also be a code word polynomial and, therefore, be divisible by $g(x)$. For closure under polynomial multiplication modulo $m(x)$ to hold, $g(x)$ must divide $m(x)$. The modulus polynomial must, therefore, be of the form

$$m(x) = g(x)h(x) \tag{7.50}$$

A code-word polynomial $c(x)$ is a multiple of some generator polynomial $g(x)$. The number of multiples of $g(x)$ in $GF(q^n)$ is simply the total number q^k of code words. We are, therefore, looking for the q^k multiples of $g(x)$ that result in polynomials of degree $n - 1$. We start by writing $c(x)$ as the product of $g(x)$ and some other polynomial $d(x)$, which we call the *data polynomial*:

$$d(x) = d_{k-1}x^{k-1} + d_{k-2}x^{k-2} + \cdots + d_1x + d_0 \tag{7.51}$$

The data polynomial coefficients d_j are scalars freely chosen from $GF(q)$, resulting in q^k possible data polynomials. The data polynomials are labels for the q^k information symbols. They can be represented by polynomials of degree $k - 1$ or less. A code-word polynomial may, therefore, be written as

$$c(x) = d(x)g(x) \tag{7.52}$$

Both sides of the equation are polynomials of like degree. It follows, therefore, that the degree of the generator polynomial must be $(n - 1) - (k - 1) = n - k$.

EXAMPLE

The Hamming (7, 4; 3) code can be constructed with the generator polynomial $g(x) = x^3 + x^2 + 1$ over $GF(2)$, as shown in Table 7-7.

The resulting binary 7-tuples all appear, albeit in a different order, in an example in Section 7.1.1.

TABLE 7-7. CONSTRUCTION OF THE BINARY HAMMING (7, 4; 3) CODE FROM GENERATOR POLYNOMIAL $g(x) = x^3 + x^2 + 1$

$d(x)$	$d(x)g(x)$	Binary 7-tuple
0	0	0000000
1	$x^3 + x^2 + 1$	0001101
x	$x^4 + x^3 + x$	0011010
$x + 1$	$x^4 + x^2 + x + 1$	0010111
x^2	$x^5 + x^4 + x^2$	0110100
$x^2 + 1$	$x^5 + x^4 + x^3 + 1$	0111001
$x^2 + x$	$x^5 + x^3 + x^2 + x$	0101110
$x^2 + x + 1$	$x^5 + x + 1$	0100011
x^3	$x^6 + x^5 + x^3$	1101000
$x^3 + 1$	$x^6 + x^5 + x^2 + 1$	1100101
$x^3 + x$	$x^6 + x^5 + x^4 + x$	1110010
$x^3 + x + 1$	$x^6 + x^5 + x^4 + x^3 + x^2 + x + 1$	1111111
$x^3 + x^2$	$x^6 + x^4 + 1$	1010001
$x^3 + x^2 + 1$	$x^6 + x^4 + x^3 + x^2$	1011100
$x^3 + x^2 + x + 1$	$x^6 + x^2 + x$	1000110

The simplest way to encode is by polynomial multiplication. A data polynomial $d(x)$ of degree not exceeding $k - 1$ is multiplied by a generating polynomial $g(x)$ of degree $n - k$. This always produces a code word of degree not exceeding $n - 1$. This approach to encoding does not really require the use of a modulus polynomial $m(x)$ to ensure closure under polynomial multiplication by reducing the degree of the resulting product polynomial to less than n.

This encoding procedure is easily implemented with linear shift register circuitry. Note that polynomial multiplication is equivalent to the convolution of the sequences of polynomial coefficients. Thus, if we multiply the polynomials

$$a(x) = a_m x^m + a_{m-1} x^{m-1} + \cdots + a_1 x + a_0$$

and   (7.53)

$$b(x) = b_n x^n + b_{n-1} x^{n-1} + \cdots + b_1 x + b_0$$

we obtain the product polynomial

$$c(x) = a(x)b(x) = (a_m b_n)x^{m+n} + \cdots + (a_0 b_1 + a_1 b_0)x + (a_0 b_0) \quad (7.54)$$

The coefficients of the product polynomial are identical to the terms resulting from the convolution of the polynomial coefficient sequences:

$$c_j = \sum_{i=0}^{m} a_i b_{j-i} = (a_0, a_1, \ldots, a_m) * (b_0, b_1, \ldots, b_n) \quad (7.55)$$

resulting in

$$c_0 = a_0 b_0$$

$$c_1 = a_0 b_1 + a_1 b_0$$

$$\cdot$$

$$\cdot \quad (7.56)$$

$$\cdot$$

$$c_{m+n} = a_m b_n$$

with the proviso that $b_j = 0$ for $j < 0$ and for $j > m$.

The close relationship between polynomial multiplication and convolution of polynomial coefficients is already familiar from the context of digital signal processing. The convolution of two signal sequences, a common filtering operation, is equivalent to the multiplication of the sequences' z-transforms, which are nothing more than polynomials in the variable z [Op 75, Ra 75].

The z-transform $A(z)$ of a sequence $\{a_j\}$ is a function of the complex variable z and is defined by the series

$$A(z) = \sum_{j=-\infty}^{\infty} a_j z^{-j} \quad (7.57)$$

when that series converges. The convolution of two sequences $\{a_j\}$ and $\{b_j\}$ is another sequence $\{c_j\}$ and can be written as

$$c_j = \sum_i a_i b_{j-i} \tag{7.58}$$

Multiplying both sides by z^{-j} and summing over all j, there results

$$C(z) = \sum_j c_j z^{-j} = \sum_{i,j} a_i b_{j-1} z^{-j}$$

$$= \sum_i a_i z^{-i} \sum_{j-i} b_{j-i} z^{-(j-i)}$$

$$= A(z)B(z) \tag{7.59}$$

Thus, the convolution of two sequences is equivalent to the product of their z-transforms, which are polynomials in z.

Any method that computes a convolution can also be used to compute polynomial multiplication. Convolution brings to mind linear finite impulse response filtering and suggests an implementation along the lines of a transversal filter. The linear feed-forward shift register circuit shown in Fig. 7-20(a) implements the convolution $c_j = \sum_i a_i b_{j-i}$, where the signal samples b_i and the filter coefficients a_i are, in general, scalars from any field. Each square box represents a unit time delay, and the circles are multiplications by the indicated field elements. This circuit is a delay-and-sum implementation and results in a convolution of the input sequence with the sequence of filter coefficients. If the convolution is over $GF(2)$, considerable simplification results because the filter coefficients are scalars from the set $\{0, 1\}$. Filter taps are needed only where $a_j = 1$. There are no taps where $a_j = 0$. The $GF(2)$ implementation is shown in Fig. 7-20(b).

Encoding by polynomial multiplication proceeds as follows. A code word polynomial $c(x)$ of degree $n - 1$ or less is formed by multiplying a data polynomial $d(x)$ of degree $k - 1$ or less with a generating polynomial $g(x)$ of degree $n - k$. We can implement this operation with the equivalent convolution:

$$c_j = \sum_{i=0}^{n-k-1} g_i d_{j-i} \tag{7.60}$$

The filter registers are initially set to zero. The data sequence $\{d_0, d_1, \ldots, d_{k-1}\}$ followed by a block of $n - k$ consecutive zeros is input to the encoding filter, as shown in Fig. 7-21. The filter outputs the code word polynomial, one coefficient at a time, in n consecutive clock cycles. This process may be repeated with new data by separating successive blocks of k data symbols by blocks of $n - k$ zeros. This produces one code word every n clock cycles. This encoding procedure is valid for any linear block code.

Note that the identity of the information symbols is not preserved by this encoding procedure. It is not possible to read directly the information symbols from a code word by inspection. Some processing is required before the data symbols are

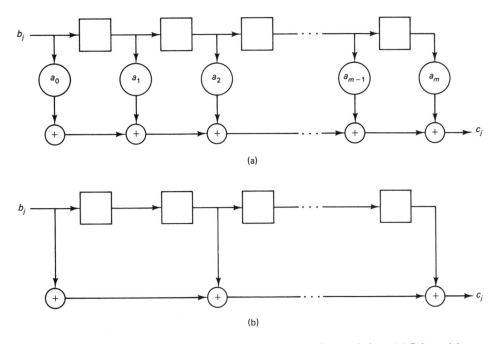

(a)

(b)

Figure 7-20. Circuits for polynomial multiplication through convolution. (a) Polynomial multiplication over an arbitrary field. The coefficients b_j are entered in the order b_0, b_1, ..., b_m so that the first multiplication to occur is $a_0 b_0$ and the last one is $a_m b_m$. (b) Polynomial multiplication over $GF(2)$.

available. In a signal-processing context, we are saying that deconvolution must be performed to retrieve the original signals. A code for which the information symbols do not directly appear in the code word is called *nonsystematic*. A code is *systematic* if k of the n coded symbols correspond directly to the information symbols. The Hamming $(7, 4; 3)$ code generated by multiplication by the polynomial $x^3 + x^2 + 1$ resulted in the nonsystematic code presented in earlier examples. Whether a code is systematic or not has no effect on its error-control performance.

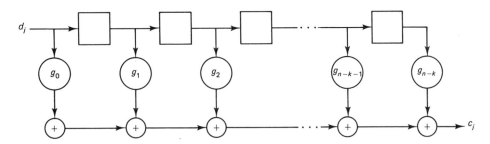

Figure 7-21. Nonsystematic encoding by polynomial multiplication by $g(x)$. The polynomial multiplication is implemented as a convolution.

It is also possible to encode systematically. The idea is extremely simple. We first multiply the data polynomial by x^{n-k}. This produces a polynomial of degree not exceeding $n-1$ and for which the coefficients of x^0 through x^{n-k-1} are all zero:

$$x^{n-k}d(x) = d_{k-1}x^{n-1} + \cdots + d_0 x^{n-k} + 0x^{n-k-1} + \cdots + 0x + 0 \quad (7.61)$$

This polynomial provides the highest powers of x in the code-word polynomial $c(x)$ we seek. The remaining lower $n-k$ coefficients of $c(x)$ are determined from the requirement that $c(x)$ be a multiple of the generating polynomial $g(x)$. Let us denote the polynomial of degree $n-k$ corresponding to the $n-k$ lowest powers of x terms of $c(x)$ by $p(x)$. We then have

$$c(x) = x^{n-k}d(x) + p(x) = a(x)g(x) \quad (7.62)$$

since a code word must be a multiple of $g(x)$. Rearranging terms, we have

$$x^{n-k}d(x) = a(x)g(x) - p(x) \quad (7.63)$$

and $-p(x)$ is recognized as being the remainder resulting from dividing $x^{n-k}d(x)$ by $g(x)$.

To encode systematically, we must, therefore, first multiply the data polynomial $d(x)$ by x^{n-k}. In an n-tuple representation, this is equivalent to shifting the data symbols by $n-k$ places. The remaining $n-k$ places correspond to $-p(x)$, the negative of the polynomial obtained after dividing $x^{n-k}d(x)$ by $g(x)$.

We saw earlier that the nonsystematic encoder can be implemented by a linear feed-forward shift register circuit that calculates the product of two polynomials through convolution or linear filtering. Similarly, a systematic encoder that follows the algorithm just described can be implemented with a linear feedback shift register circuit that performs polynomial division.

Consider the linear feedback shift register circuit shown in Fig. 7-22. The output of this filter can be written as

$$c_k = \sum_{j=1}^{m} b_j c_{k-j} + a_k \quad (7.64)$$

Multiplying both sides by z^{-k} and summing over all k, there results

$$C(z) = \sum_k c_k z^{-k} = \sum_{j,k} b_j c_{k-j} z^{-k} + \sum_k a_k z^{-k}$$

$$= \sum_j b_j \sum_k c_{k-j} z^{-k} + A(z)$$

$$= \sum_j b_j z^{-j} \sum_{k-j} c_{k-j} z^{-(k-j)} + A(z)$$

$$= B(z)C(z) + A(z) \quad (7.65)$$

so that

$$C(z) = \frac{A(z)}{1 - B(z)} \qquad (7.66)$$

The z-transform of the filter output can be expressed as the ratio of two polynomials.

To encode systematically, the procedure illustrated in Fig. 7-23 is used. Data are entered on the input line marked d_k and consist of k scalars from $GF(q)$ followed by $n - k$ zeros. The line labeled "Output" provides the systematic part of the code word during the first k clock cycles, and the remainder modulo $g(x)$ during the last $n - k$ cycles.

We now begin our discussion of the decoding process in terms of the algebraic properties of codes. Whether systematic or nonsystematic, encoding produces code-word polynomials that are multiples of some generating polynomial $g(x)$. We have already discussed decoding in general terms. We presently extend this discussion a little further, but without getting involved with the mechanical details of decoding specific codes.

A received n-tuple can be described either as an n-dimensional vector over $GF(q)$ or as a field element of an extension field $GF(q^n)$. We take the latter view and, as in our discussion of encoding, use the polynomial representation for the scalars of $GF(q^n)$. We view the transmission process over a channel as introducing errors in the received signal polynomial $b(x)$, causing it to differ from the transmitted code word $c(x)$ by some additive error polynomial $e(x)$:

$$b(x) = c(x) + e(x) = a(x)g(x) + e(x) \qquad (7.67)$$

since $c(x)$ is a multiple of $g(x)$. In $GF(2)$, the error pattern can be described as a binary n-tuple with ones at places where bits were received in error. In general, the weight of the error pattern is equal to the number of code-word symbols received in error.

Decoding is based on the divisibility properties of the received polynomial $b(x)$. This divisibility can be tested with linear shift register circuits similar to those described earlier in this section. We are specifically interested in whether or not

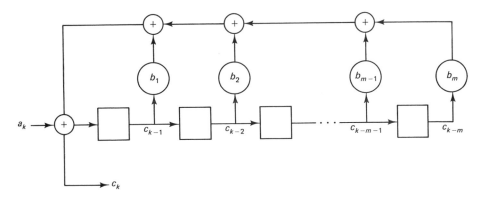

Figure 7-22.   Linear feedback shift register circuit for polynomial division.

$b(x)$ is divisible by $g(x)$. If $g(x)$ divides $b(x)$, then the remainder upon such a division must be zero. We take this as an indication that no channel transmission error has occurred. For this case, $b(x)$ is taken to be the transmitted code-word polynomial and decoding is complete.

Note that an error polynomial that coincides with one of the code words results in $b(x)$ being divisible by $g(x)$, even though a transmission error has occurred. This corresponds to undetectable errors, against which any code is powerless. If the remainder after dividing $b(x)$ by $g(x)$ is not the zero polynomial, then an error has been detected and we must examine the situation in more detail.

An arbitrary field element $b(x)$ can be expressed as the sum of a multiple of $g(x)$ plus some remainder $r(x)$:

$$b(x) = f(x)g(x) + r(x) \tag{7.68}$$

The degree of the remainder polynomial $r(x)$ must necessarily be less than the degree of the generator polynomial $g(x)$, which is $n - k$. The degree of $r(x)$ can be at most $n - k - 1$, because a polynomial of degree $n - k$ can be divided by $g(x)$ to yield a remainder of degree less than that of $g(x)$. The largest possible degree for the remainder polynomial $r(x)$ is, therefore, $n - k - 1$. There are q^{n-k} such polynomials over $GF(q)$. They can, therefore, be used to label q^{n-k} error patterns. Viewed as $(n - k)$-tuples over $GF(q)$, the remainder polynomials represent vectors with Hamming weight less than $n - k$. The remainder polynomials themselves are not the error patterns, since an error can occur in any of the n components of the code word, and not just those corresponding to polynomials of degree less than $n - k - 1$. The remainder polynomials are, in general, not the error polynomials themselves, but they can be used as unique labels for some of the errors that have occurred during transmission. For this reason, we shall refer to the remainder polynomial $r(x)$ as the *syndrome polynomial*, or, simply, the *syndrome*.

There are at most q^{n-k} syndromes, and these are not sufficient to unambiguously label all possible error patterns. In fact, since $q^n = q^k \cdot q^{n-k}$, we can allocate at most q^{n-k} syndromes to each of the q^k code words. Since there are only q^{n-k}

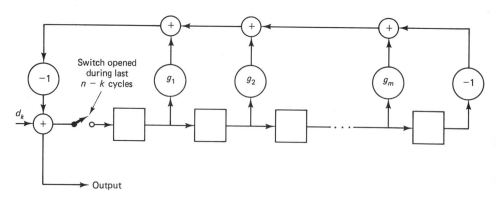

Figure 7-23. Systematic encoder using polynomial division by $g(x)$.

syndromes in all, the same set of syndromes must be reused for each code word, forcing decoding to be to the nearest code word. This results in correct decoding only if the received signal is within the decoding radius of the code. We can, therefore, decode only in the presence of the least severe error patterns, i.e., those which have the least weight, and assign (label) a unique syndrome to each correctable pattern.

The syndrome $r(x) = 0$ corresponds to the case of no transmission errors. There is only one such possibility. The least-weight error vectors correspond to an error polynomial with only one term or, equivalently, to an n-tuple over $GF(q)$ with only one nonzero entry. There are $\binom{n}{1}(q - 1)$ such possibilities, and these use up $\binom{n}{1}(q - 1)$ of the remaining syndromes. The next set of error patterns with the least weight have weight equal to 2. These can be described by error polynomials having two nonzero coefficients. There are $\binom{n}{2}(q - 1)^2$ such patterns, and these reduce the stock of available syndromes by a like amount. We can continue in this manner, enumerating error patterns of least weight, until all of the q^{n-k} syndromes are exhausted. In general, considering all error patterns with weight not exceeding t, we arrive at a familiar result, the Hamming bound:

$$\sum_{j=0}^{t} \binom{n}{j}(q - 1)^j \leq q^{n-k} \qquad (7.69)$$

By the use of a simple counting argument, we have shown that there is a sufficient number of syndromes to assign one to each of the error patterns with weight not exceeding a parameter t satisfying the Hamming bound. We will show that it is possible to label all such correctable error patterns with a unique syndrome.

We now prove the simple but important result that the syndrome depends only on the error pattern and not on the particular transmitted code word. The received signal can be represented in polynomial form that is expressed as the sum of a code word $f(x)g(x)$ and an error polynomial $e(x)$:

$$b(x) = f(x)g(x) + e(x) \qquad (7.70)$$

where $f(x)$ is a polynomial of degree $k - 1$ or less, and $e(x)$ is a polynomial of degree $n - 1$ or less. The first term on the right-hand side of Eq. (7.70) leaves no remainder upon division by $g(x)$. It follows, therefore, that $b(x)$ and $e(x)$ share the same residue modulo $g(x)$, namely, the syndrome polynomial $r(x)$.

It now remains to be shown that there is a one-to-one relationship between each of the syndromes and each of the correctable error patterns. This does not produce a specific decoding procedure, but shows that such a procedure exists. It is beyond the scope of this work to describe specific decoding algorithms and to discuss their computational efficiencies. We will prove, however, the important fact that the syndrome contains sufficient information to decode to the nearest code word.

"Nearest" in this context refers to the Hamming distance, which is the number of coefficients by which two polynomials differ. We are restricted to error polynomials having t or fewer symbol errors, where $t = w(\mathbf{e}) \leq [\frac{1}{2}(d_{min} - 1)]$. We show that a unique syndrome can be assigned to each such correctable error pattern. We arrive at this result through a method called *coset decomposition* of the elements of

$GF(q^n)$. For this discussion, it may help to visualize the received signals as n-tuples over $GF(q)$. Coset decomposition arranges all possible received n-tuples into a table having the property that the elements belonging to the same column are decoded into the same code word.

To construct this table, we first list all of the code words to form the top row. The leftmost element is the zero code word $c_1 = 0$. The other code words may appear in any order. To form the second row, we choose any element that has not previously appeared in the table and place it in the leftmost column, below c_1. The remaining column entries are determined by adding that element to the code word appearing at the top of the column. For each remaining row, we again select an element that has not been previously picked and repeat the procedure until all elements are exhausted. The result, called the *standard array*, is shown in Fig. 7-24. Each row of the standard array is called a *coset*, and the leftmost element of a coset is called the *coset leader*.

The first row of the standard array consists entirely of code words. Each other row consists of terms that are sums of a code word and some other pattern equal to the coset leader, and, therefore, represents some possibility for a received pattern. Every coset of the standard array consists of the same pattern added to a different code word. All of the elements from the same coset, therefore, share the same syndrome. There are q^k such elements, one for each code word.

We now introduce some of the important properties of the standard array. The first result is that there are no duplications in array elements: each element is unique. The standard array, therefore, lists all possible n-tuples over $GF(q)$ or, equivalently, all of the elements of $GF(q^n)$. The elements of any coset in the standard array are all distinct. This follows from the construction of the standard array, where the same coset leader is added to a different code word to form the elements of a coset. Two identical elements from the same coset would imply that the two corresponding code words at the top of the columns are equal, in contradiction with the array construction method.

We also have the result that any given element appears in only one of the cosets. If this were not so, element $\mathbf{a}$ could be represented by $\mathbf{c}_i + \mathbf{e}_r$ in the rth coset and by $\mathbf{c}_j + \mathbf{e}_s$ in the sth coset. We would then have $\mathbf{a} = \mathbf{c}_i + \mathbf{e}_r = \mathbf{c}_j + \mathbf{e}_s$, from which $\mathbf{e}_r = (\mathbf{c}_j - \mathbf{c}_i) + \mathbf{e}_s = \mathbf{c}_k + \mathbf{e}_s$, which implies the reuse of an element as a coset leader, in contradiction with the assumed construction method.

$\mathbf{c}_1 = 0$	$\mathbf{c}_2$	$\mathbf{c}_3$	$\cdots$	$\mathbf{c}_{q^k}$
$\mathbf{e}_2$	$\mathbf{c}_2 + \mathbf{e}_2$	$\mathbf{c}_3 + \mathbf{e}_2$	$\cdots$	$\mathbf{c}_{q^k} + \mathbf{e}_2$
.	.	.	.	.
.	.	.	.	.
.	.	.	.	.
$\mathbf{e}_{q^{n-k}}$	$\mathbf{c}_2 + \mathbf{e}_{q^{n-k}}$	$\mathbf{c}_3 + \mathbf{e}_{q^{n-k}}$	$\cdots$	$\mathbf{c}_{q^k} + \mathbf{e}_{q^{n-k}}$

Figure 7-24.   The standard array.

Since an element can appear in only one coset, and since all coset elements are distinct, the standard array consists of $q^{n-k} \cdot q^k = q^n$ distinct elements, which must be all of the elements of $GF(q^n)$.

We can consider the coset leaders to correspond to error patterns. Each entry in the standard array can be uniquely identified by a code word and an error pattern. Note that q^{n-k} elements are decoded in each code word. By choosing the coset leaders to correspond to error patterns having minimum weight, minimum metric distance decoding is implemented. We now show that this is always possible.

In choosing the coset leaders to correspond to error patterns of least weight, the standard array can be used as a table for minimum-distance decoding. Each column contains elements that are within a certain decoding distance of the corresponding code word. All q^n possible received patterns are decoded into the nearest code word.

For minimum-distance decoding, we choose as coset leaders error patterns having minimum weight. We can easily show that each coset contains at most one pattern with weight not exceeding $t = [\frac{1}{2}(d_{\min} - 1)]$. These are the correctable patterns we use as coset leaders. If two members of the same coset each had weight not exceeding $t = [\frac{1}{2}(d_{\min} - 1)]$, then their difference must be a code word since they share the same error pattern and since the difference between two code words is another code word. However, the difference between two patterns, each having weight not exceeding t, is itself a pattern whose weight cannot exceed $2t < d_{\min}$. This contradicts the fact that the resulting code word must have a weight at least equal to $d_{\min}$. Therefore, there can be at most one coset element with weight not exceeding $t = [\frac{1}{2}(d_{\min} - 1)]$.

Going down the list of cosets, we choose as coset leaders those coset members having the least weight and end up with a set of coset leaders that describes all vectors with weight $t \le [\frac{1}{2}(d_{\min} - 1)]$. These error patterns are guaranteed to be correctable. A unique syndrome can be assigned to each. In addition, a few more patterns may be correctable, depending on the code.

While we have developed the standard array in terms of code words and added error patterns, a similar development exists for code word, error, and syndrome polynomials. All members of the same coset share the same syndrome polynomial since they have in common the same error pattern. Furthermore, no two cosets can share the same syndrome, for this would imply that the corresponding coset leaders differ by a code word: $\mathbf{e}_r = \mathbf{c}_k + \mathbf{e}_s$, and that the rth coset leader is a reuse of a previous array element, contrary to the assumed construction procedure. Each coset leader, therefore, has a distinct syndrome polynomial.

7.2.3 Cyclic Codes

Our discussion of error-control codes began with general properties of codes. We then restricted our study to linear codes, which have useful algebraic properties. Linear codes are a subset of all codes and can be simply implemented using linear shift register circuitry. Moreover, a theory of linear codes can be built on the properties of finite fields. We now introduce a further restriction on linear codes. There is a particular subset of linear codes that lends itself to an elegant theoretical description using algebraic field theory and that can easily be implemented in digital circuitry. These are the cyclic codes.

A *cyclic code* has the following two properties:

1. the code is linear, and

2. any cyclic permutation of the code word symbols is also a code word.

The second condition means that if the code word, in n-tuple representation, is given by

$$c = (c_{n-1}, c_{n-2}, \ldots, c_1, c_0) \tag{7.71}$$

then each of the $n - 1$ cyclic shifts of c,

$$(c_{n-2}, c_{n-3}, \ldots, c_1, c_0, c_{n-1})$$
$$(c_{n-3}, c_{n-4}, \ldots, c_0, c_{n-1}, c_{n-2})$$

.

.

.

$$(c_0, c_{n-1}, \ldots, c_3, c_2, c_1)$$

is also a code word. The polynomial representation of cyclic codes is particularly simple and useful. Thus, if $c(x)$ is the code word polynomial

$$c(x) = c_{n-1}x^{n-1} + c_{n-2}x^{n-2} + \cdots + c_1x + c_0 \tag{7.72}$$

then the first left cyclic shift of $c(x)$ is

$$c^{(1)}(x) = c_{n-2}x^{n-1} + c_{n-3}x^{n-2} + \cdots + c_0x + c_{n-1} \tag{7.73}$$

Note that this can be written as $xc(x)$ modulo $(x^n - 1)$. The modulus polynomial has the form $m(x) = x^n - 1$ for a cyclic code. This establishes a congruence between the pairs x^n and $x^0 = 1$, x^{n+1} and x, x^{n+2} and x^2, and so on. Similarly, the next three left cyclic shifts are

$$c^{(2)}(x) = c_{n-3}x^{n-1} + c_{n-4}x^n + \cdots + c_{n-1}x + c_{n-2}$$
$$c^{(3)}(x) = c_{n-4}x^{n-1} + c_{n-5}x^n + \cdots + c_{n-2}x + c_{n-3}$$
$$c^{(4)}(x) = c_{n-5}x^{n-1} + c_{n-6}x^n + \cdots + c_{n-3}x + c_{n-4}$$

In general, the jth cyclic shift of $c(x)$ is simply

$$c^{(j)}(x) = c_{n-j-1}x^{n-1} + c_{n-j-2}x^n + \cdots + c_{n-j+1}x + c_{n-j} \tag{7.74}$$

and can be expressed as $x^j c(x)$ modulo $(x^n - 1)$. In a cyclic code, $x^j c(x)$ modulo $(x^n - 1)$ is a code word polynomial whenever $c(x)$ is a code word polynomial.

The motivation for using cyclic codes is purely practical. In the previous section, we have shown that each of the q^{n-k} syndromes can be uniquely associated with a correctable error pattern. We also found that the standard array could be used as a decoding table. We were not concerned with practical implementation, as our task was to present the conditions under which decoding is possible. The practicality of this approach decreases with code length, since the decoding complexity increases combinatorially. Algorithms whose complexity increases only linearly with code length can be developed if a further restriction is imposed on the code. This restriction is that the code be cyclic. Although we do not intend to discuss encoding and decoding techniques for cyclic codes, we will present a brief summary of their algebraic properties. For a more detailed discussion of cyclic codes, the reader should consult [Bl 83, Li 83, Ma 77, Ma 87, Mi 85, Pe 72].

The form of the modulus polynomial for cyclic codes imposes a restriction on the choice of generator polynomials. Recall that the generator polynomial must divide the modulus polynomial, i.e., that $m(x) = g(x)h(x)$. For a cyclic code, this restriction takes the form

$$g(x)h(x) = x^n - 1 \tag{7.75}$$

Hence, the task of generating a cyclic code starts with the task of factoring the monic polynomial $x^n - 1$ into irreducible polynomials over $GF(q)$. Since factoring is equivalent to finding the roots of a polynomial, we shall also see that roots of $x^n - 1$ in $GF(q^n)$ play a special part in the description of cyclic codes.

The modulus polynomial $x^n - 1$ can be factored as follows:

$$x^n - 1 = p_1(x)p_2(x) \cdots p_r(x) \tag{7.76}$$

in terms of prime polynomials. It is always possible to factor a polynomial in this fashion, and the factorization is unique, except for the unimportant order in which the prime polynomial factors appear in the product. We remind the reader that all these polynomials are over $GF(q)$. It is immediately apparent that a generating polynomial $g(x)$ for a cyclic code must be expressible as the product of these same prime polynomials since $g(x)$ divides $x^n - 1$. In general, there are several ways of constructing $g(x)$ from the factors of $x^n - 1$. These correspond to choosing different combinations of $p_1(x)$ through $p_r(x)$ to compose $g(x)$.

We shall limit our study to codes whose block length $n = q^m - 1$ for some integer m. These block lengths are called *primitive block lengths*, and the corresponding codes are called *primitive cyclic codes*. We have already shown that a code can be described in terms of its generator polynomial $g(x)$. We shall now show that we can also describe a code in terms of the roots of $g(x)$ in $GF(q^n)$. This will eventually lead to a simple way of specifying the construction of cyclic codes.

Some of the results needed for this discussion come from number theory. We shall use these results without proving them. We do, however, inform the interested reader that many of the properties of finite fields can be better understood in the light of the theory of numbers. Those readers needing a more thorough understanding of algebraic coding theory will find time spent studying the theory of numbers to be amply rewarding. Many good texts have been written on this subject and [Da 83, Ha 85, Lo 72, Mc 72, St 52] are highly recommended.

The field $GF(q^m)$ has $n = q^m - 1$ nonzero elements that form a multiplicative group. Any element α of that multiplicative group has an order that divides $q^m - 1$. In other words, for any nonzero element α of $GF(q^m)$, we have $\alpha^n = 1$, where $n = q^m - 1$. Now consider the polynomial $x^n - 1$, where $n = q^m - 1$. This polynomial of degree n has $q^m - 1$ roots in $GF(q^m)$. These roots are precisely all the nonzero elements of $GF(q^m)$. We can, therefore, express $x^n - 1$ in a factored form that includes all of the elements of $GF(q^m)$ as linear terms and no other term:

$$x^n - 1 = (x - \alpha_1)(x - \alpha_2) \cdots (x - \alpha_n) \qquad \text{where } n = q^m - 1 \qquad (7.77)$$

The modulus polynomial can be expressed, therefore, entirely as a product of linear terms involving its roots, which are elements of $GF(q^m)$. This provides us with a new way of describing the modulus and generator polynomials. Up to this point, we had factored these polynomials in prime polynomials over the base field $GF(q)$. Now we can express these same polynomials as products of linear terms over $GF(q^m)$. In particular, we can choose $g(x)$ to have some particular set of roots $\{\alpha_1, \alpha_2, \ldots, \alpha_s\}$ over $GF(q^m)$:

$$g(x) = (x - \alpha_1)(x - \alpha_2) \cdots (x - \alpha_s) \qquad (7.78)$$

It follows that the roots $\{\alpha_1, \alpha_2, \ldots, \alpha_s\}$ of $g(x)$ are also roots of every code word in the code, since for every code-word polynomial $c(x)$, we have $c(x) = a(x)g(x)$, and, therefore,

$$c(\alpha_1) = c(\alpha_2) = \cdots = c(\alpha_s) = 0$$

Let us now combine these ideas. A generator polynomial can be expressed as a product of prime polynomials over $GF(q)$:

$$g(x) = p_1(x)p_2(x) \cdots p_s(x)$$

with each of the $p_j(x)$ being a divisor of $x^n - 1$. That being the case, it must be possible to factor each such $p_j(x)$ over $GF(q^m)$ in terms of the roots of $g(x)$ in $GF(q^m)$. That is, for each $p_j(x)$, we can write

$$p_j(x) = (x - \alpha_{j,1})(x - \alpha_{j,2}) \cdots (x - \alpha_{j,i}) \qquad (7.79)$$

The $p_j(x)$ are the polynomials of lowest degree in $GF(q^m)$ having $\{\alpha_{j,1}, \alpha_{j,2}, \ldots, \alpha_{j,i}\}$ as roots. Such polynomials have a special name. They are called *minimal polynomials*. The set of roots $\{\alpha_{j,1}, \alpha_{j,2}, \ldots, \alpha_{j,i}\}$ associated with each $p_j(x)$ is unique to that $p_j(x)$. This is because $p_j(x)$ divides $g(x)$, which in turn divides $x^n - 1$. All divisors of $x^n - 1$ can ultimately be expressed as a product of linear terms over $GF(q^m)$. Each of the linear terms $(x - \alpha_i)$ appears in one and only one of the $p_j(x)$.

It follows, therefore, that we can specify the generator polynomial $g(x)$ of a code (and, hence, the code itself) by specifying the roots $\{\alpha_{j,1}, \alpha_{j,2}, \ldots, \alpha_{j,i}\}$ of each of the minimal polynomials $p_j(x)$ that divides $g(x)$ over $GF(q^m)$. It turns out, however, that all of the roots of a minimal polynomial are interrelated and that specifying a single root suffices to specify $p_j(x)$.

This relation between the roots is very important and is stated without proof. If β is a root of a minimal polynomial $p(x)$ of degree m on $GF(q)$, then so is β^q. Repeated application of this fact reveals that the set of roots of $p(x)$ consists of $\{\beta, \beta^q, \beta^{q^2}, \ldots, \beta^{q^{m-1}}\}$. These are the m roots of $p(x)$, leading to the following factorization over $GF(q^m)$:

$$p_\beta(x) = (x - \beta)(x - \beta^q)(x - \beta^{q^2}) \cdots (x - \beta^{q^{m-1}}) \qquad (7.80)$$

We associate the root β with the minimal polynomial $p(x)$ and explicitly express this association with the notation $p_\beta(x)$. To each element β of $GF(q^m)$, there corresponds to a minimal polynomial $p_\beta(x)$. this polynomial is unique. The set of elements $\{\beta, \beta^q, \beta^{q^2}, \ldots, \beta^{q^{m-1}}\}$ has the same minimal polynomial. The members of such a set are called *conjugate* elements.

EXAMPLE

The polynomial $x^2 + 1$ cannot be factored over the field of real numbers **R**, but has the conjugate roots j and $-j$, where $j = (-1)^{1/2}$, over the complex field **C**. **R** serves as the base field and **C** as the extension induced by the polynomial $x^2 + 1$, which is irreducible over **R**.

We can now return to the description of cyclic codes. A cyclic code has a generator polynomial $g(x)$ that can now be written as

$$g(x) = p_{\beta_1}(x)p_{\beta_2}(x) \cdots p_{\beta_s}(x)$$

where $p_{\beta_j}(x)$ is the minimal polynomial corresponding to the element β_j of $GF(q^m)$. Some of these elements may be conjugates and share the same minimal polynomial. For this reason, the generator polynomial is usually required to be the least common multiple (LCM) of the set $\{p_{\beta_j}(x)\}$:

$$g(x) = \text{LCM} \, [p_{\beta_1}(x), \, p_{\beta_2}(x), \, \ldots, \, p_{\beta_s}(x)] \qquad (7.81)$$

Actually, any multiple of $g(x)$ can serve as the generator polynomial (see Prob. 7.5). We shall use, however, the last result and show in the following section that an important class of cyclic codes can be constructed by specifying the roots of its generator polynomial in $GF(q^m)$.

The polynomial corresponding to a received signal is

$$b(x) = c(x) + e(x) \qquad (7.82)$$

the sum of a code word and an error pattern. Since $c(x)$ vanishes at the roots $\{\beta_1, \beta_2, \ldots, \beta_s\}$ of $g(x)$, we can evaluate the received polynomial at those roots to get

$$b(\beta) = e(\beta) \qquad \text{for } \beta \in \{\beta_1, \beta_2, \ldots, \beta_s\} \qquad (7.83)$$

This is reminiscent of a syndrome. Evaluating $b(x)$ at the roots $\{\beta_1, \beta_2, \ldots, \beta_s\}$ of $g(x)$ results in the s quantities $\{e(\beta_1), e(\beta_2), \ldots, e(\beta_s)\}$ that depend only on the error pattern and not on the particular transmitted code word. This procedure gives us the error polynomial evaluated at s elements of $GF(q^m)$. If the error polynomial $e(x)$ can be determined from the $\{e(\beta_1), e(\beta_2), \ldots, e(\beta_s)\}$, then correction can be simply accomplished by subtracting it from the received pattern polynomial. Under certain conditions, a polynomial can be determined by its value at certain points. The roots of a generator polynomial are chosen so that these conditions are met. A full mathematical description would take us afar from the goal of this work, but the reader is referred to books covering coding theory and its applications such as [Bl 83, Li 83, Ma 77, Ma 87a, Mi 85, Pe 72] for the details.

7.2.4 Bose–Chaudhuri–Hocquenghem Codes

We are now in a position to construct cyclic codes. We shall illustrate this procedure with an important class of error-correcting codes. The Bose–Chaudhuri–Hocquenghem (BCH) codes are good examples of the application of algebraic coding theory. These codes are both of theoretical and practical importance. This family of codes illustrates well how the theoretical developments described thus far can be applied to the task of designing codes for correcting multiple errors. Several efficient algorithms have been developed for their decoding. The Hamming codes we have already encountered are a subset of the BCH codes.

The BCH codes are linear block codes of length $n = q^m - 1$ having $n - k = mt$ check symbols. These codes have a minimum distance bounded by $d_{\min} = 2t + 1$ and are capable of correcting up to t symbol errors per code word.

The design of BCH codes begins by choosing the block length n and the number t of errors to be corrected. Once these numbers have been selected, the procedure for designing the code is straightforward. Before describing the construction of BCH codes, let us pause and reflect on what can be considered intelligent choices for n and t.

Constructing the code gives us k, which, in turn, determines the code's rate k/n. There are two conflicting forces to be balanced in the selection of a code. One is the need to maximize the ability to correct errors. The other is the desire to minimize the price paid in redundancy (a reduction in the coding rate) required to achieve error control. This trade-off should be kept in mind throughout the process of code selection.

The quantities n and t are chosen with error-correction capability in mind. We shall assume that code vectors over $GF(q)$ are transmitted one symbol at a time and that channel errors are independent from symbol to symbol. If the symbol error probability is P, then as n becomes very large, the number of symbol errors in a code word approaches nP. The probability that the fraction of symbol errors differs from P becomes smaller and smaller as n increases. Another way of putting it is that error patterns will tend to cluster in tighter and tighter shells of radius nP about each code word. We want to design a code so that these shells are within the correcting radius of the code.

In practical cases, P is usually a small number. The probability of a code word decoding error is bounded by

$$P_c = 1 - \sum_{j=0}^{t} \binom{n}{j} P^j (1 - P)^{n-j} \qquad (7.84)$$

To ensure that P_c be small, we must choose a code such that the number of probable errors per code word is less than t. This results in a code for which probable errors are all corrected. The residual errors are measured by P_c. The first step that should be taken before selecting a code is to calculate P_c and compare this with values that are acceptable to the user. This provides a range of acceptable values for n and t.

The next step is the selection of a code. Since we shall consider only primitive block lengths, we take $n = q^m - 1$. The generalization to nonprimitive block lengths involves no new fundamental principles and is algebraically straightforward. The resulting codes have symbols over $GF(q)$ and code words that can be represented as scalars in $GF(q^m)$.

In the previous section, cyclic codes were succinctly described in terms of their generator polynomial, which, in turn, was described by a set of elements from $GF(q^m)$ that serve as its roots: $g(x) = \text{LCM} [p_{\beta_1}(x), p_{\beta_2}(x), \ldots, p_{\beta_s}(x)]$. The roots of the generator polynomial for a BCH code are chosen to be the first $2t$ successive powers of a primitive element of $GF(q^m)$. That is, we first choose a primitive element β of $GF(q^m)$ and then form the set

$$\{\beta, \beta^2, \beta^3, \ldots, \beta^{2t}\}$$

The reason for this choice is stated without proof: it makes possible the determination of the error pattern polynomial $e(x)$ from its evaluation at the roots of $g(x)$. The generator polynomial of a BCH code, therefore, has the form

$$g(x) = \text{LCM} [p_\beta(x), p_{\beta^2}(x), \ldots, p_{\beta^{2t}}(x)] \qquad (7.85)$$

In some cases, this can be simplified when the applicable powers of β are conjugate elements. Only those minimal polynomials corresponding to distinct elements of $GF(q^m)$ have to be included in $g(x)$. We illustrate this procedure with an example.

EXAMPLE

We wish to construct a BCH code over $GF(2)$ with $n = 15$ and $t = 4$. The generator polynomial for this code has the form

$$g(x) = \text{LCM} [p_\beta(x), p_{\beta^2}(x), p_{\beta^3}(x), \ldots, p_{\beta^8}(x)]$$

It might appear at first glance that we need to find eight minimal polynomials. However, in $GF(2)$, the elements $\{\beta, \beta^2, \beta^4, \beta^8\}$ are conjugates, so that we need only calculate

$$g(x) = \text{LCM} [p_\beta(x), p_{\beta^3}(x), p_{\beta^5}(x), p_{\beta^7}(x)]$$

The polynomial $p_{\beta^6}(x)$ is not included because it is equal to $p_{\beta^3}(x)$ since β^3 and β^6 are also conjugates. From Table 2-1, we find that $\beta = x^4 + x + 1$ is a primitive element of $GF(2^4) = GF(16)$. With this element, we can generate all of the nonzero elements of $GF(16)$. To each element, there corresponds a unique minimal polynomial. These elements and their minimal polynomials are listed in Table 7-8.

The reader may wonder how these minimal polynomials are obtained in the first place. Recall that the minimal polynomial of an element β of $GF(q^m)$ is the irreducible polynomial of least degree over $GF(q)$ having β as a root over $GF(q^m)$. Minimal polynomials could be generated by systematic search (i.e., trial and error), or they could be looked up in tables appearing in books on coding theory, such as [Li 83, Mi 85, Pe 72].

The generator polynomial, therefore, becomes

$$g(x) = (x^4 + x + 1)(x^4 + x^3 + x^2 + x + 1)(x^2 + x + 1)(x^4 + x^3 + 1)$$

$$= x^{14} + x^{13} + x^{12} + x^{11} + x^{10} + x^9 + x^8 + x^7 + x^6$$

$$+ x^5 + x^4 + x^3 + x^2 + x + 1 \qquad (7.87)$$

The generator polynomial has degree $n - k = 14$, so that $k = 1$. This code is guaranteed to correct up to four random errors. In fact, this is the binary repetition code of odd length 15. This code can be majority decoded to correct up to seven errors. The quantity $2t + 1$ is called the design distance, denoted by d^*. The minimum distance of a BCH code is lower bounded by the design distance. There is no known general formula for the minimum distance of a BCH code.

We now turn to the performance of BCH codes. It will help the reader understand the results that follow if we first present an outline of the major conclusions. The performance of BCH codes is somewhat paradoxical. To exaggerate this point, we could state that (mathematically), the BCH codes are asymptotically worthless because their rate decreases as their block length increases. The BCH codes do not provide the road to Shannon's promise of reliable communication at the channel capacity rate. On the other hand, it turns out that on the practical side, finite block lengths must be used, and there are many BCH codes that offer an attractive compromise between fidelity and information rate.

These results may inspire the reader to question the value of Shannon's results for signaling over a noisy channel. We mentioned in Chapter 4 that Shannon's results are not constructive in the sense that they provide no precise indication on how to achieve efficient coding, other than to point toward codes of high complexity.

Shannon's results are remarkable in that they dispel a popular misconception that existed before their publication in 1948. That misconception, however, can still easily entrap the unwary. Shannon's trailblazing breakthrough radically changed the philosophical outlook on communication. It was recognized that channel limitations such as additive noise introduce degradation on communications. The erroneous generalization that followed is that noise limits the reliability of communications.

TABLE 7-8. THE ELEMENTS OF GF(16) AND THEIR MINIMAL POLYNOMIALS OVER GF(2)

Field Element	Polynomial	Minimal Polynomial
0	0	
β^0	1	$x + 1$
β^1	x	$x^4 + x + 1$
β^2	x^2	$x^4 + x + 1$
β^3	x^3	$x^4 + x^3 + x^2 + x + 1$
β^4	$x + 1$	$x^4 + x + 1$
β^5	$x^2 + x$	$x^2 + x + 1$
β^6	$x^3 + x^2$	$x^4 + x^3 + x^2 + x + 1$
β^7	$x^3 + x + 1$	$x^4 + x^3 + 1$
β^8	$x^2 + 1$	$x^4 + x + 1$
β^9	$x^3 + x$	$x^4 + x^3 + x^2 + x + 1$
β^{10}	$x^2 + x + 1$	$x^2 + x + 1$
β^{11}	$x^3 + x^2 + x$	$x^4 + x^3 + 1$
β^{12}	$x^3 + x^2 + x + 1$	$x^4 + x^3 + x^2 + x + 1$
β^{13}	$x^3 + x^2 + 1$	$x^4 + x^3 + 1$
β^{14}	$x^3 + 1$	$x^4 + x^3 + 1$

Adapted by permission from [Bl 83]

This conclusion was supported by experience with the (uncoded) communication systems of the day. However, Shannon showed that, in general, it is the information rate and not the reliability that is affected by noise. Specifically, he showed that there is a property of every discrete channel called the capacity and that error-free communication is possible at information rates that are below channel capacity. This important and counterintuitive result introduced a fresh way of approaching communication engineering and paved the way for the search for efficient coding procedures.

Error-control codes trade capacity (information rate) for reliability. The engineering problem of selecting a suitable code becomes a problem of delivering a stated communication reliability at a reasonable price. In this chapter, we consider only the price paid in redundancy (i.e., in reduced available capacity for information throughput). A complete system design should also include the implementation costs associated with the mechanics of encoding and decoding.

Returning to BCH codes, we shall first explore their asymptotic performance. Table 7-9 shows the parameters n, k, t, and d^* for the first few binary BCH codes. More extensive tables can be found in [Li 83, Ma 77, Mi 85, and Pe 72]. In general, for each block of length n, several BCH codes exist that span a range of k and t. The number of BCH codes having length n increases as n increases. Normalizing k and t by n, we obtain $R = k/n$ as the code rate, and $\tau = t/n$ as the fraction of correctable symbols per code word. We learned in Section 7-1 that R is always less

TABLE 7-9. THE FIRST FEW BINARY BCH CODES

n	k	t	d^*
7	4	1	3
15	11	1	3
	7	2	5
	5	3	7
31	26	1	3
	21	2	5
	16	3	7
	11	5	11
	6	7	15
63	57	1	3
	51	2	5
	45	3	7
	39	4	9
	36	5	11
	30	6	13
	24	7	15
	18	10	21
	16	11	23
	10	13	27
	7	15	31

Adapted by permission from [Ma 77]

than unity and that it represents the effective information rate. The parameter τ is a measure of the code's ability to correct a given fraction of channel errors.

Figure 7-25 plots R versus τ for BCH codes having various block lengths n. A similar figure can be found in [Pe 72], and the detailed discussion that can be found there complements what is presented in this section. There are two equivalent ways of interpreting this figure. We can look at the variation of R with n at a constant τ. This corresponds to the A–A cut in the figure. As the block length increases, the code rate decreases, indicating that an increasing portion of the signal is dedicated to redundancy to maintain the constant fraction of correctable symbols per code word. The decrease in coding rate represents a reduction in information throughput. The rate R approaches zero as n increases without bound. Strictly speaking, this behavior says that the BCH codes are "asymptotically worthless." This, however, is misleading because BCH codes with finite block lengths can be very useful.

Looking now at the B–B cut in Fig. 7-25, we observe the behavior of the error-correcting capability τ as n varies, keeping R constant. As n increases, τ decreases. This indicates that in order to keep R constant, one has to spend more and more redundancy on error correction as the block length increases.

Trading rate for reliability is only one way of looking at the performance of BCH (or any) codes. The signaling energy efficiency of these codes must also be considered. The measure of performance here is the energy contrast ratio per bit (γ_b) required to achieve a stated code word decoding error probability P_e or any quantity that varies monotonically with P_e. For example, we consider binary BCH codes with the binary elements of the code words transmitted over $GF(2)$ using the best possible modulation scheme: antipodal signaling. In Section 7.1, we saw that the decoded bit error rate is bounded by

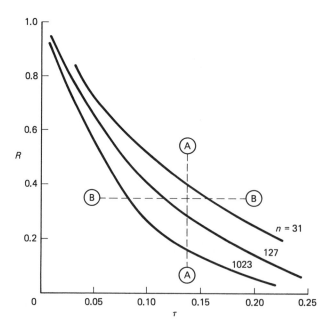

Figure 7-25. Rate-reliability trade-off for some binary BCH codes.

$$P_{be}(\gamma_b) \leq \frac{1}{2} \sum_{k=t+1}^{n} \binom{n}{k} p^k (1-p)^{n-k} \tag{7.88}$$

where, for antipodal signaling, we have

$$p(\gamma_b) = \frac{1}{2} \text{ erfc } (R\gamma_b)^{1/2} \tag{7.89}$$

with $R = k/n$. If we now set $P_{be} = 10^{-5}$, we can regard the previous expressions as determining γ_b as a function of the parameters k, t, and n. The results of such a calculation are shown in Fig. 7-26. This figure plots γ_b for $P_{be} = 10^{-5}$ as a function of the code rate R, with the code word block length n as a parameter. Calculations were made for allowed values of k, t, and n, and a smooth curve was then faired through the results.

Two conclusions emerge from this calculation. First, rates in the vicinity of $R \approx 0.4$ to $R \approx 0.8$ are the most energy efficient for BCH codes. There is a distinct minimum in γ_b for rates in this range, corresponding to a maximum in the coding gain. We also note that codes with longer block lengths correspond to smaller γ_b for the same reliability, and, therefore, to larger coding gains.

In these calculations, we used a bound for the decoded bit error probability. We could also have used a bound for the decoded code word error probability. The results would not have changed significantly. Alternatively, we could have considered another modulation for transmitting the symbols over $GF(2)$. It turns out

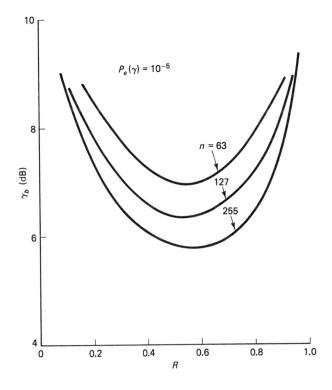

Figure 7-26. Coding gain comparisons for various BCH codes.

that antipodal signaling is a useful benchmark because it provides the best possible binary performance and is easily calculated. Finally, other reliability standards such as $P_{be} = 10^{-6}$ or 10^{-8} could have been used as well, without greatly changing the results. The conditions under which coding gain is calculated, however, must be specified along with the gain itself.

As another example of coding gain calculations, we shall compare the relative merits of sending information either uncoded or coded with binary BCH codes. For uncoded communications, information bits are grouped in blocks of k bits. Each block is then transmitted one bit at a time over a BSC channel using antipodal modulation. The block error probability is then

$$P_{\text{unc}}(k, \gamma_b) = 1 - [1 - p(\gamma_b)]^k \qquad \text{where } p(\gamma_b) = \tfrac{1}{2} \text{ erfc } (\gamma_b)^{1/2} \qquad (7.90)$$

The corresponding code-word probability of error is bounded by

$$P_e(\gamma_b) = 1 - \sum_{m=0}^{t} \binom{n}{m} p^m(R\gamma_b)[1 - p(R\gamma_b)]^{n-m} \qquad (7.91)$$

where $R = k/n$. For these calculations, we define the gain to be the difference, in dB, between the γ_b required to achieve $P_{\text{unc}}(k, \gamma_b) = 10^{-5}$ and $P_e(\gamma_b) = 10^{-5}$. The comparison is made on the basis of a probability of error for a group of k bits. The results of this calculation are shown for various values of R and n in Fig. 7-27. Codes with larger block lengths have the largest coding gains. The gain itself peaks in the vicinity of $R = \tfrac{1}{2}$.

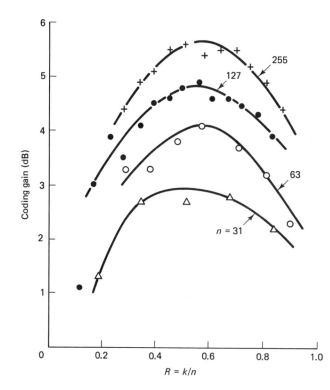

Figure 7-27. Coding gain for binary BCH codes for a code word error probability of 10^{-5}.

In addition to BCH codes, there are many other linear block codes that can be used for error control. We have already encountered Hamming and Golay codes. The BCH codes can be generalized to include the nonbinary BCH codes over $GF(q)$ and a subset of these, the Reed–Solomon codes. These and other linear block codes are discussed in detail in the error-control coding references mentioned earlier.

PROBLEMS

7.1 Show that

$$\lim_{n \to \infty} \log \binom{n}{pn} = n h(p)$$

where $h(p) = -p \log p - (1-p) \log(1-p)$.

7.2 Show that the binary repetition codes with odd code word lengths are perfect codes.

7.3 The Golay (23, 12, d_{min}) code is perfect. Show that its minimum distance is 7.

7.4 A new code is formed from the binary Hamming (7, 4; 3) code by adding an overall parity bit in the following manner: if the old code word weight is even, the parity bit is 0; otherwise, it is 1. This is called an *extended* Hamming code.

  (a) Is the new code linear? Base your answer on the structure of the code and not on a brute-force evaluation of all possible linear combinations.

  (b) How many information bits can be transmitted per new code word?

  (c) What is the weight distribution of the new code?

  (d) What are the error-detection and -correction capabilities for the new code?

7.5 Show that any of the code words of a linear code can be used as a generator polynomial for that code.

7.6 Computers handle data in byte-size chunks consisting of a seven-bit ASCII (American Standard Code for Information Interchange) character and a one-bit parity check.

  (a) How many code words are there in this code?

  (b) How many patterns are detectable?

  (c) How many patterns are not detectable?

7.7 Using the Varsharmov–Gilbert bound, find a lower bound for the minimum distance for each of the binary BCH codes of length 15. Compare these bounds with the design distances.

7.8 A form of error-control technique, called automatic repeat request (ARQ), is used in the commercial, military, and amateur radio services in which a seven-bit code is used for each character or letter. The seven-bit ASCII code is used for digital transmission. Each seven-bit channel symbol has four mark and three space bits. This four-to-three ratio is checked at the receiver for correctness. If an error is detected, a request is issued for retransmission.

  (a) How many symbols does this code contain?

  (b) Is this code linear?

  (c) What is the code's minimum distance?

  (d) What are the error-detection and -correction capabilities for this code?

  (e) Calculate and plot a bound for the probability of error detection as a function of the bit energy contrast ratio. Assume noncoherent binary FSK is used to transmit the code words over $GF(2)$.

  (f) What is the channel capacity per code word use?

7.9 A linear block $(n, k; d_{min})$ code over $GF(2)$ is used for error detection in an ARQ system. Transmission is done with noncoherent binary FSK.

(a) Calculate the probabilities of undetectable (P_{un}) and of detectable (P_d) errors. Use bounds where appropriate.

(b) What is the probability that it will take m repeats to get a correct code word?

(c) What is the expected value of the number of repeats required to get a correct code word?

(d) What is the probability that m or fewer repeats will be required to get a correct code word?

(e) How many repeats does it take to get a correct decoding with a probability of α?

7.10 The maximum allowable transmitter output power in the amateur radio service is 1500 watts. Radioteletype signals can be transmitted using a 32-ary alphabet transmitted over $GF(2)$ as noncoherent frequency-shift keyed binary tones. ARQ can be used with the following protocol. Symbols are transmitted using the code described in Prob. 7.6. The resulting 128-ary signals are transmitted using noncoherent FSK. Assume a repeat request is possible for each transmitted symbol. Discuss the ARQ coding gain and indicate the output power at which a station using ARQ will achieve the same performance (in AWGN) as a station using full legal power, but without coding. Assume the reference performance reliability is one incorrect symbol per hundred (after no more than one, two, and three possible repeat requests on ARQ). Repeat the calculation for a symbol error rate of 0.001 and up to three ARQ requests.

7.11 The automatic gain control on a receiver has a recovery time of T seconds. If the bit duration is $\tau < T$ seconds, static crashes can cause blocks of T/τ consecutive bits to be lost. As a precaution against this, bit interleaving is used prior to transmission, followed by deinterleaving and then error correction using an (n, k, d_{min}) code. The static crashes are statistically independent, and the probability that a crash occurs during a bit time interval is p. Interleaving is done by pseudorandomly rearranging the bits in time over blocks of M bits. Assume that the channel is otherwise clean.

(a) What is the mean time between crashes?

(b) What is the effect of interleaving on bit errors?

(c) Roughly how large must M be so that the code word error rate is not large?

7.12 Construct a $(7, 4; d_{min})$ code with the generator polynomial $g(x) = x^3 + x + 1$. Identify the cyclic subgroups within this code. List the code words as polynomials and as 7-tuples over $GF(2)$ according to the cyclic subgroup to which they belong, and according to their weight. What is d_{min} for this code?

7.13 Determine the condition under which the addition of the same polynomial to all code-word polynomials results in a code that is equivalent to the original code.

7.14 The discussion of cyclic codes presented in this chapter focused on left cyclic shifts. Show that any right cyclic shift can be expressed as an equivalent left cyclic shift and that, consequently, our discussion is perfectly general. Show that code words under the operation of cyclic shifts form a cyclic abelian group.

7.15 Show that the matched filter for an (n, k) coded waveform over $GF(2)$ can be implemented with two matched filters and delay-and-sum circuitry. This dispenses with the need to implement 2^k separate matched filters. What is the trade-off in this design?

RATE-DISTORTION THEORY

A bird can roost on but one branch.
A mouse can drink no more than its fill from a river.

Chinese proverb

8

In Chapter 4, we introduced Shannon's theorem for source coding. This theorem states that the coding rate, as measured by the average code word length, must be at least as large as the source entropy to allow perfect coding. Stated another way, there must be a sufficient number of code words to uniquely label all of the possible messages issuing from the information source. The information rate of the source is measured by its entropy, a function of the source symbol probability distribution. When the information rate exceeds the coding rate, there results unavoidable distortion.

There are many practical situations where it is not possible or convenient to achieve perfect coding. Sometimes, channel constraints place an upper bound on the coding rate that may be applied. In other instances, the source may be a continuous information source (such as speech) that must be approximated by a finite set of discrete waveforms. In all such cases, unavoidable distortion occurs, and it becomes the task of the communication engineer to minimize such distortion.

The motivation for this can be looked at in two equivalent ways. On the one hand, we may be interested in determining the minimum coding rate that will result in a stated average distortion. This is reminiscent of the type of approach used in selecting an error-correcting code: we attempt to satisfy user requirements for fidelity and information rate and at the same time economize on the use of channel capacity. On the other hand, the coding rate may be assumed fixed, as with an assigned digital transmission channel, and we wish to encode in such a way as to minimize the unavoidable distortion that results.

We presently continue the discussion of coding begun in Chapter 4. We shall consider information rates larger than coding rates, and complete Shannon's coding theorems by exploring what happens when the coding rate is not sufficiently high to provide exact replication of the source information. Specifically, we shall find that there is a lower bound on the distortion for any coding rate below the information rate. This lowest distortion corresponds to the best possible performance. In general, such performance is achievable only through the use of very complex codes. We shall find that such codes exist.

The branch of information theory dealing with such situations is called *rate-distortion theory*. This chapter presents the rudiments of rate-distortion theory and shows how it can be used to provide guidance in practical situations where we may be forced to compress data to the point where we start to incur distortion. We shall be interested in minimizing such distortion.

For further reading, the reader is referred to the texts [Ga 68, Ma 87a, Vi 79], the very readable articles [Sh 59, Wy 81], and the excellent but out-of-print text [Be 71].

8.1 DEFINITIONS AND FUNDAMENTAL LIMIT

With much of the mathematical principles of communication theory behind us, we may now pause and reflect on what has been accomplished thus far. Standing above all the rest are two general principles. Perhaps a more accurate statement is that these two principles lay a solid foundation upon which the rest are erected. The first principle is an intellectual triumph of civilization: the symbolic representation of information. A set of symbols is not per se the information, but only represents the information. Consequently, the nature of the symbols themselves is irrelevant other than that there has to be a sufficient quantity of distinguishable symbols to represent the information at hand. The clever originator of this revolutionary principle is, unfortunately, lost to antiquity.

It was not until the publication of Shannon's work in 1948 that a quantitative description of information mapping from one set of symbols to another was made possible. Shannon's noiseless (source) coding theorem provides the other general principle. This theorem was introduced in the section on source coding. There it was shown that with every information source, there is associated a quantity called the source entropy. The entropy measures the rate at which new information is produced by the source. Shannon's first theorem states that to encode such a source perfectly, one must use an alphabet that has, on the average, at least the same information rate as the source. Conversely, encoding with an alphabet that does not at least match the source information rate results in an irretrievable loss of information and, therefore, imperfect coding. The theorem is not quantitatively specific about the amount of distortion.

We encountered another of Shannon's theorems in our discussion of channel coding. There it was found that with every channel, there is associated a quantity called the capacity and that perfect transmission through the channel is possible only if the information rate transmitted over the channel is less than the capacity. This was further illuminated in Chapter 7, where it was pointed out that as long as the information rate is below channel capacity, the channel affects only the rate at which information is transmitted and not its reliability. Indeed, we can view the effect of the channel as that of limiting the set of symbols that can be used for transmission.

The sphere-packing argument presented in Chapter 4 is a good example of this. As the signal-to-noise ratio decreases, fewer distinguishable signals can be defined in signal space, with the overall effect of limiting the transmission rate (i.e., the capacity). This restricts the number of channel symbols that can be used to encode the information. In this way, channel coding and source coding are very similar. For information rates above channel capacity, perfect transmission is no longer possible and unavoidable degradation occurs. Again, the theorem is not quantitatively specific about the resulting distortion.

There is a striking similarity between these two theorems by Shannon. Both state that perfect communication is possible in one set of circumstances and impossible in the other. These circumstances have to do with the matching of source and representation alphabets. The differences between these two theorems become even more blurred when we choose to reinterpret what we call an "information source" and what we call a "channel." In the conventional interpretation of Shannon's noiseless source coding theorem, the information source is usually considered to be an external agent that produces symbols "at random" from some finite source alphabet $\{x\}$ and feeds these to the communication system. The communication system first performs source coding through a mapping $\{x\} \rightarrow \{y\}$ from the source alphabet onto another set of symbols $\{y\}$ that constitutes the representation alphabet and passes these along to the channel for transmission. This situation is depicted in Fig. 8-1(a), which shows an information source with alphabet $\{x\}$ and entropy H bits per source symbol, and a source coder using symbols from a representation alphabet $\{y\}$ with an average number L bits per source symbol. Note that we conveniently refer all information measures on a per-source-symbol basis. For this case, Shannon's first theorem for noiseless source coding guarantees that perfect representation is possible as long as $L - H \geq \epsilon$ for any positive ϵ. However, what we call a source coder and what we call a channel is to a large extent arbitrary. The placement of component boundaries in a communication system is largely a matter of convenience. For exam-

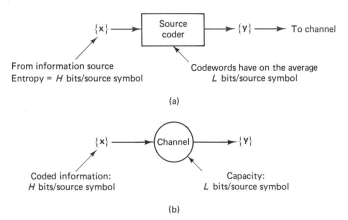

Figure 8-1. Two alternative interpretations of Shannon's source-coding theorem. (a) Conventional interpretation. Perfect coding is possible iff $L - H \geq \epsilon$ for all positive ϵ. (b) Source-coder-as-channel interpretation. Perfect coding is possible iff $L - H \geq \epsilon \, \forall \, \epsilon > 0$.

ple, we could just as well consider the source coder as a "channel" having a capacity defined by L bits per symbol in the coding alphabet. This interpretation is shown in Fig. 8-1(b). Clearly, this "channel" can perfectly pass all information having a rate less than capacity, as guaranteed by Shannon's theorem for channel coding. Whether the channel capacity is restricted by noise or other causes is irrelevant. All that matters is the finite channel capacity, which is a function of the number of distinct signals that can be formed over the channel.

By moving the source encoder-channel boundary about, we can reinterpret Shannon's first theorem in terms of his second theorem. Obviously, we can also reinterpret the second in terms of the first. What is gained by this exercise is the realization that what is going on in both cases is a mapping of one set of symbols onto another. The mapping is reversible only if the representation alphabet has at least as much capacity for information storage as is required by the source alphabet. What is lacking thus far is a quantitative statement about the amount of distortion that results when the source information rate exceeds the representation coding capacity. Rate-distortion theory fills that gap by providing a lower bound on the distortion and guarantees that there exist codes that achieve that bound, but can do no better.

This chapter concentrates on what can be done in the regime for which $H(\mathbf{x}) > R$. Having already established that some distortion must occur, we must now develop a measure of distortion. This will give us a mathematical tool with which to deal with the problem of minimizing the distortion for a given source entropy. We should find applications of rate-distortion theory in two types of situations. In the first, we are concerned with source coding where the coding alphabet cannot exactly represent the information source. This forces us to do "data compression." Here the goal of rate-distortion theory is to provide guidance in establishing a *deterministic* mapping $\{\mathbf{x}\} \rightarrow \{\mathbf{y}\}$ from a source to its representation in a way that we hope minimizes the resulting distortion. The other situation involves cases where we are forced to transmit information at rates greater than channel capacity. Here rate-distortion theory provides a measure of the distortion that occurs as the result of uncorrectable *random* transitions on the channel. This error measure can, in turn, guide in the selection of a channel coding procedure.

8.1.1 Coding Fidelity Criteria

Rate-distortion theory can be viewed as a natural extension of Shannon's coding theorems. Consider a discrete memoryless information source consisting of an M-ary alphabet set $S: \{\mathbf{x}_i; i = 1, \ldots, M\}$ of statistically independent symbols together with the associated symbol probabilities $\{p_i; i = 1, \ldots, M\}$ where $p_k = \text{Prob}(\mathbf{x}_k)$. We shall denote the symbols individually with a subscripted boldface letter $(\mathbf{x}_i)$ and collectively without the subscript $(\mathbf{x})$. Let H be the source entropy

$$H = -\sum_{k=1}^{M} p_k \log p_k \tag{8.1}$$

If the source symbols are statistically dependent, then the entropy is no longer a function of the first-order statistical properties of the separate symbols in $\{\mathbf{x}\}$. We must instead consider the joint statistical properties of a finite sequence of symbols, or, more precisely, of the Lth extension $S^{(L)}$ of S. The source entropy can be generalized in terms of the limit of the joint entropy:

$$H = \lim_{L \to \infty} L^{-1} H[S^{(L)}] \qquad (8.2)$$

where

$$H[S^{(L)}] = - \sum_{k_1, \ldots, k_L} P(\mathbf{x}_{k_1}, \mathbf{x}_{k_2}, \ldots, \mathbf{x}_{k_L}) \log P(\mathbf{x}_{k_1}, \mathbf{x}_{k_2}, \ldots, \mathbf{x}_{k_L}) \qquad (8.3)$$

a straightforward generalization of the definition introduced in Chapter 4.

Let R be the average coding rate in bits per code word. The representation code words are from an alphabet $\{\mathbf{y}_j ; j = 1, \ldots, N\}$. Shannon's first theorem states that a perfect representation of the source is possible for any positive ϵ, however small, as long as $R - H > \epsilon$. In other words, perfect reproduction is possible as long as the coding rate exceeds the information rate.

If, on the other hand, $H > R$, distortion is unavoidable. This distortion results in an information loss that is measured by the equivocation $H(\mathbf{y}|\mathbf{x})$. This information loss must be at least as large as $H - R + \epsilon$. This can be (loosely) deduced from the equation for the average mutual information $I(\mathbf{x}, \mathbf{y}) = H(\mathbf{x}) - H(\mathbf{y}|\mathbf{x})$. The average mutual information $I(\mathbf{x}, \mathbf{y})$ is the information gained about $\mathbf{x}$ from knowing $\mathbf{y}$. If $H(\mathbf{x}) < R$, then there are ways to code such that $H(\mathbf{y}|\mathbf{x}) = 0$ and $I(\mathbf{x}, \mathbf{y}) = H(\mathbf{x})$. If $H(\mathbf{x}) > R$, then $I(\mathbf{x}, \mathbf{y})$ can, at most, be R since the coding limits the information available about $\mathbf{x}$, and $H(\mathbf{y}|\mathbf{x})$ must, at least, be equal to $H(\mathbf{x}) - R$. This is not rigorous, but qualitatively describes what happens for $H(\mathbf{x}) > R$, which was not discussed in Chapter 4.

It may be helpful to visualize the source coding process as a "channel" with capacity defined as the coding rate. The goal of rate-distortion theory is to provide a quantitative description of the process of information transmission at source information rates exceeding capacity. The accomplishment of rate-distortion theory is that it can be used to define the channel properties (i.e., the input–output symbol transition probabilities) that minimize the distortion for a given rate or, equivalently, that minimize the rate for a given amount of distortion.

Since distortion is unavoidable for $H(\mathbf{x}) > R$, it is necessary to define measures of distortion in order to develop a quantitative theory. There are several possible ways to define distortion. No general rule exists. We consider the general problem of representing a set of symbols $S : \{\mathbf{x}_i; i = 1, \ldots, M\}$. As usual, we shall assume that these symbols issue from a discrete memoryless source, are statistically independent, and have probabilities $\{p_i; i = 1, \ldots, M\}$, where $p_k = P(\mathbf{x}_k)$. In general, each of the M source symbols $\mathbf{x}_i$ is mapped into one of the representation symbols $\mathbf{y}_j$ from an N-ary alphabet $S':\{\mathbf{y}_j ; j = 1, \ldots, N\}$. The two alphabets need not be identical, although they generally are in many communication systems.

We can distinguish between two possible mechanisms by means of which this mapping can take place. On one hand, the mapping can be deterministic, as in data compression. Here we have a set of fixed rules by means of which source symbols are mapped in representation symbols. The simplest example of this is analog-to-digital (A/D) conversion, where a continuous signal (and, hence, possibly an infinite amount of information per sample) is coded into one of N discrete code words. This example is a bit out of place here because the source alphabet is strictly speaking infinite, but the point to be made is that we are dealing with a many-to-one mapping that results in some distortion that in this case is quantization error. We shall have occasion to revisit A/D conversion in more detail later in this chapter.

The theoretical developments in this section are mainly concerned with the mapping of a finite M-ary source alphabet $\{x\}$ onto another finite N-ary representation alphabet $\{y\}$. This limited application suffices to introduce the basic concepts of rate-distortion theory. Other important applications exist, however, and the theory can be generalized to cover other cases such as the mapping of the real line onto a finite alphabet, as in A/D conversion.

In the same vein, we may wish to do data compression to represent, say, b_1 bit words by b_2 bit words, where $b_1 > b_2$. Obviously, this involves the loss of information. Proceeding on intuition, we might guess that if some bits have to be discarded, they should be the least significant bits. Rate-distortion theory sheds light in cases where intuition in more general instances requiring data compression may not be a reliable guide.

A deterministic mapping $\{x\} \rightarrow \{y\}$ can be completely specified by an assignment matrix or by a table with entries denoted by $Q(i,j)$, $Q(i \rightarrow j)$, or $Q(j \mid i)$ to indicate that symbol x_i belonging to the M-ary source alphabet $\{x\}$ is mapped into symbol y_j from the N-ary representation alphabet $\{y\}$. For reasons that will soon become apparent, we choose the last notation: $Q(j \mid i)$. If symbol x_i occurs with probability $p_i, i = 1, \ldots, M$, then the probability that symbol y_j occurs is given by

$$\text{Prob } \{y = y_j\} = q_j = \sum_{i=1}^{M} Q(j \mid i) p_i \tag{8.4}$$

where the $Q(j \mid i)$ represents the deterministic assignments $\{x\} \rightarrow \{y\}$. Note that if we require that $Q(j \mid i)$ have the normalization

$$\sum_{j=1}^{M} Q(j \mid i) = 1 \tag{8.5}$$

then the function $Q(j \mid i)$ behaves just like a conditional probability and, in fact, is mathematically indistinguishable from a conditional probability even though the process considered is deterministic.

The other mapping mechanism occurs when random channel errors cause one symbol to be mistaken for another during reception. Here we are dealing with a probabilistic process that assigns representation symbol y_j to source symbol x_i with probability $Q(j \mid i)$ conditioned on x_i having appeared at the system input. If symbol x_i occurs with probability p_i, $i = 1, \ldots, M$, then the probability that symbol y_j occurs is given by

$$\text{Prob } \{y_j\} = \sum_{i=1}^{M} Q(j \mid i) p_i \tag{8.6}$$

where the $Q(j \mid i)$ represents the probabilistic mappings $\{x\} \rightarrow \{y\}$. Note that this expression is identical to Eq. (8.4), which was obtained by assuming that the mapping is deterministic. We, therefore, need not make a conscious distinction between deterministic and probabilistic mappings. The function $Q(j \mid i)$ associated with the mapping $\{x\} \rightarrow \{y\}$ need not be a conditional probability. We, therefore, adopt the more general name *conditional assignment* for $Q(j \mid i)$.

We now introduce a *distortion* or *cost* function $d(i,j)$ associated with the joint event of having the symbol x_i as source and y_j as representation. The function $d(i,j)$ is a quantitative measure of the consequence of the mapping $\{x\} \rightarrow \{y\}$. The only restrictions we impose on $d(i,j)$ is that it be real and nonnegative.

EXAMPLE

A simple example of a distortion measure is the Hamming metric

$$d(i,j) = \delta(i,j) \tag{8.7}$$

between identical source and representation alphabets. Here $\delta(i,j)$ is the Kronecker delta, which is unity when $i = j$ and is zero otherwise. In this case, the distortion is zero when input and output symbols are the same and is one when they differ.

EXAMPLE

In the last example, the same weight is applied to any coding error, no matter what the source and coded symbols are. In some applications, it might make sense to define a distortion measure that is in some way proportional to the severity of the error. Thus, if x be some number that is reproduced as y, a likely measure of distortion might be

$$d(x,y) = |x - y| \tag{8.8}$$

This distortion measure has the property that it vanishes when $x = y$ and otherwise is as large as the absolute value of the difference between x and y. The selection of a distortion measure that both accurately represents the costs associated with symbol mappings and results in an analytically tractable expression is not yet a fully developed discipline.

EXAMPLE

The distortion measure $d(x,y) = (x - y)^2$ is a useful definition that has the advantage of being identical with the square of the Euclidian metric between x and y. We also associate this distortion with the energy contained in the "error" signal between x and y. In this case, the intuitive concepts of distortion and metric distance coincide.

Figure 8-2 shows the primary parameters of rate-distortion theory. The representation symbols $\mathbf{y}_j$ are obtained from source symbols $\mathbf{x}_i$ through the intermediacy of a conditional assignment $Q(j \mid i)$ obeying the normalization condition $\sum_i Q(j \mid i) = 1$. The $\mathbf{x}_i$ occur with known and given probabilities p_i. The distortion associated with the mapping $\mathbf{x}_i \rightarrow \mathbf{y}_j$ is given by the nonnegative distortion function $d(i,j)$.

The quantity $d(i,j)$ is commonly referred to as the *single letter distortion measure*. It measures the specific distortion associated with the source-representation letter pair $(\mathbf{x}_i, \mathbf{y}_j)$. We can form the statistical average of the single-letter distortion measure over all possible source and representation symbols:

$$d^* = \sum_{i,j} P(i,j)d(i,j) = \sum_i p_i \sum_j Q(j \mid i)d(i,j) \qquad (8.9)$$

where $P(i,j) = Q(j \mid i)p_i$ is the joint probability of occurrence of source symbol $\mathbf{x}_i$ and representation symbol $\mathbf{y}_j$. The quantity d^* measures the average distortion associated with source symbols $\{\mathbf{x}\}$, occurring with probabilities $\{p_i\}$, mapped into representation symbols $\{\mathbf{y}\}$ with transition probabilities $Q(j \mid i)$ and single-letter distortion measure $d(i,j)$. The average distortion depends on both the statistics of the symbols and on the definition of a distortion function. When d^* is given a specific numerical value, it is called a *fidelity criterion*.

Note that d^* is a nonnegative continuous function of the conditional assignment $Q(j \mid i)$. In particular, d^* is a linear function of $Q(j \mid i)$. Viewed as a continuous function of $Q(j \mid i)$, d^* measures the distortion associated with a particular conditional assignment (i.e., coding). The other parameters in the definition of d^* reflect the influences of the input symbol probabilities over which we have no control and of the definition of the single-letter distortion measure, which is chosen to reflect the consequences or costs associated with the various conditional assignments.

The smallest value $D_{\min}$ of the average distortion occurs by selecting the smallest distortion corresponding to each representation symbol, i.e., $d(i,k) \leq d(i,j)$, for all $i = 1, \ldots, M$, and by setting the corresponding $Q(j \mid i) = 1$ for $i = k$, and $Q(j \mid i) = 0$ otherwise. Given a measure of single-letter distortion, this scheme selects that conditional assignment that results in the smallest overall distortion. In other words, the only allowed assignments are those to representation symbols that result in the least single-letter distortion. We then have

$$D_{\min} = \sum_i p_i d(i,k) = \sum_i p_i \min d(i,j) \qquad (8.10)$$

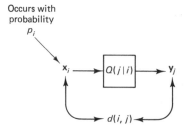

Occurs with
probability
p_i

Figure 8-2. The primary parameters of rate-distortion theory.

Finally, a conditional assignment $Q(j \mid i)$ is called *D-admissible* if it results in an average distortion that is upper bounded by D. Mathematically, we can define a set Q_D of D-admissible assignments as follows:

$$Q_D = \{Q(j \mid i) : d^* \leq D\} \tag{8.11}$$

The subset of all $M \times N$ values of $Q(j \mid i)$ that form the set Q_D satisfies the three conditions of nonnegativity: $Q(j \mid i) \geq 0$; normalization: $\sum_i Q(j \mid i) = 1$; and the upper-bounding of the average distortion $d^* = \sum_{ij} Q(j \mid i) p_i d(i, j) \leq D$.

Having defined a measure of distortion, we have at our disposal one of the two important functions of rate-distortion theory. As the name "rate-distortion" implies, the other important function is a measure of the information rate through the coding and decoding processes. We shall derive this rate function from the average mutual information between $\{x\}$ and $\{y\}$ in the following section. We shall find that the rate and distortion functions are linked through the conditional assignment $Q(j \mid i)$.

8.1.2 The Rate-Distortion Function

The average mutual information between the symbol ensembles $\{x\}$ and $\{y\}$ is

$$I(\mathbf{x}, \mathbf{y}) = \sum_{i,j} P(\mathbf{x}_i, \mathbf{y}_j) \log \left[\frac{P(\mathbf{x}_i, \mathbf{y}_j)}{p_i, q_j} \right] \tag{8.12}$$

where the representation symbol marginal probabilities are given by

$$q_j = \sum_i P(\mathbf{x}_i, \mathbf{y}_j) = \sum_i Q(j \mid i) p_i \tag{8.13}$$

The average mutual information $I(\mathbf{x}, \mathbf{y})$ can be rewritten in terms of $Q(j \mid i)$ and p_i as follows:

$$I(\mathbf{x}, \mathbf{y}) = \sum_{i,j} Q(j \mid i) p_i \log Q(j \mid i) - \sum_{i,j} Q(j \mid i) p_i \log \sum_k Q(j \mid k) p_k \tag{8.14}$$

Recall from Chapter 4 that the significance of the average mutual information $I(\mathbf{x}, \mathbf{y})$ is that it is the information available about ensemble $\{x\}$ from ensemble $\{y\}$. In Chapter 4, the average mutual information was used in defining the capacity of communication channels. In this chapter, we use the average mutual information in a similar sense: it is the amount of information about a source $\{x\}$ available from its representation $\{y\}$ through the effect of the coding process.

The situation to be considered is one in which the source symbols $\{x\}$ and their probabilities are given and where the average distortion d^* has been specified as a function of the conditional source-representation assignment $Q(j \mid i)$. The rate of information transfer between source and representation is measured by $I(\mathbf{x}, \mathbf{y})$, which is a continuous function of $Q(j \mid i)$. Varying the conditional assignment $Q(j \mid i)$ causes both the average distortion d^* and the average mutual information $I(\mathbf{x}, \mathbf{y})$ to change. The average amount of mutual information between $\{x\}$ and $\{y\}$ and the average distortion caused by the assignment $\{x\} \rightarrow \{y\}$ are related by the conditional assignment $Q(j \mid i)$. We consider this conditional assignment to be a free parameter to be varied so as to result in a minimum coding rate and distortion. All of the other quantities such as p_i and $d(i,j)$ are fixed. We emphasize the functional dependence of the average mutual information on the conditional assignment $Q(j \mid i)$ with the notation $I(Q)$.

A *rate-distortion function* $R(D)$ is defined as the least value of $I(Q)$ for which $Q \in Q_D$:

$$R(D) = \min_{Q \in Q_D} I(Q) \tag{8.15}$$

This is a compact way of saying that the rate-distortion function $R(D)$ is the smallest coding rate possible for which the distortion is guaranteed not to exceed D. We intuitively expect the distortion to decrease as the rate is increased. Conversely, tolerating a large distortion allows the use of a smaller information rate for coding and/or transmission. We shall find that intuition is correct. We can already appreciate the importance of a rate-distortion function. With it, we can make a quantitative evaluation of the trade-offs associated with reproduction fidelity (the distortion D) and the coding and transmission complexities associated with providing an information rate R. Our definition for $R(D)$ hints at how such a function might be calculated. Given the input symbols $\{\mathbf{x}\}$ and their probabilities p_i and given a definition of the single-letter distortion $d(i,j)$, we can calculate the average distortion $d*(Q)$ as a function of the conditional assignment $Q(j \mid i)$.

A brute force way to proceed might be to select among all possible $M \times N$ values of $Q(j \mid i)$ those that belong to the set Q_D, (i.e., those for which $d*(Q) \leq D$). The values of $Q(j \mid i) \in Q_D$ correspond to a range of possible values for the average distortion: $0 \leq d*(Q) \leq D$. Note that the value of the average distortion is not fixed, but may range over the closed interval $[0, D]$. Finally, we could compute all of the values of $I(Q)$ with $Q(j \mid i) \in Q_D$. Of these values of $I(Q)$, one will be smaller than the rest. The least value of $I(Q)$ thus obtained is the rate $R(D)$ corresponding to the average distortion bound D.

This statement of the rate-distortion function has been cast as a variational problem. In other words, we are to find the conditional assignment $Q(j \mid i)$ that minimizes the average mutual information $I(Q)$ subject to certain conditions imposed on $Q(j \mid i)$. This variational problem could be solved by the usual techniques of the calculus of variations were it not for the fact that two of these conditions are expressed as inequalities rather than equality constraints. By restricting $Q(j \mid i)$ to be a D-admissible function, we require that $d* \leq D$. Also, we require that $Q(j \mid i)$ be non-negative. The remaining normalization constraint on $Q(j \mid i)$ is of the constant type.

We shall for the moment neglect the possibility of the conditional assignment $Q(j \mid i)$ assuming negative values. This assumption turns out to be generally valid for small values of D and, in some special cases, for a wide range of D; see, for example, [Be 71]. If, for the moment, we simply ignore the two inequality constraints, then the analytical calculation of $R(D)$ follows in a straightforward way from its variational definition. We want to minimize $I(Q)$ subject to normalization constraints

$$\sum_{j=1}^{N} Q(j \mid i) = 1 \qquad \text{for } i = 1, \ldots, M \tag{8.16}$$

In addition, we impose the constraint that the average distortion d* be exactly equal to D:

$$d^*(Q) = \sum_{i,j} p_i Q(j \mid i) d(i,j) = D \tag{8.17}$$

In effect, we are specifying a fidelity criterion $d^* = D$ instead of $d^* \leq D$. This constrained minimization problem can be recast as an equivalent unconstrained problem through the use of Lagrange multipliers. We seek the $Q(j \mid i)$ that minimizes the expression

$$J(Q) = I(Q) - \sum_i \lambda_i \sum_j Q(j \mid i) - \mu \sum_{i,j} p_i Q(j \mid i) d(i,j) \tag{8.18}$$

The conditional assignment $Q(j \mid i)$ that causes $J(Q)$ to be stationary is a solution to the Euler–Lagrange equation

$$\frac{dJ(Q)}{dQ} = 0$$

The solution of this variational problem leads to the conditional assignment for the discrete memoryless channel. We shall solve this problem in the following section. For the moment, note that we would have arrived at the same variational problem had we set it up to minimize the average distortion with a constant-rate constraint. Had we done that, we would have arrived at a distortion function as a function of the rate $D(R)$, the inverse of the rate-distortion function. The problems of finding the minimum rate for a given average distortion level and of finding the minimum distortion corresponding to a specified rate are entirely equivalent.

It may seem more natural to state the problem in terms of solving for the minimum distortion. This interpretation would be preferred in applications involving data compression, where the representation alphabet, the storage medium, or the transmission channel has less capacity than is required by the source information entropy. In such cases, the coding rate is fixed and the problem is to find a conditional assignment scheme (i.e., a code) that results in the least amount of average distortion.

On the other hand, the user of a communication system may specify an upper bound on acceptable distortion, and it becomes incumbent on the communication engineer to design a transmission system that is maximally economical in terms of channel resources and/or coding complexity. In this case, the rate-distortion problem is more easily stated in terms of finding the least information rate corresponding to a prescribed average distortion measure.

Under what condition does the average distortion d^* attain its maximum value? What choice of $Q(j \mid i)$ results in the largest possible average distortion? Clearly, the largest amount of distortion occurs when no information about the source alphabet $\{\mathbf{x}\}$ is available for reconstruction. This happens when the source $\{\mathbf{x}\}$ and representation $\{\mathbf{y}\}$ alphabets are statistically independent. For this special case, we have $Q(j \mid i) = q_j$. The expression for $d^*(Q)$ becomes

$$d^*(Q) = \sum_{i,j} p_i q_j\, d(i,j) = \sum_j q_j \sum_i p_i d(i,j) \tag{8.19}$$

The statistical independence of the $\{\mathbf{x}\}$ and $\{\mathbf{y}\}$ alphabets results in $I(Q) = 0$ and, consequently, also results in $R(D) = 0$. The rest is a straightforward variational problem. The constraint that $R(D) = 0$ is automatically incorporated in the last expression for $d^*(Q)$ by requiring the statistical independence of the source $\{\mathbf{x}\}$ and representation $\{\mathbf{y}\}$ alphabets. It remains to find the minimum value of $d^*(Q)$, which we denote by $D_{\max}$. Minimizing $d^*(Q)$ is accomplished by finding the value $j = j^*$ for which the expression $\sum_i p_i d(i,j)$ is a minimum and then setting the corresponding $q_j^* = 1$, and all the remaining $q_j = 0$ for $j \neq j^*$. We, therefore, have

$$D_{\max} = \min_j \sum_i p_i d(i,j) \tag{8.20}$$

At first glance, this expression may appear to be very similar to Eq. (8.10), the expression previously obtained for $D_{\min}$. They are different, however, because the operation of taking the minimum value is not linear and, therefore, may not be interchanged with the summation.

What we have done is to find the maximum value of a minimum value. That this may appear confusing is excusable. Finding $d^*(Q)$ is always a minimization problem. That is, we always select as $d^*(Q)$ the least value of the distortion subject to Q being a D-admissible function, i.e., for which $Q \in Q_D$. To each D-admissible set Q_D, there corresponds a unique minimum value of the average distortion $d^*(Q)$. By changing the composition of the set Q_D by considering different values of D, the value of $d^*(Q)$ also changes. What we have done before is to look for that particular composition of Q_D that results in the largest possible value $D = D_{\max}$ of $d^*(Q)$. Thus, $d^*(Q)$ is obtained by a minimization procedure over a particular set Q_D and then by varying D until the largest value of $d^*(Q)$ is obtained.

The rate-distortion function $R(D)$ has been defined for values of the distortion D in the closed interval $D_{\min} \leq D \leq D_{\max}$. It can be shown that we lose nothing by setting $D_{\min} = 0$ (see Prob. 8.3). This can be accomplished through a suitable definition of the single-letter measure of distortion $d(i,j)$. We already know that for $D = D_{\min} = 0$, we must have

$$R \geq H_s = -\sum_k p_k \log p_k \tag{8.21}$$

where H_s is the source entropy. Recall that for simplicity, we are dealing with statistically independent source symbols. We also already know that $R(D \geq D_{\max}) = 0$ since for that case, the input and output alphabets are statistically independent. We now present a few important general properties of $R(D)$ for $D_{\min} \leq D \leq D_{\max}$.

The first property of $R(D)$ to be introduced is that it is nonnegative. To see that this must be so, recall that $R(D)$ is defined as an average mutual information, which is known to be nonnegative.

Next, we show that $R(D)$ is a nonincreasing function of the distortion D. To see that this must be true, note what happens to R as the distortion is increased. As D increases, more and more conditional assignments $Q(j \mid i)$ result in $d^* \leq D$ and, consequently, the number of elements belonging to the D-admissible set Q_D increases. Furthermore, the increase occurs in such a way as to always include as a subset all the members corresponding to $d* < D$. In other words, increasing the size of the set by increasing the distortion from D to $D + \delta D$ results in retaining previous elements since these result in a distortion that is at most D, and, therefore, less than $D + \delta D$, and adding to that set those elements that result in the additional values of the distortion allowed. Since $R(D)$ is found through a minimization procedure over the D-admissible set of conditional assignments, increasing the size of the set over which minimization is performed can only result in $R(D + \delta D) \leq R(D)$. Hence, $R(D)$ is a nonincreasing function of the distortion D.

The third important property of the rate-distortion function is that it is convex downward (written convex $\cup$). Convex $\cup$ is a stronger condition than nonincreasing. Not only is $R(D)$ nonincreasing, it is a strictly decreasing function of D. To prove this property, consider a conditional assignment Q giving rise to a distortion D and consequently a rate $R(D)$. Similarly, consider a different conditional assignment Q', with distortion D' and rate $R'(D')$. These two conditions form two points with coordinates (D, R) and (D', R') on the rate-distortion curve, as shown in Fig. 8-3. Now form a new conditional assignment $Q* = \alpha Q + (1 - \alpha)Q'$, with $0 \leq \alpha \leq 1$. This new conditional assignment behaves just like any other assignment, as guaranteed by the bounds on α. With the new conditional assignment $Q*$, we associate the distortion $D*$ and the rate $R*$. The linearity between distortion and conditional assignment results in

$$D* = \alpha D + (1 - \alpha)D' \tag{8.22}$$

Note that $\alpha = 0$ results in $Q* = Q'$, and $\alpha = 1$ results in $Q* = Q$. In general, there results $Q \leq Q* \leq Q'$. Since the distortion is a linear function of the conditional assignment, we also have $D \leq D* \leq D'$. Since the rate is a nonincreasing (i.e., monotonic) function of the distortion, this ordering is preserved and we also have $R' \leq R* \leq R$.

The rate-distortion function in Fig. 8-3 has already been drawn convex $\cup$. On it, we have joined the points (D, R) and (D', R') with a straight-line segment functionally described by the function $y(x)$. To prove that the rate-distortion function is convex $\cup$, we must show that $R*(D*) < y(D*)$. But the rate is a convex $\cup$ function of the conditional assignment, and since the conditional assignment is a linear function of the distortion, we conclude that the rate is also a convex $\cup$ function of the distortion. Therefore, for $D \leq D* \leq D'$ and $R' \leq R* \leq R$, $R*$ must lie below the straight-line segment joining the points (D, R) and (D', R'), and, therefore, $R* < y(D*)$.

It is easy to show (see Prob. 8.5) that $y(D*) = \alpha R(D) + (1 - \alpha)R'(D')$. Combining this with the previous result, we have

$$R* = R[\alpha D + (1 - \alpha)D'] < y(D*) = \alpha R(D) + (1 - \alpha)R(D') \tag{8.23}$$

Convexity implies continuity. If $f(x)$ is an increasing (or decreasing) function of x in some interval (a, b), then the limits $\lim_{x \to c_+} f(x)$ and $\lim_{x \to c_-} f(x)$ exist for every point c in the interval. We then say that $f(x)$ is *continuous* within the interval [Wh 63]. Since this argument can be applied to the rate-distortion function $R(D)$, R is a continuous function of D.

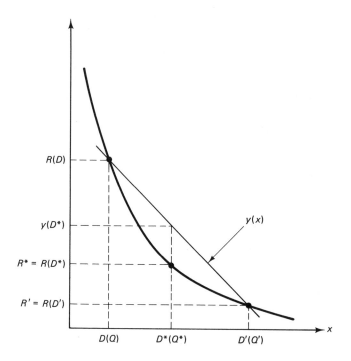

Figure 8-3. Convexity of the rate-distortion function. We show that $R(D^*) < y(D^*)$.

Summing up what we have learned thus far about the rate-distortion function, we know that it is nonnegative and strictly decreasing over the range $D_{min} \leq D \leq D_{max}$. We can define a single-letter distortion measure for which $D_{min} = 0$. No distortion occurs only if the rate exceeds the source entropy: $R(0) \geq H_s$ and the rate vanishes for statistically independent source and representation alphabets: $R(D \geq D_{max}) = 0$. Over the range $D_{min} \leq D \leq D_{max}$, $R(D)$ is a convex $\cup$ and, therefore, a continuous function of D.

A typical rate-distortion function appears in Fig. 8-4. The interpretation of this figure is that points above the curve correspond to possible (R, D) pairs, whereas points below it are forbidden by information theory. For a given D, the minimum rate required is $R(D)$. Conversely, the ordinate and abcissa can be interchanged to give a distortion-rate function, as would be obtained, for example, by minimizing D for a given rate constraint. The interpretation is that D is the minimum realizable distortion for a given R. Points above the curve are possible (D, R) pairs and points below it are not. Note that $R(D)$ is not defined for the region $D < D_{min}$.

8.1.3 The Fundamental Theorem of Coding

Having defined a rate-distortion function, we are now prepared to state and prove a fundamental theorem of coding theory. This theorem goes beyond Shannon's noiseless and noisy coding theorems, which specify the conditions under which perfect reconstruction is possible. The fundamental theorem of coding specifies a

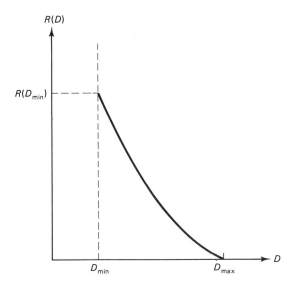

Figure 8-4. The rate-distortion function. $R(D)$ is not defined for $D < D_{min}$.

lower bound for the distortion incurred when coding (or transmission) is done at a given rate. The fundamental theorem of coding asserts that it is possible to encode a discrete memoryless source with fidelity arbitrarily close to D when the rate is arbitrarily close to $R(D)$.

   Theorem.   Let $R(D)$ be the rate-distortion function for a discrete memoryless source with respect to a single-letter distortion measure. Then, for any $\epsilon > 0$ and for sufficiently large blocks of length L, there exists a code that maps the Lth extensions of the source alphabet $\{\mathbf{x}\}$ onto the Lth extensions of the representation alphabet $\{\mathbf{y}\}$ with the coding rate bounded by $R < R(D) + \epsilon$ and with the distortion bounded by $D < D + \delta$. Conversely, if the coding rate is less than $R(D)$, then the distortion must exceed D.

   This theorem guarantees the existence of codes that achieve the lowest coding rate consistent with average distortion D. Recall that $D = 0$ is possible only when $R \geq H_s$. Since the $R(D)$ curve is a continuous nonincreasing function of D, the degradation in coding performance is not catastrophic for $R < H_s$, but rather increases gradually as the coding rate decreases.

   The method used in proving this theorem involves considering coding longer and longer extensions of the source alphabet, with the best performance being achieved in the limit of very long extensions. What we must show is that it is possible to achieve a fidelity arbitrarily close to D or better when the coding rate is arbitrarily close to $R(D)$. The argument followed is similar to the random coding approach used in proving Shannon's noisy channel coding theorem in Chapter 4. That is, we prove that for sufficiently large L, a code picked at random from the available code words satisfies the theorem when the rate and distortion are averaged over all permissible codes. There must be at least one code that performs that well.

   Consider a source alphabet $\{\mathbf{x} : \mathbf{x}_i; i = 1, \ldots, M\}$ with statistically independent symbols and corresponding probabilities $\{p_i; i = 1, \ldots, M\}$. For example, these could be the symbols generated by a discrete memoryless information source. The coder encodes by assigning a code word to each block of L input symbols. We can view this coder as a channel. It can be described in terms of a conditional assignment $Q(j \mid i)$. Consider the single-letter distortion measure $d(i,j)$ associated with that assignment. We can define a fidelity criterion, as in Eq. (8.17), and a rate-distortion function, as in Eq. (8.15).

Coding consists in making L independent assignments $\{x\} \rightarrow \{y\}$. We consider a particular case of the Lth extension of source symbols from $\{x\}$, and denote this by $\mathbf{u}_i$. To be explicit, $\mathbf{u}_i$ can be written as $\mathbf{u}_i = (\mathbf{x}_{i_1}, \mathbf{x}_{i_2}, \dots, \mathbf{x}_{i_L})$. The source extensions $\mathbf{u}_i$ belong to the set $\{\mathbf{u} : \mathbf{u}_i; i = 1, \dots, M^L\}$. Mapping the source symbols $\{x\} \rightarrow \{y\}$ is equivalent to mapping the extension $\{\mathbf{u}\} \rightarrow \{\mathbf{v}\}$, where the representation extension set is the set $\{\mathbf{v} : \mathbf{v}_j; j = 1, \dots, N^L\}$ of code words used to represent the source extension $\{\mathbf{u}\}$. The probability of a code word $\mathbf{v}_k$ is given by

$$\text{Prob}\{\mathbf{v}_k\} = \prod_{j=1}^{L} \sum_{i=1}^{M} Q(k_j \mid i) p_i \qquad (8.24)$$

There are many possible code words of the form $\mathbf{v}_k$. Each of the M source symbols can be mapped into N representation symbols by the coder. A code word $\mathbf{v}_k$ consists of a concatenation of L such representation symbols. Equation (8.24) specifies the probability for each of the N^L possible $\mathbf{v}_k$. Out of these, we shall select a subset of $K < N^L$ to be used to encode the information. Of course, it would make sense to select those code words that actually result in the least distortion. It would seem that preselecting only those code words having the best chance for good performance would make the proof of the theorem easier. It turns out, however, that trying to prove a general result that hinges on a particular code word selection scheme is very difficult, even if the selection algorithm is well-defined. A much easier approach is to select K code words at random among the N^L candidates. This random coding approach is by no means intuitively obvious, and it took the genius (and courage) of Shannon to use it in proving some of the most important results of information theory. We shall show that averaging over all possible random selections leads to the performance stated in the fundamental theorem of coding, provided L is allowed to become sufficiently large. For similar approaches to the following derivation, the reader should consult [Be 71] and [Ma 87a].

Now define the average distortion per input symbol

$$d(\mathbf{u}_i, \mathbf{v}_j) = L^{-1} \sum_{k=1}^{L} d(\mathbf{x}_{ik}, \mathbf{y}_{jk}) \qquad (8.25)$$

If the information source is ergodic, then the previous code word average of $d(\mathbf{x}_{ik}, \mathbf{y}_{jk})$ is equal to the statistical ensemble average

$$d^* = \sum_{i,j} Q(j \mid i) p_i d(i,j) = D \qquad (8.26)$$

provided the block length L is sufficiently large. We now define S_i as the set of all code words $\mathbf{v}_j$ for which $d(\mathbf{u}_i, \mathbf{v}_j) < D + \frac{1}{2}\delta$, where δ is an arbitrary positive quantity. The code word members of S_i are those that result in an average distortion that is at most $D + \frac{1}{2}\delta$, given that the sequence $\mathbf{u}_i$ was transmitted. The probability that a randomly picked code word belongs to S_i is, therefore,

$$P(S_i) = \sum_{\mathbf{v}_j \in S_i} \text{Prob } \{\mathbf{v}_j\} \qquad (8.27)$$

We shall show that for a code $\{\mathbf{v} : \mathbf{v}_k; k = 1, \ldots, K\}$, the probability that none of the $\mathbf{v}_k$ belong to S_i becomes vanishingly small for sufficiently large L. To that end, we define a set T_i having the property that members of T_i are code words $\mathbf{v}_j$ for which, given that sequence $\mathbf{u}_i$ was transmitted, have an average coding rate that is upper bounded by $R(D) + \frac{1}{2}\epsilon$, where

$$R(D) = \sum_{i,j} Q(j \mid i) p_i [\log Q(j \mid i) - \log q_j] \qquad (8.28)$$

where q_j is given by Eq. (8.13). The code words $\mathbf{v}_j$ that belong to T_i satisfy the inequality

$$L^{-1}[\log \text{Prob } \{\mathbf{v}_j \mid \mathbf{u}_i\} - \log \text{Prob } \{\mathbf{v}_j\}] < R(D) + \frac{1}{2}\epsilon \qquad (8.29)$$

for any transmitted sequence $\mathbf{u}_i$. The expression in square brackets in Eq. (8.29) will be recognized as the mutual information between $\{\mathbf{u}\}$ and $\{\mathbf{v}\}$. Equation (8.29) can be rewritten as

$$\text{Prob } \{\mathbf{v}_j\} > 2^{-L[R(D) + \frac{1}{2}\epsilon]} \text{Prob } \{\mathbf{v}_j \mid \mathbf{u}_i\} \qquad (8.30)$$

Now, since the set S_i must include its intersection with the set T_i, the probability measure of S_i must necessarily exceed that of $S_i \cap T_i$:

$$P(S_i) \geq \text{Prob } \{S_i \cap T_i\} = \sum_{\mathbf{v}_j \in S_i \cap T_i} \text{Prob } \{\mathbf{v}_j\} > 2^{-L[R(D) + \frac{1}{2}\epsilon]} \sum_{\mathbf{v}_j \in S_i \cap T_i} \text{Prob } \{\mathbf{v}_j \mid \mathbf{u}_i\}$$

$$(8.31)$$

Recall that $P(S_i)$ is the probability that given $\mathbf{u}_i$, a code word $\mathbf{v}_j$ picked at random results is an average distortion per symbol that is less than $D + \frac{1}{2}\delta$. The probability that a code of size K contains no such code word is

$$[1 - P(S_i)]^M \leq [1 - 2^{-L[R(D) + \frac{1}{2}\epsilon]} \sum_{\mathbf{v}_j \in S_i \cap T_i} \text{Prob } \{\mathbf{v}_j \mid \mathbf{u}_i\}]^M \qquad (8.32)$$

We now show that the summation in inequality (8.32) is arbitrarily close to unity when L is allowed to be sufficiently large. But, first, we separately prove that for any $\mathbf{u}_i$, we have both $\mathbf{v}_j \in S_i$ and $\mathbf{v}_j \in T_i$.

For sufficiently large L, the code-word average in Eq. (8.25) and the ensemble average in Eq. (8.26) become equal. Since this is true for any $\mathbf{u}_i$ and $\mathbf{v}_j$ provided the source is ergodic, we must have

$$\lim_{L \to \infty} P(S_i) = \lim_{L \to \infty} \text{Prob } \{\mathbf{v}_j \in S_i\} = 1 \qquad (8.33)$$

Similarly, we have, in the limit of large L,

$$L^{-1}[\log \text{Prob} \{\mathbf{v}_j \mid \mathbf{u}_i\} - \log \text{Prob} \{\mathbf{v}_j\}] = L^{-1} \sum_{k=1}^{L} [\log Q(j_k \mid i_k) - \log q_j] = R(D)$$

(8.34)

by equating code word and ensemble averages of the coding rate. Since this is true for any $\mathbf{u}_i$ and $\mathbf{v}_j$ provided the source is ergodic, we must have

$$\lim_{L \to \infty} \text{Prob} \{\mathbf{v}_j \in T_i\} = 1$$

(8.35)

Returning to the inequality (8.32), we set the summation equal to unity, which is true in the limit of large L. If we now choose $K = 2^{L[R(D) + \frac{1}{2}\epsilon]}$, the inequality (8.32) becomes, after expanding,

$$[1 - P(S_i)]^M < 1 - M 2^{-L[R(D) + \frac{1}{2}\epsilon]} + \text{H.O.T.}$$

(8.36)

where H.O.T. stands for higher-order terms in $2^{-L[R(D) + \frac{1}{2}\epsilon]}$, all of which vanish more rapidly than $2^{-L[R(D) + \frac{1}{2}\epsilon]}$ as L increases. Note that $K = 2^{L[R(D) + \frac{1}{2}\epsilon]}$ corresponds to a coding rate of $R(D) + \frac{1}{2}\epsilon$. The expansion of $[1 - P(S_i)]^M$ must converge since $P(S_i) < 1$, and the theorem is proved.

The converse of this theorem, not proven here, simply states that it is impossible to incur less distortion than D if a coding rate $R(D)$ is used. Taken together, the fundamental theorem and its converse specify the conditions under which the best coding performance is possible.

8.1.4 Rate and Distortion for a Discrete Memoryless Source

We now return to the solution of the variational problem set up in the previous section. The solution of this problem is similar to that offered by Berger [Be 71]. Substitution of Eq. (8.14) into Eq. (8.18) gives

$$J(Q) = \sum_{i,j} Q(j \mid i)p_i \log Q(j \mid i) - \sum_{i,j} Q(j \mid i)p_i \log \sum_k Q(j \mid k)p_k$$

$$- \sum_i \lambda_i \sum_j Q(j \mid i) - \mu \sum_{i,j} p_i Q(j \mid i)d(i,j)$$

(8.37)

Now let $\lambda_i = p_i \log \xi_i$, so that $J(Q)$ can now be written as

$$J(Q) = \sum_i p_i \sum_j Q(j \mid i) \left[\log Q(j \mid i) - \log \sum_k p_k Q(j \mid k) - \log \xi_i - \mu d(i,j) \right]$$

(8.38)

$$= \sum_i p_i \sum_j Q(j \mid i) \left\{ \log \left[\frac{Q(j \mid i)}{q_j \xi_i} \right] - \mu d(i,j) \right\}$$

The solution for the $Q(j \mid i)$ that make $J(Q)$ stationary is tedious but straightforward. We merely set the derivative of Eq. (8.38) with respect to Q to zero:

$$\frac{dJ(Q)}{dQ(m \mid n)} = 0$$

First, note that there are no contributions to this derivative when $j \neq m$. Consequently, only the $j = m$ term has to be considered, which disposes with the j summation. Two separate cases have to be considered with the i summation. When $i = n$, we have

$$\frac{dJ(Q)}{dQ(m \mid n)} = \frac{d}{dQ(m \mid n)} \left(p_n Q(m \mid n) \left\{ \log\left[\frac{Q(m \mid n)}{q_m \xi_n} \right] - \mu d(n,m) \right\} \right)$$

After the differentiation is carried out, this expression reduces to

$$\frac{dJ(Q)}{dQ(m \mid n)} = p_n \left\{ \log\left[\frac{Q(m \mid n)}{q_m \xi_n} \right] - \mu d(n,m) + \frac{1}{\ln 2} - p_n \frac{Q(m \mid n)}{q_m \ln 2} \right\} \qquad (8.39)$$

Finally, we consider the case $j = m$ and $i \neq n$. For this case, we have

$$\frac{dJ(Q)}{dQ(m \mid n)} = \frac{d}{dQ(m \mid n)} \sum_{i \neq n} p_i Q(m \mid i) \left\{ \log\left[\frac{Q(m \mid i)}{q_m \xi_i} \right] - \mu d(i,m) \right\}$$

After differentiation, this reduces to

$$\frac{dJ(Q)}{dQ(m \mid n)} = -\frac{p_n}{\ln 2} \left[1 - \frac{p_n}{q_m} Q(m \mid n) \right] \qquad (8.40)$$

Combining our results, we have

$$\frac{dJ(Q)}{dQ(m \mid n)} = p_n \left\{ \log\left[\frac{Q(m \mid n)}{q_m \xi_n} \right] - \mu d(n,m) \right\} = 0 \qquad (8.41)$$

which implies that

$$\log\left[\frac{Q(m \mid n)}{q_m \xi_n} \right] - \mu d(n,m) = 0$$

and, therefore,

$$Q(m \mid n) = q_m \xi_n 2^{\mu d(n,m)} \qquad (8.42)$$

The ξ_n may be determined by summing Eq. (8.42) over m, and using the normalization condition of Eq. (8.5), from which

$$\xi_n^{-1} = \sum_m q_m 2^{\mu d(n,m)} \qquad (8.43)$$

Substituting Eq. (8.42) in Eq. (8.26), there results the following expression for the average distortion:

$$D = \sum_{i,j} p_i q_j \xi_i d(i,j) 2^{\mu d(i,j)} \qquad (8.44)$$

where the ξ_i are given by Eq. (8.43). Similarly, substituting Eq. (8.42) in Eq. (8.28) gives

$$R(D) = \mu D + \sum_i p_i \log \xi_i \tag{8.45}$$

Note that since the second term on the right-hand side of Eq. (8.45) does not involve D, the parameter μ can be interpreted as the *slope* of the $R(D)$ function. Together, Eqs. (8.44) and (8.45) form a pair of parametric equations for the average distortion D and the rate $R(D)$, in terms of the parameter μ. Equations (8.42) and (8.43) form a solution for the conditional assignments $Q(m \mid n)$ in terms of the representation symbol abilities q_m, which are, in turn, defined by Eq. (8.13). A simplification of this solution results by multiplying Eq. (8.42) by p_n and summing over n:

$$q_m = \sum_n Q(m \mid n)p_n = q_m \sum_n \xi_n p_n 2^{\mu d(n,m)} \tag{8.46}$$

so that we have

$$\sum_n \xi_n p_n 2^{\mu d(n,m)} = 1 \tag{8.47}$$

where ξn is given by Eq. (8.43).

Equations (8.42) through (8.45) represent the formal solution to the rate-distortion problem for a discrete memoryless source with respect to the single-letter distortion measure $d(i,j)$. When applying this formalism to a particular case, Eq. (8.42) can first be solved for the $q_m(\mu)$. This step will generally require a numerical solution. From that point, it is an easy matter to compute the $\xi_n(\mu)$ from Eq. (8.43), the average distortion D from Eq. (8.44), and $R(D)$ from Eq. (8.45).

EXAMPLE

Consider a source for which the M symbols are equiprobable; in other words, let $p_i = M^{-1}$ for $i \in \{1, \ldots, M\}$. Let the number of representation symbols also be M. For any $i, j \in \{1, \ldots, M\}$, let $d(i,j)$ assume values from some permutation of the set $\{d_1, d_2, \ldots, d_M\}$. If this sounds artificial, consider the representation of the integers $\mathbf{x} \in \{1, 2, \ldots, 9, 0\}$ by the integers $\mathbf{y} \in \{1, 2, \ldots, 9, 0\}$, where the single-letter distortion measure is the absolute value of the difference $d(\mathbf{x}_i, \mathbf{y}_j) = |\mathbf{x}_i - \mathbf{y}_j|$. Since there are at most only M distinct values of $d(i,j)$, many of the summations are simplified. For example,

$$\xi_n^{-1} = \xi^{-1} = \sum_j q_j 2^{\mu d(n,j)}$$

From Eq. (8.47), we have

$$\xi \sum_j p_j 2^{\mu d(j,m)} = 1$$

so that

$$\xi^{-1} = \sum_j q_j \, 2^{\mu d(n,j)} = \sum_j p_j \, 2^{\mu d(j,m)}$$

from which $q_j = p_j = M^{-1}$, and, therefore,

$$\xi^{-1} = M^{-1} \sum_j 2^{\mu d(j,n)} = M^{-1} \sum_j 2^{\mu d_j}$$

The conditional assignments are

$$Q(m \mid n) = M^{-1} \xi 2^{\mu d(n,m)} = M^{-1} \xi 2^{\mu d_m}$$

The average distortion is

$$D = M^{-2} \xi \sum_{i,j} d(i,j) \, 2^{\mu d(i,j)} = M^{-1} \xi \sum_i d_i 2^{\mu d_i} \qquad (8.48)$$

Finally, the rate is $R(D) = \mu D + \log \xi$.

EXAMPLE

Now consider equiprobable binary source symbols and binary representation symbols. Using the results of the previous example, we have, therefore, $M = N = 2$ and $q_j = p_j = \frac{1}{2}$. If we now use the Hamming measure of distortion for which the distortion is zero if $x_j = y_j$ and is one otherwise, we have $d(i,j) = 1 - \delta_{i,j}$ where $\delta_{i,j}$ is the Kronecker delta. Letting $\alpha = 2^\mu$ to simplify the notation, there results

$$\xi = \frac{1}{2(1 + \alpha)}$$

$$D = \frac{\alpha}{1 + \alpha}$$

and

$$1 + R(D) = D \log D + (1 - D) \log(1 - D) = h(D) \qquad (8.49)$$

The distortion-rate function corresponding to the solution to $h(D) = 1 + R(D)$ is shown in Fig. 8-5. Note that interchanging the two axes gives back the $R(D)$ function. For $R = 0$, the maximum distortion is $\frac{1}{2}$, corresponding to the maximum "bit error rate" at the coded output. For $R = 1$, one representation bit is allocated for each source bit and the minimum distortion can be made to vanish. This problem can be generalized to the case where the source symbol probabilities are p and $1 - p$ (see Prob. 8.7).

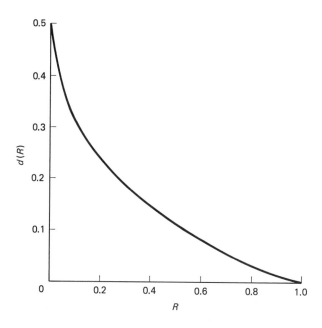

Figure 8-5. Solution to $h(D) = 1 + R(D)$.

8.1.5 Rate and Distortion for a Continuous Source

The results of the previous section can be extended to the very important case of encoding a continuous (i.e., analog) source. Consider two continuous random variables $\mathbf{x}$ and $\mathbf{y}$ having a joint probability density $p(x,y)$. Recall from Chapter 4 that the average mutual information between the continuous random variables $\mathbf{x}$ and $\mathbf{y}$ is given by

$$I(\mathbf{x},\mathbf{y}) = \int\int p(x,y)[\log p(x,y) - \log p(x) - \log q(y)]\, dx\, dy \qquad (8.50)$$

where

$$q(y) = \int Q(y\,|\,x)p(x)\, dx \qquad (8.51)$$

Note from Eq. (4.19), which is repeated here, that

$$I(\mathbf{x},\mathbf{y}) = H(\mathbf{x}) - H(\mathbf{x}|\,\mathbf{y}) = H(\mathbf{y}) - H(\mathbf{y}|\,\mathbf{x})$$

The average mutual information $I(\mathbf{x},\mathbf{y})$ is expressible as the difference of two continuous entropies. As a result, the resulting infinities discussed in Section 4.1.6 exactly cancel and do not affect the average mutual information for continuous processes. The derivations of the distortion and rate functions for continuous processes can be developed along similar lines as for discrete processes. In particular, we can define an average distortion function

$$d^* = \int\int Q(y\,|\,x)p(x,y)d(x,y)\, dx\, dy \qquad (8.52)$$

where $d(x,y)$ is a continuous distortion measure. An example of a continuous distortion measure, the squared difference $d(x,y) = (x - y)^2$ was introduced earlier. With $d*$ as defined in Eq. (8.52), this leads to a mean-square average distortion measure. As with the discrete case, $d*$ is a continuous linear function of the conditional assignment $Q(y\,|\,x)$.

Just as with the discrete case, the rate-distortion function $R(D)$ can be defined in terms of a constrained variational problem, which, for the continuous case, can be stated as follows. We seek the least rate $R(D)$ corresponding to a fidelity criterion $d* \leq D$. The same caveats concerning inequality constraints apply here also. In fact, we shall be solving this variational problem for the equality constraint $d* = D$. That is, we are looking for the conditional assignment $Q = Q(y\,|\,x)$ that makes the following expression stationary:

$$J(Q) = I(\mathbf{x}, \mathbf{y}) - \int\int \lambda(x)Q(y\,|\,x)dx\ dy - \mu\int\int Q(y\,|\,x)p(x)d(x,y)\ dx\ dy \tag{8.53}$$

where $I(\mathbf{x}, \mathbf{y})$ is given by Eq. (8.50). Note again that this can be interpreted either as minimizing the rate for a constant distortion or minimizing the distortion for a fixed rate. By defining a new Lagrange multiplier $\lambda(x) = p(x)\log\xi(x)$, Eq. (8.53) can be rewritten as

$$J(Q) = \int\int Q(y\,|\,x)p(x)\left[\log\frac{Q(y\,|\,x)}{\xi(x)q(y)} - \mu d(x,y)\right] dx\ dy \tag{8.54}$$

This result is similar in form to Eq. (8.38) for the discrete case. The solution to that problem is

$$Q(y\,|\,x) = q(y)\xi(x)2^{\mu d(x,y)} \tag{8.55}$$

Integrating Eq. (8.55) over y, we find that the Lagrange function $\xi(x)$ is given by

$$\xi^{-1}(x) = \int q(y)2^{\mu d(x,y)}\ dy \tag{8.56}$$

The average distortion is

$$D = \int\int p(x)q(y)\xi(x)d(x,y)2^{\mu d(x,y)}\ dx\ dy \tag{8.57}$$

and the rate-distortion function is

$$R(D) = \mu D + \int p(x)\log\xi(x)\ dx \tag{8.58}$$

As before, the parameter μ can be interpreted as the slope of the rate-distortion function. We shall find it convenient to rewrite the exponential term appearing in Eqs. (8.55), (8.56), and (8.57):

$$2^{\mu d(x,y)} = e^{(\mu\ln 2)d(x,y)} = e^{\mu d(x,y)} \tag{8.59}$$

where the constant $\ln 2$ term is, henceforth, understood to be incorporated in the parameter μ. This formalism is usually cumbersome to use in particular situations. The rate-distortion problem can be solved analytically only for a few special cases.

EXAMPLE

We shall now calculate the rate-distortion function for a Gaussian source with respect to a squared difference distortion measure. Let the information source generate a random variable $\mathbf{x}$ that assumes values x that are normally distributed with zero mean and variance σ_s^2. The value of the mean is actually irrelevant, as was found in Prob. 4.8.

Instead of using the previous formalism, we employ a clever bit of reasoning attributed to Shannon [Sh 48b]. We first note that

$$R(D) = \min_{Q(y|x)} I(\mathbf{x}, \mathbf{y}) = \min_{Q(y|x)} \{H(\mathbf{x}) - H(\mathbf{x}|\mathbf{y})\}$$

$$= H(\mathbf{x}) - \max_{Q(y|x)} H(\mathbf{x}|\mathbf{y}) \tag{8.60}$$

Recall again from Section 4.1.6 that the infinities in $H(\mathbf{x})$ and $H(\mathbf{x}|\mathbf{y})$ cancel, so that the difference indicated by Eq. (8.60) is indeed a measure of information. From Prob. 4.6, we find that $H(x) = \log \sigma_s(2\pi e)^{\frac{1}{2}}$. It remains to calculate the maximum value of $H(\mathbf{x}|\mathbf{y})$. Recall that $H(\mathbf{x}|\mathbf{y})$ is the equivocation between $\mathbf{x}$ and $\mathbf{y}$, and that the equivocation measures the amount of information needed to specify $\mathbf{x}$ once $\mathbf{y}$ has been measured. Restricting our analysis to finite power signals, the equivocation $H(\mathbf{x}|\mathbf{y})$ is maximized by $\mathbf{y} = \mathbf{x} + \mathbf{n}$, where $\mathbf{n}$ is a zero-mean Gaussian process with variance σ_0^2. For this case, we have

$$H(\mathbf{x}|\mathbf{y}) = \log \sigma_0(2\pi e)^{\frac{1}{2}} \tag{8.61}$$

The distortion measure is given by $d(x, y) = (x - y)^2$, corresponding to the fidelity criterion

$$D = E[(x - y)^2] = \sigma_0^2 = \epsilon^2$$

where the notation $D = \epsilon^2$ reminds us that the distortion is defined with respect to a mean-square error. The rate-distortion function is, therefore,

$$R(\epsilon^2) = \log \sigma_s(2\pi e)^{\frac{1}{2}} - \log \sigma_0(2\pi e)^{\frac{1}{2}} = \log(\sigma_s/\sigma_0) = \frac{1}{2}\log(\sigma_s^2/\epsilon^2) \tag{8.62}$$

The rate of a Gaussian source with variance σ_s^2 is given by Eq. (8.62), where the distortion is a Gaussian process with variance $\epsilon^2 = \sigma_0^2$. This is a very important result.

8.2 APPLICATIONS

We are now ready to look at some practical considerations of rate-distortion theory. In some cases, the theory helps us understand fundamental limits associated with signal representations. In others, it can help us design coding systems by providing a rational approach to data compression.

The advent of the digital computer and its capacity for fast and accurate calculations again emphasizes the importance of digital signals. Today, digital signal processing stands as one of the principal disciplines of electrical engineering. An increasingly larger proportion of communications is being done digitally. In this section, we will take a look at some applications of rate-distortion theory for cases in which it is necessary to perform some form of analog-to-digital coding.

Most applications of digital signal processing are in one way or another related to physical measurements of analog signals. In communication, the transmission of music or speech starts with a transformation of an acoustic waveform into an equivalent electrical signal. In principle, this mapping from one Hilbert space to another can be made reversible. A simple coordinate transformation suffices. If, however, transmission or storage is to be made over a digital channel, then the music or speech signal from Hilbert space must be mapped into a finite number of signal states and distortion must result. A particularly good example of this is provided by compact disks, on which information is stored digitally. This many-to-one mapping invariably results in distortion, the amount of which falls within the purview of rate-distortion theory.

This section deals mainly with waveform quantization. Much has been written on this subject and it is not possible to do justice to all the relevant material here. The interested reader is encouraged to read the well-written paper on pulse code modulation by Oliver, Pierce, and Shannon [Ol 48]. Additional information on waveform quantization can be found in the IEEE reprints edited by Jayant [Ja 76]. For examples on speech coding, the book by Rabiner and Schafer [Ra 78] is still one of the best texts.

8.2.1 Pulse Code Modulation

There are two types of approximations, and, correspondingly, two types of distortion, involved in the transformation of an analog signal into a digital representation. First, the continuous signal is represented by a finite subset of its coordinates in some signal space. There are several ways to choose these coordinates. For example, the Karhunen–Loève transformation was introduced in Section 5.1.3 to represent continuous waveforms by a set of discrete uncorrelated samples. In practice, sampling at the Nyquist rate suffices to provide an adequate representation. To the extent that the signal to be coded is band-limited, Nyquist sampling provides a perfect representation with a finite number of samples (coordinates) per unit time. The signals we shall consider can all be assumed to be band-limited, so that no degradation results from sampling. This is usually a good approximation, especially when antialiasing filters are used to precondition the analog signal.

The only degradation we shall consider is the result of coding. The samples of an analog signal are real numbers, i.e., scalars from the field of real numbers. Since there is an uncountably infinite number ($\aleph_1$) of such scalars, it is impossible to perfectly represent them with a finite coding alphabet. At some point, approximations must be made, and rate-distortion theory can help us make intelligent design decisions for these approximations.

Pulse code modulation (PCM) is perhaps the simplest way of mapping continuous signals onto a finite alphabet. We are given a real signal, i.e., a signal x defined on the real line. At this point, we shall assume that the original signal has been appropriately sampled, so that the only task remaining is that of representing these real samples with symbols from a finite alphabet. The general approach to this is to partition the real line into a number of (possibly disjoint) segments and to identify for each segment that value x' of x that, in some well-defined way, is most representative for the segment as a whole.

This procedure is illustrated in Fig. 8-6. A portion of the real line is shown partitioned into equal segments of unit length. These segments are identified by the braces above them. With each segment is associated a code word c_k. The signal x to be coded can range anywhere on the real line. The $\times$ in the middle of each segment is the most representative value of x for that segment. By this, we mean that, for example, if the particular value of x that is measured falls within the interval $-0.5 \le x < 0.5$, then we represent it with the average value $x' = 0$ for that interval. For this case, the symbol c_0 is transmitted and decoded as the scalar value $x' = 0$ at the receiver. Similarly, if $1.5 \le x < 2.5$, then the symbol c_2 is transmitted, corresponding to $x' = 2$, and so on. This algorithm completely specifies the mapping, which, in this case, replaces any scalar falling within an interval with the arithmetic average of all scalars in that interval. If the values of x are uniformly distributed, i.e., equally likely anywhere over a segment, then one would expect this approach to result in the least distortion, on the average.

This is clearly a many-to-one mapping. The source signal ranges over the field of real numbers, whereas the representation scalar values are integers. Some information is lost by the coding process. It is impossible to tell, from the representation values, precisely where within an interval the source sample originally was. We can only approximate it to the nearest integer. This coding procedure essentially rounds off real numbers to the nearest integer. It is also clear that despite this loss of information, the approximation can be made better (in the sense of a smaller Euclidian distance between coded and uncoded waveforms) simply by using more smaller intervals. As the number of code words increases, so does the representation precision. Coding devices that operate on the principle shown in Fig. 8-6 are called *analog-to-digital* (A/D) converters.

The operation of an A/D converter is customarily represented by a staircase function such as the one shown in Fig. 8-7. Here we show the same A/D converter as in Fig. 8-6, but with one important difference. Since the number of encoding steps must be finite, we can encode only a finite portion of the real line. In uniform quantization, the length of each x segment is Δ. The length of each y segment is also Δ. Just as with Fig. 8-6, the middle of each segment is chosen as the representative (i.e., decoded) value, and these are described by the y coordinate. The thick staircase-looking function $y(x)$ represents the decoder output as a function of the coder input. For the example shown, the x values are encoded with seven code words.

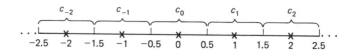

Figure 8-6. Partitioning the real line into segments for coding.

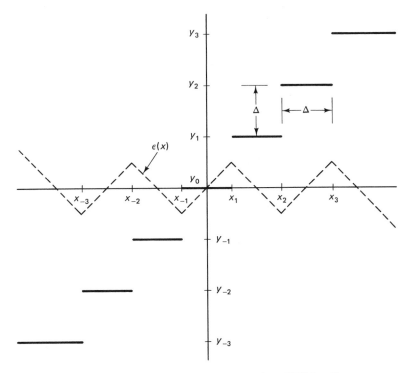

Figure 8-7.   Staircase function representation of PCM coding.

This end-to-end functional representation corresponds to the coder/decoder system shown in Fig. 8-8. Here we take the outputs (code words) of the A/D converter to be fed directly to a *digital-to-analog* (D/A) converter. The D/A converter is a decoder for the code words. The output $y(\mathbf{c}_k)$ of the D/A converter is a real quantity that is a function of the code word. For the purpose of this analysis, we disregard the code-word transmission errors that would normally occur with a real channel. This will let us concentrate on the object of study in this chapter, which is the distortion incurred as a result of representation by a code with a given rate that, in general, can be less than the source entropy. In reality, transmission errors would cause additional degradation.

In addition to the decoder output y as a function of the coder input x, Fig. 8-7 shows, as a dashed line, the quantization error $\epsilon(x) = y(x) - x$. Note that $\epsilon(x)$ vanishes only at certain values of x. In general, $\epsilon(x)$ is nonzero and exhibits a characteristic triangular-wave functional dependence on x. This form of distortion is called *quantization noise* or *granular noise*. Note that except for end effects, the maximum excursion of $\epsilon(x)$ away from zero is $\pm\frac{1}{2}\Delta$. The error $\epsilon(x)$ can be made arbitrarily small by making the step size Δ small. Decreasing Δ causes the staircase

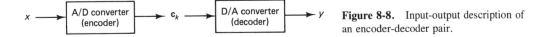

Figure 8-8.   Input-output description of an encoder-decoder pair.

function to look more and more like a 45° line, i.e., we approach the perfect coder
$y(x) \approx x$. Thus, quantization noise can be controlled by varying the quantizer step
size.

At both ends of the coding range, however, the error $\epsilon(x)$ increases without
bound. This is the result of truncation or clipping, which occurs because there is
no way to represent values of x that are greater or smaller than set limits if a finite
number of code words are to be used. For the example shown in Fig. 8-7, these limits
are $x_{max} = x_3 = 2.5\Delta$ and $x_{min} = x_{-3} = -2.5\Delta$. The range from x_{min} to x_{max} is called
the *peak-to-peak* range of the coder. The only way to control clipping is to extend
the maximum range of the quantizer. To do that without increasing quantization
noise requires more quantization steps, and, therefore, more code words.

In practical situations, physical considerations naturally limit the range of
values a signal x is likely to take, and a quantization range can be chosen to make
clipping, at most, an occasional occurrence.

The function $y(x)$ shown in Fig. 8-7 is precisely the conditional assignment
$Q(y \mid x)$ for encoding a real scalar. We shall take this $Q(y \mid x)$ to be a given quantity
for the moment. The A/D converter of Fig. 8-7 and its associated $Q(y \mid x)$ were not
obtained as the solution of a variational problem. Plausibility for the structure of this
coder is argued on the basis that, under certain conditions, namely, equally likely
x, the average value of x in a segment is the best representation for the segment.
Also, as the number of segments increases, this coder approaches (but never actually
becomes) a perfect coder.

Before getting into a quantitative analysis of PCM, we should mention that
there are two ways of structuring a PCM coder. The quantizer shown in Fig. 8-7
encodes $x = 0$ into $y = 0$. This is done by making the value $x = 0$ fall in the
middle of one of the x segments. This is called a *mid-run* quantizer. Note that for
a mid-run quantizer with an even number M of quantization levels, there results an
unbalanced output. This is because $y = 0$ is one of the levels, leaving $M - 1$ (an
odd number) levels to be split between positive and negative signals. The effect of
the resulting imbalance may be made small if M is sufficiently large. This situation
can be avoided by using an odd number M of levels, but available A/D and D/A
converters as a rule are even-M devices, with M usually being a power of 2.

The advantage of using a mid-run quantizer is that for very small signals, or
when only low-level ($x \ll \Delta$) zero-mean noise is present, the source is consistently
represented by $y = 0$. This may occur, for example, during speech coding, when
waveform $x(t)$ consists of a period of silence and only noise is present at the source.
For this case, we say that the *quiescent state* of the coder is zero. An example of a
three-bit mid-run quantizer is shown in Fig. 8-9(b).

Consider, on the other hand, the three-bit coder shown in Fig. 8-9(a). Here
the x segments are distributed evenly for positive and negative x and result in a
balanced output y. However, low-level noise is sometimes represented as $y = -\frac{1}{2}\Delta$
and sometimes as $y = \frac{1}{2}\Delta$, depending on the polarity of x. If x is low-level zero-
mean random noise, then the output y flips at random between the values $-\frac{1}{2}\Delta$ and
$\frac{1}{2}\Delta$. When speech or music is coded that way, very low-level signals are reproduced
as a buzzing noise caused by these random transitions. With a fixed step size, the
quiescent state of a mid-rise coder is characterized by random granular noise. Since

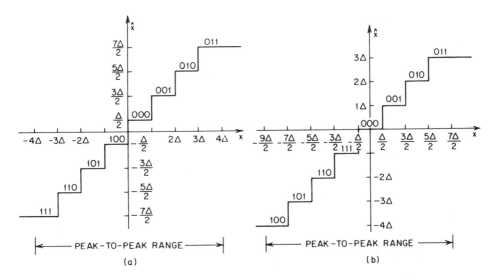

Figure 8-9. (a) Mid-rise and (b) mid-run PCM coders. Each quantizing step is labeled with a binary code word. (After Lawrence R. Rabiner and Ronald W. Schafer, *Digital Processing of Speech Signals*, Englewood Cliffs, NJ: Prentice-Hall, Inc., 1978.)

the magnitude of that noise is related to the fixed step size, it cannot be decreased. In effect, this is nonlinear amplification of the noise process. The coded values represent the algebraic sign of the noise, regardless of noise amplitude.

It is clear by now that PCM quantization always results in some degradation. This degradation can be made very small by increasing the peak-to-peak quantizer range and by using a large number of steps, but can never be made to vanish. We already have a semiquantitative understanding of this. Real signals correspond to infinite information sources and, therefore, cannot be exactly represented with a finite M-ary coding alphabet. This was studied in the last section in conjunction with the rate-distortion function of a continuous source with respect to a distortion measure. Given that we must accept some distortion, it is important to quantify that distortion and express it in terms of coding parameters. This is a first step in the intelligent selection of coding parameters.

We proceed next with a very simple analysis of PCM distortion. For this, we shall assume that the source signal $x(t)$ has been exactly represented as a sequence of scalars, for example, by sampling a band-limited signal at the Nyquist rate. We further assume that a sample x presented at the PCM encoder input contains no extraneous noise, but consists entirely of the desired signal we wish to represent with symbols from a finite M-ary alphabet. In general, the samples of x will assume different values. We make the final assumption that these values all fall within the quantization range of the encoder. In other words, we assume that distortion is due entirely to quantization noise and not to clipping. This situation may be closely approximated by choosing an appropriate peak-to-peak range for the encoder.

Let us consider a quantizer with $M = 2^b$ steps, where b is the number of bits per code word. The step size is Δ for all steps, i.e., we are considering uniform quantizer steps. If the source samples are uncorrelated and sufficiently different one from the other, and if M is sufficiently large, then each sample will access a different quantizer segment. The precise value of x reached within a segment will be random and uniformly distributed. In other words, for each of the M quantization intervals, a histogram of the values of x for that interval would tend to be flat if a sufficiently large number of samples were collected. The random variable x is uniformly distributed within an interval with a mean of x' and a variance of $\Delta^2/12$. The quantization noise process $\epsilon(x)$ is, therefore, also uniformly distributed, but with zero mean and variance $\Delta^2/12$. We now consider the D/A output to be the linear sum of the A/D input plus a quantization noise $\epsilon(x)$ term

$$y(x) = x + \epsilon(x) \tag{8.63}$$

Thus, we view the effect of the quantization process as resulting in an additive independent noise process being combined with the signal. The reproduced signal is additively contaminated with quantization noise, and we can now quantify this effect by considering the signal-to-quantizing noise ratio. An estimate of the signal-to-noise ratio can easily be made. The maximum peak-to-peak signal amplitude is $M\Delta = 2^b\Delta$, corresponding to a signal sample energy of $2^{2b}\Delta^2$. In reality, a calculation of the average signal energy should involve the probability density $p(x)$ for the source variable x:

$$\sigma_x^2 = \int (x - \mu)^2 p(x)\, dx \qquad \text{where } \mu_x = \int x p(x)\, dx \tag{8.64}$$

which results in the variance for that variable. Different densities $p(x)$ result in numerically slightly different signal-to-noise ratios, but these differences are small and do not affect the generalities we wish to point out in the result. We consider, therefore, the signal energy to correspond to the full peak-to-peak energy. The quantization noise (or variance) was already seen to be $\Delta^2/12$. The resulting signal-to-noise ratio for a PCM quantizer is, therefore,

$$\text{SNR} = \frac{2^{2b}\Delta^2}{\Delta^2/12} = 12 \times 2^{2b} \tag{8.65}$$

In decibels, this becomes

$$\text{SNR} = 10.79 + 6.02b \text{ dB} \tag{8.66}$$

The result we wish to show is that each quantization bit contributes approximately 6 dB of signal-to-noise ratio, or, equivalently, of dynamic range. The constant term on the right-hand side of Eq. (8.66) varies with the probabilistic model used for the source process x. Clearly, the simplistic model used before results in the highest signal-to-noise ratio. Instead, we could have assumed that x is uniformly distributed over all quantizer steps, and, in fact, this is more in line with our understanding of how a quantizer works. For this case, the signal variance (i.e., its energy) is $M^2\Delta^2/12$, and the signal-to-noise ratio becomes

$$\text{SNR} = M^2 = 2^{2b} \qquad (6.02b \text{ dB}) \tag{8.67}$$

Since the uniform density is the most random, any other density $p(x)$ will necessarily result in a lower SNR. Again, Eq. (8.67) brings out the universal result of 6 dB per quantization bit.

Now let us look at the quantization process as a transmission channel corrupted by additive noise. We can use the results of Section 4.2.5 to calculate the capacity of that channel per channel use. One channel use corresponds to quantizing a single sample. For this case, $n = 1$ since there is only one signal coordinate, and Eq. (4.81) for the amount of information per sample becomes

$$I = \tfrac{1}{2}\log(1 + 2\gamma) = \tfrac{1}{2}\log(1 + 2^{2b}) \qquad (8.68)$$

where $\gamma = \tfrac{1}{2}\mathscr{E}/N_0$, with $\mathscr{E} = M^2\Delta^2/12$ and $N_0 = \Delta^2/12$. If the number of quantization steps is large, then we have $2^{2b} \gg 1$, and there results $I \approx b$ bits per channel use. As we saw earlier, the signal-to-noise ratio corresponding to uniform signal density is the largest possible SNR and, therefore, yields the maximum capacity. For any other source density $p(x)$, the capacity will be less than b bits per channel use.

8.2.2 The Max Quantizer

The problem of optimizing a PCM quantizer was formally solved by Joel Max [Ma 60b]. He assumed a very general PCM structure in which, for a fixed number M of steps, all x and y intervals may assume different values. He then solved for the values of these intervals that result in the minimum average distortion for a given distortion measure and source statistics. This section closely follows the development presented in [Ma 60b].

Given a distortion measure $f(x - y)$ and a source x with probability density $p(x)$ being encoded as the scalar y, a distortion may be defined by the statistical ensemble average

$$D = \sum_{k=1}^{M} \int_{x_k}^{x_{k+1}} f(x - y_k)p(x)\, dx \qquad (8.69)$$

where the y_k are the M decoder outputs. This equation can be interpreted as follows. A source sample x falling in the interval $[x_k, x_{k+1})$ is mapped into the value y_k. For that interval, the distortion is $f(x - y_k)$ for every $x \in [x_k, x_{k+1})$. The distortion is averaged over the interval. The overall average distortion for all the steps is simply the sum of the average interval distortions. Equation (8.69) contains all that is needed to optimize the coding process: it is an expression for the average distortion D expressed in terms of the known coder/decoder structure, the yet to be determined step sizes $\{x_k, y_k; k = 1, \ldots, M\}$, the given definition of the distortion measure $f(x - y_k)$, and the known statistics $p(x)$ of the source process. With this information, it is a simple exercise in differentiation to minimize the average distortion D with respect to the unknown step sizes.

The formal solution proceeds by calculating the partial derivative of D with respect to the step sizes and by setting these derivatives equal to zero. This results in $2M - 1$ equations:

$$\frac{\partial D}{\partial x_j} = [f(x_j - y_{j-1}) - f(x_j - y_j)]p(x_j) \qquad j = 2, \ldots, M \qquad (8.70)$$

and

$$\frac{\partial D}{\partial y_j} = -\int_{x_j}^{x_{j+1}} f'(x - y_j)p(x)\,dx \qquad j = 1, \ldots, M \qquad (8.71)$$

where the prime indicates partial differentiation with respect to y_j. Setting these derivatives equal to zero, we obtain

$$f(x_j - y_{j-1}) = f(x_j - y_j) \qquad j = 2, \ldots, M \qquad (8.72)$$

and

$$\int_{x_j}^{x_{j+1}} f'(x - y_j)p(x)\,dx = 0 \qquad j = 1, \ldots, M \qquad (8.73)$$

Equations (8.72) and (8.73) form $2M - 1$ conditions that can be used to solve for $2M - 1$ unknowns: the M x interval endpoints that specify the equivalence classes used in the many-to-one encoding process and the corresponding $M - 1$ values of the decoder outputs.

If we now require the distortion function $f(x)$ to be nonnegative, even symmetric, and a monotonically increasing function of its argument, then Eq. (8.72) implies

$$|x_j - y_{j-1}| = |x_j - y_j|$$

and, therefore,

$$x_j = \tfrac{1}{2}(y_j + y_{j-1}) \qquad (8.74)$$

which can be written as a recursion for y_j:

$$y_j = 2x_j - y_{j-1} \qquad (8.75)$$

A specific example can be worked out for the optimal PCM encoding of a source with respect to a square distortion measure. Setting $f(x) = x^2$, Eq. (8.73) becomes

$$\int_{x_j}^{x_{j+1}} (x - y_j)p(x)\,dx = 0 \qquad j = 1, \ldots, M \qquad (8.76)$$

from which

$$y_j = p_j^{-1}\int_{x_j}^{x_{j+1}} x p(x)\,dx \qquad \text{where } p_j = \int_{x_j}^{x_{j+1}} p(x)\,dx \qquad j = 1, \ldots, M \quad (8.77)$$

Note that $f(x) = x^2$ is a metric. Equations (8.76) and (8.77) are valid for any $p(x)$. Equations (8.75) and (8.77) can be solved numerically for given $p(x)$ and M. The solution will be the step sizes $\{x_j, y_j\}$ that result in the least distortion for a mean-square fidelity criterion and a source probability density $p(x)$. Max solved this problem for a Gaussian source

$$p(x) = \frac{1}{(2\pi)^{\frac{1}{2}}} e^{-x^2/2} \tag{8.78}$$

with zero mean and unit variance. Numerical results for several values of M are tabulated in [Ma 60b].

The results derived thus far are for an optimized hypothetical quantizer for which the x and y step sizes have been chosen to result in the least average distortion. Commercially available quantizers do not have that flexibility. Hardware A/D converters have $M = 2^b$ equal steps, with decoded y values chosen to be in the middle of the corresponding x interval. One would, therefore, expect these devices to have a poorer performance than the optimal quantizers defined by Eqs. (8.75) and (8.77). Max then asked and answered the important question: "Precisely how much poorer is the performance of a real A/D compared to the hypothetical optimum?" For this case, Max [Ma 60b] has shown that for an even number $M = 2N$ outputs, (see Prob. 8.9), we have

$$D = 2 \sum_{k=1}^{N-1} \int_{(k-1)\Delta}^{k\Delta} f[x - \tfrac{1}{2}(2k-1)\Delta] p(x)\, dx$$

$$+ 2 \int_{(N-1)\Delta}^{\infty} f[x - \tfrac{1}{2}(2N-1)\Delta] p(x)\, dx \tag{8.79}$$

where Δ is the unknown step size. A similar expression exists for odd M. To solve for the optimum Δ, we simply set the derivative of D with respect to Δ equal to zero:

$$\frac{dD}{d\Delta} = - \sum_{k=1}^{N-1} (2k-1) \int_{(k-1)\Delta}^{k\Delta} f'[x - \tfrac{1}{2}(2k-1)\Delta] p(x)\, dx$$

$$- (2N-1) \int_{(N-1)\Delta}^{\infty} f'[x - \tfrac{1}{2}(2N-1)\Delta] p(x)\, dx = 0 \tag{8.80}$$

Again, Max obtained numerical results for $f(x) = x^2$ and a zero-mean unit-variance Gaussian source.

Max's principal numerical results on PCM coder distortion are summarized in Fig. 8-10. This figure expresses the average distortion, Eqs. (8.69) and (8.79) for the optimum and fixed-step-size PCM coders as a function of the number of steps M. As expected, the average distortion decreases as M is increased. Note that the fixed-step coder does not perform appreciably better than the optimum coder. This indicates that commercially available devices perform almost as well as an optimum PCM coder. It is probably not worth the effort to develop an optimum system.

Another comparison is made in Fig. 8-10. The solid line represents the least amount of distortion according to rate-distortion theory. This line was computed from Eq. (8.63) with $\sigma_s = 1$. The coding rate was set at $\log M$, giving a minimum distortion of M^{-2}. This limit provides an absolute basis against which to compare

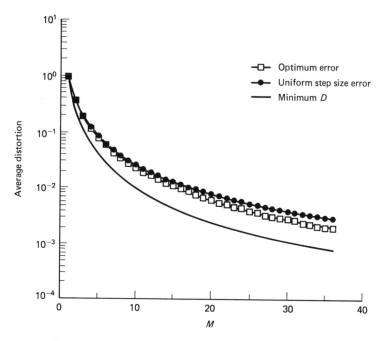

Figure 8-10. PCM distortion for the optimal (squares) and fixed-Δ (diamonds) coders. The solid line shows the least distortion allowed by rate-distortion theory.

the optimum and fixed-Δ PCM quantizers. To achieve a distortion that is closer to that limit, a quantizer would have to be more sophisticated than simple PCM. For example, a quantizer could incorporate linear predictive circuits that exploit known sample-to-sample correlations in the source signal. Other approaches exploit known spectral features. More sophisticated coders likely have distortions that fall somewhere between the PCM curves and the solid line of Fig. 8-10.

To achieve the performance shown in Fig. 8-10, the fixed-Δ fixed-M coders have been optimally matched to the source dynamic range. Given such a coder, the data must be scaled to match the source variance to the coder range. In this manner, the data are scaled to fit the coder. This is equivalent to fitting the Δ to the data variance, but allows the fitting to be done by a simple scaling operation and, therefore, allows the use of standardized PCM coders. This scaling can be done adaptively, as shown in Fig. 8-11. The coder output state is sensed and negatively fed back to a variable-gain amplifier. The feedback gain parameter is chosen to keep the coder input matched to the actual range of the coder. A similar circuit at the decoder can restore the original scaling. The insertion of nonlinearities can be used to achieve an effect similar to that of having unequal step sizes. A popular technique with speech signals is logarithmic companding [Ra 78]. The object of these signal-processing techniques is to match the source signal's dynamic range to that of the quantizer.

The coding process maps an infinite information source $x(t)$ into a finite M-ary alphabet having a finite information rate. A continuous information source is represented by a discrete memoryless source with an entropy given by

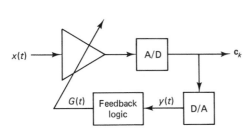

Figure 8-11.   Adaptively matching source and coder dynamic ranges. The source signal $x(t)$ is encoded into the symbols $\{c_k\}$, which are then sent to the destination. The $\{c_k\}$ are also decoded locally into $y(t)$ and fed back to the gain adaptation logic. This results in a gain control $G(t)$ that is similar to the automatic gain control (AGC) in receivers and to the automatic level control (ALC) in transmitters. Large $y(t)$ produce small gains and vice versa.

$$H_s(M) = -\sum_{k=1}^{M} p_k \log p_k \qquad (8.81)$$

where the code word probabilities p_k are given by

$$p_k = \int_{x_k}^{x_{k+1}} p(x)\,dx \qquad k = 1, \ldots, M-1 \qquad (8.82)$$

The code word entropy $H_s(M)$ is shown plotted against M for both the optimal and fixed-Δ PCM quantizers in Fig. 8-12. Also shown on this plot as a solid line is log M. The proximity of $H_s(M)$ to log M for both coders shows that a simple binary encoding of the PCM coder outputs is reasonably efficient.

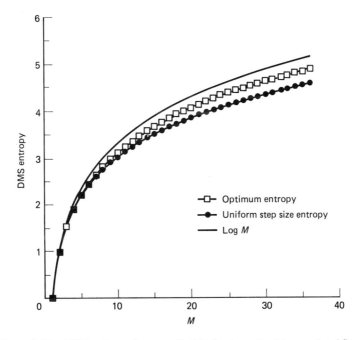

Figure 8-12.   PCM code word entropy $H_s(M)$ for the optimal (squares) and fixed-Δ (diamonds) coders. The solid line is log M, the number of bits needed to provide a binary representation for M steps.

Note that $H_s(M) \approx \log M$ implies that the code words $\mathbf{c}_k$ are approximately equiprobable. With this in mind, let us step back and take in a broader view of analog source coding. The source waveform $x(t)$ may be from any continuous band-limited process. For example, $x(t)$ may represent speech or music signals. The source signal usually has a correlation structure that is removed by a Karhunen–Loève transformation or, when possible, by sampling at the Nyquist rate. This signal-processing step removes from $x(t)$ its obvious correlation structure and presents uncorrelated samples to the encoder.

From these uncorrelated samples, the encoder produces a sequence of equiprobable code words, or at least as close to equiprobable as possible. This, in effect, removes the remaining statistical structure from the samples and results in a sequence of code words having maximum information entropy. These samples are maximally random.

Recall from Chapter 4 that the symmetric DMC capacity is maximized precisely when the source symbols are equiprobable. Our source coder, by transforming $x(t)$ into a set of equiprobable symbols, has, in effect, matched $x(t)$ to the DMC: it has represented $x(t)$ with the least distortion and in a manner that will make optimal use of the DMC capacity. This source-to-channel match is precisely what the communication engineer strives to achieve. We have approached this result piecemeal in previous chapters by considering the conceptually separate steps of source and channel coding. When we studied source coding, the goal was to obtain an efficient and reversible representation for the information source. When we studied channel coding, the goal was to make maximum use of channel capacity. For the symmetric DMC, this was accomplished by using a DMS with equiprobable symbols. In both cases, there are theorems due to Shannon that guarantee that these goals are, in principle, achievable.

Our study of rate-distortion theory is giving us a deeper appreciation of the mathematical theory of communication. We can view source and channel coding as a single operation that maps any information source signal $x(t)$ into a set of equiprobable channel symbols that simultaneously form the best representation of $x(t)$ and drive the channel at full capacity. This optimum *metacoder* structure is achievable, according to Shannon's theorems and could, in principle, be constructed as a single box that simultaneously performs source and channel coding.

The overall function of the metacoder is to transform a correlated signal $x(t)$ into a set of uncorrelated random signals. All of the source signal's correlation and statistical structures are removed by the metacoder. The metacoder output can, in fact, be considered random by the randomness criterion presented in Chapter 3. The metacoder achieves a minimal algorithm representation of $x(t)$.

It is not really necessary to consider source and channel coding as separate operations. Such a separation is fortunate from a pedagogical point of view. But the beautiful unifying structure of the mathematical theory of communication would be missed altogether if we continued to insist on this artificial dichotomy.

We note with some interest that the metacoder does nothing more than a mapping from the information source waveform $x(t)$ to a set of channel signalling waveforms. The corresponding metadecoder reverses this operation, but must do so through statistical estimation since its measurements are, in general, noisy.

8.2.3 Analog Signal Quantization Performance

Some of the practical considerations of using A/D coders were studied by Goblick and Holsinger [Go 67]. This section summarizes some of their interesting findings in comparing the limits stated by rate-distortion theory to the performance achievable by practical waveform coders.

In this section, we consider the coding of a zero-mean analog signal $x(t)$ having Gaussian statistics and variance $E[x^2(t)] = A$. As a fidelity criterion, we use the mean-square error between $x(t)$ and its reproduction $y(t)$ at the decoder output, i.e.,

$$\epsilon^2 = E\{[x(t) - y(t)]^2\} \tag{8.83}$$

The source probability density function $p(u)$ is defined by

$$\text{Prob } \{u \le x(t) < u + du\} = p(u)\, du$$

where

$$p(u) = \frac{1}{(2\pi A)^{\frac{1}{2}}} e^{-u^2/2A}$$

Three different approaches for digitally representing an analog signal $x(t)$ can be used to illustrate the relationship between performance and implementation complexity, and especially what can be achieved with available hardware. The simplest approach would be to use a uniform (i.e., equal Δ steps) quantizer with M steps and to directly represent the output symbols with b binary digits, where

$$M \le 2^b \tag{8.84}$$

Here a binary representation of the PCM output symbol is made as each sample of $x(t)$ is encoded. Of course, if M is a power of 2, then $M = 2^b$, and the encoding process is efficient. Otherwise, the inefficiency implied by inequality (8.84) results. The situation is similar to the inefficiency that occurred in Section 4.1.4 when we tried to encode various extensions of a hypothetical alphabet of 37 equiprobable letters. To represent that source in binary form, we had to use a binary code containing a number of code words that is the next higher power of 2 as there were source symbols to encode. This sometimes resulted in unused code words, an inefficiency that tended to decrease as larger and larger extensions of the source alphabet were considered.

At an intermediate level of complexity, the same sort of logic can be used in the present problem to remove this type of coding inefficiency. If the PCM output is over an alphabet of M code words, we can efficiently match this to a power of 2 by encoding a block of N PCM symbols, where

$$N M = 2^b$$

with b an integer. In other words, we choose 2^b to be a multiple (preferably the least common multiple) of N and M.

The third and best approach would be to use a code that achieves the Shannon limit. Here we consider the coder output to be a DMS with symbol probabilities $P(\mathbf{c}_k)$ and source entropy

$$H_s(M) = -\sum_{k=1}^{M} P(\mathbf{c}_k) \log P(\mathbf{c}_k) \tag{8.85}$$

This can result in a very complex implementation. We will refer to this technique as *entropy coding*. Putting aside the practical implications of finding such a code, we assume that the code is available and use it as a performance bound since no better code exists. Since the source signal $x(t)$ has Gaussian statistics and since the distortion is with respect to a mean-square fidelity criterion, the rate-distortion function is given by

$$R(\epsilon^2) = \tfrac{1}{2}\log(A/\epsilon^2) \tag{8.86}$$

bits per sample.

Goblick and Holsinger's results for Gaussian source digitization are shown in Fig. 8-13 In this figure, $R(\epsilon^2)$ as computed from Eq. (8.86) is the lowest curve shown and represents the fundamental limit imposed by rate-distortion theory. Three curves for $H_s(M)$ are shown, corresponding to $M = 10$, 20, and 40. These curves are, in general, double-valued in the data rate for a given value of A/ϵ^2. The $H_s(M)$

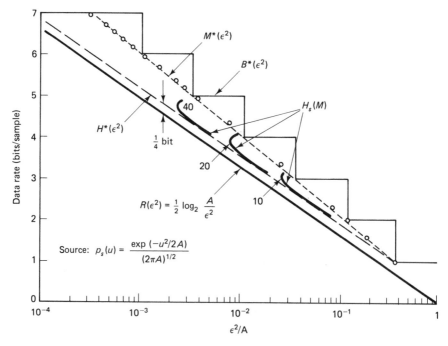

Figure 8-13. Data rates required to transmit uniform quantizer outputs as a function of the dimensionless parameter A/ϵ^2. Also shown are curves of quantizer output entropy $H_s(M)$ plotted against A/ϵ^2 for $M = 10$, 20, and 40. (Reproduced from [Go 67] by permission. ©1967 IEEE.)

curves were computed by varying the quantizer's maximum amplitude range for a fixed M or, what is equivalent, by varying the step size Δ for a constant M. The lower branches for each $H_s(M)$ curve are very well approximated by the expression

$$H^*(\epsilon^2/A) = \tfrac{1}{4} + \tfrac{1}{2}\log(A/\epsilon^2) \qquad (8.87)$$

bits per sample. Note that this is only one-quarter of a bit per sample more than the absolute minimum required by rate-distortion theory for any coding scheme. The implication of this result is that the entropy encoding of the uniform PCM quantizer outputs comes within one-quarter of a bit per sample of the best possible encoding for an analog Gaussian source.

We now take a brief aside to comment on the significance of the two branches of the $H_s(M)$ curves. These curves were generated by varying the step size Δ. At one extreme, Δ is very small and the entropy is high because the entire coder range is contained close to the center of the Gaussian distribution, where the probability density of $x(t)$ is approximately uniform. A large distortion is incurred because most values of $x(t)$ fall outside the coder range and are clipped. At the other extreme, when Δ is very large, the entire source range falls within one or at most two quantizing steps. The entropy is correspondingly low and the distortion is high because $x(t)$ is represented by only a few scalars per sample.

Somewhere in between these two extremes lies the condition that gives rise to the turning points in the $H_s(M)$ curves shown in Fig. 8-13. These points correspond to the lowest distortion achievable by matching the quantizer to the source's dynamic range. The lower envelopes of these curves are tangent to the quantity $H^*(\epsilon^2/A)$ given by Eq. (8.87). This is the minimum rate achievable for a given distortion. The optimum operating points on these $H^*(\epsilon^2/A)$ curves are the turning points where the dimensionless distortion ϵ^2/A is a minimum.

The most complex encoding scheme is entropy coding. Entropy coding is not normally used in a practical situation, but is shown here as an absolute performance limit against which other techniques can be compared. For example, the constant-Δ PCM quantizer considered by Max [Ma 60b] can be evaluated against this benchmark. The circles in Fig. 8-13 represent the rate as given by $\log M$ and the distortion as computed by Max [Ma 60b] for the uniform quantizer. The rates given by the circles correspond to the binary encoding of blocks of several PCM code words. These points are approximated by the equation

$$M^*(\epsilon^2) = 0.125 + 0.6\log(A/\epsilon^2) \qquad (8.88)$$

bits per sample. The staircase curve in Fig. 8-13 represents the performance of directly converting the PCM outputs into binary digits.

8.2.4 Coding Speech Signals

A good example of the utility of rate-distortion theory is provided by the encoding of speech signals. While it is possible to quantize speech signals by encoding successive speech samples with uniform PCM, a considerable reduction in coding rate can be realized if the spectral structure of speech is exploited. The long-term power spectral density of speech for male and female speakers is shown in Fig. 8-14. The peak in the spectrum occurs somewhere between 100 and 500 Hz. Above approximately 4 kHz,

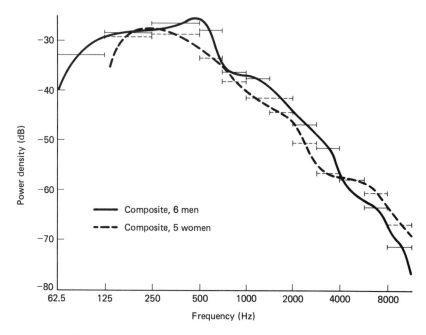

Figure 8-14. Long-term power spectral density of speech. (After Dunn and White [Du 40].)

the power spectral density is roughly 30 dB below its peak value. In many practical applications, speech spectral components above 4 kHz can be safely ignored and are, in fact, removed by an antialiasing filter prior to sampling. This leaves 8000 real samples per second, which must be encoded by uniform PCM at eight bits per sample in order to produce acceptable quality speech. This adds up to 64 kbps, which is very large. There are many ways of designing sophisticated coders to reduce this coding rate. All exploit source signal structure. This section describes one such technique, subband coding, and shows the role played by rate-distortion theory in the design of subband coders. More details on subband coding can be found in [Cr 76, Cr 77, Cr 81, and Gr 80].

The functions shown in Fig. 8-14 indicate that speech power (or energy) is unequally distributed across the spectrum. This implies that there is more signal variability at frequencies where the spectral density is high. Another way of looking at this is to consider speech as being a linear superposition of various spectral components, each having a different long-time norm. We would intuitively expect information to be apportioned in proportion to the spectral density. This becomes clearer when we examine the waveform being reconstructed at the receiver. There we can model the waveform as a linear superposition of the original source signal plus quantization noise. If we assume quantization noise to be white, then the sphere-packing argument of Chapter 4 can be invoked to argue that the speech spectral components having the largest norm also contain the most information and should be allocated more quantization bits.

In addition to being unevenly distributed in frequency, speech energy is also unevenly distributed in time. Figure 8-15 shows a spectrogram of speech obtained by plotting the time evolution of short-time Fourier spectra. In Fig. 8-15, the ordinate represents the frequency axis, from 0 to 5 kHz, and the abcissa is time. The spectral density is highest in the dark areas of the plot. This spectrogram spans 1.6 seconds of speech. The sentence spoken is "Why do I owe you a letter." What we wish to point out here is that speech energy changes at the syllabic rate, reapportioning itself over the spectrum as time advances.

Subband coding exploits this spectral structure by separating the speech spectrum into several separate frequency bands (the subbands), and then by encoding each band separately. Instead of spending coding resources (i.e., bits) uniformly across the spectrum, these coding bits are judiciously used where the information really is.

This approach is illustrated in Fig. 8-16. In this example, the speech spectrum has been limited to a range from 0 to 4 kHz by an antialiasing filter not shown in the diagram. A bank of analysis bandpass filters (F_1–F_4) is then used to separate the speech spectrum into four frequency subbands. In this example, the subbands are all shown with equal bandwidths. In general, the bandwidths need not be equal. The output of each filter is individually sampled at the appropriate Nyquist rate for that filter. The four sample streams thus formed are then passed to four separate source coders (C_1–C_4) where each stream is digitized. The coder outputs can then be multiplexed, if necessary, and transmitted over a channel.

Decoding involves the inverse of this process and is not shown in the figure. The four coded signals are first individually decoded and processed by a synthesis filter bank that reconstitutes an image of the original speech signal.

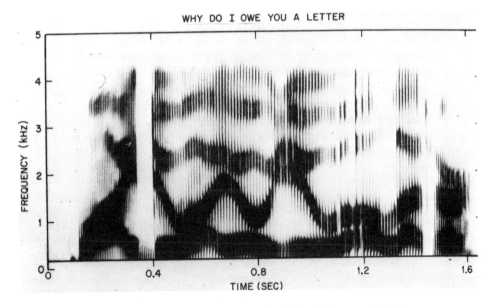

Figure 8-15.   Speech spectrogram. (After Atal and Hannauer [At 71].)

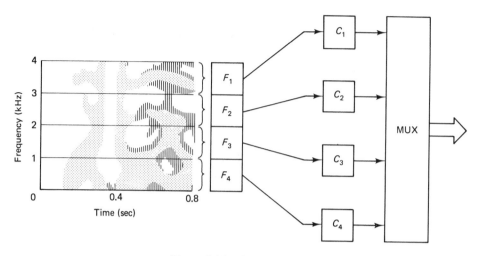

Figure 8-16.   Subband coder.

Speech is usually encoded with a fixed channel-capacity constraint. For example, a digital channel of 16 kbps may, typically, be available, and the speech coding problem reduces to finding the best way (i.e., lowest distortion) to encode speech for that fixed channel data rate.

Two strategies can be used to determine the optimal coder parameters: static and adaptive. These coder parameters include the number of bits allocated to each subband and possible linear prediction coefficients if these are used. We shall be exclusively concerned with the bit allocation across the subbands, as this is the principal parameter to be adjusted. In static bit allocation, the number of bits assigned to each subband is permanently determined by the long-term speech spectral density, for instance, the function shown in Fig. 8-14. In an adaptive coder, the speech spectrum is measured, for example, by measuring the instantaneous power in each of the subbands, and then the bits are dynamically reallocated according to the local spectral estimate.

In either case, some strategy is needed to exploit the spectral structure of speech and to convert this into a bit assignment. This strategy is based on rate-distortion theory. The rate associated with a Gaussian source with respect to a mean-square error ϵ^2 fidelity criterion is

$$R = \tfrac{1}{2} \log(\sigma^2/\epsilon^2) \qquad (8.89)$$

where σ^2 is the variance (i.e., the power) of the Gaussian source process. If we assume that speech is approximately Gaussian, then we can apply Eq. (8.89) to each of the subbands. If the M subbands are denoted by the index $k = 1, \ldots, M$, then we can express the total distortion across all subbands as

$$D = \sum_{k=1}^{M} \epsilon^2(k) = \sum_{k=1}^{M} \sigma^2(k)e^{-2\rho(k)\ln 2} \qquad (8.90)$$

The assumption that speech has Gaussian statistics in a subband can be approximately justified by invoking the central limit theorem at the output of the analysis filters. The results of this approximation can often be justified a posteriori by the performance of the coder thus designed. In any case, the derivation presented here may be repeated for non-Gaussian statistics if warranted. We use Gaussian statistics here to simplify the calculations. Note also that Eq. (8.90) assumes that the error processes are statistically independent across the subbands, and, therefore, their variances are additive.

From the user's point of view, it is the total distortion D that must be minimized with respect to the subband bit assignments $\rho(k)$. This assignment is constrained, however, by the fixed channel capacity R, so that we are dealing with a constrained minimization problem. If we denote by $w(k)$ the bandwidth of the kth subband, with total source signal bandwidth W, then we have

$$W = \sum_{k=1}^{M} w(k) \tag{8.91}$$

since the subbands do not overlap. The convention used here is that the source signal is real and, therefore, has a symmetric Fourier spectrum. The bandwidths are understood to be one-sided bandwidths, measuring the spectral widths of positive or negative frequency components. The constraint on the total rate R is expressed as

$$R = 2 \sum_{k=1}^{M} \rho(k)w(k) \tag{8.92}$$

since each subband is sampled at the Nyquist rate of $2w(k)$ real samples per second. Minimizing Eq. (8.90) with respect to the M values of $\rho(k)$, taking into account the constraint implied by Eq. (8.92) leads to the constrained minimization problem:

$$J = \sum_{k=1}^{M} \sigma^2(k)e^{-2\rho(k)\ln 2} + 2\lambda \sum_{k=1}^{M} \rho(k)w(k) \tag{8.93}$$

where λ is a Lagrange multiplier. We seek the subband coder bit assignment $\rho(k)$ that makes the quantity J stationary. The solution to this problem is

$$\rho(k) = \frac{R}{2W} + \frac{1}{2}\log\frac{\sigma^2(k)}{\theta(k)} \tag{8.94}$$

where $\theta(k)$ is given by

$$\theta(k) = w(k)\prod_{j=1}^{M}\left[\frac{\sigma^2(j)}{w(j)}\right]^{w(j)/W} \tag{8.95}$$

A similar expression was derived by Cheung and Winslow [Ch 80] for the design of an eight-band coder. The first term in Eq. (8.94) is simply the average data rate for the entire signal. The second term accounts for variations above and below this average, according to the details of $\sigma^2(k)$, the source power spectral density averaged over the subband.

What we have done, for the special case of a finite number of subbands, is to find the optimal bit allocation for a given spectral density for a Gaussian signal. For a subband coder, the spectral density is defined crudely as $\sigma^2(k)/w(k)$ for the kth subband. We can use this analytical approach to investigate the more general problem of finding how a continuous coding rate should be spectrally distributed for a Gaussian signal. This is easily solved by letting the previous derivation pass to the limit of a continuum as $M \rightarrow \infty$, $w(k) \rightarrow d\nu$, and $\sigma^2(k) = \mathscr{E}(\nu)\,d\nu$ in such a way that the total bandwidth is now given by

$$W = \int_0^W d\nu \tag{8.96}$$

and

$$R = 2\int_0^W \rho(\nu)\,d\nu \tag{8.97}$$

We now seek the continuous information-rate spectral density $\rho(\nu)$ that makes the expression

$$J = \int_0^W \mathscr{E}(\nu)e^{-2\rho(k)\ln 2}\,d\nu + 2\lambda \int_0^W \rho(\nu)\,d\nu \tag{8.98}$$

stationary with respect to variations in $\rho(\nu)$. This variational problem is solved by the information density

$$\rho(\nu) = \frac{R}{2W} = \frac{1}{2W}\int_0^W \log\mathscr{E}(\nu)\,d\nu + \tfrac{1}{2}\log\mathscr{E}(\nu) \tag{8.99}$$

The interpretation we give to Eq. (8.99) is that it represents the distribution of information rate with frequency for a Gaussian signal. The first term on the right-hand side is simply the average information rate per sample, in terms of the total rate R and bandwidth W. The sampling theorem (Nyquist criterion) requires $2W$ samples per second to uniquely specify a real band-limited signal with bandwidth W. The $\tfrac{1}{2}\log\mathscr{E}(\nu)$ term gives us the actual functional dependence of $\rho(\nu)$. The important point here is that $\rho(\nu)$ varies as the logarithm of the spectral density. The second term on the right-hand side of Eq. (8.99) is a normalization term that makes the average information rate come out to be as given by Eq. (8.97).

8.2.5 Maximum Entropy Spectral Analysis

A very interesting extension of rate-distortion theory relates to the estimation of the spectral density of a random process. This section is presented with the intent of illustrating an area where information theory branches out of communication engineering and serves to provide a rational approach for solving mathematical problems arising in other areas of applied mathematics.

Our aim here is not to lecture on spectral analysis. That subject is adequately covered elsewhere [Bl 59, Ch 78, Je 68, Ka 87, Ke 86, Ma 87a]. We assume that the reader is already familiar with the fundamentals and techniques of spectral analysis. In this section, we present an example of approaching spectral analysis from a philosophical point of view that is a natural extension of rate-distortion theory. The most difficult part of solving a problem is often the initial setting up of the available information in a way that can be attacked by known mathematical methods. The actual solution itself is usually simple, once the proper questions have been posed. Coming up with the right questions is much more difficult than answering them. Rate-distortion theory provides a formalism for formulating the proper questions.

The evaluation of the spectral density $\mathscr{E}(\nu)$ of a deterministic function $f(t)$ presents no fundamental problem, provided that the conditions for the existence of its Fourier transform $F(\nu)$ are satisfied. The density is simply given by

$$\mathscr{E}(\nu) = F^*(\nu)F(\nu)$$

Two cases can be distinguished. If $f(t)$ is defined over the interval $(-\infty, \infty)$, then it may be expressed as a Fourier integral:

$$f(t) = \int_{-\infty}^{\infty} F(\nu)e^{2\pi j \nu t} d\nu$$

where $F(\nu)$ is the Fourier transform

$$F(\nu) = \int_{-\infty}^{\infty} f(t)e^{-2\pi j \nu t} dt$$

If $f(t)$ is periodic with period T or if $f(t)$ vanishes outside the interval $[0, T]$, then it may be expanded in a Fourier series:

$$f(t) = \sum_{k=-\infty}^{\infty} f_k e^{2\pi j k t/T}$$

with the expansion coefficients given by

$$f_k = T^{-1} \int_0^T f(t)e^{-2\pi j k t/T} dt$$

and a Fourier transform given by

$$F(\nu) = \sum_{k=-\infty}^{\infty} f_k \delta(\nu - k/T)$$

There is no ambiguity in evaluating the Fourier transform or the spectral density for a deterministic function. This is because $f(t)$ is well-defined everywhere. Things are different for a stochastic process such as the output of an information source. It is not possible to know that function exactly. At best, all that is available is a measurement of a finite number of realizations of the stochastic process over a limited region of its domain.

Different realizations of the same stochastic process have different Fourier transforms. The Fourier transform for one realization contains information about that realization only and not necessarily about others. The spectral density, however, when suitably defined, is a characteristic of the process in general. Since the various realizations of a stochastic process are random quantities, so is the spectral density, which may not be known precisely in the deterministic sense, but must be estimated.

Cast in a very general sense, the fundamental problem with spectral estimation is that the estimate must be obtained from incomplete information. For example, several finite-duration segments of a process can be Fourier analyzed and the resulting spectral densities averaged [We 67]. This produces a function that captures some of the spectral features associated with the process, but at the cost of tampering with the data. To wit, this approach first requires windowing finite-duration segments, which by implication assumes that data samples outside the window range considered are all zero. This necessary condition is "justified" because the Fourier transformation is a mapping from $(-\infty, \infty)$ to $(-\infty, \infty)$. Data not measured are arbitrarily set to zero with a tapering window. The value of zero cannot be justified a priori, except possibly that it is the mean value of the process. A loose a posteriori justification can perhaps be made from the pleasing results obtained, but this takes us afar from mathematical rigor.

Another approach to spectral estimation involves first calculating the autocorrelation function of the data and then invoking the Wiener–Khinchin theorem to obtain the spectral density as the Fourier transform of the autocorrelation function. Here, again, the finiteness of the data forces us to cut corners. Strictly speaking, the autocorrelation function can only be approximated for a finite number of lag values. On practical grounds, the value of the autocorrelation vanishes for sufficiently large lag values. This is often used as a license to truncate the autocorrelation function past a certain lag and assume that it vanishes beyond that value. This, however, is an assumption about data not measured. Furthermore, values of the autocorrelation for small lags are calculated using more data samples than those for larger lags. This is a necessary consequence of using finite data sequences. The autocorrelation estimates all have different variances. In general, smaller variances are associated with small lags.

Is it possible to maintain mathematical honesty and still obtain a useful spectral estimate? And, if so, what guiding principle should be used in defining such an estimate? The wily reader, alerted by the title of this section, obviously expects that maximum entropy spectral analysis has something to do with the answer. This is so, but the treatment given here takes a different twist from what is the usual approach to the subject. Most modern discussions of maximum entropy spectral analysis heavily emphasize autoregressive time series modeling. Some of the earlier treatments [e.g., Ab 74, Bu 75] relied more heavily on the information-theoretic concept of entropy. We present still another approach, based on rate-distortion theory.

The guiding light in this problem (and others) is the principle of insufficient reason, which, loosely stated, asserts that given two equally satisfactory explanations for data, the simpler model is to be preferred over the more complicated one. A good mathematical model, like a good source code, places a premium on parsimony, the use of the minimum amount of complexity required to describe data. This concept can be compared with the notion of the minimal algorithm, encountered in Chapter 3. There we found that the minimal algorithm is the smallest algorithm capable of reproducing a data set. This concept has then evolved into source coding, which ideally is a minimal algorithm for an information source.

We are not strictly considering a source coding process here, but rather with a transformation that, when performed on the data, presents us with results that in some way are more meaningful. For the case at hand, we wish to produce a spectral estimate through certain transformations on the data. Clearly, such a transformation should distort the data as little as possible. Ables [Ab 74] puts it more clearly and gives us the first principle of data reduction:

> The Result of any Transformation imposed on the Experimental Data shall incorporate and be consistent with all Relevant Data and be maximally non-committal with regard to Unavailable Data.

Clearly, assumptions about data (or their autocorrelation) vanishing when in fact substantiating measurements are not available are in violation of the first principle. Ideally, we would like the spectral density estimate to be consistent only with the available autocorrelation values and to be maximally noncommittal with regard to data not measured.

Let us, for definiteness, assume that we are dealing with a band-limited process, whose $2N + 1$ autocorrelation values $\{\varphi_k = \varphi_{(k\Delta\tau)}; k = -N, \ldots, N\}$ are available, corresponding to the lags $\tau_k = k\Delta\tau$, and that it is desired to estimate the spectral density from these data. The lags are spaced by $\Delta\tau = 0.5/W$, the Nyquist sampling interval. To achieve consistency with the available autocorrelation values, we require that these values be derivable from the spectral estimate. If we denote the spectral density by $\mathscr{E}(\nu)$, then the autocorrelation values φ_k are obtained from $\mathscr{E}(\nu)$ through the Fourier relation

$$\varphi_k = \int_{-W}^{W} \mathscr{E}(\nu)e^{2\pi j\, \nu k\Delta\tau}d\nu \qquad k = -N, \ldots, N \qquad (8.100)$$

We wish to reconstruct the spectral density $\mathscr{E}(\nu)$ in the interval $[-W, W]$ from the data $\{\varphi_k\}$. The next step is to ensure that the spectral density is maximally noncommittal with regard to unavailable information. This has a strong variational flavor and can be restated in the language of rate-distortion theory by requiring that the rate corresponding to the spectral density $\mathscr{E}(\nu)$ be as small as possible. In other words, we wish to minimize the rate associated with $\mathscr{E}(\nu)$, but with Eqs. (8.100) as constraints to the variational problem. Note that as they stand, Eqs. (8.100) cannot be solved for a unique $\mathscr{E}(\nu)$ from a finite number of autocorrelation values. The mapping is unique from $\mathscr{E}(\nu)$ to the $2N + 1$ values of φ_k, but not the other way around. There are many spectral densities $\mathscr{E}(\nu)$ that correspond to the same set of autocorrelation values $\{\varphi_k; k = -N, \ldots, N\}$. Assuming that $\varphi_k = 0$ for $|k| > N$ results in a unique spectral density, albeit at the cost of violating the first principle of data reduction. The variational approach we are in the process of formulating simply chooses that spectral density corresponding to the least rate, i.e., which is informationally simplest while still able to accurately model the data.

We now turn to Eq. (8.99), the spectral rate associated with $\mathscr{E}(\nu)$. Actually, the first two terms on the right-hand side of Eq. (8.99) are constants chosen to make the average rate come out to the specified value for the subband coding example. These additive constants are unimportant here; we concentrate on the functional dependence on $\mathscr{E}(\nu)$ and write the spectral rate for a Gaussian process, up to a scale factor, to be

$$\rho(\nu) = \ln \mathscr{E}(\nu) \tag{8.101}$$

We write ln instead of log for analytical convenience. Since we are interested in minimizing the rate, the choice of a logarithmic base is irrelevant; only the logarithmic functional dependence on $\mathscr{E}(\nu)$ matters. The total rate is simply the integral of that quantity, so that we seek to minimize $\int \ln \mathscr{E}(\nu)\, d\nu$ subject to the constraints implied by Eqs. (8.100). This constrained variational problem may be concisely stated as the minimization of the equivalent unconstrained functional

$$J = \int_{-W}^{W} \ln \mathscr{E}(\nu)d\nu - \sum_{k=-N}^{N} \lambda_k \int_{-W}^{W} \mathscr{E}(\nu)e^{2\pi j\, \nu k \Delta \tau}d\nu \tag{8.102}$$

where the λ_k are Lagrange multipliers. The solution to this problem is

$$\mathscr{E}(\nu) = \left(\sum_{k=-N}^{N} \lambda_k e^{2\pi j\, k\nu \Delta \tau} \right)^{-1} \tag{8.103}$$

To solve for the Lagrange multipliers, we substitute Eq. (8.103) into Eq. (8.100) and obtain the $2N + 1$ equations:

$$\varphi_k = \int_{-W}^{W} \left(\sum_{m=-N}^{N} \lambda_m e^{2\pi j\, m\nu \Delta \tau} \right)^{-1} e^{2\pi j\, \nu k \Delta \tau}\, d\nu \qquad k = -N, \ldots, N \tag{8.104}$$

Following the derivation of Burg [Bu 75], we evaluate this integral using contour integration in the complex plane. Letting $z = e^{2\pi j\, \nu \Delta \tau}$, we have

$$dz = 2\pi j\, \Delta \tau e^{2\pi j\, \nu \Delta \tau}d\nu = 2\pi j\, \Delta \tau z d\nu$$

and Eq. (8.104) becomes

$$\varphi_k = (2\pi j\, \Delta \tau)^{-1} \oint \left(\sum_{m=-N}^{N} \lambda_m z^m \right)^{-1} z^{k-1}dz \qquad k = -N, \ldots, N \tag{8.105}$$

where the contour is taken counterclockwise around the unit circle. Note that in terms of the complex variable z, the spectral density is expressed as the reciprocal polynomial

$$\mathscr{E}(\nu) = \left(\sum_{k=-N}^{N} \lambda_k z^k \right)^{-1} \tag{8.106}$$

of degree $2N + 1$ evaluated on the unit circle $|z| = 1$. Since $\mathscr{E}(\nu)$ is required to be real and positive, it must be possible to express it (and, consequently, its reciprocal) as the product of the squared modulus of some complex quantity. Specifically, we write the polynomial

$$\sum_{k=-N}^{N} \lambda_k z^k = (\mathscr{E}_0 \Delta \tau)^{-1} a^*(z) a(z) \tag{8.107}$$

where $a(z)$ is the complex polynomial

$$a(z) = 1 + a_1 z + a_2 z^2 + \ldots + a_N z^N = \sum_{k=0}^{N} a_k z^k \tag{8.108}$$

and

$$a^*(z) = 1 + a_1^* z^{-1} + a_2^* z^{-2} + \ldots + a_N^* z^{-N} = \sum_{k=0}^{N} a_k^* z^{-k} \tag{8.109}$$

since $z^* = z^{-1}$. The quantity $(\mathscr{E}_0 \Delta \tau)^{-1}$ in Eq. (8.107) is a positive scaling factor. Both sides of Eq. (8.107) are polynomials of degree $2N + 1$ in z. The left-hand side can be factored into the $2N + 1$ factors $(z - z_{-N}) \ldots (z - z_0) \ldots (z - z_N)$. The roots z_k are the poles of the all-pole spectral density $\mathscr{E}(\nu)$. These same factors must also appear on the right-hand side and correspond to roots of the polynomials $a(z)$ and $a^*(z)$. Since $\mathscr{E}(\nu)$ is real and positive, these roots form complex conjugate pairs, and at least one root is real and shared by $a(z)$ and $a^*(z)$. Determining either polynomial $a(z)$ or $a^*(z)$ also determines the spectral density $\mathscr{E}(\nu)$.

Since $\mathscr{E}(\nu)$ is an analytic function, its z-polynomial representation must converge and, in particular, $a(z)$ must also be analytic. The polynomial expression of Eq. (8.108) for $a(z)$ converges for $|z| \leq 1$. This restricts the roots of $a(z)$ to lie outside the unit circle. Similarly, the roots of $a^*(z)$ are confined inside the unit circle.

Substituting Eq. (8.107) into Eq. (8.105), there results

$$\varphi_k = \mathscr{E}_0 (2\pi j)^{-1} \oint \left[\sum_{m=0}^{N} a_m z^m \right]^{-1} \left[\sum_{n=0}^{N} a_n^* z^{-n} \right]^{-1} z^{k-1} dz \tag{8.110}$$

Now consider a sum of the form

$$\sum_{k=0}^{N} a_k^* \varphi_{s-k} = \mathscr{E}_0 (2\pi j)^{-1} \oint \left[\sum_{m=0}^{N} a_m z^m \right]^{-1} z^{s-1} dz \qquad s = 0, \ldots, N \tag{8.111}$$

We now consider two cases. If $s \neq 0$, then the contour integral in Eq. (8.111) vanishes because the contour contains no singularities by virtue of the analyticity of $a(z)$. For $s = 0$, we use Cauchy's formula

$$\oint f(z) z^{-1} dz = 2\pi j f(0)$$

so that

$$\sum_{k=0}^{N} a_k^* \varphi_{-k} = \mathscr{E}_0$$

since $a_0 = 1$. Incorporating these results in the summation appearing on the left-hand side of Eq. (8.111), taking the complex conjugate, and remembering that $\varphi_{s-k}^* = \varphi_{k-s}$, we have

$$\sum_{k=0}^{N} a_k \varphi_{k-s} = \mathscr{E}_0 \delta(s) \qquad s = 0, \ldots, N \qquad (8.112)$$

Equation (8.112) can be written in matrix form:

$$\begin{vmatrix} \varphi_0 & \varphi_1 & \cdots & \varphi_N \\ \varphi_{-1} & \varphi_0 & \cdots & \varphi_{N-1} \\ \vdots & \vdots & \ddots & \vdots \\ \varphi_{-N} & \varphi_{-N+1} & \cdots & \varphi_0 \end{vmatrix} \begin{bmatrix} a_0 \\ a_1 \\ \vdots \\ a_N \end{bmatrix} = \begin{bmatrix} \mathscr{E}_0 \\ 0 \\ \vdots \\ 0 \end{bmatrix} \qquad (8.113)$$

A matrix with this banded structure, where the diagonal entries are all alike, is called a *Toeplitz* matrix. A Toeplitz matrix was encountered in Eq. (3.6). Equation (8.113) can be written more compactly as

$$\mathbf{\Phi a} = (\mathscr{E}_0 \, 0 \, 0 \ldots 0)^T \qquad (8.114)$$

where $\mathbf{a}$ is a vector of coefficients a_k, and the matrix $\mathbf{\Phi}$ is the correlation matrix.

Remembering that $a_0 = 1$, Eq. (8.114) is a system of $N + 1$ linear equations for the $N + 1$ unknowns $\{a_1, a_2, \ldots, a_N, \mathscr{E}_0\}$. Efficient techniques such as the Levinson algorithm exist for solving these equations [Bl 85b, Bu 75, Ha 86, Ma 87a].

Ables also obtains Eqs. (8.103) and (8.104) from the variational problem of Eq. (8.107), and the present approach differs from his only in the way of motivating the use of $\int \ln \mathscr{E}(\nu) \, d\nu$ as a measure of spectral information [Ab 74]. It is of interest here to go through Ables' approach.

Ables reasons (see e.g., [Ba 78] and [Sh 48b]) that the observed process may be thought of as being the output of a linear filter with spectral response $\mathscr{E}(\nu)$ for which the input is a white noise process. A process with entropy H_1, when passed through a linear filter with spectral response $\mathscr{E}(\nu)$, emerges at the output as a process with entropy H_2, where

$$H_2 = H_1 + \frac{1}{2W} \int_{-W}^{W} \log \mathscr{E}(\nu) \, d\nu \qquad (8.115)$$

Shannon [Sh 48b] presents a particularly lucid explanation of Eq. (8.115) in terms of entropy loss through a linear filter. The effect of a linear filter is to perform a coordinate transformation on a signal. The coordinate system of the input signal may be chosen to be its Fourier components, in which case, the filter merely multiplies these components by a set of scalars, with no coupling between different frequencies.

Consider, for simplicity, a signal consisting of the discrete frequency components $X(\nu_k)$. The effect of a filter with transfer function $T(\nu_k)$ is to produce an output

$$Y(\nu_k) = T(\nu_k)X(\nu_k) \tag{8.116}$$

where $T(\nu_k)$ is a diagonal matrix. In other words, the Fourier coordinates form a set of eigenvectors for the transformation matrix and diagonalize that matrix. If the input spectral density is white, then the output spectral density is given by

$$\mathscr{E}(\nu_k) = Y^*(\nu_k)Y(\nu_k) = T^*(\nu_k)T(\nu_k) \tag{8.117}$$

The filter output entropy is

$$H_2(Y) = -\sum_k \int p_Y(Y_k) \log p_Y(Y_k)\, dY_k \tag{8.118}$$

where $Y_k = Y(\nu_k)$. With the help of the transformation of a random variable given by Eq. (8.116), the right-hand side of Eq. (8.118) can be expressed in terms of the entropy of the filter input X ensemble:

$$p_X(X_k) = |T_k| p_Y(Y_k) \tag{8.119}$$

and, therefore, Eq. (8.118) can be rewritten as

$$H_2(Y) = -\sum_k |T_k|^{-1} \int p_X(X_k) \log[|T_k|^{-1} p_X(X_k)]|T_k|\, dX_k$$

$$= -\sum_k p_X(X_k) \log p_X(X_k)\, dX_k + \sum_k \log|T_k| \tag{8.120}$$

$$= H_1(X) + \frac{1}{2}\sum_k \log|T_k|^2$$

Now taking the limit as the uniform frequency spacing approaches zero, Eq. (8.120) reduces to

$$H_2(Y) = H_1(X) + \frac{1}{2W}\int_{-W}^{W} \log \mathscr{E}(\nu)\, d\nu \tag{8.121}$$

The second term in Eq. (8.121) is negative and represents the entropy loss through a linear filter with spectral characteristic $\mathscr{E}(\nu)$. The larger the entropy loss, the lower $H_2(Y)$ will be for a given input entropy $H_1(X)$. Thus, we are guaranteed an output process having the least rate by noting that such a process is indistinguishable from white noise passed through a linear filter with spectral characteristic $\mathscr{E}(\nu)$, where $\mathscr{E}(\nu)$ has the property of minimizing the second term of Eq. (8.121), subject to the constraints given by Eqs. (8.100). Minimizing that term also minimizes $H_2(Y)$, the rate of the output process. What is maximized in maximum entropy spectral analysis is the entropy loss in going through the filter and not the entropy itself.

It is now customary to treat maximum entropy as an autoregressive modeling of the corresponding time series (see [Va 71] as well as the references cited earlier in this section). In fact, the two approaches are identical. We shall not elaborate beyond pointing out that the maximum entropy spectrum of Eq. (8.103) is an all-pole spectrum.

PROBLEMS

8.1 Show that, in general, a distortion measure is not a metric, but that any metric may be used as a distortion measure. Give an example of a metric that can be used as a measure of distortion.

8.2 Consider the two alphabets $\{x_i; i = 1, \ldots, M\}$ and $\{y_j; j = 1, \ldots, N\}$ with the joint probability $P(x_i, y_j)$. For example, the x alphabet could be the source and the y alphabet the representation. For perfect coding, $P(x_i, y_j) = \delta_{i,j}$. Consider the function $\xi(i, j) = 1 - P(x_i, y_j)$. Can $\xi(i, j)$ be used as a distortion measure? Is $\xi(i, j)$ a metric?

8.3 Consider the two alphabets $\{x_i; i = 1, \ldots, M\}$ and $\{y_j; j = 1, \ldots, N\}$ with respective symbol probabilities $\{P(x_i); i = 1, \ldots, M\}$ and $\{P(y_j); j = 1, \ldots, N\}$. These alphabets are related by the conditional mapping assignment $Q(j \mid i)$. Show that the following identities are true:

$$\sum_{i=1}^{M} Q(j \mid i) = \sum_{j=1}^{N} Q(j \mid i) = 1$$

8.4 Show that we may, without loss of generality, set $D_{\min} = 0$, and that the result is to leave the shape of the $R(D)$ curve unchanged, and to translate that curve on the D axis.

8.5 Show that $y(D^*) = \alpha R + (1 - \alpha)R'$, i.e., derive Eq. (8.23).

8.6 Comment on the possibility of the digital implementation of an antialiasing filter.

8.7 Rework the last example of Section 8.1.4 for the more general case of arbitrary binary input symbol probabilities $(1 - p)$ and p. Obtain an explicit expression for R in terms of p and D only. For what value of p is the rate a maximum?

8.8 Derive Eq. (8.79).

REFERENCES
AND BIBLIOGRAPHY

[Ab 63] NORMAN ABRAMSON, *Information Theory and Coding*, New York: McGraw–Hill, 1963.

[Ab 72] MILTON ABRAMOWITZ and IRENE STEGUN, *Handbook of Mathematical Functions*, Washington, DC: U.S. Department of Commerce, 1972.

[Ab 74] J. G. ABLES, "Maximum Entropy Spectral Analysis," *Astronomy and Astrophysics Supplement* 15 (1974): 383–393.

[Ar 85] GEORGE ARFKEN, *Mathematical Methods for Physicists*, 3rd Ed., New York: Academic Press, 1985.

[At 71] B. S. ATAL and S. L. HANAUER, "Speech Analysis and Synthesis by Linear Prediction of the Speech Wave," *J. Acoust. Soc. Am.* 50 (1971): 637–655.

[Ba 78] M. S. BARTLETT, *An Introduction to Stochastic Processes*, 3rd Ed., Cambridge, England: Cambridge University Press, 1978.

[Be 60] WILLIAM R. BENNETT, *Electrical Noise*, New York: McGraw–Hill, 1960.

[Be 71] TOBY BERGER, *Rate Distortion Theory*, Englewood Cliffs, NJ: Prentice-Hall, 1971.

[Be 88] SERGIO BENEDETTO, EZIO BIGLIERI, and VALENTINO CASTELLANI, *Digital Transmission Theory*, Englewood Cliffs, NJ: Prentice-Hall, 1988.

[Bl 59] R. B. BLACKMAN and J. W. TUKEY, *The Measurements of Power Spectra from the Point of View of Communications Engineering*, New York: Dover, 1959.

[Bl 83] RICHARD E. BLAHUT, *Theory and Practice of Error-Control Codes*, Reading, MA: Addison–Wesley, 1983.

[Bl 85a] RICHARD E. BLAHUT, "Algebraic Fields, Signal Processing, and Error Control," *Proc. IEEE* 73/5 (1985): 874–893.

[Bl 85b] RICHARD E. BLAHUT, *Fast Algorithms for Digital Signal Processing*, Reading, MA: Addison–Wesley, 1985.

[Br 60] LÉON BRILLOUIN, *Science and Information Theory*, 2nd Ed., New York: Academic Press, 1960.

423

[Br 65] RON BRACEWELL, *The Fourier Transform and Its Applications,* New York: McGraw-Hill, 1965.

[Bu 75] JOHN P. BURG, *Maximum Entropy Spectral Analysis*, Ph.D. dissertation, Stanford University, 1975.

[Ca 86] A. BRUCE CARLSON, *Communication Systems*, New York: McGraw–Hill, 1985.

[Ch 70] CHI-TSONG CHEN, *Introduction to Linear System Theory*, New York: Holt, Rinehart and Winston, 1970.

[Ch 75] GREGORY J. CHAITIN, "Randomness and Mathematical Proof," *Sci. Am.* (May 1975): 47.

[Ch 78] D. G. CHILDERS (ed.), *Modern Spectrum Analysis*, New York: IEEE Press, 1978.

[Ch 80] R. S. CHEUNG and R. L. WINSLOW, "High Quality 16 kb/s Voice Transmission: The Subband Coder Approach," *Proceedings of the IEEE International Conference on Acoustics, Speech, and Signal Processing*, New York: IEEE Press, 1980, pp. 319–322.

[Cr 46] HARALD CRAMÉR, *Mathematical Methods of Statistics*, Princeton, NJ: Princeton University Press, 1946.

[Cr 76] R. E. CROCHIERE, S. A. WEBER, and J. L. FLANAGAN, "Digital Coding of Speech in Sub-bands," *Bell Sys. Tech. J.* 55/8 (October 1976): 1069–1085.

[Cr 77] R. E. CROCHIERE, "On the Design of Sub-band Coders for Low-Bit-Rate Speech Communication," *Bell Sys. Tech. J.* 56/5 (May–June 1977): 747–770.

[Cr 81] R. E. CROCHIERE, "Sub-Band Coding," *Bell Sys. Tech. J.* 60/7 (September 1981): 1633–1653.

[Cr 83] RONALD E. CROCHIERE and LAWRENCE R. RABINER, *Multirate Digital Signal Processing*, Englewood Cliffs, NJ: Prentice–Hall, 1983.

[Da 72] LEE D. DAVISSON, "Rate-Distortion Theory and Application," *Proc. IEEE* 60 (July 1972): 800–808.

[Da 83] H. DAVENPORT, *The Higher Arithmetic*, New York: Dover, 1983.

[Du 40] H. K. DUNN and S. D. WHITE, "Statistical Measurements on Conversational Speech," *J. Acoust. Soc. Am.* 11 (January 1940): 278–288.

[Fe 68] WILLIAM FELLER, *An Introduction to Probability Theory and Its Applications*, Vol. I, 3rd Ed., New York: Wiley, 1968.

[Fe 71] WILLIAM FELLER, *An Introduction to Probability Theory and Its Applications*, Vol. II, 2nd Ed., New York: Wiley, 1971.

[Fo 83] JOSEPH FORD, "How Random Is a Coin Toss?" *Phys. Today* (April 1983): 40.

[Fr 69] L. E. FRANKS, *Signal Theory*, Englewood Cliffs, NJ: Prentice-Hall, 1969.

[Ga 61] GEORGE GAMOW, *One Two Three . . . Infinity*, New York: Bantam, 1961.

[Ga 68] ROBERT G. GALLAGER, *Information Theory and Reliable Communication*, New York: Wiley, 1968.

[Gi 52] E. N. GILBERT, "A Comparison of Signalling Alphabets," *Bell Syst. Tech. J.* 31 (May 1952): 504–522.

[Go 50] HERBERT GOLDSTEIN, *Classical Mechanics*, Reading, MA: Addison-Wesley, 1950.

[Go 67] T. J. GOBLICK, Jr., and J. L. HOLSINGER, "Analog Source Digitization: A Comparison of Theory and Practice," *IEEE Trans. Info. Theory* IT-13 (April 1967): 323–326.

[Gr 65] I. S. GRADSHTEIN and I. M. RYZHIK, *Table of Integrals, Series and Products*, New York: Academic Press, 1965.

[Gr 80] CHRISTOPH GRAUEL, "Sub-Band Coding with Adaptive Bit Allocation," *Sig. Proc.* 2 (1980): 23–30.

[Ha 74] PAUL R. HALMOS, *Finite-Dimensional Vector Spaces*, New York: Springer-Verlag, 1974.

[Ha 75] N. A. J. HASTINGS and J. B. PEACOCK, *Statistical Distributions*, New York: Wiley, 1975.

[Ha 83a] RICHARD HAMMING, *Coding and Information Theory*, 2nd Ed., Englewood Cliffs, NJ: Prentice-Hall, 1987.

[Ha 83b] SIMON HAYKIN, *Communication Systems*, 2nd Ed., New York: Wiley, 1983.

[Ha 85] G. H. HARDY and E. M. WRIGHT, *An Introduction to the Theory of Numbers*, 5th Ed., Oxford: Clarendon Press, 1985.

[Ha 86] SIMON HAYKIN, *Adaptive Filter Theory*, Englewood Cliffs, NJ: Prentice-Hall, 1986.

[He 68] CARL W. HELSTROM, *Statistical Theory of Signal Detection*, Oxford: Pergamon Press, 1968.

[Ho 62] PAUL G. HOEL, *Introduction to Mathematical Statistics*, 3rd Ed., New York: Wiley, 1962.

[Ja 57a] E. T. JAYNES, "Information Theory and Statistical Mechanics," *Phys. Rev.* 106/4 (May 1957): 620–630.

[Ja 57b] E. T. JAYNES, "Information Theory and Statistical Mechanics II," *Phys. Rev.* 108/2 (October 1957): 171–190.

[Ja 74] NUGGEHALLY S. JAYANT, "Digital Coding of Speech Waveforms: PCM, DPCM, and DM Quantizers," *Proc. IEEE* 62 (May 1974): 611–632.

[Ja 76] NUGGEHALLY S. JAYANT (ed.), *Waveform Quantization and Coding*, New York: IEEE Press, 1976.

[Je 68] GWILYM M. JENKINS and DONALD G. WATTS, *Spectral Analysis and Its Applications*, San Francisco: Holden-Day, 1968.

[Je 77] ABDUL J. JERRI, "The Shannon Sampling Theorem—Its Various Extensions and Applications: A Tutorial Review," *Proc. IEEE* 65/11 (1977): 1565–1596.

[Ka 67] AMNON KATZ, *Principles of Statistical Mechanics*, San Francisco: W. H. Freeman, 1967.

[Ka 87] S. M. KAY, *Modern Spectral Estimation*, Englewood Cliffs, NJ: Prentice-Hall, 1987.

[Ke 76] JOHN G. KEMENY and J. LAURIE SNELL, *Finite Markov Chains*, New York: Springer-Verlag, 1976.

[Ke 86] S. KESLER (ed.), *Modern Spectrum Analysis II*, New York: IEEE Press, 1986.

[Kh 49] A. I. KHINCHIN, *Mathematical Foundation of Statistical Mechanics*, New York: Dover, 1949.

[Kh 57] A. I. KHINCHIN, *Mathematical Foundation of Information Theory*, New York: Dover, 1957.

[La 61] H. J. LANDAU and H. O. POLLAK, "Prolate Spheroidal Wave Functions, Fourier Analysis and Uncertainty—II," *Bell Syst. Tech. J.* 40 (1961): 65–84.

[La 62] H. J. LANDAU and H. O. POLLAK, "Prolate Spheroidal Wave Functions, Fourier Analysis and Uncertainty—III: The Dimension of the Space of Essentially Time- and Band-Limited Signals," *Bell Syst. Tech. J.* 41 (1962): 1295–1336.

[La 70] CORNELIUS LANCZOS, *The Vocational Principles of Mechanics*, New York: Dover, 1970.

[La 87] P. LAFRANCE and J. J. OUSBORNE, "Effects of Reduced SAR Azimuth Processing," *IEEE Trans. Aerosp. Electron. Sys.* AES-23/2 (March 1987): 152–157.

[Li 65] WILLIAM C. LINDSEY, "Coded Noncoherent Communications," *IEEE Trans. Space Electron. Telem.* (March 1965): 6–13.

[Li 83] SHU LIN and DANIEL J. COSTELLO, *Error Control Coding: Fundamentals and Applications*, Englewood Cliffs, NJ: Prentice-Hall, 1983.

[Lo 72] CALVIN T. LONG, *Elementary Introduction to Number Theory*, 2nd Ed., Lexington, MA: D. C. Heath, 1972.

[Ma 60a] J. I. MARCUM, "A Statistical Theory of Target Detection by Pulsed Radar," *IRE Trans. Inf. Theory* IT-6/2 (April 1960): 59–267.

[Ma 60b] JOEL MAX, "Quantizing for Minimum Distortion," *IRE Trans. Inf. Theory* IT-6/1 (March 1960): 7–12.

[Ma 77] F. J. MacWILLIAMS and N. J. A. SLOANE, *The Theory of Error-Correcting Codes*, Amsterdam: North-Holland, 1977.

[Ma 87a] MASUD MANSURIPUR, *Introduction to Information Theory*, Englewood Cliffs, NJ: Prentice-Hall, 1987.

[Ma 87b] S. LAWRENCE MARPLE, JR., *Digital Spectral Analysis with Applications*, Englewood Cliffs, NJ: Prentice-Hall, 1987.

[Mc 72] NEAL H. McCOY, *Fundamentals of Abstract Algebra*, Boston: Allyn and Bacon, 1972.

[Me 70] EUGEN MERZBACHER, *Quantum Mechanics*, New York: Wiley, 1970.

[Mi 85] ARNOLD M. MICHELSON and ALLEN H. LEVESQUE, *Error-Control Techniques for Digital Communication*, New York: Wiley, 1985.

[Ob 73] FRITZ OBERHETTINGER, *Fourier Transforms of Distributions and Their Inverses*, New York: Academic Press, 1973.

[Ol 48] B. M. OLIVER, J. R. PIERCE, and C. E. SHANNON, "The Philosophy of PCM," *Proc. IRE* 36 (November 1948): 1324–1331.

[Op 75] ALAN V. OPPENHEIM and RONALD W. SHAFER, *Digital Signal Processing*, Englewood Cliffs, NJ: Prentice-Hall, 1975.

[Pa 84] ATHANASIOS PAPOULIS, *Probability, Random Variables and Stochastic Processes*, 2nd Ed., New York: McGraw-Hill, 1984.

[Pa 77] ATHANASIOS PAPOULIS, *Signal Analysis*, New York: McGraw-Hill, 1977.

[Pa 79] SUBBARAYAN PASUPATHY, "Minimum Shift Keying: A Spectrally Efficient Modulation," *IEEE Commun.* 7 (July 1979): 14–22.

[Pe 72] W. WESLEY PETERSON and E. J. WELDON, Jr., *Error-Correcting Codes*, 2d Ed., Cambridge, MA: The MIT Press, 1972.

[Pi 80] JOHN R. PIERCE, *An Introduction to Information Theory*, 2nd Ed., New York: Dover, 1980.

[Po 84] EDWARD C. POSNER and ROBERTSON STEVENS, "Deep Space Communication—Past, Present and Future," *IEEE Commun.* 22/5 (1984): 8–21.

[Pr 83] JOHN G. PROAKIS, *Digital Communications*, New York: McGraw-Hill, 1983.

[Ra 75] LAWRENCE R. RABINER and BERNARD GOLD, *Theory and Application of Digital Signal Processing*, Englewood Cliffs, NJ: Prentice-Hall, 1975.

[Ra 78] LAWRENCE R. RABINER and RONALD W. SHAFER, *Digital Processing of Speech Signals*, Englewood Cliffs, NJ: Prentice-Hall, 1978.

[Sa 68] DAVID J. SAKRISON, *Communication Theory: Transmission of Waveforms and Digital Information*, New York: Wiley, 1968.

[Sa 83] DEBABRATA SAHA, "Q^{2}PSK—A New Spectrally Efficient Modulation Scheme," *Proceedings of the Twenty-First Allerton Conference on Communication, Control, and Computing*, 1983, pp. 954–963.

[Sa 86] DEBABRATA SAHA and THEODORE G. BIRDSALL, *"Quadrature-Quadrature Phase Shift Keying: A Constant Envelope Modulation Scheme,"* presented at the Conference on Information Sciences and Systems, Princeton, March 1986.

[Sc 66] MISCHA SCHWARTZ, WILLIAM R. BENNETT, and SEYMOUR STEIN, *Communication Systems and Techniques*, New York: McGraw-Hill, 1966.

[Sc 68] LEONARD I. SCHIFF, *Quantum Mechanics*, New York: McGraw-Hill, 1968.

[Sh 48a] CLAUDE E. SHANNON, "A Mathematical Theory of Communication," *Bell Syst. Tech. J.* 27 (July 1948): 379–423.

[Sh 48b] CLAUDE E. SHANNON, "A Mathematical Theory of Communication," *Bell Syst. Tech. J.* 27 (October 1948): 623–656.

[Sh 49a] CLAUDE E. SHANNON and WARREN WEAVER, *The Mathematical Theory of Communication*, Urbana, IL: University of Illinois Press, 1949.

[Sh 49b] CLAUDE E. SHANNON, "Communication in the Presence of Noise," *Proc. IRE* 37 (January 1949): 10–21.

[Sh 51] CLAUDE E. SHANNON, "Prediction and Entropy of Printed English," *Bell Syst. Tech. J.* 30 (January 1951): 50–64.

[Sh 59] CLAUDE E. Shannon, "Coding Theorems for a Discrete Source with a Fidelity Criterion," *IRE Nat. Conv. Rec.*, Part 4 (March 1959): 142–163.

[Sh 68] PAUL C. SHIELDS, *Elementary Linear Algebra*, New York: Worth, 1968.

[Sk 88] BERNARD SKLAR, *Digital Communications*, Englewood Cliffs, NJ: Prentice-Hall, 1988.

[Sl 61] D. SLEPIAN and H. O. POLLAK, "Prolate Spheroidal Wave Functions, Fourier Analysis and Uncertainty—I," *Bell Syst. Tech. J.* 40 (1961): 43–63.

[Sl 64] DAVID SLEPIAN, "Prolate Spheroidal Wave Functions, Fourier Analysis and Uncertainty—IV: Extensions to Many Dimensions; Generalized Prolate Spheroidal Functions," *Bell Syst. Tech. J.* 43 (1964): 3009–3057.

[Sl 76] DAVID SLEPIAN, "On Bandwidth," *Proc. IEEE* 64/3 (March 1976): 292–300.

[Sl 78] DAVID SLEPIAN, "Prolate Spheroidal Wave Functions, Fourier Analysis and Uncertainty—V: The Discrete Case," *Bell Syst. Tech. J.* 57/5 (1978): 1371–1430.

[St 52] B. M. STEWART, *Theory of Numbers*, New York: Macmillan, 1952.

[St 80] G. STRANG, *Linear Algebra and Its Applications*, New York: Academic Press, 1980.

[St 88a] JOHN C. STAPLETON and STEVEN C. BASS, "Synthesis of Musical Tones Based on the Karhunen–Loève Transform," *IEEE Trans. Acoustics, Speech and Sig. Proc.* 36/3 (March 1988): 305.

[St 88b] HENRY STARK, FRANZ B. TUTEUR, and JOHN B. ANDERSON, *Modern Electrical Communications*, 2nd Ed., Englewood Cliffs, NJ: Prentice-Hall, 1988.

[Ta 86] HERBERT TAUB and DONALD L. SCHILLING, *Principles of Communication Systems*, 2nd Ed., New York, McGraw-Hill, 1986.

[Th 69] JOHN B. THOMAS, *Statistical Communication Theory*, New York: Wiley, 1969.

[Tr 76] STEVEN A. TRETTER, *Introduction to Discrete-Time Signal Processing*, New York: Wiley, 1976.

[To 84] DON J. TORRIERI, "The Information-Bit Error Rate for Block Codes," *IEEE Trans. Commun.* COM-32/4 (April 1984): 474–476.

[Tu 60] GEORGE L. TURIN, "An Introduction to Matched Filters," *IRE Trans. Inf. Theory* IT-6 (June 1960): 311–329.

[Un 82] GOTTFRIED UNGERBOECK, "Channel Coding with Multilevel/Phase Signals," *IEEE Trans. Inf. Theory* IT-28/1 (January 1982): 55–67.

[Un 87a] GOTTFRIED UNGERBOECK, "Trellis-Coded Modulation with Redundant Signal Sets, Part I: Introduction," *IEEE Commun.* 25/2 (February 1987): 5–11.

[Un 87b] GOTTFRIED UNGERBOECK, "Trellis-Coded Modulation with Redundant Signal Sets, Part II: State of the Art," *IEEE Commun.* 25/2 (February 1987): 12-21.

[Va 68] HARRY L. VAN TREES, *Detection, Estimation, and Modulation Theory*, New York: Wiley, 1968.

[Va 71] A. VAN DEN BOS, "Alternative Interpretation of Maximum Entropy Spectral Analysis," *IEEE Trans. Inf. Theory* IT-17/4 (July 1971): 493–494.

[Vi 66] ANDREW J. VITERBI, *Principles of Coherent Communication*, New York: McGraw-Hill, 1966.

[Vi 67] ANDREW J. VITERBI, "Error Bound for Convolutional Codes and an Asymptotically Optimum Decoding Algorithm," *IEEE Trans. Inf. Theory* IT-13 (April 1967): 260–269.

[Vi 79] ANDREW J. VITERBI and JIM K. OMURA, *Principles of Digital Communication and Coding*, New York: McGraw-Hill, 1979.

[We 67] P. D. WELCH, "The Use of Fast Fourier Transform for the Estimation of Power Spectra: A Method Based on Time Averaging Over Short, Modified Periodograms," *IEEE Trans. Audio Electroacoust.* AU-15 (June 1967): 70–73.

[We 74] ROBERT WEINSTOCK, *Calculus of Variations*, New York: Dover, 1974.

[We 82] WARREN WEAVER, *Lady Luck*, New York: Dover, 1982.

[Wi 49] NORBERT WIENER, *Extrapolation, Interpolation, and Smoothing of Stationary Time Series*, New York: Wiley, 1949.

[Wh 71] A. D. WHALEN, *Detection of Signals in Noise*, Orlando, FL: Academic Press, 1971.

[Wh 15] E. T. WHITTAKER, "On the Functions Which Are Represented by the Expansions of the Interpolation Theory," *Proc. Roy. Soc. (Edinburgh)* 35 (1915): 181–194.

[Wh 63] E. T. WHITTAKER and G. N. WATSON, *A Course of Modern Analysis*, 4th Ed., Cambridge, England: Cambridge University Press, 1963.

[Wo 53] P. M. WOODWARD, *Probability and Information Theory, with Applications to Radar*, 2nd Ed., Oxford: Pergamon, 1953.

[Wo 65] JOHN M. WOZENCRAFT and IRWIN M. JACOBS, *Principles of Communication Engineering*, New York: Wiley, 1965.

[Wy 81] AARON D. WYNER, "Fundamental Limits in Information Theory," *Proc. IEEE* 69/2 (February 1981): 239–251.

[Yo 71] JOHN F. YOUNG, *Information Theory*, New York: Wiley, 1971.

INDEX